Trapped By A Psycho Doctor

A Warning to All

Jonah Jon Jefferys
&
Leo Finney

Copyright © 2023 Jonah Jon Jeffreys

All rights reserved. No part of this book may be used or reproduced by any means, graphic, electronic, or mechanical, including photo-copying, recording, taping or by any information storage retrieval system without the written permission of the author except in the case of brief quotations embodied in critical articles and reviews.

Because of the dynamic nature of the Internet, any web addresses or links contained in this book may have changed since publication and may no longer be valid. The views expressed in this work are solely those of the author and do not necessarily reflect the views of the publisher, and the publisher hereby disclaims any responsibility for them.

Any people depicted in stock imagery provided by Thinkstock are models, and such images are being used for illustrative purposes only.

Certain stock imagery © Thinkstock.

ISBN: 978-1-964283-41-8
Library of Congress Control Number: 2012905564

Table of Content

AUTHOR'S NOTE iii
PRECIOUSTHINGS iv
ACKNOWLEDGMENTS v
INTRODUCTION 1
COSMETIC SURGERY CAN BE HORRIFYING 2
THE DOUBLE MIRROR 5
MY ADOLESCENT YEARS 20
FROM ADOLESCENCE TO ADULTHOOD 32
THE ADULT YEARS 50
THE ENCOUNTER 90
TRAPPED BY A PSYCHO DOCTOR 116
ADVICE TO THE READER 199
CHECKLIST 201
PRESIDENT TRUMP VERSES THE DEMOCRAT HOUSE 218
I FOOD FOR THOUGHT 286

For the love of money is the root of all kinds of evil, for which some have strayed from the faith in their greediness, and pierced themselves through with many sorrows.

1 Timothy 6:10

Author's Note

The author has changed the names of most of the people and modified identifying features in some places of the other individuals in order to preserve their anonymity. The goal in all cases was to protect people's privacy without damaging the integrity of the story. The story is based on actual events.

PRECIOUS THINGS

There are precious things in life that we hold so dear that no one should ever take them from us. If they do, it can rob us of our dignity and leave us feeling violated and alone. When these precious things are taken from us in a careless or malicious manner it can cause us to feel ripped off and stripped of their true value and our self-worth.

ACKNOWLEDGMENTS

I would like to give special credit to my sister Marlie and to my friend Leo for their contributions in making this book a great read for people everywhere whether they are interested in having cosmetic surgery, have had cosmetic surgery or have had a botched surgery.

INTRODUCTION

This book is based on a true story. Most of the names have been changed to protect the innocent as well as the guilty. The events that negatively affected my life were a slow and painful process that I endured for years. It took many more years to completely determine everything that Dr. Butcher did to me, mentally and cosmetically.

In the right hands, cosmetic surgery is an art of facial feature enhancement, and a tremendous self-esteem enhancer for individuals. In the wrong hands it can be a powerful force that destroys a person's self-esteem and self-confidence.

When I was looking for the best cosmetic surgeon for the procedure I desired, I chose one who as I unfortunately discovered too late cared more about gaining my business than he cared about my cosmetic interests. Instead of my gaining self-esteem and an improved self-image after my surgeries I obsessed over what had happened to me.

The information presented in this book provides all the necessary tools and strategies for how to avoid choosing the wrong cosmetic surgeon. I never should have become the victim of cosmetic surgeries, and I hope that the readers of our book will never go through the devastating experiences that I have suffered.

I would like to save the readers from being victimized by an uncaring, opportunistic medical predator. I hope that our book will educate millions, but we would be pleased if it helps even one person escape the clutches of a medical doctor who cares more about professional gain than he or she does about the patient's cosmetic interests.

Jonah Jon Jefferys

1

COSMETIC SURGERY CAN BE HORRIFYING

Looking back at the way in which Dr. Butcher dealt with me, I now understand that he allowed me to come to my own conclusions that he could fulfill my cosmetic dreams for my facial features. After he built up my confidence at our initial consultation, things began to deteriorate during my second and third consultations although I didn't recognize that at the time. He did a good job of keeping me mentally off guard and stupid. This surgeon had something else in mind for me on the day of my surgeries a mental and cosmetic whammy.

How could I have known that this cosmetic surgeon was setting me up for something that was the opposite of what I'd wanted and needed cosmetically? I had hunted for the right surgeon, and he had hunted me for his own selfish agenda. These facts have become more evident to me as the years have gone by.

This doctor didn't have the skill or the discernment to correctly interpret my cosmetic interests. I was mentally worked on by an eccentric predator.

A friend told me recently, "A shark doesn't negotiate. It just comes up and takes your leg off."

The painful and devastating results became more evident with the passing of time. I have questioned myself, over and over on how this could have happened to me. I felt violated by a medical surgeon who never should have touched my nose and ears.

The doctor's approach caught me off guard on the very day of my surgeries. Post-surgeries, my mind was black and dismally blank with the powerful effects of his cosmetic heist. The reader may conclude that I was stupid for going to a cosmetic surgeon who as I realized only after my surgeries, was not listed with the American Board of Medical Specialties (ABMS). I wasn't aware of Dr. Butcher's qualifications when I went in for an initial consultation.

A woman, who works for a board-certified plastic surgeon in the Pacific Northwest, answered my phone call, saying, "Cosmetic surgery is an enhancement of a person's appearance. Plastic surgery focuses on repairing and reconstructing possibly abnormal structures."

I didn't know those facts or other revealing things about Dr. Butcher before surgery. Maybe I was naive at the time, but I thought I was being honest and proactive in my pursuit of the best surgeon who could do precisely what I desired cosmetically.

I learned, after my surgeries, that Dr. Butcher a doctor of medicine (MD) and a doctor of dental surgery (DDS) can reconstruct the face under his dental license and can practice plastic surgery under his medical license.

According to the staff member who answered my call to the Medical Quality Assurance Commission (MQAC), Dr. Butcher "has a general anesthesia permit under his dentistry." I also learned that "a medical doctor does not have to be board certified in the State of Washington to practice medicine."

I gradually came to realize that I had been royally ripped off, cosmetically and financially, by a cosmetic predator.

Years before I went to see Dr. Butcher, I learned from a woman who worked for a prominent plastic surgeon in the Pacific Northwest that when it came to plastic surgery, you want a double board-certified plastic surgeon. A board-certified plastic surgeon sent me an email that explained, "Double board certified means certified in two specialties: general surgery and plastic ophthalmology and plastic ENT and plastic reconstruction surgery."

Regretfully, I forgot that good advice when I chose Dr. Butcher. He was not a board-certified plastic surgeon listed with any of the twenty-four boards of the American Board of Medical Specialties. Unfortunately, I also found out, post surgeries, that Dr. Butcher was not the board-certified reconstructionist that I wanted for my specific facial-feature needs. He is double board certified, but he is not a specialist in the nose and ears, as the American Board of Medical Specialties' true surgeons are.

The approach Dr. Butcher took with me was like that of a smooth-talking salesman who did not want me to focus on what I was about to purchase. A slick car salesman doesn't want you to think about how you will make your payments, nor does he take the time to get to know you personally as an individual. If he is only interested in advancing his salesmanship status, he won't invest the time to learn your likes and dislikes in helping you choose the right car for you.

I had assumed that if Dr. Butcher couldn't do what I wanted and needed cosmetically, he would refer me to a more qualified surgeon. That assumption however was wrong because Dr. Butcher had his own plans and vision for my facial features. I had previous surgeries on my nose, ears, and chin, so I was very particular about finding the right cosmetic surgeon, but my cosmetic dreams were destroyed by a sociopath.

Dr. Butcher gave me only brief information before the surgeries, and he made up things before my later multiple surgeries. I realize now that he never recognized my wants or needs for my facial features that is more than scary. It was a painful and devastating experience that plunged my life into a deep sea of quandary of questions, and it slowly destroyed my self-esteem and self-image as a unique creation of God.

I watched a television program one day about plastic surgery. The narrator commented that every year there are ten thousand unnecessary cases of cosmetic surgery. I know for a fact that my cosmetic fiasco was totally unnecessary, and I now realize that it was cosmetic and financial crimes. I had concluded that my particular case was a cosmetic homicide, but for years I wasn't able to figure out fully what Dr. Butcher had done to me.

I repeatedly requested a new hearing with the MQAC, the medical board that issued Dr. Butcher's medical license, and with the Dental Quality Assurance Commission (DQAC), the dental board that issued his DDS license. Those commissions govern Dr. Butcher's license to remain in practice.

I had sent in a series of complaint letters to the DQAC, and the MQAC over several years requesting that legal action to be taken against Dr. Butcher. I also requested a reconsideration for a new hearing against the medical doctor, calling for his license to be revoked or for disciplinary action to be taken against him. I became convinced beyond a shadow of a doubt that Dr. Butcher had committed medical malpractice, and criminal actions against me and I wanted the iron will of justice to prevail against him. I assumed that after my complaints, Dr. Butcher would be held liable for his cosmetic and financial crimes against me. This was another assumption that was absolutely wrong.

Sometime later I learned from the MQAC that Dr. Butcher hadn't been asked to respond to my complaint letters or to the commission's inquiries concerning the approach that he had taken toward me. Each year that I requested an investigation regarding my cosmetic case against him I found my request was denied.

A reputable plastic surgeon had not worked on my facial features; it was medical negligence, malpractice, and utter butchery by the wrong cosmetic surgeon. I had been robbed.

2

THE DOUBLE MIRROR

I grew up in Lupine, a small town in the Pacific Northwest, with my family one brother, two sisters, and my mother and father. My Christian parents' pastorate was working among the Native American congregation at the Lupine Assembly of God Church. The Lord had blessed our family ministry in that small congregation throughout the years.

My father, Benjamin Jeffreys, and my mother, Jessica, had dedicated my siblings and me to the Lord, when we were babies for God's use and service. My mother remembers that when I was a young infant I fell off the front-row pew being fast asleep, and that I continued sleeping on the floor as the church service continued. I was remarkably comfortable in the house of prayer, and I never cried whenever I would fall onto the floor.

Mother learned from the doctor that I had been born with rickets, a disease in which the bones often are soft or even bent because of a lack of vitamin D or sunlight. Mother began giving me a bone-strengthening product called bone meal, which the doctor had recommended to help strengthen my weak bones as it contained the vitamin D that my young body needed to grow a strong skeletal structure. I had difficulties with walking as well as other children my age, and my mother was concerned about the weakness this childhood ailment caused. It was difficult for me to walk until I was approximately three years old, but with the Lord's overseeing protection and the doctor's advice to use vitamin D supplements I grew into a healthy young boy.

I had a severe ear infection as a young child, and my mother prayed for me to be healed. The Lord, our healer, Jehovah Rapha, reached down His gracious hand of compassion and healed me of my ear infection. I have continued to have excellent hearing throughout the years, and I have not had a serious ear infection since that time. My caring father and mother made sure that all their children were prayed for, regardless of what ailed them at the time. As loving parents, they wanted their children to continue to have God's strong protection and divine health for their future well-being as well.

One day, the family stopped to see the nearby rapid-flowing Selway River, with its large boulders. The rushing river was capped with white water, and as the Jeffrey's family was viewing the spectacular scenery I went back to the car and crawled onto the back seat for a nap. When the family members couldn't find me anywhere they became extremely concerned that I might have fallen into the powerfully rushing water. To their surprise and relief, they returned to the car to find me resting comfortably on the back seat, without concern for the wonders of nature.

As a young boy, I took an interest in God's creation as a visible witness to nature's wonders. God's handiwork is clearly evident in the things that He has created, and I fully enjoyed His creatures. The Holy Bible tells us that we are fearfully and wonderfully made as God's marvelous creation. When I was five years old, the Scone family moved to Clover Valley, the city where I'd been born.

One warm summer day as I was catching butterflies in a vacant field about five blocks from my home, a big bully stole the butterflies from me. It didn't matter to the larger boy that I had worked patiently to catch the butterflies, and had carefully placed them in a paper-cup bucket. The big kid decided that what had belonged to me was now his to take. I was hurt by this act of aggression, but because of my smaller size I didn't offer any resistance. I hadn't learned to fight for what rightfully belonged to me.

When we first moved to Clover Valley, I slept downstairs in the basement with my brother, Daniel. One night after we were in bed I needed to go to the bathroom. Still new to the home, I made the trek up the basement stairs, turned to the right, and opened the door, ready to take aim to fire in the hole.

Unfortunately, the hole was in our living room coat closet. My mother caught me just in the nick of time and quickly took me down the hallway to the bathroom. I was still foggy from sleep, and I needed a motherly hand to lead me down the hallway to the right "thunder mug." I never had a problem with finding the bathroom after that night.

One day, I decided to catch honeybees that were buzzing around a honeysuckle bush next to our home. I was successfully catching the honeybees and placing them into a glass jar when one of them stung my arm. I removed the stinger and was willing to have another go at catching honeybees. My mother asked me what I was going to do with the honeybees. I told her that the bees were going to make honey for me and that I was going to sell it to make some money. I never did make any money by catching honeybees, although some people are successful at raising honeybees in beehives. I have enjoyed having a peanut butter and honey sandwich now and then throughout the years. Pure honey goes well with a lot of things.

During my boyhood I enjoyed having pets. My mother bought me a turtle that I liked to play with after school. I also enjoyed my multicolored parakeet that the family named, Pretty Pete. I looked forward to coming home after school and spending time trying to teach my parakeet to talk. I would talk to him in his cage and also in the bathroom in front of the mirror. I was able to teach Pretty Pete to say, "Pretty bird." Pretty Pete grew accustomed to riding around on my shoulder inside our home.

When I worked on my homework after school, Pretty Pete would fly down and land on my pencil as I worked on my assignments. Pretty Pete liked to land on the family table or on my cereal bowl, and I would keep right on eating. Pretty Pete also stood on my head, and I could sense his feet on top of my hair. One day, Pretty Pete died from the flu, and my best friend, Treat Munson, and I gave the bird a decent burial behind our family home. Treat and I placed Pretty Pete into a plastic butter container and lowered him into his grave. After covering his plastic casket with dirt, we gave Pretty Pete a three-gun salute with my Downing Rifle BB Gun. Treat then placed a cross at Pretty Pete's gravesite, symbolizing his Christian burial.

As a young boy, I discovered that I enjoyed the female gender. God had created them to become wonderful friends with young boys. I especially liked a tall girl in my first-grade class named Connie.

I decided to stop by the corner grocery store to buy some candy before going to Connie's house to see if she could come out to play with me. I spent twenty-five cents on candy at the store, which was good money to spend on a girl back in the sixties, and it bought much more candy than it would today.

I knocked at Connie's front door, and when I found out that she couldn't come out to play I walked home, eating all the candy in my sack by myself. My mother thought that I might break a tooth by biting down on the hard jawbreakers. Thank goodness I didn't break any of my teeth, but my mouth certainly got a good workout by chewing all the candy by myself.

Although I liked to play with Connie at school I never was successful at becoming her steady boyfriend. When I grew up, I came to recognize that the Lord's will for our ongoing spiritual growth is to only date Christians.

After the Sunday morning service my friends, and I liked to shoot yellow jackets with our homemade rubber-band guns. The yellow-marked hornets, flying near the upper beams of the Weeler Assembly of God Church in the Pacific Northwest were quite daring. It was risky business to shoot one of these potentially multiple-stinging insects, but we boys found the thrill to be well worth the risk. We were able to bring down one or two of them whenever we persisted at shooting our rubber bands at them. If we got tired of this activity, we would go outside and walk down to the east fork of Silver Tip Grizzly Creek to try to catch crawdads, frogs, or garter snakes.

Another activity we young boys enjoyed doing together was walking several blocks from the church to the train tracks, where we could throw rocks at the birds that were sitting on the power lines overhead. One day, I was successful at hitting one of the birds with my quick throwing arm. These were positively fun things to do in between church services on Sundays for my friends and me.

One Sunday night after church I discovered a nicely wrapped present inside the family's front screen door. When I saw it was a gift from a nice girl named Angela, I decided to return the special favor by giving her what I considered an unusual present. I placed a large bottle of Pepsi and some hard candy in an empty shoe box, and wrapped it up the best that I could. I took it up to Angela's house at night and left it next to her front door.

After I got back home, I opened Angela's gift to me and found that she had given me a Password game. I became embarrassed as I reflected upon the difference in the value of the gifts we had given each other. After school the next day, I took a classmate friend with me to the store to buy Angela a higher-priced gift to balance out the cost of our gifts to each other. My friend picked out facial powder and some perfume. As I left these additional gifts for Angela, I hoped that would finalize our gift exchange. I didn't hear anything from Angela about whether she liked or didn't like my gifts, so I concluded that I had effectively brought the gift-giving to an end.

I had a dog named Elijah that I kept chained up outside of the house. On one occasion, my best friend, Treat came over to show his new sweater to me, and Elijah jumped up and ripped a hole in the sweater with his front claws. Treat was so hurt by Elijah's excited action that he went home early for the day. Another time, the Jeffrey's family had a dog named Leakalou. The animal wet so many times as a puppy that Marlie, my sister thought we should change the dog's name to Leakalake. The dog got distemper on Christmas Eve one year, and our father took it down to the dog pound where they put the animal to sleep.

Later, I had a wonderful solid-black dog the family called Nubbin because of his short tail. Nubbin was a terrier, but he looked like a shrunken Labrador retriever with a short tail. Nubbin grew up to be lively dog, with a big heart for me. When Nubbin was a puppy, I kept him in my bedroom at night. As Nubbin grew up, although he was still small in size my mother wanted him to be chained up outdoors. Nubbin reluctantly went along with this plan, but he loved to play and be with me all the time. Nubbin was a great pet for me, and we enjoyed spending a lot of time together.

My friends and I liked to play hide-and-seek with Nubbin. We would throw a bone or a ball down the street and then run and try to hide from Nubbin. Nubbin would find the object, retrieve it in his mouth, and then diligently track down us boys whether we were hiding in a tree, behind a car, or up a telephone pole. Nubbin had excellent tracking skills and a keen sense of smell.

One day, Treat and I threw the bone down the street and quickly hightailed it behind a neighbor's house. We continued to run through two neighbors' backyards and then across the street only to make another fast run across another street, and a dash up the alley for approximately 60 feet. Treat and I then ran into a vacant lot and hid behind a storage shed. We sat down to rest from all our running, thinking that we had outsmarted and successfully hidden from Nubbin. A short time later, we saw Nubbin slowly running with his nose to the ground. When our trail ran cold, Nubbin turned around and discovered Treat and me hiding out behind the shed.

One day the Jeffrey's family went to Sam's Lake to go boating and waterskiing. I was inexperienced at waterskiing. As I put out three separate large sprays of water, I lost my balance on the skis, sending me crashing into the lake. When Nubbin saw me fall, he entered the water and began swimming out to rescue the fallen skier. My mother called out to Nubbin to come back to shore, being concerned for his safety Treat, who was an excellent swimmer, started swimming out after Nubbin.

Treat was successful in grabbing Nubbin by the tail and getting him turned around, guiding him back to the beach. Nubbin was a great swimmer, and had he been left to swim the distance to where I was in the lake, he would have succeeded in doing so. I wasn't a good swimmer as a boy, so I ended up riding in the boat back to the shoreline where the others were looking on. Nubbin was a great dog for retrieving a stick or a ball that one of my friends or I would throw out into a lake or into a slow-moving part of the Sussan or Big Rock Rivers. As I held onto my dog's short tail, Nubbin would pull me around a lake or a pond, as I lay on an inner tube or an air mattress. Nubbin was always good about lending his tail.

Nubbin was my favorite pet and he would do anything he could for me. One winter day at my request, my mother made a halter for Nubbin to wear. I was then able to hitch Nubbin to my sled to provide a ride for me. Nubbin wouldn't pull me on the sled until I walked him up to the next street and then told him to go home. When Nubbin heard the command to go home he dug his paws into the snow, and with great effort he pulled me all the way home on my sled. I loved my special dog, Nubbin; he provided faithful companionship for me as a boy.

Just like Mary and her little lamb, wherever I went, Nubbin wished to go along with me. For Nubbin's own protection and for my personal privacy, I occasionally told my dog to stay home in a stern voice. Nubbin had been trained to obey my commands to come or to stay home, whenever I told him to do so.

Nubbin provided a lot of entertainment value for my friends and me. One afternoon, the mailman sprayed Nubbin with pepper spray. When he entered our house after being sprayed, he began rubbing his eyes with his paws to get rid of the stinging spray. Daniel and a friend of his, who had protruding ears came into the house, and when Nubbin saw Daniel's friend, he fell off the couch rubbing his eyes.

Trapped By A Psycho Doctor

My friend Treat and I were home from school, and when we saw Nubbin fall off the couch rubbing his eyes, after looking at Daniel's friend, we began to laugh. Thank goodness Daniel and his friend already had gone downstairs so they weren't offended by our laughter. Eventually, the pepper spray wore off, and Nubbin was back to being a good dog again and acting like himself once more.

Nubbin discovered that whatever I liked to eat was good enough for him to eat too. I would give Nubbin a portion of bread with peanut butter on it. When Nubbin opened his mouth to take the bite of sandwich, I would clamp down on his muzzle with my hands. After lifting my hands from Nubbin's muzzle, I would stand back and watch my dog have a challenging chewing exercise. I could be a rascal to Nubbin; he was such a good dog and he didn't deserve it. At times, I would give Nubbin a Sugar Daddy sucker to chew on. As a natural consequence, Nubbin acquired a sweet tooth. My friends and I would be amused at poor Nubbin's chewing ordeals. I discovered that Nubbin was an excellent fielder of French toast, pancakes, meat, or candies that I would toss his way.

Daniel was not fond of Nubbin watching him eat at the dinner table. He felt Nubbin keenly staring at his every bite of food until finally he couldn't take it anymore. He suddenly stopped eating and said to Nubbin, "Go on, vulture." Daniel wasn't compassionate toward Nubbin. I fed Nubbin's hungry stomach daily, but unless Nubbin was completely stuffed he always seemed ready for more food. Nubbin was able to eat a lot more than we'd expect, looking at his small size.

When Nubbin was chained up outdoors at night, the paper carrier had teased him repeatedly, unknown to the Scone family. My mother finally caught the paper carrier dangling his paper bag in front of Nubbin, just out of Nubbin's reach. Jessica later stopped by the paperboy's home to have a talk with his mother and reported his actions. The paperboy had a sudden change of behavior when he delivered the paper from then on, but Nubbin's dislike for the paperboy never went away. Nubbin continued to growl and bark at him as if he could eat him alive for breakfast.

I discovered that Nubbin had a strong dislike for the mailman as well. Nubbin instinctively knew the time of day that the mailman would make his afternoon delivery to our home. One day the front door was open, and Nubbin managed to push the screen door open. He immediately went running down to get at the mail carrier, barking and growling.

With Nubbin eagerly waiting just outside the gate to the next-door neighbor's fence, the mailman saw his opportunity to settle the score with the angry dog. He decided to cure Nubbin of ever giving him a hard time again and put a stop to Nubbin's ever biting him on the leg in the future. With Nubbin angrily growling and barking in front of the gate, the mailman kicked as hard as he could into the wooden gate which should have slammed into Nubbin's face and body. But to his painful surprise, the neighbor's gate didn't move one inch under the powerful impact of the mailman's foot the gate opened by pulling it inward, not pushing it outward.

If the gate had cooperated, Nubbin could have been seriously hurt. My father talked to the mailman about trying to make friends with the dog, but the mailman said that he didn't have time to make friends with dogs.

Nubbin could be considered a wonder-dog by today's standards. He was not only my special dog; he was the best dog I ever owned. Nubbin was a dedicated, affectionate, vigorous companion and friend to me, and he was always eager to go along with whatever I wanted to do. Nubbin was considered a part of the Jeffrey's family. One summer, we traveled to South Dakota to visit the old family homestead and our relatives, who lived on a wheat farm. Nubbin had to be given sleeping pills to subdue his nervousness for him to safely travel in comfort.

To protect the car seats from Nubbin's claws, he was given rubber boots to wear. When Nubbin was let out of the car to do his business, he looked awkward, walking or running with the rubber boots on. He seemed very uncomfortable and awkward like Pluto, the cartoon character in Walt Disney animated films. Nubbin managed to survive the trip to see our relatives though, and also to see Yellowstone National Park.

I thought it was pretty neat that a bear cub left its paw print on the window of our '69 four-door Chevrolet–a souvenir for my family to show friends when we returned home. The Scone family vacation was a good one for both Nubbin and me.

My friends and I liked to look for fun and exciting things to do. Treat and I liked to watch The American Sportsman with Curt Gowdy. After watching an exciting episode about big-game hunting, Treat and I wanted to go hunting for the Scone family's pet cat, named Bo. This good black-and-white cat became our unwilling big-game mountain lion. I told Nubbin to find the cat, and Nubbin knew what I wanted him to do.

Nubbin, Treat, and I took off hunting down Bo as if we were tracking a mountain lion in the mountains of the Scone family yard, side lot, or a neighbor's yard. Nubbin acted out his natural tracking abilities and diligently led Treat and me to Bo's hiding place. Upon seeing Nubbin, Bo ran for his life. Nubbin was in hot pursuit and did a great job of getting the cat treed, just like hound dogs treeing a mountain lion. The big-game hunting experiences were exciting for us boys after watching each Sportsman program, but it was an unpleasant experience for Bo, the family's peaceful feline every time.

One night, Nubbin had a sad encounter with a skunk. While the family was outside, talking together, Nubbin went after the animal in the dark. He might have thought it was a cat, but the animal soon sprayed him, leaving him with a foul, stinking smell. When Nubbin came back home after this encounter, my mother wanted me to give Nubbin a good bath to rid him of the stench. Mother had canned fruit for years, and she told me to open a couple of jars of tomatoes that were stored in the basement and to pour them on Nubbin to get rid of the stink.

I was concerned about the horrific stench getting on my clothes when I brought Nubbin into the house I was starting the sixth grade the next day, and I didn't want to go to school smelling like a skunk. I took Nubbin into the bathroom though, turned on the bathwater, and subsequently poured a couple of large jars of tomatoes into the bathtub. I did my best to scrub Nubbin down with the tomato juice from the canned tomatoes. I hoped my dog had learned his lesson to never to mess with a skunk again.

One day, after helping to paint my grandparents' home which my mother had inherited when her parents passed away, Nubbin and I were on our way back home on foot. Nubbin and I were quickly heading for home. Unfortunately, Nubbin was hit by a truck when we were crossing the busy Cloverdale Road in the Valley. I couldn't believe this had happened to my most loyal friend. I reached down and picked up my lifeless best friend and pet, and sadly carried his body home with me. I cried deeply over the death of my favorite pet, and requested that the Lord raise him up from the dead so that I could continue to have a loving relationship with my dog.

The Lord never answered my prayer to give life back to my dog, but He would continue to be good and faithful to me in other ways. I didn't want another dog to take Nubbin's place because I knew that there wouldn't ever be a more special pet that provided such faithful, good, and loyal companionship to me as Nubbin.

I had a self-confidence derived from my multitalented family. My father, Benjamin, was a good pastor, a barber, and an excellent musician. My older brother, Daniel, was a multitalented athlete, who worked with me to improve myself as an individual athlete. Our mother said to Daniel, "You can do whatever you put your mind to." Daniel was good in baseball and basketball as a junior high athlete. He ran in track when he was in high school but only as a means to pursue his love for the sport of basketball at Clover Valley High School. In his senior year, Daniel was voted captain of the track team, and he was voted most inspirational on the varsity basketball team.

My sister Carol became a good piano player as a youth, and she was an excellent student throughout her years in school. Marlie grew up to become an excellent piano player, who played by ear. She was also a good singer and actor when entertaining people. Marlie was especially recognized for her acting role as Ernestine at the Tabernacle Church in Graniteville. I appreciated hearing Carol, Marlie, and Benjamin sing and play gospel songs together. On different occasions, my parents either would sing a duet or sing independently at Christian Churches to which we would travel when they were invited to share in gospel and song with the congregation.

I received significance in life as an individual created in the image of God. God gave me abilities and talents that I have used for God's glory. My confidence received a real boost in life when my talent of being a good baseball pitcher was consistently validated by my coach, players, and family members.

I fondly remember the Jeffrey's family playing music together and how our family's talents were used to bring honor to God in Christian Congregations. I came to realize that I had many good qualities in my personal life. I recognized that how we see ourselves is a reflection of how we look at others. I had faith in God, and I had good qualities and good friends to do things with.

My family would hold hands and start the day by saying a prayer together. I remember one of the family prayers that we would say at the dinner table:
Come, Lord Jesus, be our guest. May this day by thee be blessed.
Amen.

As a young boy, I was not totally familiar with the family prayer, and I would pray it this way: "Come, Lord Jesus, be our guest. May this day by BB blest. Amen."

Marlie said that I was purposely getting the words wrong, but since I was young, I honestly didn't know the right words. Kids can easily misjudge one another. They may not properly understand their brothers or sisters. It's easy to believe that we are always right, as seen through our own rose-colored glasses, and that's why kids say what they say to each other. A lot of times, both children and adults have their own preconceived notions and ideas about people and their personal relationships with others.

As a boy, I needed to have more knowledge, better understanding regarding life and relationships, and greater wisdom on how to deal with my personal relationships with my family and friends. I continued to grow and increase in maturity and wisdom, before God and man, with the passing years.

My character developed as a young boy, growing up in a Christian home. Whenever I heard one of my non-Christian friends take God's name in vain by using His name as a swear word, it would bother me. My friends knew I didn't swear. I was well accepted by my family and the good Christian Congregations that I attended while growing up, which placed a high premium on and respect for biblical teachings that were to be observed, according to the laws of God.

It was understood in the Jeffrey's family that God's Word was extremely important, and that

His commands, laws, and principles were not to be broken or violated. Unfortunately, today we see the tragedies of people's broken lives because they erroneously believe that they can sin, breaking God's laws with impunity, without experiencing serious consequences in their personal lives and in their bodies.

Some powerful examples of law-breaking consequences can be clearly seen in the teenage pregnancies and the Aids, alcohol, and drug abuse crises in the United States.

As The Holy Bible says, "Do not be deceived, God is not mocked: For whatever a man {and a woman} sows, that {they} will also reap; and be sure your sin will find you out" (Galatians 6:7; Numbers 32:23). There are God's laws, man's laws, and nature's laws in this present world, and we need to respect each one of them for our own good.

One Sunday, when the small congregation was seeking God at the Weeler Assembly of God Church, where my parents ministered, Pastor Benjamin Jeffrey's concluded his sermon, urging the congregation to seek the Lord Jesus for the powerful experience of the baptism of the blessed Holy Spirit. I remember seeking the Lord in the best way that I knew by the example of others who were seeking the Lord at the same time.

Everyone knelt in prayer at the altar or on the steps that led to the platform of the church. Each one called upon the name of the Lord God in earnest heartfelt prayer. I cried at the altar at the tender age of eleven. At the time, it was an emotionally sensitive and spiritual experience for me.

I discovered, however, that once I got back home, I could tell dirty stories to my friends, just as bad as the best of them. I had not experienced the big change from my time of seeking God at the altar with the other Christians which the Lord would provide for me one day during my adolescent years.

I am grateful that my father didn't pursue his idea of having a barbershop in Weeler, located in the Pacific Northwest, to generate more income, along with his pastorate, when he was considering moving the Scone family to Weeler, even though the family, as a whole, was not in favor of moving to that small logging community, rather than living in Clover Valley.

One day, Treat Munson and I were throwing rocks at an old, black cast-iron stove in the lot of the Saint Paul's Catholic School building. I bent down to pick up some more rocks to throw, and I happened to lift my head up in the line of fire as Treat hurled another rock at the old stove. I took a hard hit as the rock slammed squarely into the center of the back of my head.

As I walked home, which was several blocks away, I kept my head down because I was bleeding from the head wound. My mother told me to let her know if I began seeing double. Thank goodness, I didn't see double after the rock-throwing episode, but I recognized that I hadn't used my head when it came to throwing rocks that day. Not using my head to think about what my friend was doing at the time is not how one gets ahead in life.

I was enjoying a new bow and arrows that my mother had purchased for me when I decided to take aim at what I thought was a rat in back of Treat's home. The creature was in a sticky bush just behind the backyard fence. I could see that the little animal had stopped moving in the bush. I let go of my arrow, and wham, it struck the creature in its side, piercing it deeply.

The animal began making a crying, screeching sound of pain. I discovered, to my horror, that it wasn't a rat but a small baby rabbit. I felt bad about shooting it, and then wished I could catch it to take home as a pet.

After I removed the arrow, hoping the rabbit would recover from its wound, the little animal didn't live long. The bunny rabbit was the only animal that I killed with my bow and arrow, and I regretted killing it. I thought it was a rat, a recognized health hazard with deadly consequences in American history.

I once took my friend Treat to a Christian evangelist meeting, where David Wilkerson was preaching the gospel of Christ Jesus. I was not gloriously saved myself, being just a boy when I heard the good news about Jesus Christ, the Savior of humankind. After David Wilkerson, the mighty man of God, had preached a powerful sermon about the good news of God's wonderful plan of salvation, he invited all who would like to receive Jesus Christ into their hearts and lives to come forward during the altar call to accept the Lord.

My good friend Treat said that he didn't want to go forward, and I didn't feel like going forward myself. When I look back on that important moment in time, I recognize that I should have responded to the invitation, especially for both of our sakes. Treat did not go forward that day when David Wilkerson gave the salvation invitation and we both didn't respond to the alter call. The last time that I shared the things of Christ Jesus with my friend years later, I found that Treat's heart was cold and indifferent to the things of the Lord.

I regret not going forward with Treat for God's free gift of salvation when the Lord Jesus was knocking at his heart's door. If only we could roll back time, things could have been different for Treat and me on that golden day of opportunity.

Jesus says,

Behold, I stand at the door and knock. If anyone hears my voice and opens the door, I will come in to him and dine with him, and he with me. (Revelation 3:20)

For He says: "In an acceptable time I have heard you, And in the day of salvation I have helped you. Behold, now is the acceptable time, behold, now is the day of salvation." (2 Corinthians 6:2)

At the time of David Wilkerson's Christian evangelistic crusade, I wasn't aware of these two powerful Bible verses that could have made a difference in my best friend's life, Treat Munson, possibly receiving the gift of salvation when the opportunity of eternal choices was given by the evangelist for Christ.

May we never let an opportunity of priceless worth leave us empty of eternal treasures, chances, and values to be seized through Jesus Christ and Him Crucified.

Keep in mind that when all is said and done, only what's done for Christ Jesus during the course of a person's life will last for time and eternity. I mentioned this one day to my friend, Bud, who said, "That can only be done through our faith in the finished work of Jesus Christ on the cross of Calvary, not only for our salvation but also for daily, lifelong sanctification. This is the only place that the Holy Spirit can operate." He later cited the following scriptures to support his comment: (Romans 6:3– 14; 8:1–2), 11; (Ephesians 2:13–18); (Galatians 6:14); (1 Corinthians 1:17–18, 21, 23); (1 Corinthians 2:2); (Colossians 2:14–15); and (Jude 1–3).

Treat and I decided to experiment with smoking tobacco. Treat's father George, smoked a pipe, and Treat liked the smell of the cherry-flavored pipe smoke. His mother, Sally smoked Marlboro cigarettes. Treat took two from his mother's pack he figured she wouldn't notice that any were missing and brought them to my house so we could experiment.

I watched how Treat smoked his cigarette by inhaling. I didn't like the thought of inhaling the smoke into my lungs, partly because I didn't think it was the right thing to do and partly because I didn't want to develop the bad habit of smoking cigarettes. Still, monkey see, and monkey do I became a willing participant in experimenting with tobacco smoking. It was not a wise thing for a young Christian boy to do, and it was also not a smart thing for a healthy athlete to do. Thank goodness I learned my lesson at an early age that cigarette smoking can be hazardous to a person's health.

My father grew corn in a family garden in our side lot. My mother had a tobacco can on our back porch that had belonged to her father, Robert so we decided to use some of the tobacco from that can in our homemade corncob pipes.

Treat took the time to bore out the middle of a corncob and make a hole in the base of the cob for the pipe mouthpiece. At first, we took turns smoking from the homemade pipe. Then I decided to fill the pipe again, but when I smoked from the pipe the second time I began to feel nauseated. I went down the alley and threw up; that sickening feeling was a negative consequence of smoking tobacco. My body was telling me that smoking was not good for me. I learned a valuable lesson that day.

Unfortunately, I tried smoking cigars but gave up that nasty smoking experiment during my adolescent years. I am grateful to God that smoking didn't become a lifelong habit.

Life is a reflection of how we see ourselves; it is also true that how we see ourselves can reflect how we look at others. I had high self-esteem and self-acceptance, and I was willing to accept responsibility for my actions when I made mistakes.

When a music teacher came to my first-grade class one day I sang out with great confidence, which caught the music teacher's ear. When
I performed well, whether singing with confidence or playing baseball, and I was rewarded by others I wanted to continue the activity.

I learned the importance of having a competitive spirit in sports. Since my older brother put forth everything with the intention of excelling, I wanted to imitate and model myself after his example. When I played baseball I tried to do my very best, and the results of my pitching performances were satisfying. I later discovered that when I applied myself to my music, my studies, or playing sports I naturally reflected the talents, gifts, and abilities that God had given to me. I later discovered that my talents and abilities could positively affect other people.

When I was a young boy and looked at myself in the mirror, I thought that I was good-looking and that the opposite sex found me physically attractive as well. I spent time in front of the mirror, making different expressions with my mouth and nose, trying to find the right look to make me appear attractive to the girls at Cloverdale Elementary School.

My older sister, Carol, and her friends thought that I was a cute boy when I was young. I was a sensitive child, and when I heard that one of my brother's friends a girl didn't think that I was good-looking, it hurt my feelings. I felt rejection from the opposite sex deep inside whenever I heard a negative comment about my physical appearance. I also felt self-conscious if a male friend or even someone I didn't know personally made a critical remark about my looks. One football coach made a cutting remark, saying that I looked like a monkey. I took mental note of the coach's negative comment, but I kept on practicing on the football field with the other players.

Any hurtful comment about my appearance caused me to become more self-conscious about my looks, but God helped me to have a healthy acceptance of myself. I could act shy around others if I felt they didn't accept me, but I would be nice toward other people who I didn't find physically attractive myself. I was willing to be kind and sensitive toward the unlovely, as Jesus had done when He walked the earth.

I came to see myself as someone who was important to other people. My step-grandmother,

Elma Jane Hillers did her level best to make me believe that I was special, and she showed it by her kind feelings toward me. Elma Jane was greatly fond of me, and she always wanted to give me a slice of my favorite cherry pie each time I visited my grandparents.

I had an affectionate relationship with my mother. I liked to pat her "pod" (her belly fat) when she made eggs for me, just the way I liked them, or made French toast on the kitchen stove. I especially appreciated my mother when she made my favorite dessert, a whipped cream salad. My mother would ask me to slice the bananas or dates or grapes and have me stir the whipping cream. I liked to express my physical affection for my mother for all the good and kindhearted things she did for me.

I had my own reward system, and I knew exactly how to show my love and affection to the family members who made me feel good about myself. When I would pat my mother's pod, she would say, "Leave my fat alone. You just wait. One day you're going to be fat." I enjoyed showing affection to my mother, and she appreciated receiving it.

I played fast-pitch baseball and fast-pitch softball and was a very good pitcher. Each step of success gave me confidence that I could succeed and achieve victories in competitive sports. My successes rewarded me with a feeling of satisfaction as an individual player, as well as a team player who was seen as a positive contribution to the team. Whenever I pitched a losing game, I would take it personally, and this would cause me to reflect heavily on my own pitching performance, and what I might have done that contributed to my team's loss. I would always endeavor to pick myself up after a significant loss in order to make a positive difference in the next game.

One of the good players on the Little Aces Baseball Team was Tommy Ray, who played second base. Tommy was an infielder who was good at preventing any balls from getting past him, and he was good as a hitter as well. I once went over to Tommy's place to see the rabbits they had outside in a large cage. They had several floppy-eared rabbits that I hadn't seen before. Tommy went to Saint Paul's Catholic School in Clover Valley, so our friendship centered mostly around baseball which included playing catch together or riding together to a game or practice.

I discovered years later that my friend Tommy had gotten into trouble with the law for vandalizing cars, and he was sent to a juvenile detention center for boys. I also learned that Tommy and his sister had been abused by their alcoholic stepfather, something I never realized at the time.

I had single-minded focus on the things that interested me. I put a great deal of concentration into playing baseball. I liked to watch the Oakland Athletics, Boston Red Sox, and the Cincinnati Reds Baseball Teams on television because I liked watching good-quality pitching by some of the best major league pitchers.

I also enjoyed watching some of the best hitters go up against excellent pitching. I liked to watch Johnny Bench catch and throw out base runners with his quick releases to first, second, and third bases. I closely watched the performances of these excellent pitchers so that I could learn to emulate their pitching styles; I wanted to be successful at pitching at every level.

One summer day while I was at the Clover Valley baseball field, a friend told me that there was talk that I might be one of the best pitchers to ever come out of the local valley.

Whenever a young pitcher shows any signs of promise, some adults and young people talk about the possibility of him becoming a future sensation in the major leagues. The general rule for intelligent adults and for each young prospect who has the hope of succeeding in a particular sport is that they must not get caught up in the emotional hype of the crowd.

There are a lot of variables that are susceptible to change so we have to expect the best, wait and see, and follow each athlete's success and progress toward emerging one day as a major league ball player. I would have enjoyed playing professionally as a major league pitcher, if things had worked out in that direction.

I had a trusting nature with regard to my relationships with other people. I grew up trusting that I could trust whatever my family said to me; I could expect them to keep their word. I had a simple, childlike faith and believed that I could depend on my family to honor their promises and keep their commitments to me and to each other.

If my father told our family that we needed to get to a church service on a certain day, the family members could expect him to take us to church that day. If my mother agreed to take me to one of my baseball practices or games, I could trust that she would get me to the ball field on time. I never learned about distrust because the local valley and the surrounding area where I grew up was still largely a safe place to live. I never learned that I shouldn't trust individuals who had questionable or negative character qualities, except for a couple of isolated cases. One case dealt with the husband of my mother's friend who wanted my Christian parents to listen to demon spirits recorded on a record album. My mom told the man to take that record home or she would break it. My mother later told me that he eventually was admitted to a mental institution.

I continued to trust in the good will of humankind for the common good of fellow individuals. The Bible warns us to watch out for wolves in sheep's clothing, but I continued to have an innocent faith, trusting good people in positions of care and trust. I would one day have my innocent trust shattered by a person in a trusted position.

One night, when my sister Marlie and I went for a ride with our mother to get some skim milk for the family, Marlie and I discovered that the back seat could be pulled back so that we could crawl behind the back seat and into the trunk of our family car, a '48 Chevrolet. As we rode along in the trunk of the car our mother didn't know what had happened to us until we came out from our hiding place.

I would go with my father to the Arthers' home to pick up a gallon of milk, and Nubbin would run along on the sidewalk trying to keep up with our slow-moving car. We could hear Nubbin's claws clicking on the pavement. Years later, our family was blessed to afford a new 1959 automobile which Nubbin found was a good-running slow-moving vehicle to run alongside.

One time I wanted to show my sister Carol my blue-tailed lizard that I had found in a sandy field on the north side of Clover Valley. I was the proud owner of that blue-tailed lizard, as they are extremely rare. Carol was reading a volume of the encyclopedia in a cushioned chair when I asked her if she would like to see my lizard. She ignored me as if she hadn't heard a word I'd said to her. I asked again if she would like to see my lizard, and once again she ignored my inquiry. I was so eager to show my big sister my blue-tailed lizard that I intentionally dropped the reptile directly on top of Carol's book. Carol became hysterical with fright, and began screaming and climbing on top of the chair to get away from the lizard. I couldn't believe that she would have such a fit over a tiny creature. I just wanted to show her my blue-tailed lizard.

When I was eleven years old Carol got married to a man named Randell Wikum.Randell was a strong tall man with wavy blond hair. They had met at the Pentecostal Bible Institute in Browerland. I was heartbroken that Carol wasn't going to marry Daniel's friend Randy they had dated before Carol left for college. I cried about Carol's decision to marry a man I didn't know very well, and someone other than a personal friend of Daniel's who had become a friend to the Jeffrey's family.

Carol decided to marry Randell because he fit the image of the tall blond-haired man she had seen in her dreams. Carol told Marlie one day, "I'm marrying a real man. He's nothing like our mealy-mouthed father." Carol didn't have the healthy respect for our dad in her heart with love and honor that she ought to have had before she married Randell.

I had to get dressed up for the wedding, and then there were the family pictures that followed the wedding ceremony. After the wedding I enjoyed having punch, peanuts, and some of the wedding cake. I found that weddings could be nice to attend provided you get to enjoy the celebration with some tasty food and drinks at the reception.

I came to know Randell as an intelligent and friendly Christian man who thought pretty highly of himself, and who was gifted with many talents that God had blessed him with. I would learn a lot more about Randell a multitalented Christian man in the future.

My friend Ernest liked for me to show my physical strength by giving him piggyback rides. If I didn't show any interest in giving him a ride on my back Ernest would offer to give me money if I would give him a piggyback ride.

Ernest liked to see what he could talk me into whenever I was with him, and one day he offered to give me a dollar if I would climb up the large locust tree that was in the yard on the south side of my house. I decided to accept Ernest's offer, and I went inside the house to put on my big green coat and gloves which could protect me from the sticky thorns on my way up the tree.

Ernest pointed to the top of the tree that was the spot I had to reach in order to earn his dollar. I got less than eight feet up the trunk of the tree when I realized that my climbing adventure was definitely not worth a dollar. I decided to give up the climb, but Ernest had a good laugh as I determinedly had climbed the big tree before I changed my mind.

One day Ernest and I took turns putting on my large green coat for protection as we shot at each other with my Downing Rifle BB Gun from across the street. On the west side of the neighbor's house were several trees that Ernest and I could use to shield ourselves momentarily from the small bronze-colored BB's that we fired at each other, and each of us kept moving along from tree to tree. Ernest never hit me with one BB, and I was glad of that since I was able to swiftly move along the lawn without being hit.

When it was my turn to shoot I took aim and had perfect timing. I hit Ernest with pinpoint accuracy on the right side of my green coat. Ernest let out a sudden cry of pain as he'd taken a direct hit from the
BB. Ernest quickly realized he didn't want me to shoot at him anymore. After Ernest's turn with the BB gun, in which he was unsuccessful at hitting me with a BB, we came to a mutual agreement to stop the playing until another day.

I learned that my brother, Daniel and his friends had gotten into a BB gunfight at the Viola Cemetery. It sounded like a real shoot-out had taken place as the older boys took turns firing BBs at one another from behind trees and various tombstones or other nearby cover.

Ernest and his brother Frank and I along with our friend Joe were shooting cows with BB guns down at Willow's Packing Company. While we were intent on shooting at the cows inside the fences some men from the packing company ran toward us. We took off over the fence to escape being caught by the men only to find ourselves running right into the police who were waiting for us beyond another fence. The Clover Valley Police Officers took all our BB guns away from us for our actions. Randell Wikum, a police officer in Union, happened to be visiting the Jeffrey's family, and he saw my knees shaking as the police officer from Clover Valley talked to my mother about the cow-shooting incident.

I learned to have a healthy respect for the law during my adolescent years. I eventually realized that I needed the life-changing experience of the Lord Jesus Christ, who alone can make changes within the human heart and conscience of individuals. We need that change of heart in America again and worldwide.

I needed to get saved by faith in the grace of God extended through the precious blood of the Lord Jesus Christ to have the ongoing love and peace of God in my heart and life.

One night when I was a boy, Marlie, Daniel, and some of Daniel's friends wanted to play Spotlight outside of our house. Carol happened to be inside doing her homework on the couch.

They were having a good time playing outside, and then Marlie decided to go inside for a drink of water. As Marlie went in the front door she spotted an intruder a man with dark hair on the back porch. The intruder suddenly went out through the back-porch screen door and took off into the dark night. Marlie told Daniel and his friends about the man, and they ran after the invader on foot as fast as they could run up the alleyway searching diligently for the person who had entered our family home.

They were unsuccessful at finding the intruder that dark night, but that frightful incident put a scare into the Jeffrey's family. We knew that something sinister could have happened to Carol if Marlie hadn't gone into the house at that moment.

The Jeffrey's family believed that the good Lord had protected Carol that night when she had been vulnerable to a potential assault by an intruder. This was the other case of evil intentions that the family was aware of.

"The angel of the Lord encamps all around those who fear Him, And delivers them." (Psalm 34:7)

I was a friendly child which made it easy for me to make friends in life. When I was friendly and showed an interest in the interests and concerns of others I found that I could make a friend of that person.

I enjoyed playing with Brian when I was growing up; our families knew each other. I considered Treat Munson as my best friend among my boyhood friends. Frank and Ernest White were brothers with whom I spent a considerable amount of time over the years, and one summer day I decided to join up with the White brothers on the east side of the Sussan River.

My mother had purchased a pair of blue swim fins for me, and Frank and Ernest began teasing me about my new fins. They told me that I couldn't catch them on their inner tubes. I swam after them as fast as I could, but when I discovered that I couldn't catch my friends who were pulling away from me farther out into the Sussan River I began to swim back toward the shore.

I was not considered the greatest swimmer in the world even with my new fins on. I stopped to secure one fin that was loose, and as I looked at the shoreline it appeared so far away. I kept swimming toward the shore, but then stopped again to secure the other fin. I soon became very tired, and wondered if I might drown before I made it back to shore. Fortunately, the next time I stopped to rest I discovered that I could touch the bottom although I was still some distance from shore.

As I walked out of the river to rest on the shore my hands cramped up on me, with my thumbs curling inward. My young life had been spared physical death, and I thank the good Lord my life was spared from drowning during that dangerous incident.

I had taken swimming lessons when I was eight years old, but I didn't pass the test on the final day at the Clover Valley Swimming Pool. I was going to be tested on swimming the width of the deep end while dog paddling without reaching up to touch or grab hold of the edge of the pool. Unfortunately, I failed the swimming class because I reached up and grabbed the edge of the pool before I reached the other side. I was disappointed with myself for failing the test, but I recognized that swimming was not my forte. I didn't desire to become a world class swimmer like Mark Spitz.

I enjoyed playing in the pool anyway. One day I was having a difficult time, and was gasping for air while in the swimming pool. I was close to the edge, but the water was a little too deep for me, and I wasn't able to pull myself up and out of the dangerous situation that I was in.

Thank goodness the lifeguard realized my predicament and reached down to rescue me. God used the lifeguard at the Clover Valley swimming pool to save my life that day.

I thank the good Lord for His protective hand on my life and for His guardian angel watching over me.

There was another time when I potentially could have drowned in a swift-flowing section of the Grand River. I had traveled up the Sussan River in a car with my friends to a section of the Grand River where the current was flowing at a faster pace. I walked out from the shoreline into a shallow but swift-flowing section of the river, and I didn't perceive the real danger until I tried to get back to shore. That's when I realized that the current was pulling me back out again. This time I gave it all I could muster and quickly swam toward the shore. Thank God I was successful at reaching the shore where I could stand up and walk onto the rocks-and-sand area.

Once again my hands had cramped up, but I had escaped drowning. God had spared my life again. My parents had dedicated me to the Lord as they had with all their children, and I know that God is the divine protector of each one of His children.

I have realized that God wants to be our Savior, rescuer, and shock absorber of the hurtful things in life. God is the giver of all good things that we have, and everything that we enjoy in this life. When we recognize these wonderful truths we can rest assured that He will watch over us concerning our best interests for us and according to His perfect will for our lives.

Jonah Jon Jefferys

3

MY ADOLESCENT YEARS

I grew up in a good Christian home in Clover Valley in the Pacific Northwest. Life was not always easy for me during my adolescent years, but I can remember many positive life-changing experiences that happened in my Christian-based home that helped to develop the foundation of my character. I experienced many constructive changes, and healthy life-changing principles that would influence the direction of my life.

Although I had a good childhood I was self-conscious about my appearance even at an early age. One day my sister Marlie said to me, "Jonah, you have a great big nose and a little bitty chin with little beady eyes." The words spoken out of the blue pierced me deeply to the core of my being, and this affected my self-image during my adolescent development.

I was quick to internalize an emotional focus on my nose more than my other physical characteristics. The negative impact of the word picture planted into my subconscious by, Marlie would remain with me throughout my youth. My emotional focus on my physical attributes would overshadow my relationship with my family members.

Marlie can't recall making that comment to me; it was years later that I reminded her of the insulting remark. Now as a grown man I don't hold anything against Marlie for throwing a negative curveball at my adolescent self-image which in turn affected my self-esteem.

I was already self-conscious about my nose in particular because I had a bulbous nose but Marlie's remark caught me completely off guard. Her words brought acute focus, emotionally and mentally to my physical characteristics.

I thank God for helping me to realize that I had natural God-given abilities and talents that enabled me to rise above the negative impacts of life that could have hindered my developmental years.

My father, Benjamin Jeffreys brought home a good-looking banjo that one of his barber customers was willing to give to me provided I would practice playing the instrument. Unfortunately, I never consistently practiced playing the banjo, and I became irritated whenever my father would ask me if I had practiced that day. In time my father gave the instrument back to his customer.

It was a lot more fun for me as a young boy to play with my friends, and eventually I tried out for the baseball team. My coach and my teammates discovered that I had a strong pitching arm that was effective in striking out the opposing team's batters. I enjoyed the competition in the game, and I became pretty good at it.

I was well liked by my classmates in Cloverdale Elementary School in Clover Valley. I was a fast runner, and I enjoyed racing against a friend or competing in playground sports activities at recess. I enjoyed talking with girls on the playground too. I also earned the reputation of being a strong fighter primarily as a good wrestler who could whip his opponent.

I am grateful that I didn't get into a scrap with a stronger adversary in grade school than my good friend Frank White. Frank fought with me in his front yard, and he put all his strength into giving me a good whipping. Even considering Frank's home-turf advantage I was surprised by his strength, and how quickly he moved to get me into a strong wrestling hold that I was unable to overcome. I was determined to increase my strength by lifting a suitcase in which I'd placed a lot of books to increase its weight until I was able to purchase my own weight set. I became a strong young boy with real potential for a future in baseball.

I was a skinny boy and was known as Skinny Jonah, but as even a slender wiry boy I was strong and earned myself a good reputation among my peers. Many people were surprised that such a skinny child could accomplish the feats of strength that I could.

Marlie and I liked to play at fighting. She would fake a punch at me, and I would grab her arm while bending down to lift her up onto my shoulder. I showed my strength in front of friends or family members by spinning Marlie around as she was bent over on my shoulder.

I showed my friend Kyle Schurman that I not only was strong, but that I had swift boxing moves when we were sparring together in my backyard. Kyle and I were only in the second grade, but I was able to come at Kyle with quick jabbing speed and hard-hitting punching power until Kyle conceded that I was better than he was at boxing with gloves on.

My brother, Daniel told me that being slender had its advantages in karate, a form of martial arts. He said that someone who was wiry could hurt an opponent in a big way. I learned that when a martial artist combines speed with being wiry, and having focus he carries tremendous punching power that can cause an adversary critical damage.

Frank White, Treat Munson, and I had a tree fort in a large maple tree on the north border of our family side lot. It had a solid wood floor with plenty of space to stand up or to sit down. We decided that we needed something to sit on so we brought up a large round stump. We tied a rope securely around the heavy stump, and began to pull it up to the fort. At first Treat and I did most of the work, but as the pulling became more of a struggle Frank added his strength to the strenuous pulling on the rope. As we were intensely focused on working together pulling up our new tree-fort furniture we were unaware that the rope had wrapped itself around Frank's leg and foot.

When it became obvious that we three couldn't pull the stump up from under the front board of our tree platform we let the stump fall to the ground. The suddenly taut rope descending quickly to the ground caught Frank's leg, and flipped him up in the air and he fell to the ground.

Frank landed flat on his back. He just lay there not moving except that his left hand began to shake from the traumatic impact with the ground. Treat and I climbed down from the tree fort as fast as we could to check on our good friend. To our surprise thank God, Frank was all right with no serious injuries. My mother ended up paying for the doctor's bill when Frank went for his doctor's examination.

By my male classmates I was voted by popular vote to be first lieutenant, and number-one flag patrolman of our crosswalk guard at Cloverdale Elementary School. My friend Joe Daniels was voted as captain, and the second flag patrolman. One day while Mr. Nelson was talking with our fifth-grade class I placed my right arm into my left shirtsleeve, and my left arm into my right shirtsleeve just for something to do in the middle of class even though Mr. Nelson was sitting on my desk as he spoke to the class. Mr. Nelson liked to share stories on various topics that he thought would be of interest to us.

Then I found myself in a real predicament I wasn't able to pull my arms back into the correct shirtsleeves. Mr. Nelson saw the pickle that I had gotten myself into, and he had me get up in front of the class to show them the difficulty I was in. The class got a real kick out of my predicament that day. I got the attention of my teacher and my classmates, but I never repeated my awkward crisscross-shirt episode again in school.

Whenever Mr. Nelson found me chewing my fingernails he would put adhesive tape on my fingers to help me consciously quit the bad habit, and it did help me to be more conscientious about my nervous habit. I was able to overcome the habit after Mr. Nelson brought attention to this nervous practice.

My brother, Daniel had an effective way of helping me to remember to chew my food with my mouth closed: Daniel told me that I sounded like I was slopping hogs. I was surprised by his remark, but it had an impact on me and I became more conscientious about chewing with my mouth closed at the breakfast table.

One Saturday, Treat Munson stayed overnight so that he could go to church with me on Sunday morning. Treat had poured himself a large bowl of cereal with some cold milk. We got our milk from the Arthers, who owned milking cows. If one of their cows happened to eat something unpleasant it could affect the taste of the milk and Treat quickly detected the bad taste after one bite.

Daniel, being the big tough athlete came into the kitchen and told Treat to hold his nose and choke it down. Daniel poured himself a large bowl of cereal, took one bite with the bad-tasting breakfast milk and said, "Oh man," and he quickly removed himself from the table. Even my tough athletic big brother, Daniel couldn't handle the sickening milk that Sunday morning.

I however had eaten my small bowl of cereal with the good-tasting homogenized milk that was in the refrigerator. I didn't want to chance having the Arther's milk with my cereal.

One Saturday afternoon I went to an activity center for boys in Graniteville, across the Sussan River to check out the club, and to see what activities I might be able to take part in. I saw that the club had a ping-pong table and a gymnasium for youth to play basketball. I didn't have any friends to play with me at the time so I decided to wander down to the basement area to check it out. A large youth suddenly seized me and took me down onto a wrestling mat, and began aggressively trying to unbuckle my pants belt.

The large boy had caught me completely off guard. I felt totally defenseless and powerless against him, and I began to cry. The big bully immediately let go of me, and took off up the stairs. There had been no way for me to avoid his attack as it had caught me unaware. Fortunately, I was unharmed, and it left no lasting impact on me. I thank the good Lord for His protection against something that could have turned into something more sinister.

Daniel was an avid sports enthusiast, and he took an interest in my athletic abilities. He worked with me to help me develop my pitching skills. Daniel's friend Randy also took me under his wing; his good-sized frame provided a larger target to pitch to which made it easier to hit the catcher's glove. The pitcher's objective is to throw to the catcher's glove regardless of the size of the catcher, but as a young boy I found it was easier to throw strikes with my fast balls to a larger-sized catcher.

Peter Sanders was a quality catcher who played for another team, and he said that I was a faster pitcher than Phil Ness, one of the league's best pitchers. Peter's comment surprised me, and it boosted my confidence regarding my pitching speed.

I was riding the wave of success as an outstanding baseball pitcher when I had a disastrous experience on the pitching mound during tournament play. I was twelve years old and had just finished pitching my team to a tremendous victory over a great team, the Aware Repeats when my coach had me immediately start the next tournament game. Early in that second game I threw my arm out due to ligament and muscle strain; my coach, unfortunately had made a bad call for me. It became my last game of the baseball season, but that turned out to be a good thing because my injured arm needed plenty of time to rest from pitching.

I played basketball with a Clover Valley Elementary School team, but I was not as good a basketball player as Daniel was. One day I took the basketball down the Saint Paul's Catholic School gymnasium floor, and made a fantastic jump shot that cleared the hoop with a swish. The only problem with my perfect basket was that I had added to the other team's score.

I eventually tried out as a freshman for the Clover Valley High School basketball team, but I got cut from the tryouts. I was disappointed that I wasn't considered good enough to play on the junior varsity team, but looking back I now can understand that I lacked the fundamental skills to be a really good player or a major contributor to the team. My brother, Daniel once told me, "You can't put in what God has left out." God didn't give me the talent and skill to play basketball as He gave to other athletes such as Michael Jordan.

I also tried out for the Clover Valley High School Football Team in my freshman year, and I successfully made the team. I managed to get into one game, and the play called for me to go out for a pass. Unfortunately, I never got to touch the football. It was a night game, and although I saw the football flying into the night air I lost sight of it, and it went sailing over my head and onto the field. I wasn't the most outstanding football player anyway, and I didn't care to watch the games from the sidelines, but I continued to attend the team's practices and to watch the games as a spectator player or to talk to a friend on the sidelines during the games. I never tried out for the football team again after my freshman year as a Clover Valley Lion.

I had inherited the Jeffrey's nose as my father had from Grandfather Jeffreys. The Jeffrey's nose was definitely more prominent, and exaggerated than the nose on my mother's side of the family. From an early age I enjoyed talking with girls at school, and I discovered that certain girls took an interest in talking to me too. The girls didn't seem to have a problem with my appearance based on their interactions with me.

Daniel had taken a serious interest in sports, and he became extremely good in track and basketball. I had already become a pretty good baseball pitcher in grade school, and I continued pitching into my junior high and high school years, after my arm was healed by the Lord. Playing sports gave me a healthy perspective on life as a team player. However, I was introverted and self-conscious about my nose it was a very sensitive subject.

One day I was playing football on the Clover Valley Lions' baseball field. I called out, "Big play, big play," before the play began. In response one of my high school classmates called out, "Big nose." This insensitive remark caused me to shut down emotionally, and I remained subdued for the remainder of our football game.

I had concluded early in my life that if anyone made an unkind remark about my nose or made fun of my appearance I would not trust that person to be my friend. That became my relationship rule for life to protect myself from negative comments about my physical appearance.

My father was a conscientious pastor at the Lupine Assembly of God Church. He desired to see souls saved and for them to be filled by the blessed Holy Spirit with power. He also was a barber in Clover Valley as well as in Graniteville Suburbs to help put food on the table and meet his family's needs.

My mother worked faithfully with my father in the ministry to prepare Christians to live for the Lord Jesus Christ. My father was extremely self-conscious and introverted as a pastor of the church. It took a lot of courage for him to stand in front of the congregation to preach to and teach them.

I had my own bouts with self-consciousness about my prominent nose. I felt it was clearly visible for all to see whether I was in church, at school, or playing baseball in front of crowds of supporting fans at the various baseball fields in Clover Valley and Graniteville.

Playing baseball helped me to focus my attention on hitting the catcher's glove, and striking out the batters or allowing my fielders to throw out an advancing base runner. Since baseball is a team sport I came to realize that every player on the team had a very important role to play in helping the team to win games.

I enjoyed playing at Destiny Ville in the Pacific Northwest in the Sons of Liberty Stadium against a really good team from Justice. The baseball stadium had a wooden fence surrounding the ball field which we weren't accustomed to playing on. When I began warming up on the pitching mound I heard one of the Justice Team offer advice to the lead-off hitter saying that he needed to swing faster.

After I heard that I reared back, and began throwing even harder to the catcher's glove. I felt a strong need to demonstrate that I was a dominating fastball thrower, and I wanted to provide the opposing hitters a really big show of pure power pitching.

I pitched for three innings without giving up any runs, and then the coach called for a pitching change. Coaches had a rule they would call for a pitching change just to prevent damaging a young boy's arm during the games. First baseman Carl Davidson pitched for the last three innings of the game.

I scored on a base hit by Carl, and our team went on to win three to two. It was an exciting game to play because the opposing team's pitcher and catcher were the female coach's sons, and they were the top team from Justice.

The mighty victory built up my confidence that what I had was sufficient to help my team win big games. My good friend Bud, aka, "Brutus Knuckles" from Pardon Ville, Missouri thought the exciting developments of the game were interesting: I had pitched three innings without giving up a run; Carl, pitching the last three innings gave up two runs; and we all realized the importance of playing with intensity, healthy competition, and full dedicated consecration had taken place during that summer game which happened to turn out in my team's favor. The team had something to celebrate knowing we had defeated a great team from Justice.

We had an important game in which I was to pitch against a strong left-handed pitcher named Gene Bradshaw at the Clover Valley High School baseball field. Gene had good speed and excellent control, something that my teammates and I, the Little Aces baseball team hadn't faced before. I gave up one unfortunate hard-earned run in the first inning, and then I found myself bearing down to do my best against the Meadowlark Baseball Team during the rest of the game.

The tall lanky hard-throwing Gene Bradshaw had given up a walk to my teammate Doug Seltzer who played first base for the Little Aces. Gene was closely watching Doug moving back and forth off first base, when he glanced toward the catcher in his side wind-up position. Gene saw Doug take a large lead off the first base bag challenging Gene to pick him off first base. Doug was preparing to take off and steal second base when Gene suddenly and quickly threw to his first baseman. Doug made a valiant effort to get back to first base before he could be tagged out, but it was too late. Doug was called out by the umpire.

Doug was our only base runner in a good position to potentially score a run for us, and it was a costly out from which the Little Aces couldn't seem to recover. I went on to shut down the Meadowlark Baseball Team from scoring any more runs against me, but the one-to-nothing loss was a disappointing game that I did not want to repeat again. I hoped that my team would win the next game should the two teams play again, but I didn't like defeat which the Little Aces weren't accustomed to experiencing. I recognized there were a number of excellent pitchers playing for other teams in Clover Valley who could give the Little Aces a tough challenge on any good day.

I know that life is a reflection of how we feel about ourselves. I have discovered that our lives consist of a lot more than the abundance of things that we possess, and especially when our lives are not totally wrapped up in our physical appearance.

The world's standards for being accepted and being considered a true success in life require that we have brains, beauty, and bucks. This standard of measurement has a strong influence on our ability to get ahead in certain success-oriented businesses, political arenas, friendships and relationships, talent contests, the arts and theater, and the movies as well as whether we may get promoted to a leadership position in a good Christian Church. This is not God's standard however for the pathway to receive promotions in any walk of life. I now realize that people look at the outward appearance, but God looks at the hearts of men and women regarding their hearts and motives for their life's pursuits.

Having good character is worth a lot more than pursuing our own self-interests at the neglect and expense of others. People have their own ideas of what makes them feel good about themselves, and having good looks can help along the course of life. Adolescents who have a favorable view of their physical appearance generally have more stable self-images.

We need to have a positive attitude toward ourselves apart from our outward appearance. If you don't believe that God has smiled upon you with natural physical beauty I want to encourage you with good news: I wasn't the most physically attractive young boy according to the world's standards, but I know that God forever loves me and that He expects me to develop other talents for His eternal purposes with His help. God's love is extended to all.

I appreciated the good times that my family and I enjoyed while doing things together. We went on camping trips and went fishing. My parents were thoughtful and considerate and were willing to reward us children with good times in the great outdoors.

We went to Soteriology Lake, which is a part of the greater Truth Lake in the Pacific Northwest. I didn't fish off the dock as my father and siblings did, but I had the good experience of going out on the lake in a motorboat. My father was good at catching bass at Sunset Index on Galloping Trails Lake. Marlie and Daniel knew how to catch trout, perch, crappie, and catfish. I wasn't considered good at fishing as the rest of my family were, and I wasn't interested in spending a lot of time trying to catch fish for lunch or dinner that is for certain.

While other family members were serious about catching fish I would look for ways to have fun by throwing rocks at birds, hoping to catch a squirrel or chipmunk, or playing in the sand. Later when I was older I tried to bag a bird, squirrel, or chipmunk with my father's long-barrel Remington .22 rifle. There were a lot of ways to have fun in the great outdoors.

I enjoyed taking a friend along on our family campouts or on one of our great-outdoors outings. It was healthy fun just to get out of town on occasion and go up to the mountains or to a lake.

I enjoyed the adventure of outdoor activities with a good friend more than hanging out with the family all the time. I went huckleberry picking in the mountains which my parents had enjoyed as a traditional activity for years. I wasn't big on picking huckleberries all day on Sparrow Mountain or any of the other berry-picking sites, but I enjoyed eating the berries as well as eating the huckleberry pie that my mother would bake. I came to appreciate my mom and dad for all the things they did for my siblings and me to give us kids an appreciation and respect for God's wonderful creation in the great outdoors.

We often went to the A & W root beer stand in Clover Valley after we got home from church. We also went to the Linguini Restaurant on the outskirts of Graniteville for spaghetti and meatballs with the delicious chicken dinner a special treat for the Jeffrey's family on a Sunday afternoon after the morning service.

I enjoyed going to the Graniteville rodeo with my family to watch all the exciting rodeo events. My family also looked forward to coming home from church on Sunday evenings to watch The Fugitive on television. Our family had many good times together.

One Sunday evening after attending a Christian Church service we watched a movie about the life of Christ. I cried when I saw them crucify the Lord Jesus on the cross of Calvary. It was a tender moment for me as a young boy as I considered the power of an event that I didn't fully understand at the time. I later had a greater understanding of the magnitude of God's great love for me and for all humanity.

My family would drive up to Franklin Mountain Water Falls, north of Clover Valley to do some sledding together. This was a great winter activity that the entire family enjoyed together. We put wax on the hard metal blades of the sled and our old wooden toboggan so they would slide effortlessly down the white-blanketed sled run. I liked to get on Daniel's or my father's back to make the long run on a fast-moving sled down the snow-covered mountain road to the bottom of the hill. Then of course we would make the long trek back up to the top of our sledding slope I didn't especially appreciate that part of our sledding adventure.

During one family sledding adventure we'd built a campfire to stay warm on a cold winter's night. I wasn't paying attention to how close I was standing to the hot fire, but my mother happened to catch sight of the tips of my rubber boot being burned by the heat from the campfire. I needed someone to carefully watch out for my careless actions when I was an innocent child.

I enjoyed making the fast sled run riding on top that required each navigator to stay focused on what they were doing all the way to the bottom of the hill to have a successful sledding experience.

Life was good for me although our family was not financially well off; we weren't in the "upper crust," but I had heard that the upper crust was just a lot of crumbs stuck together with a lot of dough. Although the Jeffrey's family was not financially rich, we were rich in talents and abilities especially when it came to the family's Godly Christian Heritage. My family had Bible devotions together, followed by a time of prayer. I didn't always appreciate this as a young boy I always wanted to get our devotional time over as quickly as possible so I could get together with a friend on a Saturday morning, yet I was required to spend time with my family and God first.

I liked reading Psalm 117 as a boy because it was the shortest chapter in the Bible. My parents saw that it was necessary to honor God by having one of us read a passage from the Word of God and take the time for prayer before we left for the day. I now can see that this traditional practice to remember God and His goodness was good for the Jeffrey's family.

I appreciate that my mom and dad set a model example for us kids by reading the Bible together faithfully on a daily basis. I remember my dad had a powerful scriptural quotes and principles he had placed on the flyleaf of his Bible which read: No Bible no breakfast No Devotions no dinner No Scripture no supper. I'm forever grateful that my parents had decided to prioritize setting a high premium of reading, practicing, and living according to the Word of God and His will for their lives.

My father, Daniel, and I enjoyed watching television together. We would get a hearty laugh out of watching, The Munsters and our family members took an interest in watching The Andy Griffith Show. These shows seemed to have good wholesome family entertainment that either struck a humorous chord, had a good family theme, or had subject matter that held our interest. We had some good times of hearty laughter and got a kick out of watching the comedy programs together. My mother, Jessica shared with me that she didn't care for Deputy Barney Fife. She thought he was too much.

My father and I had a similar sense of humor which helped us bond with each other especially in my adult years. We found ourselves laughing together whether my father was giving me a haircut or we were sitting around just talking. We especially had good times as a family when we incorporated humor into our family relationships. I liked to be funny, telling jokes, and I enjoyed making my family and friends laugh every chance I got.

One day I remember we had a young man at our home in Clover Valley, and he had a very unusual type of laughter that caused me to begin laughing so hard I wet my pants outside our home listening to him laugh. His laughter was hilariously funny and bladder busting comical.

I made friends easily because I took an interest in others, and showed that I really liked being with them. I also discovered that I could get certain friends to do things with me and for me like the time that my parents wanted me to help dig out our dirt basement. I got some of my friends to help me dig and empty the dirt out of the wheelbarrow into our large side lot. I hired my friends' help for twenty-five cents an hour for a while, but eventually they grew tired of the project and decided to use their time watching television instead of helping me finish the project. They had wanted a pay raise to seventy-five cents an hour.

Daniel and I along with another hired hand my parents paid, were the only ones willing to finish the project. My mom and dad rewarded me with a brand new Kawasaki 100 motorcycle and an orange helmet for all my hard work in digging out the basement. I enjoyed riding my new motorcycle in town and also when I rode the combination-street and dirt bike on gravel roads or dirt trails up Feather Creek north of Clover Valley.

I experienced a life-changing transformation at the age of fourteen when I had a personal encounter with Jesus Christ of Nazareth through the transforming person of the Holy Spirit, the Spirit of Christ. My father and mother were between pastorates, and we began attending Clover Valley Assembly of God Church. On Sunday, Senior Pastor Neal Adams wanted the congregation to have a time of prayer before we left the church that afternoon.

Jonah Jon Jefferys

As I knelt down for a time of prayer I sensed a warm presence come over me which caused me to realize that I needed to invite Jesus Christ to come into my heart, and ask His forgiveness for my sins. My new-birth experience brought a transforming change into my life which made a wonderful difference in my thinking, actions, and personal relationship with God and with others. God had made a new person out of me, and I wanted my friends and other non-Christians to come to know Jesus as He had so marvelously revealed Himself to me.

I became excited about the things of God, and I looked forward to reading my Bible when I came home from school. I discovered that Jesus Christ had produced a newfound meaning in my life and a reason for living. I now looked forward to going to church, and sharing my faith with others at school.

Although Jesus had made a profound change in my life, not everyone at school was freely willing or wanting to come to Christ Jesus as I had. I shared my faith with a childhood friend, and I told him how God had changed my life. My friend, Sidney said that he had seen the change in my life at the pivotal moment right between eighth and ninth grade.

"You are right," I told him. "That was the exact time when Jesus wrought a wonderful change in my heart and life."

God was doing a continuous good work on my personality, and He continued to develop Godly character with habits and traits in my life and my existence would never be the same. Now I would have a friend who would stick closer to me than a brother, living in my heart and life for all eternity. My life was now marked by my Creator for God's glory and purposes.

I learned that my new life in Christ Jesus was to reflect the life and light of God to the people of the world. Jesus is the light of the world, and when He comes into a person's life He manifests Himself to that individual who willingly loves and obeys Him. He then wants that individual to reflect His divine life, and light to everyone who does not know Him in a personal way. He is not willing for anyone to be lost. He wants all to come to the knowledge of the truth in Him and the finished work of His cross.

The devil wants to extinguish the light and life of Jesus that shines out to every person who needs eternal life through Christ Jesus. Satan, the Bible says comes to steal, kill, and destroy, but Jesus Christ came that you might have life and have it more abundantly. (John 10:10 NKJV).

Unfortunately, Satan uses people to extinguish the life and light from a Christian's heart and life through all types of tactics. The Bible is the Word of God, and His glorious promises will keep us from sin or sin will keep us from walking and living in the light of His Word.

I recognize that the Lord's divine presence reaches out to people as they sincerely call upon His glorious name, in spirit and in truth. Nothing that this world has to offer can compare to eternal life in Christ Jesus our Lord. Daniel encouraged me to improve myself in baseball and other athletics. He told me about one man who was able to do six thousand push-ups which I understood to mean six thousand consecutively in a single block of time.

For a number of weeks I had been doing push-ups and sit-ups to keep myself in good physical shape, and to mentally prepare myself for the physical challenge I was thinking of participating in. I decided to work on my own physical conditioning, and one night I was able to do 395 push-ups without putting my knees down to rest. This tremendous physical feat caused me to work up a good sweat roughly within an hour because I had paused and resumed my push-ups a number of times to meet my goal. I was determined to persevere until I reached the highest number of push-ups during one single block of time.

I didn't have a professional trainer hovering over me with a stopwatch during my rigorous, challenging feat of endurance. My chest and arm muscles became larger and harder from doing the push-ups. I was interested in muscle tone and definition for my arms and chest, but I was not interested in becoming muscle-bound which might cause pitching difficulties in the future. I decided against a goal of increasing the number of push-ups I could do in an hour because I hoped to pitch for the Clover Valley High School Baseball Team someday, if I was physically capable and if everything worked out just right for me.

I had a good deal of confidence in acting in front of people. One night at the Graniteville Assembly of God Church I participated in a church play. I was able to say my lines and then pour milk on another actor's head and the audience laughed at my performance. I was delighted to know that I had pleased the audience.

One day at school I starred as a Daniel Boone–type character and put my friend over my shoulder to present myself as a mighty frontiersman who had bagged a bear. I discovered that I had God-given abilities that only needed to be developed by consistent effort.

Daniel took karate lessons, and when he competed against a martial arts opponent he decisively defeated him. He later went on to receive his master's degree in athletic administration and has become a very successful Sports Professional.

I became pretty good at ping-pong, baseball, and picking on my five-string Deering Banjo. It took a lot of practice to become good at each hobby or art.

I didn't receive the best grades in elementary, junior high, and senior high school, but I later discovered that I had a good memory for details and for memorizing dialogue. I did receive extra credit for my memory skills in college, and I received good grades while attending Union's Theology Institute.

When I read about the six ways to make people like you in the book, How to Win Friends and Influence People by Dale Carnegie it positively influenced me to reach out to a lot of people. I was motivated to make friends with good-quality people as Dale Carnegie that provided me with good tools for making friends in the right way. I wanted to reach out to others at Clover Valley High School because I had a friendly nature, and I wanted to be friendly in a positive way for the cause of Christ Jesus; I wanted to influence young people in my school to know the giver of salvation and eternal life.

I was awarded a significant honor by the high school seniors at Clover Valley High School. I give all the credit to my personal Lord and Savior, Jesus Christ for this significant award that my classmates kindly bestowed upon me. I also won a clock radio from a drawing they had at the senior prom.

One significant moment when my personal Lord and Savior helped me was during an important baseball game. I was pitching for the Granite-Clover Valley Basic Legion Baseball Team, and I barely missed the plate with a rock-solid fastball called a ball by the umpire. The pitch missed the outside corner of the plate, and I used a four-letter swear word although I said it softly so that only I could hear it. You can hear this barnyard word blared out by an angry rancher on any given day.

I was certainly disappointed with myself for not throwing the pitch across the plate. I took time to whisper a prayer to the Lord to forgive me for my momentary transgression; I was not accustomed to using profanity on the ball field or anywhere else. I played baseball with non-Christians, but I had never taken on their bad habits of using profanity whenever they were angry or frustrated by their on-the-field mistakes.

Jonah Jon Jefferys

The Lord forgave me for saying an objectionable word that day, and I have not had another problem with uttering profanity during an angry or frustrating moment since that time. God helped me to be conscious of the words that I spoke in His presence and in the presence of other people. I was a compliant and obedient child when I was growing up in the Scone family home. My parents didn't have any ongoing disciplinary problems in raising me. I had a sensitive conscience and an easy going disposition during my adolescent years.

One night our father had a talk with his four children regarding something that he was not happy about that was happening in the home. I was very young at the time so I don't remember what the issue was, but I do remember that after our father took the time to communicate his displeasure with his children he took the belt and gave Carol and Daniel a good spanking for what he felt they had done wrong.

Marlie stood up afterward and said she thought that she also deserved a spanking too. My father complied by giving her a licking with the belt as well.

I remained sitting down and never volunteered to have my bottom spanked for what my father considered bad behavior. There were times however when I needed to be disciplined for misbehavior during my growing-up years. My mother usually did the disciplining with a lilac switch to my legs in our home. She would ask me to go out and break off a lilac stem for her to use on me. I typically would pick out a thin, flimsy lilac stem, instead of a thick one that could hold up for a number of lashings. The spankings generally were short lived this way and soon forgotten without any serious lasting pain.

The comparison between my nose and my brother's nose was made evident one day by Daniel's wife, Allison when she said that my nose was "more exaggerated" than Daniel's nose. Daniel tried to soften the negative impact of her insensitive comment even though her evaluation was accurate by quickly saying that I had a better personality than he had.

I made a mental note of Allison's comment, but I never tried to counter what she said, not at the time or since.

I allowed people to say what they felt like saying about my physical characteristics, but I didn't try to retaliate by making critical remarks about their physical features. The subject matter was too emotionally charged to get into negative mudslinging about physical characteristics that God had created and that were out of my control to change anyway. I knew that my prominent nose was physically not as attractive as my brother Daniel's, but I was not constantly focused on my physical characteristics.

I had learned and adopted a saying I found in a Christian Evangel magazine as to what true optimism is: "True optimism is having the cheerful frame of mind that enables a teakettle to sing though in hot water up to its nose." I endeavored to apply a consistent positive and optimistic attitude toward life even in the face of adverse conditions, circumstances, and negative-thinking people.

Daniel had married his lovely bride, Allison when he was twenty-five years old, and he asked me to be his best man. Naturally, I agreed. As of this writing, Daniel and Allison have been married for twenty-seven years. God has blessed Daniel and Allison throughout their years in holy matrimony, and they have four talented children.

One day my girlfriend, Cindy and I planned to meet with my parents at Trout Lake, southwest of Justice. Cindy and I went into the Trout Lake Restaurant to use the restroom before meeting them. The men's room had water on the floor, and this had left moisture on the toilet seat. I laid toilet tissue on the seat before sitting down. When I came out of the bathroom I didn't realize that I had toilet tissue sticking out of my pants. I noticed how friendly everyone seemed toward me; they all had smiles on their faces, and they seemed to really enjoy having me there. One man took an interest in my inquiry about the bears that had been sighted at a specific southern point of the lake.

When Cindy and I left to go out to my car I came to the self-conscious realization that I had toilet tissue stuck to my backside, and it was sticking out of my pants. I then realized the reason why everyone had been so friendly toward me. I told Cindy, "Let's get out of here." I was too embarrassed to stay around the Trout Lake Restaurant any longer. That was one of the most embarrassing moments in my life.

My life-changing experience gave me the confidence that I needed in life. I discovered that whenever I took the time to pray about a situation that I was facing, God would come through and answer my prayers. One particular time I couldn't find my contact lens; I thought for certain it had fallen on the floor. I searched diligently and looked in all the obvious places, but it was nowhere to be found. I then asked the Lord to help me find my contact lens. I immediately got the idea to look inside my dresser drawer. My dresser top had an inch and a half or two overhang so it seemed impossible that my contact lens could have ended up in the drawer.

I decided to look in the drawer anyway, and to my great surprise there it was. Another time the Lord helped me to find my contact lens was when it fell on the sawdust-covered floor at the Crest Forest Industries Sawmill where I worked in Graniteville. The Lord was showing me that He was interested in the little things and the big things in my life.

God continued to answer my prayers, and He would continue to be faithful, good, and kind to me throughout my adolescent years.

4

FROM ADOLESCENCE TO ADULTHOOD

When I invited the Lord Jesus Christ into my heart and life at the tender age of fourteen I found that my new life in Christ was the best decision I had ever made. Jesus Christ changed me into a new creature in Christ, and I wanted my friends to come to know the one true God as I had.

I would come home with my schoolbooks in my arms only to set them aside to spend time reading The Holy Bible. The Word of God was doing a new work in my life, and this life-changing experience was making a profound difference in my relationships with others.

One important day I made a choice for Christ that forever changed my relationship with some of my good friends. Three of my good friends and I were on our way to the Lion's Den where teenagers would gather to dance while live rock bands performed on stage. Without a word to my friends I stopped before crossing Washington Street, allowing my friends to continue to the Den without me.

I had come to a crossroads in my life: I needed to leave the world's interests and activities behind me, and take a firm stand for Christ Jesus my Lord and Savior. I felt I had to take a stand for the Lord if I was going to live for God. I turned around and walked back home recognizing I had made the right decision. That decision, however strongly affected my relationship with my good friends after that they became cold toward me but I knew that I had made the right decision.

I only wish now that I'd had the good sense to communicate to my friends that I needed to go home because I didn't feel right about going to the Lion's Den that night. Even if they hadn't understood my Christ honoring decision it would have been the appropriate thing for me to do to keep my friends from cooling off toward me.

I was a young Christian, and being a teenager I didn't have the wisdom to deal with my friends in the best way when they still wanted to maintain a friendship with the world. I learned that my friends would go to beer parties at times where they had kegs of beer to drink. I didn't want to have any association with the beer drinking crowd.

My family believed in Christian traditional family values, and drinking alcohol was not part of my family's cultural experience. The Bible and my Christian Church warned me about making friendships with the world, and warned against partaking in the things of the world which included drinking alcohol in excess. I was doing my best to make wise choices to avoid the evils in the world that could be destructive to my walk with Christ.

The Bible says:

Do not be unequally yoked together with unbelievers. For what fellowship has righteousness with lawlessness? And what communion has light with darkness? And what accord has Christ with Belial? Or what part has a believer with an unbeliever? And what agreement has the temple of God with idols? For you are the temple of the living God.

As God has said:

"I will dwell in them and walk among them. I will be their God, and they shall be my people."

Therefore "Come out from among them and be separate, says the Lord. Do not touch what is unclean, and I will receive you."

"I will be a Father to you, and you shall be My sons and daughters, Says the Lord Almighty. Therefore, having these promises, beloved, let us cleanse ourselves from all filthiness of the flesh and spirit, perfecting holiness in the fear of God." (2 Corinthians 6:14–18; 7:1 NKJV)

I wanted to maintain my relationship with my Lord and Savior, and still be able to participate in wholesome activities with my friends. I wanted to be able to play baseball and ping-pong with them, play over-the-line, go bowling, or attend one or more of Daniel's Clover Valley Lions Basketball Games. I enjoyed playing miniature golf and tennis and getting together for bites to eat with friends.

Another activity I participated in was scuba diving with my friend, Kevin and his dad in the Rock Bass River. We also did some scuba diving together across from the Crest Forest Industries Mill in Graniteville. I once reached out to touch a large fish in the Rock Bass River, when it made a sudden turn and came right at us. Kevin began to laugh, and he needed to make a quick rise to the surface as I witnessed the large creature seemingly on the attack. I then realized it was trying to escape from possibly becoming our dinner.

When my friends and I wanted to get together for good times the key word was brazos. I had learned that call word for coming together for something important from watching the movie The Over-the-Hill Gang, in which retired Texas Rangers all now senior citizens come together to clean up a town run by a crooked mayor.

Kevin, David, Scott, and I saw our getting together as something important with a lot of fun times. Our getting together was exciting and something we looked forward to because we had something significant to do. My three friends and I were talented athletes, and we all played together on the Clover Valley High School Baseball Team. Being involved in sports had helped to bring about our friendship.

I remained friendly with my good friends, although I wasn't as close with them as I had been before my Christian conversion. The Lord had brought about a significant change for the better in my heart and life, and as I continued to grow in the grace and knowledge of the Lord Jesus Christ, God continued to help me through the good times and the difficult times that I faced in life.

One summer Kevin, David, Scott, and I decided to camp out at Buck State Park. We enjoyed having dinner together around a cozy campfire, followed by playing cards inside the tent with Kevin's kerosene lantern providing good lighting for our game. The four of us had a good time being together.

The following day after having cereal for breakfast, Kevin and I decided to build a rock pathway across Feather Creek by dropping rocks into the swift-flowing water. I positioned my hard-toed boots securely on a rock that was sticking up in the creek, put my hands out, and gave Kevin the go-ahead to pass me the rock. When he did it slipped through my hands and landed squarely on my right foot. The hard-toed boot didn't protect me when the rock slammed down.

I suddenly felt intense pain in my right foot like I had never felt before. I walked right through the creek not caring about getting wet, and sat down on some smaller rocks on the creek bed. The pain in my foot was intense, and I suddenly felt like throwing up. David asked if I wanted him to build a fire, but I didn't care about having a fire built for me. I threw up on the rocks from the sheer trauma of my painful experience.

I saw Kevin and David smiling about the situation my friends didn't know the agonizing pain I was in. David and Scott helped to carry me back to the tent where I was able to get some sleep. We had no pain medication on the campout, but sleep helped to relieve my pain. I was awakened by the sound of my three friends rolling rocks down the hill into Feather Creek. When it came time to leave the park my friends took turns, two at a time, crossing their arms together to provide a seat to carry me down the gravel road. They had carried me for less than a quarter of a mile when a truck stopped and gave us a ride to Kevin's house.

We were blessed to have been given a ride at that crucial time. My foot was seriously hurt, and without the truck driver's help I might not have been able to get back home.

Upon arriving at Kevin's house I finally removed my boot and sock, and I saw that my foot and toes were swollen and black and blue. Kevin's dad gave me a ride home which I appreciated.

A doctor later x-rayed my right foot and said that I had broken my big toe, and the two toes next to it were fractured with hairline cracks. I had to use crutches for a while, but I eventually recovered without needing a cast on my foot. I am grateful that I don't have any residual pain from that rock-dropping incident at Feather Creek.

I am grateful for my good friends who took the time to help a friend in need. When my big toe was broken on that unfortunate day I was in a world of hurt. I appreciated having friends who cared that I was hurting. I learned by firsthand experience that a friend who helps a friend in need is a good friend indeed.

The powerful evangelist Dwayne Friend strongly influenced my walk with Christ when I was a young believer. I would come home after a Sunday night Church service to find my father watching Dwayne Friend preaching a sermon on television. My life was positively influenced by the powerful teaching of this spiritually stimulating Christian evangelist.

One day my parents drove over to Newtown to hear Dwayne Friend preach an exciting sermon at an evangelistic crusade. The next day I was able to go with my parents to hear the Christian evangelist myself, and to enjoy the powerful crusade service. After the wonderful service I had the golden opportunity to talk with Dwayne Friend who shared with me how to walk with Christ. He said that God had a million doors for me to walk through, and if I found those doors I would truly know what life was about. My personal encounter with Dwayne Friend made a profound difference in my life for years to come.

At age fifteen, I felt that the Lord had given me a pastor's heart. I cared about people's souls and their eternal destinies. The Bible tells us that Jesus saw people as sheep without a shepherd, needing salvation. I realize that human souls need a spiritual guide to lead them safely through this life, and I see that the Lord Jesus Christ is the good Shepherd. Through the power of the Holy Spirit He wants to protect us from all harmful predators in this life.

Christians need to guard their hearts and govern their lives for the Lord's work. People, like sheep, are easily led astray by ravenous wolves disguised as sheep. Good Christians can be misled by the big bad wolf which doesn't care about the sheep or their individual interests.

The family united acts as a shelter, a shield, and a protection for each family member from the wolves in the world who want to hurt the sheep for their own selfish interests and pursuits.

I would like to keep people from being hurt, used, and abused by individuals who are under the control of the evil one. We all must stay alert to the wolves that diligently look for souls who are alone and without protection.

When I was fifteen Kevin, David, Scott, and I decided to go swimming in the Clover Valley swimming pool late at night. The swimming pool had been closed for hours when we climbed over the wire fence that surrounded the pool area. We all took off our clothes I put my underwear and socks in a brown paper sack and then we all swam for a good amount of time. When we'd had enough of swimming on that warm summer night, we climbed back over the fence and walked together across the Clover Valley baseball and football fields.

We crossed over Franklin Street and entered Abe Lincoln Park doing our best to stay out of sight from any vehicles' headlights. We were about halfway into the city park when we saw a car coming up the alley on the south side of the park. We tried to avoid being spotted, but when we saw the vehicle make a sudden turn we knew that we had been detected by the occupants in the fast-moving automobile.

David and I ran as fast as we could across the park, across 5th Avenue, and into the driveway of Marvel's Funeral Home. Kevin and Scott jumped over a concrete wall into the yard of a home on the south side of the funeral home. David and I saw that the car was heading in the our direction, and we ran as fast as we could and run through Marvel's Funeral Home parking lot, and then quickly turning south up the alley. With every turn that we made the car with its bright headlights and noisy muffler came speeding right behind us.

We were looking for a backyard that we could dash into, but we only saw the backs of fences all along the narrow alley. David finally managed to find an opening into a backyard, but with the fast car hot on my heels I decided to wait to see who was in the car and wondering who had taken such an interest in me. When I turned around I saw it was a Clover Valley police car that had pursued us.

The police officer wanted to check my paper sack which still contained my underwear and socks. As I was detained by the officer my friends watched me through the fences in the alley. I got a free ride in the police car to the Clover Valley Police Station for breaking curfew as a minor. When my father was contacted to pick up his delinquent son at the police department he had been sleeping in his comfortable bed. He signed the release papers and drove me back to our home. On the way home my dad was pretty cool about the whole thing. When he saw another vehicle pulled over by a police car with flashing lights he said, "Don't they have anything better to do?"

As an adult I discovered that not all was well in the Jeffrey's family even after I had gloriously met the Lord. I learned that, Randell Wikum my sister Carol's husband had molested my sister Marlie when she was just a teenager. Marlie didn't know how to deal with the horrible pain and guilt from Randell's molestation. She began acting out sinful behaviors in her relationships with the men she dated. Marlie also got involved with drugs and alcohol as a teenager, and there were many times when she didn't go to school.

Daniel thought Marlie was faking being ill when she would stay home from school so often. He didn't know that Marlie had been horribly hurt by Randell.

I observed Marlie's different behaviors and attitude, but being a teenager myself I didn't realize that the best thing that I could do for her was to pray for her to be set free and healed by Christ Jesus, and to have others continue to pray that the Lord would make a significant difference in her life. She also needed the tender, healing touch of our gracious Lord Jesus Christ in her heart, mind, and emotions.

Years later I learned that Randell considered himself to be a self-made man and thought pretty highly of himself. Randell also considered himself to be God's gift to women. Throughout his marriage to Carol he was an unfaithful philanderer, and had affairs with different women. Randell had even tried to seduce Daniel's wife, Allison early in their marriage. I never knew the specific details of what Randell had done, but Allison had felt uncomfortable by his actions and words. Randell was a charmer with the ladies, and he was worldly-wise in how to win women for his own self interests.

Randell served four years with the navy, and during his military service he boxed in the ring with some hard-hitting servicemen. Randell served on the Union Police force for a number of years, and he graduated with a four-year degree from the Pentecostal Bible Institute in Browerland. One day when the Scone family had said the Lord's Prayer together while holding hands Randell turned, and punched Daniel forcefully on the shoulder. It caught Daniel completely off guard, but he knew better than to try for a payback with a solid punch of his own. Daniel respected Randell for his marriage to Carol, his intelligence, and his physical abilities.

Randell had demonstrated his physical prowess and had let Daniel know he had powerful physical strength. Randell could have been trying to shake off any Holy Spirit conviction of his sinful ways while the family held hands and said the Lord's Prayer together.

When Randell made his choice to sexually molest Marlie whether he realized it or not he made a choice for his and Marlie's spiritual deaths before the Lord.
God says,
"I call heaven and earth as witnesses against you, that I have set before you life and death, blessing and cursing; therefore choose life, that both you and your descendants may live; that you may love the Lord your God, that you may obey His voice, and that you may cling to Him, for He is your life and the length of your days; and that you may dwell in the land the Lord swore to your fathers, to Abraham, Isaac, Jacob, to give them." (Deuteronomy 30:19–20)

Death in the biblical sense means separation from God. Only the blood of Jesus Christ can take our sins away, and provide us with a way of having a new relationship with the living Lord God.

When Randell chose spiritual death for Marlie and himself, I chose life for myself with the one true God of heaven and earth as revealed in The Holy Bible.

I had respected my brother-in-law Randell during my adolescent years, and I'd looked up to him with admiration as a role model. I discovered years later that Randell had been a philanderer with other women during his marriage to Carol, but I wasn't aware of it at the time.

My family kept many things quiet as many families do when they don't know how to deal with certain family members who act out with unusual behaviors that are not recognized as Christian or normal behaviors. Many families may end up destroying the reputation of family and other associations they are acquainted with. They can gossip and slander at will. The Book of Proverbs and James Chapter 3 has many things to say about the unruly power of the tongue that is set on fire by hell. (James 3:5-6 NKJV)

Carol kept their faults from the family's attention because she was hoping that things would change for the better. She also was trying to honor the Lord by fulfilling her marriage vows before God, and she hoped to keep their marriage together by weathering the storms as a married couple. In many Christian families we assume that individual family members who have personal or relationship problems need to come to the end of themselves in order to allow Christ Jesus to take charge of their personal lives.

Coming to the end of themselves may take some Christian's years because many of us think we can make it by ourselves, and that we don't need the help of God and others who serve as guides along the course of life's journey.

Eventually Carol felt the release from the Heavenly Father to divorce her unfaithful husband, and with the passing of time choose to marry a faithful Christian man. Her marriage to Roberto Carlos is much more stable.

Randell made a crucial mistake as a Christian by getting his eyes on people instead of keeping his eyes steadfastly on Christ Jesus. Jesus is called the Author and Finisher of our Christian faith. Many believers succumb to taking their eyes off of the One who can calm the seas of our lives, and they fasten their eyes on other Christians who profess Christ Jesus as Savior and Lord. When they see other Christians make crucial mistakes or sin before God they then lose faith in living the Christian faith with confidence and faith in God's Word as the Manuel and Standard for Christian Living and Life's Principals.

Randell may have used other Christians' unfaithfulness as an excuse to pursue his own sinful course of following after the flesh by finding lonely, vulnerable, and lustful women. Randell had become another poor example of Christians who fail the Lord Jesus by loving the things that are of the world's system.

Randell should have been circumspect in his Christian walk before the Lord by watching out for the following:

"Do not love the world or the things in the world. If anyone loves the world, the love of the Father is not in him. For all that is in the world the lust of the flesh, the lust of the eyes, and the pride of life is not of the Father but is of the world." (1 John 2:15–16 NKJV)

Randell would find the door to repentance at times for his sinful ways, but then would go back to his wayward living again and again. He needed to learn to rely on the Lord, and the help of good Christian men who could hold him accountable for his actions on a consistent basis. There are far too many inconsistent Christians in the Christian Church today.

I have discovered that walking with the Lord in purity is the sure road to holiness which is the only way to life and power with God. Jesus said, "Blessed are the pure in heart, For they shall see God" (Matthew 5:8 NKJV).

I wish my brother-in-law Randell could have laid hold of eternal life and the righteous principles of Jesus Christ. A lot of Christians have good intentions of living out their Christian walk with Christ Jesus, but when temptations come knocking at their heart's door they flirt with the temptations which leads to spiritual disaster and the shipwreck of their faith in God.

The Lord's solution is spoken eloquently in Psalm (119:11), which says, "Your word I have hidden in my heart, That I might not sin against You." The way to repentance requires turning from sin and its evil ways.

Solomon says, "He who covers his sins will not prosper, But whoever confesses and forsakes them will have mercy." (Proverbs 28:13 NKJV).

(Isaiah 55:7) says, "Let the wicked forsake his way, and the unrighteous man his thoughts;

Let him return to the Lord, And He will have mercy on him; And to our God, For He will abundantly pardon."

The apostle Paul writing to Timothy says, "Nevertheless the solid foundation of God stands, having this seal: 'The Lord knows them that are His,' and, 'Let everyone who names the name of Christ depart from iniquity" (2 Timothy 2:19 NKJV)

The Christian believer who is lured into the web of carnal thinking according to the world's practices must learn to reject evil imaginations. "But each one is tempted when he is drawn away by his own desires and enticed." (James 1:14 NKJV). God also says, "I beseech you therefore, brethren, by the mercies of God, that you present your bodies a living sacrifice, holy, acceptable to God, which is your reasonable service. And do not be conformed to this world, but be transformed by the renewing of your mind, that you may prove what is that good and acceptable and perfect will of God." (Romans 12: 1-2 NKJV).

The best way to overcome persistent sexual thoughts and temptations is to recognize the following:

"For though we walk in the flesh, we do not war according to the flesh. For the weapons of our warfare are not carnal but mighty in God for pulling down strongholds, casting down arguments and every high thing that exalts itself against the knowledge of God, bringing every thought into captivity to the obedience of Christ." (2 Corinthians 10:3– 5 NKJV)

A fleshly thought may enter a Christian's mind once in a while or he or she may be bombarded with sexual thoughts, but it is imperative to cast those thoughts down and bring any carnal thinking into obedience to Christ. We can't prevent a bird from flying over our heads, but we can prevent the bird from building a nest in our hair. Christians must learn to prevent the world's way of thinking from building a nest in our thought life. Learning to exchange the fleshly thoughts of the world for the thoughts that God wants us to have must be a priority to every believer who wants to live a successful Christian life.

The Bible says,

"Finally, brethren, whatever things are true, whatever things are noble, whatever things are just, whatever things are pure, whatever things are lovely, whatever things are of good report, if there is any virtue and if there is anything praise worthy meditate on these things." (Philippians 4:8 NKJV)

One day I had a good talk with my father about my two older sisters' relationship. He had thought that by taking his kids to church they would change by having the Word of God applied to their lives in church. He didn't realize that each Christian principle and all applicable teachings from the Word of God needed to be applied to their lives just as he had taken the time to apply the Word of God to his personal life. This neglected and necessary Bible instruction had created relationship problems for my sisters later in life.

Many Christian families assume that merely going to church will change their lives so that they become the beautiful people that God wants them to be. They assume that everything will change naturally for the better and that the Bible will become their life-changing manual for every decision they make. Instead, individual Christians must learn to apply the Word of God to whatever situation they face in life in order to bring about the necessary changes that they expect, want, and need to happen in their lives. The Lord Jesus tells the unconverted, "Do not marvel that I said unto you, You must be born again."(John 3:7 NKJV)

God has only good things in mind for those of us who are willing to surrender to Him and His will for our lives. The Lord checks our hearts to see what may be hindering and holding us back from being the kind of persons that He wants us to be. God wants to mold our individual Christian lives into vessels of honor that He can use to be a blessing to others in need. When we allow Christ Jesus to sit on the throne of our hearts, God can then direct our relationships and our personal paths in the way that we should go.

We must learn to acknowledge, surrender, and submit our lives and relationships to the Lord before He can direct our lives. We also must learn to apply the Word of God to the situations we face and to our relationships in life.

I have learned from firsthand experience that things go better with Christ Jesus at the center of my personal life and relationships. Christ Jesus has made the difference in my life, and I would like to see every reader enjoy the benefits of having a consistent personal relationship with Christ Jesus, our Lord and Savior.

One-day Carol and Randell drove over for a visit with the Jeffrey's family. Randell was sitting in the family's comfortable cushioned chair, intently reading a book. I walked out from the kitchen with a small glass of water, and I poured it on Randell's head as a joke, and then quickly dashed into the bathroom and locked the door behind me.

After Randell tried the doorknob to the bathroom I could hear him moving around in my bedroom closet which had an adjoining wall with the bathroom. I thought that Randell was trying to get at me by coming through the bathroom wall from my bedroom closet.

When I couldn't hear any more stirring in my closet I sneaked out of the bathroom to see what my brother-in-law had been doing in my bedroom closet. To my surprise Randell had taken my clothes off the clothing rod and dropped them on the floor. I was not a happy camper to say the least, and I decided to pay Randell back with a mischievous favor of my own.

I looked in the kitchen cupboard and found a box of lime Jell-O mix and some ketchup. I went outside to Randell and Carol's brand-new car, and I poured the green Jell-O granules and the tomato ketchup onto the windshield. (I hadn't put the Jell-O mix and ketchup on the car's painted surface for good reason.)

When I went back inside the house, Randell grabbed my hands in his large left hand while he tried to spray hair spray into my face. I was moving my head back and forth desperately trying to dodge the sticky hair spray. I was successful in preventing Randell from spraying my face and I pulled myself free from his strong grip, but I then discovered that I wasn't prepared for everything that Randell had in store for me.

Randell went outside to my car and sprayed the hair spray onto the windows of my bronze metallic two-door Honda Civic. Randell also let the air out of two tires flattening both of them. When I discovered what Randell had done to my tires, and the windows of my car I definitely was not pleased. My feud with Randell escalated until my mother and Carol called for me to stop. They hadn't called for Randell to stop his dirty actions against me. As a teenage Christian I was unhappy with Randell's malicious actions, but I reluctantly ended my ongoing battle with him.

I had learned a hard lesson in life: that certain individuals are determined not to permit you to get one up on them, and they will do their level best to defeat you in whatever situation you may compete with them. Certain people are not willing to play fair according to the rules of the game and commonly understood boundaries of respect in relationships and human decency. Certain people are intentionally willing to hurt you. If you are not careful and on your guard, they will try to prove that they can top whatever you did or said to them. I learned the difference between a prank payback and someone doing something against you that is beyond an equal response which is way over the top when it comes to payback.

One day after I had successfully pitched my Graniteville-Clover Valley Basic Legion Baseball Team to an exciting victory in Graniteville, I decided to go on a camping trip with my friends up Feather Creek. I had previously talked with my friend Bradly Franklyn about them going to an off-the-road camping area in the woods. I planned to meet up with my friends who would be waiting for me up the creek after the game. I was looking forward to making the trip on my Kawasaki Motorcycle to spend the night in the great outdoors. I drove home after my team's win in my mother's celery-colored Rambler to load up my backpack with everything that I thought I might need for our outdoor one-day vacation.

I put my sleeping bag on the handlebars of my Kawasaki 100 Motorcycle as the character Jim Bronson would have done in the television program Then Came Bronson. Then I put on my backpack with my camping necessities. I made certain that I had a good working flashlight with me before making the long trip to the campsite.

As I was riding up the Feather Creek asphalt road my headlight suddenly went out on my bike. Even with my burned-out headlight however, I was determined to continue the long journey with the aid of my trusty flashlight. Since my Kawasaki Motorcycle was a clutch-operated five-speed heavy bike, I had to accelerate the throttle with my right hand while I shone my flashlight with my left hand allowing me to maintain my position toward the center of the roadway to avoid running off the road or having a collision with the ditch or barbed wire fence.

I made steady headway until I left the paved road and drove onto the gravel section of the Feather Creek Road. I then discovered that my method of riding slowly, steadily, and ever so cautiously on the loose shifting gravel was not as swift as my progress on the paved roadway. I tried holding the flashlight in my mouth to light my course in the dark sections of small stones and pebbles on the roadway, but my jaws got tired. I decided that it was in my best interest to stop my bike riding periodically to give myself and my jaws a break from holding my flashlight in my mouth.

Although it was a long journey and an ordeal riding through the night, I made it to the dirt turnoff that would lead me to the location where my friends were camping. The good Lord was with me as I rode on into the night on the dirt trail hoping to eventually meet up with my friends enjoying their campout. I came to the place on the dirt road where there was a large metal fence, and I was unclear on what to do at this point.

There hadn't been good communication before my ball game as to my friends' exact camping location. I couldn't see any signs of them, but I didn't realize that I needed to go through the fenced area and over a small hill on the dirt trail to reach the area where they were. Unfortunately, I wasn't aware that they were camping just beyond the fence junction area. I stopped my bike and called out to my friends, but I didn't hear a response. The stillness of the night was interrupted only by the sounds of the nearby Feather Creek. It was a spooky situation for me with Feather Creek making its flowing-water noise over the rocks as I steadily passed its banks that led through the mountain region. The large looming trees and the surrounding darkness gave me a foreboding, and I didn't feel like hanging around there any longer. I got back on my motorcycle and rode to a pull-off area close to Feather Creek and off the dirt trail thinking I would possibly camp out by myself on a picnic table for the night.

As I rode up to the wooded picnic area in the dark night I shone my flashlight on a large-eyed creature that was sitting on the picnic bench. I became frightened when the creature didn't move one inch when I aimed my flashlight at it. Its large eyes shone brightly back at me, but it didn't move toward me or run away to escape. Something was amiss here.

As I held my flashlight steady I suddenly realized that the seemingly wild animal unwilling to budge from the picnic table was only two pop cans close together. I decided to leave this potential campout area because of my personal encounter with a seemingly frightful creature; the spooky situation had heightened my imagination to the fears of the unknown in the great outdoors.

I rode back down to Buck State Park to stay there for the night. I had camped out with some friends at the park before, and now that I was getting tired I thought it was a good time to get some sleep under a covered shelter. When I turned off my motorcycle I could hear an animal barking in the pitch dark night air. I didn't know if I might meet up with a coyote or a wolf that might be in the area. I called out for the wild animal to get out of there; the fact that I could not see the creature that was making the noise had brought a fear of the unknown and unseen in the dark night.

Suddenly I heard a voice call out, "You get out of here!" I wasn't about to stay there for the night and possibly have to face people who told me to leave. I rode my bike back out to the gravel road, and I headed for my home in Clover Valley. I eventually made it back home by early in the morning when it was still dark out, and I knew that the good Lord had been with me during my challenging adventure.

God protected me from serious harm another time when I was riding on the gravel road of Feather Creek Road on my motorcycle with my friend Ernest sitting behind me. I had been showing Ernest just how good a bike rider I was by accelerating on the road and taking the turns with precision. I was doing a good job up to a certain point. I saw that I needed to slow down to make a right turn, but I was going too fast for the road conditions. My motorcycle began to slide in the gravel as I applied my front and rear brakes. As we fishtailed in the loose gravel on the heavy bike we found ourselves heading toward the opposite shoulder of the road and nearing the drop-off edge.

I brought my Kawasaki to a stop, but to my deep regret Ernest had burned his bare leg on the hot tailpipe. I was truly sorry that my friend got hurt on that unfortunate day, but the situation could have been much worse we might have fallen over the edge of the road on my heavy motorbike. I did not act as a wise teenager with a passenger aboard, and certainly I was not conservative in practicing safety on a precarious gravel road.

I placed a high premium on baseball in my teenage life. I believed by faith that the Lord had healed my pitching arm which I had hurt when I was twelve. Pastor Neal Adams prayed for my arm to be healed from the injury I experienced during a baseball tournament. I accepted that my arm had been healed by the Lord when Pastor Adams prayed for it to be healed. I was chosen to be on the fifteen-year-old all-star team as a pitcher. My teammates and I had the golden opportunity to fly to Inspiration River, Missouri to play in a baseball tournament. While I was in Inspiration River I discovered that baseball great, Tom Seaver had pitched in a similar tournament when he was fifteen years old.

I was extremely disappointed when I wasn't chosen to start the first game, and I cried tears of disappointment over what I perceived as a failed promise by one of the coaches. I was called on to start the second game, but to my chagrin, I had a poor pitching performance, which resulted in my all-star team suffering a major loss.

Sometime later, I heard that another pitcher on our team had said that the team would have won the tournament if he had pitched that important game. I would like to tell all my all-star players

Jonah Jon Jefferys

who may have had similar sentiments that I am sincerely sorry that my pitching performance resulted in our team's loss. I only wish that the other pitcher, Marvin Barnes could have pitched the game in my place and that he would have won the game for his teammates.

I was watching YouTube Videos one day MLB Greatest Throws of All Time, and it caused me to remember a one bounce perfect throw I made from right field to our catcher who tagged out the advancing base runner heading full steam for home plate. I had been relieved as the pitcher in the big game that led to a mighty victory over a highly talented team, Mountain Top Grizzly's. My perfect strike throw from right field to our all-star catcher, Calvin Colfax was a major contribution that allowed me to advance to the 15 year old all-star team. It also was a big win for our great and very talented team.

I discovered that Ping-Pong was a great game to play competitively as an intense, healthy, active sport. When I was in Inspiration River for the all-star baseball tournament my roommate and I went over to a home where some of the other team members were staying, and some people there were playing Ping-Pong. I hadn't played the game before.

When I flew back home after the baseball tournament I introduced the game to my friend Dale Andrews, who was willing to go to the Clover Valley Assembly of God Church where they had a Ping-Pong table in the basement.

Since baseball season was over I really enjoyed playing Ping-Pong with Dale after school as often as we could play. I started to develop into a good amateur Ping-Pong player; I had a quick backhand and was able to keep a consistent volley of play going against some competitive players. I have liked healthy competition in sports as a participant and as a spectator. I discovered that Ping-Pong was a great game to work up a sweat, and I could consistently improve my level of play with a lot of practice.

I played against Pastor Adams of the Clover Valley Assembly of God. He would hold the Ping-Pong paddle between his index and middle fingers, and by doing so he could apply some good English spins of the Ping-Pong ball which I couldn't counter at first to keep the ball on the table. When Pastor Adams served a ball with a good spin on it the ball would veer off my paddle and away from the table and onto the floor. Pastor Adams consistently gave me a good cleaning in Ping-Pong, but I was determined to practice until I could defeat him.

I kept practicing positioning my Ping-Pong paddle in ways that I was able to keep the ball in play. After a lot of practice I not only could compete against very talented players, but I also won a number of the games in which I competed. I have to admit though that I ran up against some top-caliber Ping-Pong opponents who I was never able to defeat no matter the number of games I played against them. I have played plenty of Ping-Pong over the years, and I still enjoy a good game whenever I find time to play.

I have played Ping-Pong as an adult against some excellent and highly skilled Ping-Pong players. I could hold my own against some good players who worked with me at the William County Carrier Company. As a shuttle bus operator I was part of a team of shuttle drivers. Operators were responsible for driving their assigned routes during their shifts which were in the morning, the afternoon, or the evening. Shuttle drivers (also called carrier operators) could choose the shifts they wanted to work, and we could make good money in any given week. It all depended on how motivated we were, how much money we were satisfied with earning, and the hours we were willing to put in each day.

I played against an excellent player named Millard Judson, who told me that he was once the

Northwest Junior Champ in Ping-Pong. He gave me a nice compliment by telling me that of all the competition he had faced with the carrier company I was the best player that he had played against. Millard could come from behind whenever I had the upper hand in the game and find a way to defeat me in Ping-Pong every time. Although Millard consistently won even when I sometimes had the lead, I was determined to continue playing against him hoping to find a way to defeat him.

One day a young man who was on my shuttle carrier told me that his picture was on a magazine because he was the third-ranked Ping-Pong player in the United States. When I heard his exciting news I offered to play Ping-Pong with him sometime I wanted the opportunity to play against one of the top players in the United States. He was interested in my challenge, but the Ping-Pong match never took place because he was busy attending Country City College.

I continued to have a strong interest in pitching baseball. I was good at it, but I came into a period when I struggled with my pitching control. As a teenager with pitching potential, and having control problems was a major disappointment for me. I had helped my baseball teams win many games over the years which had left me feeling emotionally confident with my peers. I didn't need this difficult struggle with my pitching control.

Teenagers will experience struggles, challenges, and disappointments, but it can become a very difficult time in a teenager's development when his or her disappointments become an ongoing problem. It is important for a person's mental and emotional health to overcome disappointments, challenges, struggles, and personal setbacks.

My Clover Valley Junior Varsity High School Coach, Hank Sheen once put the blame squarely on my shoulders for the team's loss of an important game. The coach suggested that I had intentionally lost the game by throwing the wrong pitch to the batter who then made the winning hit for the opposing team.

I didn't think it was all my fault; baseball is a team sport. I can see now however from the coach's perspective that my ineffective pitching caused our team to give the opposing team the advantage of scoring more base runs than we had.

I thought that the coach was out of line in his hot-tempered attitude toward me as well as with his critical remarks and his evaluation that I had blown a significant game. I was wounded when he expressed this opinion in front of the team, and I was embarrassed by losing face before my teammates.

I was silent as my coach railed at me with his angry, disrespectful, and demeaning attitude. It became obvious to me that Coach Sheen needed someone to blame for the team's defeat, and so he picked me. Some coaches take the game so personally that during their outbursts, though often brief, they lose touch with the more sensitive players on the team.

As a consequence of Coach Sheen's excessively critical remarks to me that day I lost respect for him for the rest of the baseball season. I continued to pitch to the best of my God-given abilities however, and I lettered in my Junior and Senior years of High School. I wish I could have been more of a contributing pitching force to my High School Baseball Team, The Clover Valley Lions in my Junior and Senior Years, and the team did go on to win the State Championship. The Clover Valley Lions Team was loaded with talented ballplayers and each one in his own right could proclaim, It's Hard To Be Humble When You're As Great As I Am. My parents had given me a wooden plaque with the above quote.

I wasn't satisfied with my pitching performance during my junior and senior years so I decided against pursuing a college scholarship in sports. Coach Finney had told me that he could get me a college baseball scholarship, but at the time I no longer had the heart that I once had for the great game of baseball. I felt that I needed to take some time after graduation to decide what direction my life should take.

God had good things in store for me, and I needed to find the open doors that the Lord had in mind for me. I discovered that there were wonderful things in life outside of sports.

My Graniteville-Clover Valley Basic Legion Baseball Coach, Bob Benson shared an interesting story with the players during one of our baseball practices. Bob Benson had played for the legendary great Legion Baseball Coach Tom Redmond when he was only thirteen years old. Tom Redmond coached many great-quality and talented baseball players for years as the head coach of the Graniteville-Clover Valley A Legion Baseball Team.

Bob had gone to Montana for a baseball tournament, where he watched an eighteen-year-old pitching to a batting cage. Bob said the kid's pitches kept missing the screened cage used for batting practice. He then told us that the eighteen-year-old kid was Sandy Koufax, who was having control problems when he played legion ball. Sandy Koufax went on to be one of the legendary great baseball pitchers of all time once he was able to solve his control difficulties.

This story clearly shows that if a person is willing to persevere through adversity he can look forward to bigger, better, and greater things in his pursuit of the good things in life and possibly see his dreams fulfilled.

I got the call from Coach Bob, telling me that I would pitch against Gary Holland and the Carltonville Bulldogs. Gary was a tall, hard-throwing, fastball hurler from Carltonville with excellent pitching skills and good control. He had a full head of long hair that stuck out from the sides and back of his ball cap.

Gary threw consistent high heat against the Graniteville-Clover Valley Basic Legion Team; then it was my turn to bat. I stepped up to the plate only to go down on three straight fastballs from Gary. The balls looked like aspirin tablets as they sailed across the plate and into the catcher's glove. I looked like a blind man looking for a black cat in a dark room that wasn't there. My hitting abilities were simply no match against Gary's superior pitching skills.

My teammates put up a hearty hitting scrimmage against Gary with a number of strike-outs, but we couldn't put together a string of hits to produce any runs, and Gary and his team defeated the Graniteville-Clover Valley Basic Legion Baseball Team that day five to nothing. My teammates and I were simply not fierce enough competition against this future major league pitcher.

During the game one of my teammates, Darrin Redmond reprimanded me for the lack of faith I was demonstrating as our team was not making any progress against Gary Holland. I knew that Darrin was telling me the truth about my comments and my attitude which revealed my discouragement in the face of our lack of success against Gary.

I was surprised by Darrin's truthful evaluation that I lacked a winning mind-set which had clearly diminished us against such a fierce pitching opponent as Gary. Although we lost the game it was a good lesson for me to remember: that no matter what the game, situation, or score might be, it's important to maintain a winning psychological attitude and believe that your team can make a comeback to win the game in the end. With God, all things are possible to those who believe. Hopefully your team will have a better outing the next time you face a new or same pitcher, provided you put in a lot of practice and have good talented ball players.

I discovered years later that Gary had gone on to pitch professionally in the major leagues he'd been drafted by the California Angels with a ninety-five-mile-an-hour fastball. Gary was a naturally gifted all-around talented athlete, and I thought it was pretty neat that I had the opportunity to pitch against a future major league pitcher.

One of my classmates, Glen Sims had crumpled up a gospel tract that I had handed to him, and he threw it on the floor as a demonstration of his defiance against my Christian witnessing. Glen did pick it up as if he were merely kidding, but it was probably an outward manifestation of his disgust for my consistent sharing of my faith with others whenever I had an open door to witness.

Dwayne Friend was a bold, powerful, lay-it-on-the-line, and tell-it-like-it-is evangelist for Jesus Christ. He had tremendous influence on my Christian witnessing for Christ Jesus. I desired to witness for my Lord and Savior, Jesus Christ in the hope of leading lost souls to the Lord so I also became willing to reach out to others for Jesus as Dwayne did by sharing my faith with people. An effective method of reaching others for Christ was by handing out gospel tracts. The good news of how people could be saved from their sins, invite Jesus into their hearts, and have eternal life by believing on the Lamb of God, Jesus Christ was clearly communicated in each gospel tract I handed to a prospect for Christ.

I wasn't intimidated by the rejection of the good news of salvation presented and being clearly explained in each gospel tract I would hand out.

One day I handed a gospel tract titled, "Holy Joe" to Brad Allen one of my classmates and Brad said, "You're just like him," implying that I was a similar type of a witness for Jesus Christ as Holy Joe was in the gospel tract. I accepted that as a compliment of my consistently living a righteous and godly Christian life and as a witness for Christ, of which the world needs to see more of. There are far too many inconsistent Christians in the Christian body of Christ today.

I liked to imitate and memorize certain things that Dwayne Friend said in his evangelistic crusades. Dwayne was an effective communicator for Christ Jesus during his soul-saving meetings in which he used catchy phrases and sayings to capture the attention of the audience. The following are some of his sayings:

"The man who testifies for God by the yard but lives for him by the inch ought to be kicked by the foot." "If talking were effective, there are scores and scores of men who would move a mountain off its base and move it back again. But as a language stated true and blunt, they're never worth a dime to lift 'cause all they do is grunt."

"Some Christians' faces are so long they look like a Missouri mule." [This referred to believers in Christ Jesus who didn't manifest the joy of the Lord on their faces but chose to reveal a sour and sullen

Christian appearance as a gloomy witness for the Lord.]

"Their tongues are so long you could roll a biscuit on it." "My brother Harold sings higher than a hawk's nest."

A powerful saying that Dwayne Friend used in one of his sermons was this: "Do you know that God can't use you until you admit that you're not worth a dime? When you finally admit it, God can use your life." I have remembered that great truth in my own personal life in wanting to be a witness for the Lord and in my approach with God throughout the years. Dwayne once shared about a man named Jim, who had heard some singing coming from a church on a cold winter night. Jim went into the church that night to listen to the singing, and he returned the next day.

The pastor was in his study when he saw Jim walk down the aisle to kneel in prayer at the

altar. While kneeling Jim said, "Jesus, this is Jim."
That's all Jim said. He then got up and walked out of the church.

Dwayne said that Jim got hit by a truck after he left the church, and his body sailed through the air and landed against some rocks. Jim was taken to the hospital in bad shape. The pastor of the church heard that Jim was in the hospital, and he went in to see him.

As the pastor stood near Jim he heard a voice say, "Jim, this is Jesus. I've come to heal you." Jesus healed Jim, and Jim went into the ministry.
I was touched, spiritually and emotionally by Jim's wonderful story.

The next Wednesday night I decided to share Jim's story that Jesus had healed Jim and that he had gone into the ministry with the small congregation at the Clover Valley Assembly of God Church.

As I shared the incredible story with the people in attendance that night I got emotional and began to cry. The blessed Holy Spirit was working in my heart and life as a teenager, and I was having a difficult time telling this emotionally moving story to the people.

God used Dwayne Friend's story of Jim to do something special, spiritually and emotionally, in my young Christian life. God is so good, kind, and loving to those who love Him and to the people who are willing to place their faith in Him and His finished work on the cross of Calvary. One night I drove out of state to attend a Tabernacle Christian Church service.

They had a guest speaker who shared that God had helped him and the men in his special frogmen military operation during the war against German soldiers, who were occupying a concrete fortress. The man of God had a fascinating story; that he told in detail of how God had protected him during this special operation which caught the occupying German soldiers by surprise.

After the special speaker had shared his incredible story of the events that had taken place in the dark of night I saw that this man of God was truly a man of tremendous prayer with power. I thought how great it would be to be an effective man of God like this man was. It was obvious that he knew how to get results through his prayers on behalf of their military operation which had been carried out with great success. I was impressed by the wonderful story of how God had protected this precious man of God and his men during a time of war.

On another night when I attended the Tabernacle Church the pastor did something unusual which took me by surprise. Pastor Cliff Flores pointed to me, and asked me to come forward to the front of the church as the congregation looked on.

When I stepped out into the aisle I felt the presence of the Lord meet me there before I walked forward. Once I stepped out in obedience to the calling of the man of God, the Spirit of the Lord met me in the aisle. It was surprising to me to immediately feel God's presence there, and the Spirit of God came over me before I walked to the front of the church.

Before I stepped out in obedience to the call of God, Pastor Flores said he could spiritually visualize the calling on my life. God was preparing me for the work of the ministry in whatever direction that would take. I remembered that kids at school had told me that I was going to be a preacher.

When I shared my faith with my friends, and others I was doing the work of the ministry even if I wasn't officially preaching, teaching, or ministering behind a pulpit in front of a Christian Congregation.

My good friend Jay LeBlanc invited me to go deer hunting with him. We drove from Clover Valley, up the Sussan River to hunt in the surrounding hills in the Grand River area. Since Jay had a hunting rifle with a scope I decided to leave all the shooting for him so he could bag himself a qualified deer, and one that would meet the standards of the fish and game department. Although Jay and I hiked over a number of hills that Saturday we didn't see any deer. We decided to give up hunting for the day and headed back down the Grand River road keeping an eye out for any deer sightings along the way.

Suddenly I spotted what I thought was a mountain lion on the side of the hill across from the Grand River. As we got closer to the area where I'd seen the big cat roaming the hillside, Jay recognized that the animal wasn't a mountain lion at all it was a woolly sheep with a big long tail that hadn't been cut off by its owner. I wasn't experienced at distinguishing species of large game to hunt nor was I an Eagle Scout able to spot big game for Jay. Jay recognized my inexperience at hunting, and he had himself a good laugh over my inaccurate sighting.

After Marlie had her second child, a boy named Garth she asked me if I would babysit him one day, and as his uncle I willingly agreed. After I'd been watching Garth for a while he needed his diaper changed. I wasn't the most experienced diaper changer in the world, but I was willing to do my best to make things more comfortable for my baby nephew. I laid Garth down on a newspaper, and changed his diaper the best that I could my hands were inexperienced at handling the safety pins for his cloth diaper. Finally Garth was good to go.

After Marlie returned she changed Garth's diaper, and she later told me that Garth had newsprint imprinted on his butt! (It must have made for some interesting reading.) I didn't know that laying Garth down on a newspaper for his diaper change would result in leaving behind incriminating evidence of that I had changed my nephew's wet diaper. I have come to realize that many things turn out for good in the end in more ways than one.

When Garth was a young child Marlie brought him over to our family home so we could babysit him while she ran errands. Garth was a cute little boy who would have baby boo-boos and then. That particular day Garth fell hard on the linoleum floor in the living room, and I knew it was painful by his vocal reaction. Rather than focusing on Garth's injury however which could have caused him to cry even more I focused my attention on the floor, and acted concerned that it might be damaged from Garth's fall this was to deflect Garth's focus away from his pain. I walked over to the area he had fallen, and I got down to examine the floor as if I was making sure that he hadn't left a dent in the floor.

When Garth saw me checking on whether the floor was all right he suddenly stopped crying and made his own inspection of the linoleum flooring. After Garth was sure that the floor wasn't damaged from his great fall he was ready to enjoy bigger things and better times as he explored and made new discoveries in the Jeffrey's Family Home.

When Marlie had her third child she named him Travis. He provided a lot of humorous times for their household. Travis liked to watch Tarzan on television, and one day he made an interesting comment to Marlie that caused her to laugh. Travis had watched enough of the Tarzan movies for him to conclude that something was missing from his jungle life and activities. He wondered aloud why Tarzan never went to the bathroom.

Had I been there when young Travis made his humorous observation I might have said that Tarzan probably knew how to hold it. Young Travis might not have understood the witty comeback, but it might have brought forth a laugh from the others who were watching.

One Sunday church service Travis heard, "Jesus lives big in your heart and life." When he saw a 350-pound woman named Shelley Moore who attended their church he said to her, "Shelley, I know why you're so big. It's because Jesus lives big in your heart and life." He stretched his arms out wide.

I played with Garth and Travis over the years as they were growing up. We had good times playing baseball, tennis, and board games like Monopoly and taking them out for fast food at McDonald's or to the Igloo Burgers for a tasty hamburger, French fries, and an ice-cold drink or milkshake. My two young nephews and niece, and I always took time to thank the Lord for the good food He provided for us to eat.

One Sunday afternoon I had a negative encounter with my father. I was seated on the left side of the kitchen table closer to my father. My mother and my dad were seated at the opposite ends of the table. I no longer remember exactly what I said, but I made a negative remark about my dad in front of him. I had picked up on a critical spirit that Mother had toward him, and I expressed that same critical spirit toward my father. He stood up and wanted to discipline me for my critical attitude.

I wasn't aware of it at the time, but I had dishonored my father by the negative remark I had made about him. My father tried to hold both of my hands while he tried to slap me in the face.

I was now a strong seventeen-year-old athlete who had lifted weights growing up, and I shoved my father away from me in anger and told him to leave me alone. He recognized the power in my shove, and he backed down from trying to discipline me. I left the kitchen area, and I went to my room where I had a good cry over what had just taken place with my dad.

I had a rude awakening when I realized that my father didn't appreciate my negative fault-finding attitude. I recognized that I was in the wrong. I later apologized for what I had said to my dad that Sunday afternoon.

The next day when I came home from school I asked my mother why she was bucking dad all the time. I had done a lot of thinking about Sunday's negative encounter with my father, and I was looking for an answer as to why I might be picking up on a critical spirit from her about my dad. I was still a young Christian, and I needed to grow up more spiritually in my relationship toward my father as a seventeen-year-old teenager.

Mother shared that she had seen a next-door neighbor mistreat his wife, and mother was determined that she wouldn't submit herself to any man in her life. Mother had decided to take that stand when she was only nine years old, and it had manifested itself through her having a critical spirit now as a married woman. I didn't understand everything that she said after the Sunday incident with my dad, but I woke up to the fact that my attitude toward my father needed to change for the better and especially for the Lord's sake.

I needed to have the right attitude toward my dad, and the Lord helped me to see that I needed to have a God-honoring relationship with the Lord and my father. Dad and I seemed to relate better as I grew in my understanding of the ways of the Lord and my walk with Him.

Thank the Lord that I never had another bad attitude toward my dad after that day.

I attended a Future Living class when I was going to Clover Valley High School in my senior year. My teacher, Judith Dempsy showed the class a film of a woman giving birth. As I watched the film I became queasy at the sight of blood and felt light-headed. I put my head down because I felt like I was going to faint. I never did like the sight of blood nor the sight of my own blood.

When I was in Junior High School I once felt faint during physical health class as I watched a film of a man having his chest cut open during surgery for cancer. When I saw the blood and the black cancer cells inside the man's chest I got light-headed and felt like I was going to faint. I had a sensitive nature when it came to the sight of blood that other people didn't seem to have.

In an earlier time while I was attending Jefferson Middle High School in Clover Valley I cut out a pen holder using a jigsaw blade in wood shop. One of my classmates, Tim Dickson wasn't as confident about using the jigsaw machine, but I was willing to help out a fellow classmate. I began to push the wooden board toward the thin saw blade with my left thumb. I wasn't paying attention to how close my thumb was to the blade, and suddenly I felt the jigsaw blade cutting into the tip of my thumb. I quickly pulled my hand away and tightly wrapped my fingers around my thumb. When I saw the blood on my hand from the cut I moved quickly over to my workbench to sit down on the floor.

When my teacher, Mr. Rogers saw me sitting on the floor and leaning back against the workbench feeling faint because of my bloody thumb he thought it was hilarious. I wasn't amused by Mr. Roger's attitude toward my cut thumb.

I am grateful that the tip of my thumb wasn't completely cut off in that incident, but I still have a scar on my thumb as evidence of my carelessness with the jigsaw blade in woodshop class. I didn't jig fast enough when the jig was up.

5

THE ADULT YEARS

After I graduated from Clover Valley High School I applied for summer work at Bridge Port City Foods. I was hired on as a combine operator working in the pea harvest for $3.25 an hour.

My co-workers and I would drive combines to harvest peas in large fields working a twelve-hour shift from sundown to sunrise.

I came home one morning after riding my combine. The combines had automatic levelers that helped the combines to adjust to going up and down hills, and when a combine operator was harvesting peas on the sides of the hills.

I ran my bathwater and sat down in the tub to enjoy a good bath to clean off all the dirt and dust from the pea fields. When I sat down though it seemed like the tub was moving around me. It took a while for my mind and body to adjust to sitting in the bathtub, and to realize that I was no longer riding my combine with the levelers. The motion of driving the combine all night was recorded and felt in my mind. It took me a short while to regain my mental senses and land legs.

One night when the weather was extremely cold I took my lunch break, and hovered close to the large combine engine to keep warm. It was summer, but it felt more like a cold winter night to me. One summer I was assigned to drive a swather a farm implement that cuts small grain crops for the pea harvest. Driving the swather was a lot faster than a combine for harvesting the peas. If someone was good at swathing he could take a rest as the combines kept operating at a much slower pace.

Once the pea harvest came to an end my two friends, Brett Roberts and Shawn Anderson and I decided to go on an ocean-fishing trip. Brett had been on the Pacific Ocean on a number of occasions, but Shawn and I had not. We rented an eighteen-foot runabout and headed out of the inlet of La Push, Washington to the wide-open sea hoping to land a big king or silver salmon. Brett asked the skipper of a charter boat how things were on the ocean that day. The skipper said, "Kicker boats are coming in, but I think it's all right to go out."

Brett had more knowledge of the ocean so he was the skipper, and Shawn who had driven a boat on the Sussan River and on some lakes before became the driver of our fast-running vessel.

Shawn seemed confident as he ran the boat in the inlet, but when we were ready to leave the harbor and enter the blue ocean waters a large wave came directly at us and Shawn said, "Oh, jazz."

Our boat went up into the air as we collided with the huge wave, and Shawn immediately pulled back on the engine throttle to slow our speed. Wave after wave kept coming at us and pushed our boat back toward the rocks behind us.

Brett called out, "Give it more throttle!" We needed to move away from the rocks before we were shipwrecked. Shawn gave the boat more throttle thrust to move us out into the house-sized waves, and we were on our way out to sea.

We went out on the mighty Pacific Ocean in what Brett later described as the worst weather he'd ever experienced. The large waves had whitecaps, and when we went up with one wave we saw a large cargo ship off in a distance; when we went down with a huge wave we could see nothing but sky and surrounding waves. This was my first time being on the high seas, and I vomited from all the rocking and rolling with the swelling waves.

We three amigos were determined to catch some salmon, and we kept at it. I caught a salmon, but it bit the line and disappeared into the vast waters.

After fishing for some time we decided to call it quits for a while, and head back in for a break from dealing with the powerful ocean.

Back on land I had a drink of water, and a chocolate candy bar that seemed to hit the spot. I no longer had a queasy stomach from the rolling waves; rather I was ready to go out fishing again. After an hour of break time on land we went back out on the mounting ocean waters again to do some more fishing.

My father had a plaque in the basement that read: The Angler's Prayer

Lord, give me a fish so big that even I, in the telling of it afterward, may never need to lie.

Brett, Shawn, and I hoped to catch a number of good-sized salmon that we would be proud to show the family and that would make for good eating around the dinner table.

My dad told me about a time when he and Mother had gone on a campout with Carol, and Randell and they had gone fishing. Dad caught a large rainbow trout that he was quite proud of. He brought it back to their campsite, and placed the big fish in a pail of water to keep it fresh. He then went into the tent to take a nap which he always liked to do after his fishing labors.

Later when he went to look for his fourteen-inch trout it was nowhere to be found. When he asked Randell about it Randell just patted his stomach and said, "It made for some good eating."

My father was not pleased with his son-in-law; he'd planned to bring the large rainbow trout home to show off his successful fishing to family, neighbors, and friends. Now he couldn't show off his prize fish to anyone thanks to Randell.

I let my fishing line out a long distance behind the fishing boat. I wasn't an experienced salmon fisherman, but I was up for being a good sport about reeling in a large fish that would make for some good eating later.

I caught another salmon on my hook, and this time Brett who was a much more experienced fisherman than I was took control of my pole to ensure that this salmon would not get away. When the salmon was up to the back of the boat Shawn reached down and caught the large fish in his net.

It turned out that I caught the only silver salmon that day. After fishing for what seemed like hours I threw up again. As before I put my head down as Shawn navigated the eighteen-foot runabout back toward land for the final time.

As we headed back Shawn drove rather quickly doing a good job of staying out in front of a good-sized wave that was directly behind the boat. When Shawn turned the boat sideways to make his turn into the harbor however a large wave almost capsized the boat. God was with us that day as we made the long trip back home. We had shared about a near misfortune broadsided by a big wave, but we finally were back on land again and praise the Lord we were.

That fall I applied for employment at the Crest Forest Industries which is now Timberland Forest Industries. I didn't have to wait long before being called in for an interview. I was hired and began work at The Sawmill Plant located in west Graniteville. I soon found that I didn't care for the tough working conditions at The Sawmill, and I decided to quit after only a few weeks of employment.

After working at the mill I worked with Brett for a short time putting cedar shakes on people's roofs. It was getting colder in Clover Valley, and I didn't want to continue working with Brett outdoors.

I was out of work for the rest of the year, but since I was still living at home with my parents I wasn't too concerned about being unemployed. The following year I reapplied at the Crest Forest Industries Sawmill Plant. I was grateful that I was given another opportunity to work there. I discovered that it was better being employed, working hard, and making money than being unemployed and broke.

I made good money at The Sawmill, and I was able to purchase my first car. I was able to make large payments toward my new bronze-metallic, two-door Honda Civic. I chose the car for its sporty look, and I liked having a clutch four-speed vehicle to drive to work and get around town.

God blessed me as I continued to live at home with my parents, work at The Sawmill, and attend the Clover Valley Assembly of God Church.

My friend Jay LeBlanc called me one day and told me about a Christian woman who he said was "just like you." Jay was incredibly impressed with this special Christian lady who worked at the Clover Valley Care Center with him, and he just knew his co-worker Olivia Knutson and I should meet.

Jay encouraged me to give Olivia a call as soon possible he had checked with Olivia to see if it was all right for me to call her, and she had agreed.

Olivia and I had a good conversation over the phone before we went out on our first date.

I soon discovered that I really liked Olivia's sweet personality, and I liked spending time with her. I enjoyed playing miniature golf with her which was next to the bowling alley in Cloverland.I also enjoyed taking Olivia to Wanpa Lake in Idaho, and going to her First Protestant Tabernacle in Clover Valley to see a Christian film called The Rapture. I was falling in love with this pretty brunette Christian woman. As Olivia and I were getting to know one another that summer she told me that she was going to attend a NW Protestant Institute in another state. I was saddened by the news of her leaving, but I was encouraged that she was still interested in communicating with me via letters and phone calls.

Jay recognized that I was thinking a lot about Olivia after she went away to the Christian Institute. Olivia also thought about me during her absence, and she invited me to come down to see her; she made me think she had missed me.

Jay was willing to make the long trip with me from Clover Valley to Peaceful, Oregon. After Jay and I arrived at the institute Olivia wanted me to meet with a conservative Protestant leader, Lenny Myers who was convinced that the baptism of the Holy Spirit with the evidence of speaking in other tongues was not for believers today.

I had spoken in tongues before, and I believed that the gift of tongues was for us today.

I listened carefully to what Lenny Myers had to say about his personal experience of speaking in tongues. He didn't believe it was real even though he told me that he had spoken in tongues at a Christian gathering. Lenny didn't experience the power that comes with speaking in other tongues as Jesus had promised to His disciples. It is understandable that Lenny may have doubted his experience when he found himself speaking in tongues or he already had preconceived ideas passed onto him that the baptism in the Holy Spirit has passed away and no longer for today's followers and believers in the power of God with the initial evidence of speaking in other tongues.

Lenny probably was expecting sudden power and immediate wonders to come pouring into him at that very moment of speaking in tongues, and because he had preconceived teachings thrust into him from an earlier age he refused to accept and believe in the second work of grace experience that Jesus Christ is the baptizer and this glorious experience is for today.

I disagreed with Lenny, but I didn't think it was my place to convince him that what the Bible says about speaking in tongues "God says, 'For the promise is to you and to your children, and to all who are afar off, as many as the Lord our God shall call'" means exactly that God is willing to give to all Christian believers who are open to His free gift (Acts 2:38–39).

Olivia had been influenced by Protestant leaders like Lenny and teachers of her classes at the Protestant Institute. She concluded that there was a major difference between her Protestant faith that speaking in tongues was not for today and what my Pentecostal-believing Assembly of God Church believed in.

I saw signs in Olivia's attitude toward my beliefs, and by the things she said to me it was clear that things were cooling off in our relationship.
"How can two walk together except they are in agreement?" (Amos 3:3)
Olivia, Jay, and I went on a drive together to an urban center in
Oregon that revealed how Olivia honestly felt about her relationship with me. During the course of our drive in Jay's truck, Olivia told Jay that he was cute and that she had always felt that he was handsome. She had made it perfectly clear that she didn't think that I was handsome, and when I heard her words to Jay it was very obvious to me that she didn't love me from the heart. I rode along with Jay and Olivia quietly listening to the sweet talk Olivia giving Jay while she conspicuously neglected any kind words toward me. I was hurt by the special treatment Olivia gave to Jay, and I felt that she was being disrespectful of my love for her.

The words spoken sweetly to Jay by the person I thought was my girlfriend, and who supposedly loved me were a clear indication that Olivia's heart wasn't fixed on me. Olivia had given me an open invitation to come down to NW Protestant Institute, but she clearly did not truly love me.

The trip to see Olivia was a painful one for me, but it helped me to see the obvious: that my relationship with her was not worth pursuing. Olivia made it clear that she wanted me to change my position of believing in the baptism of the Holy Spirit with the initial evidence of speaking in other tongues if I wanted to keep the relationship doors open with her. I decided not to break tradition with the Pentecostal belief of speaking in other tongues with the power of the Holy Spirit as was experienced by the disciples of Jesus Christ in the upper room in (Acts 2:4).

I realized that there were more fish in the sea than just Olivia Knutson.

When I graduated from Clover Valley High School my family watched the ceremony from the stands. It was a good graduation ceremony, and all my classmates managed to get through it in an orderly formal manner.

Jonah Jon Jefferys

After the graduation the Scone family had a picture taken with me the graduate. Once my mother had the pictures developed I was interested in taking a close look at the graduation picture to see how I looked in the photo. In particular, I closely examined how my nose appeared in the graduation picture did it appear too large, prominent, and noticeably conspicuous? If I noticed my nose, then I knew that others who saw the picture would see my bulbous-tip nose as well.

I did the same thing with all my pictures growing up and as an adult. Ever since I was in Cloverdale Elementary School I was quick to notice what my nose looked like in each individual picture and every family photo. I wanted to know if my nose looked good in the picture.

Each time that I thought my nose was too conspicuous to overlook in a family picture it caused me to become self-conscious once more. I was keenly aware that my nose was larger than most peoples' noses, and this made me feel insecure and self-conscious about my physical appearance.

My sensitivity regarding my nose would be a lifelong struggle, and I would need God's grace to sustain me throughout the years.

When I was attending Jefferson Middle School in Clover Valley my science teacher Albert Scoggins brought colored eggs to our class. He placed them in warm incubators for them to hatch as our science experiment. Later when the eggs hatched I brought home two pink baby chicks. I took an interest in raising the little chicks until I was able to give them away to the Arthers who already had chickens.

I would go out in the night to catch night crawlers to feed to my chicks. They loved to eat all the large worms, chicken feed, and bugs that I fed them until their chests would swell up like balloons.

I had my own Farmer John experience raising the chicks into full-grown chickens, and it was an interesting and good experience at that.

One day my mother took a picture of me with a baby chick on each of my shoulders, my black dog Nubbin sitting on my left side yawning, and the family's black-and-white cat, Bo lying on his back and cradled in my arms.

It turned out to be quite a colorful picture of me being close to my animals wearing my blue high-water pants. After the picture was developed I wanted to see what my nose looked like in the picture. Once again I was emotionally discouraged when I saw that my bulbous nose stood out as the most embarrassingly noticeable physical feature; this caused more self-conscious sensitivity to grow inside of me.

I hadn't yet progressed in my Christian faith in the finished work of the cross of Christ Jesus when I was in my eighth-grade science class, but I would continue to be sensitive about my physical features even after I became a genuine born-again Christian.

I later learned that God was using my physical characteristics to build character qualities in me that only He could create for my good. God's ways and purposes are not our ways, but He knows what it requires to produce good character in each of His children for His glory.

When I was working at the Crest Forest Industries Sawmill in Graniteville I was injured on the job. I was using a long push bar that looked like a metal rocket to push a large log that wasn't moving on the sawmill deck toward the cutoff saw.

I lifted the heavy push bar which had a bent metal prong underneath it into the stationary chain, and positioned in a steel sleeve on the deck. Once I had the push bar ready for the deck operator to move the chains the sudden thrust of the chain below me caused the push bar to twist, and I lost control of the torpedo-shaped push bar.

I quickly reacted and caught the falling push bar, but without thinking what I was doing my right index finger got caught between the push bar and the steel sleeve that housed the steel chain. I quickly moved around the deck reacting to the acute pain in my finger.

My lead man, Edward Eastlund took me over to the restroom to run cold water over my painful cut finger. Then he planned to take me down to the first-aid department so a nurse could bandage my finger.

Edward thought that I was all right after my injury, but to my surprise and his as I slowly walked to the restroom doorway I fainted from the traumatic experience of having cold water flow over my injured finger, and from seeing my own blood oozing from my finger.

Edward revived me from fainting, and assisted me down to the first-aid department. After the caring nurse bandaged my finger I was ready to resume my work on the sawmill deck.

I still carry the scar on my index finger which has the appearance of a fingernail trying to grow through the skin.

When I was working in the Crest Forest Industries sawmill I had an unusual and new spiritual experience. I had come to know spiritual touches from the Lord which I could physically feel. I knew what it was to enjoy the joy of the Lord, and what it felt like to experience a spiritual restoration in my heart and soul after going through a dry spell.

On this particular day I felt what seemed like a spiritual snowball or a small meteorite coming right through my silver-colored hard hat. I took mental note of this unusual sensation from the Lord and kept on doing my work at The Sawmill. I knew what it was like to have a parakeet on my head, finger, and shoulders, and now I was experiencing spiritual sensations on my head that were similar to the light parakeet-feet sensations I had felt when Pretty Pete would land on my hair.

I eventually realized that the Lord as my Good Shepherd was reassuring me that He was with me by laying His blessed hand upon my life, and by painting my life with the anointing of oil which is symbolic of the Holy Spirit coming upon a Christian's life for His service and ministry.

A couple of verses to support my thinking on the mentioned above are these:

"You prepare a table before me in the presence of my enemies; You anoint my head with oil; my cup runs over." (Psalm 23:5 NKJV)

"You have hedged me behind and before, and laid Your hand upon me. Such knowledge is too wonderful for me; It is high; I cannot attain it." (Psalm 139:5–6)

That night after work I went into the bathroom and stood in front of the mirror. With my work helmet off I checked to see if I had any impressions on my hair of what had felt like parakeet feet. I wasn't able to see any visible impressions on my hair that day, but I knew this wasn't something I was imagining. Still I wasn't quite sure what this could mean.

When I read in Holy Scripture that God had anointed David's head with oil, and that the Holy Spirit came down upon Jesus in the form of a dove I realized that these touches from the Lord were signs that God hadn't forgotten me. I was positively on the Lord's mind and He had my best interest at heart. He was showing me how much He loved me by providing spiritual manifestations of His loving and protective hand on my life.

My father and I enjoyed going hunting together. We would take Dad's Remington .22 Rifle and his Classic Sharp Shot .20-gauge Shotgun to hopefully shoot a rabbit or bag some quail and pheasants during our outdoor hunting excursions. Unfortunately, our hunting activities were not the most successful, but we liked getting out of town for the experience anyway.

My relationship with my father improved as I grew older, and especially as I grew spiritually in my understanding of the ways of the Lord as an adult. My father and I would have long talks discussing Bible related subjects about the things of God, current and end-time events (Eschatology) that we could see shaping up in what many Christians believe are the last days, interpersonal relationships between family members and their interactions with mom and dad, and how the Lord is at work in Christian lives today.

Our father and son bonding also included some hearty humorous times in which we would have hilarious laughter together over seemingly little things that would hit our funny bones and our similar senses of humor. Dad and I bonded together spiritually through times of having spiritual talks and sharing family relationships together, playing our instruments of dad strumming on his guitar, banjo, or playing the piano, sharing new songs we have been practicing on with each other or me picking the 5 String Banjo, going hunting, fishing and boating trips, going on country scenic drives together that would include campouts, huckleberry picking or going on vacations with mom and dad that would involve staying in a motel or the onetime sailing event on The Big Red Boat to the Bahamas.

My father brought home a barber chair, and placed it in the basement so he could cut hair at home. I wanted him to cut my hair "just right" because I had fine hair, and I was especially sensitive about how my haircut looked.

After my father finished cutting my hair one day, and thought he had done a good job I went upstairs to inspect my haircut in front of the bathroom mirror. When I inspected my haircut I thought that my haircut needed to be evened out and balanced so I went back downstairs to have Dad make some more precise changes.

After each correction I would inspect my father's work in the bathroom mirror, and then ask him to make another slight precision cut here or there. Finally, when my finicky attitude about my hair had caused Dad to grow weary with my haircut experience he said, "When I get through it's going to be a fifty-dollar haircut." Then he caught me completely by surprise when he said, "That's where the side of your head is caved in." We both had a long laugh about his comment; it had really struck a funny chord both of us.

One day I was talking with Isaac Nelson who was attending Union Theology Institute. I appreciated hearing about his experiences there and learning what I could expect if I decided to go to the institute. At a later time I spoke with Hal Matheson who also was attending Union Theology Institute. The more I thought about attending the theology institute the more I began to see the importance of going to a Christian school that had excellent Bible teachers with an emphasis strictly on the Word of God to learn more about the things of God.

I couldn't see myself being a lifer at Crest Forest Industries Sawmill although I was making good money at the time. I worked at CFI Sawmill for around two and a half years, and then decided to change my destiny by receiving Bible College training so that I could work for the Lord in Christian Ministry.

I took the next step by contacting Union Theology Institute and talking to the registrar, Pastor Peter Sampson who helped me to enroll for the fall semester.

I enjoyed attending the institute and soon made friends who appreciated me for who I was. I was accepted at the institute where each Bible student had his or her own reason for how he or she came to be a part of the theology institute.

I took my Bible training seriously and wanted to make good grades. The teachers were of excellent caliber, and I could sense the blessed Holy Spirit in the classrooms as I learned about the great things of God. I especially appreciated Pastor Howard Paul Jennings who became my favorite Bible instructor. Not only was Pastor Jennings an excellent professor with tremendous Bible knowledge, but he exemplified being a man of God. He knew God in an amazing way and walked with God on a daily basis. I learned firsthand from his sound doctrinal teachings, scriptural note books, sermons, and revelations found in God's Word from this great authority figure and the fact he personified being a man of God. He was a man of prayer, and he walked by faith in the light of The Word of God faithfully.

One day during our morning Bible Chapel Pastor Jennings announced a three-day fast combined with prayer. I decided to join the three-day fast which ultimately had good spiritual results for me. God was at work in my life as I attended the Bible institute, and He had greater things for me to experience as I faithfully pursued the Lord in my heart and life.

A powerful revelation came to me during one of my Gospel of John classes. Professor Ken Hendricks shared that when the Holy Spirit came upon the Virgin Mary new life was conceived in her. The spiritual truth ministered to me that day was that my desire to have the life of God in my heart and life would come about by the power of the Holy Spirit. The blessed Holy Spirit working to bring about a quickening in my spiritual life had to be done through the wonderful works of the Spirit of God. I had benefited from going on a two-day fast at home, and now while attending the Bible institute a three-day fast. Now I decided to go on a five-day fast before the Lord, and this helped me spiritually as well.

I read stories in a book by Franklin Hall titled, The Fasting Prayer which explained how God had worked in the lives of Christians who embarked on protracted fasts including a fourteen-day fast, a twenty-one-day fast, a forty-day fast, and longer. I read about ordinary Christians who saw God perform miracles through their praying and fasting before the Lord. I made up my mind to go on a protracted fast to see God work mightily in my spiritual life.

I was attending Union Theology Institute when I started on my lengthy fast. Everything was going fine until I bent down to get a book on a low library shelf. When I stood up things went black momentarily. From then on I tried to be careful about standing up too quickly when I was on a protracted fast, but I wasn't inclined to end my fast over that experience in the library. When I reached days sixteen to nineteen I felt a movement in my lower intestinal tract that felt like something was spiritually moving inside of me. The sensation I experienced was similar to the spiritual snow ball I felt come through my silver hard hat at The Sawmill I shared about previously.

When I reached day twenty-two of the fast I was dropping off an assignment when a couple of my classmates saw me, and laughed at my appearance I was very thin from fasting. After that I became self-conscious about my physical condition. I decided to end my fast, but I knew from reading The Fasting Prayer that I needed to be careful how I brought my fast to an end because I could injure myself physically, and cause myself spiritual harm if it wasn't done correctly. I decided to have only liquids like pink lemonade, hot chocolate, or a grapefruit drink from day twenty-three to day thirty. God had been with me throughout my protracted fast, and He would be with me in a greater way after I completed my spiritual fast.

When I broke my fast I happened to be with a couple of friends who were interested in watching a football game together. Mark Fleming, Angie Caldwell and I had agreed to get together, and have some snacks while watching the game on television. I ate cookies, potato chips, and drank soda pop, but I ended up vomiting afterward. Such snacks weren't the best things to take into a body that had been purged from physical contaminants, chemicals, and food toxins.

The Holy Spirit had raised up in my life as a result of my going on my protracted fast causing me to experience a wonderful spiritual restoration in my heart and life like I had never experienced before. The living God of heaven and earth had quickened me spiritually, and I grew spiritually in my theological studies and in my relationship with God and others.

When I went to my dorm room one day after the fast I felt the Lord say, "Now, let's start marching as a soldier in the Lord's army." I had never sensed a revelation like that before, and I since have realized that it had to have come from the Lord Himself.

I was so encouraged by what God had done in my life as a result of my protracted fast that I decided to go on another one during my summer break.

That summer at home I asked my mother if I could borrow the tent and go up into the national forest to camp out. She agreed and I headed to the mountains to have another visitation with God Himself through prayer and fasting. I was able to endure my spiritual camping trip for only four days because the weather was cold both day and night, and that became a distraction to me as I tried to concentrate on seeking God. I did find wonderful-tasting water in a hollow log by the roadway and I enjoyed that.

I loaded up the car and headed back to Clover Valley to continue my fast at my parents' home. I'd had only water for the first four days of my fast, and then I drank different liquid drinks from days five to forty. When I reached day forty I felt like I hadn't spiritually benefited from my fast because I was receiving nourishment from the various drinks I drank.

I decided to continue my fasting for the next seven days with only water. I persisted in wanting to experience the wonderful spiritual blessings of the Lord that comes from completing a fast. I'd already been a thin man, and now I was really skinny from the long fast that I had undertaken. On the last night of my protracted fast I couldn't seem to get to sleep. When I heard a fire engine siren I got up from my bed, and walked in the direction of the sound. After returning to my bed my mind was active, and I thought of every restaurant in which I had ever eaten in Union before coming home for the summer break. I decided I would break my protracted fast by eating something in the morning I had gone long enough without food.

I learned later that it was a good thing that I ended my fast when I did. My body was so thin from my continuous fasting that it might have begun feeding on itself. I never consulted a physician before going on any of my lengthy fasts.

I had green grapes and cultured milk to help get my stomach's acidic enzymes working again. I didn't have a powerful post-fasting experience as I was hoping, but I believe the Lord wanted to reward me for my desiring after Him anyway.

I realize that He wants us to walk by faith as we seek His face, and not by sight or feeling. The important thing for a Christian is to faithfully seek and serve the Lord, and leave the spiritual rewards and results up to Him. Great things happen when we diligently seek the Lord's face.

I returned to Union Theology Institute that fall to resume my training in theology. God was faithful to me throughout my Bible institute days, and I wanted the Lord to use me as His servant in ministerial ways wherever I found open doors to minister for the Lord.

During my theology training I was able to minister to souls during outside activities, witnessing in the downtown area of Union at the Banner Convalescent Center, on my personnel carrier routes whenever possible, and at the Golden Bells Chapel.

I also did my own personal witnessing for the Lord wherever I found someone interested in spiritual things in the hope of leading that person to Jesus Christ, the Savior of humankind. I enjoyed attending Evangel Christian Fellowship Church which had been founded by a Christian gathering.

I had many rewarding spiritual experiences while attending the Christian Church, and in classes where I sensed the precious Holy Spirit's anointing presence. The anointing is the painting or coming upon of the Holy Spirit for the Lord's work as a chosen vessel. The Lord God can use anyone anywhere that is open and available for His Divine anointing use, guidance, and equipping for ministry. It doesn't have to be in a Church building. The anointing of the Holy Spirit enables a Christian believer to do things supernaturally for the Lord that he or she would not be able to do with their own natural abilities.

The wonderful Holy Spirit's touch upon the pastors, and Bible school instructors made the difference between receiving academic knowledge in theological training and receiving experiential knowledge which the Lord wants for all His children on a daily basis. The Lord will equip all Christian worldwide to function in His will without official titles from a Christian denomination.

I had fasted so long that I looked emaciated. My mother took pictures of me from the side, and back to clearly show how skinny I had become as a consequence of my protracted fast unto the Lord.

I believe that in a chosen fast the Lord calls a person for a specific reason and purpose anywhere. I also believe that if a Christian desires to seek the Lord for a specific spiritual reason and purpose by giving himself or herself in prayer and fasting, the Lord will give that individual believer the desires of his or her heart because God is faithful.

I know that God is the giver of miracles, and that He has great and wonderful things in store for those who seek Him through prayer and fasting. Nothing is impossible for those Christians who dare to believe God for the miraculous in this day and hour. Many people do not believe in miracles any longer nor do they believe in a supreme deity. One day however they will have to give an account of their lives to the supreme deity, The Lord God Almighty who is The Living God of Heaven and Earth.

So then each of us shall give an account of himself {or herself} to God. (Romans 14:12 NKJV)

I know and believe that certain circumstances will not change on their own; they require Christians with pit-bull determination to see a miracle created, and performed through their personal lives or in the lives of others. When I was attending Union Theology Institute I learned about the Basic Youth Conflicts Seminar taught by instructor, Bill Gothard which was coming to Seattle, Washington. My brother, Daniel had told me about Bill's great Christian teachings, and so I decided to make the trip to Seattle to listen to this man of God teach on the principles of life for the Christian believer.

I was incredibly impressed with Bill's teachings. He explained life's principles wonderfully with oratory examples, great life's illustrations, and colorful pictures to help and encourage those who desired to follow Christ's life principles and to see God bring about positive change(s) in their lives and others.

I appreciated all of Bill's teachings, but I especially took note when he mentioned that one could make a change to improve one's physical appearance if it was a distraction to the Christian's focus on the Lord and the things of God.

The example Bill gave at the time was correcting a person's crooked teeth which could be a distraction to his or her physical appearance, but I quickly applied his teaching to my nose if something could be done to improve its appearance I was willing to have it done.

I felt that my prominent nose was a distraction to my overall self-esteem, self-worth, and self-image as a Christian believer. I felt that my bulbous nose was holding me back from having a positive future in Christian ministry, and marrying a wife who could join me in my Christian ministry. My thoughts were influenced by physical features I had seen glamorized on television and in the movies.

It was glaringly obvious to me that Hollywood chose handsome men and beautiful women as actors in order to capture the viewing audience's attention. I saw the emphasis on physical beauty in the entertainment industry. I would have liked to have been born with natural physical beauty that was admired by others and was attractive to beautiful women, but I wasn't born that way. Logically I knew that physical beauty was skin deep, and I recognized that God wanted me to accept my physical appearance just the way He created me.

On the other hand, I thought God would think it was within reason to have corrective cosmetic surgeries that resulted in beauty enhancements if a person's physical unattractiveness was a detriment, distraction, or loss of God-consciousness due to the person obsessing over his or her physical appearance.

One day I went to see the registrar at the Theology Institute to talk with him on how to determine which Christian woman to marry. Pastor Peter Sampson shared that he could have married five different women, and each of them had her own unique and special quality. When he met the woman who became his wife however she had all the qualities of the other five women, and she had her own unique quality as well. He said that I would have to decide for myself which qualities I was looking for in a woman.

I appreciated that Dr. Sampson had given me something to think about with regard to choosing a life partner. I had taken an interest in a couple of ladies at the institute. Britney Langley caught my interest by the way she entered into worshiping the Lord during song and worship service. She was a pretty blonde lady who really loved the Lord. She was a gifted straight-A student, but she was conflicted by my personal struggles. I needed the Lord to give me more maturity to make a wise choice in a soulmate.

With the wonderful presence of the Holy Spirit working in my life I struggled with guilt before I went on a long fast. I needed the Lord to strengthen me in the spirit of my character, and to break any bondages that hindered the spirit of my mind. I appreciated Pastor Samson sharing with me that he could read 800 words per minute, and I needed to read groups of words, and not get hung up over single words read. I desired to tell the truth; to be honest before the Lord, and in my personal relationships.

When I was given reading assignments by my different professors I wanted to honestly say that I had completed my assignments. While in Bible training I experienced an overactive conscience that kept me alert to my responsibilities before God and others. In my freshman year before going on my lengthy fast I got hung up on reading the same word or phrases over and over, to make certain I was reading my Bible and doctrinal assignments, and the lessons my teachers gave in each class. I was struggling with wanting to be a truthful and an honest student of the Bible, and doing what my conscience was telling me to do before God. I needed the Lord to help me with my overactive conscience.

After I spoke with Pastor Sampson regarding this problem I moved on to reading groups of words in phrases instead of the individual words which only hindered the spirit of my mind, and making it feel like it had spiritual viruses and slowing my reading speed down to a snail's pace. God gave me the victory over this problem with my reading assignments in the form of the sound advice from Dr. Sampson, and after a time of prayer and fasting.

I told Britney that I loved her by faith, but she wasn't encouraged by my unusual way of telling her I loved her. I wasn't positive that I truly loved her as my future wife, and eventually the two of us drifted apart.

I took an interest in another young Christian lady at the institute named Judy Clovis. I met Judy when the two of us were doing door-to-door witnessing as part of our required outside activities at Union Theology Institute.

When we were witnessing together I took an interest in Judy who was a sophomore while I was a freshman, but I never asked her out until a number of months later.

One day I saw Judy in the institute's library; she was wearing an attractive purple dress, and I took a fancy to her that day. I happened to attend church with Judy one Sunday, and I met her parents later on. I had learned that it was good to see a potential wife in as many situations as possible before you take the plunge. I realized it wasn't wise to rush into getting married as many people who do may end up wishing they would have gotten to know their spouses better before they said, "I do."

Judy's mother, Shirley Clovis was overweight, and she had ongoing marital conflicts with her antagonistic husband. Nick Clovis was nice to me, but he was argumentative with his wife. Nick seemed to always give Shirley a hard time; he lacked any sensitivity or compassion toward her.

I liked Judy she was a rose between two thorns but I decided not to marry her partly because of the discouraging marital tension and intense conflicts I witnessed in her home life.

I got a kick out of something my sister, Marlie once told me about a man who was trying to decide which of two women he could marry. One woman was unattractive physically, but she was talented and could sing like a canary. The other woman was truly beautiful, but she couldn't sing. Finally, after some consideration the man decided to marry the plain woman who could sing and play the piano. They were married and spent their first night together on their honeymoon. In the morning the husband looked over at his wife in bed, and seeing that his wife did not look any better to him after they tied the knot he said, "Sing baby sing."

I realized that I was influenced by the world's standards of beauty because I wanted to change my physical appearance. I was self-conscious about my looks even though I didn't obsess over them which was a good thing. The Lord was helping me with my physical appearance flaws, but I now realize that I had flaws in my thinking concerning my outward appearance, and I should have looked to the Lord for His help with that.

I thought about my physical appearance, and would become self-conscious whenever I looked at my Union Theology Institute yearbook pictures. They had included an embarrassing photo of me during my freshman year, and it really bothered me that they had put in the worst of two pictures that the photographer had taken. I thought my album picture was so awful to look at.

I was self-conscious about my appearance throughout my remaining theology institute years. The negative experience of seeing myself in the freshman album made me that much more self-conscious, and desirous to make a physical change provided I had a way to.

I graduated from Union Theology Institute, and I continued to sense the presence of the Lord at work in my life post-graduation.

Jonah Jon Jefferys

I enjoyed watching the Seattle Mariners Baseball Team, the only major league baseball team in the Pacific Northwest.

Alex Tucker and I were friends and classmates in the theology institute. We liked traveling to the games whenever we could find the time, but the Mariners lost so many games that we had become discouraged with the team, and we would look forward to seeing the other team win. Alex and I got a kick out of telling others that we were going to watch the opposing team win the game.

The ballgames were exciting to watch especially when the New York Yankees, the Boston Red Sox, the Houston Astros (with Nolan Ryan pitching), or the Oakland Athletics were in town.

I also liked to watch the University of Washington Huskies Football Team play on television. I enjoyed seeing the semiprofessional Thunderbirds Hockey Team play a number of times, whenever I could make the trip those games could be really exciting.

One Saturday afternoon I parked my William County Shuttle some distance from the Huskies football stadium to take a break from driving. I was sitting on the shuttle during my break when a nice couple on their way to the stadium asked if I would like a free ticket to the Huskies game they'd bought a ticket for their eleven-year-old son who no longer wanted to attend the game with his parents.

Naturally I appreciated their kind offer, and I thoroughly enjoyed watching the game from an upper-deck middle-of-the-field exceptionally fine viewing position. The Huskies won the game, and I was grateful to the special couple who had made it all possible.

Although I enjoyed watching sports my being involved in the Lord's work was a greater calling than the pursuit of a sports dreams and making big money from a lucrative contract with a major league baseball team.

I thought back to my teenage years when I had read about, Bob Feller a tall hard-throwing fastball pitcher who played for the Yankees in 1939. Bob would hold a shotput in his pitching hand for a time so that later when he held a baseball it would feel as light as a feather in comparison.

No wonder Bob was such an amazing fastball thrower during his prime years.

I also read about Johnny Bench who played for the Cincinnati Reds as an incredible catcher for years. He could throw a baseball from a squatting position up to 250 feet with pinpoint accuracy. He also could hold seven baseballs together in his large right hand. Unfortunately, I had inherited my mother's hands, and I was able to hold only four or five baseballs in one hand with my fingers hard at work to hold them in place.

I learned about the sensational African American pitcher Leroy Paige. Leroy went by the nickname of Satchel. Satchel Paige had an amazing fastball as well as other incredible pitches that he would use to surprise and catch the batters off guard. The batters experienced difficulty with trying to hit his outstanding slew of pitches. I would have liked to have seen Satchel pitch especially during his prime years. I would have enjoyed sitting next to my father watching Satchel Paige pitch against Bob Feller at Sick's Stadium in Seattle. Satchel was still pitching in the major leagues when he was fifty-nine or sixty years old. I was greatly impressed with these incredible major league baseball players who were inducted into Baseball's Hall of Fame.

Satchel had pitched against Bob Feller in an exhibition charity game in Seattle on October 7th, 1945. The pitching duel between the two sensational pitchers would have been a tremendous game to see with my father if only I had been born at an earlier time.

My father told me that he had gone to a game at which Satchel was flown into the baseball stadium in a helicopter. The helicopter landed on the field, Satchel stepped out, and he began warming up on the pitching mound. Now that would have been an exciting event to witness sitting next to my dad in the stands.

Satchel had quite a variety of different names for his arsenal of incredible pitches such as his "hesitation pitch" and his sensational "bee-ball," which was his high-velocity fastball. Satchel Paige's recipe for striking out opposing batters was a mixture of the right ingredients to shut down even the best hitters. I would have liked to have watched and learned from Satchel, chief architect of the most incredible and successful pitching talent as has ever put on a baseball uniform. Satchel was loved and admired by a great number of adoring fans not only for his pitching ability, but also for his delightful character. He enjoyed being a show-off, a role he liked to portray in life. Satchel Paige, an interesting baseball player who became a pitching legend, had a likable personality, and he was highly honored by the fans who followed his Major League Baseball career.

I have reflected on my prospects of ever pitching for a major league team, and I have recognized there were key factors that influenced that chances, and key elements for me to learn before I could pitch in the big leagues. First of all, when I was twelve the coach of my team didn't have the wisdom or insight to not have me pitch a second game immediately after I pitched a six-inning game which resulted in my throwing my arm out early on. Secondly I would have liked to have pitched on the same team as Gary Holland, and learned his pitching mechanics, proper workout, and exercise routine.

Had I pitched professionally I would have liked to have had a 105-mile-an-hour fastball with a 95-mile-an-hour change-up. My pitching arsenal would have included names like "hit this," "the shocker," "hot to trot," "total surprise," "lock bat," "clean sweeper," "don't even try," "snail's pace," "straight shooter," "cry-baby," "talk to your bat," "bat biter," "brush-off pitch," "I can't see you," "reversible boomerang," "thunderous momentum," "no catch-up," "mouth stopper," "maximum frustration," "the tumbler," "the drop-off," "turn the key," "acceleration pitch," "guess who," "I don't have all day," "peekaboo," "frost bat," "chiller thriller," and "don't even think about it."

I had good arm speed as a young pitcher, but as I grew older I needed to develop lower body and hip strength to have a greater push-off and follow-through from the mound. As a teenager I received worthwhile pitching instruction and sound advice from a knowledgeable pitching coach, but I wasn't able to raise my skill level as a growing baseball pitcher which might have thrust me into having far greater pitching potential and a much better form. The above mentioned possibly could have moved move me into a higher level of pitching performance.

I recognize now that my long-past pitching memories are part of a fading futile fantasy. Scores of good athletes reflect on what could have been thinking if they had only done this or that things could have turned out in their favor. Things of this nature however are the bumps in the road of life.

Even if I had met my pitching ideals though that doesn't mean I would have raised my skill level to be potentially qualified as a major league pitcher. I just look back on it now and think I might have had that privilege if things had worked out, and if I was physically capable of becoming a professional big-league pitcher. Possibility thinking has its good points, but God had better plans for me than the prospect of pitching in the Major Leagues could ever offer.

I was able to acquire a brand-new intermediate Deering Five-String Banjo at a music store in Union. My theology institute classmate Judy Clovis was kind enough to purchase the banjo for me, and then I made payments to her until I paid it off.

I wanted to learn to play the handsome quality banjo as soon as I could. I started out by learning to play chords with a plastic flat pick; in time I wanted to learn to play the bluegrass five-string picking style with two metal picks and a plastic thumb pick. I have taken banjo lessons from a number of banjo teachers over the years, and playing the banjo has helped me in so many ways. I have been able to sing and play my banjo at Christian churches, and at other Christian group gatherings for the Lord as well as for entertainment for friends and family.

I have had the opportunity to hear some talented banjo pickers including Butch Robins, Earl Scruggs, Ralph Stanley, Bela Fleck, Sonny Osborne, and many others at different times in the State of Washington. I also have heard Bill Monroe at the Monroe Center in Seattle playing his mandolin, and Mark O'Connor playing his amazing violin.

My father and I have enjoyed going to hear various bluegrass bands play over the years. I was especially impressed with Earl Scruggs playing his Gibson Five-String Banjo with his incredibly talented band that performed at the Benaroya Hall in downtown Seattle.

I continued to attend the Evangel Christian Fellowship Church after I graduated from the theology institute, and continued working at William County Carrier Company.

I graduated with a degree in theology, and in time I attended Sumpter Community College for additional credits which I needed to continue my college education. Sometime later I also applied to the Pentecostal Bible Institute in Browerland which was fully accredited, and I was accepted to attend the college in Browerland. The majority of the credits I had earned at Union Theology Institute were accepted by the college. My major was in biblical literature, with a minor in counseling. God continued to bless me as I continued my college education and learned to play my banjo.

I moved out of the dorm while attending Union Theology Institute, and I found decent housing in the Banner District in Union where I also lived while attending different classes at the Pentecostal Bible Institute in Browerland.

I have appreciated watching and listening to the Jimmy Swaggart's Evangelistic Ministry on SonLife Broadcasting. Jimmy has been like John the Baptizer who declared the coming of the Lord as the Lamb of God who takes away the sins of the world (John 1:29). I personally have benefited and have been blessed spiritually by the great preaching and teaching with soul-stirring messages and principles from God's Holy Word. God has anointed Jimmy Swaggart and other members of his Jimmy Swaggart Ministries (JSM) team to see souls saved, and brought into the Kingdom of Heaven through repentance of sin and turning to God wholeheartedly.

I urge and encourage every sincere reader who desires to help advance the Lord's Kingdom through JSM to faithfully support financially this wonderful soul-saving work, and see God the Blesser abundantly bless your life and family. Please keep in mind that God rewards those who diligently seek after Him by faith with all of their hearts.

"But this I say, He which soweth sparingly shall reap also sparingly; and he which soweth bountifully shall reap also bountifully. Every man according as he purposeth in his heart, so let him give; not grudgingly, or of necessity: for God loveth a cheerful giver." (2 Corinthians 9:6–7).

If the Lord Jesus Christ gave rankings as the U.S. Armed Forces does, Jimmy Swaggart certainly would be awarded as a Four-Star General in the Lord's Army. He is an inspirationally gifted musician and intelligent man of God who has written many excellent books to help Wake Up Christians spiritually, inspire them, and motivate them to serve the Lord wherever they maybe in their personal and individual walks with the Lord and whatever their maturity development in Christ Jesus happens to be. Jimmy Swaggart has used his multiple talents to glorify the Lord of Glory through inspirational songs, great teachings of Christian doctrines, and powerful sermons to win the lost.

He continues to be a voice of moral clarity in a time when the nation is in moral decline, and needs an encouraging word to turn the nation's people and the world back to the Lord Jesus Christ. I truly have appreciated Jimmy Swaggart saying to viewers, "Satan was defeated at the Cross." This powerful truth should encourage all Christian believers to hold their heads high, and look to the victorious Lamb of God as the author and finisher of our faith.

Jimmy Swaggart writes in his book, The World, the Flesh, and the Devil,
To be frank, our salvation and our victory depend on three things:
1. The Cross. 2. Our faith in Christ and the Cross.
3. That which gives the Holy Spirit latitude to work. … We are obligated to do one thing, and one thing only, and that is to ever exhibit faith in Christ and His great sacrifice of Himself (Rom. 6:3–5; 8:1–2, 11; Gal. 5–6). It is ever by faith, which refers to faith in Christ and His sacrifice.

I am truly grateful for Jimmy Swaggart and his JSM Team who are faithfully focused on the person of the Lord Jesus Christ, and what He did on the cross for us He paid our penalty to take our sins away through His shed blood and He forever purchased our glorious free gift of eternal life through Jesus Christ our Lord (Romans 6:23).

God's amazing grace unto salvation is available to all who will call upon the name of the Lord for His great mercy and loving kindness. God the Father has given us His very best, the Lord Jesus Christ. Now it is up to us to freely receive the greatest offer heaven could bestow upon the fallen human race separated from God because of our sins (Isaiah 59:1–2). Thank God that Jesus is our blessed hope who forever bridged the gap between us, and the all-powerful Creator and lover of our souls.

Jimmy Swaggart's Ministry has rich soil to plant and grow an abundant harvest in the Kingdom of God where we will lay up treasure for our future rewards in heaven.

Bud shares, "They [Jimmy Swaggart Ministries team] daily face persecution and twisting of their message of the 100 percent finished work on the cross by Jesus Christ (1 Corinthians 1:17–18, 23; 2:2). Jesus Christ did not go to hell when He left the cross. He went to Abraham's bosom which was paradise in Luke 16. The very words of Jesus tell us that hell was separated from Abraham's bosom/paradise by a great gulf/chasm."

The Oneness United Pentecostal people believe that Jesus Christ died on the cross as a sinner. Because Jesus died as a sinner He had to go to burning hell for three days wherein He suffered as a sinner for Himself. This teaching is full blown heresy because when Jesus took our penalty for our sins He didn't become a sinner that needed to become born again like we have to. And as the perfect Lamb of God who was spotless, sinless, and pure He took the keys of death and hell from the devil at the cross of Calvary, and won a total decisive victory for all who will receive Him.

Then Jesus Christ took the repentant thief with Him down into the center of the earth to Abraham's bosom which was paradise, and fully separated from burning hell fire by a great gulf. No one could cross over from either direction. The saints of the Old Testament could not be set free from Abraham's bosom/paradise because the blood of bulls and goats could not set them free.

Only the life's blood of Jesus Christ could set the sinner totally free from sin and the sin nature. On the third day when Jesus arose from the grave He emptied paradise by leading captivity captive when He ascended into heaven to be with the saints for all eternity.

You can read what Jesus said to the repentant malefactor concerning him going to paradise with Jesus Christ on the very day Jesus died on the cross (Luke 23:42–43). Those powerful words of Jesus Christ to the dying thief on the cross gave that penitent man the best news he had ever heard in all his life. Rather than going out into outer darkness for all eternity with no hope the repentant illuminated man now had a bright and joyous future awaiting him in beautiful, splendorous, and majestic Shechinah Glory in the presence of God where Jesus is the Lamb; the light of the world is the light of heaven itself (Revelation 21:23).

From the lips of the resurrection and the life, Jesus Christ this man believed in the Lord Jesus Christ and he was saved from his debt of sin, and eternal damnation separated from God for all eternity. Oh what a glorious day that had to have been for the dying thief who called on the name of the Lord to be remembered when Jesus came into His Kingdom (Luke 23:42–43). He would be forgiven and justified as if he had never sinned against God, but when it came to breaking the law of the Jewish society he had to pay the penalty for the crimes he had committed.

He was forgiven by God at that very moment that he repented on the cross, but he still had to pay his debt of sin to society which meant death by hanging on the cross. Unlike the other criminal however his destiny was to be with Jesus Christ in heaven forever.

The same thing could happen to you right now as you repent of your sins, and believe in the Lord Jesus Christ and His shed blood for the remission of your sins. Then simply look to the Lamb of God with all your heart, and place your faith and trust in Him, Jesus Christ and you too will be forgiven, justified as if you had never sinned, and saved for all eternity. What a glorious day that will be for you right now and throughout all eternity.

If you commit a crime and break the laws of the land you may need to pay your debt for your criminal actions by spending time in home confinement, a local jail, or in a federal penitentiary. If you believe on the Lord Jesus Christ as your personal Lord and Savior however you can rest assured, He will be with you during your time in confinement. If you are not a born-again Christian as an unbeliever there will be serious consequences if you break the law depending on the severity of your criminal actions unless you go before a lenient judge.

Consider the other criminal dying for his debt of sins hanging on the third cross on Golgotha's hill on that bloody darkened day. This thief did not have a revelation that Jesus was truly the Son of God, totally innocent of all charges, blameless, and didn't deserve the scoffing and mockery from the Roman soldiers and religious rulers. Instead the thief chose to join in with the world, and hurl sneering and contemptuous insults at Jesus and to provoke an accusation of blasphemy toward the guiltless Lamb of God who was dying for the other malefactor and the sins of the whole world.

This dying thief could have made the choice to soften his hardened heart, but he chose not to believe in the Lord Jesus for salvation. He was not rescued and delivered from his blackened burden of sin, and he did not put his faith and trust in the One True God who could write his name in the Book of Life for all eternity. The thief went in the other direction with the crowd (Matthew 7:13).

This dying malefactor took the broad way of the world which is the sure path to destruction. While he still had breath he stubbornly kept on the broad freeway to burning hellfire. He still had time just as all the men and women did who stood there observing the redeeming sacrifice of the Lamb of God, Jesus Christ who was paying their debt of sin. The thief chose not to make the correct decision which was to choose life, and blessing for all eternity before he took his last breath and his eternal spirit left his body.

I encourage you to read The Gospel in a nutshell which is (John 3:16) The Holy Bible gives the Basic Instructions Before Leaving Earth. (Acrostic for the Bible)

In another Bible passage, Jesus Christ the Son of God who is the resurrection and the life was scoffed at and mocked because He told the people who were weeping and crying that a twelve-year-old girl was not actually dead but only sleeping (Mark 5:35–43). In this passage the people were making a commotion, and their religiosity blinded them from the truth spoken by Jesus Christ.

These weeping people pretended to be concerned about the young girl yet they were blinded by the devil, and they mocked and scorned Emanuel God with us in human flesh. To fully know the Lord Jesus, the King of kings and Lord of lords one must have a genuine, blood-bought, born-again experience which is salvation in Christ Jesus (John 3:16–8; Revelation 19:16).

All regenerated blood-bought Christians should share their faith with their families and others; that when they got saved they knew beyond a shadow of a doubt that they were born again. The presence of God should be evident in their lives although they may not feel anything at the time of their conversion. God's presence will grow and become more experiential as they continue to grow in their faith on a daily basis.

It is imperative that we reckon ourselves dead to sin and self-interest pursuits. In turn reckon yourself alive unto God through Christ Jesus so you can pursue God and His heavenly interests (Romans 6:11; Colossians 3:1–17). A Christian should also be able to say, "I knew that I knew that I knew that I knew I was born again when I repented of my sins and received the Lord Jesus Christ into my heart and life."

I spoke with someone a number of years ago who had a Roman Catholic background. She was confident in her faith at the time. In her opinion I should be able to tell she was convinced because of what she had received from God or the Roman Catholic Church or because she had gained in knowledge through her own personal religious pursuits and studies. She insisted she was fine in her vertical position and relationship with God.

At the time I wasn't 100% confident of her personal vertical relationship with God that she felt in herself she was perfectly fine with the Lord. The Lord God knows the hearts of all men and women thank goodness. We can inspect the fruits of a person's life by the Godly measurements of their true Christian spiritual status before God and if they are truly saved.

When I think back to that conversation in which I questioned her Roman Catholic experience as an individual I wish I had asked her if she could point to a specific time, and place when she knew without any trace of uncertainty that she had met the Lord Jesus personally through the free gift of eternal life by faith in God's Word and the cross of Calvary.

It is imperative that all Christians proclaim and share their Christian experiences with their families and friends that they have genuine salvation. I regret not asking her if she could recall the specific time and place when Jesus Christ became her spiritual husband. Likewise, all married women worldwide can provide the concrete evidence when and where they were married to their earthly physical husbands in this life. Many people today have questions and wonder if they are truly saved and born again, and if they are ready to make heaven which is paradise their eternal home forever.

I would encourage all people who have serious doubts and questions regarding if they are truly blood-bought, and washed in the blood of Jesus Christ shed on Calvary's cross for the remission of our sins. A true born-again Christian that seeks the Lord Jesus, and His righteousness for the full salvation born-again experience with the added assurance they seek and need to satisfy their longings in Christ Jesus. A gentle reminder that there is a God shaped hole in the Christian's heart that Jesus Christ has filled through the finished work on the cross of Calvary, and the daily application of His precious shed blood on the cross.

Those that have a God shaped hole in their hearts prior to salvation in Jesus Christ try to fill that empty hole with all kinds of counterfeits.

I also would encourage sincere seekers those who desire to know God personally and His will for themselves and their families to pray and fast to have a more intimate relationship with the Lord Jesus. I believe the Lord Jesus will meet you at the point of your need for His grace and for faith which will help you to come into a much greater, and closer relationship with Him through the finished work of the cross of Calvary (Jeremiah 29:13; John 6:24, 33; John 7:16–17; 1 John 5:12–13).

If you truly hunger to know the Lord Jesus as your personal Lord and Savior prior to salvation in Christ Jesus with a full assurance that you are positively a born-again Christian which Jesus said you must be in order to see and enter the Kingdom of God, and know there is no condemnation upon you if will you come to know God personally and His will for your life and loving guidance (John 3:3–8, 16–19).

The people of Jairus's household were so caught up in their crying and wailing in their religious pretensions, and making such a commotion that when they heard the declaration of Jesus "The damsel is not dead, but sleepeth" they poured forth their scorn and ridicule at Him, the Author and Finisher of our faith, who can stare death in the face, rebuke it, and raise the dead by pronouncing resurrection life to all those who will believe in Him for their lives now and for all eternity. Jesus took the girl's father and mother, and they put out those who were mocking him. Then Jesus said to the girl, "Arise," and her spirit returned to her body and then she arose. (Luke 8: 53-55)

God is always so great and mighty. The gospel is good news that you can totally trust in forever.

Let's not forget:

"And I, brethren, when I came to you, came not with excellency of speech or of wisdom [worldly wisdom psychology], declaring unto you the testimony of God. For I determined not to know anything among you, save Jesus Christ and him crucified." (1 Corinthians 2:1–2)

"For Christ sent me not to baptize, but to preach the gospel: not with wisdom of words, lest the cross of Christ should be made of none effect." (1 Corinthians 1:17)

I heartily recommend watching the anointed crusades of the Jimmy Swaggart Ministries, "The Classics" from the 1980s if you enjoy Holy Spirit–inspired songs and powerful preaching by Jimmy when he was younger. I have enjoyed and benefited watching them myself.

I am forever thankful to the Lord Jesus Christ that Marlie came back to the Lord as her personal Lord and Savior. She surrendered and gave her heart to our wonderful, glorified, risen Savior, who is the Prince of Peace (Isaiah 9:6). I was encouraged that Marlie not only made peace with the God of her salvation, but that she began faithfully watching Jimmy Swaggart on the SonLife Broadcasting Network. Marlie has an incredible memory, and I was impressed when she began naming many of the Christian members featured on the Jimmy Swaggart Telecast who sang or played an active ministry role in the body of Christ on the Christian program.

The good Lord gave Marlie a tremendous gift that I recognize comes from the Magnificent,

Totally Awesome, Creator of the universe including all creatures, small and great, and all human beings known to God. All the glory, praise, and honor belong to our Lord and Savior, Jesus Christ for who He is and the great things He has done for He is the Creator and The Big Boss. The Commander in Chief of the Universe.

Bud recently shared with me concerning the Roman Catholic teachings. He went on to say,

The Roman Catholic hierarchy claims that they have the authority to change the wafer that is put on the tongues of the kneeling worshipers, into the real body of Jesus, and the wine cups that they drink from is changed into the real blood of Jesus. This teaching or dogma is called transubstantiation.

Faithful Roman Catholics claim that they have received Jesus because of the wafer and wine changing into the actual blood of Jesus. They also claim in that they were sprinkled as babies by the priests, the Roman Catholic Church claims the authority to pronounce babies Christians based on their faithfulness in attending mass and attending confessions this means perpetual mass cards.

Roman Catholic priests pray for the dead in Purgatory and the person having the perpetual mass card, the priest prays for the family member of that Roman Catholic that are in Purgatory. The Roman Catholic priest when asked if the person they are praying for is out of Purgatory yet, the priest will shrug and say, "Nobody can know that". This teaching of Purgatory like so many other Roman Catholic teachings are not found in The Holy Bible, but are based upon Roman Catholic traditions which is basically considered extra non-Biblical teachings prescribed by the Roman Catholic Church and its faithful followers.

Any non-Roman Catholic that marries a Roman Catholic, the marriage ceremony is held in the Roman Catholic Church. A legal document has to be signed by the non-Roman Catholic and the Roman Catholic that has had any children conceived in the marriage must be raised according to Roman Catholic teachings and attend Roman Catholic Parochial School. If the non-Roman Catholic chooses or refuses to raise the children as Roman Catholics the Roman Catholic spouse will take away the children from the non-believing spouse.

The Roman Catholic Church has a lot of Roman Catholic lawyers. Let the reader be aware. The Roman Catholic Church believes that Mary is the holy mother of God , she is the co-mediator and to make request of Jesus she has the ear of Jesus for them. Thus, the Roman Catholic Church does not have the Holy Trinity, but believes in the Holy quartet. The Roman Catholic Church also believes in prayers to the dead saints because the dead saints have more light than we mortals on earth do. All of these teachings are in direct violation and deviation of the Word of God as recorded in The Holy Bible.

The Roman Catholic Church teaches the Virgin Mary remained a virgin until she ascended into heaven and that she is the Co-Redemptrix wherein she is believed upon as the holy mother of God. She intercedes on the behalf of the Roman Catholics and Jesus listens to mother Mary in answer to prayers. Roman Catholic teachings which are based upon Roman Catholic traditions violate and deviate from the exegesis whereas there is no private interpretation of the infallible Word of God. The Roman Catholic hierarchy believe they are developing the Word of God by adding to, taking away from, or ignoring the finished work of the cross of Calvary.

Semiramis, the mother of Nimrod who was the founder of Babylon. The same site where the tower of Zigerot which is the tower of Babel and it stood where the people were speaking one language had gathered in what would be considered the global village thinking of that day and building it higher and higher in order to worship the sun, the moon, and the stars. This is the early form of astrology and the people were worshipping the creation and not the Creator God.

The Roman Catholic Church advocated and were part of torturing and murdering Christians, Jews, and Muslims who objected to the Roman Catholic teachings. The Christians were also in defiance against the teachings of indulgences which was the teaching of perpetual mass cards in order to ransom loved ones out of Purgatory. The Roman Catholic inquisition ordered by the Pope was against all those who opposed the Roman Catholic teachings. Thousands of faithful and devout Christians were murdered in cold blood by barbaric Roman Catholic torturers and executioners in the 15th and 16th centuries in front of yelling, cheering, and excited people. Peradventure you would like to know more about Roman Catholic doctrines and teachings of the church we recommend Catholicism & Christianity by Jimmy Swaggart.

Marlie is a multitalented gifted woman of faith. The Lord has also blessed her with a quality voice and tremendous musical talent as a gifted pianist. Marlie doesn't read music, but she receives inspiration when she sits down to play the piano. I believe God gave her the talent, and she developed her musical dedicated talent and is a skilled performer. Through continuous practicing and playing the piano by ear over the years she has reached a higher skill level as a pianist. The Lord God Almighty is the true giver of gifts and talents which He graciously bestows upon His creation, and Marlie is one who God blessed with gifts; she uses those gifts and talents to bless the Lord and the large number of people who have heard her sing and play the piano over the years.

One summer when I was at home in Clover Valley, Randell Wikum came down for a visit. He needed a place to stay because he, and Carol weren't doing very well in their marriage. While Randell was visiting, he and my dad, and I went to Feather Creek to do some fishing. Randell was engrossed in his fishing when I sneaked up behind him across an open field. Randell was just below the bank on the north side of Feather Creek which was flowing westward.

As I was creeping across the field I stayed low so that Randell couldn't catch a glimpse of me coming from behind. When I was near to Randell's fishing position I lit a Black Cat firecracker, and flicked it in his direction with a perfect finger toss. It landed right behind Randell and exploded with a loud cracking pop.

Randell was caught completely off guard, but he said, "Jonah jon Jeffreys, would you grow up?"

I was pleased with myself that I had surprised Randell with a firecracker in good sport.

Later when we were back home Randell pushed a firecracker of his own through the bathroom window where I was drying off after having a bath. The firecracker fizzled and didn't explode with the payback explosion that Randell was hoping for. Later when Randell was away from the house I short-sheeted his bed and put cornflakes in his sheets.

Randell however detected something peculiar about the bed, and he was able to thwart my mischievous plans of giving him a hard time out of good fun.

Randell was a good sport at times throughout his marriage to my sister Carol.

When I went back to Union I liked to counsel my friends, and I enjoyed sharing Christian doctrines, words of wisdom, and knowledge through my counseling insights. I liked sharing words of encouragement to friends and acquaintances.

I was witnessing in downtown Union when I saw an African American man on the sidewalk. He came up to me and my witnessing partner, Chris saying, "I know what you're down here for. On the dollar bill it says, 'In God we trust,' and as long as I have that dollar bill I trust in God."

There are a lot of characters in this world who need evangelizing for Christ Jesus, but they are too egotistically proud and wrapped up in their own head games; they have preconceived notions and ideas about trusting in God, knowing God, and how to rightly live for God. The Lord expects us to walk humbly before Him with humility and reverence of heart and mind.

"He has shown you, O man, what is good; And what does the Lord require of you but to do justly, to love mercy, and to walk humbly with your God?" (Micah 6:8)

When I was attending Union Theology Institute I applied for a job with William County Carrier and was hired by the company. I met my friend, Greg Danielson while working at William County as a shuttle carrier driver. Greg approached me one day in the carrier lot, and asked if we could get together sometime for lunch to talk. I had taken a course on pastoral care and counseling while attending the Pentecostal Bible Institute, and a counseling course at Union Theology Institute. I tried to be a personal friend, and a positive source of encouragement to Greg who seemed to have problems in his personal life. The things that bothered him had caused a great deal of emotional suffering and mental perplexity.

I looked for ways to offer my friend advice, and wisdom that he might be able to apply to his personal life and in his relationships with women. I saw Greg as an immature Christian, one who had a lot of questions without solid answers that would bring him relief, help, and genuine satisfaction that God could fulfill his needs. Greg had plenty of questions that he asked me or a friend who would come along for a lunch or for a dinner get-together. Greg didn't always have answers to his questions, and he enjoyed playing devil's advocate with me and others.

Greg said that God had passed him over when it came to having brains and good looks. He felt like he was a "seven" in the looks category, and he wasn't a good communicator with the women. I tried to encourage Greg by providing advice on what he could talk about with any potential date. Greg felt like the women weren't taking enough time to get to know him. Once they found out that Greg was a part-time shuttle carrier driver they didn't want to go out for a date with him. For a lot of women Greg would be considered the bottom of the rung.

I continued to be a positive source of encouragement to Greg over the many years of our friendship. Greg was able to have a friendship with two women who appreciated him. He played tennis with one of them and got together for talks with the other.

Greg and I did the following together: had lunches and dinners, played tennis, went bowling, played chess, ran against each other in competition, played golf, arm wrestled, attended sports events, attended a Christian gathering and Christian concert, and went on a double-date.

Greg said he would have a thousand questions for God when he got to heaven, but he liked to ask me the questions for which he felt there were no answers.

I believed that God already provided the answers for us as recorded in The Bible, and the Holy Spirit can give us answers that we struggle with intellectually and emotionally.

Greg and I were in competition in key areas of our personal lives in sports, spirituality, and relationships with women. He thought that he was a better tennis player than I was, and I said that we should let the outcome of the games prove who-was-the-better player. Over the years Greg worked hard to defeat me in tennis and in other games where we competed against one another, but in the end I defeated my friend Greg in more sporting events than he won.

When it came to spiritual matters Greg seemed to feel that God should make provisions for him as a father would provide for his son; Greg told me he had been a Christian for thirty-five years. I could see that Greg had areas in his life that he needed to work on before he could find the woman of his dreams. Greg felt that he was missing out on a lot of things that God had promised in His Word, and that God hadn't provided the fulfillment of His promise for Greg. He didn't appreciate waiting for God to answer his prayers especially when it came to finding a good woman.

One Sunday night Greg and I attended Christian Fellowship Tabernacle, a Christian gathering in Riverbend. Following the gathering service we decided to go to Cindy's Restaurant before going home. We each had our own cars, and each of us was determined to beat the other at arriving first at Cindy's. Greg had gotten an early lead in his '77 Honda Civic. I was surprised to see Greg sitting at a stop sign, waiting for the southbound traffic to clear when I pulled up in my '75 Honda Civic on the right shoulder next to the concrete bulkhead. Greg did not look in my direction when he started to make a right turn directly into my bronze-metallic Civic.

He never saw me sitting there ready to make a right-hand turn also. He never knew that I had sneaked in on his right side until he ran into my car's left front bumper and then he backed up to allow me to pull out first.

When we went inside the restaurant we had a long hearty laugh together over our amusing accident. I apologized to Greg for what I had done to cause the accident, and Greg forgave me for pulling up and moving out of the white boundary lines on the road. I thanked the good Lord that Greg didn't hold it against me for the crinkled wheel well on his car. On my car the black rubber stripe pulled loose on the left front bumper, but I was able to glue it back flush with my silver bumper which caused it to match the car body.

One day a passenger on my carrier shuttle wanted to know if I could lead him in a prayer after I had shared the love of God with him. The man's name was James Salvador, and he gave his life to the Lord as I led him in a sinner's prayer right on the carrier. James and I were alone on the personnel carrier during a winter snowstorm in 1986. I didn't have chains on my carrier, and when I tried to continue driving in the storm I couldn't get my vehicle to move due to a lack of traction.

Without chains on the tires I didn't have any traction to move the heavy carrier in the snow. I placed some ground black coal (from a plastic container on the carrier) under my tires, but I still wasn't able to drive. I had made a crucial mistake in stopping my carrier shuttle on the hill after someone had rung the chime chord. I realized too late that I should have gone to the top of the hill before stopping.

On a separate occasion I invited an African American passenger, Bill Henderson to come with me to a Christian Fellowship Tabernacle gathering to hear the evangelist James Robinson preach. Bill came with me, and he responded to the alter call, and he gave his life to the Lord Jesus. Bill was new in town, and he had to wait for his luggage to arrive the next day at the Shuttle Bug Station. I took the now-Christian man home with me, and Bill was so appreciative of my Christian kindness by taking in a complete stranger and providing food and shelter. The next day I gave him a ride to the Bug Station so that he could get his luggage.

God used me for his Christian service and ministry, and I looked for ways that I might be able to serve the Lord by bringing people to Christ Jesus those who were interested and open to receiving Him as Lord and Savior.

I went to a Tae Kwon Do Martial Arts Center in the Brocket District with a fellow carrier driver and friend, Lynn McConnell. We'd had lunch at the Queen's Wharf Buffet, and now we wanted to see a demonstration of martial arts between well-trained individuals or by someone working out by himself to improve his martial arts with precision body skills, finesse, and power.

Lynn said that he had a black belt in Karate, but he didn't want to tell the martial arts

Trapped By A Psycho Doctor

instructor at the training center about his black belt status. The instructor turned out to be a nine times grandmaster in Tae Kwon Do, and instead of giving us a martial arts demonstration he performed some of his simple moves on Lynn to show how to disable an opponent. The demonstration resulted in Lynn feeling unpleasant pain. Lynn and I walked away from the martial arts center unhappy that the demonstration had been applied directly to his unsuspecting body. We learned what to do by the demonstration on Lynn at the hands of the nine-time grandmaster how to stop an adversary.

For anyone interested in surviving a physical attack, muscle memory plays a vital part because without muscle memory an oncoming attack catches you by surprise which is horrifying and causes you to freeze up. Some martial artists have been beaten-up by an unskilled street fighter that has only one trick in their arsenal which is a sucker punch.

One day Lynn and I drove from the Rolland Carrier site, the only personnel carrier site of the William County Carrier Company to the Brocket District for lunch. We decided to go to a pizza parlor for their all-you-can-eat pizza. Instead of eating the entire slice of pizza we ate the toppings off each slice and then placed the crust on a brown plastic tray. We ate a lot of pizza toppings between the two of us, and the stack of pizza dough grew higher and higher.

After a good deal of the toppings had disappeared the manager came over to have a talk with Lynn. "You have to stop eating the pizza that way," he said, "or I'm going to call the police."

Lynn shrugged. "Do what you have to do because we aren't going to stop eating this way."

The manager refunded Lynn the money for our order; he didn't say a thing to me even though I'd been eating my pizza the same way as Lynn. In fact it had been my idea. I had learned to eat the toppings off the pizza from watching my landlord, Charlene Spencer a very special senior citizen Christian lady.

Lynn was unhappy with me for not speaking up to the manager as he had done. When the manager confronted Lynn I was as quiet as a church mouse, but I stopped eating any more pizza slices the way we had been when I heard the manager complain to Lynn that he needed to stop eating the way he was. I'm positive the cashier must have alerted the manager of Lynn's eating style, but since I was facing away from the cashier she must not have focused her attention on me eating the same way as Lynn had been.

The manager had brought our enjoyable lunch experience to a halt. It was a total surprise and seemed like an overreaction to the way we were eating our pizza. We left Joe's Pizza Parlor before the police were called or at least before they arrived.

I saw Lynn as an intellectual sort and a reasoning type of a person who appreciated talking with me about God. He intellectualized and reasoned his way to understanding God and the ways of God.

Lynn said that he saw Greg as a baby Christian with a big diaper, one who was beating up on God by complaining all the time that God wasn't meeting his individual needs. Lynn had grown disgusted with Greg's negative thinking, and continuous complaining about his unsuccessful life. Lynn didn't want to be around Greg anymore because of his negative perspective.

When Greg, Lynn, and I were having lunch one day at the Queen's Wharf Buffet Lynn told Greg, "You're going to hell."

Greg thought that Lynn had misjudged his relationship with God and his eternal destiny.

At the Rolland Carrier site, Lynn had more words for Greg. He said, "If I wasn't a Christian I'd beat the crap out of you."

Greg didn't respond to Lynn, but he did want to talk to me.

I understood that Greg and Lynn each wanted to have an ongoing friendship with me, but definitely not with each other. I had appreciated my relationship with Greg over the years, but Greg did have some erroneous thinking about his relationship with God and with women.

I continued to try to encourage Greg even when my words of wisdom, and positive advice didn't seem to make any difference to him.

Greg liked to ask me what I would do if I got married, and then my wife packed on three hundred pounds and didn't want to exercise to shed those unwanted pounds. "What if she was in a car accident, and you couldn't have sexual relations anymore?" Greg liked to think of the worst scenarios concerning marriage so he could get my perspective. I believe Greg wanted me to admit that I would grow tired of a woman that wouldn't keep herself looking good for me, and I would eventually throw in the marriage towel and divorce her for irreconcilable differences which could include weight gain issues.

I offered words of wisdom from God's perspective and an answer that Greg might think was the right way to view a committed marriage relationship. "A man should honor his marriage vows," I told him, "for better or for worse, in sickness and in health. He should remain committed to his wife."

"But what if you're not happy in the relationship?" Greg asked. "Would God expect you to stay in an unhappy relationship?"

"I can see the importance of remaining faithful before God to your loving spouse regardless of whether she was in perfect physical health or wasn't as physically attractive as she was on the day you married her." Greg had experienced so many negative circumstances and rejections from women throughout the years that he had developed a defeatist attitude in his relationships with them.

I had been dealing with Greg for years regarding his seemingly endless negative thinking about the insincere things that even Christian women were guilty of committing. Greg had been to Christian Churches and dances where he would ask a nice Christian woman to go out for coffee, to lunch, to a concert, or to play tennis. Many women would give Greg their phone numbers, but when he called them later they would say they were busy or that they had a boyfriend.

Greg couldn't understand why Christian women wouldn't merely tell him up front when they weren't interested or that they had a boyfriend. He had grown distasteful of Christian women; he felt they should be honest in their relationships with men, yet they had shown him that they didn't have good character qualities. He wondered about the Christian women's motives.

"Many women," I told Greg, "because of their emotional natures, can't seem to tell the would-be suitor who may not be the man of their dreams, that they have other plans, commitments, or a boyfriend but if they have a boyfriend what are they doing in a Christian singles group?"

Greg had made negative comments about women for so long that I thought I would provide Greg with an interesting situation and give Greg a taste of his own medicine. Greg had more than enough negative relationship situations to ask me about, but no matter what positive answer I gave to Greg he always had another negative question. So after years of his negative questions I asked Greg what he would do in a particular situation. "What if you met the woman of your dreams a beautiful figure, measured up in every way that you would want in a woman, was interested in sports, and could play tennis?"

This was very important for him. "She'll make you happy as your wife, but she has one problem." I was ready to share the big punch line to see if he would marry this wonderful woman who only had one issue to overcome. I said to Greg, "She doesn't have a vagina. Would you marry her?"

"Of course not," Greg said. I recognized the woman he wanted to marry needed to have the standard pieces of equipment.

One day as Greg and I debated an important issue I decided to let Greg read what the Bible had to say about the matter. Greg liked to play the devil's advocate when he debated or argued with me on spiritual subjects, social issues, relationship matters, political parties, and sports. He debated me with confidence regardless of the subject.

When I showed Greg the Bible passage that I believed would settle the matter, I thought he would concede that my points were in line with God's thoughts on the matter, but Greg boldly said, "I don't care what you say. I don't care what the Bible says. I've got to live in this world."

His words surprised me. I declared, "You're not a Christian." Greg was hurt by my quick evaluation of his relationship to Jesus
Christ, but I felt that Greg was in the wrong to declare his total disregard
for what God had stated as eternal truth in The Holy Bible. His Word will never be revoked by the One true God who can never lie.

There may be other professing Christians who feel the same as Greg did, but they have never said that they need to conform to the world in order to survive. Jesus told his believers that He has overcome the world by His faith, and every Christian with God's help can overcome this world by using his or her faith as Jesus has being full of the Holy Spirit.

One time I had a sleeping passenger on my personnel carrier shuttle. When I reached the designated carrier terminal I saw the passenger lying down on the seats in the back of the carrier. He didn't get up as expected, and so I thought I should wake him. I suspected he was intoxicated and that he wouldn't be fazed by what I was about to say over the intercom system. I took hold of the microphone and said, "If anyone is caught sleeping on this carrier they will be shot on sight."

To my surprise the man quickly got up, and hurried to the door wanting me to open it. The sleepy passenger seemed wide awake now, and he hastily left my carrier coach without saying a word.

I discovered that I could play the lip trumpet over my intercom system on my carrier shuttles. One early morning I was driving the shuttle route from Hoover Beach to downtown Union. As I was driving my carrier route I found out that one of the elderly passengers was going to retire soon. I made an announcement over the intercom system asking the other passengers to join me in singing "We Wish You a Happy Good Year" to the tune of "We Wish You a Merry Christmas." After the riders and I sang the song for the retiring senior citizen I played the melody with my lip trumpet. When I finished blowing into the microphone all the travelers applauded.

I continued to drive my route stopping at each designated carrier stop. When I eventually stopped at Eighth and Executive in Downtown Union, a tall African American man walked up the aisle and said to me, "I've been playing the trumpet for sixteen years. You sounded like you were playing the horn."

I accepted the compliment from the considerate passenger as an acknowledgement of my lip-trumpet talents. I enjoyed playing the lip trumpet for my clients during the Christmas season with a variety of Christmas songs.

I also transported children to their schools while driving for William County Carrier. One hot day in June a cute little elementary child was about to get off of the shuttle and I said, "Don't you catch cold out there." The small boy looked directly at me and said, "Yeah, right," and then stepped off the carrier.

I liked to communicate with my passengers by saying, "Have a good day," or "Have a good night." I frequently shared a friendly smile with my passengers to make them feel welcome on my carrier shuttles.

One day a senior citizen woman passenger got on the carrier carrying a cane. I said, "I see you're raising Cain." When she went to exit my carrier I commented with, "One good thing about a cane it makes you able." She smiled to let me know that she liked that.

I liked to tell passengers and other carrier drivers the Willie Nelson joke. I'd say, "Have you heard the sad news about Willie Nelson? I was listening to the news today, and they said that he got run over."

The passengers would say something like, "Oh no, really? Was he killed?"

Then I would give the punch line saying, "He's been playing on the road again."

Most people understood that this was a joke, but one senior carrier driver had been leaning out into the aisle to hear what had happened to Willie Nelson, and when I gave the punch line he sat back in the seat and acted like he didn't care to hear anything more what I had to say. The Willie Nelson joke was a good attention-getter. Having something humorous, kind, and considerate to say can go a long way to brighten a passenger's day. I asked my customer friend Larry who worked for the Morris Parking Company with Avista Transportation if he had caught the fight at the candy store. Then I told him, "The sucker got licked."

Larry seemed interested in hearing the gory details of the big fight, thinking that the person who got "licked" had experienced a thorough thrashing. Larry kept pressing me for more details of the fight, but I kept repeating, "The sucker got licked at the candy store."

"Which candy store?" Larry asked.

So I provided the name of a store that Larry was familiar with in Union Bristol's, a pharmacy drugstore. Time and time again I would repeat the same line about the sucker getting licked at the candy store. Larry kept insisting that I tell him the bloody description of the struggle, and I repeated over again the same line the sucker got licked.

When it was obvious that Larry didn't get my corny joke I finally let him know that it was just a joke.

Having to repeat myself to Larry reminded me of when I told a friend about two parrots named Pete and Repeat sitting on a fence together. I told my friend, "Pete flew away so who was left?"

He answered, "Repeat."

So I said again, "Pete and Repeat were sitting on a fence. Pete flew away so who was left?"

Once again he said, "Repeat."

Not everyone catches on to the funny scenario the first time I tell it; it is only meant for a joke.

One day a talented young lady named Jackie McPhearson, who was on her way home to Kismet Island rode my shuttle carrier. Jackie said that she attended Creative Designed Institute which I discovered was Charles Finney Society on Madison Ridge in Union. She graciously invited me to come to see her perform in a play in which she sang and acted like the actress Julie Andrews. I was truly impressed with Jackie's singing and acting abilities during the evening performance.

Trapped By A Psycho Doctor

Jackie had some fun with me by telling me some corny jokes while I drove my carrier route. Jackie said, "Let me hear you spell silk."

I responded, "S-I-L-K." "What do cows drink?" I responded, "Milk."

Jackie said, "Wrong. Cows drink water. Calves drink milk." I thought that was a pretty good joke.

Jackie said, "Let me hear you say roast." I responded, "Roast."

"Let me hear you say boast." I said, "Boast."

"Let me hear you say almost." I responded, "Almost."

Then Jackie said, "What do you put in a toaster?" I responded, "Toast."

Jackie said, "No, you put bread in, and you get toast back."

I was impressed with Jackie's jokes. She had caught me off guard during her carrier ride, and I caught other people on the same humorous jokes over the years.

I got together with a nice couple of carrier operators who worked at William County Carrier Company. They were married, and they wanted to share a business plan with me; they thought I might be interested in making some extra money outside of the carrier company. Rex and Cathy Bernard were kind enough to take time out of their day to share with me what they hoped would be a win-win proposition that could turn out to be a successful business opportunity.

I arrived late at the Denny's Restaurant where we were to meet, and I informed them that I didn't have long to spend with them because I had another meeting to go to.

Later in their work week Rex told me that he had shared the business opportunity with the waiter after I left, but the waiter told Rex that he had come into some money and wasn't interested in the business plan. The waiter had told Rex that he was a single father and he had a daughter. Rex assumed that the waiter probably received $35,000.00 so he kept trying to sell the waiter on the business plan. When Rex could tell the server wasn't catching fire on the business opportunity he asked the waiter how much money he had come into. The waiter said, "Forty-two million dollars."

The waiter had waited on a man for nine years, and he never knew that he had that kind of money. When the man would come into the Denny's Restaurant he would give the waiter a gift. Rex said to me, "The same man who gave that waiter forty-two million did the same for four other people."

When I was driving home after hearing Rex's story I thought to myself, Can you believe that? Here we are working as carrier driver's earning the pay we get, and this guy is freely given all of this money. When I later reflected on the story I heard from Rex I concluded, That is truly a human-interest story.

When I called to speak with the manager at the Denny's Restaurant the next Sunday I asked if the story I had heard was true and he said, "Yes". "Is the waiter going to continue to work there?" I asked. The manager said, "Yes, he's going to".

The last time I planned to follow up to see if the waiter was still working at Denny's the restaurant had closed down.

I made my usual client pickup at Seventh Avenue and Royal Diamond Street in Union to drive my carrier shuttle route out to Polo and Collard one Saturday evening. I drove my southbound trip all the way out to the city of Collard, and when it came time to pull into the Collard Carrier Center I observed a vehicle in front of me with its left turn signal on. I assumed the driver would continue turning into the parking lot without stopping, but instead I was caught off guard when the vehicle stopped for an oncoming car that was some distance ahead.

I had to make a sudden stop to avoid hitting the vehicle in front me, and when I braked suddenly an elderly woman fell backward onto the hard floor of the carrier hitting her head. A couple of men helped her up, and she sat down in the first seat across from me.

After the riders had gotten off the shuttle at the carrier center I was able to ask the lady how she was. She said she thought she was all right, but as she felt the back of her head she wasn't quite so sure. "Are you willing to remain on the carrier while I drive my next route so I can make certain you're going to be fine?" I asked.

The woman agreed to remain on the shuttle, and I was able to monitor her by listening to the things she was saying. During the course of the carrier route I heard her say, "I don't know how I'm going to be. I'm going to have my son take me to the hospital to be checked out."

When I heard that I knew I needed to fill out an accident report when I returned to the Rolland Carrier site.

At the end of the carrier line a male traveler in a brown trench coat walked to the front of the carrier, and asked me if I'd seen who had taken his bag. I could tell the man was upset about his missing bag, but I hadn't seen anyone take it.

The man continued to search around his seating area until he came up another time to ask me for my ID number that was issued to me by the carrier company. I told the man, "W-I-L-L-I-A-M."

The angry man was not amused by my answer. He got off the carrier only to return a short time later for another vigorous search for his bag followed by slamming his fist into the passenger window he broke it with a fierce blow.

Finally, I had the presence of mind to ask the frustrated and fuming man where he had gotten on the personnel carrier.

"I got on at Fifth and Cellar," the steaming rider said.

I knew that was in downtown Union. "I took over the carrier route at Seventh and Royal Diamond," I told him. "That's south of downtown Union."

I knew the angry passenger was doing his level best to hold me responsible for his missing bag, but I refused to accept responsibility for it. Finally, he admitted to me that he had fallen asleep on my shuttle carrier, and I knew the rider was responsible for his own missing bag. Each time the angry man got off my carrier after making repeated searches for his lost bag I continued my conversation with the woman who had fallen. The final time the irate traveler exited my carrier the injured woman said, "Man, he is scary. I was concerned that he might have a gun."

I made the important phone call to report the woman's accident and also reported that the man had broken the window on my carrier. Then I took the opportunity to feel the back of the woman's head where she had made contact with the floor. I was surprised to find a large bump on her head, and I realized it was probably best that she have it checked out by a doctor especially at her age.

The woman said, "I know of a woman who had got a bump on her head and ended up dying."

This was not something I wanted to hear, but she then said her son would take her to the hospital. I drove my remaining passenger back to the Collard Carrier Center where she stepped off my carrier shuttle.

As I drove my carrier shuttle route back to downtown Union, and subsequently to the Mandalay District I thought about the angry man. He was insistent on holding me responsible for his missing bag. As I contemplated the possibility of the angry traveler waiting for me at the end of the line I became concerned that he might be hiding behind a tree with a gun.

These concerned thoughts were going through my mind as I slowly drove up to the carrier terminal at the end of my shuttle route in Collard.

I peered toward the trees to see if the man was lurking behind one armed and dangerous. When I didn't see him I turned off my carrier shuttle, and rested my head on my crossed arms on the steering wheel.

A couple of minutes before I was to begin my next trip into downtown Union I heard three loud pounding sounds on the driver's side window.

I immediately looked out the window, and when I didn't see anyone I quickly looked into my driver's side mirror only to see the same angry man walking back down Twenty-Seventh Avenue NE away from my carrier shuttle. I was startled by what had just transpired the still-fuming rider pounding with his fist on the side window. When I made the loop back over to 273rd and Twenty-Ninth Avenue NE, and pulled up to a stop sign I saw the man with the brown trench coat walking away from my carrier with his back turned toward me.

As I reflected on the three hard pounds on my driver's side window I interpreted the man's pounding message as, "Bang, bang, bang. I could have shot you while you slept."

I never saw the man again, but it certainly was an unusual experience and gave me a good scare.

One night I was able to get the night off from driving three trips on my regular route 456 shuttle from downtown Union to Hoover Beach, and on the return two trips from Hoover Beach to downtown Union. Later on I would drive two round-trips on two separate late-night service carrier routes, leaving from Sixth Avenue and Frontier Street in downtown Union. (Route 876 left downtown at 1:45 a.m)., and (Route 879 left from Sixth and Frontier at 3:45 a.m.)

I later discovered that on my night off a homeless African American man had waited for my carrier shuttle to show up at Twelfth Avenue and Capella Street. When my carrier shuttle driven by a substitute driver showed up at the carrier lay-over stop the homeless man was standing there.

The driver opened the door and asked, "Are you getting on the carrier?" When the man said he was waiting for me to show up the driver responded, "Hotel Jonah jon Jeffreys. I know him. He's off tonight."

The patient homeless man was disappointed to learn that he would have to wait until the following night to catch up with me.

I had attracted quite a number of homeless individuals who looked forward to riding with me on my late-night carrier service. Unfortunately, not all my fellow carrier drivers appreciated my kindness and hospitality toward the homeless; they felt that I was setting a bad example that they would have to follow. From my perspective I was showing acts of caring compassion toward people who didn't have a home. My late-night carrier was well-known for its hospitality to the homeless, and became known as a motel on wheels. Unfortunately, my carrier had unpleasant odors that other respectable night riders didn't appreciate.

I discovered that the carrier supervisor who oversaw the late-night service from downtown Union was fully aware of my providing a helpful comfortable seat to people less fortunate than others.

One fine evening a woman named Vera Brown was on my coach. Vera had shared with me that when she was thirteen years old she had been hit by a car while walking in a crosswalk, and the impact had left her disabled for life. Vera also told me that she had given birth to two girls when she was living on the streets. Vera's mother had insisted that Vera give up one girl for adoption, but her mother was raising the other girl as her own daughter.

I also discovered that Vera had a good sense of humor, and that elevated her life and character from merely being a victim of circumstances as a young girl to an adult capable of giving and who chose not to wallow in the negative things in life. I enjoyed playing the lip trumpet for Vera using the microphone over the intercom on my carrier shuttle. She thought it was an amazing feat that I could go from an extremely high-pitched trumpet sound to a really low bass note. Any way you look at it Vera was a delightful, and a colorful individual who expressed her sense of humor with a hearty laughter that could be heard throughout my carrier shuttle.

I had driven my personnel carrier to East Union Junction, and continued on to Saint Charles Street where I stopped for the traffic light. I looked across the intersection and read the advertisement on the window of the, The Pizza Palace. Vera was sitting across the aisle from me and I said to her, "Hey Vera, the next time you think about having any more children The Pizza Palace delivers."

My words struck Vera's funny bone, and she burst out laughing. She wasn't shy in any respect about restraining her outburst of laughter. When the traffic signal changed, and I turned onto Johanson Drive. Vera was still laughing at the image of having any future children delivered to her by The Pizza Palace delivery boy.

Melody Paradise had taken a special interest in me as her personnel carrier driver in Collard. Melody, a kindhearted senior citizen had a couple of hobbies: writing poetry, and taking photographs of people and things that interested her.

I had shared Bible truths with Melody. She took them seriously and began reading the Bible. I also shared the sinner's prayer with her which Melody prayed with me over the phone, and she gave her heart to Jesus Christ as her personal Savior and Lord. She also was extremely grateful that I had shared doctrinal points in which the Roman Catholic Church had not been scripturally honest or accurate. Melody left the Roman Catholic Church after learning that many of their doctrines were not based on Bible teachings, but on Roman Catholic teachings derived from Roman Catholic traditions throughout the centuries.

I hope and pray that many other died-in-the-wool Catholics will have their eyes opened, repent of their sins, and come to know the Lord Jesus Christ as their personal Lord and Savior.

As Mary the mother of Jesus said, "My soul doth magnify the Lord. And my spirit hath rejoiced in God my Savior" (Luke 1:46–47). Mary recognized that she needed the Savior for herself. Mary was a sinner like everyone else she was born with a sin nature, and in need of having her sins forgiven through the shed blood of Jesus Christ on the cross of Calvary. To God be the glory, honor, and praise for who He is and the great things He has done by saving whosoever will call on the name of the Lord by His saving grace through an act of faith believing. Thank God for His glorious salvation which is His free unmerited gift to all humanity Worldwide.

Bud recently shared with me concerning the Roman Catholic teachings. He went on to say, The Roman Catholic hierarchy claims that they have the authority to change the wafer that is put on the tongues of the kneeling worshipers into the real body of Jesus, and the wine cups that they drink from is changed into the real blood of Jesus. This teaching or dogma is called transubstantiation. Faithful Roman Catholics claim that they have received Jesus because of the wafer and wine changing into the actual blood of Jesus.

They also claim in that they were sprinkled as babies by the priests, the Roman Catholic Church claims the authority to pronounce baby Christians based on their faithfulness in attending mass, and attending confessions this means perpetual mass cards. Roman Catholic priests pray for the dead in Purgatory and the person having the perpetual mass card, the priest prays for the family member of that Roman Catholic that are in Purgatory. The Roman Catholic priest when asked if the person they are praying for is out of Purgatory yet the priest will shrug and say, "Nobody can know that".

This teaching of Purgatory like so many other Roman Catholic teachings are not found in The Holy Bible, but are based upon Roman Catholic traditions which is basically considered extra non-Biblical teachings prescribed by the Roman Catholic Church and its faithful followers.

Any non-Roman Catholic that marries a Roman Catholic, and the marriage ceremony is held in the Roman Catholic Church. A legal document has to be signed by the non-Roman Catholic, and the Roman Catholic that has had any children conceived in the marriage must be raised according to Roman Catholic teachings and attend Roman Catholic Parochial School. If the non-Roman Catholic chooses or refuses to raise the children as Roman Catholics the Roman Catholic spouse will take away the children from the non-believing spouse.

The Roman Catholic Church has a lot of Roman Catholic lawyers. Let the reader be aware. The Roman Catholic Church believes that Mary is the holy mother of God, she is the co-mediator and to make requests of Jesus she has the ear of Jesus for them. Thus the Roman Catholic Church does not have the Holy Trinity, but believes in the Holy quartet. The Roman Catholic Church also believes in prayers to the dead saints because the dead saints have more light than we mortals on earth do. All of these teachings are in direct violation and deviation of the Word of God as recorded in The Holy Bible.

The Roman Catholic Church teaches the Virgin Mary remained a virgin until she ascended into heaven, and that she is the Co-Redemptrix wherein she is believed upon as the holy mother of God. She intercedes on the behalf of the Roman Catholics, and Jesus listens to mother Mary in answer to prayers. Roman Catholic teachings which are based upon Roman Catholic traditions violate and deviate from the exegesis whereas there is no private interpretation of the infallible Word of God. The Roman Catholic hierarchy believe they are developing the Word of God by adding to, taking away from, or ignoring the finished work of the cross of Calvary.

Semiramis, the mother of Nimrod who was the founder of Babylon. The same site where the tower of Zigerot which is the tower of Babel and it stood where the people were speaking one language had gathered in what would be considered the global village thinking of that day, and building it higher and higher in order to worship the sun, the moon, and the stars. This is the early form of astrology and the people were worshipping the creation and not the Creator God.

The Roman Catholic Church advocated and were part of torturing and murdering Christians, Jews, and Muslims who objected to the Roman Catholic teachings. The Christians were also in defiance against the teachings of indulgences which was the teaching of perpetual mass cards in order to ransom loved ones out of Purgatory. The Roman Catholic inquisition ordered by the Pope was against all those who opposed the Roman Catholic teachings. Thousands of faithful and devout Christians were murdered in cold blood by barbaric Roman Catholic torturers and executioners in the 15th and 16th centuries in front of yelling, cheering, and excited people. Peradventure you would like to know more about Roman Catholic doctrines, and teachings of the church we recommend Catholicism & Christianity by Jimmy Swaggart.

One Saturday I showed Melody a childhood picture of my good friend Treat Munson and me. We were sitting together on the couch in my house in Clover Valley, dressed up as a clown and a beautiful girl, before we went out trick-or-treating on Halloween night.

"I'm the one dressed as a clown," I said. "Could you get my picture enlarged at Bristol's Drugstore?"

"I'll do that," Melody agreed and because she like the picture, she also had a copy made for herself. Later when Melody handed me the copy of my photo, she pointed to the girl in the picture and said, "Why didn't you hang onto her? She is so beautiful."

"I did hold on to my 'girlfriend' all these years."

Melody didn't understand; she knew that I now was married to my lovely wife Lorena Scone.

Eventually I explained what I meant by telling her that I had held on to my childhood girlfriend. I was not the boy dressed up as the clown in the picture; I was the boy dressed up as Treat Munson's "girlfriend" and we were still friends after all these years.

I had taken an interest in a couple of women after graduating from Union Theology Institute. One blonde, Jennifer Berg was an attractive woman, and I thought she had a nice-looking nose. Jennifer was a Christian lady who was interested in serving the Lord in the ministry along with her future husband. Jennifer worked well with small children in the daycare, and I found that she was caring and sensitive concerning the things of the Lord. Jennifer sometimes compared herself with her sister who was already married and had children. Jennifer thought that I would make a good addition to the Berg family if we married.

We liked to talk about the Lord and Christian counseling; we listened to music, attended church together, and got together for lunch or dinner at times. Sometime later I got to meet Jennifer's parents who had come to visit their daughters in Union. I discovered that Mr. Berry Berg had a large, unattractive nose, which gave me major concerns regarding marrying Jennifer. I thought that if we had children they likely would have prominent noses too.

I also took an interest in an attractive woman from the Philippines named Phoebe Philomena, who was a passenger on one of my personnel carrier routes. One day I invited Phoebe to go church with me to the Grace Gospel Church in Union. I found out that Phoebe had grown up in a very conservative, traditional, religious home in the Philippines. When I met her she was living with her father in south Union. Her mother had remained in the Philippines where she was able to take care of their crops with the hired servants. I told Phoebe that the religious church she was attending was not in agreement with the Bible, and Phoebe listened to what I had to share, concerning her traditional religious church. In her church she wasn't accustomed to hearing the biblical teachings that I told her about.

Later on Phoebe said that when I told her that the teachings of her ritualistic traditional church were in contradiction with the Bible it had hurt her.

That night I picked her up for church, and we drove to the Grace Gospel Church service. I had heard that evangelist Peter Youngren was going to be at the church that night, and I wanted Phoebe to hear the salvation message that he would preach under the anointing of the Holy Spirit. While attending the theology institute, I had learned that the anointing of the Holy Spirit is the painting or coming on of the Holy Spirit's presence over a person's life.

Peter Youngren preached about Jesus feeding the five thousand men as well as the women, and children present during lunchtime in the Bible days when Jesus walked the earth. I sensed a powerful anointing of the Holy Spirit in the church building that night which was unusually stronger and which people could feel and sense.

I could hear Phoebe sniffling as Peter was preaching a powerful heart touching message. It seemed to touch her heart with the good news about the miracles of Jesus Christ.

When evangelist Peter Youngren had finished his preaching about the miracle of the multiplication of the fish and bread he gave an invitation for those who would like to receive Jesus into their hearts and lives.

I thought about asking Phoebe if she would like to accept Jesus into her heart, but I decided to leave it up to her and the Holy Spirit. To my surprise Phoebe raised her hand signifying that she would like to receive Jesus into her heart that night. At Peter's invitation Phoebe walked to the front of the church along with the other souls who desired to receive God's free gift of salvation through an act of inviting God into their lives in the person of Jesus Christ.

Upon repeating the sinner's prayer after the evangelist's promptings Phoebe, and the others were led to a side room to be given further instructions on how to live for the Lord each day after accepting Jesus Christ as their Savior and Lord. The new birth experience had been miraculously conceived in her spiritual heart and life by the Spirit of Jesus Christ.

When Phoebe joined me again in the congregation a member of the church named, Willard Houston came over to us. Willard said that he had seen Phoebe before she accepted Christ Jesus in the church service, and he could see that her face had lit up after she accepted Jesus into her life. Phoebe had a big grin on her face showing that she had received God's gift of salvation as found in the person of Jesus Christ.

After the service Phoebe said that when she heard that the disciples had turned their backs on the people who represented the need, and they had looked to Jesus first it really had touched her heart. Jesus met the spiritual needs of the people before He met their physical needs. Humanity worldwide has spiritual, emotional, mental, financial, social and family relationships, and physical needs that God in Christ is able to meet with abundance for those who place their faith and trust in the finished work of Jesus Christ on His cross which is resurrection-validated. The Holy Spirit had brought home to her heart and life the wonderful truths of the miracle working power of Jesus as preached by Peter Youngren.

Before I drove Phoebe home I decided to stop by Charlene Spencer's home to have Phoebe tell her the good news of receiving Jesus into her heart. Mrs. Spencer was a very precious and dearly beloved Christian senior citizen and my landlord. Phoebe walked up to her and gave her a big hug saying, "I married Jesus." For a traditional religious person to say that she married Jesus I knew that something wonderful had happened in Phoebe's heart and life.

I kept in touch with Phoebe to see how she was doing in her new walk with Jesus in her life, and Phoebe once said that she had read in the Bible that Jesus had brothers and sisters. Phoebe was learning the wonderful truths about Jesus as revealed in the Bible for herself, and God the Holy Spirit was making the difference in her new life in Christ. Phoebe was saved, being saved, and continue to be saved as she would continue to look to Jesus Christ as the author and finisher of her new found faith in Him.

After she came to Christ Phoebe thought that she could serve the Lord by becoming a pious nun. She was so sincere and precious in her new, born-again, and spiritual-birth-of-a-new-nature-in-Christ Jesus, Christian walk with the living God that she was willing to serve the Lord in any way she could. Phoebe stayed at a pious convent for nuns for three weeks. She later told me that she'd come to the realization that she could live for God without becoming a nun. Jesus was so good in His leading and guidance to Phoebe, and showing her little by little His revealed will for her life's journey.

Phoebe wanted to find a Christian church where she could grow in her new life in Christ. She had decided not to attend the Grace Gospel Church or the big Congregational Christian Church in Union. She also didn't want to make the Pentecostal Philippine Church in Union her church home. But when she found the Congregational Christian Church in Canton, Phoebe decided that was the right Christian church for her, and she made it her church home.

Phoebe had shared with me that when she was in the Philippines she had gone to a Baptist Church that emphasized the doctrine of water baptism as a requirement for salvation; that was where she first heard the words of receiving Jesus into her heart. Although she'd heard those words at the Baptist Church she hadn't responded to the invitation at the time. After she accepted Jesus Christ into her heart at the Grace Gospel Church she continued to go to the Catholic Church which is a traditional religious church with her father in Union.

It was her father's wish that she remain in their traditional faith as was observed and practiced in the Philippine culture. She heard the priest say the words, "Receive Jesus into your heart," but it wasn't the same. Phoebe said that she didn't feel she could grow in her new life in the traditional Catholic Church, and that was the reason that she began searching for the right Christian Church where she could grow in her new life in Christ Jesus.

I recognized that God the Holy Spirit was at work in Phoebe's life, and He was doing a good work by directing her steps before the Lord. I saw Phoebe at the Congregational Christian Church in Canton years later; it was good to know that she had remained faithful to the Lord by her consistent attendance to the House of God over the years.

Phoebe is a living testimony that Jesus Christ can change a person's heart, and life if that person will come to Him by faith and His free gift of salvation. It's important for the new believer in Christ to continue in their personal relationship with God by maintaining a faithful relationship with Jesus Christ and Him crucified on a daily basis. Reading and meditating on the Word of God will help the Christian to grow in their faith in God. The new or mature Christian will continue to grow in Christ as they remain faithful to the high calling of God in Christ Jesus.

I learned an important lesson from watching Phoebe come to the Lord at the Grace Gospel Church. I learned that when anyone comes to know the Lord Jesus Christ it can only happen through the power and operation of the Holy Spirit drawing that person to the Lord Jesus.

I had made the right choice in leaving the best work up to the Holy Spirit to work inside of Phoebe's heart and life rather than for me wanting to move her toward the call for salvation before the Lord had prepared her heart with His tender promptings when evangelist Peter Youngren had given the salvation invitation. I discovered that good things happen to those who wait on the Lord.

I thought about marrying Phoebe who would be a good Christian wife, but I balked at the idea when I thought about having children with her. I concluded that any children we might have together would be short in stature as Phoebe and her sweet parents were short. Phoebe was a special lady with good qualities, but once again I had certain qualities I was looking for in a wife, and being too short wasn't one of them. The Lord knew what qualities I was looking for in a wife, and I was willing to wait until I found that one special lady to marry.

I played slow-pitch baseball for the Resurrection Life Church in Union. I enjoyed pitching and playing right field on the team. One day when my team was having practice at Lake View Park I happened to throw a ball in from center field. It took one bounce and hit my teammate on the right buttocks. I called out to my Christian team member, "Turn the other cheek!" To that my teammates booed in unison. I'd made the witty remark on the spur of the moment, but they wanted me to know that my remark wasn't the best thing for a Christian ballplayer to say.

One day I had the opportunity to play slow-pitch against the Fairview Believer's Worship Center Baseball Team at Mountain View Park in Union. I had good control that day when I found myself pitching to a former professional football player named Mutu Swains.

Whenever I was ahead on strikes I liked to throw a high pitch that was above the strike zone before it made its descent right into the catcher's glove. Mutu waited on one of my high-pitched out-of-the-strike-zone throwaway pitches and he knocked the ball completely out of the park. The ball sailed so high and long that it cleared the Mountain View Park fence and sailed into the tall trees, a long way past the home run fence.

I had given up five home runs to the big man in the two-game double-header. When I saw him standing at home plate again for his turn at bat I turned around to see if my coach, Jerry Alpha wanted me to pitch to Mutu or give him a free walk to first base. Jerry gave me the signal to go ahead and pitch to Mutu. Once again the Mutu taught me a lesson on how to hit a fat juicy pitch out of the ballpark for home run number six.

Thank goodness he was on the Lord's side, but it wasn't a pleasant day in the park for my teammates and me.

I surrendered two losing games to Mutu and the Fairview Believer's Worship Center Baseball Team that day. I later discovered that Mutu Swains had played for the Seattle Seahawks before being traded to the San Francisco '49ers. He then played for the '49ers as a defensive lineman. I decided to join the William County Carrier summer softball league, and I played for the Casaesar Carrier Softball Team for a couple of years in the nineties. I pitched every game that first year during our scheduled play for coach, Kent Martin. During the first year that I pitched for the Casaesar Carrier Baseball Team, the team won the regular season play with the most wins, but when it came time for tournament play at the end of the season, my team lost the opening game to the Rolland Carrier Softball Team at Alexander Hamilton Park in East Union.

We found ourselves out of the tournament disappointed with the crucial loss but determined to rally the troops and play again the next softball season. The following year I once again pitched every game on our schedule. I had excellent control when I threw my pitches with the back of my hand facing home plate. When I released my pitches with my right arm extended high in the air the softball tended to have plenty of backspin on the pitch. This seemed to create problems for the hitters which gave me success on the mound. When I pitched the softball with the palm of my hand facing home plate however I couldn't control my pitches.

In the second softball season my teammates and I lost the regular season play, but we won the tournament championship. During the tournament my teammates and I came alive with consistent play at every position, intensity, and power at bat. We produced more runs than the opposing teams to win the William County Softball Tournament. When the team later had a victory celebration at the coach's home, Kent Martin honored me by acknowledging that I was the reason the team had won the championship and I appreciated his kind remark for our success.

One late night I decided to drop off several paper bags full of leaves into the woods south of Union. As a single man I looked for ways to save money, and since I hadn't set up the extra yard waste service with my garbage collection account I thought I'd take the leaves into the woods, and nobody would be the wiser. I drove down the steep street and pulled over to park near the curb across from a secluded wooded area. There was a cement bulkhead on the north side of the street which was opposite my parked car that was an ideal area to empty the leaves.

Hoping I was inconspicuous I dropped the contents of the bags over the side of the cement barrier. As one of the sacks fell from my hands onto the ground below I suddenly worried that the paper sack I'd dropped had my fingerprints on it. I anxiously decided to retrieve the sack just in case someone found it, and turned it in to the police which could reveal my sneaky save-some-bucks-in-the-cool-of-the-night actions. I was wearing a long-sleeved jacket that protected my arms as I dropped over the side of the cement wall. Once I picked up the sack now empty of the leaves I discovered I wasn't tall enough to scale the wall by myself.

After repeated vain attempts of grabbing on to the flat top of the tall barrier, I decided to pile the leaves on the grass next to the wall, hoping this would give me the extra height I needed to get over the wall. The piled-up leaves, however, did not help. All my efforts were futile in the cool of the dark night air. I was fortunate that no police came along to investigate my parked vehicle.

I was now faced with a real dilemma: how was I going to get back home? There was the concrete wall I couldn't scale, and there were the blackberry vines along the tall barrier that also hindered my escape. I decided to work my way to the street below by going down the hillside through the tall dense thicket which ran along the side of a local park, but I soon got hung up by the thorny thicket that grabbed at my clothes, and I had to retrieve one of my tennis shoes when I got stuck in the soggy muddy soil. I had thoughts of the fire department coming to my rescue to save me from the sticky clutches of the long-armed thorny thicket, with a camera crew filming the rescue that would be shown on the daily news.

I finally realized that I wasn't going to escape my predicament by working my way down the hillside so I worked my way back up to the side of the cement wall slipping in the mud a number of times. In desperation I worked my way along the side of the wall on the short lip of ground that had blackberry vines protruding in a menacing manner hindering my progress.

I thought of the time I'd spent already in trying to escape my ordeal in the woods. I was grateful that there were streetlights which provided enough lighting for me to see as I slowly made my way. Once again though I realized I couldn't walk away from my sticky captivity the blackberry vines were too thick. This was a serious predicament.

Finally, I realized my way of escape from the blackberry vines was to work my way back to the pile of leaves. Painstakingly and slowly I got back to the pile of leaves in front of the cement barrier. I took more time to build up the pile of leaves into the tallest possible mound, and then tried again to use it to get over the concrete wall. The extra time I'd taken by working on other ways to break free must have recharged my energy level. This time although my jacket got scrape marks from my brushing against the concrete wall I was finally free.

My freedom was the real reward for my persevering in difficult circumstances. I had kept myself busy though that was partly out of fear of being found by a police officer or by the fire department who might question why I'd abandoned my vehicle and what I was doing in the woods late at night that would have caused suspicion.

When I got home I lay down on my bed worn out from my experience, and called my girlfriend, Bobbie Jo to tell her about my predicament in the woods.

While I was talking to her I heard a loud piercing scream from the cat that I was taking care of for a friend. The male gray-and-white tiger-striped cat was named Sneakers because all his feet were white as if he was wearing white tennis shoes. Sneakers had a powerful dislike for my female cat,

Fluffy. I was keeping Sneakers in the spare bedroom away from my two female cats, but somehow when I was on my night outing Sneakers had escaped from the small bedroom.

I immediately jumped up from the bed to go to the rescue of my long-haired gray cat, Fluffy. I knew from the angry mountain lion–like screams that Sneakers had Fluffy trapped. I grabbed a plastic coat hanger to scare Sneakers away from my mild-mannered pet. I turned on the light in the short hallway and headed directly toward the screams. I saw Sneakers in the dim light that came from the partially opened door of the entertainment room.

I took two swipes with the plastic hanger at Sneakers at which point Sneakers leaped up and dug his claws into my arm. The sudden painful attack surprised me. I was in shock that Sneakers would attack me as violently as a fierce tomcat. I freed myself from him and got him to go back up the stairs. When I looked at my right arm I saw the bloody wounds.

After saving Fluffy from Sneakers I called Bobbie Jo again. When I told her that Sneakers had attacked me she said, "I think you might need to go to the Fairmont Medical Center in Collard for a tetanus shot."

I appreciated her concern, but I decided against going to the hospital so early in the morning; it was still dark outside. I concluded that Sneaker's care at the Scone residence was now over with; he needed a home where he could be cared for by someone without other cats that would compete for attention. I was able to get Sneakers back into his bedroom with the aid of a trusty broom, and that put an end to my night of terror and scary encounters.

The next morning, I spoke with Jake Williams who assured me that he knew of a woman who could provide a good home for Sneakers. Jake had done a lot of yard work for me so I trusted him, and his promise of a caring home where Sneakers could be the king of his own domain. Later when I checked with Jake to find out how Sneakers was doing Jake said, "Once you give a pet away you shouldn't inquire about the pet."

I was surprised by Jake's response to my simple question, and I later concluded that Jake had disposed of the cat even though I couldn't prove it one way or the other. I at least had tried to find another caring home for Sneakers, and Sneakers had taught me a lesson about the unpredictability of domestic animals that can become aggressive.

One day as I was listening to the radio while driving my car I heard an advertisement for a cosmetic surgeon who practiced at the Open Door Surgery Center in Champus. I called the phone number that was given over the radio and made an appointment to see Lowell Piper MD, who did facial surgeries. I also went to see Alfred Thompson MD, a double board-certified plastic surgeon in Union. Double board certified in this instance meant he was certified in two specialties: in general surgery and in plastic ophthalmology, plastic ENT, and plastic reconstruction surgery. Dr. Piper wanted $2,900 for a rhinoplasty a nose job and Dr.

Thompson wanted $5,000 for the same procedure. I came to what seemed like a no-brainer conclusion: go for the less expensive one.

In the nineties I had my first rhinoplasty with Dr. Piper which cost me $3,100 including tax. I wasn't satisfied however with my results, and at a later date in the nineties I had my second rhinoplasty. Dr. James Evans a double board-certified plastic surgeon reduced the bridge of my nose to evenly balance my nostrils, and he reduced the tip of my nose a little bit more.

I didn't like these post-surgery results either initially, but in time when my nose had softened and relaxed I decided that I liked the doctor's cosmetic work. Later however I became self-conscious that my left nostril was somewhat higher elevated than my right nostril due to missing cartilage. This made me self-conscious when people would talk to me while standing on my left side.

I had my ears and chin worked on by a plastic surgeon named, Christopher Smith MD also in the nineties. I was under a local anesthesia and felt the pain as Dr. Smith was cutting on my ears. During the otoplasty surgeries Dr. Smith persistently flirted with the nurse in the surgery room trying to get together with her at a later time.

Sometime later I learned that Dr. Smith was nearing the end of his career as a plastic surgeon, and I believe he primarily was interested in adding me to his professional statistics. I wasn't pleased with my cosmetic results post surgeries, and I asked if Dr. Smith could perform a second surgery on my right ear to evenly balance the contour with the left ear. Unfortunately, the second surgery on my right ear wasn't successful either. I now recognize that Dr. Smith didn't have the cosmetic skill level that I needed and wanted.

I now wish I had not had any surgeries on my ears because they were fine to begin with. At the time I wanted to have my ears brought in closer to my head somewhat, and to give them a good-looking natural shape like the actors I'd seen on television. Like so many other would-be cosmetic consumers I was influenced by the physical beauty glamorized in Hollywood and portrayed on television and in the movies.

I know I can't blame Hollywood for my poor cosmetic results, but I was influenced to have cosmetic surgeries because physical beauty is recognized as valuable in being accepted by other beautiful people. I realize now that the world has a lot of fool's gold that people seek, but that will leave them feeling empty, used, and abused by profiteers and exploiters if they are not careful.

Over the years I've appreciated my mother's different quips and quotes. She learned one particular quote from her cousin Ralph Jorganson who used to live in Phoenix before he passed away. It goes like this: "I know how handsome I are. I know that my face is no star. But my face I don't mind it. It's the folks in front that gets the jar."

Any potential surgical patient and cosmetic consumer needs to ask a lot of questions regarding the medical doctor before ever proceeding with having cosmetic surgery. A female staff member at a medical center that includes plastic surgeons told me to ask a couple of excellent questions of a cosmetic or plastic surgeon: (1) "Who are you board certified through?" and (2) "What are your qualifications?"

If you are contemplating plastic surgery ask the doctor or his office staff for names and phone numbers of satisfied patients so you can get a good idea of what you can expect for post-surgery results.

Be specific regarding the cosmetic procedure and post-surgery results because when it comes to your face you want to have a qualified cosmetic or plastic surgeon working on your facial features.

I was informed before surgery that Dr. Lowell Piper, who did my first rhinoplasty was an ENT, meaning he specialized in the ear, nose, and throat. That gave me confidence to choose him. I realize now though that I should have had my nose work done by Dr. Alfred Thompson who is a double board-certified plastic surgeon in Union. I wish I had paid the five thousand dollars for the extra qualified plastic surgeon in the first place rather than to go for extra surgeries to have my initial nose work corrected at a later time. I now realize the importance of finding the right plastic or cosmetic surgeon from the start.

I caution you to do your homework before you make an appointment with a cosmetic surgeon for physical beauty enhancements. Your future happiness depends on finding the right plastic surgeon for you. That is very important for your mental health so that post-surgery you can be confident that your surgeon was the right one, and you can move forward in life with a bright future feeling successful. You never want to live with regret as I have done throughout the years. I now realize I wasn't properly educated or informed, and I did not have a complete understanding of what to expect with each of my procedures and results. Cosmetic surgery can be a scary proposition in the wrong surgeon's hands.

    I know from firsthand experience that there are cosmetic surgeons who are willing to use you as a guinea pig, and exploit you for their own self-interests, professional gain, and personal profits.

    Move forward with cosmetic surgery only after being properly educated and well informed of each step the cosmetic or plastic surgeon will take.

Jonah Jon Jefferys

6

THE ENCOUNTER

I saw an advertisement in the Yellow Pages on how to find the right cosmetic or plastic surgeon. I had patiently waited for nearly five years after my last procedure, and now I was interested in seeing if there was anything that a plastic or cosmetic surgeon could do to bring down my left nostril so it could be equal with the right nostril. I had been self-conscious about it long enough. If anything could be done to correct the imbalance of my nostrils it was worth having it surgically corrected.

When I saw the full-page ad for Thadeaus Damon Cutter, MD DDS in the Yellow Pages I had completely forgotten about the advice I received from the woman who had worked for Dr. Alfred Thompson a double board-certified plastic surgeon in Union. She had told me that if I wanted nose surgery I should have it done by a double board-certified plastic surgeon. I concluded based on Dr. Cutter's full-page ad that if he couldn't do what I was interested in having done he would refer me to another doctor who could do what I wanted.

When I called Dr. Cutter's office I told the receptionist, Alice that I had two previous nose surgeries.

"Dr. Cutter frequently has patients who come to him after having previous surgeries with other doctors," Alice said.

"I saw another doctor's ad in the Yellow Pages on how to find the right surgeon for cosmetic surgery," I said. "I saw listings for both plastic and cosmetic surgeons in the Yellow Pages. What's the difference between the two?"

"They are basically the same," she said.

Without further consideration I made my appointment with Dr. Cutter.

When I went to Dr. Cutter's office I met with a woman who was his photo technician and nurse before I met with him. She seemed a little nervous, but I didn't ask her about her demeanor.

She said, "If I could have cosmetic surgery on my nose over again I would have Dr. Cutter perform the surgery."

I understood her comment to indicate her satisfaction with her first-time rhinoplasty procedure. She never said she was waiting for Dr. Cutter to perform another rhinoplasty, and that it was only a lack of money to pay for the surgery that had delayed her second rhinoplasty. She was only making a statement which I now see was her way of building up my confidence to proceed with having my third rhinoplasty this time with Dr. Cutter. She took a number of photos of my face, and then I waited to meet with Dr. Cutter.

When I met with him I said, "I'd like to see if my left nostril could be brought down to be equal with the right."

Dr. Cutter stood up, turned around, and faced the wall. He didn't say anything.

I broke the silence by saying, "It must be hard to bring it down once it's up?"

Dr. Cutter turned around and sat back down across from me. He began by saying a couple of nonpertinent things that didn't address my cosmetic concerns. Then he looked right at me and said, "I see ten different things wrong with your nose."

When I heard Dr. Cutter address my nose in such a way I thought, at last I've found the right cosmetic surgeon for me. I had my hopes built up by Dr. Cutter's assistants who informed me that he was "good with noses," and by Dr. Cutter himself. Dr. Cutter had a team of women working for him his receptionist, the nurse/photo tech, and even the blonde woman who had spoken with me before I filled out my credit card information to pay for my surgeries.

Each one had a role to play in building up my confidence in how good he was with noses and facial features. Post-surgeries I realized that Dr. Cutter's female employees had positively had a direct influence on my thinking that I could expect beauty enhancements for my facial features.

Dr. Cutter then moved me to his computer imagery room where my left side profile was clearly visible on his computer monitor. With a click on his computer mouse Dr. Cutter said, "How about this?"

The monitor screen revealed my nose having a subtle change with a straight bridge and a minimal reduction to the tip of my nose. The corrections that Dr. Cutter's monitor suggested were to be corrected in the same position as he had found my nose as was clearly shown on his computer screen. He never mentioned that he might need to elevate my nose in order to straighten my "banana-shaped nose" as he referred to it.

I was focused on what Dr. Cutter was suggesting to me because of what my nose would look like post-surgery. I didn't know that he planned to raise and reposition my nose (something I discovered to my abject horror only after surgery).

I have learned that doctors who are not board certified will use computer imagery to capture the attention of a potential patient, but the cosmetic results may be painfully contrary to the imagery portrayed on the doctor's computer screen.

When I saw the subtle change to my nose on the computer monitor which I found appealing I said, "Yeah!" After all Dr. Cutter wasn't suggesting a major change; there was no reason for concern. He and his assistants led me to believe that he was a specialist in nose and ears. I would have appreciated hearing from Dr. Cutter that he was not a board-certified plastic surgeon or a reconstruction cosmetic surgeon, but he did not tell me that he was not board certified by any of the twenty-four boards of medical specialties.

I might not have understood his outpatient board certification, his American Board of Oral Maxillofacial Surgery status, and his unrecognized American Board of Cosmetic Surgery status, but Dr. Cutter should have informed me exactly how that medical training he underwent had prepared him to do additional cutting on my nose and ears above and beyond what Dr. Piper, Dr. Evans, and Dr. Smith had done. Had Dr. Cutter been more forthright with me I might have had a little more respect for him post-surgeries.

Dr. Cutter's storming-the-brain tactics included a blitzkrieg of new information that caught me mentally off guard, and I questioned in my mind why he hadn't explained his plans before the day of surgery. My mind felt paralyzed and subdued, and I felt I had no options to consider on the day of surgery.

Dr. Cutter had appeared to provide me with options during my initial consultation and my second consultation, but he made certain that there were no other options for me but to have the surgery he chose to perform on me after I received the anesthesia.

I explained everything to Dr. Cutter in my post-surgery desired-results notes, a copy of which Dr. Cutter had requested, but he never discussed whether he could or couldn't fulfill my specific cosmetic interests and post-surgery expectations.

The long and slow process that I had to painfully endure gradually allowed me to come to a full realization years later of what Dr. Cutter did to me pre-and post-surgeries.

During the initial consultation Dr. Cutter took me into a separate room where I asked if he could correct the bent curve in my nose. Dr. Cutter said he could do that. I don't know if my nose had a natural bent to it when I was born or whether the bridge of my nose was bent when I had a collision with a catcher at home plate during a baseball game when I was a teenager.

"My first rhinoplasty was with Dr. Piper," I told him. "He's an ENT," Dr. Cutter responded.

"My second rhinoplasty was with Dr. Evans." "He's a plastic surgeon."

During my second consultation Dr. Cutter said, "Your nose and chin will be easy, but your ears will be tricky because they might relapse back inward when I try to bring them out away from your head."

Still I was willing to have this surgical procedure to evenly balance my ears resolving the imbalance created by Dr. Smith's two separate otoplasty (cosmetic ear surgery) procedures on my right ear, and one otoplasty on my left ear as a consequence of the ear surgeries I'd had years previously. I thought I was dealing with a specialist in the nose and ears at this point, and not a cosmetic con artist trying to deceive and scam me as an unsuspecting patient with cosmetic fantasy images dangled before me.

I left Dr. Cutter's office thinking I had finally found the right surgeon to correct my physical characteristics.

I talked to my co-worker Denise after the initial consultation telling her I had found the right cosmetic surgeon.

"Does he have a qualified anesthesiologist?" she asked.

"I'm sure he does," I said. I assumed that Dr. Cutter's professional practice was in proper order, and that he had qualified assistants working for him. When I came back for my second consultation I intended to make certain he could do what I wanted and needed. I wrote out specific desired results post-surgery notes for my nose, ears, chin, and I wanted Dr. Cutter to tell me whether he could do what I was truly interested in.

Dr. Cutter held a photo album open several feet away from me, and he told me about a male patient on whom he had performed surgery. Dr. Cutter never handed the photo album to me so I could examine the cosmetic results for myself. In retrospect I can see how Dr. Cutter set me up to perform cosmetic surgeries on my nose, ears, and chin. It was something that I would come to regret for years that I spent in agonizing mental and emotional pain, humiliation, self-consciousness, embarrassment, and shame.

When I showed Dr. Cutter my notes during our second consultation he said, "I want to make a copy for myself. This gives me something to work with." He started to walk away, but stopped three quarters to the doorway, turned around, and said, "I'm a perfectionist."

When Dr. Cutter came back into the consultation room where I was patiently waiting he gave me my notes back, but we never discussed my desired results of whether Dr. Cutter could do what I wanted and needed. I now see that Dr. Cutter didn't say a lot. He should have clearly communicated with me from my perspective and told me exactly what he planned to do he knew his next move, but I didn't. Had Dr. Cutter been a better communicator during our initial consultation he would have lost my business, but he would have gained my respect.

Too late I realized that Dr. Cutter had only wanted my cosmetic, and financial business so he kept his communication with me to a minimum. He was adept at keeping me mentally off balance and mentally starved for more detailed information.

Still I left Dr. Cutter's office that day trusting that he knew what I really wanted from my surgeries. As my surgery date approached I realized I still needed additional assurance that the Dr. Cutter understood the results I wanted, needed, and expected.

Since I was going to have three surgeries for my nose, ears, and chin on the same day instead of paying $12,000, I would pay $11,400. I was pleased to get a financial discount on my cosmetic surgeries.

I looked forward to my new look with anticipation, and I had something important to show Dr. Cutter. I brought in a videotape of The Accidental Tourist, starring the actor William Hurt to let Dr. Cutter take a look at the actor's nose.

A male passenger on one of my William County Carrier shuttle routes had commented that I looked like William Hurt which I accepted as a compliment because I considered the actor to be a handsome man with a good looking nose.

I wanted Dr. Cutter to view the videotape to see the actor's nose, but Dr. Cutter said, "I don't want to see the video; I know the actor."

I was very disappointed and perplexed that he wouldn't take the time to observe the actor's nose on the video especially because I felt he had left a lot unmentioned.

Dr. Cutter stood up and moved directly behind me saying, "Well, I better go about building up the bridge."

That was a mental whammy, and I wondered why he hadn't said this to me before the day of my surgeries. I followed Dr. Cutter into the next room which was darkened, and I bumped into him and my mind went suddenly blank. I didn't expect to be deceived, and mentally assaulted by a professional using hypnotism and trickery clever tactics on me.

It wasn't until years later that I eventually figured out precisely how I had become a patient of Dr. Cutter's. I asked myself why Dr. Cutter hadn't told me of his plans to build up the bridge of my nose which was not in my notes the same notes that Dr. Cutter had made a copy of for himself so he'd be sure to know what I wanted. Dr. Cutter's mental whammy directly had preceded my receiving anesthesia for my surgeries.

I woke from surgery while I was still on the surgery table and Dr.
Cutter said, "You're going to like it."

I was mentally dull after my surgeries; my coworker Denise Montgomery gave me a ride home.

Ten days post surgeries I came back in to have my stitches removed at Dr. Cutter's office. His assistant removed two sutures from my nostrils and the stitches from my nose saying, "I was in the surgery room on the day of your surgeries." Then Dr. Cutter's assistant left the room.

Jonah Jon Jefferys

I was sitting down with my legs resting on Dr. Cutter's dental chair when Dr. Cutter entered the room and said to me, "See it as a sculpture. I tore it down, beat it up, and built it back up." He then left the room.

I reflected on his words especially the way in which he had described his actions during the surgeries I tore it down, beat it up, and built it back up and I wondered over and over again why he had said I should, "see it as a sculpture." There seemed to be a total disconnect between the cosmetic surgeon and the patient.

I eventually realized that something had gone horribly wrong with our communication. Why hadn't he told me the total truth of his plans and what he had envisioned for me? I couldn't believe that a medical doctor would ever tell a sensitive multiple-surgery patient such bizarre things which seemed totally insensitive and callous. I realized much too late that I had chosen the wrong medical doctor for my cosmetic needs. If that's what he envisioned doing I thought why didn't he tell me that up front during our initial consultation?

The more I thought about Dr. Cutter's words in his office when I came to get my stitches removed the more his comments began to bother me. I racked my brain wondering why Dr. Cutter had done this to me. Why did this happen to me? And how could something as horrifying as this cosmetic nightmare have happened? Why did Dr. Cutter say what he did but not clearly communicate with me before my surgeries?

I was constantly thinking, reflecting, rehashing, and rethinking again and again how I had chosen Dr. Cutter when he did the opposite of what I had wanted, needed, and expected for my nose and ears.

My experience was devastatingly painful and mentally confusing. What type of a doctor waits until after their surgeries to say, "See it as a sculpture. I tore it down, beat it up, and built it back up?"

I found myself looking in the mirror at the changes to my facial features, but I didn't recognize all the detailed changes at first. I videotaped myself so I could see the changes Dr. Cutter had made to my nose, ears, and chin on my large-screen TV. I closely examined, scrutinized, and inspected Dr. Cutter's cosmetic work over and over for long periods of time.

I had begun to carefully examine the changes that Dr. Cutter had made to my facial features after the adhesive-taped plastic molding fell off of my nose while I was taking a shower one day. I tried to determine if the changes I could clearly see in the mirror or on the videotape were an improvement in my looks or a detriment to my overall appearance.

Within the first couple of months following my surgeries I realized the cosmetic changes were not what I wanted, needed, or expected. I experienced painful mental and emotional agony, and suffered incredibly because of the postsurgical results; I experienced a nasty case of deep emotional depression and mental consternation. The post-surgeries results eventually became horribly revealing my nose had been raised and repositioned making it look like a turtle-shaped nose. My ears initially appeared to have been brought out away from the side of my head, but within weeks they relapsed closer to the side of my head than their pre-surgery position.

The skin pigment on my chin was no longer flesh-tone, but now it had a reddish color which caused me to want to grow a beard to cover my embarrassment of a chin with reddish skin pigment.

I became painfully aware that not only had I chosen the wrong surgeon, but these cosmetic crimes should have never taken place. Had the policies of the medical boards been upheld and enforced, restricting such surgical procedures, particularly on a multiple-surgeries patient to only board-certified plastic surgeons who were recognized by the American Board of Medical Specialties I would never have had any surgeries performed by Dr. Thadeaus Damon Cutter.

I am an advocate for preventing medical malpractice by doctors as well as medical negligence by professional personnel in hospitals throughout the country. The legal and medical authorities need to Wake Up to the physical atrocities taking place against innocent victimized patients throughout the U.S.A. The laws and policies supposedly being upheld by the health commissions in each state should recognize that there are predators disguised as caring medical doctors. It's time for every medical commission in this great country to see what is happening under their presumably caring eyes.

I examined and re-examined my physical appearance repeatedly, and the more I examined my facial features the more displeased I became with the results of my surgeries. Each day caused me to reflect on Dr. Cutter and his actions on the day of my surgeries. When I would see my reflection in the mirror I became increasingly saddened by what I saw.

I decided to make an appointment with Craig Cranberry, MD to get his professional opinion on my results. I had seen Dr. Cranberry before having my surgeries with Dr. Cutter, and I was interested now in hearing what he thought about my post-surgeries results.

During my appointment Dr. Cranberry said, "I think your nose is better than what you had before surgery."

This surprised me but I later learned that Dr. Cranberry was a friend of Dr. Cutter's. Dr. Cranberry had told me during my first consultation that he was not a plastic surgeon, but that he had worked with a plastic surgeon. I looked through some of Dr. Cranberry's photo albums of his work and thought his post-surgery pictures showed that he did good quality work.

I left Dr. Cranberry's office feeling dissatisfied with what he'd said regarding my post-surgery results. I decided to get a second opinion from another cosmetic surgeon I'd seen prior to my surgeries with Dr. Cutter.

I made an appointment to see Chris Kirtpatrick, MD who told me that he was a triple board-certified cosmetic surgeon. I showed Dr. Kirtpatrick the notes I'd given to Dr. Cutter regarding the results I wanted, and after he read through them he said, "There must have been a misunderstanding." I told Dr. Kirtpatrick exactly what I wanted him to do, and he understood that I wanted to have my left nostril brought back down to be evenly matched and balanced with my right nostril.

I wasn't interested in having the bridge of my nose built up or the tip of my nose raised to correct the imbalance with my nostrils so I never mentioned those two separate aspects to Dr. Kirtpatrick. When I heard Dr. Kirtpatrick say that he would build up the bridge and raise the tip of my nose I decided not to have nose surgery with him. I left Dr. Kirtpatrick's office that day determined to continue my search for the right cosmetic or plastic surgeon.

I had mentioned to Dr. Kirtpatrick that I was thinking of suing Dr. Cutter, and I immediately wondered if I shouldn't have mentioned that as it might get back to Dr. Cutter. Dr. Kirtpatrick however asked if I wanted him to act as a mediator between me and Dr. Cutter, and so I signed a consent form for him to act in that capacity.

I initially thought that Dr. Cutter had taken my nose in the wrong direction. Now was a good time to hear what other doctors had to say about my cosmetic results.

I had made my appointments to see Dr. Cranberry and Dr. Kirtpatrick before going back in to see Dr. Cutter approximately three months after my surgeries. Once again Dr. Cutter's nursing and photo assistant took pictures of my post-surgeries new cosmetic look. My coworker Denise had come with me to the appointment I had wanted a witness when I talked to Dr. Cutter and we waited patiently to see Dr. Cutter. He eventually came into the computer imagery room and sat down next to me.

As I was pointing out that my left nostril had been raised during surgery Dr. Cutter abruptly cut me off saying, "You are this close to terminating the doctor/patient relationship. You went to see a couple of my colleagues without my permission. That was unethical." "I have a lot of critics. Do you want their phone numbers?"

"No," I said. He caught me completely off guard by his reaction. I still felt mentally dull and wanted him to explain to me what he had done to my nose.

Dr. Cutter then stood up, walked over to the doorway, and while facing the upper doorway he said, "You can sue me. You can blackmail me. I don't care what you do. You're not getting your money back."

When he said that, I immediately realized that was what I wanted at the time so I said, "I'd like my money back."

Denise saw that Dr. Cutter was acting unprofessionally, but she calmly said about me, "He has difficulty going out into public places because of his appearance."

I appreciated that Denise had spoken up to Dr. Cutter on my behalf. Her remark was accurate, succinctly stated, and most appropriate to say to this doctor on the attack. I was totally devastated by the results of the surgeries on my facial features. It absolutely was extremely painful and difficult for me to go out in public places where anyone could look at my abnormal facial disfigurements caused by Dr. Cutter.

Dr. Cutter responded to Denise, but when he spoke he was staring right at me. "Well, if I had known he had mental problems I never would have done it."
"He videotaped himself with his camcorder," Denise said.

"Then he needs to throw his camcorder away," Dr. Cutter sniped. He stood next to me momentarily, but then walked across the room, looked up, and said "No-o-o-o!"

I didn't know what Dr. Cutter was doing at the time, but in retrospect I'm convinced Dr. Cutter had a sudden revelation that he had made a big mistake. I am convinced that at that moment Dr. Cutter knew he had hurt an innocent, unsuspecting patient, but he also knew that he couldn't retract what he had done to me.

Dr. Cutter took me into a separate room his dimly lit pre-surgery room and said, "Didn't I show you a right-side profile of your nose and tell you what I was going to do?"

"No you didn't," I said boldly, and Dr. Cutter seemed surprised by my response. "You showed me a left-side profile of my nose, and then clicked your computer mouse and said, 'How about this?'" I found myself stumbling over my words so I stopped talking. It wasn't worth continuing to explain what had happened next to me.

I did tell Dr. Cutter that I had gone to see Dr. Thompson who was double board certified, and that I had seen Dr. Kirtpatrick who was triple board certified. I said, "I never let them touch my nose. I don't even know what your qualifications are."

With that Dr. Cutter became silent. He never explained his qualifications to me for doing additional cosmetic work on a multiple surgery patient.

Before I left my consultation with Dr. Cutter I looked up directly into his face and said, "I do not like it."

"You have ruined my night" he responded, "because I have a meeting to go to."

Dr. Cutter had clearly and unequivocally proven that he wasn't the skilled plastic surgeon that I had needed. Dr. Cutter had used hypnotic tactics on me such that I couldn't consider my options of having multiple surgeries or not having surgery or respond in a normal manner. He had gone to extreme lengths and drastic measures just to get my business.

It took a full seven to nine years of meditating and cogitating over and over in my mind on my dark encounter with Dr. Cutter before I finally worked it through, and broke free of the mental restraints in my thoughts. I completely figured out what had happened to me when I followed Dr. Cutter into that dimly lit room I had experienced a sudden mental blankness under his hypnotic mental manipulation tactics.

Dr. Cutter's hypnotic assault on me was like having a mental straitjacket placed on my mind to restrain me from thinking clearly and freely. It kept me from figuring out exactly what Dr. Cutter had done to me mentally, and how he was able to get my business in the first place. His actions were a waste of my mental, emotional, spiritual, and physical being; they became utter torment inflicted on this innocent unsuspecting patient.

I finally realized that as a multiple-surgery patient with the suffering I experienced by the mental manipulation and surgical actions of Dr. Cutter I had been violated and victimized by a sadistic medical predator. Dr. Cutter's haughty arrogance and braggadocio was on clear display when he triumphantly said as if he was the master of my cosmetic destiny, "See it as a sculpture. I tore it down, beat it up, and built it back up."

I had not asked Dr. Cutter to tear down the previous doctors' work nor was that stated in the notes I gave him regarding what I wanted from my surgeries.

Dr. Cutter had misinterpreted who I was as a person. I clearly was not a man on whom Dr. Cutter could take malicious liberties with my physical characteristics; Dr. Cutter was not a specialist in the nose and ears. He thought he could get away with his cosmetic violations, butcheries, and deviations, and I was supposed to sit idly by and do absolutely nothing about it. I didn't appreciate Dr. Cutter's bold remarks to me or his insensitive actions before my co-worker Denise.

He must have thought his malicious actions would escape the watchful eye of the medical and dental review boards and the investigator unit, but I slowly realized that Dr. Cutter needed to be stopped in his tracks, and the medical and dental boards needed to be warned of his insensitive actions against me.

In the nineties I experienced an AC separation in which the collarbone separates from the shoulder blade when my car did a complete rollover after losing its right rear tire. I was driving home from my parents' place heading back to work on the highway approximately eight and a half miles outside of Granted Orchards, and listening to a Christian music station on the radio.

Suddenly I heard a thud and a strange grinding noise coming from my car. I slowed down my compact Toyota just a little, and turned down the volume on my radio to listen for the noise coming from my car. I drove along intently listening for the sound coming from my vehicle. When I heard a loud braking sound I pressed down firmly on my brakes, and my car veered to the right and onto the gravel shoulder of the road with rapid speed. Everything moved in fast motion for me. I continued to apply the brakes as my Toyota headed directly toward the embankment.

I said, "Oh dear Jesus" as I tightly held the steering wheel. My car caught a mound of dirt at the beginning of the embankment which caused it to do a complete rollover, and ended up facing northeast. I literally saw stars on that sunny day as the dust flew high into the air around my car. I realize now it was a life threatening situation. I hadn't been wearing my seat belt at the time, and it proved to me the Divine protective hand on my life by the LORD. As I remained sitting in the driver's seat some people stopped to check if I was all right. To their inquiry I responded, "I think I'm all right, but could you call a tow truck when you get to the next town?"

They assured me that they would and then drove away from the scene of the accident. Other people stopped as well, to see if I was okay, and I believed I was going to be just fine. After I had recovered my banjo and song books that flew out of my damaged vehicle's trunk, I remained in the driver's seat post-accident, however, I came to recognize that my left shoulder blade had an unusual awkward tension, and it didn't feel like it should have.

As I waited for the tow truck another man stopped and said he had somewhere to go, but if I was still there when he came back he would stop for me. Later when I still didn't see a tow truck or even any police or state patrol car I became concerned about my physical situation.

With darkness coming on I pressed down on the brake pedal causing my brake lights to come on which would show my whereabouts for someone to stop and help me. Finally a car stopped on the shoulder of the road, and I didn't know if it was the same guy who offered to stop by if I was still there on his return. Sure enough it was the same man, and he did a good Samaritan deed which I believe the Lord blessed him for helping me out.

At this point I could feel that the dull knot in my collarbone area was not getting any better, and the kind man whose name was, Ken Princeton he took charge and gave me a ride to the hospital in Foggy Meadows which was forty miles away. I accepted his kind offer, and Ken drove me to the Foggy Meadows Hospital where a doctor checked me out for any sustained injuries. The doctor requested two x-rays of my shoulder area anyway.

The x-rays confirmed the doctor's suspicions, and he had me lie down while he pushed my clavicle bone down flush with my shoulder blade. I could feel the clavicle bone go back into place, and it felt perfectly fine. The doctor had informed me that it would require having it stitched together to correct the problem.

After laying there for a while I thought that I was ready to go, but when I got up off the table to leave the room I felt the clavicle bone pull away from my shoulder blade. I was given a ride to a motel by a hospital personnel where I stayed the night, taking the medications that the doctor had prescribed for possible consequential pain. I was grateful for the pain pills because I would have been in terrific physical pain if I hadn't had any pain medication during the night.

The next day I called a car rental agency, and a representative provided a ride for me to the agency. After renting a car I drove back to the area where I had my accident. I could see the skid marks in the gravel and where my car had made contact with the lip of the embankment. I looked for my right rear tire which had come off my vehicle, and I thought it had to be in the area somewhere. I spent some time searching for the missing tire, but I was never able to find it.

I got back into the rental car and drove to Granted Orchards I'd learned my car had been towed there. I discovered from the tow truck operator who was also a mechanic that the spindle in the center of the right rear tire had broken off. He agreed to take out my tape player and AM-FM radio, power booster, and the speakers from my car all of which were still in good condition. I thanked the tow truck operator/mechanic and paid him for his towing and labor services.

I drove back out to the highway and once again headed for home. I had put a lot of miles on my

Toyota Supra, and I knew that I was going to have to purchase another car. First though I needed to have my AC shoulder separation fixed. My surgery was scheduled with Dr. Harvey Crandon and Dr. Stanley Martinez at the Fairmont Medical Center in Collard. They used a metal screw to fuse my shoulder blade together with my collar bone, and then I was wheeled into a room for the night. I learned that my roommate who was making some painful noises on the other side of a blue partition had his foot crushed in eight places.

A nurse came in and gave me half a sandwich and some juice. As I lay in bed, watching television, I kept hearing the steady moans coming from my roommate. I knew I wouldn't get any sleep when he was continuously moaning so I asked the nurse if I could be moved into a different room where I could have some peace and quiet. The nurse had sympathy for my plight and kindly moved me into a room where I could be alone.

I liked having a private room, and when the nurse came back in she brought me a whole sandwich a couple of cookies and more juice. I was able to relax in peace while I enjoyed my early morning meal and watched television.

I felt so good after the surgery that I asked the nurse if someone could give me a ride home. If I needed to recover from surgery I figured I might as well do it at home, but the nurse said there wasn't anyone available to give me a ride.

After the nurse left the room I thought about walking home; it was only a three-to four-mile walk. As I thought on the prospects of walking home feeling comfortable from the delicious food I'd eaten I eventually fell asleep around four thirty in the morning.

(At 7:25 a.m). I got up to use the restroom, and I began to break out into a sweat and feel faint. After using the facilities I crawled back into bed and took a couple of the pain pills that were left for me. I realized that it was a good thing I hadn't taken off for home in the morning hours on an extremely cold winter night. The morphine that was still in my system after my clavicle surgery had prevented me from feeling pain in a serious way. I wisely waited for my ride at noon which my good friend Leroy O'Hara would provide for me.

I appreciated that Leroy sacrificed his time to give me a ride home from the hospital. I had to wear a sling on my arm to protect my collar bone and to keep the screw safely in place while I gradually healed from my surgery. After my shoulder was healed I made an appointment to see Dr. Harvey Crandon to have the screw removed. When I arrived for my appointment Dr. Crandon told his receptionist, "He's been screwed, and I have to unscrew him."

I eventually returned to work after I'd been off for nearly two and a half months.

After my car accident I made an appointment to see Dr. Cutter once more. I was still interested in receiving a periodic cortisone injection from Dr. Cutter who administered it directly to my nose to help reduce the swelling caused by the neoplasty.

Dr. Cutter had learned of my AC shoulder separation injury, and he apparently wanted to inject some levity into the situation. When I came in for another cortisone injection Dr. Cutter referring to my shoulder surgery said, "Well, at least it helps to take your attention off of your nose." He chuckled, and so did his nurse. I found myself lightheartedly chuckling along with them although I believed the nurse was present in the consultation room to provide Dr. Cutter with a witness to anything he said to me.

I took note of Dr. Cutter's attempt to take my focus away from my devastating rhinoplasty results. His effort however was futile because I was totally overwhelmed and consumed by my experience with this ominous character disguised as a cosmetic specialist. I slowly realized that Dr.

Cutter was going to have his way with my facial features whether I liked it or not.

On the next appointment, I wanted to communicate my disappointment about my surgeries, and I wanted to hear Dr. Cutter's opinion of the results. When he entered the room, I was standing, looking sideways at the wall, but in my peripheral vision, I saw him stop and look at me before entering the room. As he walked past me, he ambled sideways toward his desk with his back facing me. As he took a seat at his desk, he appeared to be self-assured.

I sat down across from Dr. Cutter and said, "What happened to my nose? It looks like a turtle nose."

Dr. Cutter immediately stood up, turned around and with his back facing me he looked up at the wall and said, "If something could be done we'd have to wait a year. I hope it will come down." He acted extremely disappointed, as if he had just missed an important hole in a game of golf.

The doctor finally got the courage to turn around and sit across from me once more. He looked directly at me and said, "It didn't turn out as I had envisioned." I responded to his remark by saying, "My complaint is not only that it didn't turn out as I had envisioned but also with the way you went about getting my business." Dr. Cutter stared at me for a moment but then looked down as if he didn't want to deal with the subject any longer.

I was glad that I'd communicated with him how I felt about my cosmetic debacle. He had seriously hurt my appearance in the most horrifying way.

I set up an appointment to see Dr. James Evans who had practiced in Union and then moved to Browerland. I was curious to get Dr. Evans's professional opinion on my cosmetic results as he was the plastic surgeon who had done my second rhinoplasty.

Dr. Evans had taken photos of me prior to the consultation so he could study my results. When I met with him for my appointment he was blunt in his opinion of Dr. Cutter. "He thinks he's a plastic surgeon," Dr. Evans said. "He didn't have to raise your left nostril that high."
"Would you be willing to testify against Dr. Cutter?" I asked.

Dr. Evans shook his head. "I must decline. I can't help you with a formal complaint against Dr. Cutter."

I understood why Dr. Evans wouldn't want to testify against another medical doctor especially since he continued to practice in Browerland, although his medical practice used to be in the same city where Dr. Cutter had his medical practice.

I went to see Dr. Dwight Marshall to get his professional opinion on my results. When Dr. Marshall saw me he said, "I don't know of any surgeon in the extended area who could be of any help to you."

I finally realized that I wasn't going to find any medical doctor in the surrounding area of Union and the suburbs who would help me with plastic surgery reconstructive work.

Dr. Marshall then mentioned a surgeon in Los Angeles. "I believe Dr. Raymond Rockwell might be able to help you," he said and he gave me the doctor's phone number.

Once again I was encouraged with new hope, and I looked forward to making an appointment with Dr. Rockwell.

I had tried to explain what Dr. Cutter had done to me to a number of people who worked for cosmetic and plastic surgeons in the Union area. In doing so I found out about Dr. Donald Philbert in San Diego, California. I had been advised by a woman who worked for a plastic surgeon in Champus that I shouldn't complain about my post-surgery results when I met with the Dr. Philbert; instead, I should see if he might be able to help me. I was encouraged by what I heard about Dr. Philbert, and I made an appointment to see him; he charged a two-hundred-dollar consultation fee.

To my disappointment Dr. Philbert said he didn't think that he could help me cosmetically although he thought he might have been able to help me if I'd seen him before Dr. Cutter had performed surgery on me.

Dr. Philbert looked at my pictures which I had brought with me, and he arranged them in chronological order closely examining my pre-surgery and post-surgery photos. He then said, "I think your nose looks okay for a nose job, but he didn't do what you wanted." When I showed him Dr. Cutter's business card he said, "He is a dentist. I don't know why a dentist would want to do it."

I left Dr. Philbert's office and drove from San Diego to Los Angeles to see Dr. Raymond Rockwell for a $120 consultation fee.

Dr. Rockwell didn't greet me in the standard manner saying, "Hello Jonah jon Jeffreys. My name is Dr. Rockwell. How can I help you?" Instead Dr. Rockwell looked at my elevated nose and immediately said, "You're not bringing it down."

Still I was confident that Dr. Rockwell could make the necessary changes to my appearance based on what I had heard about him, and his qualifications as a plastic surgeon. I had met with Dr. Rockwell's assistant in a private consultation room, and she shared relevant information about him. Dr. Rockwell was recognized by the American Board of Medical Specialties (ABMS) and was board certified by the American Board of Plastic Surgery. He also was a specialist in the nose and ears, and as a plastic surgeon he could perform reconstruction surgeries for facial features. Dr. Rockwell had the credentials and qualifications to produce good-quality cosmetic and reconstruction results for his patients.

After making the lengthy trip to see the two doctors in California I returned to work in Union satisfied that I had found the right doctor who could correct the devastating results that Dr. Cutter had caused to my nose and ears.

Dr. Rockwell performed multiple surgeries on my nose, ears, and chin. Unfortunately I was not completely satisfied with my corrective revisions, and I eventually realized that Dr. Rockwell was not the god of creative miracles who could make my physical characteristics completely whole or restore them to their original physical image.

Dr. Rockwell had to cut under both of my breasts to remove cartilage to help bring my nose down from the elevated position where Dr. Cutter had placed it. Dr. Rockwell performed three separate corrective revisions for my physical characteristics, but as I've mentioned I was not satisfied with my overall appearance.

The most important rule to remember is to find a qualified surgeon by doing your homework. Learn all you can about the surgeon by asking questions before you go in to talk with the surgeon. Be informed and equipped with the appropriate information on how to find the right surgeon which will help to eliminate any future regrets like those I have endured.

So many negative thoughts came to mind post surgeries that I found the mental and emotional anguish was difficult to deal with, socially, professionally, personally, and spiritually.

I told my co-worker Denise that I was not pleased with my post-surgery results and I was concerned about the negative thoughts I was thinking about Dr. Cutter.

Denise told me to write down my thoughts, and I appreciated Denise for her wise advice.

I ended up contacting the various medical boards with which Dr. Cutter was licensed, and I went on the record and made my complaints known to each of the licensing boards. I also sent a series of complaint letters to the state legislators in Olympia, Washington.

I came to realize that the cosmetic violations to my nose and ears were not an accident, but the cruel, callous, and cold-hearted actions of a malicious cosmetic surgeon disguised as a caring medical doctor. As the days ground mercilessly by I became increasingly disappointed and devastated, and I was convinced that I had been victimized by a predator who cared more about gaining my cosmetic and financial business for his own professional gain and personal profits than about delivering the results that I wanted.

I would like to be a spokesman against medical malpractice and encourage lawmakers to change the existing laws which benefit the predators, attorneys, judges, and legal system while the victims continue to suffer needlessly. I know that if the doctors or anyone in the legal system experienced what I did they would join with me to see that the
U.S. Congress, and state legislatures throughout this great United States of America would enact laws to immediately put a stop to all medical malpractice victimization and rule in favor of the victim. Let all medical malpractice victimization be a thing of the past, and not an active practice now or in the future.

I googled "medical malpractice" and found a relevant definition, but I appreciate the following definition provided by my sister Marlie:

Medical malpractice is an act of extreme injury to a patient. This medical negligence shows up in different forms, such as infections cultivated in failure to monitor the patient's vital signs, surgical errors, misdiagnosis, and failure to follow up with treatment.

I encourage you to contact a medical malpractice agency or a medical negligence lawyer if you have been a witness to or a victim of medical malpractice. I advocate putting an end to all forms of victimization through medical malpractice, and medical negligence whether intentional or unintentional by doctors and hospitals. I advocate that all medical doctors who are not recognized by the American Board of Plastic Surgery and the American Board of Medical Specialties remain within their respective specializations when performing cosmetic procedures on patients. Some doctors may see their patients as guinea pigs, but I assure you they are real people.

Medical policies must be changed now or there will be a steady stream of medical malpractice cases submitted to the medical commissions throughout Victimized, U.S.A., and medical commissions throughout Victimized, Worldwide. More medical boards will review complaint after complaint against doctors who are suspected of committing medical malpractice crimes.

My encounter with Dr. Cutter resulted in medical malpractice assaults resulting in my mental and emotional anguish, and contrary changes to my nose and ears. Such malpractice could have been avoided if the medical boards had restricted an unrecognized doctor who had a specialty in dentistry (not cosmetic surgery) as the "DDS" behind his name in the Yellow Pages showed.

My problem was that when I was searching for the right doctor after having had previous surgeries on my nose, ears, and chin I didn't know or understand what DDS meant. Dr. Cutter should have clearly explained that his specialty was in dentistry and not in the nose and ears, but he absolutely did not!

When I first met Dr. Cutter I didn't know that the American Board of Cosmetic Surgery, the American Board of Oral Maxillofacial Surgery, and being board certified in outpatient surgery was not recognized by the American Board of Plastic Surgery (ABPS) or the American Board of Medical Specialties (ABMS). When I first encountered Dr. Cutter I wasn't familiar with those boards mentioned above. I didn't know why the boards were not accepted by the ABMS and the ABPS or how those boards had helped qualify Dr. Cutter to perform surgeries on a multiple-surgery patient like me. My experience with Dr. Cutter was a scary cosmetic nightmare, physically dangerous, and painfully devastating for me mentally and emotionally.

I feel that my complaint letters to the various licensing boards merited having disciplinary or termination action or a criminal investigation against Dr. Cutter. I discovered that the MQAC the medical board with which Dr. Cutter has his MD license and the DQAC which licenses Dr. Cutter's dental practice does have an investigation unit that determines whether a complaint merits having disciplinary or termination action taken against a medical doctor. I also learned that the MQAC does not have a criminal investigation unit. The chief investigator, Arnold Richards informed me that the MQAC is the one board that authorizes reviews and investigations, and they also make the decisions.

I am convinced from what I have personally experienced and from what other medical doctors have said to me regarding my results of Dr. Cutter's surgeries that I had a legitimate case. I most certainly qualified as a cosmetic and financial victim, and my case warranted having a thorough criminal investigation into Dr. Cutter's professional medical malpractices against me. When I was violated and victimized by Dr. Cutter in such a careless, ruthless, and malicious manner I felt that I had been robbed of the valuable physical treasures that God alone had royally given to me.

It seemed totally outrageous and unexpected that a medical doctor in a position of trust had deviously taken my priceless possessions through mental manipulation, and unrecognized surgical procedures on my facial features. I had tried to be so careful about choosing the right surgeon for my special cosmetic needs before I gave my permission to any surgeon.

When I least expected it however in a secluded, dimly lit room, an unqualified medical thief, Dr. Cutter decided to rob me while I was on the road to finding a qualified specialist in the nose, ears, and chin. I am authorizing the lawful authorities to find the notorious thief named Dr. Cutter and carry out justice against the notable criminal described, and found guilty of crimes committed against me. I leave the legal prosecution of Dr. Cutter to the proper authorities as I was never able to bring a lawsuit against him myself.

Dr. Cutter referred me to Dr. Salmon Pride for consultation by saying, "Sometimes we need to receive counseling which can be of help during difficult times."

When I went to see Dr. Pride he was sitting in a chair looking tired, and he didn't say anything. I didn't know what to think at that moment. I'm pleased Dr. Pride broke the silence in his office between us. I knew that he was aware that I felt seriously hurt by Dr. Cutter's actions against me, and eventually Dr. Pride responded to my disappointment with my cosmetic results by saying, "There was a woman who had her nose worked on a second time, and it was worse than before. I won't say it wasn't Dr. Cutter."

Dr. Pride didn't think he could do anything for me cosmetically, but the short time I spent with the kind doctor was a good thing for me. I appreciated talking to him, and in retrospect I think Dr. Pride was giving me information that I could use should I bring a case against Dr. Cutter or report him to the proper authorities.

I didn't have the mental wherewithal post surgeries to do much other than to suffer needlessly day in and day out. It was a slow, agonizing, painful process that I was forced to endure, and I wrote down my negative thoughts toward Dr. Cutter. I eventually began to send in my complaints which I had patiently prepared to the licensing boards Dr. Cutter was licensed with.

Although I experienced mental difficulties post-surgeries I took the time to write down what I could remember that Dr. Cutter had done to me. I was confident that the medical review boards would take disciplinary action against Dr. Cutter upon receiving my complaints, but I found out later that they never did.

When I discovered the MQAC hadn't even required Dr. Cutter to respond to my complaints I couldn't believe their inaction; I knew that Dr. Cutter had committed sinister criminal actions against me. I continued to suffer mercilessly personally, socially, and professionally as the days rolled slowly and agonizingly by.

The consequences of my experience with Dr. Cutter drastically affected my performance in my profession and the quality of my personal life. My professional and personal lives were devastated by the cosmetic results of Dr. Cutter's surgeries and by the cold reaction I received from the general public. After my horrifying ongoing developments, and the repercussions I didn't feel safe in pursuing further corrective surgeries with Dr. Cutter.

I have appreciated my co-workers and every person who has shown me acceptance in society with my physical imperfections. I have tried to rise above the negative reactions from a lot of the general public wherever I've been. Due to my embarrassing cosmetic results I have had to deal with many difficult situations on the job and in life. I also experienced doing my level best adjusting and dealing with negative thinking people in various environments in the Christian churches when they observed my adverse physical characteristics.

I flew down to Dallas/Fort Worth Airport to meet my longtime friend, Bud Finnigan from Pardonville, Missouri back in the early 2000s. Bud saw me at the airport as I was waiting for my luggage, but at first he didn't believe it was me because of my facial changes. After Bud got over the initial shock of my new appearance and after we awkwardly got reacquainted again after being separated for years we made our preparations for the lengthy drive to the Pentecostal Christian special services gathering, being held at Lake Job featuring a famous evangelist who has since gone home to be with the Lord.

I would listen to the evangelist on the radio in Union, and I enjoyed listening to his sermons. He was a powerful man of faith who had witnessed and experienced many miracles in the evangelistic and healing tent crusades throughout his ministry not only when he traveled with A.
A. Allen, but also in his own Christian evangelistic ministry.

When Bud and I walked into the sanctuary we saw that women were greeting others, but when they looked my way they suddenly seemed very critical of my appearance and became aloof. The two door-greeting women did not approach us, but remained stand-offish toward us. When they didn't greet us personally we found seats inside the sanctuary by ourselves. You might think that Bud and I should have walked up to those women, introduced ourselves, and been friendly toward them. My response to that would be have you ever tried approaching and hugging an iceberg or a porcupine? When we reflect on the moment back then that was how we thought about the situation.

We were not disappointed with God or His ability to perform miracles, but I left there without experiencing the divine, creative, miracle anointing to restore my nose in particular that I was hoping for from the Lord. Missing out on a divine miracle from the Lord didn't shake my faith in God in the least. I kept walking in faith with God and hoped for a future miracle which I knew the Lord was fully capable of performing with a unique manifestation from the Lord's tender hand or a spoken Rhema Word from the Lord.

Bud was a good student when he attended Union Theology Institute. One day he informed me that he used to be an atheist. I didn't ask him how he came to know the Lord, but now Bud is not ashamed to share his faith in Christ, and he has a firm belief regarding the finished work of Christ Jesus who made the ultimate sacrifice by freely giving his life to pay for our salvation. He shed his sinless blood on the cross of Calvary to take away our sins and provide us with eternal life. This is the good news that anyone can know for a fact they can repent of their sins, turn to God in repentance and faith, and receive the free gift of salvation from God Himself, and inherit eternal life in Christ Jesus.

After Bud's first child was born he told me that he'd named his son, Jonah jon Jeffreys after me which I appreciated. When Jonah jon Jeffreys grew up he enlisted in the U.S. Marine Corps and served in the armed forces for four years as a protector of the United States of America. Bud said that Jonah jon Jeffreys had ambitions of re-enlisting after serving his initial four years and to become a sergeant as he rose in the Marine Corps ranks. Unfortunately, Jonah jon Jeffreys's plans of continuing his service as a defender of our country were cut short by a decision by President Obama to bring our troops home and put an end to the war with Iraq and Afghanistan's Taliban Islamic fighters and Al-Qaeda terrorists.

Bud told me that President Obama did not totally back off his Middle East agenda; rather he cut back on the troops there. His policies leaned toward tolerance of the Muslims, and even to the United Nations' hostility toward Israel and its prime minister.

Jonah jon Jeffreys and his fellow marines received their honorable discharges from the Marine Corps, and he is now serving the U.S.A. as a good-standing, nonmilitary civilian in a small city in a southern state. I commend Jonah jon Jeffreys and all the men and women who have faithfully served our great country in each of the armed forces regardless of the active service role they provided and performed for their platoons or squadrons. They all deserve our support, blessings, commendations, and respect with dignity and honor.

These brave and courageous men and women took an oath that they are willing to die and make the ultimate sacrifice to keep us safe from harm in our great country. They are willing to lay down their lives to keep Americans free. Freedom comes at a great price, and we thank each and every person who has served in the armed forces. May God continue to bless our military troops for their services at home, and may God continue to bless our U. S. Customs Agents and all U.S. Borders Protection Policies. 2 (Chronicles 7:14) and Romans Chapter 13 applies to all U.S. citizens of various offices and functions.

Bud became a diligent theology student of the Word of God, and he knew how to rightly divide the Word of God. He also became an avid Bible scholar, and a tremendous historian in his own right. Throughout the years I have listened and learned, and benefited from his vast knowledge in many fields of various study. One day out of the blue I asked Bud how he became a believer in God when he'd formerly been an atheist. I was so taken by Bud's dynamic testimony as he told of how he had become a Christian, and how God had found him at a point of sheer desperation in his life and had rescued him from taking his own life. This was nothing but a miracle of the Lord, and amazing grace manifested and revealed to Bud by the divine presence of the risen glorified Lord Jesus Christ.

I would like to share Bud's personal testimony for the world to know just how great and awesome the Lord Jesus Christ truly is. Because Jesus did it for Bud he will do the same for others, revealing and manifesting Himself to as many as call upon the name of the Lord for salvation, and deliverance in a state of desperation when calling upon the Lord from a person's free will being drawn in cooperation with the power and operation of the Holy Spirit's drawing of searching for lost souls. God's amazing plan of His salvation is unearned and is offered to all which was fore ordained before the foundation of the world. (1 Peter 1:20).

It's the goodness of God combined with a total surrender of repentant sinners to believe in Jesus Christ, and God's finished work on the Cross of Calvary that give us the daily and ever increasing total victory over the world, the flesh, and the devil. Faith in Jesus and the Cross of Calvary gives the Holy Spirit permission to operate in our hearts and lives as He so desires.

Once the unconverted receives the Lord Jesus Christ into their heart and life the Holy Spirit begins to apply the finished work of the Cross into their total spirit, soul, mind, and body. Only the Lord can fill the God shaped hole in everyone's heart and life through the total finished work for which Jesus paid for on the Cross of Calvary. Keep in mind there are two most important events in a person's life which are, when they are born and when they find out the reason for their birth.

The following is Bud's powerful and awesome testimony that I captured on my audio cassette recorder along with a brief conversation between Bud and myself after Bud finished giving his glorious testimony.

American singer-songwriter Bob Dylan recorded a song with the lyric, "Knock, knock, knocking on heaven's door." This phrase was taken from a letter that a GI in Vietnam had written to his mom because he was disgusted by experiencing the war firsthand, and he was terrified when he saw people die around him including his own buddies. He felt that his time was short and he wrote, "I'm going to be knocking on heaven's door soon because there is a bullet with my name on it out there."

There was a period when I was a total atheist. I didn't believe in God, and I didn't believe that God even existed. I went partying, getting drunk and smoking marijuana, and people I hung out with felt the same way.

Two ladies, Betty Ortiz and Donna Ellora lived in in the Melody Apartments in Harmonyville, Idaho and both of them prayed for my salvation. I would go out partying, and they would pray for me although they didn't tell me they were praying for me; they just did it. After a time I started feeling conviction, but I kept partying. When the conviction came on me I just felt like a spring was tightening up inside my chest, and I felt driven and I was running from it.

I would go to the bars and get drunk. I also would buy marijuana, but at some point I no longer could find the people who sold me the marijuana. It was as if they had dropped off the planet. I didn't recognize it at the time, and I couldn't see God's handiwork, but the Lord was at work in my life and on my behalf before the manifestation came.

And as time went on I would go into a bar, and order a schooner of beer which held about fifteen ounces. One night I just had picked up the beer schooner when someone put a quarter in the jukebox and played Bob Dylan's song, "Knockin' on Heaven's Door." At that time the message of the song really got to me. I didn't want to hear it, and it made me as mad as a wet hornet. I stormed out of there, jumped into my pickup, and peeled out from the gravel parking lot to go to the next bar down the line.

This happened to me as I was leaving from three or four bars that night, and the same thing happened when I went to a biker party I almost got killed that night; I came within inches of dying. I got into a fight, and some of the bikers jumped on me. One of them choked me on the floor, but the rest pulled him off. I had been badly beaten, but I went home to my apartment at the Melody Apartments in Harmonyville.

And as the days rolled on I was depressed. I had lost my job the place had closed down and things had happened in my life. I didn't understand the conviction I felt on me because I didn't believe that God existed.

I was in my apartment on January 3, 1976. I had a .357 Magnum Colt Trooper in my hand. I had shut the door to the hallway and was alone in my apartment. I was getting ready to kill myself, just to end it all, because a lot of things had piled up on me. I just wanted to grab the emergency brake and pull the lever to stop the world and say, I'm getting off.

As I got ready to pull the trigger all of a sudden through that locked apartment door I felt the presence of God come into that apartment. The presence was heavy, heavy, heavy; there was no denying it. I could feel His presence as I stood in the bedroom. I felt His presence boldly come in. He just strolled in like He was the boss. I didn't know what to say. I just dropped my gun and dropped to my knees beside the bed. I didn't know how to pray. I just blubbered and wept. God understood my heart's cry.

I cried out to the Lord. I didn't have a copy of The Four Spiritual Laws in front of me, but I cried out before the Lord, "Please forgive me. Please forgive me." I didn't know all the words to say, but I do know that when I got up approximately an hour later I felt like I was standing suspended in the air. And I felt like rushing out into the street and hugging everybody in sight.

In the days and weeks that followed God confirmed Himself to me over and over again. And I went to a Bible bookstore just a small hole in-the wall Bible bookstore and I told the sales clerk what had happened to me and that I needed a Bible. She reached up to a high shelf behind her, hauled down a copy of the Thompson Chain-Reference Bible, and put it in my hand. Back then that Bible cost about forty dollars; today it's around $150.

When I held that Bible in my hand and opened it up I thought it was the most precious book I had ever held in my life. And from that point on I read and read and read the Bible. That was my first Bible, and after all these years I have never forgotten when the Lord Jesus Christ came into my heart and life. That was very real; as I said I could feel His presence come into my apartment. I could feel it. It wasn't my imagination; I knew what it meant to imagine something, and this was not my imagination. The presence of God came in there to me alone in that apartment, and when He did it was Him dealing with me.

Although I have failed God at times over the years since God has never failed me. And as I've learned the Bible I've learned that it is the finished work of the cross of Calvary. What Jesus Christ did at the cross of Calvary is what paid the debt for our sins which we could not pay. He came into my heart and life, and no matter where I go or where I've been I've never forgotten that experience.

I believe that the Bible teaches the doctrine of the Holy Trinity and speaking in other tongues. I believe in the Word of God and the blessed Holy Spirit who is the third person of the holy triune God. Within the nature of the one true God exists every split second throughout eternity three distinctives, three offices, and three personages; the Father, the eternal logos; the Word of God that became flesh, the Son of God, Jesus Christ; and the Holy Spirit. These three are the one God because they cooperate in unison throughout eternity.

Jonah jon Jeffreys added to Bud's testimony saying, "Very good Bud. The three personalities or persons in the triune God the Holy Trinity are the one true God."

Bud added, "Yes, and not only that, but I can prove from scripture that each member of the Holy Trinity has intellect, emotion, and will or volition. Each one has the distinguishing elements mentioned that reveals the mark of intelligence and the mark of personality."

"Very good," Jonah jon Jeffreys said. "And what about the finished work of the cross?"

"That's what I was talking about," Bud said. "He finished the work at the cross of Calvary. His resurrection was a given because He finished the work totally. There is not one sin or anything that was not paid for our sin debt of sin past, present, and future if we submit to His finished work on the cross for us. Don't add to, take away from, or ignore His finished work on the cross. At the cross our sin debt was paid in full by His precious shed atoning blood by the Lamb of God who is totally and eternally sinless."

"The blood of animals through the past centuries could not stop the wrath of God against people who sinned against Him. Only briefly could the animal sacrifice which had to be done over and over again, would stop God's anger against sin and its deadly consequences. Then came God's chosen sacrifice the Word of God who became flesh, the Son of God, Jesus the Christ. He came to this earth to go to the cross."

"But before the foundation of the world it was already in God's mind what He was going to do to bring us to God as new creations in Christ Jesus so we might make heaven our eternal home after the Holy Spirit draws and woos us to Him, but we still have the option of receiving or rejecting Him."

"We could not be justified by the law (Romans 3:23–24). In (John 19:30), Jesus let us know it is finished, and to ignore it, add to it, or take away from it is an insult to God Himself. Psychology, a part of psychoheresy takes away from, adds to, and ignores the completed work of Jesus Christ on the cross of Calvary for our sins. And when it comes to the sin nature everyone since the Garden of Eden has had the sin nature passed on to them through the steady transference of the genetic part and parcel of the human race."

"Non-Christians are controlled by the sin nature whether they know it or not. Christians, born-again new creatures in Christ Jesus need to maintain faith in the finished work of the cross of Jesus Christ every day. When we accept Jesus Christ into our hearts and lives we become part of Jesus's death on the cross and His resurrection. Our continual faith in the finished work of the cross of Calvary guarantees our own resurrections to be united with Jesus Christ in our resurrected glorified bodies. When Christians' spirits leave their bodies they take on a glorified body to live with the Lord Jesus in heaven for all eternity. In (John 11:25) Jesus says, "I am the resurrection and the life: he that believeth in me shall never die. Believest thou this?"

"Physical death does not mean spiritual death to the Christian. Physical death for the non-Christian means eternal damnation in burning hell (Luke 16:19–31). The Holy Bible does not make provision for Roman Catholics who have their hearts right with God at the time of their deaths to go to purgatory for a time to burn off any venial sins or mortal sins of the person's body and soul. This teaching of purgatory attacks the finished work of Jesus Christ on the cross."

"That's right," Jonah jon Jeffreys said.

"And regarding the works of God the Holy Spirit," Bud said, "when Baptists and others say it is blasphemy to speak in tongues that it is of the devil they just blasphemed God the Holy Spirit. It's not something to be winked at." Every believer in Jesus Christ that claims Christ Jesus as their Lord and Savior should recognize the spiritual danger they place themselves in when speaking against the operation of the Holy Spiritin the lives of Christians operating in the gifts of spiritual tongues which the Holy Spirit interprets.

Jesus said, "Wherefore I say unto you, All manner of sin and blasphemy shall be forgiven unto men: but the blasphemy against the Holy Spirit shall not be forgiven unto men. And whosoever speaketh a word against the Son of man, it shall be forgiven him: but whosoever speaketh against the Holy Ghost, it shall not be forgiven him, neither in this world, neither in the world to come." (Matthew 12:31-32 KJV).

We admonish you to search the scriptures concerning this wonderful free gift called a second work of grace from God. We recommend contacting SBN Broadcasting Network and request the booklet on the receiving the Baptism of the Holy Spirit. Many other full gospel ministries can also help you to be open minded to seek the Baptizer Jesus Christ so you also might be filled with the Holy Spirit and with power to live for the Lord and follow Him in righteousness and holiness all the days of your life in victory focusing on the finished work on the cross of Calvary. (Acts 1:8; 2:1-4, 38-39; 10:44-48; 19:1-7 KJV).

"And then concerning our salvation," Jonah jon Jeffreys said. "God the Father thought it and planned it, the Lord Jesus Christ bought it, and the Holy Spirit sought it and applied it"

"Amen," Bud said.

"To our hearts and lives," Jonah jon Jeffreys added.

Bud verbally agreed. "To our hearts and lives and only because of the finished work of cross of Calvary."

"And then we become a new creature in Christ Jesus."

"That's right," Bud said. "His resurrection becomes our resurrection too because we will be resurrected later with glorified bodies because of our faith in the finished work of Calvary. We'll only be in heaven because of what the Lamb of God did for us on the cross."

"Very good Bud. All right. Thank you for giving your testimony. I better wrap things up."

I recorded Bud's personal testimony while on a break at work. I love and appreciate Bud as my brother in Christ Jesus and my personal long-time old friend.

Bud shared, "Keep in mind that the Lord Jesus spoke more about hell than He did about heaven. Roman Catholic teachings that depend on a place called purgatory to erase people's sins deal with a total fabrication of the Roman Catholic Church which is perpetual mass cards not recognized by the Protestant Church or other Christian Churches. A text out of context becomes a pretext to biblical and scriptural error. Roman Catholic priests cannot tell you when someone gets out of purgatory no matter how much money is offered (called indulgences) by a concerned family member for the soul of a deceased person."

We live in a generation when it is easy for a Christian pastor to say during a funeral service or at a burial service that Sally or Johnny has gone to a better place rather than telling the mourners that the sinful individual went to outer darkness into hellfire because of the sinful life that he or she led. Sorry to say, but Sally and Johnny never repented of their sins and invited the Lord Jesus into their hearts and lives.

The subject of being eternally separated from the loving God revealed in The Holy Bible, and the heavenly paradise He promised to all believers is a powerful subject to deal with. God Almighty has chosen for everyone those who repent of their sins, die to the sin nature, and are reconciled to God will receive the free offer of eternal life and will inherit a new nature in Christ Jesus if they determine to live righteously in Christ Jesus until the day they are called home to be with the Lord forever.

Since the Bible is its own commentary I will let The Holy Bible record speak for itself on the matters of life and death, and also on weightier matters concerning heaven and hell. Any Christian who speaks to a soul concerning eternal hellfire should share the subject with a tender, loving heart and weeping, agreeing with the Lord's will that they also are not willing that any should die without knowing the Lord or perish without making peace with God. No caring Christian wants to see the lost end up in a place of eternal torment separated from their loving Lord and Savior Jesus Christ. God has better plans for you and all your family members.

The following scripture verses and passages in the next paragraph are taken from The Holy Bible which I have chosen to share with you so that you will know the will of God regarding how God looks at things. The heavenly Father offers grace, mercy, and peace through Jesus Christ our Lord and His Word, and your faith believing the truths found in The Holy Bible settles the matter.

May everyone be encouraged and made wise in the Lord Jesus Christ as believers and potential believers, and be warned should you not know the living God and His will for your life.

Take the time to read the verses below to become enlightened on the mind of God regarding the plans He has for you, and have a concerned heart for those who don't know God and choose to reject His plan of salvation. I also hope you will take God's Word seriously and stand firm on His great and precious promises believing by declaring, "God said it: God meant it: I believe it, and that settles it!" (John 3:16; Jeremiah 29:11–13; Acts 16:31; Luke 16; Mark 9:42–50; Romans 5:1; 1 Peter 3:8–10; Hebrews 2:3; 9:27; 2 Thessalonians 1:7–12; 2 Timothy 3:16; 2 Peter 1:20–21).

God has a plan for every person who was conceived before we were born into this present world. This proves the sanctity of human life; thus abortion is an abomination to the Lord God Almighty (Psalm 139:13–16; Jeremiah 1:5; Proverbs 24:11–12).

As a negative outcome of Dr. Cutter's surgical actions I had to deal with victimization by self-centered people in spite of my having attempted corrective surgeries with Dr. Raymond Rockwell. I have refused to give in to society's pressures expressed through various behaviors to give up my job. Post-surgeries the general public seemed to have difficulty looking at my new appearance. Some people stared at me and then quickly looked away when I looked in their direction. Other co-workers also stared at me as if they were bum-fuzzled at my changed appearance. Some of the customers on my job showed by their uneasy actions that their evasiveness became immediately apparent. They would become uncomfortable looking at my appearance and quickly depart.

After my surgeries many people weren't as friendly or accepting of me as they had been previously, and they lacked courtesy and acceptable social etiquette. I was unaware of what I would be left to deal with, and so my performance on the job and in difficult social settings has been reduced by adverse gossip and rude comments. Overall people tend to show a lack of concern for my feelings, and social interactions often prove that I am an object of ridicule.

I have chosen to be a man of principle over popularity. I have decided to weather the storms of social rejection and adversity, and to withstand the steady pressure of people's persistent objections. Instead I have chosen to see the good that comes to those who persevere through the storms of social oppositions of life, resistance, and rejections by the general public. In fact I thank God for His love and grace to help me endure and persevere through those trials of life.

My friend Sean Ridpath once said, "I'm like mold. I grow on you." Through many years of safe, friendly, and courteous job performances I have adopted a philosophical attitude regarding the travelers who suddenly have stopped riding my personnel carrier: "Let them come, and let them go."

My mother once said of visitors who came to our home, "I like the comers-and-goers, not the comers-and-stayers."

Another philosophical attitude I have adopted toward customers who quickly exit my coach without thanking me or acknowledging me for my driving services is, "Let them come on quick and get off faster." Bud shared, "Feliz Enchiladas."

I appreciate the good times I have experienced on the job and the customers who have brightened my day with a humorous comment. One day a kindly man was exiting my carrier and he asked me, "Where can I put a homeless chicken?" When I didn't have an answer for him he said, "Foster Farms." He smiled and walked away leaving me with a good joke to share with other people and, in turn to brighten their lives and leave them with something to think about.

One day I was finishing my early morning carrier route and was on my way back to William County Base when I saw a semi-truck ahead on the freeway. I thought I could pass it so I sped up to overtake it. I suddenly realized however that the semi was traveling at the same rate of speed as I was. There was no way I could pass him and make the next exit as I had originally thought. I decided to let the semi take the lead, and I would pull in behind him making every correct lane change so I could take the exit in a safe manner. I happened to look over at the side of the truck as I was slowing down to let him get ahead of me, and as I did I saw the large colorful advertisement on the side of the truck that read "Foster Farms."

I thought that was pretty good for me to actually see the punch line to the joke on the side of the truck. I have gotten a lot of mileage out that joke asking people, "Can you tell me where my wife and I can place a homeless chicken?" Someone responded, "In the pot." Another said, "An animal shelter." What simple, reasonable, and logical answers for my question. I have enjoyed listening to people's responses and then following up with, "Have you ever considered Foster Farms?" Some people have started laughing when I've told them the punch line. I've found that joke is an ice-breaker, and a good way to enter into a friendly dialogue with someone I don't know. It's also become a good way to end a conversation over the phone.

I recognize that God always causes those who place their faith and trust in Him the Lord Jesus Christ to triumph through tough times, difficult situations, and every unpleasant circumstances. Glory to God for His victorious intervention in the face of tough situations that Christians face in this life.

The following is the June 5 1997, letter that Dr. Cutter sent me recommending a consultation with Dr. Pride and suggesting that I seek counseling help:

Dear Jonah jon Jeffreys:

This letter is a follow-up to your recent postoperative visit in my office Wednesday 6/4/97. As you know, (you had a 5:00) appointment. We had you stay in the library until Cindy seated you at (approximately 5:30), at which time she took images. I spent from (approximately 5:45 to 6:45) with you in consultation in the imaging room. It should also be noted I examined you clinically in one of the exam rooms, with particular attention paid to the nasal exam.

Examination that day and review of the images show the following findings:
1.   The chin is healing well with good position, though the patient is somewhat concerned

about some asymmetry. However, the full beard makes it difficult to judge the symmetry at this time.

2. There is still a small patch of resolving alopecia on the chin and some minor skin irregularity over the corrected crease in the chin. The patient was told that there probably will be further resorption of the area, and most likely the alopecia will continue to resolve itself.

3. Good position of the ears with some very minor asymmetry. Overall, improvement was noted with regards to their position.

4. Intranasal examination showed a patient airway on both sides. The patient reports somewhat restricted airflow on the left side. Some scar tissue was noted in the left anterior nose that may be contributing to some of the airflow issues. The nasal mucosa was noted to be slightly erythematous.

5. External nasal examination showed the nose to be healing well with good overall symmetry. There still is some fullness in the nasal tip which is to be expected at this relatively early postoperative oint.

Jonah jon Jeffreys, I spent approximately 1 hour with you and Denise in the imaging room as we reviewed and discussed your progress. You had some concerns that the tip had been lifted up somewhat; however, I pointed out that your tip was still swollen. This is very normal postoperatively, particularly for someone who has had 2 previous rhinoplasties to the one that I did. A large part of your concern seems to resolve around the augmentation of the dorsum. You told me that I only discussed this with you on the day of surgery. I pointed out to you in my progress notes, which were dictated at our initial consultation in February 1997, that I clearly delineated that your dorsum was overreduced and that part of my treatment plan was to augment the dorsum. If somehow I failed to communicate that to you clearly at that time, I sincerely apologize. However, I also showed you the changes on the computer imaging which I had done for you at your initial consult. The images clearly indicated that I had treatment planned for you to have the dorsum built-up. Again, I apologize if there was any misunderstanding.

Over the last two months you have been concerned about your appearance. I know that you have seen at least two of my colleagues for consultation with regard to your early surgical results. You expressed your concerns to them and both of them have indicated that you are doing well and have no significant problems. You are certainly free to see anyone you wish with regard to your surgical outcomes; however, I would have appreciated being informed about your specific concerns. I feel I could have been of more assistance with regard to your issues. After our discussion on Wednesday, I do not believe that you are satisfied with your surgical outcome to date. I would encourage you to seek further consultation.

One individual that I would recommend that you see is Dr. Salmon Pride. He has a national reputation for lecturing on nasal surgery and is very well respected in this community. In order to facilitate this, I have enclosed a copy of your pre-and post-operative photographs in case you will need them. I would also encourage you to have Dr. Pride call me so that I can discuss your case with him (with your permission, of course).

With regard to giving your money back, I believe that was an inappropriate request. You are progressing well in your postsurgical course. Two other surgeons have stated that to be true and I have stated that to be true. I will be glad to remain your doctor and do everything I can to help with the healing process.

Finally, Jonah jon Jeffreys, I am concerned about your overscrutiny of yourself. It is not normal to have a one-hour postoperative visit that you were "totally devastated" over the last few months because of your surgery. Three highly qualified surgeons have looked at you, and all have said you are healing well. I would be remiss as a physician not to be deeply concerned about this situation, and therefore I am recommending that you seek some counseling help in order to deal with some of your concerns. Jonah jon Jeffreys, please don't take this recommendation in a negative way. All of us need someone to talk to at some point in our lives. I am very concerned about you, and I believe that counseling would be of benefit for you.

I hope this letter helps clarify some of the issues. I will continue to be your doctor. Jonah jon Jeffreys, I like you as an individual, and I hope that we can work together in the future. I did tell you that I would like to see you in 1 month for further follow-up care and evaluation, and you agreed to make that appointment. Again, thank you for your attention to this letter. I look forward to seeing you in early July.

Sincerely,

Thadeaus D. Cutter, MD

In early 2000 I sent in a complaint against Dr. Cutter; it turned out to be the first in a series of complaints. I was so devastated by Dr. Cutter's mental and cosmetic violations against me that I sent in a volume of paperwork to the medical boards instead of one or two pages because I felt I needed to prove my case against Dr. Cutter, providing substantial and hard-hitting evidence that I clearly was victimized although I wasn't able to pinpoint the exact moment of my victimization until years later.

With all the convincing evidence I could supply I did my level best to persuade the medical and dental review teams to take disciplinary or termination action against Dr. Cutter.

I threw Dr. Cutter a negative curveball when I sent my complaints to the review boards as to the predatory treatment that I had experienced at Dr. Cutter's hands. I decided to use my sharp cutting ax expressed in my negative word pictures and numerous illustrations as to the way I saw Dr. Cutter.

I also tried to warn the medical and dental boards that they had a dangerous medical doctor on their boards who would end up hurting other unsuspecting patients and he has if his predatory cosmetic practice was not stopped.

I sent in a series of complaint letters to the different licensing boards with which Dr. Cutter was licensed as well as to Shay Schual-Berke, a legislator in the House of Representatives in Olympia, Washington against Dr. Cutter in November.

I was making the trip to see my parents in the early fall one year when a young deer suddenly darted out from the side of the road and ran into the left side of my car. After I was able to stop I'd been traveling at a fast speed I turned my car around in the dark of the early morning hours, and in my headlights I could see the deer lying down on the shoulder of the road. I thought for sure that I had killed it as it wasn't moving. I got out of my car to take a closer look, and I noticed that the deer's side was going up and down with every breath it took. I saw white spots on its coat and realized the deer was a fawn. It had taken a hard hit when it ran directly into my car.

I placed my hand on the young deer's side, and I prayed for the Lord to heal it and raise it up. As I kept praying for the fawn it eventually raised its head. I could see blood on its mouth and nose. I petted the deer as I again prayed for the creature to be healed, and to enjoy the life that God had created it for. After a while it finally was able to stand up with my assistance. The fawn was still stunned from the trauma of hitting its muzzle above the front left wheel wall of my vehicle.

I was pleased to see the deer making gradual progress in response to my prayers for it. The

Jonah Jon Jefferys

Lord God helped the fawn to make a full recovery from its stunning collision with my car.

For years I had made the lengthy drive to Clover Valley to spend time with my parents by taking the highway north and traveling west on Foggy Mountain Pass through the busy thoroughfares and beyond. After I drove across the Sacajawea River bridge I continued heading west on the highway until I reached another little town. There are a lot of small towns in the Pacific Northwest. After driving through Donny Brook Lair on my long highway travels I came to the turning point that would take me home to Clover Valley; I would soon be on the road again and homeward bound.

God had answered my prayers for the young deer as it tried to make it across a ditch onto an embankment. The deer fell on the knoll on the other side of the ditch, and it lay there momentarily. As I contemplated helping the fawn continue on its journey it managed to regain some strength and make it through a barbed wire fence to the other side.

As the deer stood in the tall yellow weeds of the field it looked back at me as if to take one last look at a good Samaritan who had taken time to help a wounded friend in the battle of life. Once again God gets the glory for answering prayer and coming through to facilitate the life of one of His creatures.

I got back on the road again and once I reached my parents' home I contacted the Price Police Department to see if a ranger or a game department official could go to the location where I'd last seen the fawn and check on its wellbeing. I later found out that a ranger had gone to the location, but didn't see the young deer which was a good sign that it had fully recovered.

One day while taking some riders on the Tumbling Hills county road when I saw an extremely handsome reddish-colored buck raise up his front hooves two to three times, and then forcefully pound them on the road as he saw my carrier approach. The magnificent buck got my immediate attention, and I applied my brakes to allow him to cross the road. He had a dignified manner about him as he crossed behind my carrier.

As I look back on that moment it seemed as if the buck was communicating to me: "I'm ordering you to stop that motorized vehicle now because I have places to go and things to do. You will not interfere with my destiny and plans for the day."

This royal leader of the deer family in his prestigious reddish coat was laying down the law to let me know he was in charge of his own destiny, and I was subject to his demands. I immediately obeyed and stopped the carrier. The buck strolled majestically behind the carrier, and crossed over to the other side of the road where there was a housing complex and plenty of green grass for him to feed on.

As a personnel carrier driver I was under the authority of the William County Carrier Company, but I likewise was subject to the laws of nature, and I dutifully obeyed the magnificent buck who was in complete charge of the road at that moment.

Social suffering should not be the consequence of cosmetic surgeries by doctors who show a lapse in good judgment when performing cosmetic procedures on patients, and especially if the patient has had previous surgeries on the face as I had on my nose, ears, and chin. Precision-quality cosmetic procedures with subtle changes to a patient's physical appearance is in the patient's best interest, and should be the positive goal and result of a doctor's work.

No patient in his or her right mind wants to encounter a buzz saw, a butcher, or an unrecognized cosmetic surgeon who is not specialized in the nose and ears especially when he or she has had previous surgeries on the nose, ears, and chin.

From a patient's perspective any unrecognized cosmetic surgeon willing to do additional cutting on a multiple-surgery patient is a full-fledged criminal, butcher, and money-greedy predator.

The medical commissions throughout Victimized, U.S.A. must stop this nonsensical madness and stop turning a blind eye to the growing horror of medical malpractice. Real people are being hurt by medical doctors and by hospital negligence. Real people are being victimized by self-interested doctors, and many patients die each year as a painful reminder of this serious subject.

The legislators, medical commissions, doctors, and attorneys must recognize that there are predators disguised as medical doctors who want them to believe that patients who complain about being victimized by a doctor are simply hypochondriacs trying to smear a good doctor's reputation. They seem to suggest it's the patient's fault that he or she got hurt.

My friend Bud asked me, "Would a fan who was assaulted by a baseball bat–wielding thug be at fault simply because he or she attended a baseball game? I don't think so! This same principle applies to a patient who encounters a medical doctor in a position of trust and is maliciously victimized as a consequence of trusting that surgeon who was motivated by greed, power, and self-interests."

You can draw your own conclusions regarding medical malpractice in the United States. I have concluded that medical malpractice is a blight on society that must be stopped immediately.

As a positive consequence of my painful experience I have come up with a plan to help put a stop to this horrifying threat to so many innocent lives.

It was a long, slow, and painful process for me to solve the criminal actions that Dr. Cutter took against me. It's one thing to be viewed by other people as an oddity or freak of nature, and thus be ostracized, discriminated against, and not warmly accepted for who I am as a human being. It's quite another thing to be coldly rejected because of cosmetic procedures that left me physically disfigured and cosmetically damaged due to the self-interests of an uncaring cosmetic surgeon.

Dr. Cutter discovered that I was not hyper-suggestible or hypnotically programmable after surgery with regard to the devastating changes to my nose, ears, and chin. I was cosmetically violated by a nonspecialized cosmetic surgeon. A cosmetic predator, using devious, sinister, and criminal tactics who ran roughshod over me.

How could I support this fact with solid evidence? I sent in my complaints about Dr. Cutter's dishonest and dishonorable approach with me to the different medical boards with which he's licensed. They repeatedly informed me they were not going to take any disciplinary action against Dr. Cutter. They also did not open a criminal investigation against him as I had requested.

After nearly seven years of making my requests and appeals for some type of action to be taken against Dr. Cutter all to no avail I received a letter informing me for the last time that the MQAC was not going to reopen my request for a reconsideration. The MQAC had already decided not to take any action against Dr. Cutter based on my request after one or two years from the date of my first complaint. The medical board had not informed me of this ruling up front, and I thought I still had a chance of having my request honored for a reconsideration against Dr. Cutter right up to the last day for appeals.

7

TRAPPED BY A PSYCHO DOCTOR

The cosmetic changes that negatively affected my facial features were horrifying and painfully devastating to my self-image and self-esteem. The reactions to my new appearance from the general public were negative, judgmental, and cold.

I came to believe that the cosmetic changes to my facial characteristics were not an accident. When I sent in a series of complaint letters to the different boards they never required Dr. Cutter to respond to my complaints. I couldn't understand why the boards didn't take disciplinary action against the surgeon who had messed up my facial features.

The cosmetic changes were the opposite of what I wanted, needed, and expected specifically for my nose and ears. Dr. Cutter copped out by responding to my complaints with the excuse, "He has psychological issues." In my mind his brusque and uncalled for analysis didn't come close to the horrible mental and emotional anguish I was facing on a daily basis.

The deviations to my cosmetic blueprint were too glaringly pronounced to be trivial slips of the doctor's scalpel. I slowly realized that I had been victimized, without mercy, by a cosmetic butcher. As the days and weeks ground mercilessly by I continuously reflected on my experience. I pondered the different remarks Dr. Cutter had made to me after my surgery. You might remember he said, "See it as a sculpture. I tore it down, beat it up, and built it back up."

Dr. Cutter never mentioned that cosmetic plan of action before my surgeries. If that was his cosmetic agenda why hadn't he clearly communicated this to me?

Dr. Cutter thought I might have psychological issues because my co-worker Denise in whom I often confided told Dr. Cutter that I had difficulty going out into public settings post-surgery.

This was how Dr. Cutter responded to the medical boards, but was his response an accurate evaluation of my mental perception of my facial features or was it something more sinister that Dr. Cutter used as a smoke screen to cover his predatory actions against me? Did the cosmetic damages occur to my nose and ears because of my persistent obsession with my physical appearance or were they caused by the unskilled actions of a cosmetic predator?

The lines had become blurred in my mind. I suffered needlessly because one cosmetic surgeon forged strongly ahead with his cosmetic surgical plans. I was left confused, numb, and perplexed as to what had actually happened to me mentally, and cosmetically because of this unrecognized cosmetic surgeon.

My post-surgeries suffering continued for years despite three corrective revision surgeries for my nose and ears by a renowned board-certified plastic surgeon. I know now that Dr. Cutter did not correctly interpret my cosmetic needs, and by his actions and comments to me post-surgeries it's clear that Dr. Cutter didn't think that I would have a strong and accurate recollection of details.

I was violated by a cosmetic predator, violator, and butcher but how would I ever prove it to the licensing boards? I tried to warn the medical boards that I had been seriously hurt by the unrecognized cosmetic surgeon, and I was convinced there was a good chance that Dr. Cutter would hurt other unsuspecting consumers for professional gain and personal profit.

I found out sometime later that the medical boards never required Dr. Cutter to respond to my complaints. What an outrage and an insult to me!

I had been powerless to stop Dr. Cutter from making painfully scary changes to my facial features. The board-certified plastic surgeon Dr. Raymond Rockwell while doing his very best to make positive cosmetic revisions for me was not able to perform total miracles on my nose and ears. Dr. Cutter already had damaged and violated my facial features in a way that Dr. Rockwell couldn't correct or undo.

I spoke to a woman who worked for a recognized plastic surgeon in Union. She said that Dr. Cutter told people that he was triple board certified. A plastic surgeon who practiced in Browerland told me that Dr. Cutter "thought he was a plastic surgeon." Even if I thought of myself as a rocket scientist or a presidential candidate I would never take steps of action to position myself as a rocket scientist for NASA or as the next president of the United States. If I were to place myself in either position I could cause a lot of repercussions in various ways.

I concluded that Dr. Cutter knew the system in which the medical boards work, and so he did everything possible to avoid detection by abusing an unsuspecting consumer. My personal and social life was destroyed by a sociopathic cosmetic surgeon and narcissistic medical opportunist.

Dr. Cutter communicated things to me post surgeries that he did not communicate pre-surgeries. Although I didn't realize it at the time Dr. Cutter knew precisely what he was going to do in each step that he used on me without my consent. Pre-surgeries I didn't have a clue what he might have in store for me.

Since Dr. Cutter had left so many things unsaid, unmentioned, and non-communicated I was ignorant and uncertain what was going to happen to me next.

I was naive in my attempt to understand exactly what he did not communicate, but I didn't deserve to be treated in such a ruthless and abusive manner especially when Dr. Cutter had taken a sacred oath to not do anything that would compromise the trust of the patients under his care.

If any board member had experienced what I underwent at the hands of Dr. Cutter the board member would make a judgment ruling that this was cosmetic and financial crimes.
I was in his dimly lit pre-surgery room.

Dr. Cutter wanted me to be a blank slate, a basket case, and he especially wanted for me to be a specimen of radical and unrecognized cosmetic changes. He knew exactly when to catch me mentally off guard to psychologically deceive me into believing that my extreme cosmetic changes were merely my own psychological issues. The steady stream of social and professional rejections was abusive and personally destructive to my wholeness as a person.

I worked on isolating myself from group and social settings. I had a sad case of an inferiority complex, and a worse case of feeling totally inadequate in terms of looking and feeling normal. I had incredible stress because of Dr. Cutter's cosmetic violations. I was diagnosed with having hypertension by a medical doctor during this time, and I had to take prescription medication for high blood pressure.

I am quite certain that many cosmetic clients would have killed themselves had they been subjects of painful, and devastating cosmetic violations to their God-given facial features. Without God's saving grace to sustain a cosmetic victim many may resort to the unthinkable and unredeemable act of self-murder.

Cosmetic surgeons who commit criminal acts of cosmetic violations may want to put a lot of distance between themselves and their cosmetic crimes and deeds, but no crime is 100 percent perfect. The medical community is filled with psychotic doctors who are extremely intelligent, but they are not necessarily in touch with the needs and feelings of their patients. Many of these medical doctors live in their own ivory towers of narcissistic fantasies of power, control, and invincibility. These medical doctors think that they will get away with their cosmetic crimes. The review boards may repeatedly turn a deaf ear to the patients' pleas for a criminal investigation.

My cosmetic surgeon waited until the actual day of surgery to psychologically take over and do the unthinkable and unimaginable on my nose and ears. My cosmetic concerns meant absolutely nothing to Dr. Cutter, and he didn't even have a good answer post-surgeries for the cosmetic deviations he had made to my facial features. He had conquered me psychologically pre-surgeries, and he was on a power trip post-surgery until I began to question what had happened. I had no understanding in Dr. Cutter's dimly lit pre-surgery room.

I communicated to him in the conscious realm, but Dr. Cutter wanted to make cosmetic changes after he had impaired my mental faculties in the unconscious dimension. He made a call for changes on the day of my surgeries as a quarterback of a professional football team would call for a change of play at the line of scrimmage.

Pre-surgery Dr. Cutter said, "I'm going to raise and reposition your nose." It was a long and painful process for me to come to the realization years after my surgeries just how Dr. Cutter's call came for the changes he was going to make after he had utilized hypnotic paralysis to neutralize my brain. With me as his subdued patient he could now have total control of my cosmetic outcome.

When I was waking up after my surgeries still on the surgical table Dr. Cutter said, "You're going to like it," but I was not hyper suggestible to Dr. Cutter's hypnotic suggestion post-surgeries as the doctor was expecting.

It was not my doing to alter my appearance in the way it was done. My wife, Lorena wondered why I didn't leave my nose the way it looked in my pre-surgery photo. After all I was only interested in having subtle changes to my nose to improve its overall appearance instead of experiencing the major drastic changes caused by Dr. Cutter's surgical actions.

I explained to my spouse, "I would have left my nose the way it looked pre-surgery had Dr. Cutter not caused such drastic and scary violations to my nose and ears, and had I known that Dr. Cutter was not a specialist in the nose and ears."

Before my surgeries I wanted detailed information from Dr. Cutter to ensure that we were on the same page cosmetically, and that he could fulfill my specific and desired needs as I had explained in the notes I gave him. Unfortunately, Dr. Cutter decided to ignore my notes although I don't know whether he could or couldn't do what I had requested. After Dr. Cutter had subdued me mentally through hypnosis he took over and forced changes on my nose and ears that were totally against my will and cosmetic interests.

Dr. Donald Philbert's evaluation of Dr. Cutter's cosmetic work on me was, "The miscommunication with the oral surgeon was sad."

Dr. Raymond Rockwell said to me, "I see a lot of poor results. A lot of poor results."

I have suffered immeasurably to an extent that is inconceivable to the general public. Average citizens judge my appearance without an understanding that when they look at me they are witnesses to criminal cosmetic changes that were totally out of my control.

Dr. Raymond Rockwell performed heroic cosmetic revisions on my nose and ears, but he could only do so much to reverse the disfigurement caused by Dr. Cutter.

As I've mentioned I requested a criminal investigation by the review boards against Dr. Cutter, but they refused to take action against him. I know that Dr. Cutter should have served prison time for the false representation of his credentials, and for the cosmetic violations to my nose and ears. Dr. Cutter allowed me to believe that he was a board-certified plastic surgeon before he made cosmetic changes on me, but he was not. Dr. Cutter did not allow me to continue my search for another surgeon. He took advantage of my innocence, naivete, and trapped me in his dimly lit pre-surgeries hypnotic room.

It took me years to completely figure out what the medical review boards were looking for to bring disciplinary action or criminal charges against Dr. Cutter. I had been trapped and victimized by a ruthless and uncaring cosmetic surgeon.

My friend Bud told me, "I believe that medical predators are able to recognize their potential victims and seem to know when and how to strike. In their professional field they have learned how to hide themselves beyond the reach of the law, and away from the criminal justice system. Predators typically cloak themselves with treachery in order to avoid being detected and arrested. People who call in complaints are made to look like a drooling and bamboozled hypochondriacs."

I was an innocent victim of a psychopathic mastermind disguised as a medical doctor who wanted to advance his cosmetic credentials and medical career into an accelerated position far beyond his cosmetic training.

Dr. Cutter skipped the detailed dialogue with me, and quickly placed me into a mental state in which I would have no chance to change my mind about the cosmetic changes he was about to make on me. I know unequivocally that Dr. Cutter wasn't going to allow me to say no to the totally inappropriate and unnecessary cosmetic changes he was going to make on my facial features.

It's important to know that there is a big difference between a board-certified plastic surgeon, and an un-recognized board-certified cosmetic surgeon. There is an even bigger difference if the plastic surgeon is double board certified and has training in the specific facial feature for which you desire cosmetic improvement. Cosmetic surgeons may be able to perform the same cosmetic procedures that the board-certified plastic surgeons can do, but if you are a multiple-surgery cosmetic patient you may experience dire results caused by a medical surgeon's negligence and lack in skill set which can be destructive to your physical appearance.

The nature of my job demanded daily contact with multitudes of customers. The true impact of the cosmetic violations to my nose and ears led to years of professional and social rejection by my fellow co-workers and customers. The hurtful cosmetic deviations negatively affected me and my abilities to constantly fully function in a professional and courteous manner.

There are professionals in different fields who have a slipshod attitude, and do not service the customer according to the customer's specific wants and needs and what the consumer expects to pay for. This situational equation applies to the medical field as well.

Jonah Jon Jefferys

My father was a wonderful barber and an old-school barber who hadn't kept up with all the new barber school techniques that can provide tailor-made specifications for haircuts. His customers appreciated his barbering expertise; he worked with finesse which resulted in many satisfied returning customers. He never needed new barbering techniques to deal with the demands and expectations of our modern society. Dad had naturally gifted barbering talent and razor cutting skills that he had honed and perfected over the years with a lot of practice.

My father had many customers because of his skill set and the precision he used on each of his consumers. Some barbers however regardless of what the customer's instructions may be concerning his or her haircut, and likely due to a lack of proper barber training skills may get the unsuspecting customer's haircut wrong. We all know that a person's hair will eventually grow back if the haircut is a disaster, but a person's facial features cannot expect the same good fortune. Be cautious of barbers, medical doctors, and all professionals. Never assume that all professionals will always get it right according to your specifications, and that the results will always be to your liking.

To use an old Roman phrase, "Let the buyer beware."

I recognize that I ran into a medical doctor who was on a power trip where it was what the doctor ordered that mattered and not what the patient ordered and expected. Dr. Cutter and all other delusional doctors who are on a power trip are willing to run a slipshod practice if need be to get the patient's business at all costs. Even if the unsuspecting consumer gets hurt in the process these power-trippers are going to have things done their way. The patient is forced to accept whatever the doctor has ordered.

No reputable medical doctor would intentionally wait until the actual day of surgery to catch an unsuspecting patient mentally off guard unless that doctor doesn't care about the patient's cosmetic interests and expectations and he or she positively does not care about the patient as an individual.

What I experienced at the hands of Dr. Cutter was nothing short of cosmetic and financial heists with evidence of sinister crimes.

Based upon my experience I know that Dr. Cutter is not specialized in the nose and ears. Dr. Cutter's specialized training is in dentistry he is a DDS and a dentist without being a board-certified plastic surgeon should not have performed cosmetic procedures on me particularly as I was a multiple-surgery patient for the nose, ears, and chin.

I have discovered that a certified American Board of Plastic Surgery medical doctor undergoes specialized training in reconstructive surgery for patients' faces. Dr. Cutter was certainly aware that he had not undergone such specialized training.

From my personal experiences I know that delusional medical doctors are slackers who will not mentally Wake Up until they have been confronted regarding their irresponsibility. I know that every delusional medical doctor is a slacker when it comes to the specialized medical training that the American Board of Plastic Surgery requires doctors to complete.

I was clearly victimized by Dr. Cutter's irresponsible actions. Until victims just like me are willing to complain to the medical boards and stand firm regarding our legitimate complaints the victimization will continue. Now is the time for all victims, friends of victims, and potential victims to make our voices heard by taking a firm stand against victimization of our fellow men and women. We must answer a swift call to action to put an end to all forms of victimization in Victimized,

U.S.A. and Victimized, Worldwide.

Dr. Cutter utilized mental trickery and thuggery to gain my cosmetic and financial business. In order to achieve this he needed to ultimately deceive me, and the medical boards in his professional career. I discovered post-surgeries that I was not the only one hurt by Dr. Cutter.

Medical doctors who are not recognized by the American Board of Plastic Surgery know that they are on a power-trip express train with a one-way ticket to cosmetic derailment with unsuspecting patients' having cosmetic expectations, but they will not stop their express train because there is big money to be made along the way. The only successful way to stop these power-trippers is for the medical boards to stop their cosmetic surgeries on all multiple-surgery patients. Without the medical boards' restrictions for these power-hungry medical doctors the unsuspecting patients will continue to pay the ultimate price cosmetically and financially. These power-trippers must be stopped at all costs.

I am convinced that Dr. Cutter quickly moved me to surgery in an manipulative manner not only as a professional status-maker for himself, but as a way to signify that he had ultimately conquered, deceived, and achieved the pinnacle of true cosmetic success even though he was a cosmetic slacker who had cut corners regarding the extra training required for board-certified plastic surgeons.

My former brother-in-law, Randell Wikum is now serving time in Lurch State Penitentiary for killing his second wife. Whenever I tried to get one over on Randell he would always do his level best to top whatever I did to him. In the same way Dr. Cutter ignored all my cosmetic wants, needs, and expectations believing he could manipulate me into accepting his cosmetic agenda, and I would be none the wiser for it. The effects from this mental manipulation have had long-lasting consequences for me.

Any medical doctor cruel enough to use the painful, and mentally stunning tactic that Dr. Cutter used on me is a true predator from our perspective. The mental and emotional anguish that I suffered was beyond the scope of Dr. Cutter's calculated, insensitive, and cruel comments post surgeries.

If Dr. Cutter had come across as a sensitive and caring cosmetic surgeon pre-and post-surgeries he might have succeeded in his cosmetic and financial heists against me. Based on the facts and solid evidence however Dr. Cutter's approach toward me was cruel, criminal, and immoral. In the right hands plastic and cosmetic surgery can be an art of enhancing facial and physical beauty. In the wrong hands cosmetic surgery can be scary, painfully devastating, and mentally and emotionally abusive.

I went for a haircut one afternoon at Supercuts in Fedora Fair. The barber asked me what kind of work I did, and I said I was a carrier operator. I wondered why the barber would ask me this personal question and concluded that he was motivated by my physical appearance primarily my nose and ears which have an unusual look. Of course it's possible that the barber was naturally nosy and liked to get to know his clients by asking personal questions, but my mind-set at the time made me think he wanted to gain an understanding as to why my physical characteristics had such a different look which to the natural eye was out of the ordinary.

I didn't have any choice of the family into which I was born. Dr. Cutter didn't give me a choice in the matter regarding my cosmetic destination. Once he took charge on the day of my surgeries back in the nineties I was cut out of my cosmetic blueprint. I have suffered and continue to suffer. I want to reach a point in life where the suffering from professional and social rejections, and humiliating and embarrassing situations will forever end. This may be an unrealistic hope in an increasingly cold and indifferent world.

I can continue to look to my Creator the Good Shepherd to give me faith and hope for creative miracles for my nose and ears. I know that nothing is impossible with my wonderful God.

I am a living testimony against a malicious cosmetic predator who disguised himself as a caring medical surgeon. Dr. Cutter has an outpatient surgery certification, American Board of Cosmetic Surgery certification, and American Board of Oral Maxillofacial Surgery certification. I assumed that if he couldn't do what I wanted cosmetically he would kindly refer me to someone who could meet my needs. I later discovered however that the medical doctor I was dealing with had other plans for me.

I never expected to be dealing with a professional predator who would set me up to be deceived prior to my surgeries. I never expected to be dealing with a professional con artist who would force major cosmetic changes to my nose and ears that were absolutely undeserved, inappropriate, and unacceptable. Such painful cosmetic misery and malicious cosmetic failures are destructive to a person's mental and emotional health.

Dr. Cutter's actions toward me were clearly below the standard of care. You might remember that of the twenty-four boards of the American Board of Medical Specialties, Dr. Cutter was not listed on any of them. My cosmetic results became a horrifying nightmare that I have endured since my surgeries in the nineties.

I was left in mental darkness for years as to the actual truth of my cosmetic deviations. The results were more than scary for me. Dr. Cutter had done very visible damages to my nose and ears. My cosmetic results were painfully destructive in nature and in scope to my self-image and self-esteem. The adverse cosmetic changes were devastating and destructive to my unique facial features designed by my Creator Jesus Christ.

My physical characteristics were designed to carefully reflect and mold God-given character in me. The painful cosmetic changes had the opposite effect upon my personality. My unique physical characteristics created to exemplify my Creator's wonderful craftsmanship were now agonizingly abnormal in appearance.

My faith in God has sustained me during difficult days, weeks, months, and years. My faith in God has sustained me during many hours of suffering in silence, as normal-looking people kept doing the everyday things that they enjoy. I was clearly victimized by Dr. Cutter, but I continued to believe in God and I have hope for a better future. I continue to see the good in people even though I know that I was victimized by a cosmetic predator who should have never touched my facial features with his scalpel when he didn't have the specialized training in the nose and ears as an American Board of Plastic Surgery surgeon.

Post-surgeries although after the fact I asked my co-worker Denise to call Dr. Cutter's office and ask him what his qualifications were. Denise didn't do exactly what I asked her to do. Instead she identified herself to Dr. Cutter's receptionist by her middle name, April and she said, "If I have surgery on my nose I want someone who is board certified."

"There are a lot of boards out there," the receptionist said. She then handed the phone to Dr. Cutter.

Dr. Cutter thinking he was talking to a potential cosmetic patient named April said, "If you want a board-certified doctor you'll want Dr. Joseph Finney, MD ABPS in Champus."

I had the opportunity to meet Dr. Finney one day after having another corrective revision under my chin area by Dr. Raymond Rockwell.

Dr. Cutter won me over as Mr. Hyde, and he cut me up like Dr. Jekyll. Although Dr. Cutter took an irresistible cosmetic gamble on my facial features my resilience to life's expectancies were not quickly forthcoming. God was still my life-sustaining source, but now I had persistent negative memories concerning Dr. Cutter.

When I was out walking one day with my wife, Lorena a man who we walked past looked at me and said, "Scary."

For me it was another sad commentary, confirmation, and painful reminder of what Dr. Cutter had done to me. Dr. Cutter tore down my cosmetic blueprint and rebuilt it with something that was unrecognizable to me and was not beautiful and normal-looking to the general public. My cosmetic results were not caused by my incessant pursuit of any medical surgeon willingly eager and able to perform surgical procedures.

I knew that I was a cosmetic surgery victim, but I couldn't figure out what the boards were looking for to take disciplinary action or termination action against Dr. Cutter. I knew that the cosmetic violations were nothing short of cosmetic crimes, but I never was successful in bringing a lawsuit against Dr. Cutter, and the paralegals and attorneys continued to remind me of the statute of limitations whenever I sought for legal help.

Post-surgeries after I had met with an attorney within a two-year time frame to find out if I could bring a lawsuit against Dr. Cutter the attorney said I didn't have a case to pursue legal action against the doctor. That attorney caused me to miss out on bringing a lawsuit against the psycho doctor I had encountered. I chose to persist in pursuing a verdict, judgment, and ruling by the medical and dental boards with which Dr. Cutter was licensed. I felt that I needed closure concerning what I had endured at his hands.

I had a good recollection of events that led up to my cosmetic and financial piracy, but I had difficulty psychologically putting my finger on when and where the crimes occurred. To make my points as hard-hitting as possible I continued to utilize numerous illustrations of what I could remember had happened to me, and the way I perceived the cosmetic violator. For years I wasn't able to precisely pinpoint the exact moment the crimes took place. I needed more time to get it exactly right.

I was let down by the legislators, the investigation unit, and the courts which initially made the ruling regarding the statute of limitations in The State of Washington. I was let down by the attorney representing the legal system who didn't recognize that I might have more time to prepare for a lawsuit against Dr. Cutter I learned that if a patient experienced a loss of memory surrounding the medical malpractice event he or she is then given an additional year to bring a lawsuit against a medical doctor beyond the three-year statute of limitations.

I experienced difficulty retrieving specific detailed memories after my dark encounter with Dr. Cutter. I was not able to fully figure things out with precision and clarity on exactly how Dr. Cutter had been successful at pulling off his cosmetic heist against me. I was let down by the medical and dental boards which did absolutely nothing to take legal action or bring disciplinary action against Dr. Cutter except in one isolated case.

Dr. Cutter had ten complaints against him that I am aware of regarding his medical board status. All of them have been closed by his medical board. He has six closed complaints regarding his dental board status. Of the sixteen complaints the dental board brought disciplinary action against Dr. Cutter only once for negligence. A liposuction patient died under his care due to his professional negligence.

The laws need to be changed to allow the medical boards to have a criminal investigation team in each medical and dental board with strict enforcement powers. There must be strict enforcement against medical doctors who violate the doctor/patient trust. The laws need to be changed so that if a patient cries foul play at the hands of a medical doctor the medical or dental boards will order an immediate aggressive investigation by the criminal department, and leaving the investigation open until the victimized patient feels 100% satisfied. I never did call for my case to be closed by the medical boards.

There should not be any delays by the medical boards or the dental board waiting for years so that the patient can have adequate time to spiritually, mentally, and emotionally thaw out to have some semblance of internal equilibrium to understand everything that happened to him or her.

If the legislators, judges, and medical and dental boards recognized this needed and required standard of care safeguard to protect the consumer it could help to deter any medical doctor from thinking that his or her medical license and good standing were totally protected by the law. This would help to ensure against any medical doctor feeling narcissistic, powerful, and invincible concerning the medical, dental, and cosmetic patients who are under his or her care.

I learned the hard way that there are predators in the medical field. Dr. Cutter's professional move to apprehend my cosmetic and financial business was completely unacceptable, destructive, and devastating to my

person and mental health. I believe that Dr. Cutter was a blight on my life, and he has become a blight on the lives of other clients that he practiced on to improve his cosmetic skills.

I wish I had asked Denise who provided a ride for me to and from surgery to never leave my side until my surgeries were completely finished. By taking that added step of added security I might have been spared the malicious victimization by Dr. Cutter. I now wish that I had done my homework before coming in to see Dr. Cutter which would have spared me needless suffering. This move became a costly mistake for me. I was still asking questions of Dr. Cutter on the day of my surgeries when he made the bold move to place me in his dimly lit pre-surgeries room. I like multitudes of others wanted to trust a medical "expert," but I had the trust factor totally stripped from my life.

Dr. Cutter became an ominous cosmetic nightmare of the worst kind for me. I believe Dr. Cutter knew he was a bona fide cosmetic predator. No cosmetic surgeon would have used the malicious tactics that Dr. Cutter used on me unless he knew how to exploit the system that the medical boards operate under to increase his professional advantage.

My friend Tommy Ray used to work the casinos in Las Vegas, Nevada and he told me that he saw himself as a predator. He saw everyone else as his victims when they were sitting at the card tables. I assumed that Dr. Cutter had the trust of the medical boards, and the good character to rightly inform me during our initial consultation of everything that he could or couldn't do cosmetically.

Dr. Cutter told me, "I see ten different things wrong with your nose," and then he said, "How about this?" With a click on his computer mouse he showed me an image during our initial consultation. During our second consultation Dr. Cutter stated, "I'm a perfectionist." Post-surgeries after he messed up my nose and ears Dr. Cutter said, "It's what the other doctors did," refusing to accept responsibility for the outcome of his horrendous surgeries on me. It was the beginning point of the realization that I had become a victim which took time for the full impact to settle in, and over the years to figure out I had been dealing with a self-centered, ruthless, and abusive cosmetic surgeon.

My individual complaint case against Dr. Cutter was not properly investigated by the medical review boards or by the investigation unit; I'm sure of that. There should have been a criminal investigation by the investigation unit and the medical review boards. But it never happened. Bumbling TV Detective Colombo would have persisted until the case was solved no matter how long it took.

My case was put into limbo status. Although I have repeatedly requested a reconsideration for a new hearing by the medical review boards my case has continued to remain closed. I hope to change that situation one day. If I can do so I finally might find closure to Dr. Cutter's criminal assault on my mind which produced difficulties for me in retrieving memories post-surgeries, and the cosmetic actions he performed against me on the day of my surgeries. The inactions of the medical review boards in not informing me of my rights effectively denied my constitutional rights as a patient.

I needed help from a representative sent out by the medical review boards, and the investigation unit to help prepare the paperwork to pursue criminal charges against Dr. Cutter and to rightly evaluate the cosmetic damages he had caused.

I contacted Robin at a referral service for cosmetic surgeons. I was told that cosmetic and plastic surgery are basically the same. I had heard similar statements in the past.

I shared with Robin the information I had on Dr. Cutter's certifications or his lack thereof. I did not know how the so-called boards not recognized by the ABMS and the ABPS had qualified Dr. Cutter to perform surgeries on a multiple-surgery patient like me. Dr. Cutter specialized in dentistry. None of his board statuses was as a board-certified plastic surgeon.

I told Robin that I wasn't satisfied with the results and she explained, "The difference is the board certification of the doctor."

"Might you know about a doctor having a secondary in plastic surgery and a general in cosmetic surgery?"

"I don't know what that means," Robin told me. "Nothing else really matters; it's the board certification. If you want a specialist in plastic surgery you must find a doctor who is certified by the American Board of Plastic Surgery. There is nothing equal to that. The American Board of Medical Specialties is the board that oversees the subspecialty boards. They're like the top one that oversees the boards. There is only one that is governed by them, and it's the American Board of Plastic Surgery."

I thanked her for the information and then asked, "Anything else to add?"

"The general public is much more informed than they were ten years ago," she said. "People still need to do their research because some people are still not aware of the differences between the board-certified plastic surgeons and the unrecognized board medical doctors. This is where the horror stories come from: people going to doctors who are not specialists in that field of specialized training."

"Why would a doctor who is not a specialist in that particular field do surgery on somebody other than for the money?"

"It is about the money," she said, "We don't have laws that control that."

"It has to start from the legislation and the courts if we're going to see a change."

"I agree."

"Otherwise people are going down a precarious road," I said.

"The medical boards have to make that change a change in policy." That meant that only certified American Board of Plastic Surgery (ABPS) surgeons and certified American Board of Medical Specialists (ABMS) doctors will be allowed to do any additional cosmetic or reconstruction work on a multiple-surgery patient. Furthermore that no unrecognized board-certified medical doctors or unrecognized board-certified dentists or any other medical providers will be permitted to do additional cosmetic surgery on a multiple-surgery patient no matter how qualified they may think they are because of their years in practice.

"It's amazing that we don't have laws that govern this medical dilemma," Robin said. "Some doctors take a weekend class to learn how to do a procedure, and then they can go and do it. That's why it is so important to make sure you are dealing with a specialist."

"Do you know of any books out there to recommend to the average cosmetic consumer who wants to find the right surgeon, and one who can do precisely and exactly what the patient is asking for?"

Robin said, "No, there are no books for that. You just need to meet with the doctor. You start with the certification, and you go from there. You want to look at the before-and-after photos of previous patients. A reputable doctor will tell you if he can do what you're asking. If you've had a rhinoplasty and now you want a revisionary type surgery he will be honest with you and tell you whether he can meet those expectations." "Other than just asking the doctor how would you be able to know if he has gone for that weekend training?"

"You want to make sure they are certified by the American Board of Plastic Surgery and that they are specialists in that field."

Robin then mentioned the name of a double board-certified plastic surgeon who had a good reputation. "I'd highly recommend you go to him for your revision surgery."

I thanked Robin for talking with me on the phone. I never told her that the double board-certified plastic surgeon she had recommended; Dr. James Evans was the doctor who performed my second rhinoplasty. I thought Dr. Evans did a pretty good job on my nose at that time, but the surgery left the left nostril somewhat higher positioned than my right nostril because of missing cartilage.

It was an extremely scary situation when Dr. Cutter decided to skip the subtle-revision work that I had asked for. He simply tore down the previous doctor's work and rebuilt my nose in a higher-elevated position not what I wanted or needed. Dr. Cutter also raised the right nostril to match my raised left nostril totally against my cosmetic blueprint.

I recognize that Dr. Cutter has done some excellent cosmetic work as a woman who works for a plastic surgeon in Champus told me. Another woman who works for a cosmetic surgeon told me that the difference between plastic surgeons and cosmetic surgeons is that the plastic surgeon deals more with reconstruction surgery while the cosmetic surgeon primarily does surgery to enhance a patient's physical beauty.

I contacted the MQAC to inquire about Dr. Cutter's complaint status. I was informed that one patient had died under his care. The representative then said that another patient complaint had ended in injury or death. The representative could not disclose to me the exact status of the other victimized patient.

I curse the day that Dr. Cutter received his license to practice cosmetic surgeries.

I know that Dr. Cutter was delusional with grandiose expectations that his unrecognized board status could possibly produce fantastic cosmetic results for me. Had I been a first-time patient of Dr. Cutter my cosmetic results might have been different with more positive consequences, but since I was a multiple-surgery patient I didn't need the mental trickery or thuggery forced on me by Dr. Cutter's manic tendencies.

The thought that my results might have been more to my liking as a first-time patient of Dr. Cutter's is merely speculative relative to his noncertified board status with the ABMS and ABPS. I believe that Dr. Cutter may have been on cocaine the day of my surgeries. Dr. Cutter had to have turned off the analytical center of his brain or he had a seared conscience for him to have carried out such his malicious and sinister attack on me.

In my mind only a predator would have committed such heinous cosmetic crimes against an innocent patient. I hope I can save others from the victimization that I have endured all because I made some crucial assumptions that turned out to be major disastrous mistakes.

Dr. Cutter was purely motivated by his own power and greed. He had to have concluded that it was permissible to do some additional cutting on me from the power base of his outpatient board certification, American Board of Cosmetic Surgery, and his Oral Maxillofacial board certification status rather than from the proper certification of the American Board of Plastic Surgery.

Had the medical board and dental boards adopted and enacted a stiff law with hard-hitting penalties for any medical doctor who violated a rule of not performing surgeries on any multiple-surgery patient without being a qualified American Board of Plastic Surgery surgeon such doctors would be immediately subject to termination. I would not have been mentally, emotionally, and cosmetically violated by Dr. Cutter.

The medical and dental review boards must Wake Up and smell the cosmetic coffee. They must open their eyes to objectively see that they cannot continue in the business of safeguarding unsuspecting consumers without taking on a criminal enforcement team.

Dr. Cutter would not be hiding behind his medical licensing boards had there been a criminal enforcement team ready to take action when any patient called foul play by a medical doctor. Dr. Cutter would have been rooted out and prevented from ever practicing his medical and dental surgical procedures again.

Dr. Cutter's delusional thinking motivated by greed and power would get cleared up and eliminated in a hurry. Dr. Cutter's delusional thinking had opened the doors in his mind to erroneously think that there are a lot of boards out there. Dr. Cutter's thinking had infected his receptionist's thinking as well as proven to Denise my co-worker over the phone post-surgeries.

If we were living in a perfect world where every surgical procedure would produce 100 percent perfect results I could agree that every medical doctor could perform multiple cosmetic procedures on any patient at any time and in whatever manner the medical surgeon deemed necessary. If we were living in a totally accepting world I could agree to allow medical malpractice crimes and abuses to continue in Victimized,

U.S.A. If ugly in were in and beauty were out I could agree to permit numerous cosmetic surgeons to carve and cut at will on any unsuspecting patient because it wouldn't matter what the doctors did. The results would always be in the doctor's favor regardless of his needing to be a specialist in the field or certified by the ABMS or ABPS. We could allow the power-hungry, abusive, and greedy surgeons to make all the money that they wanted to without any medical restrictions and financial caps.

But we are not living in a perfect world or a totally accepting world. That's why we must shut down and eliminate all the Dr. Cutters of Victimized, U.S.A., and World Wide. As Bud would say, "And stop making excuses for them."

I came to the powerful realization that certain medical doctors believe that they are masters of their own cosmetic universe, and we as their unsuspecting patients are puppets in their world. We are forced to go along with their cosmetic agendas and accept the results however troubling, chaotic, or devastating. As puppets we are forced to deal with the painful consequences, and the mental and emotional issues relative to these abnormal cosmetic changes.

I was seriously hurt by Dr. Cutter, but I was not willing to accept the violations, deviations, and abnormal changes to my nose and ears. I was going to fight back against Dr. Cutter by complaining to the medical licensing boards and lawmakers. I was not going to be Dr. Cutter's puppet, and foolishly accept his devious trickery and thuggery without objecting to these troubling changes. I objected to Dr. Cutter and to the medical boards, and to the legislators in Victimized, U.S.A.

The medical boards has done nothing regarding Dr. Cutter's termination nor has it brought disciplinary action against him. If it were up to me I would shut down the entire medical board system at the MQAC and the Quality of Health Operation Commission in Olympia until Dr. Cutter was fired, and had his license suspended so he could not practice under his medical and dental licenses until he confessed to his cosmetic crimes and abuses against me.

I am dead serious and determined as a survivor of heinous crimes committed against me by Dr. Cutter yet the iron will of justice has not been applied to him or his license status by the medical boards, MQAC or the dental board under the DQA Commission. From my perspective of being victimized by an uncaring doctor I felt the entire health care operation should be shut down until justice prevailed against Dr. Cutter.

I was listening to a guest on Michael Medved's nationally syndicated radio talk show on my way to work as I regularly do. I hadn't heard of Michael's guest who was talking about how politicians see the rest of us nonpoliticians as puppets of their universe. As I listened to Michael's guest share his insight with the listening audience his words caught my attention, and I made the powerful connection to medical doctors like Dr. Cutter and others who are driven by self-interests as gods of their own worlds. It became crystal clear to me that medical doctors like politicians force their subjects to go along with their self-interests, agendas, and greedy pursuits to follow the way they see things in their own universe and the world they live in.

Being the masters of the Jewish people the Nazi SS officers saw themselves as gods who literally held the power of life and death over their Jewish slaves. It didn't matter how heinous and sinister their acts of mistreatment against their Jewish subjects were. Their delusional thinking empowered these SS officers to commit horrible atrocities against the Jewish captives because they were masters of their universe, and they believed that the will of their Fuehrer, Adolf Hitler would last for a thousand years.

In like manner Dr. Cutter's delusional thinking led him to believe that his cosmetic surgeries forced on my facial features would last me the rest of my natural life. Instead the cosmetic changes became my worst nightmare which I still have to deal with today. Dr. Cutter had already hurt another man who felt he had been butchered by him, and then Dr. Cutter was willing to cosmetically violate me on top of that. Can Dr. Cutter's delusional thinking be any more obvious to the medical boards, investigation unit, and legislators?

The legal authorities must Wake Up to the atrocities being committed under their questionable eyes of mental well-being and health protection. Unsuspecting consumers who are real people are being victimized, abused, and hurt by medical doctors.

Dr. Cutter's delusional thinking led him to believe that his scalpel was quicker than my mind could perceive and faster than I could move my nose and ears out of his way. You've heard the old saying, "The hand is quicker than the eye."

Based on my experiences under Dr. Cutter's care the evidence clearly shows that I was victimized by a medical doctor who knew that he did not have American Board of Plastic Surgery certified training to qualify him as a specialist in the nose and ears. Yet Dr. Cutter played me for a fool who didn't have a brain in my head to rightly discern and properly evaluate what happened to me, pre-and post-surgeries.

Dr. Cutter made cosmetic changes that were scary, cruel, and devastating to my nose and ears. He knew that he deviously hurt me when he deceptively introduced mind-altering, hypnotic tactics and a chemical process or extreme form of radiation that would destroy my sense of discernment. By what I experienced post-surgeries having blankness and blackness in my memory bank with mental tension I suspect that Dr. Cutter used either a chemical process or a form of radiation that caused me to have mental paralysis or neutralization to prohibit me from retrieving detailed information from my memory of what led up to my surgeries and to prevent my mind from functioning in a normal manner.

This was Dr. Cutter's attempt to destroy my powerful memory, and it indicates just how spiritually sick Dr. Cutter is to stoop to criminal actions against me. Such actions clearly demonstrate just how cruel, criminal, and inhumane Dr. Cutter is as a medical doctor that he would victimize me for professional gain and personal profit.

It was a long process for me to figure out exactly what Dr. Cutter did to me. I wanted to be fair in my personal judgment of him, and I wanted to be honestly accurate in my evaluation of what I experienced at his hands. I do believe that Dr. Cutter acted alone in the mental trickery and thuggery he used on me. He wanted to use me to make the medical boards believe that his unrecognized board-certified status was just as qualified as an American Board of Plastic Surgery surgeon which would keep the surgical doors open for other unrecognized board-certified medical doctors to continue performing surgeries that they are not qualified to perform.

Based on my personal experiences Dr. Cutter used me as a sheep led to surgical slaughter for the love of filthy lucre, and to keep the surgical doors open for him. Dr. Cutter had to have known that there was a lot at stake if I reported that the medical boards had another charlatan to reel in.

I see these kinds of medical doctors as brutes lacking compassion who are willing to surgically carve up an unsuspecting patient after mentally stunning him which they know will leave that patient in a mental fog for years. These medical doctors are extremely afraid that their unrecognized board membership will be exposed as being a made-up board by certain medical doctors. They erroneously think that it would be better for all of the unrecognized medical doctors to continue performing cosmetic procedures on gullible patients knowing that because of their ignorance of the many past practice-damaged patients the percentages are on the side of these loose-cannon medical doctors.

These particular practitioners fear having their certifications yanked and their medical board status restricted so they can't perform multiple surgical procedures on unsuspecting patients. The MQAC needs to change its medical policies to state that no board-certified medical doctor other than one with an American Board of Plastic Surgery certification is allowed to perform surgeries on a multiple-surgery patient.

If the legislators, medical and dental review boards, judges, and courts of Victimized, U.S.A. don't enact new laws to put an immediate stop to the victimization many more delusional predators will eagerly wait to begin surgical procedures on innocent and unsuspecting patients. We will see many more complaints of medical malpractice crimes and abuses by certain medical doctors who are intoxicated with power, greed, and self-interests if these laws are not implemented.

They need to pull together to enact and enforce stiff laws and high penalties to discourage predators from exploiting the trusting and unsuspecting public.

I am not opposed to plastic and cosmetic surgery practice as a physical-enhancement business operation. I am also not against the doctors who have diligently earned each of their board certifications from the American Board of Cosmetic Surgery or the American Board of Oral Maxillofacial Surgery or listing themselves as board certified with nothing added.

The above-mentioned are legitimate boards with unique specializations in their own right. These boards are recognized by their own membership, and they would fall into the category of "There are a lot of boards out there," as Dr. Cutter's receptionist said.

Carrie Barkley the deputy executive director at the MQAC asked if I would like to talk to a medical doctor on hand at the MQAC in Olympia. The doctor said the same thing to me as Dr. Cutter's receptionist had said: "There are a lot of boards out there."

Keep in mind that the above boards are not recognized by the American Board of Plastic Surgery and by the American Board of Medical Specialties. I strongly recommend that all doctors and the medical and dental commissions governing each medical doctor's licensing come to recognize their shortcomings and limitations in regard to cosmetic specifications on unsuspecting multiple-surgery patients. The medical and cosmetic surgery procedure policies must be changed now or there will continue to be a steady stream of physical, emotional, and mental devastation that is avoidable and needless. The painful and physically devastating consequences on unsuspecting patients are too scary to contemplate.

Unfortunately, I will not have the opportunity to take Dr. Cutter to court over his cosmetic and financial crimes committed against me because the statute of limitations has run out for me. My compelling case presented in this book however will be heard by the entire world which can render its verdict against Thadeaus Damon Cutter, DDS MD. I never had the chance to explain the crimes committed against me before a judge and jury in the William County Courthouse in downtown Union. I want to share the honest truth and present the facts based on my experiences to support my story of how I was victimized by an unrecognized cosmetic surgeon.

You the reader can render an honest judgment giving your opinion of my victimization. I am encouraged to think that my case could help set a precedent to bring about a belated but needful change in the current medical policies to abolish all forms of medical malpractice and medical negligence in the United States and throughout the world.

Dr. Cutter took advantage of this discrepancy in the lack of policy matters by the MQAC, and he exploited me in every way possible for his own self-interests at my expense. I am a real person who encountered a medical doctor who had delusional and mental fantasies of grandiose cosmetic achievements for which he was not specialized. Dr. Cutter completely misinterpreted my cosmetic interests for my nose and ears, and he totally misunderstood what I wanted, needed, and expected.

I have been misunderstood by a number of my carrier colleagues and by the general public, but Dr. Cutter utilized a psychological blitzkrieg of bamboozlement to my mental perception to advance his cosmetic agenda against me. I know that the medical licensing boards and the chief investigator along with the investigation unit were completely fooled and deceived by Dr. Cutter's actions against me.

I can understand Dr. Cutter's actions in light of writer Jon Meacham's quote in Newsweek of December 29, 2008: "From Plato forward, philosophers have struggled to define power which is at heart the capacity to bend reality to your will."

According to my friend Bud, "This quote could also apply toward people's perception of reality which can and has been bent to their detriment by the media and social planners."

I became another victim in the long history of the abuse of power at the surgical hands of a predator disguised as a specialist in dentistry. I was unable to prevent the cosmetic surgeon from exploiting me on that unfortunate day. If the legislators, medical boards, dental board, judges, and courts of the United States of America do absolutely nothing to create and enact laws to prevent medical malpractice crimes and abuses then scores of medical doctors who are waiting in the ranks of the medical boards will continue to victimize other unsuspecting patients.

When I received my first letter from an insurance company concerning my injuries post-surgeries with Dr. Cutter I didn't know what to do with it. The insurance company provided insurance claims for hospitals and doctors I was told. After some consideration I sent back the letter providing my information regarding what I should be compensated for. My request for financial compensation was denied by the insurance company. Post-surgeries I had shared my unhappiness with Dr. Cutter's secretary over the phone, and she told me that I needed to talk to Dr. Cutter. Each day I was in the middle of dealing with a constant state of mental barriers and blockades from Dr. Cutter's stunning mental whammy against my mind along with the physical cosmetic devastation and negative reactions from a lot of the general public.

I also talked to Frances Fergeson, who dealt with medical malpractice in the Lone Star State of Texas. When I was talking with Frances and asking if I had any legal recourse to pursue a lawsuit against Dr. Cutter it became obvious to me that Frances had a good understanding of my predicament regarding the three-year statute of limitations in Washington State. Frances mentioned that in Texas they had a two-year statute of limitations.

I knew from personal experience what Frances was talking about when she said, "When a patient begins to thaw out," referring to the mental trauma and shock a stunned patient goes through during a medical malpractice experience. Any medical doctor who has to resort to committing medical malpractice by storming the brain with dirty mental, hypnotic neutralization tactics should be banned from ever performing cosmetic surgeries and stripped of his or her medical license.

My sister Marlie informed me of a conversation she had with an attorney, Paul Davis, in Clover Valley. Paul told Marlie that there will be forty thousand fewer doctors by the year 2020, and the reason for the shortage will be medical malpractice suits and fewer doctors choosing to go into the medical field.

What I experienced at the hands of a medical doctor who was willing to exploit and take advantage of me, mentally, cosmetically, and financially, when he lacked the cosmetic and reconstruction expertise of a qualified surgeon certified by American Board of Plastic Surgery is in my perspective 100 percent evil.

When power-trippers and delusional medical doctors are willing to commit cosmetic and financial crimes against innocent, and unsuspecting patients it's high time to pull the plug on their licenses to practice cosmetic surgery before they have another opportunity to hurt, abuse, and victimize other unsuspecting patients. My victimization was purely about Dr. Cutter's show and not about my personal cosmetic interests.

Keep in mind that there are psychotic predators in the medical field with smiling faces waiting for you to enter their psycho web. These medical predators haven't had the specialized training as have members of the twenty-four boards of medical specialties. These medical doctors may have delusional thinking possibly using you to add to their cosmetic statistics and financial gain to prove to themselves that they can deceive you and fool the medical boards.

These medical doctors are slackers and predators; they are delusional, psychotic, and power-tripping thinkers who are ready and willing to victimize unsuspecting patients for personal profit and professional gain. They are not about to be stopped until the medical boards recognizes that these delusional power-trippers operating as medical doctors are on a runaway train with someone's cosmetic and financial business at stake. They must be stopped in their tracks immediately with the stroke of a pen by the legislators in Olympia and by the U.S. Congress through enacting laws that have real teeth to them.

The object of these unrecognized board-certified doctors is to catch the unsuspecting patient mentally off guard on the day of surgery. They purposely play along with the unsuspecting patient who may be explaining what he or she wants, needs, and expects regarding the results. The cosmetic surgeon then says something like, "Well, I better go about building up the bridge," as he mentally pushes the patient over into the unconscious realm so that the patient is incapable of reversing his or her cosmetic tracks.

The patient then follows the doctor into a dimly lit pre surgery room where the medical doctor now demonstrated his cosmetic agenda. The patient is now at the mercy of the malicious medical doctor, who cares more about capturing the patient's business than he cares about the patient's self-interests.

When Dr. Cutter said, "Well, I better go about building up the bridge," I now know that was his call for me to go into a prehypnotic altered state of mind. I remember wondering why Dr. Cutter hadn't told me during our initial consultation that he planned on building up the bridge of my nose which I clearly didn't want. I wasn't interested in having my nose bridge built up. As I was thinking on this situation I followed the doctor into a dark room and my mind suddenly went blank.

I was powerless to stop Dr. Cutter's mind control tactics and his taking charge of my cosmetic destiny. Dr. Cutter did not play fair with me every step of the way. I was caught in and swallowed up by Dr. Cutter's psychoheresy web which means as Bud explained it, "psychological or mind deception tactics which is the integration of mind-altering techniques and theories. It's like Christ-centered ministry versus problem-centered counseling. There is a world of difference."

I found the mind-deception techniques of Dr. Cutter were not pleasant, and yet the consequences are totally avoidable provided the MQAC changes its governing policies to restrict unrecognized medical doctors from performing surgeries on multiple-surgery patients like me.

At this juncture Dr. Cutter pushed me over mentally into the unconscious dimension where he could program me subconsciously for his cosmetic agenda. Dr. Cutter knew what he was going to do to me, but I didn't know. Things were moving at a rather fast pace which caught me mentally off guard. Dr. Cutter did not give me time to think it through or time to mentally digest what he was about to do to me. In fact Dr. Cutter didn't permit me the consideration of making a decision for or against his plans.

I bear scars under both of my breasts giving testimony and providing evidence that Dr. Raymond Rockwell had to remove cartilage from my rib cage to help lower my elevated nose. Dr. Cutter had purposely raised my nose and repositioned it against my will in a way that looks abnormal. That is scary. I unknowingly entered the doctor's mental and cosmetic playground wherein the maze of post-surgeries conscious and unconscious mental confusion blurred the mental lines as to what happened to me mentally, cosmetically, and financially.

The psychotic, delusional, and power-tripper doctor had me exactly where he wanted me to be. He knew that it might take years for me to figure out what had happened to me at his hands. How could I prove what had happened to me to the medical boards, an attorney, or the judicial courts?

How long would it take to for me to know within myself that I was mentally incapable of explaining what the psychotic, sociopathic, and delusional doctor had done to me? Things got turned around in my mind, and I felt violated by a medical doctor who shouldn't have touched my facial features in the first place. After explaining what I could remember had happened to me to the people who I could trust I had to work my way through various surges of depression, trauma, and the persistent mental whammy that Dr. Cutter had dragged me into. He dragged me into the web of as my friend Bud put it psycho "deception techniques; that is psychoheresy deception tactics. In fact it is a self-esteem centered religion."

The bottom line reason for why a medical doctor would do something like what I went through is clearly for his self-interests, greed, and power over a subdued patient.

Dr. Cutter is another pathetic coward who was ready and willing to do more cutting and rearranging on my nose and ears because he was not restricted by the medical boards to stop performing surgical procedures on ultiple-surgery patients even though he was not certified by the American Board of Plastic Surgery. Because Dr. Cutter was not restricted by clear guidelines set down by the medical boards relative to his lack of medical specialty training I was cosmetically and financially ripped off by a predator, violator, and terror intruder disguised as a medical doctor.

Dr. Cutter's tactics need to be exposed so he never can use them again on an unsuspecting patient. I thank God I was given an opportunity to tell of my horrible cosmetic ordeal to save others the painful mental, emotional, and cosmetic misery I have experienced.

I have seen a Christian counselor on and off for years regarding my agonizing cosmetic ordeal at the hands of Dr. Cutter. I also have seen a professional psychologist, Willis M. Dunken PhD ABPP who is certified by the American Board of Professional Psychology and the American Board of Psychological Hypnosis.

I wanted to see if a professional psychologist could recognize that I had been hypnotized by Dr. Cutter in his dimly lit pre-surgery room. I gave Dr. Dunken a description of some of the things that I remembered experiencing on the day of my surgeries when Dr. Cutter took charge of my cosmetic destiny.

Dr. Dunken said, "From your description I wouldn't know if you were hypnotized or not."

I know within myself however and it has taken me years to figure it out that Dr. Cutter did use some form of hypnosis and some form of radiation or a chemical to cause memory loss for a long time. It took me seven to nine years to come to the complete understanding and fully know what happed to me with absolute certainty. My friend Tommy Ray who served in Vietnam believes that Dr. Cutter used something chemical related on me based on what I told him about the things that I experienced under Dr. Cutter's care.

Tommy is not an expert or an authority on the use of chemicals or radiation; it was only a thought that came to his mind when I shared my experience with him.

Dr. Dunken told me that if he used hypnosis on me to regress my mind it would ruin my testimony in the courts as the opposing attorney would argue that Dr. Dunken had influenced me to think such things. I told Dr. Dunken that I hadn't thought of having him use hypnosis on me. I don't need a psychiatrist or a psychologist to determine what I underwent at the hands of Dr. Cutter.

I know that Dr. Cutter was on a power trip to move out of his medical specialty which is in dentistry to want to take on a multiple-surgery patient like me. To preserve his own ego Dr. Cutter must have been in an altered state of mind such as a predatory or a criminal mindset to do what he did to me. Dr. Cutter had to have turned off his conscience or turned off the analytical center of his brain to commit his cosmetic and financial crimes against me. I know that Dr. Cutter was too wrapped up in his self-interests to think clearly of the consequences his overall predatorial actions would have on me.

I spoke to a woman who used hypnotism in her therapy practice in the Banner District in Union. I asked her if as a consequence of hypnosis there would be any residual blackness or blankness left in a person's memory bank?

The female therapist said, "Oh no, you have been watching too many late-night movies." She answered my questions concerning what I experienced post surgeries with Dr. Cutter. I was convinced beyond a shadow of a doubt that I had been victimized and that criminal actions were committed against me by Dr. Cutter both pre-and post-surgeries.

A man named Sid Advice who works for the MQAC told me, "If it still bothers you, why don't you seek legal help?"

From my perspective I thought that Sid offered poor advice to a patient who was continuously suffering from victimization by a malicious predator. I realize that Sid didn't understand everything I had been going through post-surgeries. I had sought legal help from attorneys but to no avail. I would have appreciated it if Sid out of a sincere heart of understanding and caring had showed me some respect and consideration concerning my desire to hear that the medical and dental boards had taken disciplinary or termination action against Dr. Cutter. That never took place.

I would replace Sid Advice if I had the power to do so for his insensitive remarks to me a cosmetic victim who was clearly victimized by Dr. Cutter. I would also shut down the MQAC if I could until they instituted new policies regarding unrecognized cosmetic surgeons, and they told Dr. Cutter to pack his bags and hit the road for his ruinous actions against my nose and ears. The nonaction verdict by the medical review boards against Dr. Cutter was pathetic, and I firmly believed that their lack of decisive action gave Dr. Cutter the green light to continue hurting other unsuspecting patients.

I called up and voiced my disappointment for their decision against taking disciplinary action with Dr. Cutter. I needed a positive verdict by the boards to show that I truly was victimized, and that it was not a mere slip of Dr. Cutter's scalpel that caused irreparable damages to my nose and ears. I know that Dr. Cutter's actions against me were not an accident but cosmetic and financial crimes.

Trapped By A Psycho Doctor

His actions were destructive to my total being, dignity, and character; these hurtful and abusive actions have wasted years of my life, and this could have been avoided if Dr. Cutter had told the truth during our initial consultation. Instead Dr. Cutter chose to exploit me by using deception for his personal and professional gain, and I have suffered for it throughout the years.

I did not need Dr. Cutter's mental trickery and thuggery which led to my cosmetic surgeries causing me irreparable damages to my nose and ears. Dr. Cutter's actions on the day of my surgeries were not in my cosmetic and financial interests.

I want to repeat an earlier statement that I know to be 100 percent true: if any one of the medical board members had experienced what I endured at the hands of Dr. Cutter they wouldemphatically say, "Truly this was positively cosmetic and financial crimes. Such actions committed against an unsuspecting patient are classified as medical malpractice facts."

The reason why the medical boards hasn't closed the doors on unrecognized cosmetic surgeons who have committed medical malpractice is greed.

I had another talk with Robin on why the medical boards haven't intervened in this problem of unqualified medical doctors. I said, "They're leaving the doors open to medical doctors who are not qualified to work on certain patients. Why haven't they come up with stricter laws concerning this serious situation? Why haven't the medical boards enforced strict guidelines for irresponsible doctors and surgeons who commit irresponsible acts on their patients?"

"That's a good question," Robin said. "I don't know why they haven't. That would be a good question for a doctor to answer."

I want to see complete and thorough action taken immediately by the U.S. Congress, legislators throughout the land, courts and judges, and the medical and dental boards to ensure more legal recourse for patients who have been victimized. The patient's costs of legal action should be absorbed by the doctors who have committed the criminal actions against the patients. That would be reinforced by the state.

I have discovered a lot of things since I first encountered Dr. Cutter. The cosmetic deck was stacked against me from the outset of my meeting with Dr. Cutter during our initial consultation. I later discovered that Dr. Cutter was not a specialist in the nose and ears as an American Board of Plastic Surgery surgeon; I was searching for such qualifications when I first came in to see Dr. Cutter.

Dr. Cutter did his level best to tear down the previous doctor's work and rebuild my nose with a substitute and imitation; he raised and repositioned my nose causing it to appear abnormal. My nose and ears were altered with irreparable damages.

I discovered that the statute of limitations was running out for me to pursue a lawsuit against Dr. Cutter due to the medical boards not informing me about all my rights and the steps I should take to see justice served. The juries are not sympathetic toward injured, abused, and victimized multiple-surgery patients, and because of that I know there will be many more victimized and unsuspecting patients until the medical boards stops pandering to delusional and power-tripper medical doctors with an insatiable desire for money, professional gain, and personal profit.

Dr. Cutter made some strong statements when he set out to victimize me. He made a powerful statement by his actions that he didn't need to have the extra training that the American Board of Plastic Surgery requires and that he could use mental trickery and thuggery on me, and still produce positive physical enhancements when operating on unsuspecting multiple-surgery patients.

Dr. Cutter was clearly making the statement that he could do whatever he wanted to do to me cosmetically because the medical boards have left the doors wide open for him to have his way with patients cosmetically with as many unsuspecting patients as he wants to until they put a screeching halt on his insatiable appetite for power, greed, and personal self-interests. He was making a statement: "I am going to have my way with Jonah jon Jeffreys because he is a simpleton. He was the one who came into my cosmetic practice, and he will accept my deranged cosmetic violations and deviations because I have the power to do so with impunity.

I am smart enough not to repeat the same criminal actions so I won't get caught and come under the scrutiny of the medical review boards because they are my puppets too." Dr. Cutter knows that no one on the medical review boards will act as spies to report criminal wrong doings to the police.

Medical doctors who are sinister predators look for weaknesses in the system, and they look for ways to exploit unsuspecting patients to avoid detection of their criminal actions against innocent victims. They criminally assault the brain of unsuspecting patients so that they are left mentally short-circuited, impaired, and confused for years as to what happened to them during surgery. If those patients complain to the medical review boards they can end up looking like mentally deranged patients.

Dr. Cutter like many other unrecognized board-certified doctors will not stop making additional cosmetic changes to unsuspecting patients because they haven't been caught or stopped in their conniving tracks. Therefore they are permitted to repeat their deranged, sinister, sociopathic actions against any number of unsuspecting patients until the victimized patients fight back by reporting them to the medical boards, investigation unit, and Better Business Bureau.

The medical board, MQAC will then be forced to put a stop to the doctors' criminal victimization by recognizing that these delusional doctors are setting a pattern of malicious cosmetic butchery that is totally below the standard of care as set forth by the health departments throughout our country and the MQAC.

I want to alert the reader to the dangers that are in the medical and business communities as I experienced major pitfalls because of my questioning and trusting attitude. Trust in human relationships is important, but this does not mean having blind trust. The same goes for a doctor/patient relationship. While searching for the right cosmetic surgeon I never expected a medical doctor in a position of trust would betray my trust. The trust factor was violated by a medical doctor acting as a cosmetic specialist in the nose and ears, but in actuality he was a wolf in medical garb. Apparently it's in Dr. Cutter's understanding that an unsuspecting patient who is used, and abused is better than one who walks away from his office and out of his dimly lit pre-surgery room.

How can you know if you encounter a sinister predator disguised as a medical doctor as I did? Here are some signs: His cosmetic credentials do not add up to the ABPS and ABMS qualifications. The cosmetic surgeon stays close to you mentally to crowd your thinking. He doesn't want you to think about what he can and can't do for you. You are allowed to come to your own short conclusions, and then he continues to work on your mind to keep you mentally starved and off balance to catch you completely off guard with his cosmetic scam.

Once you think you've been allowed to come to positive cosmetic conclusions regarding your desired results he suddenly runs a reverse psychological whammy on you by telling you something that may not be in your specific and detailed cosmetic blueprint (such as when Dr. Cutter told me, "Well, I better go about building up the bridge"). Not in my cosmetic notes, and desired results which he stated it gave him something to work with.

As I considered Dr. Cutter's plan to build up the bridge of my nose my mind went blank within a second or two as I followed the doctor into the darkened room. I bumped into Dr. Cutter directly after I entered the room, and my mind suddenly went blank. Dr. Cutter had succeeded in allowing me to come to my own conclusions that he was qualified to meet my cosmetic interests only to pull a whammy on me by informing me of his agenda for my nose shortly before my mind went blank, and shortly after anesthesia was administered for my surgeries.

Dr. Cutter didn't tell me the specific details of his plans for me upfront because he knew that if he had done so I would have walked out of his office and never come back. Instead Dr. Cutter used me for his own professional statistics, personal profit, and cosmetic agenda by purposefully withholding vital information only to offer poor excuses after my surgeries. By the time I woke up to the fact that there were cosmetic violations and major deviations to my nose and ears it was too late; my cosmetic business was under Dr. Cutter's control. After subduing me mentally Dr. Cutter filled in the blanks post-surgeries.

As I've mentioned before Dr. Cutter said, "See it as a sculpture. I tore it down, beat it up, and built it back up."

His words surprised me, and I wondered why he hadn't told me of his plans up front. I felt used, abused, ripped off, and violated. Dr. Cutter then revealed the truth of how he saw the results: "It didn't turn out as I had envisioned." He also said, "It's what the other doctors did."

Dr. Cutter frequently had his nurse/photo technician in the room when I met with him after my surgeries. I think she was there as his witness to catch anything I might say that would benefit or protect him should I pursue a lawsuit against him.

I was a victim of dirty cosmetics as Dr. Cutter didn't correctly interpret what I'd said I wanted. I was victimized by a predator, a psychopathic and sociopathic cosmetic surgeon who made excuses post-surgeries. I have come to the inevitable conclusion that it was his intention to keep me mentally starved, and off balance so that he could then fabricate answers for me post-surgeries to cover himself.

By not informing me of the details of the cosmetic procedures up front is strong evidence that he lacked the training that a board-certified American Board of Plastic Surgery surgeon has.

Remember that there are medical predators who care more about gaining your financial and cosmetic business than they care about you as an individual.

Dr. Cutter's approach was a one-way street it benefited him but not me. About three months after my surgeries I asked Dr. Cutter a question about my nose in front of my co-worker Denise. Dr. Cutter acted like he was on a power trip. When I came in for a consultation approximately six months after surgeries without a witness he acted like a guilty eccentric doctor who had extreme difficulty handling any questions from me.

As I've previously mentioned when I asked Dr. Cutter what had happened to my nose ("It looks like a turtle nose"), he turned away from me, stared up at the wall and said without looking at me, "If something could be done we'd have to wait a year." He then added, "I hope it will come down." Dr. Cutter finally turned around to sit down behind his desk and that's when he said, "It didn't turn out as I envisioned."

"My complaint is that it not only didn't turn out as I envisioned, but also with the way you went about getting my business."

Dr. Cutter just looked at me for a short time, but then dropped his head as if he didn't want to deal with what he had done to me any longer. He never responded to my comment.

I eventually realized that Dr. Cutter pushed his cosmetic agenda on me because he needed to deceive the medical boards as well as the investigation unit about his mental trickery and thuggery he utilized. What I had experienced at his hands wasn't surgical accidents but real crimes with horrible irreparable nose and ear damages along with post-surgeries emotional anguish. I continuously reflected on the kind of medical doctor he was, and how he had violated me mentally and cosmetically unnecessarily. For days, months, and years I thought about the events that led up to his cosmetic crimes.

I could sense the psychological whammy in my mind clouding my thoughts and preventing me from figuring out exactly what Dr. Cutter had done to me mentally and cosmetically.

Dr. Cutter's actions negatively affected the chemistry in my brain. I knew within myself that Dr. Cutter had committed crimes against me, but I found it hard to bring any convincing evidence to the medical boards. If I had been the chairman of the medical or dental boards I would have told Dr. Cutter to pack his cosmetic bags; his medical and dental licenses would be revoked immediately.

Dr. Cutter now has twelve closed complaints against him with the medical boards. My experience and a series of complaint letters which included a series of requests for a criminal investigation were placed with his medical board. He has six complaints against him with the dental board, and complaint number five ended in death. I strongly feel that once a medical doctor is accused and convicted of a crime in one of his medical or dental categories he or she should not be allowed to practice under another license indefinitely.

Dr. Cutter didn't allow me to choose whether I would submit to hypnosis. He just took over as a cosmetic shark without discussion, and began cutting and carving on me like I was a piece of meat. He aggressively did additional cutting on my nose and ears without my knowledge and consent. He ruthlessly and maliciously did additional cutting on my facial features totally against my wants, needs, expectations, and desired interests. These were all gradual realizations that I came to as the years went mercilessly by.

I contacted the Disclosure Department at the MQAC to check up on Dr. Cutter's complaint status. I previously discovered that Dr. Cutter had ten complaints under his medical license which were all closed except for one open complaint that was pending. This time when I inquired his complaint status had changed from ten to twelve closed complaints. He had six closed complaints under his dental license, and one open that was pending prior to my last check. He had one under his general anesthesia license that was open and pending.

I can only hope that Dr. Cutter and other predatory medical doctors are stopped from hurting victims in the course of their professional practice. Perhaps Dr. Cutter has modified his predatory actions on unsuspecting patients to comply with the policies of the medical boards, dental board, and the commission's rules. Possibly his unrecognized board-certified status has caught the full attention of the medical boards he is licensed with, and maybe he has reached the maximum complaint status without drawing more scrutiny to the list of injured patients.

Dealing with Dr. Cutter was like dealing with a phantom. The day before my surgeries in the 1990s my nose and ears were doing just fine; I only wanted cosmetic enhancement for them with subtle cosmetic changes. On the day of my surgeries I was subjected to a malicious assault by an unqualified cosmetic surgeon who was a greedy opportunist; he was an MD DDS who didn't have specialty training in the nose and ears. I understand now exactly why Dr. Cutter was malicious with me; I wouldn't have stayed if he had told me the truth. I would have said, "I don't feel comfortable with your approach, and I would like to leave here now."

Dr. Cutter mentally desensitized me so that I became nonreactive to what he planned to do. He impaired my mental perceptions so that I was rendered ineffective at discerning the doctor's actions and his deceptive approach which resulted in painful and irreparable damages to my facial features. I am convinced that I was cosmetically and financially victimized by Dr. Cutter. I know without any doubt that crimes were committed against me. When I asked Dr. Raymond Rockwell if he considered Dr. Cutter's cosmetic work on me to be a crime Dr. Rockwell responded, "If Dr. Cutter had left an orange peel or a peanut shell inside your nose then I would consider it a crime."

I shared some of the things that Dr. Cutter did to me on the day of my surgeries but Dr. Rockwell didn't have firsthand experience like I did with the horrible post-surgeries consequences. I know that Dr. Rockwell is not a forensic criminologist who could prove that I was victimized by Dr. Cutter so I simply allowed Dr. Rockwell to share his professional opinion without trying to convince him otherwise. After all I was only interested in hearing what his professional opinion would be.

I was still unable to pinpoint the exact moment when Dr. Cutter committed the actual crimes against me. When Dr. Cutter pushed me over into the unconscious realm I was unable to respond or react in a normal way to what Dr. Cutter planned do to me.

Dr. Cutter knew what he was going to do during surgery, but I didn't know; I had no knowledge of Dr. Cutter's cosmetic agenda and plans. I realize now that Dr. Cutter reversed his cosmetic agenda on me without my knowledge or consent after desensitizing my mind. This provides convincing evidence that he knew that he wasn't a nose and ears specialist, but he wanted my business anyway. Therefore the medical boards need to come to a mutual decision, and a unanimous verdict that crimes were committed against me.

Before my surgeries I frequently asked whether Dr. Cutter could do what I wanted and needed, but he took charge of my cosmetic destiny like a shark which doesn't negotiate with its victim it just comes up and takes the leg off its victim without discussion.

Dr. Donald Philbert's evaluation of Dr. Cutter's cosmetic work on me was, "The miscommunication with the oral surgeon was sad."

The MQAC needs to take immediate action against any unrecognized medical doctor who has stated that there are a lot of boards out there. The surgical doors have been left open to untold potential butchery on multitudes of unsuspecting cosmetic patients, and the medical boards will be held accountable for that. The medical boards should not wait for more than one complaint against a medical doctor before they enact new laws that prohibit unrecognized medical doctors from committing cosmetic crimes against unsuspecting patients.

I request that the MQAC terminate the current investigation unit chief, Arnold Richards who refused to open a criminal investigation against Dr. Cutter, and hire a new one who will be aggressive with regard to investigating any call for a criminal investigation from a victimized patient as I repeatedly did without any action being taken. I was truly victimized, but I had difficulty coming up with the winning combination of answers to satisfy the medical boards and the investigation units and its chief.

The medical boards failed to communicate what they needed from me to prove what Dr. Cutter had done to me, and I believe they should have called for a criminal investigation because I had requested one. To satisfy any suspicions and all possibilities of criminal actions taken toward the patient the boards should have the investigation unit meet with the medical doctor to eliminate any criminal wrongdoing provided there is good evidence for an investigation. Besides being cosmetically violated and personally devastated I dealt with ongoing confusion and perplexity for years.

God says in His Word, "God is not the author of confusion but of peace" (1 Corinthians14:33).

Dr. Cutter did a masterful job of assaulting my mind with mental blockages and blockades most likely with a chemical of some form to make certain that I had difficulties with solving the crimes he committed against me. I know that Dr. Cutter found a way to desensitize my mind so that he could help himself to my cosmetic and financial spoils without getting caught. Dr. Cutter was a slacker and con artist, driven by power, greed, and control issues that motivated him to deceive, fool, and redirect the review board's and investigation unit's attention away from the fact that he committed highly calculated and sinister crimes against me.

It took me between seven to nine years to fully understand exactly what Dr. Cutter had done to me. He was driven to devour my cosmetic and financial business like an anaconda when faced with an unsuspecting rabbit. It attacks the rabbit to devour it whole without any hesitation. I wanted my cosmetic blueprint fulfilled, but Dr. Cutter wanted to add me to his medical statistics by fulfilling his cosmetic quota. It suddenly became the unskilled, unqualified, and nonspecialized cosmetic surgeon working on a multiple-surgery patient. His work ended in deplorable cosmetic results for me that were scary.

Dr. Cutter knew that he was putting me in the extremely difficult position of proving that he had committed crimes against me so that the investigation unit and medical review boards would take decisive action against him. Dr. Raymond Rockwell told me that he would consider it a crime if Dr. Cutter had left an orange peel in my nose. That led me to realize that the key thing the review board teams, and the investigation unit are looking for is if a doctor leaves something in a patient an orange peel, a scalpel, a screwdriver. Then they will determine it to be a crime. That let me know that medical doctors are allowed to get away with various types of medical malpractice provided they don't leave behind any evidence to prove and substantiate their crimes.

If the patient isn't able to prove his criminal case to the medical boards he must find a doctor who is willing to go on record to say that the surgeon didn't do what the patient wanted. Most medical doctors however are not willing to testify in court against another doctor especially if the doctor's practice in the same state.

Because of Dr. Cutter's insatiable drive to deceive the medical boards he became oblivious to my interests. He had to have concluded, how can I go wrong with this simpleton? He is a multiple-surgery patient. If I mess up no one will notice.

Dr. Cutter was hell-bent on duping me into believing that my raised and repositioned nose was normal just like a shark's victim accepts his missing leg. The victimized patient has to deal with the aftermath all the mental, emotional, and irreparable cosmetic damages if a qualified surgeon can't repair those damages with surgical revisions.

Dr. Cutter told me twice, "I like you." I didn't need counterfeit affection from Dr. Cutter as a means of deflecting my questions. The more I experienced rejection from my co-workers, customers on my personnel carriers, churchgoers, and the general public the more I became obsessive in my thoughts about Dr. Cutter.

I continuously thought about Dr. Cutter and his sinister approach. I talked to myself about Dr.

Cutter at times, and I became angry about Dr. Cutter's slipshod methods. I shouldn't have had to deal with the agonizing pain and misery just because Dr. Cutter deceived me and operated on me when he clearly was not qualified to do so.

I was pleasant and friendly toward my family, friends, and the customers on the carrier routes I drove, but the quality of my life after my surgeries was significantly reduced. Dr. Cutter's actions were far off the mark when it came to meeting any standard of quality care and cosmetic procedures. Simply put Dr. Cutter's approach was cruel, criminal, and immoral.

I obsessively thought about Dr. Cutter's slipshod work on me and his approach with me which was not normal for a medical doctor. Even if Dr. Cutter's, "Slam, bam, thank you Jonah jon Jeffreys Scone for your business" had turned out as I'd hoped it still would be a crime because of the inappropriate approach that Dr. Cutter took with me. Because of Dr. Cutter's aggressive approach I felt mentally and cosmetically violated no question about it.

I believe that my obsessive thoughts about Dr. Cutter twice brought an evil presence into my home. If I had entertained having the negative spirit to bring harmful consequences to Dr. Cutter I would have crossed the line with God and His righteous standards. I realized the evil presence that was near was not planning great harm to all people involved. I rejected the evil spirit and his ultimate bidding and his alluring thoughts of harming Dr. Cutter.

God had to help me with my thought life. I have discovered exactly what Dr. Cutter did to me thanks to the Lord. I know what the medical boards are looking for to prove medical malpractice. I have suffered unnecessarily, and it caused years of foggy focus because Dr. Cutter wasn't willing to tell me the truth during our initial consultation.

I went on a protracted spiritual fast, and I am convinced that the Lord allowed me to see Dr. Cutter's actions in his dimly lit pre-surgery room. I saw Dr. Cutter turned sideways in a chair rocking back and forth with a big grin of triumph on his face while I sat in a chair mentally impaired. I witnessed Dr. Cutter moving about his pre-surgery mental-desensitization room, and strategically placing himself in different positions while I was only able to look on in silence. My recollections were like an old movie projector that would start and stop.

I was frozen in my seat totally unable to move when Dr. Cutter placed himself in his final pre-surgery position to the right of where I was sitting. He intently stared at me as if to say, I told you what I'm going to do. Now what are you going to do? I suddenly jumped up trying to mentally grasp what Dr. Cutter was going to do to my nose. When I couldn't comprehend his plans for me I closed my eyes in mental blankness and tension.

I eventually solved Dr. Cutter's crimes he committed against me with persistent mental evaluations; I continuously pressed forth to figure out the strange experiences I've had. Dr. Cutter used mental blocks that prevented me from coming to an early and decisive conclusion. I finally solved the puzzle of my surgeries. Dr. Cutter had waited until he moved me into an altered state of consciousness before he shared that he was going to raise and reposition my nose two things that I absolutely didn't want. This scary, painful, and devastating move against me an unsuspecting patient was clearly sinister and a devious crime in no uncertain terms. With God's help I eventually solved Dr. Cutter's criminal case that the medical boards and investigation unit had willfully missed.

I was under Dr. Cutter's hypnosis and mind-control tactics. I would call this mental desensitization being in la-la land. God allowed me to see negative images that were imprinted in my memory when Dr. Cutter hit me with his psychological whammy. I didn't recall seeing those mental images when my mind first went blank, but God gave me a vision of Dr. Cutter's pre-surgery actions during a time of prayer and fasting.

When I shared this information with the medical review boards they turned a blind eye and a deaf ear to me with regard to taking action against the surgical predator. It would require more time for me to know exactly what I had experienced at Dr. Cutter's hands and what the medical boards were looking for before they would take action against Dr. Cutter. In my personal experience it felt like Dr. Cutter had shoved his plans directly into my subconscious mind which became elusive to my analytical and inquisitive mind for years.

Scientists have discovered how to split the atom and how to put a man on the moon. Had humankind been faithful to the will and plan of God Almighty, the Lord God would have made certain that we achieved far greater accomplishments than what humankind has been able to achieve. I am convinced that Dr. Cutter believed in his grandiose, and narcissistic fantasies that he could tear down Dr. Lowell Piper's cosmetic work and Dr. Chris Kirtpatrick's plastic surgery work and rebuild my nose in the way he saw fit.

Dr. Cutter repositioned my nose alright which was excruciatingly ugly to look at and painfully embarrassing and offensive to me, and for the general public to behold. Dr. Cutter also tore down Dr. Christopher Smith's plastic surgery work on my ears and chin which also was against my interest for my ears. My chin was the one part of my facial features that fell into Dr. Cutter's specialty, and I had to admit that after I shaved off my beard about a year later my chin looked pretty good. But Dr. Cutter was not a specialist for my nose and ears as a plastic surgeon would be. Dr. Cutter's results were a horrifying nightmare for me to experience.

My wife, Lorena, and I began watching the TV series A Haunting together. Although we were Christians in our faith in Jesus Christ, and I knew that we shouldn't be watching reenactments of true events that we were curious to watch these programs and see what unsuspecting people experienced. This paranormal anthology series portrays the demonic activities that have occurred in peoples' homes and lives. Lorena and I watched this program on a regular basis until I had a dream in which a demonic manifestation of a person was laughing at me in a mocking manner.

I shared my dream with my sister Marlie and then said, "I remember seeing Dr. Cutter in a spiritual vision from the Lord, and he was doing this same type of mocking with a sinister grin on his face as if he had conquered me. I asked the Lord to help me know what Dr. Cutter had done to me."

Marlie said, "The devil is using that program to come against you just as Dr. Cutter did on the day of your surgeries. You need to stop watching those programs."

Thank God Lorena and I closed the door on the devil's work by putting an end to watching the scary reenacted programs together.

I thought about what Dr. Cutter had said to me at my appointment for a consultation about three months post-surgeries. Denise had come with me to have a talk with the doctor about the adverse changes he had made to my facial features.

Dr. Cutter asked me, "Didn't I tell you that I was going to raise and reposition your nose?"
I boldly responded, "No, you didn't."

Dr. Cutter looked surprised that I'd spoken to him in such a forceful manner. I now understand that the first half of Dr. Cutter's crimes took place in his dimly lit pre-surgery room his psycho-deception, hypnotic-whammy room; the same room where we now were having my consultation where he assaulted my brain before my surgeries. Post-surgeries, Dr. Cutter wanted me to have a hypnotic flashback wherein I would recall words he spoke to me on the day of my surgeries that's why he'd taken me to the same dimly lit room on this day. Dr. Cutter found however that using suggestive words and actions did not work on me.

I know now that when Dr. Cutter conducted his psycho-deception tactics of hypnosis on me he was in league with spiritual darkness that was willing to hurt me in a destructive way. Dr. Cutter was not going to play fair with me just like the devil doesn't play fair with his victims.

Satan rules in spiritual darkness. The Bible says he is the god of this world and the prince of the power of the air. He is the spirit that works in the sons of disobedience, says the apostle Paul in Ephesians 2. I now realize that Dr. Cutter didn't act alone whether he knew it or not because he became a tool of the devil to seek, steal, and if possible destroy my life which had been dedicated to the Lord by my parents.

God wanted to be the only one who brought true satisfaction into my life and character by having me look to Him to make something beautiful in my life. God wanted to do a good work in me, and He didn't want me to be hurt by the selfish actions of a cosmetic surgeon. It was not God's will that I was victimized by an unqualified cosmetic surgeon; rather it was God's will to keep me from predators that will cause harm.

I realize that Dr. Cutter like so many other criminals has been able to escape man's justice on earth, but if he doesn't repent of the error of his ways he won't be able to escape heaven's justice. There is a day of reckoning coming which the Bible speaks of wherein each person will give account of himself or herself to God for the life that he or she has lived.

Humankind may not like to think about the fact that we are all accountable to a powerful, all knowing God, and we are responsible for our actions toward our fellow humans.

God says in His Word, "He is not willing that any should perish, but that all should come to repentance" (2 Peter 3:9).

Dr. Cutter's actions against me have not been ignored or overlooked by our loving God who is the ultimate judge of the people of this world. I do not wish God's wrath on Dr. Cutter or His judgment in the future. I would like to see Dr. Cutter repent of his sinister actions, and become a God-fearing man who treats his fellow humans with respect, dignity, and honor. I recognize that Dr. Cutter applied his own will to my facial surgeries, and I would like to see the iron will of justice applied to Dr. Cutter for his criminal wrongdoings.

My co-worker Denise encouraged me to write down notes of things that came to my mind regarding Dr. Cutter. I began writing copious notes of what I could remember had happened to me, pre-and post-surgeries. I knew that Dr. Cutter's approach was not ethical, but it was even something more devious in nature than that. As I've mentioned it took me years to determine what the medical boards and the investigation unit were looking for with regard to my experiences with Dr. Cutter. I know now what they require from each victimized patient, but I also know that when the medical and dental boards hear that a medical doctor isn't a recognized cosmetic surgeon with the right certification and credentials they should immediately call for a criminal investigation against that doctor.

If the patient complains that he or she was violated by a medical doctor, the medical board should instantly check on that charge, as well as checking the surgeon's credentials. If the doctor isn't board-certified by one of the twenty-four boards of medical specialties defined by the ABMS the medical review board should begin an immediate criminal investigation against the surgeon because they then will have full knowledge that something of a sinister nature has happened to that unsuspecting patient.

I realize that certain medical doctors are willing to desensitize and mentally stun the minds of patients in order to get a quick confession from an unsuspecting patient. This is exactly what I experienced at the hands of Dr. Cutter who tried to prevent the medical boards and the investigation unit from taking any action against him. After I was duped and scammed Dr. Cutter pulled himself back in line as a caring physician who followed the ethics board's policies while I was left in a sea of mental confusion as to what happened to me. When I made my formal complaint to the medical boards I think they had a negative perception of me possibly that I was a hypochondriac or a lunatic. Dr. Cutter has carried on his professional practice as if he did not commit heinous crimes against me.

When the medical boards reviewed my complaint letters with Dr. Cutter he suggested that I had psychological issues, and the medical boards bought into his evaluation of my mental health although he was not a qualified psychologist or a psychiatrist and they simply closed the case. Dr. Cutter recommended counseling for me to cover his criminal actions and to deceive the investigation unit and medical boards into thinking that he was a caring physician. I know better because of Dr. Cutter's actions toward me; I know that Dr. Cutter recommended counseling for me only when I began to question what had happened to me. His recommendation was reactionary as an effort to cover his crimes; it was not proactive as a caring physician toward me personally.

I did certain things post-surgeries that momentarily helped me to forget about my cosmetic victimization by Dr. Cutter. I isolated myself from many social settings for years, and I wrote many complaint letters to the medical boards about Dr. Cutter. Talking with friends helped me to forget about the pain of my disfigurement and horrible victimization. I didn't tell my family what had happened to me until years later because it was too painful, embarrassing, and humiliating to talk about such sensitive personal issues.

It also helped me to listen to Christian, bluegrass, and country music to take my mind off my suffering. I played my banjo for long periods to help me concentrate on something other than my mental, emotional, and cosmetic ordeal. I read in Dr. Katharine A. Phillips's book, The Broken Mirror about individuals who have serious preoccupations and obsessive thoughts over the slightest physical flaw which most people simply overlook. A lot of people become reclusive and purposefully avoid making wholesome relationships because of their obsessive preoccupation with their physical imperfections and their looks in general. A lot of people suffer on a daily basis because of their difficulties with their physical appearances.

Many people also suffer unnecessarily because of what unqualified medical doctors have done to them cosmetically. These medical doctors want to improve their limited skills so they practice on their patients and end up making some extra money at the same time. The patient then is left to suffer unnecessarily possibly for years due to botched surgeries.

I purposely remained on certain carrier routes for William County Carrier Company because the customers were familiar with my post-surgeries physical appearance. If I had chosen new routes the customers would have to get over the initial shock of seeing me for the first time on each of my routes.

I have experienced a life-changing inferiority complex which has had negative effects on my personal, social, neighborhood, and professional relationships. I would like to thank all the customers, clients, and general public who have accepted me with my physical characteristics just the way they are. I would like to offer my humble and sincere apology to all my professional co-workers, customers, and the general public for any disconcerting and disfigured physical features that have caused them to recoil or simply look away because they were uncomfortable and embarrassed when looking at me.

I know that I have been misunderstood by different groups of people over the years. They have misunderstood my friendliness, and my smile which are a positive reflection of the life of Jesus Christ in my heart and life. My friendliness and smile are outward signs, expressions, and manifestations of the inward work of the Spirit of Christ. I have also used my smile to compensate for the cosmetic changes that have been painfully difficult to live and work with.

The truth of the matter is that I have enjoyed being friendly and talking with people of all ages if they are open to having a conversation. I recognize that certain individuals are non-communicative, and they come onto my carrier and exit without saying a word of thanks for my transportation services. I recognize many carrier drivers do not like striking up a conversation with their customers, and many carrier drivers choose to keep a low profile and not communicate with the clientele as to avoid being distracted while driving.

Many of my co-workers at William County Carrier Company avoid making eye contact with me. I have had fellow co-workers at William County Carrier Company give me a look over when I sign in for work, and different people over the years have wondered what my ethnic background is. My superior at Rolland Carrier wondered if I was Italian. I was caught off guard one day when he asked me that unusual question when I was signing in for work. I said, "No, I have a Roman nose."
Lukas my supervisor said, "Roman is Italian."

I didn't tell Lukas Palmer of my Norwegian ethnicity on my father's side and Scottish and Irish heritage on my mother's side. Many people seem puzzled by my physical appearance; I know this is based on the things they have said to me over the years.

I am a real work of art with medical doctors taking my nose in one direction, and Dr. Cutter elevating my nose and rearranging it in a way I didn't expect or appreciate.

I went to see an attorney who worked for an established law firm in Union. The attorney asked a female employee what she thought of my nose job and whether she could see any problems with it.

She was evasive about whether she could see any problems with my nose. I realized she was trying to spare my feelings; she could not say truthfully, "It's a good-looking nose. I don't see anything wrong with it. He should be very pleased with the cosmetic surgeon's work."

I didn't care for the attorney's approach of seeking a positive or negative response from the female employee without asking me whether I was open to the woman's evaluation.

When I called the same attorney at a later time to tell him that I believed that Dr. Cutter had hypnotized me he said, "Tell me how Dr. Cutter did that."

I couldn't describe at that time exactly how Dr. Cutter had gone about hypnotizing me. The attorney came across as rather cold and psychologically pushy, and he pressed me for answers that I hadn't completely figured out at that point. I never called the attorney after that. I am sure that Dr. Cutter knows that most victims will give up the struggle to pursue justice to its final conclusion. He knows that a victimized patient has to persevere through the maze of mental confusion to persuade the medical review boards and the investigation units to sit up and take notice of criminal acts of true victimization.

I had a good talk with my friend Leroy O'Hara concerning Dr.
Cutter's motivation for committing cosmetic crimes against me.

Leroy said, "The doctor would have to be crazy to do so." I responded, "He was crazy."

I am persuaded that Dr. Cutter was cunning in his actions on the day of my surgeries knowing he lacked the appropriate qualifications, and yet he performed cosmetic surgeries on me regardless of the consequences. No patient wants an unrecognized medical doctor performing surgery that results in the complete opposite of what he or she wants, needs, and expects.

I spoke with a woman who worked for the MQAC a number of years ago. I told her, "I feel like I was cosmetically raped by Dr. Cutter. Although I am not a woman I know what it feels like to be raped." I had experienced a mental, cosmetic, emotional, and financial violation to my whole person by Dr. Cutter, but I wasn't able to explain or describe everything to the woman at the time.

She was silent at first as she listened on the phone to my horrible experience, but she quickly got off the phone after she heard my negative description of my violations.

My friend Leroy couldn't understand why I allowed this experience with Dr. Cutter to trouble me for the last seven years. My friend never experienced the psychological, spiritual, and emotional suffering that I have in my social and personal relationships.

I don't fault the woman at the MQAC or Leroy for not understanding my ordeal at the hands of a greedy and uncaring cosmetic surgeon. I have come to realize over a number of challenging years, that my experiences with Dr. Cutter had the results it did because I was deceived, duped, scammed, and conned by Dr. Cutter cosmetically and financially. I only wish I could have seen what the medical review boards were looking for a lot sooner, but I was so devastated, mentally and cosmetically besides being in mental confusion for years that I had great difficulty trying to pinpoint what the medical boards were looking for.

I believe that I made a number of good points that should have moved the boards to call for a criminal investigation, but they needed me to emphatically say that I didn't have an understanding, partial or full, of what Dr. Cutter was going to do to me and that is 100 percent true.

How many patients will be allowed to die under the care of a physician before someone takes action? One of the complaints against Dr. Cutter filed with the dental board was from a patient who later died. I asked for more information on that case, but the disclosure unit couldn't do that. It is scary to deal with a doctor whose patient has died under his or her care and scarier to find this out only after my own facial feature devastating surgeries.

I am convinced that Dr. Cutter and other unrecognized medical doctors are malpractice cases, lawsuits, injuries, and even deaths just waiting to happen. They hold the power of life and death over their patients. Whether they know how to control that power or not depends on a number of factors. A big factor is whether they have a qualified anesthesiologist or they choose to save money by not hiring a qualified anesthesiologist.

If you plan to have cosmetic surgery I encourage you to ask a lot of questions of your chosen surgeon, and talk to a number of patients who have had cosmetic surgery on the same body part on which you will have surgery.

The MQAC informed me that they can't judge medical malpractice on the basis of cosmetic results. I urge the medical commissions, societies, and review teams throughout the land to change their rulings which are upheld by the medical boards to include cosmetic results as evidence for a criminal investigation. Where there is smoke there is fire. If a unrecognized medical doctor elects to perform cosmetic surgery, and the results are recognized by one or more medical doctors as a misunderstanding, misinterpretation, miscommunication, "not what the patient wanted or needed," and so on then the medical review teams need to call for an immediate criminal investigation especially if the patient is experiencing post-surgery symptoms of short-term or long-term confusion, difficulty in retrieving memories, and difficulty when thinking about what transpired with a medical doctor.

On the day of my surgeries I was not experiencing mental confusion. Post-surgeries I experienced the above mentioned symptoms along with mental tension for years as a result of my experiences with Dr. Cutter. Post-surgeries I told a friend that my brain had been freeze-dried in blackness. These symptoms are not normal, and the MQAC and the William County Medical Society need to recognize that there are predators in the medical field who are out to deceive the medical review teams and every investigation unit put on each individual case.

The social and professional rejections I have suffered over the years are powerful evidence that Dr. Cutter committed cosmetic and financial crimes against me. Juries are not sympathetic toward multiple-surgery patients in the State of Washington, and neither is the general public sympathetic regarding cosmetic victims who suffer in silence when others stare at them as they carry on their daily business.

I discovered that the general public in Union and the surrounding area many times had a negative reaction to my physical appearance. I know this isn't due to psychological issues on my part. I have done my own tests by acting cool, calm, and collected when out in public places versus having a psychological stigma due to personal issues which made me feel uncomfortable when out with the general public because of my being rejected or stared at in public. Being in social settings has not been a pleasant experience for me. In most cases since my surgeries with Dr. Cutter and subsequent post-surgeries revisions with Dr. Rockwell I have preferred to remain at home and not go out in full view of the general public.

Each time I underwent a cosmetic revision by Dr. Raymond Rockwell I had to go through the revision changes to my physical appearance. I had to endure the post-surgery swelling, and any new facial changes that others hadn't seen before.

I thought that the general public which had seen what I looked like before any revision work must have grown weary of each variation that became noticeably objectionable to my physical appearance. It was especially difficult if I observed that the revision change to my facial characteristic didn't enhance my new look or even appear normal. It didn't help matters if I noticed that people were uncomfortable with the physical changes I now possessed.

I have placed my hand directly under my nose while driving my car to prevent other motorists or people on the street from noticing my unpleasant appearance. I also have held a plastic or paper cup to cover my nose while driving to keep from being noticed by the general public. You might think that I shouldn't care about other people's opinions of my physical appearance maybe you would feel that way if you were cosmetically victimized but I do care what people think and how they react to any new variation in appearance.

Dr. Rockwell wanted $17,700 for the initial set of cosmetic revisions. My initial $120 consultation fee was included in the total cost for the corrective revisions. With having to pay for my airfare, rental car, and motel costs for the out-of-state consultation and subsequent surgery it ran into big bucks for me each time I had a revision surgery after my encounter with Dr. Cutter.

I have had to deal with the embarrassment, shame, and humiliation with every new change to my face. This has added to my difficulty in being seen by the general public under various circumstances and by the customers who ride my carrier routes. I have been careful not to offend, embarrass, or hurt any customer regardless of his or her skin color. I have made an attempt to be kind, considerate, and polite with all my clientele. But my actions (or lack of action) on my personnel carrier routes have been seriously and negatively affected by what I have suffered psychologically, emotionally, and cosmetically at the hands of Dr. Cutter. I sincerely apologize to anyone who has been offended by my uncharacteristic mannerisms and actions on all my carrier routes.

I have relied on my good friend Richard Dandy to help me with personal business and shopping. I have suffered with inferiority and self-image issues besides having a psychological stigma that has characterized my personal life as not being seen as normal to the general public.

I know that my victimization by Dr. Cutter was not an accident, but cunningly planned crimes by a sinister medical doctor. I wasn't supposed to Wake Up to such a troubling ordeal; I should not have awakened to Dr. Cutter's deranged actions against me. I continued having mental illness in which I went back and forth between periods of mania and periods of depression. I had manic-depressive psychological issues, and I wasn't intended to mentally Wake Up to Dr. Cutter's sick cosmetic scheme and scam.

I was meant to remain in the dark concerning the cruel, criminal, and immoral crimes forced on me by a psychotic sociopath. That way Dr. Cutter would slink back into his normal role as a caring cosmetic physician who didn't do one thing wrong during his professional practice against his patients. I know better, but the medical boards and the investigation unit have refused to recognize the evidence of the criminal elements in my case. I have heard that Dr. Cutter has a dental practice in the city where he currently resides. I was informed that he has been on probation for four years although I don't know the reason for his probation.

Perhaps this is the year that I will finally receive news that justice has been served that the medical boards has rendered disciplinary or termination action against Dr. Cutter. I know that justice has not prevailed as of this writing.

From a Christian perspective I know that Dr. Cutter was used by the devil on the day of my surgeries as a tool to assault my spiritual man and my physical body. I recognize that my real enemy is the devil according to Jesus Christ the greatest historian and authority on spiritual matters and on earthly matters. (See John 8:44.)

The Bible records in (Ephesians 6:12), "For we do not wrestle against flesh and blood, but against principalities, and powers, against the rulers of the darkness of this age, against spiritual hosts of wickedness in the heavenly places." I realize that the devil used Dr. Cutter as a vessel to try to destroy my life with abusive cosmetic surgeries. I know that the devil is the real culprit and scoundrel who committed the cosmetic and financial crimes against me through Dr. Cutter.

I recognize that Dr. Cutter who was not specialized in the nose and ears was willing, and ready to do more cutting on me because he believed he could get away with it. I would like to see the iron will of justice applied to Dr. Cutter's actions and lack of subspecialty training in the nose and ears which he applied cunningly against my physical characteristics.

Dr. Cutter was adroit at keeping me mentally confused and starved for more detailed and specific information pre surgery. I felt abused and victimized when I thought about Dr. Cutter's words and actions after my surgeries. I know that he felt pretty sure of himself when he committed his crimes against me, and he didn't expect me to remember his actions against me. I know that Dr. Cutter was going for a quick confession from me, and then he could simply move on as a caring cosmetic surgeon for first-time patients only. He would also continue to specialize in dentistry, and no one would be the wiser including the medical boards and the investigation units with regard to his cosmetic and financial crimes committed against me and others.

I see Dr. Cutter as a dangerous spectator at the 2008 Summer Olympic Games in Beijing, China who would intentionally trip an Olympic runner out of spite because he thought he could get away with it. He would then pull his leg back quickly before it was seen by other spectators while the injured athlete would lose out on his quest for Olympic gold.

I threw a monkey wrench into the operational gears of Dr. Cutter's cosmetic surgery machinery when I sent in my complaints against him. I painfully realized that Dr. Cutter's cosmetic approach was unethical and that he needed to be investigated for committing cosmetic crimes against me. The investigation never took place, but I felt that I needed to warn the medical boards about Dr. Cutter's cruel professional practice and scary cosmetic results so that other patients wouldn't be victims.

Post-surgeries Dr. Cutter acted like he couldn't believe I could remember his actions toward me. He also seemed to be pretty sure of himself post-surgeries as if he was pleased that he had the opportunity to work on me. Of course Dr. Cutter should not have had that opportunity in the first place.

I know there is a crisis in Victimized, U.S.A. concerning medical malpractice cases wherein medical doctors who are not skilled or qualified to perform specialized plastic surgery procedures on patients who need careful reconstructive cosmetic work are still allowed to operate on unsuspecting victims. The medical boards has allowed these unqualified medical doctors to make some extra money by working on multiple-surgery patients who do not want, need, or expect first-time cosmetic work repeated over again (such as my nose being elevated and bridge built up). The time is long overdue for the medical boards to change their policies to prevent cosmetic surgeons who have an unrecognized status from hurting unsuspecting patients.

My friend Tommy Ray has said that a surefire way that the medical boards could eliminate the medical malpractice problem is to have all doctors record their consultations on a DVD. This way every trusting patient would be guaranteed that the medical doctor will treat the patient with respect, dignity, and utmost care. By recording the consultations the medical doctors will have to be on their best behavior at all times and won't be allowed to get away with outright medical malpractice.

The patient would be given a copy of the DVD for review prior to the patient's scheduled surgery. The medical doctor who might want to alter the DVD to his advantage would be prevented from doing so when the doctor, patient, and the patient's family, attorney, or adult guardian all have the opportunity to review the exchange between the doctor and the trusting patient on the video. The medical boards, review teams, and investigation units would be sent a copy of the agreed-upon type of surgery before the medical doctor would be permitted to proceed with the patient's surgeries. Had the above policy been adopted by the medical boards and the legislators in the state of Washington I would not have been victimized by Dr. Cutter.

Over the years I have enjoyed the many attractions that Union has to offer. I have enjoyed Christian events, sporting events, concerts, musical events, parks, and parades. I have appreciated watching the Blue Angels perform their amazing flight patterns and routines when they have been in the greater Union area. I have enjoyed the wonderful creations of God and people throughout my many years.

The one situation that I haven't appreciated is dealing with negative repercussions from the general public. I know they don't understand what I have on my mental, emotional, and relationship plate. The social and professional repercussions have not been a total consequence of my own actions, but I realize that I am partly to blame for my social rejections because I have been far too open, free, and trusting of people in a negative environment where to be socially indifferent and apathetic is acceptable in society.

I have come to know many of my carrier passengers by name over the years, and they know me as a caring, compassionate, considerate, and kindhearted carrier driver. I appreciate the people who have made me feel accepted just the way I am, the way I look, and the way I act as a man in a negative world.

After my surgeries with Dr. Cutter my customers reacted negatively toward me. When I would look in their direction as they waited to exit the carrier many seemed repulsed and quickly exited my coach without saying a word of thanks.

From a worldly perspective I know the world loves its own and seeks to glorify, approve, and worship physical beauty. From a Christian perspective I know that my fight is not with the customers who do not approve of my physical appearance, but with the principalities of darkness that influence clients to think and react negatively toward me. I understand that I shouldn't take their negative reactions personally.

I contacted KOMO 4 a TV news station in Seattle to talk with Joey Cunningham about my victimization story. Joey told me that he was willing to air my story provided the MQAC had found that the medical doctor was in the wrong. Once again I found myself stuck in my victimization from telling my story, and I was not able to tell my account of true events in which I was used and abused by a medical doctor.

To my knowledge I knew I was blocked from moving on with my life because the MQAC and the DQAC had not even requested that Dr. Cutter respond to my complaints against him. I needed closure to my victimization by Dr. Cutter's own actions, but the medical review boards and the investigation units had closed my case against Dr. Cutter even after repeated requests for a reconsideration and another hearing to reopen it.

To my knowledge the medical boards granted me a reconsideration to open my case against Dr. Cutter only to have it closed after sometime. I am a victim of a cosmetic predator, and my case warrants having a reconsideration based on all the evidence I have provided to the medical review boards. Perhaps my book will bring some attention to my sad case, and I will find myself closer to the end of my long ordeal as a cosmetic victim.

I know that actual crimes were committed against me by Dr. Cutter, but the MQAC and DQAC representing the state I reside didn't see it that way nor did they believe his actions were actual crimes. Obviously their investigation was not very thorough. I dare to differ on the commission's investigation unit's ruling and stand up for what I firmly know for a 100 percent fact that definite crimes were committed against me by Dr. Cutter's intentional criminal acts of medical malpractice.

I don't just feel that crimes were committed against me; I know that crimes were committed against me even though the state, commission, law, police, or the highest courts in the land of Victimized, U.S.A., stated otherwise. I am a survivor of medical malpractice crimes committed by Dr. Cutter, and I challenge anyone to prove otherwise.

I contacted a number of libraries regarding medical malpractice from a patient's perspective and was informed there aren't any books not a single one from a patient's perspective. I contacted an attorney's office out of the Yellow Pages to see if they knew of a book that was written from a patient's perspective. The paralegal who answered the phone didn't know of any such book, but she said she would ask her attorney.

When she came back on the line she said, my attorney doesn't know of any such book either. There are plenty of books written on medical malpractice to which doctors and attorneys refer concerning different case procedures, but none is written specifically from a patient's perspective.

I decided that it was high time that a good book was written from a patient's perspective on medical malpractice because of all the innocent people who are being hurt, used, abused, exploited, and victimized by medical doctors who are taking advantage of naïve and unsuspecting patients.

Unsuspecting consumers may lack the knowledge of what to expect in regard to post-surgery cosmetic results. Regardless of the surgeon they choose they want excellent results such as they would get from an American Board of Plastic Surgery–certified doctors. The unrecognized medical surgeons not certified by the ABMS and the ABPS want financial compensation as their more skilled colleagues do.

It wasn't my field of expertise to know all of Dr. Cutter's fields of specialized training when I first saw his full page ad. If I call 911 I safely assume I'll find qualified trained personnel who are competent in their field whether an ambulance, police, or fire department personnel without having to check their credentials. When they respond to the emergency call I don't stop them and make them tell me all their training before they proceed. It is only reasonable to expect that the professional personnel who respond to an emergency call are well qualified to handle the serious circumstance(s) they encounter.

The unskilled medical surgeons can only hope for the best or they have to become masters of their own cosmetic worlds, and simply tell their cosmetic subjects that they are going to like it. Whether the patient likes the cosmetic results is up to the individual patient.

I painfully discovered that Dr. Cutter's cosmetic results were horrid and horrible for me, and for the general public to look at. I hope to save others from the same unpleasant fate as befell me from the cosmetic surgeon who disfigured my nose and ears. I gradually realized these painful cosmetic results after my surgeries, and then I repeated what had happened over and over in my mind day in and day out for years.

Each time Dr. Raymond Rockwell a plastic surgeon who is a genuine expert in the field of cosmetic and reconstruction surgeries did a corrective revision I was again reminded that Dr. Cutter was not the skilled cosmetic surgeon I had been searching for in the nineties, but he still performed triple-play surgeries on my nose, ears, and chin with painful post-surgeries results.

I saw Pastor Alvarez on Trinity Broadcasting Network one day, and I heard about the creative miracles that were taking place in his church in Miami, Florida. I decided to fly down to Miami to get in on the wonderful things God was doing by His Holy Spirit in real people's lives during these current times. I put in for my vacation at work in the spring. I initially flew to Chicago, and then I caught my second flight to Miami. I rented a car at the Miami Airport, and I drove around Miami for a while before driving to the Resortville Motel in east Florida where I had made reservations.

It was a good experience for me to attend the large Apostolic Faith Center on a number of occasions during my time in Miami, and Pastor Juan Alvarez actually prayed for me outside of the large edifice on the church property. I appreciated that Pastor Alvarez listened attentively to my request for my nose to come down, and the man of God prayed a straightforward prayer that my nose would come down. He called for it to happen as he spoke prophetically in the presence of witnesses.

I didn't see my nose come down as a small mountain moving from one elevated position to another lower position as I was hoping would happen while I stood in front of Pastor Alvarez. God however would use Dr. Raymond Rockwell to fulfill the prayer of the man of God during a surgical procedure in Los Angeles in a partial way. Since Dr. Rockwell is not masterpiece worker of supernatural restoration he could only fulfill my creative miracle hope in a partial sense through a series of corrective rhinoplasty revision procedures.

I thank God for the reconstruction surgeries from which I benefited. I recognize that God uses creative miracles to accomplish His will on earth, and He also uses the surgical skills of reconstruction plastic surgeons to bring about healing and wholeness into the realm of human suffering.

While visiting Florida I took time to drive through the Florida Everglades National Park, and I also drove down to Key West on a separate beautiful spring day. I took in the state's amazing scenery while traveling on Highway 1 south of Florida City. I enjoyed the beautiful blue waters of the Atlantic Ocean, and I drove across the seven-mile bridge that stretched above the vast ocean. I kept driving south until I eventually reached the quaint city of Key West with all its attractive shops and businesses. I was very much conscious of my appearance so I decided to remain in my vehicle while taking in as many of the pleasant sights that Key West had to offer before heading back northeast to the Resortville Motel.

On my final day at the Resortville Motel I checked out of the motel and drove north to connect with Highway I-75. I continued driving through the state of Florida on I-75 all the way to Atlanta, Georgia. A semi-truck barreled along right behind me on a dark Georgia night. I wasn't going to allow the truck driver to intimidate me into driving above and beyond the posted speed limit. Of course the truck driver couldn't know that I was a professional carrier driver who wasn't going to become overly nervous as had Dennis Weaver's character in the movie Duel, because of the truck driver's intimidating actions.

Eventually I made a pit stop in a rest area. Once I was back on the road I stopped for gas in Atlanta where a helpful African American woman gave me directions to Pastor Creflo Dollar's church in College Park, twenty minutes from Atlanta I had appreciated listening to Pastor Dollar on Trinity Broadcasting Network. I discovered the church was closed that night, but a security guard invited me in to the large impressive administration building of Dollar's ministry. The guard was very kindhearted to me, and gave me a couple of ministry audiocassette tapes to listen to. I appreciated the security guard's cordial personality. He represented World Changers Church, and he extended a kind invitation to stay in Atlanta for a few days so I could take in an inspirational church service. I decided though to continue my drive north and not stay any longer in Atlanta. Before leaving College Park and Atlanta I drove around the large megachurch estate area, and saw Dollar's 8,400-seat congregational church before I headed back to I-75 North.

Once I was back on I-75 I kept driving north until I decided to get some sleep in a rest area outside of Chattanooga, Tennessee. I woke up to a warm sunny day and continued my scenic drive up to Nashville. I drove around Nashville for some time experiencing the city's sights such as Music Row and other interesting landmarks. I drove around for quite some time, but I never was able to find the Grand Ole Opry or Opryland U.S.A., as I had hoped. I needed to have someone with the Country Music Hall of Fame show me exactly where I needed to go to see the famous country music entertainment hall that has been the center of scores and scores of talented musicians and entertainers.

As I drove out of Nashville on Highway 24 I saw the massive traffic congestion heading back into Nashville and beyond. When I saw the extended lineup of semi-trucks in traffic I was grateful I was leaving town rather than trying to work my way into the big city during rush hour. I continued driving to Paducah, Kentucky. I then worked my way eastward over to Highway 60 to Springfield, Missouri where I stayed in a motel for the night.

I was doing my very best to take in all the scenic sights of this great country that I could during my trip back home to the Pacific Northwest. I would look to my right and then to my left not wanting to miss any of my traveling scenic adventures. I drove around Springfield for a long time trying to locate the Springfield Assembly of God Headquarters; my parents had paid tithes to the Christian organization throughout the years. Unfortunately I never did find the Assembly of God Headquarters as I drove around the beautiful city. While I drove around Springfield I could understand why so many people wanted to live there; it appeared to be a lovely city. As I was heading out of town I saw the large James River Assembly of God Church with its rather impressive edifice.

I headed south on Highway 65 to Branson, Missouri where I drove around the city looking at all the entertainment centers where live shows were held at different times throughout the day. I never took in any of the entertainment shows which I could have, and I didn't even go into the Roy Rogers Museum where Roy's horse, Trigger reared up high in the air out in front of the museum. My mother always hoped that our family could go to Branson together someday to enjoy a great time of entertainment. Unfortunately my father passed away at ninety-four years of age. He is now in heaven with Jesus whom he preached about and whom he wanted men, women, boys, and girls to meet and know. Dad is now forever in the presence of God, the holy angels, and all the saints above. He will be missed by his family who loved and appreciated him.

When I left Branson I headed south to the little town of Pardonville, Missouri to spend some time visiting with my longtime friend Bud (aka Brutus Knuckles). Bud introduced me to his longtime friend Steven Stockton who is quite the historian, and knowledgeable of many historical events that have taken place in that part of the country. Steven was kind enough to drive Bud and me around the area one day during my visit, and tell us about a hard-fought battle that involved a heated skirmish between the North and the South during the Civil War. I learned that a lot of soldiers died during the fierce battle in the area. Later on Steven took Bud and me to a drive-in fast-food place called Sonic Drive-In for a bite to eat.

On a separate occasion Bud took me to an old cemetery; slaves had lived and died in the area. There was a marker inscribed with the name of a man who settled in the area with his family. He was a veteran of the Revolutionary War. The individual slave gravesites had a solitary rock to mark the site with no name written on it where each slave was laid to rest. Bud said, "There were also a lot of white people who when they died had an unmarked rock placed at the head of the grave."

On another day Bud drove me to an old cemetery a number of miles from, Pardonville to look at old tombstones. The names of people with their birth dates and death dates were still visible on the old markers. There was a small creek flowing near the cemetery that sunny April day, and Bud and I had a good time being together again and looking at the historical cemetery's tombstones of people long forgotten in this ever-busy world.

Bud said, "The very first church built in Washington County in 1824 was right next to where the cemetery is today. There's a bronze plaque marking where the cemetery is and where the former church stood behind the plaque."

After having a five-day visit with my good friend, Bud Finnigan I left Pardonville, Missouri and drove west to Tulsa, Oklahoma to see Oral Roberts University. I saw the giant praying hands as I entered the university campus. I also saw the prayer tower where hurting people's prayer requests are prayed over on a daily basis year-round. God has answered Christians' prayer needs with amazing miracles down through the years as His people ask and believe Him for great things.

From Tulsa I drove south on Highway I-44 to Oklahoma City to see where the federal building had been bombed killing 168 innocent people. The walls surrounding the federal building have been turned into a memorial honoring the people who died there, and now there are flowers, American flags, and pictures of fallen heroes. Inside the walls the area has been turned into a cemetery, with tombstone markers for the ones who lost their lives inside the federal building. The sad news of the bombing sobered America to the reality of terrorism in its most evil form in our homeland as well as on foreign soil. Real people are killed by malicious and ruthless villains, and are taken from us violently which is pure evil.

When I left Oklahoma City I headed west on I-40, and continuing through Oklahoma and right through the Texas Panhandle. I stayed on Highway I-40 into New Mexico where I decided to spend the night at a rest area. The following day I drove west until I reached Albuquerque, New Mexico and I drove around parts of the city to see the area, and so that I could say that I had been there. After leaving Albuquerque I kept driving west on I-40 right through New Mexico and directly into Arizona. I appreciated each state of the union that I drove through, and each with unique characteristics of national pride and qualities of scenic beauty.

I saw the sign to the Grand Canyon, but I continued my travels onward until I passed Hoover Dam on my way into Las Vegas, Nevada. There I drove around the big city for a while and stayed in a park's parking lot for a good part of the day. I then saw the city of Las Vegas at night with all its tinsel and glitter from the dazzling lights of entertainment centers. Las Vegas is a showcase of entertainment with live shows during the day and into the night as well as a host of gambling casinos which attract millions each year.

I drove around Las Vegas looking for the establishment where my nephew Travis worked. During his stay in Las Vegas he met a lot of famous celebrities. I never found my nephew that night, and I never did go to any of the entertainment venues during my stopover in Las Vegas. My lovely wife, Lorena and I flew to Las Vegas as a married couple on a mini-vacation on a November day. We enjoyed seeing the sights and entertainment centers with some of Lorena's family members.

After leaving Las Vegas I traveled south on Highway 15, and then I took 127 North into Death Valley where many souls never survived their experience with the desert heat. I wanted to see Death Valley for myself including the land with its varied terrain that had attracted visitors which some of whom never came out alive. Although I had an excellent rental car with a good air-conditioner I was mindful that this area could get extremely hot, and especially during the summer months.

I drove for some distance into the desert before I stopped to use a pay phone to call the Scone family home in Clover Valley. I told my mother where I was, and she was somewhat surprised that I would be there of all places in the United States. She later told me that after we hung up she had called my sister, Marlie in southern Idaho and told her where I was. Marlie had heard that day on the news that the hottest place in America that day was Death Valley.

I continued my drive through Death Valley; I didn't experience a lot of vehicle traffic in the desert region that day. I pulled into the visitor center to check it out. Inside the center I learned that every year one or two people die in Death Valley. I also heard about a honeymoon couple the husband decided he wanted to walk across the desert. He made the long hike across the desert to the mountain range, and on his way back he died shortly before reaching the road where their car was parked. I also learned about an older gentleman who walked out on the sand dunes in the desert and expired in the desert heat.

The people who do not survive are those who are not properly equipped to deal with the desert's unrelenting and intense heat. The sun beats down on the head of the desert traveler. It's best to always wear a hat and bring plenty of water whenever you take a long hike or even a short walk in Death Valley. Be well prepared to protect yourself from the extreme elements which you would not normally deal with on a walk in the woods.

I was aware of the other visitors who looked over at me as I talked to the representatives at the visitor center. People looked at me with disdain as if they didn't like what they were looking at or that they had a problem with my appearance. I knew that my cosmetic surgeries had left me with an unusual physical appearance, and so people usually didn't look at me with pleasant smiles on their faces. I was dealt a cruel hand, and I had to deal with it on a daily basis.

When I pulled out from the Death Valley Visitor Center I continued my drive through the Death Valley National Park. I drove to the area where the sand dunes were located and pulled over to the side of the road. I got out of my rental car, and off in the distance I saw three hikers on their way back to the main road where I was parked. I also saw two hikers walking across the sand dunes away from me toward the west side of the valley. I took time to try to catch some lizards which with amazing quickness darted among the wild desert sagebrush. I came awfully close to getting hold of the long tail of one of the desert speedsters, but when I was ready to pinch the end of its tail between my thumb and index finger it suddenly darted off to safety among the desert thicket.

After experiencing a portion of the dunes I headed back to my rental car, and continued driving through the national park. I saw the signs for Furnace Creek and Ghost Town, but I decided to continue my drive through the desert valley and head north to Reno, Nevada. I drove through Carson City and Virginia City and made the drive up to beautiful Lake Tahoe. I also saw the sign for Ponderosa Ranch, a theme park based on the television series Bonanza. A staff member of an environmental agency told me that Ponderosa Ranch was seventy-five miles, and approximately an hour and a half from Lake Tahoe. I drove around the lake and stopped in a private park where I took it easy, and relaxed for hours in my vehicle. At one point I got out of the car and walked over to take a look at the beautiful lake waters from the sandy beach viewpoint.

I noticed certain individuals who seemed to wonder what I was doing in their private neighborhood park, but I tried not to take it personally. I eventually drove out from the parking lot and headed north to see the city of Reno on a beautiful spring night. Again I never went into any of Reno's entertainment venues, but I could see people inside, and I knew the gambling casinos had their usual crowd of players seeking their luck and wishing they could win the jackpot and score by beating the house odds. I have learned from experience that most people end up with fool's gold of bad luck, and go home poorer than when they entered the casino with the hope of striking it rich.

After driving around Reno for a while and seeing the sights I drove southwest to I-80 toward Sacramento, California. When I saw the sign for I-5 North I continued my journey toward home in the Pacific Northwest.

I stopped for gas whenever I needed to and for a bite to eat at a fast-food joint when I was hungry. I was determined to drive at night, and throughout the day unless I physically couldn't continue without getting some sleep. I wanted to get home where I could relax in my own ed, and hide out in isolation from the scrutinizing eyes of unfriendly people.

I drove through the northern part of California and up into the Pacific Northwest. I eventually made it to my humble abode where I have enjoyed seeing raccoons, squirrels, blue jays, and hummingbirds in a quiet residential neighborhood without an incident of unfortunate circumstances which I could have encountered during my cross-country marathon journey. God protected me from harm on my solo trip and gave me safe traveling mercies to reach my home.

I finally met a lovely lady named Lorena Gonzalez whom I asked to marry me after a long courtship. I knew I'd better not let this beautiful woman who was willing to marry me get away. I met Lorena on one of my William County personnel carrier routes one night while I was waiting to start my route. When I opened the door of the carrier in walked an attractive woman with jet-black hair. She sat down on the customer side in the middle of the carrier.

"Will you be leaving soon?" the lovely lady asked.

"Yes," I said. "Where are you from? I notice you have an accent." "Colombia!" she responded in a spirited manner.

"Como estas?" I said in my limited Spanish although I should have used the more formal, "Como esta usted?"

In response to my question she told me she was fine.

We continued talking together, and when it was time to leave on my next carrier trip I said, "Andale! Andale!" which means "hurry up" in Spanish. The sweet Latina lady said, "Andale is used by Mexican Spanish-speaking people whereas rapido is used by Spanish-speaking people for the word hurry."

I found out that rapido can be used for the words quick, fast, or hurry up. Lorena said goodbye as she got off my bus, and I responded "Buenas noches" good night.

The third time that Lorena came on my personnel carrier she gave me a Spanish-English dictionary to improve my Spanish vocabulary. On the inside of the cover she'd written and wrote me a note: "Jonah jon Jeffreys: If you have any questions about Spanish you can call me." She included her phone number for me to call. She signed it, "Lorena," with the date included.

Lorena had mentioned that maybe we could get together sometime for lunch or for coffee. I contacted Lorena at the phone number she left with me, and we had a pleasant talk in spite of her limited English and my limited Spanish. I told Lorena that I was seeing someone at the time, and so we decided not to pursue a romantic relationship with each other at that time.

Three years later when I realized that my relationship with my lady friend wasn't heading toward marriage I called and left a message on Lorena's answering machine saying, "Feliz Navidad and Feliz Año Nuevo." I didn't know if she was still living at the same place or even still living in Union.

When Lorena heard the friendly message I had left for her she called me. We talked on the phone for several weeks before we decided to get together in person. At that point Lorena spoke much better English, but I hadn't improved much on my Spanish. I discovered that Lorena came from a family of traditional religious beliefs which she had observed while growing up in Bogota, Colombia South America. Lorena wanted to learn more about God while living in the United

States, and I found myself sharing the wonderful truths of Jesus Christ and His free gift of salvation with Lorena.

Lorena had seen Christians on television preaching, and sharing about the power of God with their viewing audience. Lorena had even witnessed the power of God being manifested in the lives of the Christian people through the scenes on her television. Lorena wanted to experience that same power for herself, but at that point in her life she felt she desired something that seemed elusive in her own existence.

One day I happened to pray for Lorena for the Holy Spirit to touch her life and show Himself mighty on her behalf. I prayed with power as I laid my hands on her head in earnest prayer. The Holy Spirit manifested Himself to Lorena in a special way while she knelt in prayer, and she went limp as if she were fainting in the Lord's presence. Each time I prayed with heartfelt intensity for the power of God Almighty, the Holy Spirit which is the Spirit of Christ manifested Himself to Lorena in His own special way and with power. I praise God Lorena experienced the wonderful touch of the Lord in waves of supernatural glory.

Lorena discovered the wonderful power of the Lord gloriously manifested on and in her life that special night. Lorena now wanted to become a born-again Christian and to live her life for Christ Jesus as observed in the Christian faith. Lorena discovered that God's truths for a Godly Christian life were revealed in The Holy Bible, and not according to the traditions observed in her traditional South American church.

The Lord has been faithful to Lorena and me throughout the years. We were married at a Christian Protestant Church. We went to Kauai, Hawaii for our honeymoon. Our flight to the Hawaiian Islands was long, but our flight took place on a beautiful spring day. When we arrived at the resort in Kauai we decided to go for the upgrade which was a deluxe hotel suite that we enjoyed. Unfortunately the weather wasn't as conducive for outdoor activities as we would have liked during our maiden voyage as a married couple; on honeymoons you would like to have the most perfect and memorable experience with your spouse.

Lorena and I never went into the Pacific Ocean during our honeymoon because of the windy conditions and the rough waters; we didn't want to have any disasters while on our honeymoon. I remember listening to the news in our deluxe hotel room, and hearing about the possibility of a tsunami heading toward the Hawaiian Islands. That never happened thank goodness. I didn't want a hundred-foot wall of water slamming into our hotel suite during our stay. Just hearing about the chance of a tsunami threatening to destroy our pleasant vacation was not enjoyable.

Lorena and I drove around the island wanting to take in the scenery in all its tropical beauty. We went to the beach on a windy day, and we went shopping on a number of occasions together. For Lorena and me just being together on our first vacation as husband and wife was well worth the honeymoon trip. I decided we should go to Kauai rather than any of the other Hawaiian Islands to avoid the crowds on the other islands, and to have the opportunity to get to know one another in romantic solitude. The good Lord provided Lorena and me with a wonderful honeymoon, and when it came time to leave the tropical garden island we flew home to the Pacific Northwest to continue growing, working on, and experiencing our married life together.

Lorena and I flew down to Las Vegas one year to join her family members, Blanca Ellen, Jacob, Boris, and Roger Lee Gonzalez. For fun I decided to make an announcement to the family with my lovely wife present in a hotel room. I spoke in Spanish so they would get the full impact of my message. When I had the floor I took full advantage of the serene moment. With all eyes looking in my direction I said, "Mi familia. Mi feliz esposa. Estaba virgin," which translates as, "My family. My happy wife. She was a virgin."

We all had a good laugh together over my announcement spoken in jest. Lorena and I had a good time together as a married couple and also with her family during our stay. Unfortunately for Lorena and me we left Las Vegas poorer than when we arrived due to losing at the slot machines. I was able to enjoy myself during our vacation getaway. I was still self-conscious about my physical appearance, but the vacation helped to divert my attention from my outward appearance to marital and family values and being involved in outside and indoor activities.

When Lorena and I visited her family in Bogota, Colombia in 2007 we witnessed the people of Colombia protesting the long struggle with the guerillas. The people were carrying white flags and honking their car horns throughout Bogota, the capital city. They were longing for peace in all Colombia, and they were tired of the fighting between the democratic Colombian Government, and the guerilla rebel groups. I wanted to videotape the historic moment of seeing the large groups of Colombians out in force demonstrating their hearts' desire for a peaceful resolution to the evil atrocities and the conflicts of war with the rebels. Unfortunately I discovered I had left my battery pack at my sister-in-law's (Blanca Ellen Gonzalez's) apartment. I was disappointed that I had missed out on recording the historic moment.

When Lorena and I were in Bogota in 2007, Margarita Romero a friend of my sister-in-law Melony Garcia asked for me to pray for her son John. I anointed John's body with oil, and I prayed the prayer of faith over him. As a positive result God healed John, and he felt better afterward. In 2009 Margarita called Lorena in North America asking that I pray for John's heart to be healed. John was facing the possibility of open-heart surgery, and he needed a miracle healing touch from the Master's hand. I prayed over the phone for John's heart to be healed and to be made whole. I prayed that Jesus Christ who is the same today, yesterday, and forever would reach down His healing hand of virtue and heal John from the top of his head to the soles of his feet.

The latest I heard concerning John's heart condition is that his heart is doing just fine. I know that I am only a vessel through whom God has worked when I have prayed for people, and that Jesus is the Healer. I could not heal a flea with a migraine headache, but Jesus is perfectly able to heal all those who call upon His blessed name believing in faith. All the glory, praise, and honor belongs to Jesus Christ.

Margarita Romero invited Lorena and me to have lunch with her, and her son John while we were in Bogota in 2009. She shared with us that she had seen Pastor Alvarez on television, and she learned where he was going to be speaking when he was in Bogota. Margarita went to the Christian Church where he was ministering to the people, and she went up for special prayer concerning herself. Margarita gave a check to his ministry, and she told him she would like to talk to him. He asked her to wait outside the church for him. Later on Pastor Alvarez came outside to give Margarita his Miami cell number, and when he was back in Miami she called the number he had given to her.

The man of God prayed for her over the phone to be blessed and prosperous, and as a benefit of his prayers she had faith to believe God would make provision for her to buy a beautiful apartment where she and her son now live. She also purchased a car. The Lord adds His blessings beyond measure in ways that are best for His people. He only asks for us to believe in Him for a harvest of souls. What we need in life we must expect in faith, and when we give tithes and offerings unto the Lord we should be cheerful givers.

Lorena informed me that her nephew Denton Garcia wanted to sell his grandfather's stamp collection. Melony Garcia, Denton's mother had brought the extensive stamp collection with her when she came up for Lorena's and my wedding, and Lorena had stored the collection in our bedroom closet.

I heard that Denton wanted to sell the stamps, but I wasn't aware they were sitting on a shelf in our closet. Lorena was waiting for Denton to come to the United States so that I could help her nephew sell the collection, and hopefully make some good money. Denton told Lorena when we were in Bogota to sell the stamp collection and give him whatever she wanted to.

When I became aware that the stamp collection had been sitting on the closet shelf I was excited because I thought the collection as a whole was possibly worth thousands, if not millions, of dollars. Lorena thought that we now could pay off our credit cards, and she would be able to buy some things that she wanted and needed for herself.

We looked at the dates of some of the stamps which were well organized in a large book designed for a stamp collection. It was obvious that Denton's grandfather had spent a lot of time on his hobby collecting foreign, United States, and Vatican stamps both used and unused. I was convinced that this eclectic collection of stamps if sold at an auction or to certain stamp investors would bring in millions of dollars. The possibilities raised our hopes with lofty dreams of becoming rich, retiring, enjoying a leisurely life of Riley, and traveling whenever and wherever. I thought we were going to be rich after selling the stamps so I made certain I kept the stamps in the same sack she had originally placed them in, and I kept them in our bedroom to ensure the stamps were safe.

On the day that Lorena and I decided to take the stamp collection for an appraisal she had a doctor's appointment. I made sure I had the stamp collection with us when I drove Lorena to her doctor's appointment. I didn't even leave the stamps in our car while it was parked in a parking garage during Lorena's appointment. I thought I was carrying a fortune with me.

When Lorena and I went to a stamp collection store in Canton to see if the historical stamps had any real value, Jeff Thurman who looked through the large book told us that the stamps had been damaged by the way they were handled. Lorena and I learned the cold hard truth that day: Denton's grandfather who had taken the time to place them carefully in the book had used white tape on the underside of each stamp. In doing so he had damaged the stamps so that they lost their monetary value. The reality of hearing the disappointing news from Jeff dispelled any hope for a future fortune and the fulfillment of our dreams.

Jeff concluded that he wasn't interested in examining any more of the stamps which were also inside a lot of envelopes, and he wasn't interested in purchasing the damaged collection although many of the stamps seemed to have historical value to novice stamp collectors.

Lorena and I drove out to Rowen to get a second opinion concerning the stamp collection's possible value. Once again we received news that the store was not interested in buying what we had to sell. For all our efforts I was able to sell three Reichsmark bank notes for a total of one dollar and one South Korean ten-dollar bill for two dollars to a coin collection store in Keeler.

It had not turned out to be a profitable day for selling things, but at least we had satisfied our curiosity. I thought about going through the old stamp collection at home just to see if perhaps the professional stamp-collection experts might have missed something by not taking the time to examine the entire collection. As of this writing I've not taken the time to do so, but I hope some rare stamps might be hidden in the mix and not damaged by the beginner stamp collector who had collected the stamps as a hobby and probably hadn't thought about giving them to his descendants one fine day.

Just as stamps and coins can be rejected due to physical damages because they have been improperly handled so real people can experience undue hardships in life because of improper training in medical and cosmetic specialties.

Lorena thinks that I would need to look like a monster for me to write my own book. I know that she loves me, but she hasn't gone through all the unnecessary suffering that I have undergone mentally, emotionally, socially, and physically so she doesn't fully understand the need for me to write a book on medical malpractice from my perspective. Innocent patients are being hurt by unqualified medical doctors who are driven by power and greed to perform unnecessary cosmetic changes which do result in cosmetic violations.

When Lorena looks at my nose she sees my physical characteristics in her evaluation as perfect; it's now down from its previous elevated position where Dr. Cutter placed it against God's creative cosmetic blueprint for me. I recognize the superior skills of the certified American Board of Plastic Surgery surgeon who performed reconstruction revisions to my damaged physical characteristics. I can still see a noticeable gap between my nose, and the outline of the top of my mustache where Dr. Rockwell worked surgically to bring my nose back down.

When I initially went to see Dr. Rockwell the first thing that he said to me was not, "It's nice to see you, Mr. Scone. My name is Dr. Rockwell. How can I help you?" Instead, Dr. Rockwell looked at my elevated nose position and said, "You're not bringing it down."
I have had to pay through the nose in more ways than one.

When Lorena and I flew into the El Dorado airport in Bogota, Colombia in 2007 a large number of Lorena's wonderful family members were waiting for us. Due to heightened security all those looking for their family and friends anxiously waited on the outside of the airport for their loved ones to come out of the building. Lorena and I were like celebrities from America with adoring fans peering in through the windows of the airport hoping to catch a glimpse of the special married couple who were received as romantic stars from a distant land.

I had brought my music horn and battery-operated speaker along on the trip to greet my new Colombian family. Once outside the airport where Lorena's family were eagerly waiting, for fun I spoke through the speaker to my loving Colombian family by saying, "Hola, familia. Pancho Villa aqui en Bogota, Colombia," which translated into English means, "Hello, family. Pancho Villa is in Bogota, Colombia."

Lorena and I provided some star status to the family who were incredibly accepting, warm, kind, loving, generous, inviting, and hospitable in every way to Lorena and me during our two-month stay in Colombia. While visiting with our family, Lorena and I went to Santa Marta, Cartagena, and San Andres with, Papi Martin Gonzalez and Blanca Ellen Gonzalez my father-in-law and sister-in-law. The four of us had an enjoyable time each time we went on a mini vacation getaway to the Colombian resorts in the summer of 2007.

Lorena and I were having lunch with Papi Martin and Blanca Ellen at the dining area near a swimming pool at the Hotel Caribe in Cartagena when we observed a young three-toed sloth moving ever so slowly down a tall palm tree. The beautiful long-armed sloth worked its way to the ground, and it was great for us to watch it in its natural environment rather than in a zoo. Situated behind the Hotel Caribe were colorful parrots, iguanas, dwarf deer, and sloths, and a number of small monkeys in cages. The Hotel had twenty-four sloths living in the long-leafed trees on the Hotel Caribe complex when we stayed there in 2007. It was incredible for us to see all the various animals in their natural habitat.

Lorena and I enjoyed being in the warm Caribbean waters at Santa Marta, Cartagena and San Andres.

When we were on another mini vacation on the island of San Andres I said to Papi Martin in Spanish, "Papi, no bueno. No monos titi."
Papi Martin agreed saying, "No bueno."

Later I saw Papi Martin standing tall on a rock, and he stood towering above the Caribbean waters. I called to Lorena and asked her how to say, "King of the rock" in Spanish.
Lorena answered, "El rey de la roca."

I then repeated those words to Papi Martin: "Papi, El Rey de la Roca."

Papi seemed thrilled by his elevated position over the Caribbean waters that day. We all had a wonderful time experiencing the warm sea, great food, beautiful scenery, and the entertaining shows at night.

I love and appreciate my Colombian family because they are such loving, accepting, kindhearted, generous, and hospitable people. These precious people have made me feel loved, admired, and accepted as part of their extended family. I thank the Lord Jesus for my close Colombian family.

Lorena and I went to an all-boys orphanage with our Colombian family in Bogota, a first-time experience for Lorena and me. We wanted to make a difference in the lives of the boys at the home by providing shoes for them. Lorena's brother, Joshua made a special contribution to the boys with clothing items they could use such as underwear and socks.

We ate a variety of the delicious foods that Colombia had to offer. I enjoyed the churrasco (grilled beef) and carne asada (grilled steak sliced thin); huevos a la cazuela (an egg casserole); various soups, like Santafereño; and healthy salads. I also enjoyed many tropical fruits, Colombian candies, Colombian coffee, and delicious juices which helped to reduce the sugar in my diet.

Lorena and I enjoyed our visits to Colombia in 2007 and in 2009. The one negative aspect was that the taxi drivers drove extremely fast which could be a scary experience to us foreigners. I thank Dios (God) that Lorena, and I were never involved in an accident during our numerous rides in taxis while visiting Colombia. Some travelers were not as blessed.

One sunny day, Lorena and her sister Abby, and I went on a long country drive with a couple of Abby's friends, Rebeca and Sofia to Bojacá in the Western Savanna Province. We visited a large Roman Catholic Church, and the large edifice was impressive with its craftsmanship and beautiful design. While we were walking around inside the historic church I needed to use the men's room so I approached a young man, the priest's assistant to ask where I might find a restroom ("Donde esta el baño?"). He gave directions to me, and when I entered the men's room area I saw a number of priests in various forms of undress. They looked in my direction as I continued to walk straight into the restroom.

I took care of personal business and then joined Lorena and the three ladies again. We enjoyed our visit to the large church, and then resumed our journey to another Colombian city. I liked seeing the countryside, and seeing the number of people who lived in the rural areas.

One evening back at home, Lorena and I met up with my friend, Larwin Curry from Panipat, India. I met Larwin on one of my carrier routes, and we have kept in touch ever since then. The three of us went to the Brocket District in Union where we enjoyed a pleasant experience at a small

Indian cuisine restaurant. Lorena and I appreciated having Larwin take control of our dining experience as he spoke Hindi to the waitress.

He ordered the type of Indian delicacies and desserts that he knew we would enjoy eating.

Larwin was a terrific host to Lorena, and me on that special night as he was right at home with the Indian cuisine. Everything he ordered for us tasted good, and we enjoyed sharing the various foods with our friend from India. Lorena and I looked forward to getting together with Larwin in the future.

When I later spoke on the phone with Larwin, he mentioned another restaurant he had in mind where he had once worked there so he was very familiar with the good-tasting Indian foods they served. Based on our previous dining experience I knew our future get-together with Larwin had the promise of another enjoyable cultural experience; Larwin is a considerate, thoughtful, and a kindhearted man and a good friend.

Lorena and I went out for lunch with her sister Julieta Westwood and her two sons, Timothy and Jonathan. Jonathan was sitting across the dining table from me when he spoke up saying, "Chad said that Duke was his god." Chad was Jonathan's uncle by marriage; Duke was Chad's dog.
"Well, if Duke is his god," I said, "then his god died."

Chad Conners, Lorena's brother-in-law once shared with me that if Duke didn't go to heaven when he died then he didn't want to go there either. Whether Chad realized it or not no person or animal is worth missing out on going to heaven to spend eternity with our Creator, who is willing to prepare a place in heaven for whosoever will believe and call on the Lord Jesus Christ as their personal Lord and Savior. God will positively prepare, and make a beautiful mansion in heaven for them to live in throughout all eternity. What a powerful price Jesus Christ paid for our salvation so that no one would miss out on inheriting a place in heaven with the King of Kings and the Lord of Lords. Now that will be glory!!

I went to a bowling alley in Bogota with Lorena's cousin, Mark Garcia and his son, Gabriel where we played Ping-Pong. I provided both Mark and Gabriel with healthy competition although it was rather usual to have to chase the ball each time one of us missed the ball as the Ping-Pong table was in an open area. Colombian spectators could watch us play an intense game of Ping-Pong if they were interested.

I was able to beat Mark in most of the games we played, and I defeated Gabriel every time. As we started to wrap up our Ping-Pong competition I issued a challenge to Gabriel.

I placed a flashlight pen on the Ping-Pong table and told Gabriel, "If you can beat me I'll declare you the winner of all the games we've played, and I'll reward you with this flashlight pen as well."

Gabriel became highly motivated to defeat me in my challenge, and he elevated his level of play. He was determined to defeat me, and he decisively won the game and became the new owner of the flashlight pen, and he was declared the champion of the series of games we had played.

I once played Ping-Pong against Caleb Garcia when he was living in the Pacific Northwest while attending El Salvador Community College. Caleb is Mark Garcia's other son, a gifted, multitalented young man. When we played Ping-Pong against one another he showed me just how talented he truly was by defeating me time and time again on that night. I won three games; Caleb won eleven games.

I was greatly impressed and amazed by just how gifted Caleb was especially as he was a teenager, and his lean slender physique didn't give the impression of his being particularly athletic. He however had both an excellent backhand, and forehand deliveries and was successful at keeping the ball in play no matter how many times I tried to put him away, mix it up from side to side, or cause him to make a mistake during our volley at play. We both remained focused during our intense battles, but his overall style of playing was that he was much more relaxed and focused than I was. Caleb played tremendously at a higher level of play than I was able to muster. I had difficulty winning any games against him that night.

Caleb and I later got together for another series of intense competition at the William County Base which had a recreation area for William County employees. I again gave it my very best to defeat Caleb at Ping-Pong, but I was not serious competition to Caleb's superior playing style, and I came up short in the number of the games we played that night. In fact, Caleb beat me at least eleven or more times whereas I defeated him only once in our second series of games. I liked playing Ping-Pong, and I wished I'd been able to give Caleb a better challenge than I delivered during the two occasions when I had the favorable opportunity to compete against him.

The Lord Jesus offered a spiritual analogy that the good sheep who hear His voice which is found in His Word, and do His will by entering through the Lord Jesus, who is the door will be saved and find good pasture (good places) to dwell in. This includes who comes to the Heavenly Father in the name of Jesus Christ. The same analogy could be said in the natural realm every day in America.

President Trump wants to build the wall to keep out the illegal immigrants who seek to enter the United States through the southern border points, and many of them are found to be criminals, murderers (like the MS-13 gang members), and other dangerous elements that come to America and commit crimes and even murder against our citizens. President Trump wants to keep American citizens safe from the predators, terrorists, murderers, and other dangerous and harmful elements that accompany the illegal immigrants who enter our country through the southern border.

Our national leaders and ICE security agents want to safeguard our country by separating the illegal immigrant families from the harmful illegal immigrants who will hurt, and bring great harm to the innocent boys and girls who accompany adults who have evil intentions against unsuspecting families. It is extremely important for us as adults to keep safe every child in the United States of America from the harmful element that has evil plans and intentions to influence and corrupt the minds of the youth in America to use drugs, and alcohol so they might fall prey to drug peddlers, pedophiles, and sexual perverts who are the true exploiters of innocent children and young people in our great nation.

There also are educational exploiters who would seek to indoctrinate every illegal immigrant to vote for, and support progressive Democratic candidates in November 2020, and have them continue to vote for Democrats in every election held in the United States of America.

I encourage every legal and illegal immigrant to consider where the politician stands on the issues you are thinking about voting for and whether that political candidate loves the God of The Holy Bible, loves Jesus Christ and is willing to testify of his or her love for Him, loves and knows God personally, and loves America and what America stands for and symbolizes, and not that he or she is only interested in getting your vote without caring about you as an individual.

Where do the political candidates stand, and do they agree with the principles of having traditional family values, faith in God, and the principles of making America great again? Or do they only see you, and this great nation humbly uniting and joining the masses however poor or rich as long as we are all part of the state government? Then there will be free national health care, universal child care, and everything else will be free they promise, and the rich will certainly pay for it. I encourage you to watch out for these types of freebie politicians. They are wolves in sheep's clothing, and willing to bankrupt America.

Many female sheep invite the wolves dressed like a sheep into their midst. The male sheep then go right along with the female sheep in order to get along with them.

The last time Mark Garcia was visiting Lorena, and me in the Pacific Northwest he asked me a very thought-provoking question as we waited for the others before they went to the airport for his flight back to Colombia. At the time I didn't have a good answer to his insightful inquiry. He asked me, "Would Jesus build the wall?"

"I'll have an answer for you the next time we get together," I said.

Now I have the information he was seeking; I would answer Mark by telling him this: Jesus has already built the wall if we have spiritual eyes attuned to it. The Lord Jesus said,

"Not everyone who says to me, Lord, Lord, shall enter into the kingdom of heaven, but he who does the will of My Father in heaven." (Matthew 7:21)

"Most assuredly, I say to you, I am the door of the sheep. All who ever came before Me are thieves and robbers, but the sheep did not hear them. I am the door. If anyone enters by Me, he will be saved, and will go in and out and find pasture. The thief does not come except to steal, and kill, and to destroy. I have come that they may have life, and that they may have it more abundantly. I am the good shepherd. The good shepherd gives His life for the sheep." (John 10:7–11)

It makes perfect sense to use common sense as a good homeowner to protect your home and premises. I believe Mark also recognizes the importance of protecting his home and family by placing a lock, and a dead bolt on the door of his home to protect his family and his valuables from would-be burglars and thieves (ladron o ratero in Spanish). He would see the extreme importance of having every safeguard to protect his family from being murdered by any dangerous criminal.

There are Socialist Democrat candidates who are willing and eager to take guns away from the American citizens because they firmly believe that is the answer to stopping the mass shootings and terrorist killings by individuals who have automatic weapons in their possession these individuals are often willing to "go postal" against their boss, foreman, manager, etc., because they were fired from their jobs although they probably deserved being terminated for a negative cause.

Mark is trained in martial arts, and if any dangerous person or individuals working as a team ever posed a threat to him or his family they would be met with lethal consequences. President Trump wants to build a wall to prevent our great country from being overrun by illegal immigrants who feel they are entitled to free things for which American citizens have worked hard to support themselves and their families.

American citizens also look forward to receiving a pension and having a retirement fund from their many years in the work force. President Trump sees the importance of putting American citizens first and not just giving goods, and services away to every illegal immigrant who feels they are entitled to the free things offered to them by Socialist Democrats when they haven't worked a day in their life for those benefits. I remind you that most Progressive Socialist Democrats want the votes of illegal immigrants, and they are willing to promise the immigrants free things and services so they can remain in power.

Mark also believes in the importance of keeping the walls up, and the doors locked in his apartment to keep criminals and harmful elements out. Yes Mark, Jesus recognizes the importance of building walls, spiritually, to keep out everyone who doesn't qualify to enter the kingdom of heaven, and you and I both agree that to keep our lives safe from spiritual and bodily harm it is extremely important to lock our doors and keep the walls of our homes strong and secure.

If necessary we may need to galvanize the walls of our homes with added strengthening and supporting materials, and if you still don't feel completely safe then put bars on the windows of your home.

When I was in Bogota, Colombia I saw that building contractors had put bars on the windows of most of the homes and buildings in the capital city. I also saw other city premises with bars on their windows to prevent any intruders and thieves from breaking in to the apartments and businesses. Darrel Banjo worked for William County Carrier Company as a part-time driver, and he also worked for the United States Postal Service. Darrel had two black belts in Kung Fu a Chinese martial art, and he had trained soldiers in Kung Fu in Vietnam. Darrel invited me to his home one day, and I was hoping he would show me a demonstration of his Kung Fu technique and fighting skills, but he wouldn't give me a good demonstration that day of what he could do in an actual fight against an opponent who wanted to cause him bodily harm.

When I asked him if he had ever needed to use Kung Fu in America he said, "One guy came against me, but when I gave him one kick he ran away." Apparently this would-be attacker recognized Darrel's abilities and decided it wasn't worth coming physically against Darrel.

"Who would win in an actual fight between someone who knows Kung Fu and another martial artist with fighting skills?" I asked.

"Whoever got that first punch in," he said. That was an interesting martial arts analysis.

I realize that bad and angry people use guns that can kill people. I also realize that guns in the hands of good people can stop a cold-blooded killer with a gun in his hands. It would be a good thing to arm every qualified, skilled, and trained teacher at a local school district to prevent any rogue student willing to kill innocent classmates and fellow students at any school in the United States.

The Lord Jesus wants to keep every baby lamb, and adult sheep from the predators who would seek to steal, kill, and destroy the flock. In like manner, President Trump wants to keep every student and citizen safe from harm in the U.S. and to prevent the rogue killers who want to cause great harm in a mass way against the student body and teachers who try to stop them. Instead of taking automatic weapons away from law-abiding citizens we need to arm well-trained teachers who will stop a misdirected student from going postal against innocent young people inside of school buildings. Metal detectors in every school in America as a preventive measure would be a good thing too.

The Bible has a good answer to this dilemma:

"Let every soul be subject to the governing authorities. For there is no authority except from God, and the authorities that exist are appointed by God. Therefore whoever resists the authority resists the ordinance of God, and those who resist will bring judgment on themselves. For rulers are not a terror to good works, but to evil. Do you want to be unafraid of the authority? Do what is good, and you will have praise from the same. For he is God's minister to you for good, But if you do evil, be afraid; for he does not bear the sword in vain; for he is God's minister, and avenger to execute wrath on him who practices evil. Therefore you must be subject, not only because of wrath but also for conscience' sake. For because of this you also pay taxes, for they are God's ministers attending continually to this very thing. Render therefore to all their due: taxes to whom taxes are due, customs to whom customs, fear to whom fear, honor to whom honor. Owe no one anything except to love one another, for he who loves another has fulfilled the law." (Romans 13:1–8)

I believe President Trump would like for the immigrants who come to America to have job skills so they can find employment. In this way the U.S. taxpayers won't solely support the families, and individuals seeking refuge or asylum by their going on welfare and needing food stamps. I realize that not all Mexicans are bad individuals who can't be trusted, and I believe President Trump also recognizes this important fact. I believe most illegal immigrants want to find employment in the

U.S. to support their families in their home country, and that is perfectly fine with most American citizens. Many Mexican immigrants are willing to do manual labor that a lot of Americans would rather not do.

Most people living in this natural world are living in a fantasy of some kind whether they recognize it or not. It's easy to get lost in our own self-interests, self-grandeur, narcissistic tendencies, and social media and television images that can shape us and cause us to conform to Hollywood images. It is so easy to get caught up with the world's view of things of importance, with all the mental and emotional hype of personal icons, heroes, and one of the biggest attention-getters athletes who are considered national heroes because of their tremendous athletic abilities in the boxing ring, football or soccer field, basketball court, hockey rink, etc., and place them on a high pedestal where they are greatly admired and applauded.

The natural beauty or cosmetically enhanced features of handsome men and beautiful women capture our attention with magnetic attraction we can't deny. You might be seeking that perfect body to have the right muscle mass and definition. Perhaps you love cars or boats, plants and flowers, or a million other things in this world that have captured your love, affections, and fascination.

The world has so many fascinating things of great beauty and natural wonders that can capture our minds, and hearts and have a lasting effect on our lives. Recognizing a person's abilities and talents or the wonders of this world for its natural beauty, peculiarity in appearance, or uniqueness is perfectly fine as long as we don't go overboard and worship that person or thing above loving and worshipping the living God our Creator.

Anything and everything of the world, the flesh, and the devil can cause people to take their eyes off their need of a Savior, the Lord Jesus Christ. Jesus said,

"For where your treasure is, there your heart will be also." (Matthew 6:21)

"And the cares of this world, the deceitfulness of riches, and the desires for other things entering in choke the word, and it becomes unfruitful." (Mark 4: 19)

Keith Green wrote a special song that Phil Keaggy sings which I very much like. It's titled "Your Love Broke Through," and the chorus of this powerful song says,

Like waking up from the longest dream, how real it seemed Until your love broke through

I've been lost in a fantasy, that blinded me Until your love broke through

Keith's song also says,

I've been blind all these wasted years and I thought I was so wise But then you [God] took me by surprise

Wow! Those insightful words make me realize that we all have been blind to seeing and coming to the Truth, the Lord Jesus who truly loves us for who we are. He wants so badly to make a regeneration in our hearts and lives so His Kingdom might live and dwell in us, and we then can become lights to the world.

You, like Keith Green may have been searching for that crazy missing part in order to find yourself or to find God in your own way, when in reality, you can do even better for yourself by being found by the Good Shepherd and become born again so His Holy Spirit may abide with you in this life and for all eternity. There isn't anything better that you can do than to come to know God personally, and to know that you are saved from sin, and know that the Lord Jesus Christ now lives sweetly within your heart and life. Know that you have made peace with God so you in turn can have the peace of God living in you.

The last time I was in Colombia, Mark came to the apartment complex where Blanca Ellen Gonzalez lived. I was able to reserve the rec room where they had a Ping-Pong table set up, and Mark and I had an opportunity to play together. Mark's unorthodox style of play including mixing up his game on me which caused me difficulty in successfully countering what he was doing to win the games. I had troubles with my mobility during each game which hampered my overall ability to match the competitive edge he had that night.

Mark was able to defeat me every single time. I give Mark full credit for playing a high-energy, and confident game play with superb strategy that created problems for me. I couldn't overcome his arsenal of attack weapons which he used to effectively whip me into an inferior position. Mark was positively the Ping-Pong champion, and the superior player for the entire night. I congratulate him as my opponent as he nullified any possible threat that I had used against him.

I wasn't able to move around as quickly, and as easily as I had when I weighed less and when I was younger. I just didn't have the mobility or the ability to position myself correctly to overcome Mark's onslaught of intense Ping-Pong fury throughout the night. He was the powerful Ping-Pong champion for the night, and I was totally inferior and unable to overcome his unorthodox Ping-Pong style and his strong forehand and what he was hitting back to me across the table.

The last time Mark Garcia and his two sons, Caleb and Gabriel came to the United States we played Ping-Pong at the William County Base in Union. From the get-go, Mark and the boys showed me they were the superior players, and I was simply no match for their strong style of play. It was obvious that Mark, Caleb, and Gabriel had been practicing an aggressive offense on a regular basis which I hadn't been doing. I still gave it my all trying to defeat them at their superior level of play, but once again I was not able to gain the upper hand or overcome their powerful performance.

The only way I was able to defeat Mark and Caleb individually was when they chose to spot me five points up in advance, and they willingly accepted five points down before commencing each game. All I had to do to defeat them was to reach eleven points before they overcame my advanced five-point lead and their five-point trailing deficit. I did my level best to defeat Mark and Caleb by being as consistent as I possibly could without being too eager to use my strong and quick-hitting backhand to put them away without their being able to return the ball, and before I began making critical mistakes I couldn't afford to make to win any game.

For each Ping-Pong game we played we followed the rule that each player takes two turns to serve the ball. Whichever player reaches eleven points before their opponent does has to win by two points. In the end I was able to defeat Mark in one hard-fought battle by reaching eleven points before he did. In a separate game I defeated Caleb in another one-and-only game victory against him for the night, and using the same five-point system I'd used with Mark which definitely increased my chances to defeat them both. I hope to play Mark, Caleb, and Gabriel Garcia sometime in the future when I hope to gain the upper hand without using my five-points-up/five-points-down advantage. I'll wait to see what happens during the next series of games between the Garcia family and me.

Bud told me one day that when he was at work he heard young women discussing that they were quite proud that they could have an abortion any time they wanted one. One woman on the job with him said, "Well, it's my body."

Bud immediately said to her, "No, it's not. It's the bodies of innocent baby boys and baby girls that are being murdered."

I realize that many millions of women today are being influenced, encouraged, and forced by our paganistic society to participate in the unthinkable atrocity of committing the cold-blooded murder of their babies and may end up being killed by an abortionist, a hired assassin who goes by the cover of being a medical doctor. If a woman, educated or uneducated wants to keep her baby she will say, "I want to keep my baby." If the woman doesn't want to keep the precious life living inside of her womb she will then say, "I don't want to keep my fetus," as if the blob of tissue living inside of her womb is not a fully developed human being at the time of its development.

The feminine gender is unfortunately rationalizing away the hard reality that they are participating in having their babies ruthlessly slaughtered by the abhorrent, barbaric, and invasive act of killing a totally innocent and vulnerable human being. When abortion was legalized evangelical theologian Francis Schaeffer said, "We have started a toboggan slide downwards."

My friend Bud said, "This eliminates the role of the man as an extension of the family line, and he is cut off. God is the Creator of the human family, and He is the Author of the institution of marriage regarding families and procreation. When the babies are conceived the seed of the man is planted in the egg of the woman. God takes the act of marriage which results in conception and creates the members or physical body parts of the human baby."

I appreciate what evangelist the Reverend Billy Graham had to say concerning America's moral decline:

Some years ago, my wife, Ruth, was reading the draft of a book I was writing. When she finished a section describing the terrible downward spiral of our nation's moral standards and the idolatry of worshiping false gods such as technology and sex, she startled me by exclaiming, "If God doesn't punish America, He'll have to apologize to Sodom and Gomorrah."1

Bud and I agree that when the abortionists decide to abort a living human being they do so to profit financially so that they might live a lucrative lifestyle of the rich and famous.

Bud once said, "The pharmaceutical industry pays Planned Parenthood for the body parts of the human babies. They use it in their products advertised over cable television for scores of women's facial and skin creams. Planned Parenthood makes a lot of money by harboring and selling baby parts, and they receive federal government funding through various sources."

It's a sobering thought when we as a nation Wake Up to realize there have been over 62 million cold-blooded abortions committed since January 1973, when the United States Supreme Court ruled in Roe

v. Wade which became the law of the land. Christians were there, but they were not allowed in the room when the Supreme Court Justices passed the abortion law. The Christians were ordered to remain in the antechamber which is another part of the Supreme Court building. The Christians who were present had medical and biblical evidence that the fetuses are human boys and girls.

This divisive law declared that if a woman didn't want to keep the life living inside her body she was allowed to have that living tissue removed[1]

Billy Graham Evangelistic Association, "My Heart Aches for America," and destroyed by an abortionist, and in many cases these life-destroying procedures are committed inside a Planned Parenthood clinic or facility.

I am forever grateful that President Donald John Trump changed his political position on this most sensitive issue from pro-choice to pro-life before he took the Oval Office as the forty-fifth Commander in Chief of the United States of America. I firmly believe President Trump's and Vice President Mike Pence's strong stance on this divisive life-or-death issue has helped to save lives by awakening the conscience of millions of men and women in the United States. Thank goodness society's voice of moral clarity has said that it is far better to choose life, and save the most innocent and vulnerable who can't defend themselves from determined abortionists willing to commit savage acts of heartless murder by using this invasive surgical technique.

I appreciate every pro-life supporter who goes all the way forward to support and protect human life, and every other group that seeks to protect the most innocent and vulnerable among us who choose to be born in today's world with all its dangers and challenges awaiting every human life. Thank God for the human family that will do everything within its power to save life and protect each human born which includes babies and the elderly. Let every human life be allowed to pursue life, liberty, and the pursuit of happiness to the best of their ability. May God continue to bless the human families, and each member of the family unit that He has wonderfully created with life-sustaining qualities.

If you have had an abortion, God in the Lord Jesus Christ doesn't condemn you for this most grievous act, but He condemns the sin. God is absolutely against the sin of abortion, but He loves the sinner. If you come to God with a sorrowful heart, and are weighed down needing forgiveness in repentance to the Lord God in Christ Jesus will forgive you.
In fact, His Word says,

"For God so loved the world that He gave His only begotten Son, that whoever believes in Him should not perish but have everlasting life. For God did not send His Son into the world to condemn the world, but that the world through Him might be saved." (John 3:16–17)
See yourself as God sees you.

"Because you say, I am rich, have become wealthy, and have need of nothing and do not know that you are wretched, miserable, poor, blind, and naked." (Revelation 3:17)

I encourage you to approach God with humility and to see the Lord Jesus as your Savior, Lord, Master, and personal God. There is truly forgiveness and hope for every repentant soul.

I appreciate President Donald Trump's slogan, "Make America Great Again," which helped promote and support his run for the presidency in 2016. Unfortunately, the Democratic Party strongly opposed President Trump's run for the presidency that same year and have come to despise him as a person, and his family as well. Ever since President Trump began declaring his long-term goals for this great country and what he planned on doing to fulfill his campaign promises to his Republican Party base the House Democrats have been extremely anxious regarding impeaching President Trump to stop him from actually achieving the promises he envisioned for

---

[1] https:// billygraham.org/story/billy-graham-my-heart-aches-for-America.

every U.S. citizen.

There are definite reasons why society may be questioning the sheer number of murders that have been committed in the recorded past and are taking place today in America. One key factor is the large number of abortions that have been committed since the Supreme Court of the United States ruled in January 1973 that it was legal to have an abortion, in the case of Roe v. Wade.

I heard that when a fifteen-year-old kid was asked why he killed someone he responded, "I don't know why you are questioning me about killing another person when babies are being killed every single day." Also, every aborted baby's blood cries out to God for justice in the spiritual dimension, and there is a direct and adverse connection and consequence that adult human life will be killed in today's society.

Whenever there is a lack of the fear of God in the human heart and a lack of respect, decency, and sacredness for human life in general, the likelihood increases of people being murdered at the hands of ruthless murderers. Paul the apostle wrote, "Do not be deceived, God is not mocked; for whatever a man sows, that will he also reap" (Galatians 6:7).

Society may think that when a human baby is murdered in cold blood by an abortion assassin commonly known as an abortion doctor that includes rationalization in their thoughts. When it comes to killing a baby and disposing of it in a disgusting dumpster then it's out of sight, out of mind, but the memory of that innocent life snuffed out is remembered by the Lord God Almighty as well as by the woman who had the abortion.

They may think, I wonder what color eyes the baby would have had. I wonder if the baby would have looked like me or the father of the baby. I wonder what the baby would have chosen for a profession, had the baby lived? Nagging questions can come back to haunt the mother or father of the baby or any number of family members who just wanted to dispose of the unwanted baby for a number of incalculable reasons, but it's colossal in any measurable way that human loss can't be calculated.

We must keep in mind that America is facing some menacing threats as a nation because we had a Christian foundation, but as a nation we have chosen to put God out of our public education system and the nation overall. One serious threat is China, a Communist regime that is an authoritarian government with nuclear weapons. There is also North Korea which has nuclear weapons; as a nation they live under a dictatorship and a Communist government. The only god the people of North Korea believe in is their supreme dictator, Kim Jong-Un.

The constitution defines North Korea as "a dictatorship of people's democracy" under the leadership of the Workers' Party of Korea (WPK), which is given legal supremacy over other political parties."[2]

And then there is Russia, a superpower with nuclear weapons which poses a serious threat to America as well. According to the New York Times, Russia today doesn't seem like "a properly run dictatorship."

Iran also poses an imminent threat to our U.S. forces in the Middle East. With all these serious threats to America it's very important that we make prayer a high priority, praying for President Donald Trump and Vice President Mike Pence and also remembering to pray for our national leaders in the armed forces and throughout our great nation.

Wikipedia,"PoliticsofNorthKorea."wikipedia.org/wiki/Politicsof
NorthKorea#:~:text=The%20constitution%20defines%20North%20
Korea,supremacy%20over%20other%20political%20parties.&text=Elections%20occur%20only%2

Trapped By A Psycho Doctor

0in%20single, selected%20beforehand%20by%20the%20WPK.

Bud told me that he saw some Iranian men who said they felt America was already theirs. That very real prospect could be multiplied with so many Muslims living in America, and abroad who want to see the destruction of American society so they can establish a Muslim dictatorship and fly an Islamic flag from the White House.

I chose to bring these menacing threats against America to your attention, not wanting to frighten American citizens but to raise America's consciousness that we need to return as a nation back to God for His divine protection, and so His sovereign kingdom will rule over this great nation again.

In order for America to turn back to God with all our hearts we need to have a mighty Holy Ghost revival in repentance and faith. We must believe in God that His protective, and powerful hand will intervene and stop every menacing enemy and opposing threat before a nuclear weapon can penetrate America's homeland security and military force shield by softening the hearts of hardened dictators who are bent on wiping out this country with a first-strike nuclear weapon combined with a payload of nuclear-tipped guided missiles aimed at America before we have time to defend ourselves with a counterattack.

As a positive return to our Christian Godly Heritage Foundation we need to recognize that American's great need is to live up to what America symbolizes to the nations of the world, and especially in the eyes of our enemies. It is imperative that we remain strong, courageous, kindhearted, benevolent, and generous to the downtrodden, destitute, and hungry.

We must recognize America has many enemies within our borders, and many outside of our national borders that want to see America collapse and go the way of another fallen empire that got too big for its own britches. There are well-funded individuals and groups that anticipate America's having open borders and uniting with Mexico, where we become a global village one day and eventually have a one-world dictatorship under the Antichrist who will one day rule the entire world as the supreme dictator. According to the Bible, he will govern the world causing every man and woman to take his mark on the back of their hands or on their foreheads.

No man will be able to buy or sell unless he receives his mark for his daily commerce in America as a member of the world's population and as one of the masses that choose to take his mark (Revelation 13:11–18). This future event described in the book of Revelation, will one day become a reality because God's Word is more up-to-date than our daily
U.S. and international newspapers.

Then there are people like billionaire George Soros and others who want to see America go bankrupt, and cause America to become part of the global village and no longer be a free country where capitalism is practiced and allowed to flourish. I thank God for the free enterprise system where products, prices, and services are determined by the market and not by the U.S. Government. I also appreciate living in a country where capitalism is practiced, and it has caused American citizens to thrive, prosper, and succeed financially to not only bless themselves, but also to bless their families.

I would like to see people like George Soros, who would very much like to see America become a "liberal wasteland," just drift away into a far-distant country and to envision changing that different country (instead of America) into whatever he wants that political region to become.
For your information:

As the so-called migrant caravan gathers at the U.S.-Mexico border seeking asylum, an open borders group that is funded by leftwing billionaire George Soros launched a smartphone app to help illegal immigrants avoid federal authorities.

Judicial Watch reports the app, Notifica, which means "Notify," is described as a tool that allows illegal immigrants with the click of a button to alert family, friends, and attorneys of encounters with federal authorities.

The group behind the app is called United We Dream, a project of the National Immigration Law Center (NILC) both of which get big bucks from Soros' Open Society Foundation. Using taxpayer dollars, Soros groups have pushed a radical agenda that includes promoting an open border with Mexico and fighting immigration laws, among other efforts.[2]

Am560 The Answer, "Soros Group Launches App to HelpIllegalsAvoidFeds,"
-group-launches-app-to-help-illegals-avoid-feds.

So the evidence is in that George Soros and others are helping to fund the illegal immigrants entering at our U.S. borders. I recommend that we as a nation continue to support President Donald Trump to make America great again to defend American borders, and to build that wall. God wants to defend, protect, and preserve America, and He is doing that very thing by giving President Trump a vision and wisdom on how to do that very thing, and how to fulfill the vision of making America great again.

I have a word of advice for all the people who would like to change America: Love America or leave America, but don't think you will change America into the philosophical and political ideal you may want her to become according to your worldview or perspective. Just leave America the way you found America or I'll make you a cordial offer to exit America and go to another country where you are free to exercise the thoughts of your imagination to make that country into the kind of nation that would make you very happy. So love it or leave it, but don't change it.

I recognize that President Trump is not your typical run-of-the-mill politician, and most people have come to appreciate his candid, straightforward, tell-it-like-it-is manner, but he does tell the truth to the American citizens whether the Progressive Socialist Democrats, and the leftist media sources like it or not. President Trump has worked at and has been successful at shutting down the leftist media that tries to smear him, and his presidential actions in a forceful manner. He will strongly call them out and identify the sources of false information by what he calls "fake news."

The phrase covers any reporter, journalist, or leaker of disinformation that tries to spread false information about President Trump which may include his cabinet and family, and all the other leftist media news sources willing to spread lies and deception to the American citizens. I like the fact that President Trump has that winning psychology, and as our Commander in Chief he knows how to get the job done that is set before him each day. The Progressive Democrats are hypocrites in many ways, and I won't vote for any of the Democratic candidates running for president whom I observed debating on CNN this year. I do not believe or trust any of them in any way, shape, or form no matter what they advocate or say they will do as the next president of the United States.

I'll go on the record to say the Progressive Socialist Democrats have an evil platform so no matter what they have to say or how polished they may appear on stage during the debates I don't trust them as they try to convince American citizens that they are well qualified to become the next U. S. President. Don't believe a word they say now in 2022 or in 2024.

The Progressive Socialist Democrats have spent their time focusing on bashing, criticizing, and

---

[2] https://560theanswer.com/content/all/soros

disrespecting President Donald Trump during his first term in office instead of focusing on supporting the president and offering the president good ideas that reveal their respect and honor for the United States of America and its citizens. Instead they choose by their own stubborn volition to spend their time protesting, obstructing, and hindering the president at every right decision he makes for the good of America.

I do not support or respect the House Democrats in power today because they dishonor President Trump regardless of the number of correct moves he has made for America. Instead they chose an impeachment inquiry based on emotionally charged assumptions, but they weren't able to present solid evidence whereby the Congressional Republican Senate was convinced of any actual crimes committed by President Trump during the impeachment trial televised for the entire nation to watch. I do not support or respect the Progressive Socialist Democrats who debated one another on CNN as presidential candidates in 2019 as they tried to convince America they are qualified to be the next U.S. President and are capable of defeating President Trump.

The Progressive Socialist Democrats have made their collective decision as a liberal party of Congress to oppose helping to make America great again in agreement with President Trump's rallying declaration to the Republican Party base, and to all American citizens. Rather than providing great ideas themselves on how they would fix the border crisis, and the major problems we have with illegal immigrants storming our southern border points and entering illegally into our country at the expense of the taxpayers, the Progressive Socialist Democratic Party chose to ignore the border crisis until it was obvious they couldn't intentionally disregard it with their reprehensible complacency and the blatant and glaring evidence that was so conspicuous.

Everyone could see for themselves on a national or local news stations if they wanted to know what was happening at our southern border with the illegal immigrant crisis.

President Donald's Trump one term in the Oval Office was earmarked by bills that he had gotten passed to building up of the border wall between the United States and Mexico which was to protect America from a further influx of the illegal aliens and drug traffickers. A further bill the U.S. Congress was able to pass that was alerting women to the fact that when a woman happens to be pregnant their pregnancy are real baby boys and girls in their wombs, and any abortions committed does deprive their lives and God given liberties and the God calling and purposes for their lives in this life. With their babies lives snuffed out it means that God had to intervene and take their spirits to be with Him in heaven forever.

The Progressive Socialist Democrats support Planned Parenthood, and abortion rights and are opposed to pro-life supporters and issues relative to the life of the unborn. I agree with Donnie Swaggart, who stated on Francis and Friends, a popular Christian program on the SonLife Broadcasting Network, "No born again Christian can vote for a Democrat for the president of the United States." Donnie Swaggart recognizes that a true born-again believer must stand for life, liberty, and the pursuit of happiness for every human being conceived and born into the human family. There are no exceptions when God Himself is the Author and Creator of life for all human beings.

Anyone who votes for the next president of the United States of America must stand for, support, and vote for a presidential candidate who fully declares and endorses choosing pro-life issues, supports traditional family values and beliefs, and stands for honoring the God of the Bible and valuing the citizens of this great country.

Pro-life supporters stand for a woman's right to keep her baby, and they honor God, country, and traditional family values. When President Barack Obama was the president, the New York Times of January 8, 2016 reported, "Obama Vetoes Bill to Repeal Health Law and End Planned Parenthood funding." Remember that President Obama was the abortion president, and he supported more than once the botched abortion bill. The Progressive Socialist Democrats remained silent to President Obama's pro-choice botched abortion bill.

You can read Jennifer Rubin's article from July 16, 2012, titled "Obama the Leftwing Ideologue." For many Progressive Socialist Democrats Obama became a champion of the radical left ideology which greatly motivated their home-base supporters. The Democrats also support homosexual and lesbian rights, the LGBT agendas, and their lifestyles which are contrary to biblical principles prescribed in The Holy Bible.

The Progressive Socialist Democrats have shown themselves to be anti-Semitic which is clearly against the Jews right to exist in their homeland as a free democratic country given to them by the God of Abraham, the God of Isaac, and the God of Jacob. Israel was recognized by the United Nations as a State in 1948, and ever since that date which marked their right to exist as a State in the annals of historic significance Israel has existed as a free people and country (John 10:10; Genesis 12:3; Psalm 122:6).

The House Democrats have also revealed their agenda of standing against the Second Amendment, and they are seeking ways to take our Second Amendment rights and freedoms of owning, possessing, carrying, and using a gun as a weapon to protect and defend ourselves and our families away from the American citizens. Lorena's brother-in-law, Chad told me that the Democrats are not anti-Semitic, but I told him there hasn't been one Democrat who has said anything against the Democrats who speak against Israel.

The media will allow any Democrat who has anything to say that counters what the Liberal Socialist Democrats have been saying against the nation of Israel, and its rights to govern itself as a free and autonomous country. Israel is the United States' only ally in the Middle East, and we need to defend her at all costs for our own good, and that the blessings and protection of God to remain on America.

I read that U.S. Representative Alexandria Ocasio-Cortez will not be going to Israel until the two U.S. Representatives, Ilhan Abdullahi Omar and Rashida Tlaib, are allowed to go. Representatives Omar and Tlaib were banned from traveling to Israel due to Israel's policy of preventing anyone from entering Israel who speaks against the Jewish established Democratic Nation and of Israel's peoples within its existing borders. President Trumps says Representative Omar and Representative Tlaib hate Israel and all Jewish people.

Israel later changed its policy to allow Rashida Tlaib to come to Israel to visit her ninety-year-old grandmother as long as she didn't promote boycotts during her stay. I firmly support Israel's right to take a strong stand against the people who could use anti-Semitic inflammatory rhetoric which means to "arouse or intended to arouse angry or violent feelings." May the Lord God Almighty continue to bless, strengthen, and protect Israel and every country that recognizes Israel's right to exist as a free democracy, and to make the decisions that are truly in her best interest as a sovereign nation and a great ally to the United States of America.

Harry S. Truman, the thirty-third president of the United States of America had the Christian biblical conviction to recognize the creation of the State of Israel on May 14, 1948. In fact, on that same day the United States under President Truman, "became the first country to extend any form of recognition" to the State of Israel.

On May, 14, 1948, David-Ben-Gurion, the head of the Jewish Agency, proclaimed the establishment of the State of Israel, U.S. President Harry S. Truman recognized the new nation on the same day.4

I believe that one of the most important events in American history was Harry Truman's recognition of Israel on May 14, 1948. America's friendship toward Israel has not been perfectly consistent, but America has been Israel's greatest friend in modern history, and that is significant. God told Abraham, the father of the Jewish nation,

"And I will make of thee a great nation, and I will bless thee, and make thy name great; and thou shalt be a blessing: And I will bless them that bless thee, and curse him that curseth thee: and in thee shall all families of the earth be blessed." (Genesis 12:2–3)

On this authority there can be no doubt that one of the chief reasons for God's blessings on America has been her blessing of Israel.

I am forever grateful that President Truman made the bold decision to recognize the State of Israel when there was mounting pressure by the State Department of the United States for him to succumb to the fear of the Muslims.

Although the United States backed Resolution 181, the U.S. Department of State recommended the creation of a United Nations trusteeship with limits on Jewish immigration, and a division of Palestine into separate Jewish and Arab provinces but not states. The State Department, concerned about the possibility of an increasing Soviet role in the Arab world and the potential for restriction by Arab oil producing nations of oil supplies to the United States, advised against U.S. intervention on behalf of the Jews. Later as the date for British departure from Palestine drew near, the Department of State grew concerned about the possibility of an all-out war in Palestine as Arab States,[3]

U.S. State Department, Office of the Historian, "CreationofIsrael,1948," threatened to attack almost as soon as the UN passed the partition resolution.

Despite the growing conflict between Palestinian Arabs and Palestinian Jews, and despite the Department of State's endorsement of a trusteeship, Truman ultimately decided to recognize the State of Israel.5

I thank the Lord God that President Truman recognized the State of Israel, and I also thank God that America has been forever blessed as a positive consequence of President Truman's strong decision to recognize God's chosen people.

"Blessed be the Lord God of Israel, Who only does wondrous things! And blessed be His glorious name forever! And let the whole earth be filled with His glory. Amen and Amen." (Psalm 72:18–19)

The Progressive Socialist Democrats are pushing a socialist, Marxist agenda that will steal, kill, and destroy our country and the freedoms we enjoy. They also attack the rights of Christians to speak up and to declare the name of Jesus Christ, and very much want to stifle U.S. citizens from communicating and expressing free speech in the market place. If the House Democrats could have their way they would want Christians to keep silent, to disobey, and to deny the clear instructions of Jesus Christ to go into all the world and preach the gospel which is good news to every creature created in the likeness and image of the living God identified in The Holy Bible (Matthew 28:18–20; 1 Corinthians 1:27–28; 2:2).

---

[3] https://history.state.gov/milestones/1945-1952/creation-israel.

The Progressive Socialist Democrats fight against capitalism, and promote and advocate socialism, but they are hypocrites because they enjoy the benefits and become rich themselves through the principles and practices of capitalism. Senator Bernie Sanders, who himself is a millionaire and there are other Democrats in the same upper-crust boat has benefited and prospered from capitalism and the free enterprise system.

Every born-again Christian needs to use godly wisdom, discernment, and a good dose of common sense when they listen to the Democratic debates because the Progressive Socialist Democrats try to sway the television audience to their Progressive Socialist ideology, bias, and agendas that they have in mind for changing America to their way of thinking. They will continue to persuade the viewers that President Trump is a racist, and that he has been dividing America with his racist attitude. Their propaganda messaging is totally untrue. The truth is the Democrats are the real racists.

They like to say that President Trump has been dividing families as families have been separated, children from the parents at the border. These Progressive Socialist Democratic presidential candidates put the full blame for this separation policy on President Trump, and don't dare point out that President Barack Obama did the same thing with the illegal immigrants when he was president.

The Democrats haven't been down to the border themselves, but they like to blame and criticize President Trump for the good that ICE, and border patrol agents who are at the border to protect our country from the harmful element among them. ICE (Immigration and Customs Enforcement) needs to be supported, respected, and honored for what they do to help facilitate the immigrant families and individuals entering our country.

The bottom line is that the Progressive Socialist Democratic presidential candidates do not love the families, and the children who come to the U.S. border. They only want the votes of the immigrants entering our great country so they can remain in power from the vast numbers of illegal immigrants crossing over from Mexico into the United States.

I encourage every Christian not to be deceived or swayed to join the critical ranks of the Progressive Socialist Democrats, and their sinister agenda to remove by your vote to oust President Donald Trump in November 2020.

I encourage every Christian to pray for President Trump and Vice President Mike Pence and their cabinets every single day. Pray also for America to Wake Up, and recognize what the Democrats have been doing to convince the American citizens that we have a racist president and that he needs to be removed from the Oval Office through impeachment. Please don't fall for their steady stream of lies and their evil agenda by siding with them. Be aware there is a lot of racism in America against white men and Christians happening today.

May God help us all, and may God continue to bless America. May America continue to bless and honor God by staying spiritually alert and prayed up every single day. We are in a spiritual battle for this great nation and for President Trump, who is doing his very best to make America great again. We can't let up, give up, or relinquish the power of the presidency to the Progressive Socialist Democrats, who want to remove God from the Democratic platform; if they had their way, they would remove God from America's political and government institutions and from our way of life. We can't let this happen.

If they do not love America and the living God of heaven and earth that has made America great, then let them go to another country where they can practice the Progressive Socialist agenda to their hearts' content, but leave America's citizens to continue to be strong and free to exercise their faith in God as they please.

When men and women of the faith put their faith and trust in the One True God and choose to believe and follow His Holy Word, and His godly principles then we can know for certain that God will bless us and heal our land (2 Chronicles 7:14).

I read where two-thirds of college-educated Democrats want to remove the words "In God We Trust" from the U.S. currency, but thank God the Republicans didn't agree with their socialist decision.

The Progressive Liberal Democrats are far too radical to defeat President Trump in November 2020 by pushing and advocating a Progressive Socialist Democratic agenda which is totally contrary to the will and plan of the Lord God and His creative designs for all His people. God's thoughts for us are thoughts of peace, not of evil, to give us an expected end. His plans and a good future are for America, and every other country that will faithfully believe and honor their covenant relationship with the Lord God Almighty so we can continue to enjoy our relationship with the Lord God of The Holy Bible.

We can receive and have an expected end as the Lord has promised us in (Jeremiah 29:11–13) as we faithfully walk, and work out our covenant relationship with God by grace through faith. This will be accomplished in the finished work Jesus paid for on Calvary's Cross.

God and the Republican Party have much better plans for America than what the radical Progressive Socialist Democrats are advocating. They want to bring about changes that they want the American citizens to believe and accept so they can once again regain the power of the presidency. We have to stop the Democratic Progressive Socialist Party in its tracks as they had two terms of President Obama, who in my opinion brought about negative changes that didn't make America great as President Trump envisions for America.

Adolf Hitler knew that if you tell a lie long enough to the German people, they will believe it. And now, I believe the socialist.

Democrats are seeking to deceive American citizens into following their socialist agenda for America as the Nazis deceived the German people, and took over Germany by great deception and the power of propaganda films and speeches by Adolf Hitler, as the Fuhrer their leader and guide.

The Democrats have accused President Trump of being a racist who is dividing America. The vocal Democrat women were silent when Obama did the same as President Trump at the border. They have accused him of acting like a dictator, and the latest accusation by the Democrats is that President Trump is not a patriot. These Progressive Socialist Democrats who are accusing the president of not being a patriot need to be ousted and removed immediately from congressional authority, and sent to live out their remaining days as a civilian in their local cities or towns.

These poor deceived people who want to lead and guide us as the premier Democrats of this great country, and to become the next president of the United States of America will stop at nothing to regain the presidency so they will continue to lie, bash, criticize, and accuse President Trump of anything and everything as long as they think it will strike a resounding chord that the American citizenry will believe, and then they will choose to have the U.S. Congress impeach the president.

We must not let this happen to a great president who champions making America great again, and who makes wise decisions for our country with the wisdom and good advice of strong and decisive leaders from every field. The real dictators today are the vocal Democratic women, and the men have a yellow streak and have spineless backs as they are not willing to stand up for and with President Trump on so many critical issues that we as a nation continue to face.

I appreciate President Trump for his economic, business, and financial knowledge and experience which has provided him the wisdom to help move our economy into a higher level which gives American citizens more spending power than when President Obama was the president. President Trump made the decision to help move Israel's capital to Jerusalem which other presidents who preceded him could have done but refused to do. So many previous presidents feared the Muslims.

President Trump received good advice before making this strategic geographic move for the good of the Nation of Israel. I appreciate President Trump for his leadership skills, and qualities that he has been blessed with in the Oval Office for leading our country during his first term and for relating to and with world leaders. I appreciate President Trump for how he deals with and outsmarts his enemies on the Democratic and liberal side of the congressional aisle.

I also appreciate that President Trump has shown himself to be a strong leader as Commander in Chief, and he is not a pushover whom the Democrats can get to cave in, surrender, throw in the towel, or call it quits as the president of the United States of America. President Trump loves America too much to compromise his firm convictions; he is willing to forge ahead to get the presidential job done every day for the good of American citizens.

President Trump is the president of all the United States, including Democrats, Republicans, Independents, and every other U.S. citizen whether they choose to do their patriotic duty by voting in the presidential elections, and midterm elections or choose not to exercise their constitutional right to vote. They can vote or not vote for whichever candidate they choose; they can decide to join or side with a particular political party that they think correlates with their Christian or non-Christian beliefs, conscience, or national, personal, and political convictions. Keep in mind that at the polling places, all absentee voters will be marked down as supporting the Democrats.

President Trump has been able to defeat his enemies through his use of tweets and presidential speeches such as when he gives the State of the Union Address; when he speaks and encourages his base during Republican rallies; or when he speaks to an unbiased reporter or journalist with the local or national news.

I encourage you to vote in November 2020 for the very best presidential candidate and the person you want to become the next president of the United States of America, the one you believe will represent, lead, and govern our nation to the best of his or her ability. I choose to vote for the current forty-fifth president, the Commander in Chief, President Donald Trump, for four more years. I encourage you to do the same.

If you are a generational Democrat who calls yourself a born-again Christian you need to change your political stance to a conservative Christian position, divorce the Progressive Socialist Democratic Party, and stand with the Lord Jesus Christ and agree with The Holy Bible and its Biblical principles. As a Christian you are a citizen of the kingdom of heaven first, and a citizen of this earth's kingdom second. Recognize that God's kingdom and laws supersede all earthly political parties, and laws which are subject to God's Heavenly Kingdom and His Laws that are not suggestions.

You may think to yourself, well, my grandparents were Democrats, and my parents were Democrats; therefore, I should also vote for a Democrat as the next president of the United

States. That may have worked just fine in former presidential elections when Democrats in a previous generation were typical Liberal Democrats; for example, when President John F. Kennedy or Dwight D. Eisenhower served as presidents of the United States.

The Progressive Socialist Democrats who were running to be the candidate for the next presidential election whom I observed debating on CNN were not your typical Liberal Democrats with a more mainstream ideology and conservative philosophy; they seemed to be more far-left, radical socialists, such as Bernie Sanders, and their political views are radical left as they seek to bring about fundamental changes to our free enterprise system, our present economic system, and our health care system. I believe they would seek to control every U.S. citizen from the cradle to the grave or from the womb to the tomb if they had their way. The U.S. citizens of America must stop their agenda by making your vote count for the right reasons!!

There will be vast and scary changes to the American way of life that we know and enjoy if society continues to be stupid enough, and is willing to trade the life, rights, and freedoms we enjoy to elect a Progressive Socialist Democrat to the Oval Office. It would be so pathetic if America listens to the steady stream of lies and deception broadcasts every day on fake-news media sources like CNN, which has political disseminators who offer intentional disinformation, and seek to tell the American people that we have a racist president who colluded with the Russians which is totally a fabrication by the Democratic Party.

The Democrat Party wants us as a free nation and democracy to believe that President Trump is not a true patriot, and that he is a despicable human being. Therefore, we as American citizens need to go along with their idiotic impeachment inquiry and move to have him viewed as an unelectable Republican Party Presidential candidate. I believe the American citizens are more intelligent, wiser, and more politically savvy than the Democrats realize. They think they have duped the "deplorables," according to Hillary Clinton when referring to the voters of President Trump. The Progressive Socialist Democrats have worked feverishly to mentally persuade, deceive, trick, and corrupt the minds of the American citizens through an arsenal of weapons geared to prevent them from knowing the truth about our current president. I encourage every citizen of the United States of America to vote for President Donald Trump for four more years in November 2020.

President Trump offers and promotes making America great again. I have not seen the Democrats come up with any winning ideas or great solutions; they don't have any real answers for the American citizens other than they are coming for our money with every great brain-storming plan they have like the Green New Deal, universal health care, or universal child care for everyone including illegal immigrants. They want to remove President Trump, who has been a successful president for a great number of American citizens including what he has done to strengthen our economy and provide jobs for every known nationality and ethnicity in the United States.

President Trump knew the real reason the Progressive Socialist Democrats have attacked him and his family throughout his presidency was they are coming for all of us. They want to radically change America into their vision of a socialist utopian society that requires their need to destroy our way of life and our U.S. history.

On the other hand there are radical-thinking Democrats like comedian Bill Maher, of HBO's Real Time who are willing to have America go into a recession in hopes of getting rid of President Trump. The Democrats are desperate for a power grab of our divided country, and they are on the road to being powerfully defeated in November 2020. I hope you see the light regarding what is happening to our country and agree with me. Let's Vote Them Out!!

Crazy-thinking Democrats can produce radical-thinking ideologies which we heard from the Democratic candidates running for president. Far too many young people do not use any real wisdom in their search for a leader. When Lorena and I were in Bogota, Lorena's nephew Mateo shared with me that he loved left-wing documentary filmmaker Michael Moore.

As I look back it now makes perfect sense to me why he loves Michael Moore. In the number of times Lorena and I have traveled to Colombia, I have never watched anything on TV other than CNN; that was their major news source for U.S. and world news. Fox News which is considered a fair, and balanced news source that I listened to in the Pacific Northwest was virtually nonexistent in Bogota, Colombia.

The Progressive Socialist Democrats are ushering in a great evil upon our sitting president. They have been pushing one narrative after another that has been revealed as total fabrications by the Progressive Democrats, and their supporting liberal news sources which Donald Trump calls out as "fake news," and rightly so. If you are a sincere seeker of truth, fact-check any stories you hear on any news outlet CNN, NBC, CBS, ABC regardless of the media source and make absolute certain the story from a Democrat left-wing ideologue is 100 percent factually based and correct. Never assume the storyteller is telling the whole truth, and nothing but the truth for the listeners' sake.

The heart, mind, and soul of this great nation is at stake so be careful how you hear, and interpret what is reported and broadcast on any U.S. or world news television station. The Progressive Socialist Democrats are not about to give President Trump any approval or congratulations for real achievements, success, or well-deserved and vigilant accomplishments such as keeping a careful watch for any potential dangers coming through every entry point of the United States.

I watched ABC News anchor George Stephanopoulos when he interviewed Barack Obama during his presidency. When President Obama said that then-senator John McCain "doesn't know about my Muslim faith," George didn't act as an unbiased interviewer by saying, "Would you care to enlighten the listeners concerning your faith as a Muslim?"

Rather, he interjected what he wanted the listeners to hear by saying, "You mean your Christian faith?" George gave the cue for President Obama to change the subject to the Christian narrative that most Americans were familiar with President Obama quickly said, "Yes, I mean my Christian faith."

This proved to me that George Stephanopoulos, former Demo-cratic political adviser to the Clintons was not an unbiased political commentator. Rush Limbaugh once referred to George Stephanopoulos as George "Step-on-all-of-us." George contributed $75,000 to the Clinton Foundation. There had to be a quid pro quo"a favor or advantage granted or expected in return for something." Left-wing political advisers and journalists know how to reward their own for future favors given directly or indirectly by the same or other Democratic-leaning individuals or groups.

I encourage you to follow the money trail, and pay close attention to every biased reporter and exactly how he or she communicates, and the message of the information they want the listeners to know and believe in order to persuade you that his or her narrative is true. Be especially in tune and critical of what you hear, and be circumspect with regard to the biased reporters trying to sway you to their political persuasion.

I believe George Stephanopoulos knew it was important to continue to conceal the real identity of the former United States president who identified himself as a Muslim on YouTube videos. Also the people of Kenya, Africa know that Obama was born in Kenya. How many American citizens still don't know that? Yet millions of Americans still hold former president Obama in high regard as a great president.

I listened to Michael Savage's radio program before President Obama was elected; Michael referred to Obama as a Socialist Marxist and a revolutionary. After Obama was elected president in 2009 I once again tuned in to Michael Savage's show. He also mentioned that of the thirty-one different types of communism he didn't know where President Obama fit into the mix. I had listened to Michael Savage's radio program on my midweek day off, and the next day I listened again to hear the subject matter he might be talking about this time.

Michael told the listeners that he had an expert on President Obama on his program, and that really got my attention. I heard the authoritative voice of the man who Michael Savage had called an expert give a succinct and concise definition of President Obama, and it clarified what I needed to know for how I should view the president. The expert said, "President Obama is a Neo-Marxist, and he was elected by a Neo-Marxist Media."

After hearing the expert on Savage's radio broadcast describe Obama in a nutshell, whenever I would listen to President Obama give speeches I would listen intently to his words and the content of his typical lengthy speeches. Whatever he would say expert analysts would later reveal to be untrue. President Obama's so-called truths were incorrect, and the opposite of what he had communicated to the American viewers. President Obama was chronically lying to America, but he wanted us to believe that he was telling us the truth. My personal opinion is that President Obama was one of the worst presidents who ever served America from the Oval Office.

Your vote is extremely important. Never underestimate the significance of your individual vote as it is part of the collective vote of the American citizens that will hold the power for the direction of our great country.

I recognize President Donald Trump is not perfect as a man or in all his ways or the decisions he makes. He fully recognizes that the proclamation of the gospel of the Lord Jesus Christ must not be restricted or hindered by House Democrats who do not place a high premium on the proclamation of the gospel of the Lord Jesus which is the good news that the Lord Jesus Christ came this earth, and became a man to die for our sins on the cross of Calvary so that we could have our sins forgiven and be restored to a right relationship with God.

I don't believe that any of the Democrats who were running for president are believers in the Lord Jesus Christ as their personal Savior and Lord. That is a known fact by the things they personally believe, advocate, and share with the American viewers.

Warning: The Progressive Socialist Democrats are not just coming; they are present in the here and now poised to take over the presidential election. President Trump recognizes the Democrats are corrupt, and I'll add that they spell trouble for all American citizens. I encourage you to watch The Death of a Nation by filmmaker Dinesh D'Souza which is a great eye-opener that reveals what the Democrats are up to. He exposes hidden history and truth in a very candid way.

The Progressive Socialist Democrats are mentally and psychologically delusional, and they are very sick individuals with President Trump syndrome. My household will not be voting for a Progressive Socialist Democrat to replace President Trump.

There are far too many baby boomers who were raised by their parents and are still living at home where their moms and dads continue to support them unless they have a job, and contribute towards household expenses and monthly bills. Unfortunately, many of these baby boomers because they've had the comfort of living at home for most of their lives right into adulthood are easily deceived and gullible. They swallow the Progressive Socialist Democrats' rhetoric that they should receive free things as Americans and they adopt this entitlement mentality that only the rich should pay for the things they want in this life.

They don't realize that nothing is free; someone has to pay for what we want except the free gift of eternal life through Jesus Christ. Everyone needs to accept responsibility for the lifestyle they would like to live, and go to work and develop job skills to support themselves instead of depending on their parents' income or some else's.

Jimmy Swaggart once told of a man talking to a crowd of people at a gathering. The man said, "Socialism will put a coat on every man in America."

There happened to be a Christian man in the crowd, and he spoke up saying, "Jesus Christ can put a new heart in every man in America."

I thought that was pretty good that the Christian was willing to speak up. Rather than recognizing what socialism could do for America he brought the focus quickly to the greatness of what Jesus Christ could do for all people in America. Glory to God for all His greatness.

The Lord Jesus said,

"But as the days of Noah were, so also will the coming of the Son of Man be. For as in the days before the flood, they were eating and drinking, marrying and giving in marriage, until the day that Noah entered the ark, and did not know until the flood came and took them all away, so also will the coming of the Son of Man be." (Matthew 24:37–39)

As a Christian if I can't win the lost for Jesus Christ then it is my spiritual duty and responsibility to warn the lost of their eternal destiny either being saved from their sins in Christ Jesus or being separated from an eternal relationship with a loving God and being eternally lost, without love, and hope for all eternity.

I pray that you will make your eternal decision for the Lord Jesus Christ by repenting of your sins, and turning to God with all your heart by faith. Then simply place your faith and trust in Jesus Christ, and what He did for you on the cross of Calvary where He paid your debt of sin that you could not pay yourself. Oh, what a powerful price Jesus Christ paid for your eternal salvation. Now it is up to you to say and believe, "I choose life and blessing by receiving God's free gift of eternal life, and by placing my faith and trust in Jesus Christ who I now make Savior and Lord of my life. Jesus is now my Boss."

I would like to help bring about restoration of the breach and any major divisions among our nation's people at this time. This generation has groups of people that call evil good and good evil. For example in the book of (Isaiah 5:20 God says), "Woe to those who call evil good, and good evil; Who put darkness for light, and light for darkness; Who put bitter for sweet, and sweet for bitter."

I encourage you to watch singer Carman's YouTube video, "America Again." I agree with Carman's lyrics in the chorus of the song if we want to see positive changes in America it will come about when America returns to God in repentance and faith. Carman's powerful video captures the very reasons why we need to have God in America again because America's sins are destroying us from within. The chorus lyrics say, "The only hope for America is Jesus. The only hope for America is Him. If we repent of our ways, stand up and say, we need God in America again."

I encourage you to pray for a mighty revival where we return to God with all our hearts and are reconciled to God, and to one another in a spirit of love, peace, and unity correlating with the

Bible and the Holy Spirit. (2 Chronicles 7:14)

People can get caught up in so many things in this life's journey that started out as a small fantasy. Solomon recognized this: "Catch us the foxes, The little foxes that spoil the vines, For our vines have tender grapes" (Song of Solomon 2:15). As Christian believers it is extremely important to remain faithful in our walk with Jesus Christ and to continue to practice living in the spirit of His Word, for therein we will truly find abundant life in all its fullness and liberty, and we will find the fulfillment we seek.

Solomon also said, "There is a way that seems right to a man {and women}, But its end is the way of death" (Proverbs 14:12). Living in real time, if we are cautious of the devil's devices and are not lost in false teachings, and we continue to take up our faith in the Cross of Calvary regardless of the trials of life and follow after Christ Jesus who is the true vine, and we are the branches we then will be able to bear fruit to the glory of God the Father.

We can't do anything for the Kingdom of God without first being in Him by being born again, wherein Jesus is born in our hearts through the Word of God when we receive Him as Savior and Lord and receive the free gift of eternal life. Then we will know the Lord Jesus Christ is true life and that living for Him will make a positive difference, in and through us, for time and eternity. Only what is done for Jesus Christ will last forever; what is done for this world, devoid of Jesus Christ, will all pass away.

The Lord Jesus said,

"I am the true vine, you are the branches. He who abides in Me, and I in him, bears much fruit; for without Me you can do nothing. If anyone does not abide in Me, he is cast out as a branch and is withered; and they gather them and throw them into the fire, and they are burned. If you abide in Me, and My words abide in you, you will ask what you desire, and it shall be done unto you." (John 15:5–7)

Jesus Christ's promises are powerful and binding. Yes, and amen, to every believer who firmly believes every promise in the book and stands on those promises until he or she sees the fulfillment of God's promises manifested and harvested in their personal hearts and lives. Our gracious Lord God provides His precious promises so that we, as believers, can claim them for ourselves and forever be blessed, in this life and in the next life to come.

I met with a couple of atheists, Benny and Barry, in a local restaurant to have a bite to eat. That particular night, our get-together included other family members, and I had prayed over the meal for us as a group. When I ended the prayer with the name of Jesus, neither atheist raised any objections. In fact, we had a good time sharing with each other since we had all worked for William County Carrier Company, although they both were retired.

Benny had changed his religious beliefs. He'd had faith in Islam but then changed to have faith in Bahai. Eventually, he abandoned both faiths and decided he did not believe in the existence of a supreme being. In essence he believed in self.

Barry, for his own reasons, did not believe in a supreme being we might know as the God of the universe and the Creator of all creatures, small and great, living on the earth. These two atheists had reached a point in their lives where they seemed to be quite content, and pleased with the belief system in which they had come to believe in.

From my perspective I enjoyed talking with them on a number of topics, and there didn't seem to be any conflicts regarding the things we discussed that night, and things we agreed on, but God in the Lord Jesus Christ was not the central theme of our conversation. We didn't speak of the weighty Bible subjects with real-time application, like Bible doctrines regarding the existence of heaven or hell; whether heaven is on this earth or somewhere in the heavenly distant realm; or eschatology, which is the part of theology concerned with death, judgment, and the final destiny of the soul and of humankind.

Barry and Benny had no fear of the Lord in their hearts that I could discern during our evening conversation. (Proverbs 1:7 and 9:10) tells us the fear of the Lord is the beginning of knowledge and of wisdom.

I was listening the radio one day when I heard a man's voice say, "I'd be willing to go to hell for it." My mind hadn't been focused on the radio at that precise moment so I didn't hear what the male speaker was willing to go to hell for. I just recognized there is nothing in this life for which I'd be willing to go to eternal hell, and suffer for all eternity in burning hellfire because of making a decision to go against God's will.

We are living in a generation when it seems so easy for a large number of people to become atheists, agnostics, infidels, and outright unbelievers who would say things like, "I don't believe God even exists," or "I don't know if there really is a God or I believe Jesus was a good man or a good moral philosopher, but I don't believe He was born of a virgin, and that He was God incarnate and died for my sins nearly two thousand years ago."

God's Word says, "But the cowardly, unbelieving, abominable, murderers, sexually immoral, sorcerers, idolaters, and all liars shall have their part in the lake which burns with fire and brimstone, which is the second death" (Revelation 21:8).

To all the people who say, "I'd be willing to go to hell for it," Bud would say, "Talk is cheap."

Spiritual forces are at work that seek to destroy America and the Christian foundation and Biblical principles this nation was founded on. David the psalmist wrote, "If the foundations are destroyed, What can the righteous do?" (Psalm 11:3). These spiritual forces are actually supernatural spirits in high places that use the carnal weapons of the world. They fight by coming against the body of Christian believers that uphold the high standards of God's Kingdom on earth, coming against American citizens, and coming against America's Godly Christian Heritage on which this great nation was established.

There is a spirit of psychology, secular humanism, tolerance, socialism, communism, and compromise in America that has been and is continuing to steal and destroy America from within. Thank God the Bible has the answer for the Christians to use to fight against the evil forces that seek to destroy us, America as a nation, and the freedoms we take for granted in this great country.

"For the weapons of our warfare are not carnal but mighty in God for pulling down strongholds, casting down arguments and every high thing that exalts itself against the knowledge of God, bringing every thought into captivity to the obedience of Christ." (2 Corinthians 10:4–5)

The religion of Islam in America has become a subject of controversy. Some American citizens are suspicious of Muslims living in America because we, as a nation, have been fighting Muslims in Iraq and Afghanistan for years. Other Americans think that the religion of Islam's values are not compatible with American values or Christian values. Bud has studied Islam for years, and he told me that the ancient Egyptian moon goddess is where ISIS gets its name.

I recommend the American-Lebanese author Brigitte Gabriel if you desire to know more about the Islamic faith in America, and whether its beliefs are compatible with Christian and American values. I also recommend author David Barton, if you would like to know more about America's Godly Heritage and America's founding fathers and what they truly believed, and what our founding fathers envisioned for America, if we continue practicing Godly Christian principles in America, or what they might have envisioned if America didn't stay the course of continuing to practice Godly Christian principles in today's society.

So many young people today don't know what true socialism is because they haven't experienced having their property, possessions, and freedoms taken away from them. They are convinced that socialism is a good thing. If these same young adults went to Cuba and Venezuela, and saw firsthand how socialism is really practiced in those countries, I'm certain they would have a change of heart very quickly.

If we, as a nation, continue to tolerate and compromise with the evil spirits of darkness which are corrupting our nation which will destroy us. If we continue to allow them to defile, corrupt our youth, weaken America's freedoms, strong character, and resolve we could lose our unique American exceptionalism which apparently Barack Obama didn't recognize.

America's adults and the next generation growing up in America today must decide which direction we will choose to go in. Will we choose Godly Christian principles and the freedoms of capitalism and the free market enterprise system that President Trump firmly practices and believes in or will we choose a loss of our freedoms, and follow a pathway of socialism that Bernie Sanders or Elizabeth Warren practices and believes in?

America's Democratic base of young and old are facing a big decision and so are the Republicans and Independents, young people and older people, with the next presidential election. The power of the critical decision is in your hands to prevent the next presidential election from being stolen again in 2024.

As a nation, we must stop allowing major divisions that prevent us from being wholly united as a country. In concept or in theory, we may be divided and have different opinions and beliefs, but convictions are what we as individuals are willing to die for. America must persevere and have the resolve and determination to know and take the right course of action in voting for the right person for the presidency, and remember the things we most treasure and value as Americans.

Whether we like to think about it or not, God's Word says, "So then each of us shall give an account of himself to God" (Romans 14:12). Those who choose not to believe in Him who the Heavenly Father sent into the world will face the judgment on that final day. God Himself will be the judge, sitting on the great white throne on that day. I encourage you to make absolutely certain your name has been written down and recorded in the Lamb's Book of Life (Revelation 20:11–15).

"He who believes in the Son of God has the witness in himself; he who does not believe God has made Him a liar, because he has not believed the testimony that God has given of His Son." (1 John 5:10)

"And this is the testimony: that God has given us eternal life, and this life is in His Son. He who has the Son has life; he who does not have the Son of God does not have life. These things have I written to you who believe in the name of the Son of God, that you may know that you have eternal life, and that you may continue to believe in the name of the Son of God." (1 John 5:11–13)

For He says: "In an acceptable time I have heard you, And in the day of salvation I have helped you. Behold, now if the accepted time; behold, now is the day of salvation." (2 Corinthians 6:2)

God's commands and laws, as recorded in His Holy Bible are critically important for us to follow, as the rules of life and death lay before us on our spiritual journey with Him. For God says,

"We know that whoever is born of God does not sin; but he who has been born of God keeps himself, and the wicked one does not touch him. We know that we are of God, and the whole world lies under the sway of the wicked one. And we know that the Son of God has come and has given us an understanding, that we may know Him who is true; and we are in Him who is true, in His Son Jesus Christ. This is the true God and eternal life. Little children, keep yourselves from idols. Amen." (1 John 5:18–21)

I hope you can spiritually understand that God's great and precious promises are for whoever may come and experience the Son of God. The Lord Jesus, in all His splendor and glory, will be resurrected in your heart and life if you will surrender your life to Him right now. The transformation will begin to grow in your heart and life, and it will develop into something beautiful that He will work out in His time. Trust and obey, believe Him, and say, "I believe; I believe God."

Radio broadcaster Paul Harvey once told of a man who couldn't understand the incarnation of Jesus Christ His becoming a man, someone the churches talk about around Christmas. I recommend listening to this great Christmas story titled "The Man and the Birds." It's only five minutes and thirty-eight seconds long, and Paul Harvey beautifully narrates the story about the man who decided not to go with his wife and family to church on Christmas Eve. He remained home to read his newspaper. The man heard thuds against his large landscape window, and when he opened his front door he found birds on the ground in the snow.

The man tried to lead the birds into his lighted barn by shooing them, and leaving bread crumbs on the ground so they might find warmth and shelter but to no avail. He finally had a revelation if only he could become a bird, they might follow him into the barn. And when he heard the church bells ringing in the distance, he then sank to his knees in the snow.

This beautiful story needs to be heard every Christmas so everyone might come to believe in the incarnation of the Lord Jesus Christ, and how He came into this world so all humankind might come to know Him, the true God, and eternal life. (John 1:12–14; 1 John 5:20).

Lorena and I both opted to have surgery with Dr. Raymond Rockwell in Los Angeles. It was Lorena's first time to have surgery with Dr. Rockwell. I decided to have a chin revision, hoping to have my left side of my chin evenly matched with the right side. Dr. Rockwell's surgical procedure included placing a silicone device under the left side of my chin to augment my chin so it looked more evenly balanced with the right side. My chin swelled up post-surgery due to the surgical procedure, and I hoped the swelling would disappear before Lorena and I left for Bogota, two and a half months later. Unfortunately, not all the swelling in my chin had subsided within that time. The silicone object inserted under my chin covered a portion under my left jaw area and gave the unsightly appearance of a protruding tumor.

During the three-week vacation to Colombia, Lorena told me that family members and friends of the family were wondering what I had inside my good-looking face. Lorena informed them that a medical doctor had placed something in there, and he was going to remove it when I went back home. It was not in my cosmetic interest to have a protruding device appearing under one side of my chin to provide me with an unevenly balanced chin. Lorena agreed with me that I should have the necessary corrective surgery to remove the hard silicone device that Dr. Rockwell had put under my chin.

Dr. Rockwell had mentioned that he couldn't figure out why my first doctor had put screws in my chin since the procedure he did was a routine chin implant. When I thought on the matter, I couldn't recall that Dr. Smith or Dr. Cutter mentioned putting screws into my jaw for any medical or cosmetic reason. I began to suspect that Dr. Cutter had possibly put the screws into my jaw as a way to let me know that I had been "screwed" by the malicious medical doctor. I knew that Dr. Thadeaus Damon Cutter had truly victimized me, but I was not in a position to say that Dr. Cutter was the doctor who had placed the screws into my chin.

Later, when I decided to pursue a valid answer to my nagging suspicions concerning Dr. Cutter, Dr. Rockwell provided me a more logical explanation that put my inquisitive mind to rest. Dr. Rockwell said that although he didn't have the old pre-op reports regarding my chin implant, so he didn't know who had done the procedure, he knew that whoever did the first chin implant would have broken my chinbone to slide it forward known as an osteotomy, and then would have put in a screw to hold it in place.

Dr. Rockwell's explanation made perfect sense, but I had been hoping to hear that he suspected the second doctor put the screw or screws in place; that would have clearly pointed back to Dr. Cutter as the real culprit. I had good reason to suspect Dr. Cutter with fraud regarding my chin, along with the work on my nose and ears, but I was willing to listen to Dr. Rockwell, a cosmetic expert who knew the procedures and medical terms.

Later, I was able to locate the pre-op report at home, and I sent a copy to Dr. Rockwell. He now had the pre-op report as evidence that Dr. Cutter had put the screws in my chin, the evidence I had wondered about which showed that Dr. Cutter had been the medical doctor who put the screws in my chin. I thought to myself, I was literally screwed by Dr. Cutter, and I took it on the chin.

I was able to find Dr. Cutter's release of records, including an operation report for me. I read:

Once the horizontal cut had been completed, the chin distal fragment was advanced forward. An Osteomed bone plate using a 10 mm chin plate was adapted to create a 9 mm advancement graft of the chin and secured with four 6 mm screws. Care was taken to keep the midline in the correct position.

I planned to send the operation report to Dr. Raymond Rockwell for his own medical information. For me, this was verification that Dr. Cutter had put the screws into my chin; it was in Dr. Cutter's medical operation report.

I discovered firsthand that history has a way of repeating itself. When I thought back to my experience as a teenager when I was at bat against a future major league baseball pitcher named Gary Holland, even though I could see a white streak hurtling toward me, it was like a blind man looking for a black cat in a dark room that wasn't there. My experience with Dr. Cutter was like a repeat of not beating the competition. At the time, I didn't realize I was competing with Dr. Cutter. My experience with him was once again, like I was a blind man looking for a black cat in a dark room that wasn't there. I simply was no competition for the two people I faced in both situations.

No patient wants or expects to go through the horrifying cosmetic experiences that I went through; I dare to say that not even Dr. Cutter himself would. I am convinced that Dr. Cutter, with the conniving approach that he took against me knew that he had hurt an innocent cosmetic patient because he didn't have the specialized training that was necessary. Based on Dr. Cutter's actions pre-and post-surgeries, I know that he realized the surgical damages that he had inflicted on my mind, nose, and ears. For this reason, I know beyond a shadow of a doubt that Dr. Cutter didn't try to contend with the licensing boards to continue practicing cosmetic surgeries on patients who had more than one surgery on their noses and ears.

If Dr. Cutter would volunteer to have a cosmetic surgeon, with primary skills in cosmetic surgery and secondary skills in plastic surgery, work on his nose and ears after he had undergone numerous surgeries on his nose and ears, would he consider that equal treatment and being fair-handed for what I underwent post-surgeries? Or would he consider facing a nonspecialized cosmetic surgeon after having multiple surgeries on his physical characteristics an unfair deal and a more accurate description of cosmetic crimes of a deranged, delusional, and psychotic medical doctor?

It is obvious to me that Dr. Cutter didn't expect, care, or consider that post-surgeries I would Wake Up from his horrifying cosmetic nightmare and decide to pursue a maximum course of action by complaining to his licensing boards which holds his medical and dental licenses to be revoked, and that the licensing boards would totally revoke his medical and dental licenses for his sinister criminal actions taken against me.

I truly believe Dr. Cutter optimistically predicted in his twisted psychotic mind and hoped I would pursue a lawsuit against him which would result in a total failure, and I would appear as a complete imbecile, idiot, and mentally incapacitated thereby having a short circuited memory of anything other than what he had stated to me in an unconscious or altered mental state in his pre-surgeries dim lit room. I believe he falsely assumed I would not be mentally able to function as a normal person and be hyper suggestable and programmable if he had spoken any words to me through his defense attorney to cause me to accept as his so called truth and relinquish, succumb, and concede that I was wrong in my assumptions and he was 100% right in performing cosmetic surgeries with his dental specialty as a DDS on a multiple surgery patient. I am certain that Dr. Cutter expected for me to be like Pavlov's dog.

I believe that Dr. Cutter expected for me to be delusional in my post-surgeries thinking, and he believed that he could control me, a subdued patient who was mentally not all there. Dr. Cutter discovered however, that I still had certain mental faculties remaining that came back to haunt him in his cosmetic practice.

It is obvious to me that Dr. Cutter didn't expect, care, or consider that post-surgeries I would Wake Up from his horrifying cosmetic nightmare and decide to pursue a maximum course of action by complaining to his licensing boards which holds his medical and dental licenses to be revoked, and that the licensing boards would totally revoke his medical and dental licenses for his sinister criminal actions taken against me which they never did. This applies to all patients who have been or currently being victimized worldwide.

I am convinced that Dr. Cutter moved out of town to distance himself from his cosmetic crimes that he committed against me, and other unsuspecting patients. He has made victims of his patients, and he covered it up by putting distance between him and his victims.

A day of reckoning is coming for every power-tripping medical doctor who is willing to abuse, exploit, and victimize unsuspecting patients, if not in this world, then on judgment day when they meet God as their judge. I say, "Let Justice Prevail."

I sent in my first series of complaints to the different medical boards with which Dr. Cutter was licensed. In my first complaint letter, I said that I had trusted that Dr. Cutter could do what I wanted him to do, which he hadn't. I was so horribly traumatized, devastated, and agonizingly cosmetically violated that when it came to sending in my complaints over a number of years after my surgeries, I still hadn't fully comprehended the total magnitude of Dr. Cutter's incalculable damages to my total person.

I realize now that Dr. Cutter completely destroyed any trust in my soul when he boldly took charge of my cosmetic destiny without my consent or understanding, and he helped himself with his attack on my mind, nose, and ears for which he had no specialization. It has been a long, painful process for me to exist in a world where people are judged on the basis of whether they physically meet the world's standards of acceptance, approval, and success.

I contacted Arnold Richards, chief investigator of MQAC, and asked if I could find out how long the medical board and the investigation unit had kept my case open against Dr. Cutter. "How could I find that information?"

"It went to the archives of the state," he told me. "You can find that information through public disclosure."

I cordially thanked him and hung up the phone. I waited a short while and then called back, hoping to speak to a different representative who might give me the information I was seeking. The woman who answered the phone on my second call transferred me to another representative, who in turn transferred me to Arnold, chief investigator.

Arnold said, in no uncertain terms, "I already told you what you need to do. You can find the information through public disclosure. I don't want you talking to my staff, trying to get information from them. I've already told them not to respond to you. We're willing to work with you, but you need to find what you're looking for through public disclosure."

By the sound of Arnold's determined tone of voice, I realized I had pushed his buttons by talking to his staff. I didn't know I was talking to Arnold's staff members when I called the second time. I'd just hoped someone could give me the information I wanted over the phone, instead of my waiting for state personnel to search for my files that now were in the state archives. Arnold's rebuke over the phone made it clear I'd made a nuisance of myself by calling the MQAC too many times over the years. I also realize that I was suffering from post-surgeries trauma for years, resulting from Dr. Cutter's abusive actions against me.

Arnold had reminded me that the necessary information was not in his office, but in the state archives. I didn't need Arnold's overbearing, irritated, authoritarian attitude when I called back. I wasn't pushy with the representative I spoke with. The emphasis should not have been on me being persistent about finding answers, but on their losing patience with me and how they failed to take corrective action against Dr. Cutter. My persistence over the years was prompted by their lack of action against the sinister medical doctor. Arnold's attitude showed me however, that he and his staff did not care about people in my predicament. I thanked Arnold a second time and hung up the phone.

From my perspective I believe the medical boards were involved in a massive cover up.

I know that Dr. Cutter committed crimes against me, not based on a sad case of hypochondria, mere speculation, or guesswork, but based on experiential knowledge, Dr. Cutter's own admission, eyewitness accounts, hard-hitting negative experiences, and hard evidence. I realize that God knows, the devil knows, Dr. Cutter knows, and I now know that Dr. Cutter committed medical malpractice crimes against me. And now the entire world knows that the Dr. Cutters by various names in different places all over the world, by their own track records, consistently violate and victimize unsuspecting cosmetic patients.

Just as it is in the animal kingdom, if one is viewed as weak, odd, strange, or abnormal, it is picked on or rejected by the rest of the group. Psychology and evolution agree with this because they promote it. But God's Word is very clear that the problem abides in the fallen human nature that began in the Garden of Eden. I have experienced the coldness of social rejection by the general public, and I am convinced that it was largely caused by the cruel, criminal, and immoral actions of a malicious cosmetic surgeon disguised as a medical doctor.

Dr. Cutter wanted to express the desires of the god of this world's fallen system toward my facial characteristics, according to his own specifications, and prove to me and the general public that he could tear down and rebuild my physical features to my original specifications, as detailed in my post-surgery desired-results notes, which I don't know if he had copied for himself.

The god of this world's system is the devil, according to The Holy Bible, and I now realize how Dr. Cutter committed his crimes against me on the day of my surgeries. I was talking to my counselor, Norman Dodson, and he shared with me that he had learned in his counseling training to conduct instant hypnotism on another person. I knew that I wasn't delusional in my thinking about what I had experienced at the hands of Dr. Cutter.

I wondered for years why a medical doctor would move out of his specialization of dentistry, and perform surgery on my nose and ears without any specialization in the nose and ears. Dr. Cutter was so in love with himself that he wanted to play God with my facial characteristics. It started as a fantasy in his mind, and ended up as a horrible cosmetic travesty for me.

The reason why Dr. Cutter hadn't connected with me, pre-and post-surgeries, was for him to play out his cosmetic fantasies with my physical characteristics. Law officials will acknowledge that many crimes start out as a fantasy in the minds of the criminal, and then are acted out in real-life situations that end in the victimization of an unsuspecting person. This explains why I didn't have any understanding of Dr. Cutter's change in plans on the day of my surgeries and why I heard Dr. Cutter say, while I was coming to on the operating table, "You're going to like it."

The last thing I thought about before blanking out on the day of my surgeries was Dr. Cutter saying, "Well, I better go about building up the bridge."

As I went into unconsciousness I thought, why didn't he tell me that up front?

I am persuaded in my own mind that Dr. Cutter committed his crimes against me to prove to himself, as well as to any doctor I might see afterward and to the general public, that he could tear down the previous doctors' work on my nose, ears, and chin, and rebuild them to my satisfaction just as a traumatized victim would be satisfied with the results of a shark attack on his or her amputated or mutilated body part.

Apparently, the review boards had to wait for me to realize that I didn't have any understanding of what Dr. Cutter intended to do to me during my surgeries before they would take action against Dr. Cutter. Provided I am correct on my assumption mentioned above.

Dr. Cutter should be included in the United States', and the international community's Dumbest Criminals list because he gloated about victimizing me. Loose lips sink ships, and had Dr. Cutter presented himself to me as a caring medical doctor, post surgeries, he would have been able to cloak his crimes. But Dr. Cutter couldn't resist gloating about his victory over me by saying, "See it as a sculpture. I tore it down, beat it up, and built it back up." I never said in my desired-results notes, of which Dr. Cutter had a copy, that I wanted him to tear down the previous doctors' work and rebuild it. The results of Dr. Cutter's cosmetic hacking have not gone unnoticed by the general public, who have shunned me.

I have seen my counselor, Norman Dodson for a number of years, primarily to deal with the aftermath of my experiences with Dr. Cutter. Norman identified Dr. Cutter as a con artist, similar to a stereotypical used-car salesman, who gets slicker and slicker.

Norman said, "Since you never encountered that, you didn't know what hit you. Since you're not a con artist, you don't think like a con artist. You have a hard time identifying it. So it really catches you off guard, like a slick car salesman."

During one of our counseling sessions, Norman used the word rape in reference to Dr. Cutter's actions against me.

I could identify with what Norman described, and I shared with him that I was affected mentally by my experience.

"How were you affected mentally?" Norman asked.

"I could feel the pressure in my brain," I said. "I felt like I had mental blocks, preventing me from remembering certain things that I had experienced. I think Dr. Cutter's cosmetic plans were literally shoved up into my brain, but they became elusive to me when recollecting in detail what actually happened on the day of my surgeries."

Norman said, "You had difficulty retrieving memories."

I reminded Norman that as I was waking up after surgery, I heard Dr. Cutter say, "You're going to like it."

"Those words were a mental suggestion that Dr. Cutter gave you," Norman said.

I also reiterated that Dr. Cutter had said, "Well, I better go about building up the bridge," and I had wondered why he hadn't told me that up front.

This was when Norman mentioned he had learned hypnosis during his educational training. The participants had practiced the technique on each other during the training.

I know that Dr. Cutter used hypnosis on me before my surgeries, which led to the irreparable cosmetic damages to my nose and ears.

I've mentioned that I read in Katharine A. Phillips's book The Broken Mirror, which deals with body dysmorphic disorder or BDD, a mental illness involving obsessive focus on a perceived flaw in appearance. Patients with BDD don't want to be seen by other people. They have acute feelings of being rejected by others because of their physical appearance. Many people who suffer from BDD have minor physical flaws, but they avoid human contact because of a fear of being rejected; they want to hide from an often cynical public, so they stay at home most of the time.

I am all too aware of this painful disorder, which can steal, kill, and destroy a person's relationships with fellow human beings. BDD can hold its victims in an agonizing grip of mental and emotional bondage. Other people make them feel self-conscious and fearful of being seen. I have worked at isolating myself from most of my neighbors because I don't want to be seen due to the cosmetic damages caused by Dr. Cutter. I have suffered needlessly in my personal, social, and professional relationships because of the predatory actions of one cosmetic shyster who used mental trickery and thuggery on me when I was seeking only subtle reconstructive work by a board-certified plastic surgeon.

I cried as I drove my shuttle route out to Fedora Fair with a carrier half full of passengers. My horrible disfigurement caused by Dr. Cutter, combined with my mental and emotional suffering, had made me reach another breaking point in my life. My devastating experience with the ruthless and malicious cosmetic surgeon was something I didn't need in my life, but I had to deal with the abusive victimization by Dr. Cutter on a daily basis.

I wish I could have held back the tears that rolled down my cheeks during my drive, but I found myself thinking about my unnecessary, hurtful cosmetic experiences; and some customers could see my grief. I was overcome with grief and sadness from the social rejection by the general public, which made me feel that I was unacceptable and unlovely, even though I was accepting but businesslike to them when they entered my coach.

I am saddened when I think of all the victims who painfully suffer throughout the world because of certain medical doctors who are pursuing narcissistic power and greed for filthy lucre.

God's Word says, "For the love of money is the root of all kinds of evil, for which some have strayed from the faith in their greediness, and pierced themselves through with many sorrows." (1 Timothy 6:10)

Psychotherapy uses hypnosis, and many professionals have learned psychotherapy and use it in their various fields of endeavor. I am convinced that Dr. Cutter wanted to see what he could get away with when he decided to pull off his cosmetic heist against me. I am convinced that Dr. Cutter used his cosmetic practice as a surgical weapon to deceive me, and the end result proved to me that Dr. Cutter was not a board-certified plastic surgeon. Dr. Cutter showed me by actual demonstration that he could use hypnosis on my mind to cosmetically serve up a counterfeit interpretation on my nose and ears.

To me, Dr. Cutter's actions provided convincing evidence that he was not a plastic surgeon. Because of his narcissistic tendencies, Dr. Cutter quickly moved me to cosmetic surgeries on my nose, ears, and chin, only to force painful devastating cosmetic changes on my face. Dr. Cutter then forced the plastic surgeon who would perform any revision work on me to make his own professional evaluation as to whether his cosmetic work were crimes or simply a misinterpretation or a misapplication of the surgeon's cosmetic agenda.

You might remember that my friend Lynn and I wanted to see a martial arts demonstration, but as it turned out, a Tae Kwon Do nine-time grandmaster actually demonstrated on Lynn which I had witnessed. I compare that experience to Dr. Cutter demonstrated his cosmetic techniques on me by tearing down the previous doctors' work on my nose and ears, and starting from scratch to rebuild them into something that I didn't want, need, or expect. Dr. Cutter clearly was a power-tripping, delusional cosmetic surgeon in love with himself, which is why he dared to try such bold cosmetic procedures on a multiple-surgery patient like me.

It is pathetic to think of all the unsuspecting patients who have been seriously hurt, abused, and victimized by unrecognized cosmetic surgeons over the years. Many victimized patients would have self-destructed into a world of drugs and alcohol if they had gone through what I have endured since my surgeries in the nineties. Most people would not be able to endure the social rejection by the general public, and by their colleagues in their work environment. Many, it's sad to say may resort to suicide with such a disadvantage and being cut off from the road to successful living.

I wanted to be fair in my evaluation of Dr. Cutter, who never took the time from my initial consultation with him to our third consultation to properly interpret my cosmetic blueprint. He was too obsessed with gaining my business to slow down, and appropriately interpret what I wanted and needed from him. I'm convince he knew what I wanted and needed cosmetically, but he was too absorbed with demonstrating his own cosmetic agenda which clashed with what I desired.

Dr. Cutter wanted to replace the image I had for my nose and ears with his own cosmetic agenda. The results were painfully scary for me.

I recommend that health departments, medical boards, and investigators throughout the country place a security check against unrecognized medical professionals, but they also need to communicate fully to the victims of medical malpractice, verbally and in writing the steps to resolve the tragedy of their victimization so that the victims are fully compensated both physically and financially. To do anything less is to dishonor the very reason that the health departments, medical boards, and investigators exist in the first place. I also recommend that representatives from the health departments and medical boards contact the victims and personally help assist them in filling out all the necessary paperwork correctly in order to be fully compensated by the victimizing party.

They should not simply wait until the victims have provided the detailed information if they can remember everything that happened to them, and eventually work through their horrible victimization. If the physical evidence of cosmetic surgery is such that other doctors do not judge it as good, normal, or quality cosmetic results then there needs to be an immediate criminal investigation into the surgeon's practice. The victim should not have to undergo years of counseling or listen to psychobabble in order to be financially compensated and have physical damages corrected.

Bud and I advocate and urgently appeal that the United States of America Supreme Court, and Congress to pass laws guaranteeing the right of Christians witnessing and prayers made to Father God in Jesus Christ's name, by Christians for the salvation and healing of patients and residents in hospitals, nursing homes, convalescent centers, and hospices. Eternal hell is easy to get into, but impossible to escape from or get out of.

We don't like to hear that people went into burning hell because the professional staff were prohibited by state laws against anyone wanting to share, witness, or pray for patients that need to hear the good news of the gospel of Jesus Christ crucified for them that they can have eternal life through their faith placed in Jesus Christ's precious shed blood on the Cross of Calvary, as the perfect Lamb Of God. Every patient deserves a chance to receive salvation instead of passing away into eternity, and ending up in burning hell fire eternally banned from the eternal presence of God.

Heaven is a beautiful place of harmony of love, joy, and peace in the presence of God, and for all those who have accepted Jesus Christ as their Savior and Lord prior to their spirits leaving their bodies. May the Holy Spirit rest and move on the hearts, souls, and spirits of those that pass anti-Christian laws and everyone that read these words.

My friend Tommy Ray is a survivor of abuse by an alcoholic father, and he has written a book titled, No More. Tommy discovered lot of horrifying abuse cases concerning children in the United States, and he saw the serious need to raise the consciousness level of every public citizen who is outraged by abuse and victimization of little ones throughout our wonderful country and blessed by a loving God.

Tommy has talked to me about the horrible victimization that is taking place in America by unrecognized medical doctors who abuse their positions of trust, and victimize innocent unsuspecting patients with medical abuse. Tommy thinks that from the medical board's position, it would take a lot more than a victimized carrier driver like me to bring down a medical doctor, who is one of their own, committing cosmetic abuses and cosmetic crimes against the trusting public.

I know I had better have my facts straight before accusing a medical doctor like Dr. Cutter. I am not just convinced Dr. Cutter committed cosmetic crimes against me. I know that I was victimized by an unrecognized cosmetic surgeon, and I am a survivor of cosmetic crimes that he committed against me.

I had legitimate fears and concerns that because Dr. Cutter, MD DDS, seriously victimized and hurt me, if he was not stopped by the medical boards he would continue to hurt other unsuspecting patients.

My brother, Daniel left a message for me on my answering machine saying that David Boze, a conservative talk show host, was talking about a medical doctor named Thomas Laney who had lost a patient. Dr. Laney was a practicing dentist in Moses Lake, Washington and a cosmetic surgeon. Daniel knew that I would be interested in a case about a cosmetic surgeon who had a dental board license just like Dr. Cutter.

I listened intently as David share with his listening audience. "Dr. Laney would have to be a genius, or something wasn't right with him, having different boards like that."

David had mentioned that there was an article about Dr. Laney in the Seattle Post Intelligencer newspaper dated Monday, November 10th, 2008. I was able to get a copy of the article from a kindhearted passenger since I didn't take the paper myself.

I read the well-written article by investigative reporter Vanessa Ho, which stated the following:

The [Post Intelligencer] found that Laney was doing full-body cosmetic surgeries without having done a residency or fellowship in the subject. Instead, Laney trained through sporadic classes. His surgeries led to many malpractice lawsuits and complaints with the state.

The entire article was fascinating, as it described the lawsuit against the dentist and oral surgeon, Dr. Laney including his botched breast reduction surgery performed on a woman when she was fifteen. After reading Vanessa's sad report about the woman, who claimed Dr. Laney disfigured her during breast surgery, I contacted the Collard Library to ask the reference librarian if Dr. Laney had been featured in the Seattle Post Intelligencer or the Seattle Times before the November 10th, newspaper article in the PI.

The reference librarian suggested that I go online to http://www.seattlepi.com/ and type in "Dr. Laney" in a search. As a result, I found another article written by another investigative reporter, Michelle Nicolosi. Her well-written, researched, and informative article told of the death of David Scott Kelley. His death in 2000 was a consequence of his cosmetic surgery in Dr. Laney's office.

Based upon the second article it seemed clear that Dr. Laney's training was rather questionable: "Like many practitioners now performing cosmetic surgery," the article read, "Laney did not get medical school, residency or fellowship training to do many of the cosmetic procedures he now performs."

Dr. Laney was trained as an oral surgeon, and completed a dual-degree program that gave him both a medical and a dental degree. For the most part, he said he learned below-the-neck cosmetic surgeries in weekend and weeklong courses held around the country sometimes in surgical suites and sometimes in hotel rooms where demonstrations were done on cadavers.

I was particularly fascinated with one paragraph under the subheading, "Death cases closed quietly," which stated the following:

Laney said he does have a "high" number of lawsuits, but said that "goes with the territory" when you're dealing with patients with high expectations, and with area doctors who are disgruntled that you're working in an arena they consider their territory doctors who in some cases urged patients to sue. "Regrettably, litigation is typical and expected in this type of work," he wrote in a response to questions. Laney said his number of lawsuits is "near the industry standard." See Dr. Laney's complete written response.

When I read Dr. Laney's responses to the questions he was asked, it gave me the impression that Laney had a cavalier attitude about the high number of lawsuits he had dealt with. To me, Laney's answers clearly revealed that he was in competition with better-trained and more-skilled medical doctors, and he wanted to physically demonstrate that his cosmetic skills were just as qualified as his medical competitors. I could see that Dr. Laney's delusional thinking had caused him to place himself into an arena of surgically victimized, seriously hurting, and devastated unsuspecting patients' lives.

In my evaluation, he was a delusional power-tripper, and a cosmetic surgeon who should be stopped from practicing cosmetic surgeries by the medical boards immediately. How many Dr. Laneys and Dr. Cutters is the medical boards going to allow to butcher unsuspecting patients?

If Dr. Laney is in any way like Dr. Cutter, then the general public is in grave danger of being cosmetically victimized, irreparably physically damaged, and exploited financially. I discovered that the MQAC deals primarily with licensing of medical doctors and not with medical specialties issues. My experience with making my complaints against Dr. Cutter was that I didn't feel that I was taken seriously by the medical review boards and the investigation unit.

I understand now that if the medical boards don't take disciplinary or termination action against a medical doctor within the first two years after you lodge a complaint, then you will be pleading your case to deaf ears to groups who see things entirely differently than what you know to be true. The policies need to be changed to fully protect the patients' care so that there will never be another victim of a medical doctor out to advance his or her professional career, and pad his or her financial coffers at the patients' expense. There are real people, like me, who are being victimized by unrecognized medical doctors that the medical boards must stop now.

The evidence demands a verdict by the legislators in Olympia, Washington, the MQAC in Olympia, the William County Medical Society in Union, and the Oral Maxillofacial Surgery Commission in Chicago, Illinois, that there is a medical doctor who is mentally delusional on their licensing boards. He is not adequately trained to do the cosmetic surgeries that his professional colleagues do, as they are better trained and superior in their medical specialties and have the board certification to sufficiently support their surgical skills.

The Dr. Cutters of the world are willing to surgically proceed, and practice carving on unsuspecting patients without having a medical specialty in plastic surgery and reconstructive surgery. This can be very scary for the patient when his cosmetic interests are botched by a medical doctor who led him to believe that the doctor was a medical specialist. Then, post-surgery, after he is physically disfigured he learns that the doctor who surgically worked on him was not listed on any of the twenty-four boards of medical specialties.

This clearly is a strong case for stricter surgical guidelines of qualified surgeons, with excellent judgment of their medical training and surgical skills, and limitations in light of their board-or non-board-certified status. The laws need to be changed to protect the general public by requiring that the doctor provide his or her medical history to all his or her patients of every surgery botched due to a lack of medical specialties board certification.

I contacted Patricia Walters at the MQAC, who was the person I needed to go through to send in a letter requesting a reconsideration by the medical review board of my closed case against Dr. Cutter. Patricia was the program manager who became acting deputy executive director of the MQAC. She informed me that they had been in the process of moving to a new building, and the commission would not be revisiting an issue that the commission closed some time ago.

"It's been standard procedure for some time," she said, "that the commission doesn't review cases for reconsideration after a year or two. If you have new issues in regard to Dr. Cutter, you can submit the new issues, but for something that happened so long ago, I don't feel they would accept your request for a reconsideration at this time. I assure you however, that the commission reviewed your case thoroughly."

She further informed me that she no longer dealt with the disciplinary work, as she had a new position with the MQAC. I thought it was particularly interesting that Patricia also told me that there were orders based on my previous letters that they were not to respond to me anymore because apparently I had contacted the MQAC far too many times in my quest for answers and wanting them to take action against Dr. Cutter.

I received my final letter from Patricia Walters, informing me that the commission would not be reopening my case against Dr. Cutter for reconsideration. I was not terribly surprised or disheartened by the final verdict by the MQAC. I know the medical review board, and the investigation unit made a huge mistake when they didn't take disciplinary or termination action against Dr. Cutter in my individual case.

I have decided not to send the MQAC any more requests for a reconsideration hearing of my case against Dr. Cutter. I'm going to let them find the additional information in this book.

The verdict did not deter me from going forward with our book so that the readers may benefit from my troubling victimization. I don't just believe I was victimized by Dr. Cutter; I know for a 100-percent fact that I was. I can appreciate that the medical review board heard my second complaint for reconsideration, but they need to change their policy to allow the patient to fully figure out what happened to him or her, which may take years, and never close the doors to each hurting patient until they solve each individual case of victimization by a medical doctor especially if the medical doctor is not recognized by any specialty board, such as the American Board of Plastic Surgery and the American Board of Medical Specialties.

I also contacted Carrie Barkley, the deputy executive director of the MQAC in Olympia. I asked her why the MQAC would allow unrecognized medical doctors to perform surgeries on multiple-surgery patients. I shared with Carrie the story of a medical doctor who advertised as an American Board of Cosmetic Surgery surgeon, which is a made-up board not recognized by the American Board of Plastic Surgery or the American Board of Oral Maxillofacial Surgery. "His specialties are in dentistry," I told her.

Carrie gave me the same answer that Dr. Cutter's receptionist had given to my co-worker, Denise years earlier: "There are a lot of boards out there." She didn't provide me a good explanation why unrecognized cosmetic surgeons should be recognized as qualified medical doctors to conduct surgical procedures on multiple-surgery patients.

"Would you like to talk to a medical doctor concerning this matter?" Carrie asked, and I answered, yes.

A short time later, a medical doctor at the MQAC told me the same thing that Carrie had said to me: "There are a lot of boards out there."

Dr. Cutter and other unrecognized medical doctors are exploiting the medical boards' lax policy guidelines regarding cosmetic procedures on multiple-surgery patients, which should be performed only by certified American Board of Plastic Surgery surgeons. Without a change in policy, surgeries will remain too scary to contemplate for the trusting patients who desire cosmetic specialty work.

I know that I was stonewalled from the beginning regarding my complaints against Dr. Cutter.

I did my level best to bring my complaints to the various medical review boards against Dr. Cutter, but I was met with cold, apathetic responses from the medical boards and the investigation unit reviewing my case. I was a multiple-surgery cosmetic bonanza for Dr. Cutter, but it was at my expense.

It doesn't matter how long my botched surgeries were ignored by the authorities. My complaints against Dr. Cutter should have never been closed; they should have been earnestly pursued until my case was dealt with by the medical boards resulting in the correct judgment and resolution. I have discovered to my agony that the proper authorities in the medical community are not willing to budge from their complacency when it comes to allowing surgeons to practice by medical doctors who have other board certifications that are not recognized by the American Board of Plastic Surgery and the American Board of Medical Specialties.

These doctors show by their track records that they do not qualify to be recognized by the specialized boards through proper residency training to recognize each patient's cosmetic interests with precision detailed work with perfection and excellence. The above mentioned fact is worse than scary!!

I know that Dr. Cutter had neither board certification mentioned, and I know that I was a victim of a malicious medical doctor who took advantage of my naïveté when it came to his lack of recognized board certification which I expected and needed.

I contacted a woman named Beatrice Carlson, a staff member knowledgeable in plastic and cosmetic procedures, who listened patiently as I explained in detail, the precarious and dangerous cosmetic ordeal I'd gone through with Dr. Cutter. I asked if she could answer my question of why the medical boards did not restrict medical doctors from performing multiple-surgery procedures without a board certification from the American Board of Plastic Surgery or the ABMS.

Beatrice gave me a list of relevant points that someone could use to find the right surgeon, but she said, "I don't feel that I can answer your question because there are different boards that have different requirements, and there are many of them out there that overlap one another and others that don't. You have to do a lot of checking and rechecking. You have to ask a lot of specific questions about training, experience, who does the doctor's certification, and how many surgeries the medical doctor you are considering has done. Your questions are huge policy questions, way beyond the scope of my office, but I think you could start by contacting the American Board of Medical Specialties."

I have already done so.

I heard on the news of a military instructor who had been training soldiers for forty years on how to survive on the battlefield when facing the enemy. I listened intently to the news reporter, who said that the instructor tells the troops he is training to have faith in God. I was impressed with the leader's advice on how to survive when you're facing full-fledged combat with an enemy that wants to kill you.

I want to pass on the same good advice to readers who have experienced hurtful, painful, and devastating cosmetic surgeries, which have been so destructive and a major setback to your dreams of a better-looking new you, and which have led to unforeseen cosmetic-related physical damages. Have faith in God, and do your very best to remain positive, with supportive, faithful, and loyal friends and family who love and care about you personally. Look on the bright side of life, and be a positive contributor to all those around you.

I am a survivor of sinister cosmetic crimes, scam, and heist. I have decided that I would like to move from "Victimized, USA" to "Justification City, USA."

I now realize that encountering the wrong medical doctor is hazardous to your mental, emotional, and physical health. Corrective cosmetic revisions can be very costly as the plastic surgeon reconstructionist tries to undo as much as is medically and cosmetically possible. For the whole series of corrective revisions to my nose, ears, and chin by Dr. Raymond Rockwell, my total payments came to $24,150.

I would be pleased to know that our book, which is based on true events has helped to inform, educate, entertain, and equip the reader to avoid the mistakes that I made in trying to find the appropriate cosmetic surgeon. The one I chose exploited me for his own professional gain, self-interests, financial profit, and he clearly was not qualified to perform cosmetic surgeries on me after I had multiple cosmetic surgeries.

I wish I had done my homework and had more education about the subject before trying to find the right cosmetic or plastic surgeon for me. I wish I had found a certified American Board of Plastic Surgery surgeon who would have done what I wanted, needed, and expected of him or simply left my nose and ears the way he found them when I walked into the doctor's office.

I wish the reader all the best in finding the right cosmetic or plastic surgeon. I appeal to you to urge your legislators, congressmen and women, judges and courts, and medical boards to put a stop to all medical malpractice crimes, exploitation, and abuses by changing the laws of the medical boards to make certain that they have a criminal enforcement team in each MQAC in the country. We can make a difference in the battle against medical malpractice victimization if we make our voices heard that we will not tolerate medical malpractice victimization in our United States or in any other country in the world.

Stricter enforcement laws and policies, and real prison time for all surgeons that take advantage and commit medical malpractice against unsuspecting innocent patients of which other patients have experienced as well.

As I've mentioned, Dr. Cutter eventually moved out of town. He's now living in Lake Placid. I believe my complaint played a role in Dr. Cutter's decision to move to another region.

We wrote this book with a long-range goal that the trusting public will no longer be victimized by those in positions of trust. Medical malpractice by medical doctors must be stopped.

May my victimization as well as that of other unsuspecting cosmetic consumers be immediately put to an end. May the malicious actions of all medical doctors never be repeated on any innocent unsuspecting person ever again.

I would like every citizen to appeal to his or her congressman to pass a law stating that once a medical board or dental board complaint is submitted or reported to the police, medical boards, legislators, or insurance companies, the statute of limitations immediately is extended for the lifetime of the victimized patient. I hope there will no longer be a three-or four-year statute of limitations ruling for every victimized consumer.

I sincerely would like to thank everyone who can identify with what I have painfully experienced. I hope that many have been encouraged, inspired, and motivated to take action to help put an end to all forms of hurtful and destructive victimization as a positive consequence of reading our book.

8

ADVICE TO THE READER

If you or someone you know has been victimized by a medical doctor, please pray for those who have harmed you.

Jesus tells us in the Gospel of Matthew that we should pray for those who spitefully use us. That would include a medical doctor using a patient as guinea pigs in a cruel or malicious way for professional gain and personal profit.

Beloved, do not avenge yourselves, but rather give place to wrath; for it is written, "Vengeance is Mine, I will repay," says the Lord. (Romans 12:19)

You might say, "But I'm not a Christian or a believer in Jesus Christ, so what am I supposed to do with my angry, vengeful, and bitter feelings toward those who have harmed me?"

Never give up on yourself. Take your hurt feelings, and try to go through the motions of surrendering them up to God. Although you don't believe in Him, this practice is still a healthy way to free yourself from becoming a bitter, critical, discouraged, and a depressed person. God will lovingly accept your efforts to free yourself from painful feelings as a result of your suffering needlessly at the hands of a person you trusted. If you can believe with a small measure of faith in a great big loving God He will absorb your pain as your shock absorber.

Be an encourager to others; do not be a discourager in life. Be part of the solution in this negative world, not part of the problem. Holding on to negative feelings is destructive to your mental, emotional, and physical well-being.

Remember your goals in life. Report any doctor who causes you pain in any way, shape, or form to the Better Business Bureau, the attorney general, and the medical boards and commissions with which the doctor may be licensed. If you know that a crime has taken place contact the legal authorities, and report the crime whether the crime took place against you or someone you know.

I have done many other things during the course of my life so many that if they were all written down it would require another book. The events recorded in this book are intended to equip you with information that will help you to avoid the wrong doctors and the major pitfalls that I fell into in my search for the right cosmetic or plastic surgeon.

I hope you will now be able to find the right medical doctor, one who will be a good, honest, and truthful communicator; a compassionate medical doctor who will interpret exactly what you want, need, and expect from your surgery; one who has the special skills to provide the best-quality cosmetic results. Best wishes in finding the right cosmetic or plastic surgeon who can meet your needs to your satisfaction.

9

CHECKLIST

The following is a checklist for those searching for the right cosmetic or plastic surgeon for their cosmetic interests:

1. Make certain that the medical doctor is a board-certified surgeon with the American Board of Plastic Surgery and has strong experience in doing the procedure(s) you want to have done.

2. Make certain the cosmetic surgeon is listed with the American Board of Medical Specialties (ABMS), a recognized board.

3. Have the medical doctor explain in detail what he is planning to do to your physical characteristics or body part. Make sure that explanation correlates with your cosmetic or reconstructive expectations.

4. Have a friend or family member with you during your consultations.

5. Ask if a friend or family member can videotape your consultations with the cosmetic or plastic surgeon.

6. Find out what kind of training the doctor has received with regard to the surgical procedures he or she will perform on your physical features or body part.

7. Ask for names of patients who have had similar cosmetic surgery by this doctor and who had similar pre-surgery conditions as you.

8. Do your homework before you begin searching for the right cosmetic or plastic surgeon.

9. Ask if any complaints have been filed against the medical doctor with the health department and medical boards with which he or she is licensed in your state.

10. Have the friend or family member who provided the ride for you remain with you until you have been prepared for surgery. You may even request to have that person stay with you during surgery, to be a witness for any last-minute changes the surgeon may state out loud in front of his assistants or whisper to you before you go under anesthesia.

11. Have a good attorney selected prior to surgery, should the surgeon change plans on you on the day of surgery and leave you mentally dazed, confused, and perplexed, pre-or post-surgery.

12. Inquire what the doctor's qualifications are to perform your cosmetic procedure with

precision skill.

13. Ask what the medical doctor's specialty and subspecialties are.

14. Ask a lot of questions of the medical doctor because your future happiness, mental health, and peace of mind depend on your whole person being satisfied and that you were not used, abused, and victimized for the medical doctor's professional gain and personal profit.

15. Don't be concerned with or think that you'll embarrass yourself by asking too many questions relevant to your cosmetic interests.

16. If a medical doctor hedges, hesitates, or refuses to communicate with you to your satisfaction, do not pursue a cosmetic relationship with the medical doctor. If you are in the cosmetic surgeon's presence leave the doctor's office immediately.

Dr. Cutter lacked the two-year residency that is required of plastic surgeons. He lacked the essential medical credentials and the specialized training to qualify him to perform plastic or cosmetic surgeries on a multiple-surgery patient like me. He also lacked the confidence to support the cosmetic training and necessary skills he needed; otherwise, he wouldn't have resorted to mental trickery and thuggery to gain my business. This self-centered predator did not have the supportive care and interest of his patient as his primary focus. The horrifying nightmare left me lacking any admiration or respect for Dr. Cutter.

Dr. Cutter's words and his actions, pre-and post-surgeries, as well as the disastrous cosmetic results I experienced at his psychotic and predatory hands, and that his medical credentials included his having a weekend training in a hotel room on how to perform cosmetic surgeries, add up to his being guilty of the cosmetic and financial crimes he committed against me. Add to that my experiences with my memory bank post-surgeries it was blank and in total blackness. I know beyond a shadow of a doubt that Dr. Cutter is as guilty as sin, and I hold him 100 percent guilty as charged. A key factor is that no leading, notable, and reputable cosmetic or plastic surgeon recognizes Dr. Cutter or his surgical work.

He doesn't meet the high standards of surgeries completed or superior-quality surgeries conducted to place him in the same league as cosmetic surgeons who are fully capable of performing surgery on a multiple-surgery patient such as myself.

I believe I have provided all the evidence you need to come to the same conclusion as I did that Dr. Cutter is guilty of committing cosmetic and financial crimes against me. This isn't only my opinion; every board that holds Dr. Cutter's licensing should revoke all his cosmetic licenses and deny him any future requests to practice cosmetic surgeries on anyone.

I reiterate: we must stop all victimization by medical doctors worldwide on unsuspecting patients who hope for positive results in the unpredictable world of cosmetic and plastic surgeries. May God help the boards to make the right decisions; the patients' safety must be the highest priority.

Bud shared some interesting facts with me concerning America's educational system which all Christians and American citizens should understand. Everyone must guard their children's minds, and affections from the hostile bombardment of the devil, the father of lies, which uses secular humanism in prevalent ways. The child protection agencies by enlarge penalize Christian parents who want to raise Godly Christian children.

Bud said, "The taxpayer-supported secular humanism views humans as accidental animals and as creatures of nature, coming from nowhere and going nowhere. Self-centered focus on self has no need for a belief in a God. Secular humanist manifesto number 1933 and secular humanist manifesto number 1973 both documents were signed by prominent leaders and scientists who totally rejected the belief in God and instead lifted up self. In 1960, the United States Supreme Court declared that the taxpayer-supported religion of secular humanism rules America."

God's Word counteracts this humanistic religion (Acts 5:29 and Proverbs 25:26).

The politically correct silence of the Christian Church is interpreted as an endorsement for all the state government does. Values clarification and situational ethics rule in school classrooms and churches. Pastors and Christian congregations honor graduating students, thus placing their endorsement on what the government is doing in the United States educational system.

Bud learned what the educational system was doing when he looked into what his two sons were learning in their Head Start Program. They were taught things like "Father Moon" and "Mother Earth." You will not find such cockamamie and absurd teachings in the Bible, but we know that proud men and women profess themselves as the all-wise ones. The apostle Paul writes, "Professing to be wise, they became fools, and changed the glory of the incorruptible God into an image made like corruptible man and birds and four-footed beasts and creeping things" (Romans 1:22–23).

I recognize as a Christian Conservative American and a registered Republican voter, that I am willing to do my patriotic duty which is my privilege and constitutional right to also remember the fallen heroes who made the ultimate sacrifice in the discharge of their duties; they laid down their lives in defending and protecting the citizens of America. These heroic individuals never considered themselves as actual heroes during acts of war or times of emergency. I recommend the following patriotic songs to watch and listen to on YouTube:
- "Have You Forgotten" by Darryl Worley
- "I'm Proud to Be an American" by Lee Greenwood
- "Courtesy of the Red, White, and Blue" by Toby Keith

As we remember and reflect on America's historic beginnings as a Christian nation and where we have come from, and our current downward spiral may we as a nation pause and reach up in humility and prayer to our Lord God Almighty and Creator. The Lord has provided us with an answer when we go through times of trouble: "Call unto Me, and I will answer you, and show you great and mighty things, which you do not know" (Jeremiah 33:3).

The Socialist Liberal Democrats presented a fraudulent case to the United States Senate and the American citizens to impeach President Trump which turned out to be a total fabrication based on false premises with a faulty foundation based on lies and deceptions. Each Socialist Liberal Democrat had a pathetic, and sad case of President Trump delusional deranged syndrome with rose-colored glasses that could only see President Trump in a despicably negative light. They were only able to convince their membership through listening to the Socialist Neo-Marxist Media broadcasters who are disseminators of falsehood sources with biased ideologies that side with the Socialist Liberal Democrats.

The saying, "Birds of the feather flock together" is very apropos with their biased views, distorted thinking, and thoughts dead-set against the Lord God Almighty, the American Christian values and principles, and Christian faith-based teachings. The Socialist Liberal Democrats focus on President Trump and The U.S. Constitution as primary targets to keep in their sights.

I heartily concur with President Donald Trump when he says that the Democrats are absolute hypocrites. President Trump is 100 percent correct and spot-on accurate when he boldly speaks of them being hypocrites. I might add that they use taxpayer dollars to support their cause and lies.

Since they control the media outlets, Americans are mentally dumbed down.

May all American citizens Wake Up to the sobering, solid facts that the Progressive Socialist Democrats have, as their party's agenda, an expansive, all-out pursuit for total control. America is being taken over by the dominating control factor for the mind, heart, and soul of this nation. The Socialist Liberal Democrats do not love America, which courageously stands as the land of the free and the home of the brave. We must remember that God Almighty blessed this nation because of the American people who loved, honored, and kept their faith and trust in the Lord God, who blesses those who believe and honor the living God of The Holy Bible and its Holy Principles (2 Chronicles 7:14). The Progressive Socialist Democrats do not subscribe to or believe, trust, and honor the above-mentioned facts and truths, and the Neo-Marxist Media is in their hip pocket. The Progressive Socialist Democrats use taxpayer dollars to support their cause.

The U.S. Education System and the Neo-Marxist Media, are involved in the global village programming, and the one-world order system. American citizens must continue to be extremely cautious not to merely listen to and wholeheartedly believe and accept, hook, line, and sinker, everything the U.S. educational system and the media shares. I recommend that all Americans do a fact-check on whatever the media sources broadcast on the local and national news outlets.

I recommend that you follow the money trail of who is supporting and funding the liberal media system. Americans have grown accustomed to believing that what they hear is the gospel truth. When you do some fact-checking, you may be surprised to discover that the media commentators you have been listening to for years has been telling lies consistently, and they are no longer worthy of your listening time. Recognize that it is time for a positive change in who you are listening to.

The Progressive Socialist Democrats are all like hard-boiled eggs in the same basket. It's very sad to think that a large number of intelligent American citizens have allowed themselves to be conditioned to listen to and accept what they say and that they choose to think that the Democrats have the correct national and international answers, solutions, and views that society needs to follow and accept. American citizens need to open their eyes and see the truth that the Progressive Socialist Democrats have the wrong mind-set for this nation, and they do not have a vision to make America great again, as President Trump and the Republican Party does.

The American people have been watching and seeing for themselves that the Progressive Socialist Democrats do not have the answers for America, so they continue to spend their time attacking President Trump. It proves to me and to a lot of American citizens that the Progressive Socialist Democrats have lost their focus for this great country and have failed to consider or meet the needs of the American citizens, who are in desperate need of help, answers, and financial support. No Progressive Socialist Democrat will get my vote in a presidential election, and I hope you feel the same way.

It is imperative that American citizens remember that the Socialist Liberal Democrats are only interested in advancing the cause and ideology of the Democratic Party. It doesn't matter whether they use Socialism, Communism, or any number of humanistic causes and endeavors to brainwash society with the ideology of the global one. It is their way or the highway, and anybody standing in the way will be viewed as an enemy that needs to be targeted and disposed of.

The Socialist Liberal Democrats hate America and its God-fearing and God-honoring Christians with fait hand family traditional values, who attend Christian Churches that believe in the Lord and carry their Bibles. These Christian believers also believe in the Second Amendment.

They believe it is their fundamental right to own and possess a gun permit to defend and protect themselves, their family, and their neighbor, if they are threatened by a bad person with evil intentions possessing a gun.

American citizens are persuaded to believe the lies of the Democratic Party. I highly recommend an excellent book by Michael J. Knowles, Reasons to Vote for Democrats. The book is unique in its approach to the subject at hand, giving examples of how empty the claims of the Democratic Party are. The Democratic Party is determined to obstruct and defeat President Donald Trump and win the November 2020 presidential election and God forbid. It is vitally important to stand in solidarity as a Christian Nation and not allow this to happen. America will pay a heavy price if they choose a Democrat President.

We recommend using strong caution regarding giving or sending money to those that solicit your money donations on the phone or through the mail which most likely are of the Progressive Socialist Democrat Party. Even if you ask the caller if the political persuasion is of the Democrat Party they could very well "LIE" to you. The request for donations could be a smoke screen to hide their real intentions of where the money will go.

We recommend using strong caution regarding giving or sending money to those that solicit your money donations on the phone or through the mail which most likely are of the Progressive Socialist Democrat Party. Even if you ask the caller if the political persuasion is of the Democrat Party they could very well "LIE" to you. The request for donations could be a smoke screen to hide their real intentions of where the money will go. I also recommend Dinesh D'Souza's book, United States of Socialism.

All Christians and American citizens must muster spiritual and moral courage, with Holy Spirit conviction, to urge the United States Supreme Court and the United States Congress to reenact and pass laws against human trafficking, the harmful effects of pornography, and every form of obscenity, including incest and alcoholism and drug abuse that victimizes human life, regardless of the age of the person, with its destructive forces to the human soul, mind, body, and emotions. These evil forces have reached pandemic proportions, and I pray that the United States Congress and President Donald Trump encourage all international countries involved in human trafficking of adults and children to immediately stop and ban this from continuing to take place in every country worldwide.

Any number of international countries are actively involved with using white adults and children as sex slaves. They are horribly abused and victimized while these countries are openly accepting of children being used as sex slaves for adult services and their pursuits and pleasures.

The countries that are known as perpetrating the horrendous, wicked, and evil practices of human trafficking are the United States, Mexico, the Philippines, Pakistan, Thailand, China, India, Bangladesh, Russia, Belarus, Iran, Turkmenistan, North Korea, Venezuela, and all Islamic countries. Many more have the same sinister stains of sins committed against white adults and children. The Lord God, their Creator loves and cares for them dearly. Every individual soul being sexually abused and victimized by the sexual predators of this world is more valuable than the whole world.

Jesus Christ paid their debt of sin, past, present, and future when He was crucified on the cross of Calvary nearly two thousand years ago. Jesus became their substitute, and He places a high premium on each innocent and vulnerable precious human life. I know for an absolute certainty that every sexual predator will stand before God in judgment.

You may frivolously think that God doesn't care one bit about the human tragedies and hideous atrocities being committed against adults and children who can't defend themselves, and that those who sexually harm these precious souls will not escape the wrath and judgment of the Lord God Almighty. All sexual predators need to hear what God says concerning evil practices:

"Vengeance is Mine, I will repay, says the Lord." (Romans 12:19) "Do not be deceived, God is not mocked; for whatever a man sows,

that he will also reap." (Galatians 6:7)

Remember that all sin is against God's holiness, and those who lead people astray down the wrong road, contrary to the finished work of the cross of Jesus Christ, will face the serious consequences of their actions if they haven't repented of their sins. People need to turn from their sins to escape the judgment of God and to avoid a painful harvest of bad seeds sown into their personal lives.

If you have been involved in human sexual trafficking, I encourage you to stop your predator behavior against the bodies and souls of precious lives, who are created in the moral likeness and image of the Lord God. Ask the Lord to forgive you by confessing your sins of violations and crimes of wicked assaults, which are opposed to God's commandments and His will for your life. Especially ask the Lord to forgive you for the innocent ones you have damaged for your own selfish and self-centered lustful pursuits. There is real hope and true freedom for the worst kind of offenders.

God's Word says:

"If we confess our sins, He is faithful and just to forgive us our sins and to cleanse us from all unrighteousness." (1 John 1:9)

"He who covers his sins will not prosper, But whoever confesses and forsakes them will have mercy." (Proverbs 28:13)

The federal government recognizes alcoholism as a disease, and they collect revenue for its purchase by the consumers. The federal government also collects revenue for taxes from tobacco use and from drug abuse and pharmaceuticals relating to medicinal drugs or their preparation, use, and sale.

It is quite interesting that the government methadone program of a few years ago became a total failure, and they used taxpayer dollars to fund it. There are so many things that America's Government does that can leave you scratching your head from questioning the decision-makers and the funding of all kind of programs that we may totally disagree with. We wonder if these programs are truly worth the money and effort to make them work, and in most cases, the taxpaying American citizens are left to pay the bill.

A lot of people believe the U.S. Government has many secret government programs whereby they are making the American citizens fund programs that they do not believe in, and they feel they are being cheated and forced to use their taxpayer dollars to support and fund these unknown programs. Many Americans also do not like the U.S. Government's continuing to borrow money from other countries which results in compromising America's sovereignty to govern itself without the interference, and involvement of another strong country seeking to spread its dominance and infringe upon and control us. The territorial disputes are challenging equations that our leaders have to face and deal with.

May God continue to bless our national leaders to ask God for His wisdom, guardianship, and guidance for the strength they need every day to look to the Lord to help America stay the course of the vision our founding fathers had when they boldly signed the Declaration of Independence in 1776. God has great plans for America, if we will turn from our sinful and selfish ways and seek the Lord as He requires and asks us to honor His Word as individuals and as a nation (2 Chronicles 7:14).

Hollywood likes to depict teenagers and young adults as eager to lose their virginity and as that being a cool thing to do. I acknowledge from God's point of view that a person's virginity is placed at a very high value. King Solomon speaks that a woman's virtue is valued higher than the worth of rubies (Proverbs 31:10). I encourage all men and women and boys and girls to vigilantly guard your virginity as if it was gold, and choose to remain pure before God and man because the stakes are far too high. Your soul, your life, and your reputation depend on your choice to keep your sex life with discipline and self-control. Your eternal destiny weighs heavily on keeping your spirit and body clean before the Lord, who alone is holy. God expects us to remain holy and clean from the lusts of the flesh in this contaminating world's system and to keep our lives free from the unclean things of this world and He says, He will receive us (2 Corinthians 6:17).

The Lord Jesus says, "The thief does not come except to steal, kill, and to destroy. I have come that they may have life, and that they may have it more abundantly" (John 10:10). This speaks of Satan and his emissaries, who pedal false ways of salvation.

"Then Death and Hades were cast into the lake of fire. This is the second death. And anyone not found written in the Book of Life was cast into the lake of fire" (Revelation 20:14–15). This speaks of eternal separation from God.

Jesus also says, "I am He who lives, and was dead, and behold, I am alive forevermore. Amen. And I have the keys of Hades and Death" (Revelation 1:18).

I recommend that everyone come to know the Lord Jesus as Savior and Lord, as He is the only One by whom we can come to God the Father. (John 14:6 says), "Jesus said unto him, 'I am the way, the truth, and the life. No one comes to the Father except through Me." Remember that the devil is a poor loser, and the Lord Jesus is the biggest winner. Stay on the winning side because everything goes better with Jesus Christ.

I am determined to follow the Lord Jesus and place my faith, trust, and hope exclusively in Jesus Christ and Him crucified, which is what Jesus did for me when He suffered and died for my sins on the cross of Calvary. Jesus willingly shed His blood for me and the whole world, that we might have our sins forgiven and receive eternal life in Christ Jesus.

I am a fanatic for Jesus. Before coming to the Lord Jesus I cared for the things of this world which was part and parcel of this world's system which is focused on self and where I fit into society. I thank God that I have made my choice to be a fanatic for Jesus because I want to please the Lord and be accepted by Him. I want to abide in Jesus Christ, be a fruit-bearer, and make heaven my home one bright glorious day. I cordially invite all who will choose to make the Lord Jesus the Savior and Lord of your lives to become a fanatic for Jesus Christ, where you are not ashamed of the gospel of Jesus Christ. (Romans 1:16 says), "For I am not ashamed of the gospel of Christ, for it is the power of God to salvation for everyone who believes, for the Jew first and also for the Greek." Glory be to Jesus.

Jesus also says, "For whoever is ashamed of Me and My words; of him the Son of Man will be ashamed when He comes in His own glory, and in His Father's, and of the holy angels" (Luke 9:26).

I give special tribute to the unsung individual heroes who have involved themselves in

saving, rescuing, and defending human lives in all types of dangerous circumstances and situations. I recognize First Responders, Coast Guard Rescue Teams, Law Enforcement Agencies and Police Officers, Fire Department and the EMTs, Medical Doctors,
U.S. Military Corpsmen, Mountain Rescue Teams, and the Army Corps of Engineers.

I also recognize everyone who has played a significant role or a small role in helping to fight against COVID-19. I recognize and give special credit to President Donald Trump and Vice President Mike Pence, and all President Trump's Administration Team, and the medical doctors who took part and played a significant role in addressing the corona virus pandemic, which is prevalent over the entire country. God loves and cares about all American and international citizens, and He is more than able and willing to extend His tender hands and loving arms to everyone who has been negatively affected by this unseen enemy, which has enveloped the whole world. God's love reaches every corner of the world.

Spring and summer are when people are out mowing their grass; they pick up allergies, and this corona virus is in the grass too. The lawnmower picks up the pollen particles, which can stir up allergies that people suffer with throughout the day. This corona virus can be carried by tiny particles in the grass that the lawnmower sends up into the air. The wind then takes these particles and blows them into the faces of people.

I recommend that all lawn mowing be done while wearing a medical or homemade mask to protect yourself from contracting COVID-19, the corona virus. Also remember that there will be many souls in heaven who never mowed their lawns. I'm sorry, ladies, but God is the author who will make heaven their home on that glorious day, and it is not up to the female gender, who especially like to have a neat and well-trimmed lawn and a home that they love to keep neat and tidy. During these troubling times, due to the corona virus, I'd like to encourage everyone not to be so critical and judgmental of your neighbor if he or she chooses to neglect mowing the lawn, which may appear unkempt and uncared for. They may not want to spread or send harmful virus particles your way; they may be merely considering their neighbors.

As the Christian Church of Jesus Christ, which is the universal body of born-again believers we need to fervently pray, as individuals and corporately as the church body, for our nation that the Lord will heal our land and remove this pandemic, COVID-19. We also need the Lord God to help us overcome the frightening scare that people have been subject to, concerning the pandemic, which has caused so many people worldwide to fear that they might contract the virus or unknowingly pass on this unseen enemy to family members when they return home after being exposed to other people who haven't practiced social distancing.

Americans need to follow the recommendations of the Centers for Disease Control and Prevention to ensure the safety of every U.S. citizen, so that the Coronavirus doesn't negatively affect any American life in a harmful and lethal manner. We need to continue to take all the beneficial safety precautions necessary to remain healthy and to help our family members and friends to practice Coronavirus liberation and remain germ-free. I have read the signs that advise people that to stay home is saving lives. I'm not in full agreement.

There has been a lot of civil unrest throughout American cities and communities over the unfortunate death of George Floyd, an African American who was beloved by his family. I also have seen what the media shows us concerning the massive protests against police violence and brutality and racial injustice that many are feeling, with signs raised stating, "Black Lives Matter." To be fair and balanced, white lives matter too, and I also recognize that all lives matter in the eyes of

God and true Christians.

There are extremists, such as Antifa and other extremist groups, that have hijacked the protest movements, and they have caused a great deal of damage and destruction to businesses, have defaced national monuments, shops, restaurants, and other state-owned buildings throughout our nation.

During this time of civil unrest in America, where there is peaceful and angry protesting, rioting, and looting going on, we need to stay anchored in the ark of safety, the Lord Jesus Christ, who is the Prince of Peace. The apostle Paul says, "If it is possible, as much as depends on you, live peaceably with all men" (Romans 12:18). America is experiencing a civil war at this time for the very heart and soul of our nation. I call for cooler heads and calmer attitudes, in the name and cause of Jesus Christ, to receive a spirit of God's love, peace, and reconciliation by those on the police force, those in authority, and every kind of protester in America and worldwide.

Every American citizen needs to recognize that America's future and destiny is at stake. Our economic future and the vision our national leaders foresee for our great country does not look right during these times of civil unrest. American citizens need to look beyond the passing of George Floyd and the arrest and criminal charges against the four Minneapolis, Minnesota, police officers. American citizens must come to accept the sobering reality of what kind of society and world we want to live in after all the protesting has come to its final stage. Some deceived people are demanding the defunding and reforms of police departments that serve and protect U.S. citizens to the very best of their abilities.

I realize there are good, bad, and corrupt police officers on the police force, but I believe it is only right to give credit where credit is due that there are far more of the police department's finest who are courageous, kindhearted, gracious, and thoughtful officers who serve this nation's cities and communities as public servants. Most police officers do not want to accept or surrender to the dictates of the deceived mob of people calling for surrender of the American society.

Law Enforcement Agencies have accepted a com-promising position, forced on them by political entities, yet before the massive protests began, police officers were viewed as deputized agents, with the power and the backing of the United States Government, to enforce the laws of the land. The general public accepted Law Enforcement Officers as the authority that American citizens recognize to apprehend individuals of major crimes and minor misdemeanors, such as for speeding or other traffic violations. Unfortunately, because of the massive protests taking place all over our nation, the Law Enforcement Agencies and police officers, as a whole, have taken a big black eye, and now the anarchist protesters have come to view police officers as violent racists, prepared and ready to kill for small or petty crimes.

I realize there are racist police officers who see the color of people's skin regarding the motorists they pull over for one reason or another. I also realize that good police officers, who are compassionate and honest, with excellent communication and negotiation skills, are subject to change for the worse over time after dealing with African American gang members and drug dealers and users who live a hard life of crime and violence.

From a spiritual and soul-centered perspective, a prayed-up Christian Law Enforcement Officer can remain color blind with the Lord Jesus in his heart and life. He has the ability to see the needs of the people in reality, whom he confronts and arrests for the crimes they commit. The unbelieving police officer will have more difficulties dealing with different ethnic, and various cultural groups because rather than relying on the power of the Lord in his life, he has to depend on his own natural skills and abilities to fight crime and violence.

The Lord is willing to help any police officer who has been struggling with racial tensions because of the kind of cliental and criminal element he is assigned to work with on his beat each day. God has the answer for the humble police officer who faces difficult challenges when serving people of color, who view things differently than he or she does on the streets. The American citizenry, as a whole, will never tolerate or accept racist police officers, whether they are black or white Law Enforcement Officers.

There is one significant issue that I do not see the protesters crying out for during the great demonstrations of mostly peaceful protestors throughout the nation, and it needs to be addressed and acknowledged by every protester who wants his thoughts received and remembered by those in authority. I don't see African Americans or white Americans or any other ethnic group protesting against black-on-black violence or black-on-white violence and crimes committed against other American citizens nationally.

We need to look at the national statistics that show that there are far more deaths from African Americans killing African Americans, and African Americans murdering white Americans, than what we are witnessing on media sources, which confine police violence and brutality against African Americans only. Where is the anger against the black-on-black crime and black-on-white crime that faces American citizens throughout our nation? Where are the protesters tearing down the statue of the angel Moroni, which supposedly visited Joseph Smith on many occasions?

Where is the anger that should be directed toward those who murdered the police officers? As a nation, we need to recognize that all the righteous indignation and anger aimed against the four police officers who were charged in the death of George Floyd is because the people are ignoring spiritual reason and wisdom, and this has caused the adding to, taking away from, or ignoring the finished work of the cross of Calvary, where Jesus paid the debt of sin for the whole world.

The rioting, looting, and protesting with violence throughout the country is causing the devil's destruction, lies, and mayhem in America. Satan is the one that comes to steal, kill, and destroy, Jesus said, and the crowds are following Satan's will to totally destroy America and usher in socialism and communism. The Neo-Marxist News Media is leading the way in the destruction of the nation. The young people crying and calling out for Socialism in American society cannot point to or declare where socialism has ever successfully worked, where the people have been happy with their dictators and evil regimes.

The protesters demand that America submit to their demands throughout the nation and that society's citizens need to go along with the socialist revolutionary reforms they are forcing on this nation. The Black Lives Matter movement needs to recognize that if Socialism, which is the doorway to Communism, ever takes root in American society, there will be far more African American lives lost, and every other ethnic groups will suffer under the heavy, oppressive tactics on the masses, prevalent cruelties, and deaths caused by the Socialist soldiers, trained in Socialist-Marxist boot camps, which show no mercy for their subjects.

These deceived protesting adults and young people desire free things from Totalitarian Socialism, but they are not using any wisdom in their search for a national leader who will lead them to this so-called Utopian Society that they are yearning for and seeking. They are demanding to transform and reform America into what they envision this new Authoritarian

Socialist Society should become, corresponding with the deceived dictates of their leaders and funders of this Utopian Society. They cannot show us one country that has been a beacon of hope to the nations of the world, yet America has been held up as a beacon of hope for centuries, and the immigrants were protesting the countries they migrated from.

Jesus's ministry was a 100 percent success, which was verified by His resurrection, and the devil is always busy, bringing in his demonic deception and counterfeits and the other counterfeits around the world. We need the free gift of salvation, which the Lord Jesus offers to everyone who will call upon the name of the Lord, to clearly see, with spiritual eyes, the kind of demonic spirits stirring up the people to protest, despise, and look with anger at Law Enforcement Officers in American cities and towns. Let's remember that the media knows how to stir up the people by constantly showing American viewers the police brutality and violence against black people, along with angry and peaceful protesters. We absolutely need God in America again.

The devil has done a good job bringing about division throughout our American society by using angry, misguided souls who are bent on destroying America, and changing this nation into something that the majority of society will end up hating and despising. We need for every Law Enforcement Agency, counterintelligence, and knowledgeable, informed police officers to find out who are the groups of people funding all the protesting, rioting, vandalism, and looting taking place in major cities, communities, and towns, that seek to eliminate America's properties and our way of life.

I recommend that George Soros, who supports these dissident groups and every other anti-American extremist movement, like Antifa, be arrested and charged for causing all the destruction of businesses, properties, and tearing down of our national symbols and historical statues. And that he be given something more than a slap on the wrist. This is a total disgrace to everything that has made America great. What gives them the right, freedom, and liberty to destroy the history of the United States that they do not understand or appreciate?

We need to stay ahead of the Society Curveballs toward a revolutionary change of America becoming a Socialized Communist Society, where big government is in charge of everything pertaining to our lives. The Liberal Socialist Democratic Party wants to take the power, remain in charge, and be in full control of America's citizens and to order every aspect and detail of our individual existence, from the cradle to the grave, because they think they know better how to plan, run, and set the schedules for our lives. The Democratic Party is absolutely determined to obstruct and defeat President Trump in November 2020. We appeal to all citizens of America not to let this happen.

The Liberal Socialist Democratic Party is just itching to get back in power, and they cannot wait to scratch that itch they have been feeling ever since President Trump took office. This is a reflection of what is going to happen in the future at the battle of Armageddon, where all the people and the armies of the world will be united in their denial of the Lord Jesus Christ.

I have known for years that there are people who want to destroy our nation, and they are going by the playbooks of Socialists and Communists that exploit societies' strengths and vulnerabilities. The angry rioters, looters, and those who have caused all the violent vandalism, destruction, and mayhem have caused America a great deal of damage that will take years to recover. This revolutionary movement in our nation's cities and communities proves the total discontent and anger of the outraged, massive number of protesters, who are doing their level best to change America.

The revolutionary tactics they use to eliminate America's Christian and capitalistic society, which has made America great, as One Nation under God, needs to come alive at this time, rise up, overcome, and recover all that the devil currently is stealing from us as a Christian Nation during the massive protests on American soil. I encourage all Christians and American citizens to do whatever they can to help to Wake Up the deceived people involved in this revolutionary movement, which they firmly believe will bring them the new United States of Socialism. The revolutionary-movement ideology of deceived people think they are going to be part of the global village, which is the global, united, one-world order, because they think they are ushering in the reorganization of the human family. They are totally deceived.

For all the protesters of the Black Lives Matter movement, there is something I would like for you to consider. The Liberal Progressive Democratic Party has failed you in your cities and communities over the years, and now you want to take all your anger out on the Law Enforcement Agencies, and the national and local police officers who have answered the call to stop criminals and violators against senior citizens, teenagers, and children, who are vulnerable to the gangs and drug peddlers in your neighborhoods.

The Progressive Socialist Democratic governors and mayors of so many cities and towns in America are leading the way to move you away from God, Country, and traditional family values, which is only leaving you angry at Law Enforcement Officers in American societies. Rather than focusing on being angry at the four responsible Minneapolis, Minnesota, police officers who were charged with George Floyd's death, they blame the Law Enforcement Officers who are employed to protect and defend the lives of the cities, communities, and towns they serve.

In 1860 President Abraham Lincoln warned against the Democrat Party in very strong words. Abraham Lincoln also warned American citizens that if the Democrats are in power then you know what the farmer's plant they will take the most of it and they will tax the American people and give you the remains. Abraham Lincoln warned very strongly that if the Democrats took power in the Oval Office it would become the plantation house for the whole nation that day. Abraham Lincoln warned strongly the American citizens, if the Democrats take power they will tax you, take most of your crops, and let you have a little bit to live on.

It is for the above mentioned powerful words of warnings to the American citizens by the 16th President of the United States of America the very reasons and there are many more why I literally can't understand the reasons for American citizens would ever want to vote for a Democrat for the Presidential Oval Office of this great U.S. Nation when the Socialist Democrat Political Party are known for taxing and spending the American citizens. Out of concern for the welfare of the people of this nation and based upon the events of November 3rd, 2020 we remind you and know that the Socialist Democrat Party stole the election from President Donald Trump.

President Trump and thereby the American citizens were robbed of their voting rights. We believe and know if the Democrats had their way with the American citizens they would spend us into oblivion and leave us with change in our pockets. I appeal to all Americans to Wake Up, become wise to the Socialist Liberal Democrat Parties sinister agendas for all American citizens, and come alive to faith in God like never before.

It's time to rise up with a new inspired vision for what is the best course of action for America as the land of the free and home of the brave with the Lord God's Divine Help through Jesus Christ and His Cross of Calvary, and remember the awesome price he paid for the forgiveness of our sins and receiving the free gift of His glorious eternal salvation.

President Andrew Jackson a staunch Democrat who persecuted the Cherokee Indians and drove them from their lands and gave their land to the American farmers and settlers. There were several thousand

Cherokee Indians frozen to death on the long series of their winter's journeys, and there were other various Indian tribes involved in that trails of tears. The American soldiers forced marched the American Indians with rifle butts and clubs on the long arduous marches into what was called Indian Territory which later became Oklahoma, which means the land of the Red Man.

I gently remind you that the ones doing all the violent and peaceful protesting along with causing a great deal of destruction to American statues, historical buildings, and businesses in American cities and communities in 2020 were the misguided youth and young adults like Antifa protesters and the Black Lives Matter Movement which are contributors and supporters of the Progressive Socialist Democratic Political Party.

I seriously realize these totally deceived, unwise, and radical groups of people are revealing their real hatred, scorn, and contempt for America's Godly Christian Heritage and its powerful image of a successful, prosperous, and ever increasing national status that the world looks to as a symbol of strength to the nations. When America is strong the nations of the world can remain strong.

If America becomes weak then the result would be the nations of the world would become weak structured. The same thing happened when the Roman Empire fell. Before the Roman Empire fell there were gangs of homosexuals and lesbians roaming the streets and molesting children. A lot of the perversions of the day were adopted by the Greeks. The disciplines of the Roman army had fallen apart. There were things happening at the public baths that had not been happening before with such frequency.

I was listening to a morning radio broadcaster as I was on my way to get some gas, and he happened to mention the Black Lives Matter movement. He mentioned two things concerning the movement that caught my attention. He said that they are Marxists, and he said that he was going to provide that information on the next morning's broadcast, using their own words. I have since learned that the Black Lives Matter movement, Antifa, and other extremist movements are helping to fund the Democratic Party.

Bud and I know that the Liberal Socialist Democratic Party has been very successful at corrupting the minds of American citizens with anti-American rhetoric for years. I encourage everyone to examine the evidence I have provided with other authors that informs and warns citizens of this nation of their extreme, poisonous doctrines, philosophy, and ideology.

President Abraham Lincoln was well acquainted with the evils of the Democratic Party and their radical agenda, which is 100 percent contrary and opposed to everything America believes in and stands for. I warn America to stay clear, avoid, and do not associate with the current Democratic Party and its Progressive Socialist, Marxist, and sinister strategies.

If you are interested in knowing the honest and real conservative truths of historical and current cultural events, with precise accuracy, I recommend you watch Life, Liberty & Levin on Fox News, as well as Mark Levin's radio program. Mark Levin is a very popular voice of authority who speaks about traditional, premium principles and the core values that have made America great and an exceptional nation, which has been the envy of the world from its founding. Levin's communication skills are truly amazing, and he reveals to his listening audience, every time his program is aired, the power he has to articulate the truths he wants to concisely convey to the minds of the American citizens.

He can clearly define concepts and ideas which captivate the minds and hearts of each guest or group, with the positive, influential information he wants to impress upon everyone who listens to him. Levin is an impressive broadcaster who knows how to dumbfound his enemies and critics. Be sure to watch and listen to this outstanding TV host and radio commentator.

You can see how the events of the protesting narrative have been planned out by the Liberal Socialist Democratic Party for years. They are master manipulators who know how to exploit a crisis to their advantage to bring about the social reforms and progressive changes that suit their cunning, sinister, and crafty schemes to regain presidential power, for which they cannot contain themselves until their overall agenda for this nation has been fulfilled.

The socialist media sources that have aligned themselves with the Democratic Party are primed and ready to follow the dictates, demands, and orders of the national leaders of the Liberal Socialist Democratic Party and to do their bidding whenever called upon to act. Both of these groups of progressive socialists and social reformers think they are so clever, knowing how to manipulate the masses to do the things they want them to do. They are determined to achieve their agenda by hook or by crook, and, without question, they will prevail in the end, if they are not stopped.

I recommend watching the YouTube video "Hegel's Dialectic: Key Concepts-PHILO-notes Whiteboard Edition," which is nine minutes and thirty-seven seconds in length. You will receive an education on the philosophy of Georg Wilhelm Friedrich Hegel. After watching the video, you can understand the reasons why so many young people are anti-God and anti-America. They also despise free enterprise, and love Socialism, and free things. They join the protesters, rioters, and looters as revolutionaries of social reform. Many are destroyers of property, like Antifa and other radical extremist groups who are willing to tear down historical buildings and statues.

The virus scare and the protests, combined with rioting, was preplanned by the social planners and the Socialist Democratic Party. They were not going to allow a good crisis to go to waste, but rather use it to their advantage, in hopes of hurting President Trump's chances of being re-elected in November 2020.

We are witnessing and it's being played out on our TV screens a nation's misguided people gone bonkers, in living color, demonstrating violent and peaceful protests. As an observer, I see there is mayhem of violent disorder and chaos, coupled with rioting and looting, which is creating a lot of damage throughout the country. This is not the country I grew up in that is for sure. I, along with so many others, recognize that we must turn back to God, in faith and repentance, for America to be restored and healed of the civil unrest and ugliness in what were good relationships in the past.

I recommend you watch a great video on YouTube titled "Can't We Get Along." I agree with Pat Robertson of CBN Ministries that this video should go viral. It is so touching and memorable that it could melt your heart with emotion and should motivate you to encourage others to watch it. It shows how God can work healing in the lives of divided groups of people. It is incredible to watch police officers hugging men and women of different colors in the aftermath of protesting, violence, and graffiti.

I remind you of chocolate and vanilla, which are two different flavors, but both are sweet. God can provide healing from out-of-control heated emotions. The sign of demonic activity is when we see people lashing out at one another, just as we are witnessing on TV people with flared-up emotions from strained relationships. People have scars from life in general. Scars remind us of where we have been, but they don't have to dictate where we are going in life.

Other black lives have been needlessly murdered by police officers in various cities and communities throughout America, which is an outrage. I understand and do not blame people for their fierce anger over the criminal injustice that led to the death of George Floyd, as well as all the other African Americans' deaths throughout American history, caused by trigger-happy police officers. I also recognize there have been far more African Americans killed by other African Americans, and then there are African Americans who have killed white Americans and other ethnic groups, which were caused by police violence and brutality. I recognize as well the justified anger that white Americans have toward black Americans who have murdered white Americans.

Bud recently shared with me that he was victimized by a group of five African American youths when he was six years old in Oakland, California. He said, "They threw me down on the sidewalk on my back, and they urinated on my face and clothes. They laughed while they were doing it."

Many white Americans can recall being victimized by someone of another color, and many African Americans can recollect being victimized by someone of a different ethnic group. It is never right, fair, or justified to be exploited and mistreated by anyone, regardless of the color of a person's skin.

I pray that you will ask the Lord to help you to forgive people. With the Lord's grace and power, it may result in bringing about the Lord's healing of your broken and injured heart and life. Corrie Ten Boom, who, with her family, helped Jews escape the Holocaust, described what happened to her when she forgave the Nazi guard who killed her sister, before she herself was rescued by American soldiers from the concentration camp where she had spent years. You can view her powerful testimony on the YouTube video titled, "Corrie Ten Boom Forgives Nazi Guard."

I was watching Francis and Friends on Jimmy Swaggart Ministries, and a woman caller shared what she had witnessed and experienced in Cuba. "What is going on in America is the same thing that happened in Cuba and Venezuela," she said, "The people are being deceived."

She was referring to the protesters being taken over by the Communist Party of Cuba, which takes and takes from the people and rules with cruelty, causing the deaths of so many people in Cuba. I believe the Liberal Progressive Democratic Party, which has failed the people whenever they are in power, is once again seeking political power to regain the presidency. Please consider that all your hostility and anger that is directed toward the four Minneapolis, Minnesota Police Officers is rightly justified, but all the other bad and corrupt Law Enforcement Officers who have committed violence and brutality against blacks in American history doesn't compare to the vast number of deaths caused by black-on-black and black-on-white violence that needs to come to an end as well.

We need to pray for the salvation of the nation's news media that have stirred up the hatred and animosity, which led to the outrage of the protesters who direct their disapproval toward all Law Enforcement Agencies throughout America. The news media overemphasizes the killing of George Floyd, but they underemphasize the shooting of white police officers because the news media purposefully slants the news coverage to their biased political view in order to sway American citizens to see things from their disinformation point of view.

America and all Spanish speaking nations needs fair and balanced news media such as Fox News, and NewsmaxTV that is known to American citizens as conservative news coverage and not what President Trump refers as fake news, which CNN, NBC, CBS, and other media sources present. American citizens and international citizens need to hear the truth and nothing but the truth, without the biased slant that certain news media sources are known for.

I recommend that American citizens do consistent fact-checks on what the media sources broadcast and warn us about. What the world is saying to society is important, but it is of much more significance to follow what Jesus said to do:

"Therefore take heed how you hear. For whoever has, to him more will be given; and whoever does not have, even what he seems to have will be taken from him." (Luke 8:18)

The absolute certainty of how to be successful in life is to live by the Word of God, faithfully, every day of your life. The Virgin Mary was God's temporary chosen vessel. Through the power of the Holy Spirit, He implanted in the womb of the Virgin Mary the embryo that God fashioned into the whole human baby body of the Lord Jesus. The Word took upon Himself the limitations of the human body (2 Corinthians 5:19; John 1:29), to which God was in Christ Jesus, who reconciled the world unto Himself. Mary recognized the power of Jesus Christ when she told the servants at the wedding in Cana, which Jesus had attended, "Whatever He says to you, do it" (John 2:5).

"Behold, a virgin shall be with child, and bear a Son, and they shall call His name Immanuel, which is translated, God with us." (Matthew 1:23)

America is being set up for another power grab by the Liberal Socialist Democratic Party, and they want to use the angry, focused protests as a smoke screen for Authoritarian Socialism to take over this nation, otherwise known as Communism. On Michael Savage's radio program, he mentioned there are thirty-one different types of communism, and he didn't know where Barack Obama fit into the mix.

I pray that the people involved in the protest movement will Wake Up and come to their senses and not allow themselves to be deceived by the Liberal Progressive Democratic Party. It's time for them to reconcile with the Law Enforcement Agencies, step up, and set a good example by helping the American people to reelect President Donald Trump for four more years with a great and excellent president.

President Trump will not allow anyone to usher in Socialism and Communism into American Society while he is the president and Commander in Chief of the United States of America. I encourage all protesters in America to consider a much better option for the right leaders for America, which will produce loyal followers with the most reasonable choices to bring about the blessing of God on this nation's citizens.

President Trump is doing a great job as the forty-fifth president of the United States of America and is doing his very best to help every individual and groups of people in American cities and communities to raise their socioeconomic status. I cordially invite you to join the American President Trump Rallies to Make America Great Again and help us to re-elect President Trump in November 2020.

Talk show host Dennis Prager has said, "I was wrong. Trump is a great president, according to the American Experiment."

I encourage everyone to read Dennis's comments on why he believes President Trump is a great president. I also recommend reading the opinion piece by Don Buckingham on TimesLeader.com, titled "Your View: Here Is Why Donald Trump Is a Great President."[6]

I remind America this nation maybe suffering as a whole, but remember that America's setbacks pave the way for mighty comebacks. America has rallied and overcome a lot of negative setbacks throughout our history.

America, it is high time to Rise Up and take back everything the devil has taken from us and to return to the Lord God, in repentance and faith, so we might experience peace with God, followed with the peace of God (Romans 5:1; Philippians 4:7).

I encourage people everywhere to experience true revival in your personal lives and in your nations before the Lord. We desperately need to enter into a time of personal repentance by coming before the righteous and holy Lord God Almighty, in humility and brokenness of heart over our sins that have separated us from the Lord. The prophet Isaiah called out Israel's sins:

"But your iniquities have separated you from your God; And your sins have hidden His face from you, So that He will not hear. For your hands are defiled with blood, And your fingers with iniquity; Your lips have spoken lies, Your tongue has muttered perversity." (Isaiah 59:2–3)

By demonstrating our genuine, heartfelt act of repentance before God through confessing our sins, renouncing our sins, and forsaking our sins, we, in turn, can experience God's mercies on our lives and our nations. As a positive consequence of our personal confessions and forsaking of our sins, the Lord God wants us to experience His divine presence in our hearts and lives. Walking with God by faith on a daily basis is true Christianity, in living reality before God and other human beings. We can know and experience true love, joy, and peace in Christ Jesus, every day of our lives. When we possess these fruits of the Spirit, we must guard them vigilantly and diligently.[4]

view-here-is-why-donald-trump-is-a-great-president.

America must experience a mighty Holy Spirit revival in humbleness of heart and brokenness before God Almighty and come to realize that God cannot bless sin. America loves to be blessed by God. May America remember that we need to repent of our sins and bless the Lord God (2 Chronicles 7:14).

May you make the Lord Jesus Christ your personal Savior and Lord of your life today, and may this be the best year of your life.

"For He says, In an acceptable time I have heard you, And in the day of salvation I have helped you." Behold, now is the accepted time; behold, now is the day of salvation. (2 Corinthians 6:2)

May this be the most glorious day of your life as you give Jesus Christ charge of your heart and life at this decision making moment in time.

One fine day, an elderly woman shared with me the interesting day she had spent with four men. She said, "I got up with Will Power. I went for a walk with Charley Horse. I took a nap with Arthur-Itus, and I went to bed with Ben Gay."

I liked the way she related her interesting day to me.

---

[4] https://www.timesleader.com/opinion/letters/765965/your-

10

PRESIDENT TRUMP VERSES THE DEMOCRAT HOUSE

The Democrat House with their obsession in attacking President Trump while having Trump deranged syndrome have decided to impeach President Trump after he has freely chosen to step down as the 45th President of the United States. Although the Socialist Democrats have been informed that they cannot impeach a president once he is out of the Oval Office according to The U.S Constitution, it is conspicuously obvious the Progressive Socialist Democrats want to make absolutely certain President Trump will never have another opportunity to come back to their abject horror and triumph with his powerful Trump's Let's Make America Great Again supporter base and serve as the United States President once more.

The Progressive Socialist Democrat Party unanimously dread this come back mighty one man force to preside as one might refer to him as, Resurrection Trump as Commander in Chief of this great nation, but instead the Socialist Democrat Party want him to be forever eliminated from serving politically so he can't come back politically of ever serving in any political office or capacity.

The Socialist Democrat House impeachment committee was unsuccessful endeavoring to persuade and convince any Republican Senator with convicting evidence against President Trump during their 1st impeachment failed Congressional proceedings. Thank God the U.S. Senate voted to acquit President Trump from being impeached after he had left the U.S. Oval Office, although the Socialist Democrat Party voted 57 to 43 to impeach President Trump.

It is very obvious the Socialist Democrat Party want to disqualify President Trump from ever serving as President of the United States in the near or distant future, and to discredit all of President Trump's re-election voters and supporter base called deplorables, a term used by Hillary Clinton referring to President Trump's supporters. Now the Democrats think President Trump supporters need to be deprogrammed of all such good thoughts and possibly voting for President Trump again in 2024.

We know instead of President Donald Trump being impeached the ones that should be impeached is every member of the Socialist Democrat Political Party that never spoke up, condemned, and voiced putting a stop to the months and months of the protesting, rioting, burning, and tearing down of America's national symbols and historic heritage. These very individuals seriously need to be impeached and prevented from ever serving in a national political office and capacity for the United States of America.

The Progressive Socialist Liberal Democrats want to rule and reign as elite leaders as a ruling class over America's citizens having complete power and control of every aspect of our nation's citizens of the United States. Bud and I agree we happen to see things totally opposite of the way the Socialist Democrat House Party perceive and view President Trump. The Socialist Democrats have a bad case of President Trump delusional and deranged syndrome thinking.

We believe and know President Trump greatly loves and cares about America and we do not believe the Socialist Democrat Party truly loves and cares about the people of America and the illegal immigrants that seek to enter the U.S. border points lawfully or unlawfully. Where was the Socialist Democrat Party when the rioters were looting and burning down scores and scores of business owner's stores, shops, and small and large business owners businesses went up in flames burnt to the ground throughout our nation? Where were the Socialist Democrat Senators when Law Enforcement Officers on duty were murdered while protecting and serving America's citizens?

Bud and I know what the Progressive Socialist House Democrats are up to that should be seen as just another smoke and mirrors charade by the unforgiving Democrat House. President Trump has been scorned and has become one big obstacle as seen through the Socialist House Democrats eyes throughout his first presidential term, and they want to totally erase President Trump from the minds of the American citizens and I might add the world's citizens for time and eternity. The Socialist Democrats are bad to the bone.

We positively believe and know that the Lord God Almighty hasn't forgotten all of the good, great, and wonderful things President Trump has done for the good of America, its citizens, and for Israel as well. God has not forgotten all of the abusive attacks the Socialist Democrat Party has committed against President Trump and his family, and we believe God has and will give President Trump an expected good future that heaven and the entire world will hopefully witness in the near future. As a reminder, during President Donald Trump's 1st term in the Oval Office he was continuously mocked and made fun of by the ungodly biased news media's pundits, comedians, and talk show host pundits.

The ungodly attacks against President Trump and his supportive wife, Melania and their family has not been overlooked by The Lord God. He can fully reward President Trump and his family with sweet and precious peace from all of the days of having to deal with their enemies on a daily basis. We will leave how God will deal with President Trump's enemies up to the Lord, and in His capable hands and in His time.

Keep in mind President Trump and his legal team has been willing to present their diligent preparation of illegalities of the Democrat Party supporters and show the U.S. Federal Judicial Judges all of the evidence they have in their possession, provided the federal judges of American courts in key states just how this past presidential election on November 3rd of 2020, where the presidential election experienced voter fraud on massive scale nationwide through the mail in voter ballots wherein the switch and bait voter ballots were tampered with by the Democrat monitor election officials reviewing ballots which were counting the incoming votes through the mail and election prepared teams of people that were behind closed doors while video cameras happened to capture their sinister actions after Republican election officials had left the voter locations. Captured on videotape, they show and reveal how this last election was clearly stolen from President Trump being able and willing to serve out his 2nd Oval Office term as President of the United States of America.

The above mentioned, President Trump's Legal Team have the evidence in their possession that former Venezuela's dictator Hugo Cheves' Dominion voter machines were discovered in America's voting electoral precincts and how they were used in voter locations in the United States to switch and over turn any votes for President Trump, they would automatically change any vote for President Trump to Joe Biden the incoming presidential elect candidate.

We know fully that there was election voter fraud and it has unfortunately resulted in having election fraud criminals that are now serving and erroneously have hijacked the presidency of the United States of America rather than President Trump rightly being able to serve out his 2nd Oval Office term. What has happened to President Trump is an outrage to President Trump as America's President and every American citizen that voted for his re-election.

The Socialist Democrats think they are so politically sophisticated and clever to have used social planners and the Neo-Marxist Media to help them steal America's most recent election from President Trump and our slowly eroding freedoms we take for granted. There are 3 countries Bud and I would recommend for the Socialist Democrat Party members that are bent on changing America and our right to worship God freely and openly which Christians have cherished for decades.

We realize rather than loving and leaving America to remain a free and open society the Socialist Democrats have done a good job of bringing in Socialism and Communism into America's economic commerce of buying and selling of goods, America's Educational System, and spiritual and social political affairs.

So far since we do not agree or like the opposite direction President Elect Joe Biden and his administration is taking our great nation which is far left, we request that every Christian at home and worldwide to urgently pray for America with mighty fervency and Holy Spirit power for God to have His will to be done in American politics.

We recommend the Socialist Democrat Party members fly out from or take a proverbial boat that floats and move to Iran, Venezuela, or Cuba where they would feel more comfortable with their radical ideologies, agendas, and policies of progressively and fundamentally changing America into the Socialist Democrat Utopian Nation and society which they have envisioned and would love to their satisfaction. Sean Hannity on Fox News would even help support and fund your departure trip out from our American shores by plane or by boat.

"The Democrats are constantly redefining terms" was a warning to America by Kevin Sobro's wife, Author Sam Sobro and we recognize the Socialist Democrat Political Party communicate their ideologies and agenda's for the American citizens. We recommend reading her book, "Words for Warriors" as a must read so every concerned and patriotic Christian and conservative American can keep up, stay ahead, and be constantly aware of every Democratic agenda and political move they make, and all of the new plans they have in store for the ever changing American society. Would you like to be on top and in the know of what America will look like should the Socialist Democrats continue to bring and have their political way with the direction and guidance they think is best for every American citizen's future? It is not a pretty picture!!

The Progressive Socialist Democrats are bringing their radical ideology into American society via the Socialist News Media and Education System. Every American citizen will be able to see for themselves that Socialism, Marxism, and Communism does not agree with the Godly Christian Nation that our founding Fathers' envisioned for this great country which was the land of the free and home of the brave.

America always will be a Godly Christian Nation provided American citizens choose to unite against the stealing, killing, and destructtion that Socialism, Marxism, and Communism will inevitably bring and do to our divided nation much harm unless things change in the near future.

I realize that the Progressive Socialist Democrats want to federalize America's election voting process so they are the only party that would be elected as future presidential candidates in the United States of America. They want to totally eradicate a two party presidential system in American politics.

These people are radical hardboiled hard-liners which are positively out to radically transform America into a Utopian Socialist Human Family World Order while stripping, gutting, and stealing from America's citizens, and from the next future generation of youth grow-ing up in today's society, they will be heavily burdened with a huge financial load of debt whereby they will never be able to enjoy true capitalism, and its liberating prosperity and golden opportunities it could open up for them in life, and go on to genuinely experience the American dream.

The Socialist Democrats are only focused on how they can self-serve their progressive revolutionary reformations when they erroneous-ly want to put America back onto their so called right path they believe is the right course for this nation and the American citizens. So far from our perspective the revolutionary political and societal changes the Progressive Socialist Democrat Party have been making has shown that their radical strategies and tactics have been scary, frightening, unpleas-ant to watch and hear on TV, and not something that the American citizens as a whole were expecting, desiring, and looking forward to should they elect anyone else than President Trump.

President Joe Biden said he was going to work on uniting us as a nation, and yet we see him making decisions which continue to divide America besides signing executive orders that are truly bad, painful, and costing American citizens good paying jobs. Instead of President Joe Biden showing that he really loves and cares for every American citizen's best interests, protection, and security we see President Biden continue to make decisions that are more partisan radical far-left and left-wing political policies that are opposed to the majority of Americans.

President Joe Biden needs to step up and put an immediate stop to the illegal immigration crises at our U.S.-Mexico border now not only because it is the right thing to do, but because men, women, and children of the illegals are being violated, painfully used and abused, and mistreated by the Mexican drug cartels involved in human trafficking and drug smuggling of "cocaine, heroin, methamphetamine, and other illicit narcotics to the United States". I heard on Newsmax TV that 1 in 3 women are being raped and 1 in 6 men are being sexually assaulted.

The Cartels are hardened criminals that are ruthless, barbaric, and severely brutal. Stopping the U.S. building the border wall policy by the Socialist Democrat Party-President Joe Biden's executive order has become a total failure, and caused a serious crisis at our U.S-Mexico southern border, and they want to distract the American citizen's focus which is engaged fully on the U.S-Mexico border crises, by flying illegal immigrants to further northern states to be absorbed into American cities. The Progressive Socialist Democrat Party needs to be eradicated, banned, shut down, and told to immediately cease their radical harmful tactics by the United States Supreme Court which is the highest court in the U.S. Nation.

The nine member judicial Supreme Court must become emboldened to rise up and enforce the laws of the land for all American citizens, and not just for one partisan left-wing Socialist Democrat Party, but also stand up for the Christian Churches, every conservative voice, and every non-U.S.

citizen, otherwise large numbers in these groups of citizens may although erroneously think that the United States Supreme Court, and the majority of Americans have decided to agree with the Socialist Democrat Party's Marxist Revolutionary Socialist Reformation policies in America whereby they want to continue making Socialist Marxist political changes to our health crises conscious weakened and vulnerable
U.S. Nation.

President Biden has decided to put Vice President Harris in charge of the U.S.-Mexico border crises, and the illegal immigrants are being flown into U.S. Northern states to cover up their illegal immigrant crises from the citizens of America who are visibly seeing the horrendous and outrageous human trafficking crises being played out on their Cable TV's every day that they can clearly see for themselves.

Most likely President Biden put Vice President Harris in charge of the borderless immigrant policy because he knew she would not get anything done with the illegal immigrants surging into America because of her past null and void and do nothing sanctuary city policy of San Francisco since she was good for the God forbid that this radical takeover by the policies of the Socialist Democrat Party continues to be played out on the American open border policy that will negatively impact and financially effect every citizen living in the United States of America, and the future generations growing up in this nation eventually. Thanks to President Biden and his freewheeling spirit and invitation for the illegal immigrants to come at will and apply for asylum.

Are the real supporters and voters for President Biden and Vice President Harris truly happy now with the radical policies and changes the Progressive Socialist Democrat Party is making to this nation, and the economic and financial jeopardy they have already, and will continue to put America in as a nation?

Citizens of America, we must hold President Joe Biden fully responsible for the human trafficking, and the horrible sexual abuse crises against adults involving the child abuse crises taking place at the southern border points of the United States of America. The Progressive Socialist Democrat Party is using President Joe Biden with his mental gaffes and memory losses to continue to distract the American citizens from seeing and grasping the radical Socialist Democrats agenda that want to flood America with illegal immigrants because they want the extra illegal immigrant votes to remain in power far beyond 2024, but also well into decades of future elections. It's time to Wake Up America!!

Keep in mind it was President Joe Biden that had made a statement that was captured on live Cable TV back in 2019 that they {the Democrat Party} were going to be more soft on the illegal immigration policy when he became the next president of the United States as he was looking forward to the 2020 presidential election.

President Biden said that he had never taken a single penny from any foreign country in my life during the 2020 presidential election debate with President Trump. President Biden outright lied to America, on what he had said during the presidential election, and he just like President Obama is, has, and will continue to lie to the American people who can do fact checks on President Biden's past practices when he was the Vice President of the United States.

Citizens of America and all non-U.S. citizens, I implore you to stay alert of everything President Biden is telling America as a nation, and see for yourselves the shady business dealings President Biden and his son, Hunter were involved with in, the lies, untruths, and you will uncover and discover a lot of corruption in the Biden family that America needs to hold President Biden and his family ties accountable for in every way by The U.S. Constitutional Laws, Rule of Law, and the United States Supreme Court needs to implement everything possible to stop what the Socialist Democrat Party wants to bring into American politics, and radically stop the sick mind-bending and all the radical changes they want to make to the citizens of America as a whole.

America, the Progressive Socialist Democrats are a radical bunch of "astoundingly pigheaded" politicians that had a bad case of Trump deranged syndrome for four years when President Trump served out his one term presidency. Now their ongoing troubles with President Trump have boiled over onto American citizens, and they are more than willing to use the U.S. Government to bring pressures against Christians and every conservative American and all non-U.S. citizens as well.

I heard on Newmax TV that President Joe Biden was asked about Russian President Vladimir Putin and President Biden responded that he is a killer. President Putin challenged President Biden to a debate, and he also stated that he didn't believe Biden had a soul. Apparently Joe Biden and this current Presidential Administration has shown they know how to get certain people angry with their remarks and comments about them, and they need to use more prudence in how they relate and talk relative concerning particular political world leaders.

Before President Joe Biden gets himself and America into more trouble or continue to have problems with any world national leaders he needs his team of administration protectors to teach him some good Biblical etiquette, and social graces when encountering or speaking regarding world political adversaries especially if they are a national leader of a superpower nation such as Russia, China, Mexico, India, Brazil, Japan, and Indonesia.

The Bible has the answer for President Biden, and his oral slips of the tongue whether he says things intentionally or simply a verbal mishap by accident he needs to be especially more careful how he speaks concerning world leaders. Under the inspiration of the Holy Spirit David the Psalmist penned, "Set a guard, O Lord, over my mouth; Keep a watch over the door of my lips." (Psalm 141:3 NKJV). "Even so the tongue is a little member and boasts great things. See how great a forest a little fire kindles! And the tongue is a fire, a world of iniquity. The tongue is so set among our members that it defiles the whole body, and sets on fire the course of nature; and it is set on fire by hell." (James 3:5-6 NKJV).

I heard on 770 am radio in the Pacific Northwest one conservative political pundit talking about President Biden not working with Republicans and Democrats and {Independents} on national issues as a president is expected to. He referred to President Biden acting like a dictator using {the stroke of} a pen in order to achieve his policies which we recognize are not good for the citizens of America or America as a whole, but are acceptable to the Left-Wing Democrat Party and their radical push towards Socialism, Marxism, and Communism in America.

I was able to capture this on Fox News when Steve Doocy was interviewing The North Las Vegas Mayor John Lee who had switched from the Socialist Democrat Party to the GOP Republican Party. Steve says, "You say the Democratic Party is now being run by admitted Socialists and that is why you had to get out". John Lee, "I'd say card carrying Socialists. We had a recent election in Nevada, and the Democratic Party had an election for leadership and four out of the five people were card carrying members of the Socialistic Party. It's not the party that I grew up with twenty-five years ago in this environment, and it's not the party that I can stand with anymore. It's not what we want out West and we're not going to accept it anymore".

Steve Doocy, "And the Democrat Party you grew up with were the party of the workers class, but you don't see that anymore". John Lee, "No, the worker class of men and women of this country and also the small business owners are not part of the conversation anymore. It all has to do with the elitists, and it has to do with the Socialists. That is not the agenda that I have in mind for this country of the future". John Lee added, "We are not out for expanding the government to even bigger and more intrusive into our lives. That is not what we want out West and we're not going to accept it anymore".

I saw the following on Newsmax TV and dated 31 March 2021. Rep. Jim Jordan@Jim Jordan. President Bidens' Infrastructure plan. "-Higher taxes -More spending -Job losses in the energy sector such a deal".

It is imperative that we the people choose to collectively and corporately stand strong as united American citizens, and not be double minded citizens, whereby half of the nation is uncertain if they desire to live and serve the Lord God as revealed in The Holy Bible. The Bible speaks to Christian brothers and we could apply the passage recorded in the book of (James 1:5-8 NKJV), to all men and women that need wisdom from God. "If any of you lacks wisdom, let him ask of God, who gives to all liberally and without reproach, and it will be given to him. But let him ask in faith, with no doubting, for he who doubts is like the wave of the sea driven and tossed by the wind. For let not that man suppose that he will receive anything from the Lord; he is a double-minded man, unstable in all his and ways". The scriptural passage refers to any man or woman that is double-minded, and following doctrines and teachings of this worlds system contrary to the Word of God.

We the people of the United States of America must choose to unite, agree with, and stand on the sure word of prophecy found in the Holy Word of God and its guiding principles and promises of faith, family, freedoms, love, joy, and peace that passes all understanding that will keep our hearts and minds through Christ Jesus. America, we all can obtain through Christ Jesus what He provided on the Cross of Calvary for all of mankind if we will simply believe, claim, accept, and receive God's grace and goodness He extends to all through His precious shed blood for which He freely continues to give to all those that will believe on Him as the Son of God and manifest in the flesh which means incarnate "having human nature and form" as recorded in His Word.

Joshua as the chosen leader of the nation of Israel rightfully made a declaration that the people had to make a decision whom they will serve. "Now therefore, fear the Lord, serve Him in sincerity and in truth, and put away the gods which your fathers served on the other side of the River and in Egypt. Serve the Lord! "And if it seems evil to you to serve the Lord, choose for yourselves this day whom you will serve, whether the gods which your fathers served that were on the other side of the River, or the gods of the Amorites, in whose land you dwell. But as for me and my house, we will serve the Lord." (Joshua 24:14-15 NKJV).

America, we must make the same declaration to all of America's citizens. Whom will you serve, the false gods you believed on in the country you had migrated from or will you serve the true God that has shown Himself mighty time and time again throughout America's founding beginnings to the present time in American history, and throughout the world's system no matter what country you are from? Regarding our choice as American citizens, we declare with Joshua the man of God, but as for me and our houses we choose to serve the Lord.

We encourage all American citizens to take a bold stand for the true and Living God the Creator which our founding fathers believed in and the Pilgrims and Puritans chose to traverse the high seas and the dangerous Atlantic Ocean in hopes of finding a place to worship and serve God with religious liberty in the new land where they would be separate from the Church of England. We know that now is the time for this great nation to return and serve the God of The Holy Bible, and earnestly return to America's founding principles based by faith upon the Judeo-Christian values and principles that the Lord God will bless and honor through Jesus Christ and the cross of Calvary.

We encourage all Christians and true conservative patriots to pray and seek the Lord for his direction and guidance for our national leaders, that there would be peace and harmony among Congressional leaders so that God's will would be done in our nation spiritually, morally, and civically with all of America's citizenry, and the U.S. Supreme Court as well.

We need to urgently pray for America's spiritual strength to be given to our national leaders on the Republican and Democrat side of the Congressional aisles, salvation for all, and put an end to being spineless and refusing to stand up for God, the Bible, The U.S.-Constitution, and begin making right decisions for everything that will make America great again and stop rationalizing, making excuses, and compromising America's Christian character and role America must play out for God in this world as a mighty lion with courage, strength, faith, and hope for its citizens and choose not to slink back as a mealy-mouthed mouse afraid to stand up to the radical Progressive Socialist Democrats, as the bullies that they are and fight for the rights and freedoms of all of our nations citizens.

It is time to get tough and do the right things to protect and preserve what America has fought for throughout our American history, and never back down or compromise on the principles that made you a great leader in the first place, for which American citizens thought you were a highly qualified U.S. Senator that deserves a seat in the government and should have a Congressional role and position to serve as a state Senator worthy of fulfilling a Congressional seat marked as a strong national leader representing the state of the union you represent and were elected to serve in. We especially need every Republican Senator to stand strong and not compromise for all of America.

Bud shared with me that it use to be on the school ground in America we could recognize the bullies on the school ground and people tended to not like those bullies. The news media during the President Trump's Presidency proved to be bullies as chickens in a chicken pen. So many American citizens that were programmed and bullied into going along with and joining the mockery against President Donald Trump which included the media and the educational system all played a part in attacking President Trump to get the American citizenry distracted to what the Socialist Liberal Democrats were doing with the media's help, the Socialist Democrats fulfilled their plans on stealing the presidential election from President Trump.

Jim Nations on Francis and Friends with SBN Broadcast program pointed out that he heard, Nancy Pelosi mention that President Trump will not be our new president. She had to have known that there was a calculated sinister plan to topple President Trump with their radical agendas from within America's states of the union and everything the National Democrat Political Party was going to do to upset the voter's ballots election system, and unseat President Trump from serving out his 2nd Presidential term.

Many Christian people and conservative patriots were left wonder ing how and why this could ever happen in a Christian Nation, and why God had let the Christians down to the agony of defeat to the high pitched shrill of triumph to the National Democrat Party with their Progressive Socialist crazy radical ideologies, agendas, and policies that are bad for America on all fronts and corrupt in nature and scope? God has been monitoring everything the Socialist Democrats have been up to, and He didn't fail America in their hopes and desires to continue to stand with President Trump's, Let's Make America Great Again.

Bud and I recommend that everyone watch the YouTube Video on President Joe Biden admitting that 500,071 million dead from the virus. President Joe Biden also says, "now we have over 120 million dead from Covid" referring to the health pandemic Coronavirus disease also named Covid-19. Vice Kamala Harris says, "We're looking at over 220 million in the last several months died." We appreciate YouTube Videos for they knowingly capture on video the truths and oral gaffes politicians make as well as ordinary citizens.

We recommend everyone watch President Joe Biden Admits To Voter Fraud in 0.24 seconds on YouTube Videos. He says, For the people that do not have the YouTube Video app President Joe Biden says, "We're in a situation where we have put together and you guys did it for President Obama's Administration before this, we have put together I think the most organized extensive and inclusive voter fraud in the history of American politics".

We hope President Biden and Vice President Harris embrace and accept their admissions or learn from their oral mistakes and begin telling the American citizens the whole truth and nothing but the truth which we need to hear, and nothing else they have to say that might cause people to lose their grip on reality, trigger a fear button in the minds and hearts of many American citizens, and commence a large scale panic in the lives of large numbers of American and non-U.S. citizens, that could bring on wild, crazy, and abnormal thoughts and behaviors.

I spoke recently with Lorena's cousin's son, Bentino who happens to be a teenager that hasn't reached the voting age yet. I asked him if he preferred President Trump or Biden and Harris referring to President Joe Biden and Vice President Kamala Harris. He leaned over to speak to me since he is a tall young man and he spoke to me in a soft voice that he went with the least of the worst, which was Biden and Harris. America, Christians failed President Donald Trump because Christians failed to vote God. As a nation we failed President Trump because we the people failed to vote the Lord Jesus Christ, the Author and Finisher of our faith. Keep in mind that the Lord Jesus Christ was using President Trump in his 1st Presidential Oval Office term, and He was ready to use him again had President Trump succeeded in winning the November 3rd, 2020 presidential election.

You might ask, how was Jesus Christ using President Trump in his 1st presidential term and you might wonder just how Jesus was ready and willing to use President Trump in his 2nd Oval Office term? Well, Jesus had protected President Trump and He had preserved and protected President Trump from the Neo-Marxist News Media that had been attacking President Trump day in and day out.

The Lord Jesus was giving President Trump wisdom from God how to deal with his enemies, and Jesus had given President Trump a fighting spirit to know how to fight back against an onslaught of verbal and oral mean spirited attacks that many U.S. Presidents might have buckled under.

The Lord Jesus also had protected and preserved President Trump from social planner attacks, Big Tech Companies, corrupt politicians, socialist university and college professors and their deceived, brain washed, and programmed secular humanists and Progressive Socialist Democrat students. President Trump had a lot of enemies that came against him from all sides to get him to relinquish and give up his presidential position as Commander in Chief, and his re-election to serve out his 2nd Presidential Term.

The Lord God Almighty was using President Trump to protect us from the bullies, thugs, tyrants, and terrorists among Socialists, Marxists, and Communists. Bud would call the Democrats the Digressive Party. God was also protecting America from the Progressive Socialist Liberal Democrat National Party with all of their radical ideologies, agendas, and crazy policies that do not agree with God's plans and objectives to preserve our Republic as a Godly Christian Nation with peace, harmony, and prosperity financially for all. This means spiritual, mental, emotional, and total well-being of our nation. American citizens were being blessed financially that could be measured in every ethnic groups and sub cultures under President Trump's economic agenda with low taxation rates.

President Trump's, Build the Wall Bill that the U.S. Congress had approved of and passed, the wall between the United States of America and Mexico, this same wall was also protecting and preventing U.S. citizens from being harmed by an influx of terrorists and enemy combatants that have more of a sinister terrorist minded agenda on his or her mind to cause criminal, terrorism, or pure evil devastating attacks on American citizens.

The bottom line America, Christians failed President Trump when Christians and American citizens failed to vote the way God wanted them to. Many Christians and non-Christians sided with the crowd rather than using spiritual wisdom and Godly discernment to absolutely determine which presidential candidate is the right one that God the Father, God the Son, and God the Holy Spirit had chosen and decided upon for the November 3rd, 2020 presidential election. With this last presidential election now behind us, was God even in the voting picture for most Americans? Something to reflect upon and think about as you consider everything that went into your decision to vote for the presidential candidate that you did vote for.

Christians and American citizens had failed President Trump because they failed to vote Jesus Christ. Christians and American citizens had failed President Trump because they had failed to vote according to the Word of God, The Holy Bible. You know that a good contractor and the carpenter that wanted to build a house would positively use a plum line to make absolutely certain that the house they're building is 100% accurate according to the blueprint design plans, along with their building alignments and measurements. Bud added, "Built on a solid concrete base or foundation".

This is absolutely crucial. It is positively needful to use a plum line, and it is also crucial to have building alignments when constructing a house or any other building you might be planning on constructing or building. Christians and all U.S. American citizens and non-U.S. citizens failed President Trump because we as a nation didn't have the mind of Christ when it came time to cast our votes. "Let this mind be in you which was also in Christ Jesus," (Philippians 2:5 NKJV).

The United States of America's citizens failed President Trump because "Biden received 306 electoral votes", and we hold each of the electors fully responsible that constitutes the Electoral College which cast each of their individual and collective votes for President Elect Joe Biden had also let President Trump and the American citizenry down big time.

We recommend and encourage every presidential elector to repent, renounce, and revoke your decision to cast your Electoral College vote for presidential candidate Joe Biden in order to help him obtain and win the presidential election back on November 3rd, 2020. Our nation is suffering in so many ways as a consequence of your anti-God and carnal thinking and voting. I can assure American citizens the Electoral College voters did not base their voting rights on who God wanted them to vote for.

American citizens are being killed and left behind in Afghanistan including Afghan interpreters, translators, journalists, the Afghan interpreter that rescued U.S. Senator Joe Biden in 2008, and many Afghan
U.S. Visa applicants were left behind by President Biden's call for our
U.S. Armed Forces to pull out from Afghanistan before making certain all non-U.S. citizens and Afghan U.S. Military supporters, and all of our U.S. military equipment has been removed that could be subject to being seized by the Taliban terrorists.

May your decision be directed and guided by the Lord God Himself, and let your individual and collective determination produce helping the Citizens of America to begin to experience great rejoicing by continuous joyous celebrations throughout every state, city, town, and community that the bands of wickedness and the shackles of tyranny have begun to be broken off America through the control of Socialists, Marxists, and the Communists rule of thinking without their belief in God and the freedoms we enjoy in this nation. May Jesus Christ regain the Supremacy of Kingship He alone deserves on the thrones of our hearts and over all government rule.

We recommend for everyone reads John Nolte: "WE ALL KNOW WHY JOE BIDEN IS HIDING OUT TWO WEEKS FROM ELECTION DAY"

"Democrat presidential candidate Joe Biden has been in hiding for days and intends to remain in hiding at least until Thursday night's presidential debate, and I think we all know why…
Think about this…

Joe Biden's mental frailty, his position on packing the Supreme Court, and his son Hunter's emails are so bad, he and his campaign believe he is better off hiding from the public than going out and campaigning during the final two weeks of the election.

First, though, let's talk about how outrageous it is for Biden to be so smug and secure in his victory, so smug and secure the national media will campaign on his behalf, that he thinks he can sit it out, hug the ball, run out the clock, while President Donald Trump is out there doing two and three events a day while being president.

Never before in my 54 years have I seen anything like this. Okay, nothing about how corrupt and evil the national political media are in any way surprises me. Nothing. The media have embraced political terrorism… Not a surprise. The media are basically running Joe Biden's campaign against Trump… Not a surprise.

No joke if we find out the media have hired assassins to take out their political opponents that would not surprise us in the least. Same with Big Tech.

So the media's behavior does not surprise me. But Biden almost entirely removing himself from the campaign trail for days and days and days this close to an election… Amazing. Who would have ever thought the 2020 Democrat nominee would make Hillary Clinton look like a workhorse.

Biden thinks he can win this thing with TV ads and media coverage only… I mean, on top of making almost no campaign appearances, he has almost no ground game. No one's knocking on doors for Joe.

But we all know the main reasons why Biden is hiding…

First off, Biden's scared of being asked questions about his obvious desire to pack the Supreme Court with additional justices which would mean the end of democracy. That's not hyperbole. If you appoint a bunch of unelected Democrats to the Supreme Court with lifetime tenure, that's the end of democracy that's turning the court over to an unaccountable legislature.

You see, if you intend to pack the court, it is better off to remain in hiding than to admit that. Then there's his son Hunter's emails."

Grant you there is more to what John Nolte has to say, but we were hoping the readers liked what Nolte had to say and will want to read Nolte's entire article. From John Nolte's excellent analysis and explanation of the presidential campaign candidate Joe Biden before he was elected as President Elect Joe Biden and we encourage all to read his insightful article.

We all can thank the media and Big Tech companies for not allowing presidential hopeful Joe Biden the hard questions that he needed to be asked, and he needed to provide the answers for the American citizens to hear his answers whether he is the best presidential candidate to be elected as America's United States President or whether he should be viewed as only a presidential hopeful. Citizens of America, you have the right to hold the media and the presidential debates moderators responsible for letting President Trump, the American citizens, and all non-U.S. citizens, down which is totally a disgrace, shameful, and pathetic that President Joe Biden is now America's Commander in Chief.

President Joe Biden is really not fit to be America's current president, not only because of his cognizant decline, but also due to his radical policies which are not acceptable to millions and millions of American citizens that strongly believe in God, The U.S. Country, The U.S Constitution, The Christian faith and family traditions and values.

We recommend reading John Hudak's article on, "For presidential candidates' bold ideas, debate moderators must demand details and realism". Friday, April 5, 2019.

We recommend everyone watch the YouTube Video entitled, Trump-era official says 'we have rookies in ch" on FOX BUSINESS with recorded time of 6: minutes and 46 seconds long.

We encourage U.S. Congress to vote no on H.R.1 and SB1. Josh Rosenstern on Insight with SBN Broadcasting Network who is a very wise and an intelligent man of God was talking about making the voting system easier for the American citizens, and he recognizes "…the fact that people stand in line to vote for hours, that's wrong. They need to fix that. So how about instead of federalizing the election process, and making it to a wide open basically anyone can go and vote, you can mail in your ballot without requesting it, there's no means of verification. Instead of that changing that let's focus on addressing the true problems.

When you've got people that have to go thirty minutes to a voting location, they got to stand in line for three hours, there needs to be and this bill and this law in Georgia, would address that. They would say wait a minute. We've got people in this precinct, in this county, that are having to wait for hours to cast their vote. They're having to go thirty minutes, and then on top of that wait for hours.

We got to do something about this, that needs to be addressed, making it more {easier} giving people a greater ability to get in to vote, but we should not change the reality that people need to demonstrate, that they are who they say they are, when casting {their vote}.

I'm talking through this ladies and gentlemen and many have heard me explain this before, but we so quickly forget about it, yet H.R.1 and
S.B.1 and our Congress seeks to totally change everything, so they can have more power. We got to combat that, about the coming in forms, and looking for what the problems that exist that are really there and then address those".

We appreciate the words of wisdom and great wealth of knowledge that John and Josh Rosenstern have regarding the serious issues that Christians and the citizens of America are facing in these troublesome times, especially with the President Biden's Administration, the Neo-Marxists and Left-Wing radicals that he is receiving advice from to guide and direct his presidency completely opposite of God's will for the country, and what the Godly citizens of America truly need, desire, and want for this nation.

The Lord God, the Christians, and all President Trump's supporters and voters forbid all the different forms of Socialism, Marxism, and Communism from growing, increasing, and spreading on our watch in the United States of America.

We recommend watching 5 Questions To Ask "Democratic Socialists" by Liz Wheeler on YouTube Videos. Below the title it mentions, "Young America's Foundation". Below that it states, "Leftists use the phrase 'democratic socialism' to try and disguise the truly destructive policies that they support".

I happened to listen to the exchange between Josh {John's son} and John Rosenstern one morning on Insight an SBN Broadcast Network program, and the following is what they had to say: Josh, "… so do I count as an immigrant? I want to count as an immigrant. I am an American citizen", Josh said. John responded, "You were born in America, you are an American citizen". Josh, "So and then in bringing up what took place in a segregated South, in segregated schools all of that which was wrong has now been righted. There is no extra segregation that is happening like, especially like what was happening then. There is segregation that is starting to come back, but in the other direction like were reversing course in so many ways.

Josh, "Dad, this frustrates me because this is what is being said about our nation to the UN Body, and to the world". John, "They want to dismantle our Constitution. That's their goal. Eliminate the Constitution, eradicate it, amend it in ways that it is no longer effective because it's racist, but their goal and this is what the people got to understand it's not about race they could care less, it's about Communism. They want to bring about a power that will control not only what you do, but what you think.

Josh says, "Can I say this is Marxism, the premise Marx was also a Communist, but his version Marxism the difference in it factor I heard all kinds of arguments on this, but this is what it boils down to the difference Marxism as compared to paganism which is more of a peaceful means of bringing it in quote and quote. Marxism is this, you have to identify an oppressed class it's called the proletariat class John, grievances, yes.

Josh, and uh, that's correct, they have grievances with the system. John, "Mm-hmm, that's right". Josh, "and they have to be um, really riled up to come together under this cause to overthrow a system, John finishes Josh's thought. John, "a system by violent means." Josh, "a force." John, "a revolution." Josh, "a power." John, "revolution, that's right." Josh, "OK, you said it right the agenda is a Communist agenda, but here's what they need, they need a proletariat group."

John, and they are creating many, and the revolution is not with war and weapons, it's a culture revolution. Josh, that's correct. John, "they are changing the culture, and now trying to back date that which was begun in this country, and bring it back, but in a reverse status".

Josh, "here's, here's the thing. The issue of race and racism, segregation, and all of these things has been addressed in our nation, but here is how it ultimately has been addressed, here's where it started. It started with God working in the hearts of men and ultimately women as well. It was God working in the heart of Abraham Lincoln", John, "that's right" Josh, "and it was Abraham Lincoln consulting the scripture". John, "that's right". Seeing what is going on, but understanding what was happening from a heart where the righteousness of God had touched his heart". John, "that's right". Josh, "And I know that {Josh became emotional at this point as he continued} was the case for that man, President Lincoln".

John, "Yes". Josh, "And many that came after that, that God touched their hearts. Were they perfect, no, no, and you aren't either, I'm not either, but touched the hearts where there was wrong and injustice, His righteousness and His Holy Word touched the hearts of men and women, and He helped them to bring about changes.

That how this came, it was not through political activism. It was through God touching the hearts", John, "exactly". Josh continues, "and through revival coming. That's the only answer for our nation". John, "that's it alone". Josh, "If there are injustices being done right now, and wrongs happening in our nation, only I can't fix that. I can only point you to the One that can, that is Jesus Christ". John, "Amen". Josh, "That is what we must have. We don't need our nation torn down by ambassadors and others, and I haven't even gotten to what the Vice President said". John, "Yea, we need to share that tomorrow", Josh, but the answer is God touching the hearts".

Josh and John Rosenstern provide good insights in the following exchange which is taken from their Insight Program on SonLife Broadcast Network 4/1/2021. John says, "…we have to be very careful with what we identify with, what we participate {with}, who we vote for, who we don't vote for, and why are we voting and why are we not voting for a particular individual.

Psalm 94 says this, verse twenty, so the throne of iniquity have fellowship with thee which frameth mischief by the law. Let me read on, they gather themselves together against the soul of the righteous and condemn the innocent blood. The very thing you say they do.

They frame laws like abortion. A bunch of miserable old Republican men in black robes determined that life doesn't begin at conception or don't believe that let's put it that way and allow this ridiculous disgusting murder some "(context dated English) murderous.,
{"US Characterized by or given to murder, capable of killing, deadly, fatal."}, event to take place that women, they call if free choice, but it's not free choice, it's no choice for the human being that's in their womb, and no they don't have according to the word of God a decision to make about that individual whether they live or die.

We've now made women judges over humanity whether they live or die. That's God's place to do that. In other words we have put women in a position of godhood by putting them in a place where they can now choose the life or death of a human being, according to the word of God. Verse 23, And He shall bring upon them their own iniquity, and shall cut them off in their own wickedness; yea, the Lord our God shall cut them off.

Do you realize the danger that politicians are in especially our Congressional leaders both in the Senate/House if they frame mischief by law. This is where it gets crafty, and I know the time is running and I have a few other points that I want to make".

Keep in mind that John and Josh like to quote from the King James Version of The Holy Bible.

"Think of this, most of the time a bill is brought forward they will add twenty-five things that are good to it to get the one bad one passed or they will take something good and add something bad to it so if you're trying to do something good you have to have the other bad things come in. That's how they craft these laws and create mischief is because they frame mischief by a law that's what that means you put into place you structure something that you can't have one without the other. By doing so that is the highest level of deception so you're a conservative you are trying to give something good that your people it's an emergency and they want to add bad things to it.

Can you vote for those bad things, if you don't you get ostracized and criticized, well you didn't vote for what the people needed, but the reality is they couldn't because of the other harm that it would bring that would be in the long run far worse. That's why it's not good to be a politician, advice for my son. Josh chuckles at his father's inference to himself.

Is God, {does} He oppose government? Absolutely not" "Interesting enough, in the United States of America, this may not be true of other countries you have to be an American citizen and American born on this continent so to speak or this country I should say. To become president of the United States. Am I correct? Josh says, Natural born citizen. John says, "…you have said correctly on other programs that 80% of our founding documents were either found directly or the principle of scripture was used to frame those foundational laws of our country".

Josh shares, "either directly or indirectly to the words found, there were several scholars and other works that were referenced by our founding fathers in framing our Constitution and our founding documents and um, what's interesting though those scholars those who were experts, legal experts and so forth, their quotes their thoughts were shaped by the Bible. So "yes" directly or indirectly were 80% of the wording in our founding documents derived itself from scripture, so that shows you the tremendous weight". John takes over at this juncture.

John then shares some additional thoughts to compliment what Josh had to share in his contextual scriptural account regarding America's foundational laws for the good of the citizens of America pertaining to the paragraph above, and the principle to prolong a king's life. John then adds, "… now that had to do with the kings of Israel, but politicians that understand that principle that if they abide by the statutes and the commandments of God, and do that which is right it will prolong their days and will also be a blessing to their brethren…". John continued with his ending remarks, and thanks to the Lord we can all learn a great Biblical lesson by observing, obeying, and forever practicing honoring the Lord in all of His ways that we also may benefit from having our lives prolonged provided we live and abide in accordance to the laws of God, and by choosing life for ourselves and our prosperity.

The following is John Rosenstern's accurate account of the Progressive Socialist Democrat Party recorded on 4/29/2021 from Son Life Broadcast Network. John shares, "uh, many of you know my opposition, and I don't say this entirely, this is not a personal attack it's a policy attack. I don't look at these individuals as enemies, now some of you might and you're wrong. Talking to my uh, extreme right Republican friends. I'm not Republican or Democrat, I'm Christian, but my point is this. I don't hate Biden, I don't hate Kamala Harris, I don't hate Nancy Pelosi, I don't hate Chuck Schumer, I pray for them.

I'm asking God to change their hearts. They're going in the wrong direction. They are leading our country in the wrong direction. They're are being under the influence of demonic powers, that's right. We need to pray and take authority over those demonic influences in their life, those satanic powers of darkness.

You can read about what they are in Ephesians chapter 6, these hierarchy of demon powers that influence humanity. They're taking us away from the things of God, away from the things of freedom of choice, more towards a bigger, fatter, uglier government that wants to control every aspect of your life, redistributing what you earn and hard work, and now telling you what kind of work you can or can't do, creating the kind of jobs that they want to fulfill their policies, their agenda which has nothing to do with racism, it has nothing to do with the betterment of individuals, it has everything to do with Communism and power.

That's strong John! Yes it is! And the reason it's strong is because the policies that they're implementing are using the tool of Socialism that ultimately end up in Communism.

That is what Karl Marx taught. For those of you that can I encourage you to read the Communist Manifesto and Capital. Those books tell you very clearly the process of it. The means of implementing those were little bit uh, how can I say it, unable to be accomplished by Marxist concepts of revolution so, the culture revolution is the way they do it. They do it with gradualism. Little by little over the last thirty-forty-fifty years throughout my life I've watched how these policies have been implemented, and really they began going much further back into the 1915-16-17-18, etc., years it began. Woodrow Wilson brought in progressive ideas, and before that Teddy (Theodore) Roosevelt was a progressive."

We recommend for the readers to sign up with SonLife Broadcast Network to watch and learn all of what John had to say concerning the deceptions which the Progressive Socialist Democrat Party have been doing to bring about the changes they have already implemented against the citizens of America, and to be more informed how you might join the Christian and conservative resistant team to help put a stop to their ever expanding takeover of our American way of life by growing a bigger and extensive government to control the nation's population.

John also has more to say about the absentee ballots and voter fraud in the elections, Planned Parenthood which John calls Planned Murder hood, and the goal of the Obama/thee Biden Administration and others like it, and how they want to give everyone crossing the borders amnesty, place them in strategic places in the country and in so doing gain the votes of the people because we will in turn give them the goods. That is what they are doing, John recognizes.

I contacted Son Life Broadcast Network Ministries at 1+800-288-8350, and spoke with a representative about how someone could listen to and access some of their past programs. The kind spoken represent ative explained that one could go to SonLifeTV.com and under the flashing banner of watch, and it will ask you for a login and pass word, and that will let you in to watch a Message in the Cross, Francis and Friends, they've got a lot to type in there she said. We recommend the readers to go to SonLife Broadcasting Network concerning finding past programs of Insight, etc., they are available for you to watch, view, benefit from, and enjoy.

I was able to learn the following things from a conservative news station on Cable TV, and the broadcaster wanted citizens of America to know that it is important that we recognize President Biden's Administration wants more U.S. citizen's dependent on the U.S. Government. They want us to think we are a racist nation which is untrue. They want to put an end to photo identification and change the Voter ID Laws and requirements.

Bud and I can clearly see that the Progressive Socialist Democrats will continue to persevere until they have totally changed the United States of America from a Judeo-Christian founded Republic to a Progressive Socialist Marxist Democrat run government, to radically destroy our Republic and Christian Nation by every ungodly means at their disposal. President Biden's Administration, the Neo-Marxists, and Left-Wing radicals that he is receiving advice from to guide and direct his presidency need to realize that they are offending the God of The Holy Bible, the Christians, and all of President Trump's supporters and conservative voters our message resonates loud and clear with a mighty impact, With God's Help Let's Make America Great Again.

God and all President Trump's supporters and voters forbid this from ever happening to America, such a time as this, and during this time in American history. It's high time President Biden Wakes Up from his cognizant decline, and his Neo-Marxist advisors arouse themselves from the Neo-Marxist radical fantasies they are obsessed with and focused on to fundamentally change the United States of America into what they envision, and recognize you are fighting against the Lord God Almighty and He is the protector, defender, and lover of America and all of its people.

We command that the demon forces controlling President Biden, his Neo-Marxist Democrat advisors, and the evil forces, radical ideologies, strategies, agendas, and policies to be cast out from your lives, silenced, and cease from your evil designs on this nation which is the land of the brave.

We say, take your dirty hands off of this nation now and hear the Word of the Lord, "Let God arise, Let His enemies be scattered; Let those also who hate Him flee before Him. As smoke is driven away, So drive them away; As wax melts before a fire, So let the wicked perish at the presence of God. But let the righteous be glad; Let them rejoice before God; Yes, let them rejoice exceedingly." (Psalm 68:1-3 NKJV).

"According to their deeds, accordingly He will repay, Fury to His adversaries, Recompense to His enemies; The coastlands He will fully repay. So shall they fear The name of the Lord from the west, And the glory from the rising of the sun; When the enemy comes in like a flood, The Spirit of the Lord will lift up a standard against him". (Isaiah 59:18-19 NKJV). The Lord God knows how to settle your hash and shake you till your teeth rattles.

I remember my mother telling me that when men {and women} get their eyes on man {or woman}, God will show them that they have feet of clay. Citizens of America, this nation has rebelled against the Lord and His Words, "Because they rebelled against the words of God, And despised the counsel of the most High, Therefore He brought down their heart with labor; They fell down, and there was none to help. Then they cried out to the Lord in their trouble, And He saved them out of their distresses." (Psalm 107:12-13 NKJV). We as a nation have rebelled against the Lord and His Words in many ways, and as a consequence this nation is in perilous times like we haven't seen before.

I bring the following scriptural example to your attention: re-member when the disciple Peter which Jesus recognized of having little faith walked on the water in response to the Lord Jesus, "So He said, Come. And when Peter had come down out of the boat, he walked on the water to go to Jesus." (Matthew 14:22-33 NKJV). The point I would like to convey is that as long as Peter kept his eyes focused on the Lord Jesus, he was able to walk on the water as the Bible text so implies, and when the disciple Peter took his eyes off of the Lord Jesus, "But when he saw that the wind was boisterous, he was afraid; and beginning to sink he cried out, saying, "Lord, save me!" (Matthew 14:30 NKJV).

I remember my former brother-in-law, Randell Wikum who had fastened his eyes on people, {students, etc.} when he attended the Pentecostal Bible Institute in Browerland, and when he chose to place his natural eyes and focus on people, their actions and behaviors whereby he was observing which {I surmise were different people whether they professed faith in Jesus Christ or not, and how other believers worked out their salvation with fear and trembling and walk of faith in God}, whether he knew or perceived it or not, he was beginning to sink in his Christian walk with the Lord.

America, as a whole we can see the same thing happening to groups of people, and individuals when they take their spiritual eyes off of the Lord, they also will begin to sink into the troublesome waters of worry, doubt, fear, and the cares of this life. Jesus said, "and the cares of this world, the deceitfulness of riches, and the desires for other things entering in choke the word, and it becomes unfruitful." (Matthew 4:19 NKJV).

The Gospel of Matthew also says, "And Jesus went about all the cities and villages, teaching in their synagogues, preaching the gospel of the kingdom, and healing every sickness and every disease among the people. But when He saw the multitudes, He was moved with compassion for them, because they were weary and scattered, like sheep without a shepherd." (Matthew 9:35-36 NKJV).

Citizens of America, it is sad to say that many have fallen away as Isaiah "the evangelical prophet" appropriately says, "All we like sheep have gone astray; We have turned, every one, to his own way; And the Lord has laid on Him the iniquity of us all." (Isaiah 53:6 NKJV). We all need to be extremely grateful, appreciative, and thankful for the Lord Jesus Christ, and the price He paid and atoned for on the Cross of Calvary as a means so that we can have our sins forgiven and cast into the sea of God's forgetfulness {whereby they are gone, gone, gone and totally erased from our past and remembered against us no more}, for which our founding father's believed in, fought for, and endangered their very lives whereby they had based their faith in the Divine Providence {the Lord and Savior Jesus Christ} that was guiding them.

They placed their faith in the Judeo-Christian principles found in the Word of God, and the principles of the Declaration of Independence and The Constitution of the United States of America.

Bud added, "Thank God our founding fathers didn't tell Paul Revere to tone it down, and stop disturbing their wives and children's sleep. Paul Revere, you need to give your horse a rest, and give the local colonists and militias a break from your incessant declaration the British are coming. Have you seen them yourself or have you been conjuring things up again in your mind in order to bring attention to yourself? In no way should Paul Revere had slowed his horse down, but we know it was needful that he brought the warnings to Patriots John Hancock and Samuel Adams who were in Concord that there was 700 British troops that were on their way to arrest them."

It is a known fact, "During the American Revolution, Paul Revere rode his horse through villages yelling, 'the Redcoats are coming, the Redcoats are coming to alert the people that the British soldiers were coming to take over their lands…. And more bills are coming as the new day Redcoats are persistent."

We are forever grateful for The U.S Constitution which is the guiding document for our U.S. laws, and the governing principles and regulations of the United States of America. Citizens of America, we have a message we would like to provide to President Biden, Vice President Harris, and all the believers and supporters of the U.S.-Mexico borderless wall policy which President Trump had the U.S. Congress pass into law the building of the wall policy. We have a 100% excellent answer and a great solution that will put an immediate stop to the influx of all of the illegal immigrants flooding into the United States of America.

I remember when I was a teenager that if you had a puppy that urinates or defecates on the linoleum or carpet floor of the home, you rub the male or female puppy's nose in the urine or poop that the family pet leaves or deposits on the floor, and the puppy will from then begin to learn whenever the puppy feels the urge out of habit to leave a bodily function leak or a dirty mess of fresh poop on the house floor, they will learn that whenever they need to relieve themselves they will look to you to open the front door or rear door of your home so they can take their potty break outside and not in the house. This effective training method and treatment applies to both males and female puppies and dogs.

This strong proven method approach and treatment may appear mean or cruel to sensitive people, but know your favorite puppy or dog for training purposes, this will effectively help the family dog recognize by mental response not to relieve themselves on the home floor anymore. Please let us know if this proven method helps you train your faithful loyal companion and your precious pooch or doggy however you desire to refer to your three or four-legged friend.

We recognize using a folded newspaper with a swat application to the puppy's rear end will also produce a favorable mental response whereby the puppy or dog will learn it is much better to follow your stimulus application and directive to stop leaving their bodily deposits on the home floor, and decide it is better to meet your approval by taking their bodily elimination outdoors, and it is a good and healthy family puppy practice to remain with them during their outdoor excretions, and especially until they are effectively house broken and fully trained. You can find YouTube Videos and Google for more puppy and dog effective training methods to be of help.

Now for the elites and other parties mentioned in this workable and hypothetical paragraph, we the people, for the people, and by the people choose to serve notice by a U.S. Congress signed executive order or an amendment, and by the authority of an ordered mandate that President Biden, Vice President Harris, and all of the Socialist Democrat supporters and voters of the U.S. borderless policy to immediately fly or drive down to the U.S.-Mexico borderless border, and get a full view of the illegal immigrant crises taking place under your questionable eyes {peradventure you have seen the illegal immigrant crises taking place on the U.S.-Mexico border in living color shown on Cable TV}, and you shall remain there until the U.S.-Mexico open border crises is fixed and you are now hereby ordered by the U.S. Supreme Court, all Citizens of America of the people, for the people, and by the people, and every other non-U.S. citizen order you by the signed U.S Congress, signed mandate enforced by The United States Military Armed Forces to hold you fully accountable to continue to live with the illegal immigrants you so love, cherish, and want a better life for.

Do not think you will be allowed back into any U.S. State or city until the U.S-Mexico borderless crises, open border policy is 100% absolutely permanently fixed, and you will stay put while this binding court order by the parties mentioned herein shall remain in effect until the illegal immigrant crises is forever repaired and corrected, and if it so requires to produce the lasting results for the good, betterment, and lasting improvements of America and its citizens, you are then so ordered to remain with the illegals for the remainder of the number of your days on earth.

The binding court order mentioned above can only be fully enforced and recognized peradventure the U.S. Supreme Court passes their own constitutional court order mandate that the American citizens can fully back and support to its final judgment and rendered as done and carried out in the eyes of the law.

We understand that if the U.S. Congress shall pass an executive order or a signed mandate, the president has ten days to veto or approve of the executive order or the signed mandate shall then and only then will it be considered passed into law.

Let's all pray that President Biden and his Neo-Marxist advisors will be preoccupied with other presidential interests and concerns for an eleven day pause so the U.S. Congress with the signed mandate of the people, by the people, and for the people of the United States of America will recover themselves, return to God, and know for a certainty that the Lord God has given this nation a great victory of triumph over the evil forces of revolutionary Socialist and Marxist tyranny, and all radical changes to the U.S. which are totally opposite to America, The U.S.

Constitution, U.S. values and principles, the bill of rights, U.S. governing rules and regulations in every state and city in the union, all U.S. laws and all guiding and governing principles observed in this nation.

May there be great prayer on behalf of this ongoing U.S.-Mexico open border crises whereby U.S. Border Patrol Agents have also found a couple of known terrorists from Yemen that had crossed into American territory due to the open border policy currently taking place. These two male terrorists are on the State Sponsors of Terrorism as classified by the United States Department of State.

At this time there is no way of telling how many other terrorists and criminals have decided to come to America with our weakened president in mental decline, and the weak and vulnerable borderless crises where there is no end in sight to being stopped by President Biden or the U.S. Congress or by the United States Supreme Court.

This open U.S-Mexico open border policy is truly a pathetic mess created by President Biden and his co-conspirators, and a whole lot of people are being painfully victimized and hurt through all of the illegal human, sexual, and drug trafficking crises that could be stopped peradventure President Biden signs an executive order into law that the illegal immigrant crises at our U.S.-Mexico border crossings must stop immediately, and we the people, for the people, and by the people would then concur with the signed executive order that the U.S. open border crises for now shall be forever stopped.

We have a message to all the believers and supporters of the Progressive Socialist Democrats that firmly stand with the U.S.-Mexico borderless crises, and want to tear down the U.S. more and more of the influx of the illegal immigrants to flood and pour into the United States. Would you agree to the tearing down of the walls of your home, condominium, townhome, or apartment that you currently live and reside in, and remove the doors off of your living accommodations and allow the illegal immigrants to help themselves to your wife or girlfriend, grandparents, and children that live with you or to help themselves to anything and everything they choose to like, have, want, or desire any of your personal possessions in your home? Or possibly you might answer, there is no way under God's heaven that I would allow or permit any illegal immigrant from helping themselves to my living quarters or anything else in my home?

If your answer is "Yes" I am willing to have the doors removed, and the walls taken out from my home so the illegal immigrants can come and go as they so please, then we recognize you and you alone are truly a rare individual and a special someone that truly cares for the illegal immigrants that also desire and want a better life for themselves and their families.

Peradventure your answer is, No way Jose, Absolutely not, or Not a chance in heaven then you are a double-minded hypocrite that says and believes one thing, but turns around and expects for America as a whole to follow a U.S.-Mexico borderless policy which they do not fully believe in or embrace. Everyone that falls into the double-minded hypocritical camp mentioned above needs to have a rude awakening by seriously waking up to everything that is happening, experience a reality check, and smell the coffee with the horrendous tragedy and ongoing human trafficking atrocities of the U.S.-Mexico borderless crises that President Biden created.

For the people that understand and believe the valid points we are endeavoring to make here with the ongoing U.S.-Mexico borderless illegal immigrant crises that is ever growing, increasing, and spreading itself daily, hopefully you also recognize that we need to help President Biden and Vice President Harris, and their co-conspirator advisors to see the growing crises tragedy and hold them fully accountable.

Citizens of America and non-U.S. citizens, you can consider this our rally cry for the nation to see the great need to Wake Up and push back against the radical Progressive Socialist Democrat ideology, agendas, strategies, and policies that are designed to steal, kill, and destroy this "constitutional federal republic", and totally eliminate this great nation of the United States of America.

We recommend for every American citizen to listen to Francis and Friends on SonLife Broadcast Network operating April 29th and April 30th, 2021 to receive an excellent and valuable education with updated information which the panel discussed about President Biden regarding taxing the rich and other issues. Francis shared with the viewers that, "It's not the rich that is going to be hurt, it's the middle class that is going to be hurt". I would like to add, the poor of America right along with the middle class are going to be hurt as well under President Biden's Administration's tax and continue to spend policies.

They also discussed topics about the government stealing money from the others and how they try to give it to somebody else, the education system, slavery to the government, unbelief in God as the number one problem in America, systemic problem of stupidity, to keep hate going in America the narrative of the whites against the blacks which the media and other people are forming for the people one way and look another way.

The above mentioned reasons and other valuable points of interest are talked about, and we recommend for all American viewers to watch these programs over and over to fully digest everything the U.S. Government is doing to take America in the wrong direction against the Lord's desire and plans for this great country. It is always wise, peaceful, and safe to follow the Lord's paths of righteousness and holiness all the days of our lives (Luke 1:74-75), and to avoid the rocks and pitfalls of the known facts of Socialism, Marxism, and Communism that only lead to colossal tragedies, catastrophes, and other unforeseen disastrous events known to mankind throughout human history in the countries they are observed and practiced to the detriment of suffering humanity.

I recognize there are a lot of young adults that have come to willingly accept and adopt a favorable view of socialism because of the message of free health care, free daycare, free college education, free cell phones, free cars, free money with checks in the mail, and free welfare. For those that have a proclivity and consider themselves open-minded, and have a leaning towards socialism Bud and I recommend for every reader to watch Jack Van Impe Presents October 3, 2021 to receive the real truth concerning the dangers facing American society that is more accepting of socialism in our nation of today on YouTube Videos.

The truth is I don't hear Bernie Sanders a full-fledged socialist nor any other Progressive Socialist Democrat Party members touting and advocating God in our lives and in our homes throughout America, a Christ centered life, Judeo-Christian Biblical teachings and principles, faith, family, and traditional American values. We also encourage all readers to watch Jack Van Impe: Socialism Exposed on YouTube Videos before the government takes it down and has it removed.

President Biden talks about free things to the American people, and millions of U.S. citizens and non-U.S. citizens are receiving free checks from the U.S. Federal Government as if President Biden and the U.S. Government is Santa Claus without economic repercussions what so ever. Please keep in mind that once the U.S. Government runs out of using other people's money whereby the redistribution of the income and wealth of American citizens through taxation, President Biden will then offer Americans the system of Socialism which the citizens of America will then be governed by the U.S. Federal Government.

Now that radical Progressive Socialist Democrat Party President Biden as a drunken sailor has been giving away free money, and suggesting other free things to the citizens of America, and to other non-
U.S. citizens including the illegal immigrants crossing our southern border points of entry, Bill O'reilly says, the end game will be President Biden offering Socialism in place of Capitalism to free America.

We recommend watching Bill O'reilly's YouTube Videos on " O'reilly: Biden Overspending Will Cause Economic Collapse, O'reilly: Biden Will Shatter Our Economy, and all the FREE STUFF Biden Wants to Hand Out, and Capitalism Should be Taught in Every American School". These YouTube Videos mentioned need to be watched and shared with every citizen in America along with all students regardless of their educational level.

Sad to say, so many young people have been left totally ignorant of the true and accurate American history with its Christian founding and Godly Christian American Heritage. The Progressive Socialist Democrat Party and the secular humanistic educational system are directly and indirectly to blame for the dumbing down of the U.S. Educational System, and the students of America when they choose to exclude and leave God out of the picture.

There are some Biblical thoughts that have come to my mind that I would like for every American citizen and non-U.S. citizens to consider when it comes to the love of God and our future as a nation. The Bible tells us, "For God so loved the world that He gave His only begotten Son, that whoever believes in Him should not perish but have everlasting life For God did not send His Son into the world to condemn the world, but that the world through Him might be saved."(John 3:16-17 NKJV). "Beloved, let us love one another, for love is of God; and everyone who loves is born of God and knows God. He who does not love does not know God, for God is love." (1 John 4:7-8 NKJV).

It's quite interesting that before Jesus was crucified by the Roman soldiers, He was questioned by Pontius Pilate who asked Jesus a thought provoking question that even he didn't have the right answer for, having come from a confused background of idol worship. Pilate asked Jesus, "What is truth?" (John 18:38 NKJV).

I realize Pontius Pilate wasn't aware of what Jesus had told Thomas one of Jesus' disciples who wanted to know the way that Jesus was going to take, and Jesus responded to him by saying, "I am the way, the truth, and the life. No one comes to the Father except through Me." (John 14:6 NKJV). When Jesus was praying for His disciples unto His heavenly Father He said, "Sanctify them by Your truth. Your Word is truth." (John 17:17 NKJV).

When Jesus spoke to answer what the Pharisees had say about Him Jesus made a powerful declaration regarding kingdoms which could be applied to a nation divided or house divided. "But Jesus knew their thoughts, and said to them: Every kingdom divided against itself is brought to desolation, and every city or house divided against itself will not stand." (Matthew 12:25 NKJV).

Citizens of America and non-U.S. citizens, it is imperative that we unite as a Christian Nation with our allegiance to having faith in God, Country, and put an end to being divided as a nation, and a people with double-mindedness and divided hearts.

Jesus also taught the multitudes how the kingdom of heaven operates for which His disciples came to the Lord when He sat down to teach the large numbers of people that day and He said, "Therefore whoever hears these sayings of Mine, and does them, I will liken him to a wise man who built his house on the rock: "and the rain descended, the floods came, and the winds blew and beat on that house; and it did not fall, for it was founded on the rock. "Now everyone who hears these sayings of Mine, and does not do them, will be like a foolish man who built his house on the sand: "and the rain descended, the floods came, and the winds blew and beat on that house; and it fell. And great was its fall." (Matthew 7:24-27 NKJV).

To clearly define and clarify who The Lord Jesus truly is The Holy Bible says, "In the beginning was the Word, and the Word was with God, and the Word was God. He was in the beginning with God. All things were made by through Him, and without Him nothing was made that was made. In Him was life, and the life was the light of men." (John 1:1-4 NKJV). The Lord Jesus is the Eternal Logos which literally means He is the Word of God who took on human flesh and became a man. The name of Jesus Christ literally meant "Jesus the Messiah" or "Jesus the Anointed", and the title Christ means the Anointed One.

From Jesus Christ the Lord of Glory you have His Word on whatever you need in this life, and in the next life which is eternal life found in Jesus Christ and Him Crucified. Give Jesus Christ charge of your life today, and you can charge it to the Bank of Heaven for a glorious bright future with persecutions. Under the inspiration of the Holy Spirit the Apostle Paul writes, "Yes, and all who desire to live godly in Christ Jesus shall suffer persecution." (2 Timothy 3:12 NKJV).

To add definition and clarity to who Jesus Christ truly is The Holy Bible says, "And without controversy great is the mystery of godliness: God was manifest in the flesh, Justified in the Spirit, Seen by angels, Preached among the Gentiles, Believed on in the world, Received up in glory." (1 Timothy 3:16 NKJV). The following Holy Bible Scriptures found in the book of John, chapter, and verse which are intended to shed more light on the 2nd person of the Holy Trinity of God, co-eternal, co-existent, and co-equal in essence with God, and in the divine nature of God this was revealed in three persons or personalities.

To add clarity with proper definition to the Holy Trinity simply means God in three beings, distinct personages within the One Divine essence or nature of God. "God is Spirit, and those who worship Him must worship in spirit and truth." (John 4:24 NKJV). "It is the Spirit who gives life; the flesh profits nothing. The words that I speak to you are spirit, and they are life." (John 6:63 NKJV). The Lord Jesus is the Word of God. (John 1:1 NKJV).

It is totally awesome, inspiring, and uplifting when you stop and think about everything that God has revealed to us in the Holy Scripture who the Lord Jesus Christ truly is. We would like for everyone to consider not only having intellectual head knowledge or a mere mental assent who Jesus Christ says that He is, but actually giving Him an invitation and literally receiving the Lord Jesus into your heart and life today which now is the accepted time.

We encourage you to ignore any preconceived notions and ideas that you may have from your church attendance and upbringing as a youth or as an adult, and just surrender and open your heart this moment and simply invite the Lord Jesus into your heart and life by saying with meaning the words of this prayer by Jimmy Swaggart:

"Dear God in heaven. I come to you in Jesus name. I'm so sorry for my sins, the way I've lived, the things that I've done. I ask you to forgive me and cleanse me with your precious blood from all unrighteousness according to your Holy Word. Romans Chapter 10 verses 9 &

10, with my mouth I confess Jesus Christ in my heart right now. I believe that God raised Jesus from the dead and He is alive, and because He lives I can live also by His grace and the price He paid at Calvary I will make heaven my home. I accept Jesus Christ as my Savior forever, and I'll follow Him and according to His Word I believe I am saved. Well Glory! Hallelujah! Hallelujah!

I was listening recently to the radio minister, Dr. J. Vernon McGee on 820 am in the Pacific Northwest, and he happened to share about a liberal preacher that communicated he and McGee had the same Jesus. One thing McGee inquired of the listeners, "Have you ever stopped to think that the Jesus today of liberalism, the Jesus that the world thinks of actually never lived? The Jesus of the Bible and the Jesus of liberalism are just two different individuals, and the Jesus of liberalism never lived".

McGee asked the liberal preacher, "If the Jesus he preached was he virgin born?" The liberal preacher answered McGee, "Of course not". McGee responded, "The One I preach is virgin born". McGee inquired, "If the Jesus he preaches does he perform miracles? The liberal minister said, "I do not believe in miracles".

McGee answered, "The Jesus I preach performed miracles". McGee asked the liberal clergyman, "The Jesus you preach did he die for the sins of the world on a cross?" The liberal preacher said, "He died on the cross, but not for the sins of the world". McGee responded, "The Jesus I preach died a substitutionary, vicarious, death for the sins of man".

McGee then said, "Do you believe that Jesus rose bodily?" The liberal preacher answered, "Oh, he said, no of course not". McGee responded, "Obviously then, you and I are not preaching about the same Jesus. McGee asked the liberal minister, "Where are the documents for the Jesus you preach?" The liberal just laughed off McGee's question and answered, "Of course we don't have any". McGee went on to say, "Let me say to you my friend, the Jesus that the world believes in today doesn't even exit".

I appreciated what Dr. McGee had to say about, "the Jesus of the Bible which is completely opposite of the Jesus that the liberals and the world believes in today". I also liked McGee's oral interaction with the liberal preacher, and their dialogue concerning Jesus and the Bible.

According to the Apostle Paul in 2 (Corinthians 11:2-4 and Galatians 1:6-9) it is possible to receive another Jesus, another gospel, and another spirit that seeks to steal our hearts away from Jesus Christ, and capture our minds with deception, lies, and corruption against the Word and will of God for our lives. Who do you say that Jesus Christ truly is?

The Apostle Paul was very concerned for the Christian Churches that false teachers would creep into their midst, which are the internal threats of wolves in sheep's clothing {dressed and perceived as Christians}, whereby they would corrupt their minds from the simplicity in Christ Jesus (2 Corinthians 11:3 KJV).

We need to keep in mind and recognize that the Lord is a jealous God, and the Apostle Paul also says that He is jealous for the Corinthians with a godly jealousy, and He wants to present the Corinthian Church as a chaste virgin to Christ Himself. (Exodus 34:14; 2 Corinthians 11:2 KJV). This truly speaks of the awesome love God has for every believer in Jesus Christ, and He strongly desires for us to be completely in love with Him and the very and only One He gave that could redeem and pay for our debt of sin which we could not pay ourselves.

Oh, what a precious atonement, incredible, and amazing price He paid when He shed His Life's blood, and paid for our salvation on the cross of Calvary. Knowing this mentioned fact should bring a great shout of jubilation, triumph, and victory to all Christians throughout the United

States of America and Worldwide in every tongue, tribe, and culture.

Although America is divided as a nation with so many points of view, have various religious belief systems as individuals which is contrary to the Word of God, and by their defining ideology which clarifies and explains who we happened to vote for in this last November 3rd, 2020 presidential election, and who we supported because of the things that each presidential candidate promised what they would do for America, and also what they said that they would achieve or accomplish while serving in the Oval Office as the next Commander in Chief, and yet we can still choose to unite as a Godly Nation and rise up to defeat this radical force of opposition against America's core values and faith based principles fully opposed to that which the Progressive Socialist Democrat Party is ushering in.

I'm positive that if American citizenry was polled today and asked the following question, when you voted in this last presidential election were you aware that President Joe Biden was a radical Progressive Socialist Democrat that if elected he would listen to the radical left-wing or far-left progressive political advisors that would certainly usher in elements of Socialism, Marxism, and Communism into our American way of life, and endeavor to change America into a nation that has less freedoms you enjoy now?

This would include the freedom of worship, knowing they will add higher taxation, allow a massive influx of illegal immigrants, and pursue more government control of parts of your life you would like to remain in control of?

Were you aware the Progressive Socialist Neo-Marxist advisors would also utilize greater mind control tactics against your family and your children of which American citizens had only learned of since President Biden was elected, and knew these types of tactics existed in totalitarian government systems in other countries beyond the U.S. borders?

Most certainly the American citizens who took the time to answer the poll in an honest and truthful way would soundly respond, No way Jose or Absolutely Not. We recognize that the people who took part in stealing the ballots and votes from President Trump by duplicating voter ballots, etc., in order to support the Progressive Socialist Democrat Party need to be fully held accountable for their sinister, illegal, and criminal actions.

My friend Richard Dandy shared with me an effective way to stop and prevent voter ballots theft, and from voter fraud ever taking place in America, especially during a presidential election that sounded good upon hearing his idea. Richard talked about using people's finger prints that are individually unique, and unlike any other human beings finger prints on the planet.

I thought his idea was excellent which another friend of his agreed with, and provided the U.S. voter election officials would accept this concept right along with presenting their driver's license with photo ID, America would have a full proof and safe voting and election system which the citizens of America could be proud of.

I took the time to enlighten my friend concerning the Counter Culture Groups that reject good common sense ideas, suggestions, and healthy thoughts which go against their agendas and policies they find objectionable to their radical programming of the mind as they seek to control our way of thinking to agree with their twisted thinking which they want applied to every citizen in the United States of America.

It is imperative that the citizens of America pushes back against the radical takeover of the Progressive Socialist Democrat Party, and their agenda to fundamentally change America's laws and rules of regulations into their ideas of the utopian country and society they envision for the citizens and non-U.S. citizens of this great nation.

They want to destroy The U.S. Constitution which stands in their way and prevents them from fulfilling their totalitarian radical plans and policies, but as we are seeing today they are determined to implement their crazy Socialist, Marxist, and Communist ideology, goals, and objectives and show to the world that Socialism actually works in America unlike in failed countries like Venezuela.

We must let these radical advocates and believers in Socialism emphatically, decisively, and powerfully know that America will not tolerate, and become a show case to the world for Socialism which is the gateway to Communism.

Christians are encouraged to compare scripture with scripture to receive a more accurate interpretation of a Bible text or passage they want to have a more precise and complete understanding of the text they want to fully grasp in the spirit of their mind. Bud shares, "A text out of context becomes a pretext for spiritual error." Pastor Timothy writes under the inspiration of the Holy Spirit, "Study to shew thyself approved unto God, a workman that needeth not to be ashamed, rightly dividing the word of truth." (2 Timothy 2:15 KJV).

The apostle Paul writes, "Examine yourselves, whether ye be in the faith; prove your own selves, how that Jesus Christ is in you, except ye be reprobates?" (2 Corinthians 13:5 KJV).

Please understand I like the wording of the KJV Bible although it is in the King James Elizabethan English that uses ye which means "you" and thyself for "yourself" and so forth.

Had Christians used The Holy Bible as a carpenter uses a plum line for a true and accurate vertical reading or position, and had the Christians came out in force as they needed to especially for those that call themselves Christians, I would like to think there would have been a better vote count for President Trump than what we saw in the results from the November 3rd, 2020 presidential election.

Christians failed President Trump because just as the Nation of Israel when they didn't have any king ruling over them the people did things according to what they wanted to do. (Judges 21:25 NKJV), "In those days there was no king in Israel; everyone did what was right in his own eyes." We are living in a time when a lot of Christians do not vote according to what God says to live by or what their conscience tells them, but many vote Democrat so that the Socialist Democrat Party will provide them with food stamps so they can buy whatever they want to purchase.

There are a lot of African American Pastors and white pastors too that voted for a Democrat president and they encourage their parishioners by example to vote the same way they do in order to receive money or compensation from the Democrat Party when in power. Although these same pastors know better and are aware that the Democrat Party are in league with Planned Parenthood and the abortion industry they seem to have no problems that African American young people are choosing to have their babies slaughtered by abortion assassins which are slaughter houses to state it bluntly.

Large numbers of Christian couples and American citizens are choosing not to get married in this day and hour, but are shacking up together and simply living jointly without the blessing of the Lord in holy matrimony, that is honored by God and before witnesses represented by two distinct families and their friends coming together to honor their holy union. America has become spiritually, morally, and socially dysfunctional in so many respects, and sin has become acceptable in today's society as a standard of life.

The Lord saw things differently than the way Israel saw things in the Old Testament. "For My people are foolish, they have not known Me. They are silly children, And they have no understanding. They are wise to do evil, But to do good they have no knowledge." (Jeremiah 4:22 NKJV). John the Apostle wrote, "And we know that we are of God, and the whole world lieth in wickedness." (1 John 5:19 KJV).

Bud recently shared a good insight he had thought of relative to the use of our mouths, and I would like to share some additional Biblically based thoughts to support our theological revelations and insights with the Holy Scripture as our examples. Bud shared, "The human mouth is not designed by God to be a toilet bowl or a thunder mug", a receptacle which has been used for hundreds of years and kept in the bedroom so family members might relieve themselves of bodily waste {defecate and urinate} whenever needed by the elderly or the sick.

To add clarity to Bud's insight, when Bud was an atheist living in Harmony Ville, Idaho he had a Roman Catholic girlfriend, Isabella that wanted to give him oral sex and he told her not to. Keep in mind the human mouth carries hundreds of unhealthy microorganisms of different types of bacteria, and the human body eliminates waste.

From a normal health related perspective oral sex is positively not a safe sex practice for the human body because of the elimination of waste and body poisons, and certainly not morally right in God's eyes. This is especially true from a Godly Christian's perspective and a health conscious society's perspective. Bud shared with me there are prostitutes that have murdered men that have wanted the women to perform oral sex on their male organ.

Oral sex is something that is practiced and conducted by prostitutes on their clients or johns. Isabella had left Bud after a period of time, and he was left alone without a female companion and caring helpmate in his life. I remember Jimmy Swaggart's teaching and sharing on an audio cassette that I was listening to years ago, and he taught that there are two places that faith is located. One location for faith is in your heart, and the other place for the Christian that exercises his beliefs in a powerful and supernatural Deity who alone is the Lord God our Creator as revealed in Holy Scripture, is in your mouth.

You can find Biblical support for the Lord's scriptural revelation regarding believing in our hearts, and the confession of our mouths in relationship to our glorious salvation in (Romans 10:8-10). The same mouth we praise and glorify the Lord with can be used to take His name in vain or to curse Him. This ought not to be.

The Lord's will is for the Christians who were redeemed with the precious blood of Christ, as of a lamb without blemish and without spot is to remain pure in their thought life and in their daily conduct. "Blessed are the pure in heart, For they shall see God". (Matthew 5:8); "but as He who called you is holy, you also be holy in all your conduct, because it is written, "Be holy, for I am holy." (1 Peter 1:15-16; 2 Corinthians 7:1 NKJV).

Bud shared with me that he saw a woman who was in a Walmart store and she had a shirt on with the words in bold lettering that stated, "LORD keep your hand on my shoulder and your other hand over my mouth". (Psalm 19:14) Bud was able to speak with this woman and compliment her that he liked the message on her shirt who was with her husband by their vehicle outside the store, and he found that she attended a church where he used to go.

I appreciated hearing about Bud's experience recently when he went shopping, and the great printing method this Christian woman had used to share with the world a powerful message how we need to set a watch and guard over our mouths that can easily say unruly words that contradict the word of God in regards to the finished work of the Cross of Calvary, whereby we could end up speaking unwise words that can be hurtful, uncaring, insensitive, and inconsiderate.

It is a good thing to ask the Lord for His help throughout the day that we might speak and communicate words that encourage and uplift the human heart with love, kindness, and thoughts of caring and empathy towards others. It's always a good policy to say the kind of things you would like to hear from your family members and from society's people we live with. Jesus said, "Therefore, whatever you want men to do to you, do also to them, for this is the Law and the Prophets." (Matthew 7:12 NKJV).

We would have a much better world, nation, cities, and communities if only we would begin practicing the good things the Lord has prescribed right from God's manual for all real life and godliness, The Holy Bible which is "God's Instruction Manual", the best manual for our earthly life and existence, and for the next life following our earthly existence which is eternal life. Always remember our life on earth is only a dress rehearsal for eternity.

"Sometimes we just need an eternal perspective. We need to be reminded that this life is not all there is." Yes, we only live this life once – but there is in fact a whole world waiting for us beyond this fractured life, free of tears, death, and mourning." We thank God for the Lord Jesus Christ, and for the price He paid for our eternal salvation, and for everything else He bought and paid for on the Cross of Calvary.

On a lighter note, I remember there were different times I would have something to share with Bud about a particular subject matter and he would respond jokingly, "I'll take the matter under constipation". I came to recognize Bud's responses to the various things that I wanted to share, inform, educate, enlighten, or to get his opinion and ideas on certain Biblical based and theological teachings, or matters pertaining to
U.S. and World News events as his way of showing me his light hearted sense of humor.

I thank God that Bud has a good sense of humor, and for all of the incredible, tremendous, and great things he has shared with me over the years that I have used to make this book a much greater and much more powerful read so the entire world can benefit from his words of wisdom and knowledge, and the great wealth of the historical figures and events that have changed and impacted the United States of America as well as the world we live in.

Bud had another good message he shared with me recently, and I know the readers will want to know what he had to say this time. For the Christian sharing their eternal hope in heaven it is extremely important to be careful of how you say and communicate your eternal hope in Jesus Christ.

So no one misconstrues what you are saying about your eternal hope in Christ Jesus to mean you are suicidal or wanting to commit suicide, there are psych doctoric trained counselors which could misinterpret your words to mean that you are suicidal and decide to put you on (a suicide watch), whereby they would put people as your legal guardians that you do not want and they could take charge over your funds, finances, home, and legal affairs and have you strapped to a bed in a ward under suicide watch.

This is happening in our psychologized system today, and many Christians of different ages are being deprogrammed by psycho-blasphemy dogmas, which are man-made or woman-made teachings of human beings that go against the word of God.

From the Bible itself we learn some powerful lessons of God's truths, that the mouth is used for communication with God Himself, and to our family members and other fellow human beings for the use of spiritual edification and encouragement. The Lord has also designed our hearts and minds as powerful components in the human body that we might store and retain His words of wisdom and knowledge, spiritual revelations, and supernatural enlightenment and illumination as sources to help direct and guide our steps and the paths we happen to traverse and journey on during the course of our life time.

We must do our diligent part to guard our thought life and our hearts from becoming garbage and trash receptacles of the devil that could steal, kill, and destroy the wonderful plans and dreams God has in store and in mind for us. God plan's and intentions are for our good that we might press on to obtain and achieve spiritual victories, and have business success and prosperity, faithfulness to Him and obtain the pleasures {and spiritual treasures} forevermore."

God Himself has set before us everything we may need for life and godliness, and as the Lord my shepherd who has prepared "a table before me in the presence of my enemies". (Psalm 23:5; 16:11; 2 Corinthians 10: 5; Proverbs 4:23; Jeremiah 29:11-13; John 10:10; 2
Corinthians 7:1 NKJV).

Bud had another good thought that he recently shared with me, and I thought it would be a good thing to share it with the readers. He shared, some might say you are so heavenly minded that you are no earthly good or valued. The truth of the matter is that there are many Christians that are so earthly minded they are not heavenly good as they need to be.

The very best example of someone that was heavenly minded, and yet He knew how to effectively deal with earthly matters better than any known man or woman throughout the span of all of mankind's recorded history, The Lord Jesus Christ; "how God anointed Jesus of Nazareth with the Holy Spirit and with power, who went about doing good and healing all who were oppressed by the devil, for God was with Him." (Acts 10:38 NKJV).

Matthew's Gospel records, "And there are also many other things that Jesus did, which if they were written one by one, I suppose that even the world itself could not contain the books that would be written. Amen." (Matthew 21:25 NKJV).

We recognize that there are a lot of Christian pastors and congregations that have compromised their Christian faith in this generation, and many are not in right relationship with the Lord Jesus Christ and having their hearts right with God. It takes the need of placing faith exclusively in Jesus Christ and all he had paid for on the Cross of Calvary.

Many Christians are not hearing the Word of God preached in power with the Holy Spirit and Fire, but they have become dull in hearing boring sermons that do not bring true conviction to produce true humility to show them that they need to repent of their sins as they should, and by getting their hearts right with God by returning to the Lord of Glory in faith and righteousness with holiness all the days of their lives.

Every Christian needs to have a right vertical relationship with God before the Lord and a right horizontal relationship with their fellow earthlings. We realize there are a lot of social issues the American society is facing today like mental and emotional issues among adults and teenagers, a humanitarian and illegal immigration crises at the U.S-Mexico southern border, homelessness and hunger issues, joblessness or job instability, economic uncertainty, fears and doubts creep and crowd into many American citizen's minds whether President Biden's economic policy will cripple or greatly damage a healthy economy that was thriving under President Trump's presidency.

There are so many issues Christians are facing and society as a whole that could cause a major crisis in America if we do not right our
U.S. American Ship ASAP.

There are a lot of Christians that have compromised their faith in the Lord, and sad to say this has caused the natural consequences of complacency and apathy in many Christian's hearts and minds. There are far too many Christians that have gotten too close to the world, and the world has also crept into the Christian Church throughout the United States and Worldwide.

There are people in many world nations that are wondering what has happened to America that we would ever elect a weak president that cannot stand up and push back against the radical left-wing Progressive Socialist Democrat Party, but instead he gives authorization for the far-left ideologies, left-wing political activists, and every other radical left-wing political party that is able to influence President Biden and his administration in the opposite direction to what America symbolizes, represents, and stands for as a Christian Nation and a Republic.

I was listening recently to the radio station 820 am in the Pacific Northwest, and the afternoon speaker shared that in 1956 the U.S. Congress made it official that we trust in God, and had that central message imprinted on our U.S. currency. We need to make that our central and unifying message as a center piece of our conversations with the ought to people and the ought not citizens of America today.

Keep in mind, "in god We Trust" (sometimes rendered "in god we trust") is the official motto of the United States of America [1][2][3] and of the U.S. State of Florida. It was adopted by the U.S. Congress in 1956, supplanting E pluribus unum, which had been the de facto motto since the initial 1776 design of the Great Seal of the United States. [4]

Citizens of America, it's time to Wake Up and see that they want to allow Socialism, Marxism, and Communism to take root and play a significant role in the American way of life which is abjectly appalling.

Citizens of America, once America's educational system that had opened the door to a psych blasphemy position from a mindset of thinking that men like Freud, Jung, Maslow, and Carl Adler who were psychologists and psychotherapists which many Americans have studied about concerning their psychoanalysis theories and practices that helped to educate and influence large numbers of our university students which have followed their theories according to their system of ideas and beliefs that they adhered to.

Then as a whole America has fallen into and sadly vulnerable, and susceptible to follow the teachings of Margaret Sanger the Planned Parenthood founder. She had taught getting rid of useless eaters which Adolf Hitler and the Nazi German Party had adopted in their holocaust mass elimination of the Jews during World War ll. The results were human babies are being murdered for greedy profit by abortion assassins, and the elderly who are being murdered and their lives snuffed out which is euthanasia.

In the case of babies and the elderly being murdered in America, follow the teachings of Margaret Sanger who was a racist and you'll find the final results how she advocated getting rid of unfit babies that in her mind never should have been born in the first place. The unfit babies Sanger was thinking about that needed to be eliminated and disposed of were African Americans babies which she believed should be aborted rather than allowed to live in America.

When I consider President Joe Biden's presidential policies, his administration knows how to turn enemies into friends and friends into enemies. For example, President Biden's nuclear agreement with Iran that John Kerry endeavored to secure with the Iranians during President Obama's presidency.

If President Biden and the Democrats regain the 2015 Nuclear Deal with Iran as they would like to, we believe the words of Jesus could literally come alive in our known world's historical reality base, "Men's hearts failing them for fear, and for looking after those things which are coming on the earth: for the powers of heaven shall be shaken." (Luke 21:26 NKJV).

The nuclear agreement with Iran may provide former U.S. President Obama, and the current U.S. President Joe Biden the thrill of victory in securing an award of making a nuclear treaty between the U.S. and Iran.

It may give President Obama and President Biden, and John Kerry, a U.S. diplomat and politician warm sensations whereby they've really achieved positive safety measures in which the U.S. and Israel could monitor Iran's nuclear activities and performance of nuclear duties, but it doesn't produce real peace of mind, national security, and a good feeling which brings warmhearted fondness wherein all of the nation of Israel feels 100% protected for all of the citizens of Israel as a whole. Israel has been a true friend, and a strategic ally to the United States of America ever since its founding as a democracy in 1948, and a nation state to the Jewish people.

The Lord Himself identifies and describes Himself as the God of Israel. Although the U.S. has provided and given military help to Israel with military assistance, the true defender and protector is the Lord God Himself. "O God, You are more awesome than Your holy places. The God of Israel is He who gives strength and power to His people." (Psalm 68:35 NKJV; Psalm 94:22; Zechariah Chapter 9-10 NKJV).

Bud and I recommend to great books to read titled Modern Warriors by Pete Hegseth, and 13 ½ Reasons Why Not To Be A Liberal: And How to Enlighten Others by Judd Dunning.

"President Biden won the White House because the Coronavirus let him stay hidden in his basement, protecting his campaign from its biggest liability the candidate himself, a new book says.

The Biden camp ran partly on the strategy of "you put your dumb uncle in the basement," referring to the Democratic candidate, according to "Lucky: How Joe Biden Barely Won the Presidency."

"Even former President Obama initially refused to support his 78-year-old ex-vice president and friend, worried he could become a "tragicomic caricature of an aging politician having his last hurrah" if not protected from himself, the book says." The Authors are Jonathan Allen and Amie Parnes.

"Biden's team converted his basement of his home into a makeshift studio from which he could safely issue statements."

The city and state which I was curious about where Joe Biden was doing all of his hiding during the presidential race was located in Wilmington, Delaware.

I remember wanting to express my disapproval of voting for presidential candidate, Joe Biden when I happened to make an announcement over the intercom on my personnel shuttle carrier one day, "Don't vote for Joe Biden who needs to go back into hiden." I don't recall any remaining passengers making any approval or disapproval for my humorous announcement.

My dad and mom, Benjamin and Jessica Scone got married the old fashioned way. They both wanted the blessing of the Lord on and in their marriage ceremony which was small in extent and before witnesses. Lorena and I followed our parent's steps by getting married in a Christian Church. In fact, you could say we doubled up on doing things the right way according to American wedding traditions, we were married twice. Once by an attorney the 1st time, and the 2nd time in a Christian church before God and witnesses, and this was done officially and ceremoniously prior to our living together.

We as a nation need to get back to the basics of life and what gives and produces life that the Lord will bless and honor. I thank the Lord for giving the human family the institution of marriage which is the bedrock of a solid foundation, and meaningful covenant relationship between a loving committed husband and wife who desires to securely rest their joint lives together, and have the blessings of the Lord upon their devoted union.

Keep in mind there were people that were being programmed sub-consciously by the constant barrage and blitzkrieg of the Democratic Progressive Socialist Neo-Marxist Media because their Cable Network TV's were continuously on. Citizens of America you were being indoctrinated to think and believe anti-President Trump who was fighting for everything American's value, need, and desire for with a healthy economy for all.

Timothy Treadwell, 46 known as the Grizzly Man and his girlfriend, Amie Huguenard, 37 had visited Alaska for 13 seasons when a great tragedy occurred. We realize that Timothy had become familiar and comfortable being around the Grizzly Bears of Alaska believing he was a protector of the wild bears. Amie I understand listening to a YouTube Video didn't feel comfortable being around the bears, but she did share with a friend(s) that it was quite an experience being in the creeks with the bears. Amie was planning on putting a stop to going to Alaska with Timothy for the last time because apparently she had other ideas what she wanted to do with her life.

Timothy actually admitted he wanted to mutate with the bears and he was willing to die for the bears. He also admitted on a YouTube Video, if anyone else was doing what he was doing they would be killed. David Letterman asked Timothy one day when he was on Letterman's Late Night Show if one day they would hear that Treadwell had been killed by a bear to which Timothy responded, "Oh, no".

Well, the unfortunate incident took place one night when an old mean Grizzly Bear got a hold of Timothy because he was hungry and needed to fatten up for its wintery hibernation in a dormant condition and state. Not to offend anyone that admired Timothy Treadwell and Amie Huguenard for they ended up wearing bear skins because they were really close to the bears then. Timothy and Amie were not ever expecting to wear a fur coat in their seasonal trips to Alaska.

My father, Benjamin Scone shared a good story with me about a pastor that decided to go hunting for a bear one Sunday. The pastor was wanting a fur coat and when he saw a bear on the country road during his hunting trip he raised his gun to bag himself a bear in order to have the fur coat he was interested in. When the bear saw that he was going to be shot by the pastor he stood up and raised his paw to signal the pastor that he desired to have a talk with the man of God. The pastor lowered his gun. When the bear asked the pastor why he wanted to shoot him, the pastor explained to the bear that he wanted a fur coat.

When the pastor asked the bear what he was interested in, the bear shared with the pastor that he desired a free meal. Then the bear and the pastor sat down in the middle of the road together and when they rose back up together simultaneously, the bear had his free dinner and the pastor had his fur coat.

From this simple story it is obvious that pastors of the gospel of the Lord Jesus Christ should not consider going hunting on Sundays which is the Lord's Day, but choose to remain faithful to their calling and carry on the ministry to their unique congregations that depend on devoted pastors ever willing to abide as a good shepherd of the flock.

Bud shares, a pastor sat down with a secular humanist or he spoke to a group of secular humanists and later when the pastor got up he had been converted by their lies of falsehood and deception. Unfortunate reality, but the above example has been played out in the minds and hearts of multiplied millions of Christians and well intentioned believers that were beguiled by the devil through the subtlety of human philosophy and the deceptive reasoning of men and women.

Deceivers come in many forms and with smiling faces. Although they may take the time to explain their intellectual reasoning behind their beliefs and the belief system they adhere to, you can test the spirits whether they of God, from Satan, or of this world's system. "Beloved, do not believe every spirit, but test the spirits, whether they are of God; because many false prophets have gone out into the world. By this you know the Spirit of God: Every spirit that confesses that Jesus Christ has come in the flesh is of God, and every spirit that does not confess Jesus Christ has come in the flesh is not of God. And this is the spirit of the Antichrist, which you have heard was coming, and is now already in the world." (1 John 4:1 NKJV).

Bud shared a good word with me recently that he gleaned from his reading from, The Expositors Word for Every Day. Taken from (Joshua 2:1-9 and Numbers 35:9-15) which the Bible tells us that there were 6 cities of refuge that if someone killed someone in self-defense or by accident, it was lawful for the perpetrator to go to one of the 6 lawful cities to find refuge from a vengeful relative. A City of Refuge is "a city in ancient Israel appointed as a place of asylum for unintentional murders."

Significant names provided for the 6 cities which the murderer could escape to as recorded in the Bible were Kedesh, Shechem, and Hebron to the West, and 3 cities to the East which were Golan, Ramoth, and Basor.

The murderer could seek refuge from relatives seeking revenge. They lived there until the death of the High Priest. The only deliverance from the death sentence for the deliberate murders was a different story. All the people that reject and does not respect the proud, nor such as turn aside to lies." (Psalm 40:4 NKJV) refuse to come to the Cross for salvation are guilty of the blood of Jesus Christ that is on their hands. "Nor is there salvation in any other, for there is no other name under heaven given among men by which we must be saved." (Acts 4:12 NKJV).

Always remember anything that adds to or takes away from or ignores the finished work of the Cross of Calvary where Jesus paid for our debt of sin, makes the people that do so, guilty as charged.

Bud and I recommend a couple of good books, 1st Trump VS China America's Greatest Challenge by Newt Gingrich and 2nd America's #1-Adversary by John Poindexter Robert McFarlane Richard Levine. All American citizens must stir themselves and know for an absolute certainty what we are facing as a nation at this critical hour. Right now is the time to recognize we have serious enemies from within and then there are ever increasing enemies from without.

We agree with Carman's song, America Again found on YouTube Videos. Christian America we are more than conquerors in Christ Jesus and He will help us to win our spiritual battles as we stand on the victorious promises of God's Word, resist the devil, and he will flee from us. (James 4:7)

Bud shares a good insight stating, "The Constitution of the United States of America, in it is the clause separation of church and state. The reason for that was because the people that migrated to this continent were escaping religious persecution against freedom of worship by the Roman Catholic Church which was in control. The Framers of The U.S. Constitution and the Declaration of Independence, the goal was for the government by the people and for the people that all political leaders be responsible to the people.

In 1960 The United States Supreme Court over through the {separation of church and state} by their decision to put into law that secular humanism is the religion of America which is tax payer funded. This is totally against the {separation of church and state}, and the emphasis of the {separation of church and state} is that the church should not be controlled by the type of government that was in England previously". Our founding fathers wanted to make absolutely sure that the U.S. Government stays completely out of the churches freedom of worship and church policies.

The Democrat Political Party does not focus on America's core essentials like strengthening our borders between the United States of America and Mexico as President Trump and his Make America Great Again supporter base did. Rather than majoring on jobs for American citizens the Democrats led by President Elect Joe Biden focus on changing America and the redistribution of the wealth of American citizens. These same claims were made by Joseph Stalin, Lenin, and Karl Marx that ended in tyranny and bondage for the Russian People with mind control tactics for millions of the people of the Soviet Union, Poland, Hungary, and the Slavic Nations.

President Elect Joe Biden is a globalist, and he doesn't recognize America's exceptionalism just like his former boss, Barack Hussein Obama II, America's 44th President didn't when asked if he believed in America's exceptionalism to which he responded, "I believe in American exceptionalism, just as I suspect that the Brits believe in exceptionalism and the Greeks believe in Greek exceptionalism."

As Mitt Romney put it in his book, this "is another way of saying he doesn't believe it all." But Obama was just getting warmed up. His very next sentence was: "I'm enormously proud of my country and its role and history in the world." Obama continued: "If you think of our current situation, the United States remains the largest economy in the world. We have unmatched military capability. And I think that we have a core set of values that are enshrined in our Constitution, in our body of law, in our democratic practices, in our belief in free speech and equality that, though imperfect, are exceptional."

I typed in the message on google, "Obama's lack of recognizing America's exceptionalism" to receive the above quotes about President Obama.

I wanted to bring to your attention that, "U.S. President Barack Obama nominated over 400 individuals for federal judgeship during his presidency. Of these nominations, Congress confirmed 329 judgeships, 173 during the 111th & 112 Congresses and 156 during the 113th and 114th Congresses. Even while Democrats still controlled the Senate (2009-2015).

Republicans blocked the confirmation of some nominees by filibustering up until 2013. Senator Chuck Grassley commented that more nominations could have been confirmed had Obama respected recess appointment precedent by not making recess appointments to the National Labor Relations Board while the Senate was in session. The Supreme Court later unanimously ruled these January 2012 appointments illegal, and they created much ill towards Obama among Senate Republicans."

We will leave the American citizens to do more fact checking and research on how many federal judges President Obama appointed and just how many President Trump appointed that might be siding with the Progressive Socialist Democrat Party, and preventing President Trump's legal team from being able to present all of the evidence they have that would show and reveal that there positively was election ballot tampering and voter fraud which stole the presidential election from President Trump. It would be a good thing to at least explore all of the legitimate and lawful case evidence.

From my Google search I learned, "There are four types of evidence by which facts can be proven or disproven at trial which include: "Real evidence, Demonstrative evidence, Documentary evidence and Testimonial evidence". As I continue to examine further on my Google searches I discovered there are plenty of other types of evidences that can be presented to prove a case.

Knowing the critical fact base information could help President Trump's legal team win or at least be able to present their case before a
U.S. Federal Judge or U.S. Judicial Court in America, and hopefully before The United States Supreme Court one day.

Something of interest for our readers to consider from my Google search. "The Norwegian Nobel Committee has decided that the Nobel Peace Prize for 2009 is to be awarded to President Barack Obama for his extraordinary efforts to strengthen international diplomacy and cooperation between people. The Committee has attached special importance to Obama's vision of and work for a world without nuclear weapons."

When I shared with Bud that President Obama had been given the Nobel Peace Prize Bud said, "To award the Nobel Peace Prize to a man that represents the religion of Islam which is not a religion of peace, which is a total sham to the emphasis Nobel Peace Prize".

I remember watching a video on YouTube Videos where President Obama was speaking to a group of people and he admitted to the audience in attendance, "You know I wasn't born in this country", and yet President Obama went to all the trouble to reveal on Cable TV a birth certificate that stated he was born in the United States. My sister Marlie told me one day that the people of Kenya know that Obama was born in Kenya.

We recognize there positively is something wrong with President Obama's true country of origin identity, and yet if he wasn't born in America then he should have never been elected as a U.S. President to serve out his 1st presidential term, and not at all for a 2nd presidential term which he positively did perform and provide as America's Commander in Chief. Lorena and I have watched YouTube Videos sufficiently, and we heard President Obama acknowledge that he is a Muslim.

Michael Medved didn't believe that Republicans were going to win any strong political points by mentioning or arguing the point that President Obama wasn't a U.S. born citizen. I tend to side with the Kenyans concerning the citizen of origin controversy.

One evening I asked Chad Conners, Lorena Scone's brother-in-law, now that Joe Biden has been the President and he has signed a number of executive orders, are anyone of them good for America and he responded to my question by answering, "None of them". America, for your information President Elect Joe Biden is a radical and corrupt politician of the Socialist Democrat Party who says, China is a friend of America.

Now that Joe Biden is America's 46th United States President you can expect to see different forms of Socialism, Marxism, and Communism taking root in the political arenas of America that will erode, tarnish, and corrupt America's good image and way of life, freedoms, its God given wisdom, and the great potential it has exemplified and shown to the world with all of its mighty strength, courage, and premium high qualities of every good thing that God and His called out people which is His Bride, The Church of Christ, and many loving and dedicated American citizens have made her to be as a beacon of light, love, and hope to the nations of the world.

I am so sorry for the many deceived American citizens, but there are large numbers of our American society that were duped and deceived by biased political pundits and commentators that you have been listening to on Cable TV. These political broadcasters having been steadily sharing their political opinions, analysis, lies, mockery, and evaluations totally contrary to American values which were aimed against the 45th United States President Donald Trump who told you the truth about Joe Biden before he became our current 46th President of the United States of America, and what the Socialist Democrat Party would do to us if they ever took power in the Oval Office.

The Progressive Socialist political pundits like what many women and I suspect many senior citizens had been listening to on The View, CNN, and other Fake News Media sources in particular are good examples why so many American citizens were led away from Christian virtues and the need for prayer, using Godly wisdom from above, needing to seek spiritual guidance and understanding and having a spirit of Godly discernment during the last presidential election.

American citizens, I'm positive we are going to be and should be learning some hard lessons of being programmed by the emotional acting women and men that feed the public with their readings of the teleprompters, and then the American public was spoon fed all of the Anti-President Trump rhetoric which were broadcasted day after day right into the homes and minds of many vulnerable and gullible deceived Americans.

The Progressive Socialist Democrat Party think, have been using President Trump as their whipping boy to show by example their cruel power and just how mean spirited, antagonistic, and vicious they can be toward anyone that stands in their way while going for a power grab of this great nation, to be able to control the American citizenry the way they believe they should be controlled which is totally contrary to American principals. The Socialist Democrat Party think they need to deprogram President Trump's supporters and how they must be controlled or else.

The deprogramming of President Trump's supporters and voter base must happen in accordance to their way of radical thinking which is contrary to God's thoughts, plans, and future for all who will simply believe on Jesus Christ and Him crucified.

Bud shares, "Back when the Berlin Wall was torn down there were thousands and thousands of East Berliners that were celebrating and also the people in the nearby nations. If Communism is so great why were the people so excited to see the tearing down of the Communist Wall? The multitudes that hadn't seen their family members and loved ones in years were hugging, ever so grateful, and glad to see one another again. This was all caught on camera during that time.

Another example is the country of Venezuela. If Communism and Socialism are so great as many deceived people believe these days why do thousands and thousands of Venezuelans risk their lives to brave and travel through dangerous jungles to get to Colombia that they might find the freedoms, they so desire?"

Bud has personally met and spoke with a man from Czechoslovakia years ago and he shared with Bud, "he was excited to be in Seattle, Washington. He was born and raised in the Communist block nation, Czechoslovakia. He was excited to be in America, and he personally experienced and seen Communist Russian soldiers take youths out of their homes and away from the parents.

He said they would throw them into the backs of canvas covered Army trucks. While their dads and moms pleaded with the Russian soldiers and cried with great distress, they took the youths out from the trucks on mountain roads and put packs on the youths backs, loaded the packs with great big rocks, and they forced marched them up the mountain sides. If they became tired and wanted to rest, they were given blows from the soldier's rifle butts. The Czechoslovakian man waited for an opportunity to escape, and he was finally able to make his escape. It took him a month of traveling at night and hiding during the day".

American citizens, President Trump is and was an honest and truthful communicating President of the United States of America. We personally believe President Abraham Lincoln would have spoken and boasted about President Trump's truthfulness and honesty in his presidency, policies, and way of life.

I believe President Trump deserves and demands our respect, commitment, and voter support to be able to serve out his 2nd term as our U.S. President, and I do not agree with what the Socialist Democrat House is endeavoring to do in their pursuing to impeach President Trump for a second time although he stepped down after serving one term as our president.

It's sad to think about President Trump having to step down all because of the persistent lies and denials of Presidential Elect Joe Biden during the Presidential Election Debates. America was deceived into believing Senator Elect Joe Biden was telling the truth, and the citizens of America allowed President Trump to continue to be a target of the Progressive Socialist Democrat Party from that day, during his presidency, and until this very day.

President Trump as America herself is a symbol of faith, courage, leadership, and hope with freedoms as no other nation and liberties for the rights of all of its citizens. The fake news pundits deceived many American citizens into believing their fake and fraudulent news sources, and unfortunately now America is Waking Up after being duped by what we know was played out by the left wing media sources that works hand and hand with the Socialist Democrat Political Party.

I heard Mike Huckabee voice on YouTube Videos that the Democrats policies are illogical and irrational. Mike also said that the Democrats do not understand the fundamentals of an economy. When you seriously think about what Mike Huckabee told us about the economy with the crazy thinking Socialist Liberal Democrats in power that could mean wrecking, ruining, and destroying the economy we all have come to love and enjoy, but contrary to the Democrats economic agenda we need to see it remain strong and prosperous which we came to appreciate with President Trump's low taxation policies.

The dire consequences of having the radical Progressive Socialist Democrats in power over America's economy if they do not understand the fundamentals of an economy it could result in higher taxation for not only the rich, but also the middle class as well which would be a bitter pill to swallow for every hard working American citizen. We all like to keep more of our hard-earned dollars after taxes have been taken out, and spend our money on the things we freely choose to or absolutely need to like paying bills.

When you seriously stop and think about President Biden's Administrations unwise, unhealthy, and impulsive spending habits besides their war on energy and tax and spend policies, borrowing from China's Communist Party and any other nation willing to loan money to the United States as a future investment business venture, Mitch McConnell knows exactly what he is talking about when referring to the Progressive Socialist Democrat Party he says, "Democrats want to keep digging deeper. They want to try to inflate their way out of inflation". Bud shares, this also is a double negative.

Bud and I recommend reading Mitch McConnell's entire: Americans Paying Dearly for Democrats' Inflation Nightmare

Bud shared with me that his Assembly of God Pastor taught the congregation that Christians needed to forgive themselves of sin that they commit. His Pastor had stated that they have to forgive themselves of sins they commit to get rid of any strongholds which he stated numerous times during the evening church service.

Bud could see many in the congregation demonstrated approval to what the pastor had stated. After the service Bud confronted the pastor explaining the Cross is the only place Christians should go for forgive ness of sins, and we go to the heavenly Father in Jesus Name. The pastor responded by trying to avoid the issue. Telling people to forgive themselves is a double negative. (Romans 3:23) is a continuous verb of action in the Koine Greek.

The next day the pastor called Bud, and he basically said over the phone, "We are not having theological problems in this congregation". Bud told the pastor that psychology messes with the psyche of Christians because it adds to, takes away from, or it ignores the Cross. The resurrection of Jesus Christ validated the fact that the preaching of the Cross is the gospel message.

I recognize Bud provided his pastor an excellent theological answer that he looks to God to forgive his sins whenever he sins. Christians need to ask the Lord God to forgive their sins through an act of repentance and humility before God by the shed blood of Jesus Christ and what He had paid for on the Cross of Calvary. We simply cannot say, "I forgive myself" which is a double negative in theological terms.

Bud recognized there is no Biblical Scripture that supports forgiving ourselves when we sin against a righteous and holy God for all sin is against God's moral law, and He alone can forgive our sins. We cannot clear our moral law sin record, and free ourselves of the sin nature before God by the corrupted simple act of forgiving ourselves. In the Christian faith Bud had very clearly and effectively gave his pastor an apologetic answer to the double negative sermon point by providing a strong defense of the hope that we have in Christ Jesus with a solid Biblical response. We can forgive others whenever they transgress against us in the righteous, holy, and just name of Jesus Christ.

Bud related to me on another day that his pastor had preached on the Cross of Calvary before he had taught the congregation that they had to forgive themselves although there isn't one single scriptural basis or support with any Bible verse(s) found in The Holy Bible for forgiving ourselves.

As Bud was enlightening me regarding the context of the two distinct and separate sermon revelations his pastor had introduced to the body of Christ in attendance during the evening service, I remember-ed how the Apostle Peter who gave the perfect answer to the Lord Jesus when the disciples were asked by Jesus, "But who do you say that I am? Peter responded, "You are the Christ, the Son of the living God. Jesus answered and said to him, "Blessed are you Simon Bar-Jonah, for flesh and blood has not revealed this to you, but My Father who is in heaven." (Matthew 16:15-17 NKJV).

Then we find the Lord, "Jesus begin to show His disciples that He must go to Jerusalem, and suffer many things from the elders and chief priests and scribes, and be killed, and be raised again the third day. Then Peter took Him aside and began to rebuke Him, saying, Far be it from You, Lord; this shall not happen to You! But He turned and said to Peter, "Get behind Me, Satan! You are an offense to Me, for you are not mindful of the things of God, but the things of men {and women}." (Matthew 16:21-23 NKJV).

From the two separate revelations mentioned above that the disciple Peter had stated we find the first revelation Jesus Himself told Peter it was from My heavenly Father, and the second revelation Peter had was given to him by Satan. Likewise when Bud's pastor had preached about the Cross of Calvary he was ministering to the congregation attendees a divine revelation from the heavenly Father, and the second revelation he taught the church members concerning having to forgive themselves with no scriptural evidence to support such teaching, was actually coming from the devil self-inspired psychology.

The first revelation was given from God the Father with grace and mercy by faith in Jesus and the Cross, and the second revelation came from self-motivation of works which is human fleshly thinking or the carnal reasoning of psychology. It is imperative for the Christian to remain anchored to and in the sure Word of Prophecy, Jesus Christ who is the Word of God incarnate, the Ark of our Salvation and Safety. When you hear a Christian say, "Get into the Ark" they are referring to being in Christ Jesus, and Jesus Christ living in our hearts and lives which is the only true source of obtaining and having eternal security as the Christian remains saved, sanctified, and Holy Spirit filled.

Bud and I recommend for everyone to read Matthew Chapter 6 in its entirety, and read concerning the oral exchange and dialogue between the Lord Jesus and His disciples. Especially endeavor to mentally focus as you read on the dialogue between Jesus Christ and His disciple Peter. You will find the rock Jesus is referring to that He said He would build His church on that the gates of hell should not prevail against it, is the confession of his faith that Peter stated to the Lord Jesus Christ and that is, "You are the Christ, the Son of the living God." (Matthew 6:16-19 NKJV).

The spiritual revelations that God gives unto the followers of Jesus Christ are truly spiritual treasures given to men and women from our heavenly Father, "that the kingdom of the gospel would be preached in all the world for a witness unto all nations; and then shall the end come." (Matthew 24:14 KJV).

We recognize that the American citizens who place their faith and trust in the faith based principles in The Holy Bible, the Word of God, they found that their lives were blessed and enriched with God's abiding presence and goodness. The American citizens who put their faith in the Lord Jesus Christ as their personal Savior and Lord which is the basis for people coming to believe and value Capitalism whereby they could prosper and succeed to financially benefit themselves and their families in an ever increasing healthy economic system.

America wasn't based upon Voodoo economics that is for certain, but was based and founded on the Judeo-Christian principles solidly founded on the Bible itself.

God has and will continue to bless and honor the people that will believe, value, and honor His Word. As a special blessing the Lord will give revelations and insights with added wisdom to the wise men and women of faith that will seek Him, Jesus Christ. The honest fact concerning these truths is, wise men still seek Him {Jesus Christ} which is a great and constant truth to live by.

America, we need to face the hard facts that the Socialist Democrat Party is at the helm of the U.S. Government right now, and they desire to pilot The U.S. American Ship as they so desire, and they will very likely steer America's economy into the rocks of economic disaster unless they are forced by the American voters to demand a presidential recount, and force the U.S. Activist Federal Judges nominated and appointed by President Barack Obama and President Trump to steer America's U.S. Ship back into safe job producing capitalism harbors, where American citizens can become economically prosperous, successful in business, and financially stable enough to support themselves and their families in ever increasing secure and peaceful waters.

We recognize this would require that President Joe Biden stop listening to his anti-American mind control programmers, and through an act of faith in God's amazing grace help to turn this great nation back on course right onto the righteous paths of the Lord God Almighty.

Bud and I recommend Donnie Swaggart's Letter to President Trump on YouTube Videos, which clearly reveals how appreciative and grateful Donnie is for President Trump and we fully agree and concur with his special letter he shares so candidly with President Trump. The video shows his great thankfulness and appreciation in a loving way addressed to President Trump should Donnie Swaggart ever decide to send President Trump a letter providing his gratefulness for the good things he did for America and Israel.

It is imperative that America Wakes Up spiritually and recognizes that Satan himself is America's and every Christian's number 1 enemy. Satan uses spiritually deceived people to do his bidding against God's creation the human race, and throughout the nations of the world.

I was listening to Donnie Swaggart on one of their SBN Broadcast Programs and Donnie happened to share that he had read an article about a former KGB agent that had defected from the former Soviet Union and this agent tells about America being compromised from within.

The former KGB agent communicated that America through its universities is already a Communist Nation. The agent went on to say, they just don't know it and their freedoms are slowly going to be evaporating. Donnie went on to share with the congregation and viewing audience that Joseph Stalin said the 3 greatest hindrances of the Soviet Union taking over America is 1. their patriotism, 2. their morality, and 3. their spirituality.

Bud and I know that America's faith in God can turn things around for all of the American citizens provided America is 100% determined to remain faithful to the Lord God Almighty, and choose to serve Him and Him alone, and the citizens of America fully stands for God and on His Holy promises found in His Holy Word.

We know God will then fight for America and show Himself mighty on behalf of the American people that has been taken captive by a hostile takeover by the Progressive Socialist Democrat Party. They stand fully opposed to God's will for America, The Holy Bible, The Constitution, The Christian Church, and the freedoms American's have enjoyed and taken for granted in many respects. America, it is time for us to unite, rise up, and take this nation back from the radicals in power, and take our nation back from the brink of disaster and destruction out of the bondages of Socialism, Marxism, and Communism.

We will be victorious in Christ Jesus as a nation, and delight in the triumphant power of God to deliver and set us totally free. "You shall know the truth, the truth shall make you free." (John 8:32 NKJV).

Citizens of America, for those that weren't aware we had top U.S.-China diplomats that were engaged in public talks at the Alaska summit. I happened to listen in again to Newsmax TV, and I was able to capture on cassette tape and recorded the following: "To be clear China BLM is a Marxist Organization.

China wants nothing more than for BLM to continue to infect the minds of the Americans, and pushing this Communist Marxist agenda and so that's the first thing, but besides from that it is really interesting to have China of all places talking to the United States about race relations while they have Muslims in concentration camps and while they are completely on a regular basis guilty of practicing inhumanity. So I look at this not only as an interest disrespectful exchange, and let me be clear I do not support China, but at the end of the day we have a weak leadership, weak president, and ultimately they are going to use our own media against us.

Might I also mention that China was also expecting money with adds in advertisers in the media to persist propaganda, so China double exchange disrespectful interfere in it, and by the way BLM for those that are watching, it is a Marxist Organization and of course they are going to push it".

I recorded Anna Paulina Luna's statements on Newsmax TV as mentioned above. I heard Jim Nations one morning on Francis and Friends say that he heard Black Lives Matter evoke demon spirits.

Citizens of America, that is 100% not the American Spirit this nation was founded with, and we would encourage everyone involved and associated with the Black Lives Matter movement to repent and renounce your association with demon spirits and any anti-American activities, and turn to the Lord Jesus with heartfelt contrition and genuine repentance, and by faith allow the Lord Jesus to help you to nail your sins to the Cross of Calvary, and find the forgiveness you most desperately need at this time and hour. Jesus will meet you at the Cross as you kneel in prayer with Godly sorrow.

Bud and I encourage everyone that was caught up in, and involved with the Black Lives Matter movement to do some personal exploring and investigate where all the money went that was raised to support the Black Lives Matter Movement. You might be surprised to find out who actually profited and benefitted from the funds being raised. Were all your social media energized efforts good for the cause of the BLM Movement, the African American race and people, and for yourselves as individuals or a big waste of time and energy?

Mike Pompeo speaks with authority on the nation of China. "Their capabilities continue to grow. Their economy grows, they continue to act as a colonial power in Africa and South America, even in the Middle East they're trying to buy off political leaders. Their capabilities grow, their military capabilities grow too, and now they've made clear their intent. Their intention is on a bigger face they talk about this. They use to say, bide your time and hide your strength, and now they're showing us their fist, they're showing us their strength.

They're doing it in Hong Kong, they are doing it with the massive human rights violation in Western China. Make no mistake about it The Chinese Communist Party believes that America is in decline. That they are on the rise and they intend to take full advantage of that. Call them an enemy, call them an expert, call them what you will, but it is their intention to be the dominant power in the world, and they intend to do so quickly".

"Michael Richard Pompeo is an America politician, diplomat, business man, and attorney who served under President Donald Trump as Director of the Central Intelligence Agency from 2017 to 2018 and as the 70th United States Secretary of State from 2018-2021. Pompeo is a former United States Army Officer according to Wikipedia."

We recommend watching John and Josh Rosenstern on Insight which is just one of the excellent Son Life Broadcasting Network programs. Citizens of America, conservative Americans, and every non-
U.S. citizen it is imperative that everyone must remain alert, circumspect, informed, and continuously educated on exactly what the Progressive Socialist Democrat Party is up to regarding their agendas, strategies, and policies which are totally against and contrary to God, The U.S Constitution, and what America symbolizes, represents, and the standards this nation embodies.

We need to be proactive, be willing to fight, and push back against everything the Progressive Socialist Democrat Party endeavors to pass which are contrary to everything America has been historically and is today as a nation.

The Lord God is more than willing to fight for us if we will unite as one nation under God, and return to the spirit of America which is having a Godly Spirit founded on the Judeo-Christian faith and righteous principles. Then we will know and understand that we are no longer divided as a nation, but we the people for the people and by the people are The United States of America.

If America fails to unite, and put an end to our endless divisions which are a big waste of time, filled with distractions, and spending useless energy on any number of unnecessary things which we could be using to help our fellow men and women in a spirit of love, kindness, and compassion, then the end result could spell the collapse of the nation.

We recognize the Progressive Socialist Democrat Party want to continue defeating and distracting American citizens by using racist, sexual identity tactics, and a number of other means to distract the American citizenry and prevent any meaningful and purposeful dialogue and progress which America makes to regain and recover itself from getting off track spiritually, morally, and causing American citizens to have socially dysfunctional behaviors and societal and family disorders, whereby even families do not function rightfully and normally the way God would have them to.

When the family knows how to make a home run the way God designed the family unit to be successfully operated with the father and mother in a harmonious relationship with the Lord as the two heads of the household, the scheduled Bible devotions and family meetings with good discussions as far as who is responsible for doing their household assignments and choirs besides participating in the nuclear family activities as asked for and expected of them.

Then you can expect to have all of the family members compatible and working together as a team producing a series of triumphant home runs wherein each family member fulfills God's will and what the family expects of them after experiencing a grand slam of praying together, staying together, and loving each other in obedience to the Lord's will and they follow His commands for the family as a whole.

The family unit can then celebrate and rejoice simultaneously know ing the last home run produced the victorious tiebreaker wherein a couple of family members are no longer experiencing friction between themselves, and everything now is running smooth again as before the conflict that caused a rift in their relationship in the first place.

When each family member knows the Lord Jesus Christ personally themselves, He will help them make wise decisions how they can be reconciled with their father or mother, brother or sister through a simple act of humility, and asking for forgiveness if they are the one or not the one that caused a disruption in the family unit which can help to restore dynamic relationships.

Bud added, the news media and the education system needs to come aboard The Christian Gospel Ship which the Christian family lives on, and surrender to God through the Lord Jesus Christ and the Cross of Calvary. Let there be an end to all the gossip, slander, and lying against one another in the Christian family and against all humanity.

It is imperative The U.S. American Ship must right itself, and become God centered in Christ Jesus. The Progressive Socialist Democrat Party seemingly want to take this nation in a direction completely off course, and in the opposite direction President Trump was taking the country which his policies were causing America to be economically prosperous whereby the American citizens were blessed with having good jobs, healthy families, and peace of mind along with precautions and safety measures despite the pandemic Covid-19 Coronavirus.

The Lord God was blessing this nation under the presidency of President Trump, and the American citizenry was benefiting and profiting in predictable and measureable ways because President Trump's economic team were following successful principles of capitalism which are designed to produce economic and financial successes in business and small business practices. America needs to stay with normal and healthy business principles, and what works in life's relationships and business practices, and never veer off course which President Biden's Administration has been doing to this great nation.

It is conspicuously obvious that The White House would rather take America down and upset the apple cart of the best course for America contrary to the good, sensible, and acceptable life's success practices by doing things completely opposite of President Trump's principles to Make America Great Again.

Are the Democrats that voted for President Biden truly happy now with the current president or having major regrets, or are they also beginning to see for themselves that voting for President Biden was the biggest colossal mistake of their lives? We hope every Democrat President Biden supporter and voter is willing to honestly and truthfully answer the above mentioned question as if their life depended on it knowing God knows your heart and He knows your objectives, subjective thoughts, and motives.

On YouTube Videos: "McCarthy: Biden's own words stating that immigrants should "surge to the border", McCarthy says Biden spoke those words in the first primary debate. McCarthy added, "...He's created this crisis, that he won't acknowledge, that he won't even visit to see, and now he is denying press from even to watch and see what is happening in the border stations".

Citizens of America, we all need to be praying for President Biden and the Progressive Socialist Democrat Party that has already caused so much trouble to America, that they also will Wake Up and begin to see the errors of their ways before it is too late to reverse course. From what I have been hearing and learning all that President Biden's Administration has been up to and doing to America as a whole, it has become obvious they are fully committed to their radical agenda to destroy The United States of America to fit their ideology, agendas, and intentional plans. They are Big Trouble to America!!

Lisa Boothe a Fox News Contributor had this to say post-President Biden's speech before The U.S. Congress on April 28th, 2021: "Well I mean we're basically China or North Korea here, we don't {need} a media, but did it really matter what Joe Biden said or even the delivery, we already knew what they were going to say, we already knew how they were going to spin this.

The fact checkers have been on vacation over the past 100 days, well just think about all the lies he told Wednesday night including saying that January 6th was the worst attack on our democracy since the Civil War. Well, maybe Pearl Harbor, maybe 911, but it doesn't matter because this guy gets away with everything because they're all on team Biden, they're all just a bunch of propagandists".

The Progressive Socialist Democrat Party seemingly want to destroy the very foundations this nation was founded on. God speaks to us as Christians and as a nation we need to Awake to His words of warning, matter of fact, and Godly wisdom, "If the foundations are destroyed, What can the righteous do?" (Psalm 11:3 NKJV). We recognize it has been a bitter pill to watch and learn all the things President Joe Biden and his radical administration has been doing to this great nation and its Judeo-Christian foundation.

It is truly sickening and pathetic that China's Communist Party leaders see America in decline, and coming from a position of weakness when China and other world national leaders only recognize strength. This same principle of brutal rule applies to the cruel and barbaric acts of the Taliban in Afghanistan towards their subjects.

They only respect leaders who deal with them strictly from a position of strength, and never from a weakened position of an inept and incompetent President of The United States who shows full well how to create chaotic and disastrous withdrawal operations from Kabul, Afghanistan that has resulted in thousands upon thousands of U.S. Armed Forces and the Afghans who helped our U.S. Armed Forces stranded and desperate to get out of the sand box desert terrain of the Taliban terrorists now with superior weapons and planes left behind by The U.S. Armed Forces.

When any national leader of The United States no matter their political office who speaks as a representative of the United States of America, each U.S. national representative must come from a position of strength, conviction of principles, and boldness as a lion to put fear into the hearts of America's enemies.

China sees President Biden as a weak president which has sent a signal to all of America's enemies that America is in a weakened condition, and they can commit folly against American citizens because The United States President is in mental decline, and they can play America for the fool that it is to ever vote and put this feeble man in a position of power as Commander in Chief of The United States of America.

President Biden meets regularly with, speaks to, and consults alongside President Obama according to The White House, and we're certain the advice he is receiving from former President Obama does not have America's best interest in mind since Obama's father was a Communist. Let us all pray for the U.S. President Joe Biden and Vice President, Kamala Harris every day for their salvation, Godly wisdom to reverse their radical course, and lead America back to the safe harbors of life, liberty, and the pursuit of the will of God. Citizens of America, we need to go with God and God will go with us, and remain with us provided we remain with Him.

America has great potential to resist the Progressive Socialist Democrat radical agendas if we will stand the test of the forceful pressures that the radical Socialist Democrat's want, intend, and plan to bring against the Christian Church and all conservative voices throughout America. Let us unite for God and Country and stand against their Neo-Marxist goals for America.

I appreciated what the CPAC speakers had to say at the Republican Convention. I recognize that the speakers which included former President Donald Trump didn't make any proud or happy acknowledgements regarding anything President Joe Biden or Kamala Harris and the Socialist Democrat Party have been doing to America during their short time in the White House. Bud and I recommend for the reader to continue to gain a lot of good information you can watch and hear for yourselves about CPAC on YouTube Videos.

We realize it is critically important for every Christian and conservative patriot who loves God, The U.S. Constitution, and American principles of faith, family, and traditional family values to carry on with staying informed and abreast of the news concerning what the Socialist Democrat National Party are doing at each new development they think of doing and decide to implement. They are going to be using big government to come against the American citizens at every turn of their political agendas and endeavoring to control every aspect of our lives if they possible can do so.

This will include applying their mind control tactics to achieve their goals of endeavoring to change society that it might change, grow, and develop into what they envision America should be like and become as a nation. This includes taking away the 2nd amendment rights of American citizens, and leaving us defenseless against the gangs and thug that possess guns which are willing to use them against U.S. citizens.

The Constitution states: "A well regulated Militia, being necessary to the security of a free State, the right of the people to keep and bear Arms, shall not be infringed." The Progressive Socialist Democrats are more than willing to infringe on the rights of the American citizens, and dismantle The United States Constitution if the citizens of America do not stop them from doing so through an act of rising up and taking America back.

Ivan Duque Marquez was elected as the youngest president of Colombia, and he was of the Democratic Centre Party in the presidential election of 2018. We urgently appeal to all citizens of Colombia, and especially the young people and older citizens of Colombia to become better educated about the deceptive lies of the Democratic Party that is being used by the Communist Party to usher in Socialism which is the gateway to Communism.

We encourage all Colombian citizens to continue to pray for Gustavo Francisco Petro Urrego ODB ODSC, the current Colombian President that he and his administration will always choose Free Market Capitalism for all of the citizens of Colombia during his presidency. God is very much interested in helping to guide, guard, and govern national presidential leaders who are open to His spiritual wisdom, insights, and knowledge regarding all of their important governmental subject matters including their cabinet decisions, domestic and international trade significant choices for the citizens of the country, remaining strong militarily, and every other need each president must make during their presidency for the good of their nation Worldwide. Nothing is impossible with God as you live and walk by faith, and to them that will stand on the Lord's promises and abide in Him who is love.

The Socialist Democrat Party is very adroit at using rhetoric that agrees with your words and thinking on a particular subject matter or issue, but they are also good on delivering things that do not line up with their communication that sounds so plausible which you might go right along with when you first listen to their speech and line of reasoning.

Rush Limbaugh knew how the Socialists will tell you things that sounds really good on the surface, but it's based on lies to get you to accept the kind of things which they want you to go along with. In other words, don't just believe and accept the things they say, but watch what they do to find the real truth of what they intend to sell you on.

The Progressive Socialist Democrat Party are master manipulators and they are very good about twisting, deceiving, lying, and scamming intelligent thinking people to accept things they initially thought sounded true, but the end results end up hurting, stealing, killing, and destroying our nations dreams, prosperity, and future success.

We know what we are talking about because the identical same thing happened to the good citizens of America, which many have awoke to the sobering reality of the kind of things the Socialist Democrat Party are forcing onto the citizens of America, and we do not want to hear and see the same things happening to our good friends of Colombia.

May there be much prayer to God to change the hearts of President Marquez, and now current President Petro Urrego and all of the other national political and spiritual leaders, and may the truth spoken and shared among the citizens eliminate and prevent a takeover of Socialism which leads to Communism in Colombia.

We pray and hope the citizens of Colombia will push back, resist, and prevent the seeds of Socialism from taking root in their great nation. Now is the time for all Colombians to take action.

It is great news to know that President Donald Trump was acquitted from being impeached by the Socialist Democrat House, and he is not running away from the Republican Party and the idea of being elected as the President of the United States of America in 2024. When Mitch McConnell was asked by a reporter if he would support President Trump if he ran as the President of the United States in 2024 and I heard Mitch McConnell say on Cable TV, "absolutely yes."

I appreciate knowing that President Trump has not gone away, but he is sticking around and watching what the Progressive Socialist Democrat Party have been doing and planning on doing to this great nation.

I'm positive President Trump is not happy with everything that President Joe Biden and his radical administration has been doing against America, and all of the executive orders he has signed so far which we recognize none of them are good for America's Christians and conservative foundations, and every U.S. citizen and non-U.S. citizens that only desire and want what is in the best interest for America as a whole.

"KT McFarland 'stunned' by Biden's national news. Former deputy national security advisor says Biden taking credit for Trump achievements is 'shameful' on 'The Evening Edit'." She went on to say, "Biden is taking credit for everything".

I received a letter from the American Center for Law and Justice which was positively an attention getter. It reads, Dear Friend, Brace yourself. A fight for your freedoms – the likes of which we have never seen before – is coming fast. The Biden/Harris-led Left is willing to push its radical agenda as far as it can – to limit your liberties as much as it can. The only BARRIER standing in the way is the Constitution … which the ACLJ resolutely works to protect at every turn. The Constitution must be followed to protect the integrity of our Republic.

Look no further than California where the radical Left has BANNED SINGING IN CHURCH – an unconstitutional and reckless abuse of power. We all want to keep America safe right now, and the ACLJ has been hard at work to do that. But NOTHING should be allowed to trample your rights.

We are fighting back. We won't allow this blatant violation of the First Amendment to stand – not in California, not in ANY state in this great nation. We will take this case all the way to the Supreme Court of the United States if necessary, arguing for your freedoms, against the Left's extreme agenda. Liberals have made their intentions abundantly clear: They are willing to leverage and weaponized the pandemic to advance their tactics – but with your support, the ACLJ is on the cutting edge of this fight. We are already seeing victories.

The Supreme Court recently BLOCKED the enforcement of Governor Cuomo's hyper restrictive and highly discriminatory rules for in-person religious services in New York. As the Supreme Court noted:

"Even in a pandemic, the Constitution cannot be put away and forgotten. The restrictions at issue here, by effectively barring many from attending religious services, strike at the very heart of the First Amendment's guarantee of religious liberty." Now, more than ever, the ACLJ must fight to ensure the recent wins at the high court are applied nationwide. As you generously support our efforts, we will continue to take a stand against authoritarian discrimination practiced by the global elitists who disdain religion – and your free exercise thereof.

At the same time, we have just filed an amicus brief urging the Supreme Court to hear another case where a state is wrongfully clamping down on religious worship.

The governor of Illinois issued a discriminatory order singling out churches with irrational restrictions – exploiting the pandemic to impose previously unimaginable limits on religious worship. With your help, the ACLJ will continue to fight the erosion of religious liberty – and to uphold your constitutional right to worship freely. There is no doubt, your freedoms will be threatened more than ever in 2021. But the ACLJ will be there to stand.

I appreciate the ACLJ willing to go to battle against the radical Left that is more than willing to steal our religious liberties away from us at every turn. Jay Alan Sekulow, Chief Counsel also mentioned in his letter, "NOW, MORE THAN EVER, WE WILL HOLD THE LEFT ACCOUNTABLE TO THE CONSTITUTION AND TO YOU."

He says, "Please stand with us. We are battling for your freedoms, for your family, for your future. We will not allow your religious liberties to be crushed – your constitutional freedoms suppressed. At the same time, we're engaged in numerous intense legal and legislative battles this winter – for life, for our ally Israel, for school choice, and more.

Your support is needed and valued. Thank you. God bless you! Jay also mentioned: P.S. The incoming Biden-Harris Administration is NOT a friend to religious liberty. The ACLJ is on alert, ready to guard your freedoms and protect the U.S Constitution. We cannot do it alone." We recommend that every Christian and American patriot to stand with them and help strengthen and support their legal team, the ACLJ with your most generous donations as encouraged to do so by Jay Sekulow. We also recommend receiving their news letter's which are very informative and impacting with insightful information we need to be aware of so we might help support their legal cases they're battling continuously. The ACLJ direct phone number is: 1+ (757) 226-2489.

I remember hearing on ACLJ 820 am radio in the Pacific North west that they {Democrat Party led by President Biden/Vice President Harris-Left Wing political team} want to bring us under the United Nations control, and some of the countries in the United Nations are some of the worst violators of human rights on the planet.

We must stand up and push back as a sovereign nation against relinquishing our rights and independence to come under the control and authority of this international organization that was founded in 1945. We assure you as an international governing body they would seek to manipulate America to go right along with their policies and procedures.

I appreciated hearing what Ford O'Connell, a GOP Strategist had to say on Newsmax TV one day in 2021. He shared with the viewing audience, "To Democrats the Constitution is really only a suggestion and essentially they don't believe in American exceptionalism. They want one party rule and they understand how to get this, and that is by controlling the flow of information, censorship, and by controlling the narrative, and rewriting history.

We can argue about all these little things, but if you don't see the overall game plan to the Democrat, it's not to have power. It's to make sure that {they're} the only game in town, and too many Republican's like Senator Lankford and what President Trump sees that if you have a working class focus, we it is the only way were going to grow back power, and make sure we're going to uphold American exceptionalism and capitalism."

I liked hearing the GOP Strategist´s straight forward analysis of the Democrat Party whereby he described it like it is, they want to be the only game in town which means the total exclusion of any other party competing with their overall game plan".

I happened to watch Life, Liberty, & Levin this weekend and he had a special guest, Jason Whitlock who I was really impressed with. Jason is truly an amazing African American commentator and he has a wealth of knowledge, insights, wisdom, and information that as an American sports journalist he told Mark Levin in an interview, "Too many Americans have taken for granted the freedoms that previous generations won."

Jason sees the dangers of Big Tech in America and the dangers of the social media apps produced out of Silicon Valley, produced out of northern California. He went on to share, "the American discourse is controlled by Facebook and Twitter and they are in control of this highly divisive highly racist conversation that we´ve moved into on line, and so what you´re talking about because I started seeing this 4, 5, 6 years ago like you'll follow my twitter feed and you would think that Oh, my god all these people hate Jason online of the twitter social media matrix, but in the real world when I go out when I would visit other cities I´m treated like, 'Oh, my god I love you, and can we hang out, can I get your autograph, can I get a picture with you?

The real life experience is completely different than the social media experience, and what has happened in my view, the Democrats in their fight for power, they can´t win in the real world." The video had stopped on YouTube Videos. There is a massive difference between a northern California Liberal and a New York Liberal. The whole media used to dance for the approval of New York Liberals now they dance for northern California Liberals and that is a much more radical.

Socialist, Marxist, anti-American group of Liberals that they are tearing this country down and public discourse down and creating this racial divide that has people that are unaware at each other throats they can't see that working class American's are being manipulated, and the elites are using racial division to maintain power and uh, even on old media".

Jason's final comments on Mark Levin's show, "Well, they're using race to build Marxism into American culture and I got to hand it to them it is working wonderfully. Uh, but look Mark we can look at from the summer of 2020 we can see buildings burning we can see police officers assassinated and they created this false world in the corporate authoritarian media you can't even talk about that you can't discuss you can't say, hey, this isn't appropriate the rioting, looting, the killing, the violence the burning of buildings this isn't, this aint a appropriate reaction you can't say that because you will be accused of racism, but the events at the Capital which I'm just so sorry far less than it", (the recording was interrupted momentarily then), "it's not American. It's just not fair."

Mark Levin takes an opportunity to thank Jason Whitlock for being on the program he looks forward to having Jason back in the future. Mark finishes with, "God bless you sir."

We recommend watching Jason Whitlock on Useful Idiots in Sports and other YouTube Videos with Jason Whitlock that you will be astounded by his impressive knowledge on subject matters, his communication skills, and the tremendous ways he is able to make connections and draw conclusions on what is going on in our American society today. He clearly understands that it is because of Jesus Christ and Judeo-Christian principles why America has been blessed with the economic principles of Capitalism.

Jason came across as a very knowledgeable Christ centered journalist on Mark Levin's show and he made that known by what he had to share with Television talk show host, Levin and the viewing audience.

I was watching the YouTube Video on Waters' World, regarding President Joe Biden missing in action and the gaffes, mental lapses, and brain freeze or lock brain moments which Joe Biden was making on TV when he would address the nation before a microphone concerning important information the American citizens need to hear. It is really pathetic to watch President Joe Biden have these mental melt downs when he should be mentally sharp especially since he is representing The United States of America as our chief diplomat, and really the leading symbol of our nation, and he needs to be on top of the issues facing our nation, but that is simply not the case with our current president.

Joe Biden is truly out to lunch mentally in so many respects, and the crisis at the border concerning the large numbers of illegal immigrants crossing our southern border points is out of control with the vast groups of humanity wearing shirts that read, Biden Please Let Us In. Apparently President Biden made a phone call advising the migrant people not now, but I understand the president's words fell on deaf ears, and all of the eager illegal immigrants decided to cross into our U.S.-Mexico southern border crossing states with 330 ports of entry just as they were whether physically healthy or unhealthy.

The Cartel don't care one bit about ICIS and The Border Patrol Agents. They only care about getting the money for each immigrant they bring to our U.S. border points which are being allowed to enter into numerous sections of The United States of America.

The Cartel do not care at all about the illegal immigrants, The U.S. Border Patrol Agents, and The United States of America's laws since President Biden had already promised the illegal immigrants that they would be issued the steps to amnesty in The United States once they arrived and crossed into American territory. American citizens, you can thank the Progressive Socialist Democrats for all of the illegal immigrants flooding into America because socialists are anti-America, anti-God, anti-U.S. Constitution, anti-Christian, and they don't care what the will of God is or what the American citizens are truly concerned with and really care about.

President Biden was asked by a reporter if he would commit to transparency on this issue regarding some of the facilities where some of the illegal immigrant children are being packed together so the American people can see for themselves what is really going on. President Biden responded, "I will commit to transparency and soon I'm in a position to implement what we are doing right now". The reporter asked President Biden, just to be clear how soon will that be Mr. President? President Biden then responded, "I don't know just to be clear".

David Harowitz the Author of, Dark Agenda The War to Destroy Christian America followed with, "The President is a disgraceful human being. I'm not worried about what questions were asked why bother. Every time he moves his lips he's lying". Harowitz recognizes that people are packed like sardines he adds, "It's just terrible what he has done, and then he blames Trump for dismantling, Trump set up a secure border we didn't have this problem with Trump, so all created by Biden.

The idea that we're discussing you know a nice guy he is a very nasty human being, and yet he had the opportunity to bully a steal worker that is what he did, but he can accuse Trump of murdering people he doesn't. He went on to say in reference to Biden, "he just lies about everything".

Harowitz recognizes, "the worst thing the collusion of CBS, NBC, and the lying AP referring the American Press, he says, "they are all covering for him". Harowitz recognizes, "we're in a stipulated dictator-ship. He accused Trump of killing every Coronavirus base during the campaign. He is lying", he said. He also recognizes that he {Biden} "makes Trump look like a boy scout when it comes to the truth".

He added that he {Biden}, "ran a whole campaign saying he was going to represent everybody and he was going to work with Republicans that didn't vote for him as well, but the Democrats who did. Then he comes in and signs 35 executive orders, and every one of them is a poke in the eye of every, of all the seventy-five million people that voted for Trump. It's just crazy and he gets away with it because you know people are polite, and maybe they are embarrassed, uh, we don't have a president, who is in charge to make up this stuff.

I appreciated David's candid, truthful, and tell it like it is account regarding President Biden who is now at the helm of The U.S. American Ship as the chief pilot of our national affairs, and with him in the Oval Office America is heading into some of the most frightening times and excessive turbulent waters that has many citizens of America extremely concerned, fearful, and absolutely uncertain of the dark days that lie ahead. It is positively certain we cannot put our faith and trust in President Biden because of his chronic lying to America just like his former boss President Obama had done and his administration.

We cannot trust even The U.S. Government with our incessant need of help in troublesome times including the national and worldwide pandemic Covid-19, and everything else facing this nation which is a 100% factually true.

We as the people of America need to run back to God in repentance and faith, and cry out and call on the Mighty Name of the only True One, the Lord Jesus Christ who has the answers and solutions to all of our nation's problems, challenges, difficulties, and dilemmas that the Progressive Socialist Democrat Party has gotten this great nation into in such a short amount of time being in charge of America's national decision making.

I saw on Newsmax TV the following: "New York Post Biden lies, and the media doesn't question it: Goodwin". Below that it stated, "Three big things stood out in President Biden's first press conference.

1. The leader of the free world is often lost at sea and says many things that are blatantly false. 2. The media is in the tank and cannot be trusted to hold him accountable. 3. Because of Nos. 1 and 2, America is in serious trouble." I was able to capture the above mentioned facts of interest on the Chris Salcedo Show aired on Newsmax TV.

The Progressive Socialist Democrats reveal and demonstrate by their radical ideology and policies that they do not fear the Lord. The Holy Bible tells us the fear of the Lord is the beginning of wisdom which the radical Progressive Socialist Democrat Party do not believe, instead they believe in self-centeredness. (Proverbs 9:10; 14:12 NKJV).

This is positively the reason why our U.S. American Ship has gotten radically off track and heading into troubled waters, and heading on a navigational course that a large segment of American citizens do not approve of their ideology when they can see for themselves the high pressure rocks of Socialism, Marxism, and Communism that inevitably will cause The U.S. American Ship total ruin if not abandoned and forsaken in rapid fashion.

Citizens of America and many non-U.S. citizens also failed President Trump because they voted out of a strong motivational force of peer pressure, and what society wanted instead of casting their vote concerned with what the will of God is concerning the right presidential candidate from God's spiritual point of view and perspective. They needed to be seeking what God's will is strictly based on the Word of God since He knows the hearts of all people, and whether the presidential candidate has God's will in mind for the nation which President Trump did or whether they are following the ideology and agendas of the Progressive Socialist Democrat Party.

"And they prayed and said, You, O Lord, who know the hearts of all, show which of these two You have chosen." (Acts 1:24 NKJV). "But Jesus did not commit Himself to them, because He knew all men, and no need that anyone should testify of man, for He knew what was in man." (John 2:24-25 NKJV).

We can pretty much assure the citizens of America, and especially the ones that voted for

President Elect Joe Biden that they were swept along with thinking more about getting rid of President Trump by essentially base motives of disliking his tweets, and what they heard from the left-wing Socialist Neo-Marxist Media sources which are propaganda biased filled rhetoric broadcasters, with their more Socialist activist politically biased pundits that you saw and heard from on the Fake News Stations on Cable TV.

"Fake news is false and misleading information presented as news. It often has the aim of damaging the reputation of a person or entity, or making money through advertising revenue."

From this 100% accurate mentioned political definition of Fake News as President Trump called it, you can clearly see and know exactly the person and identity that became and was the target of the Neo-Marxist Media throughout his four years serving faithfully, diligently, and conscientiously in the Oval Office as the Commander in Chief in the White House, President Donald Trump. We hold all Fake News Media sources fully responsible for your steady stream of sinister lies, biased journalism and broadcasting, and deceptive activist reporting.

The Lord God Almighty has been watching and monitoring your cunning broadcasting behaviors and actions, and keeping track of all your biased reporting to help influence vulnerable American citizens to side with, and vote for a Progressive Socialist Democrat as the next U.S. President, Joe Biden in the November 3rd, 2020 presidential election. America got what they voted for.

We have a good question for each Fake News journalists, biased presidential moderators, and socialist leaning news broadcasters, was money the deciding factor why you continuously attacked President Trump, and told the American viewers that President Trump was bad, a racist, hated Mexicans and brown colored illegal immigrants, involved with Russian Collusion although Mueller found no evidence of Russian Collusion against President Trump supposedly in the hip pocket of Vladimir Putin as many American citizens came to believe?

How and why did many of American citizens come to the erroneous notion and development closure, even before Mueller's President Trump Russian Collusion Conspiracy conclusion, and the grand finale celebration by many brain locked Socialist Programmed Democrats that President Trump was involved in Russian Collusion because of Fake News pundits broadcasting slanderous allegations and dangerous propaganda continuously against President Trump?

Do you believe and feel now that this was fair for all American citizens or was it more to fulfill the Progressive Socialist Democrat Party's political agenda contrary to how the citizens of America felt and thought about the false premise of the Russian Collusion conspiracy? God will hold all deceivers responsible for their deceptive ways and lies to the citizens of America!! You can count on it!!

When I spoke with Denton, Lorena's nephew in Bogota, Colombia over the phone he had commented that when he would see Joe Biden on TV, he appeared weak and sickly. I agreed with Denton's sentiments concerning our current Commander in Chief of The United States of America, President Joe Biden.

I pray for President Joe Biden and Vice President Kamala Harris will see their great need to be saved by a personal encounter with the Lord Jesus Christ, and turn from their radical ideology which is totally contrary against God, The U.S. Constitution, and The United States of America.

Let us all pray for President Joe Biden that very soon he will have a divine revelation and see a bright light from heaven, brighter than the sun at the White House while sitting in the Oval Office from the Lord Jesus as the Apostle Paul did on the road to Damascus. I would like to hear the Lord

Jesus say to President Biden, Joe, Joe, "why are you persecuting Me? It is hard for you to kick against the goads." May President Joe Biden respond to the Lord Jesus like Paul did, "Who are You, Lord? And He said, I am Jesus, whom you are persecuting." (Acts 26:14-15 NKJV).

President Joe Biden and the Progressive Socialist Liberal Democrat Governors and Mayors have used the Covid-19 pandemic to move forward their strategies and tactics to hold the Christian Church captive to their socialist objectives in order to control the people.

President Biden and the Socialist Democrats do not show that they care that He and they are persecuting the Lord Jesus when they throttle the Church of Jesus Christ by preventing the Christians from gathering together for times of worship and prayer for our nation that is in serious trouble, unless America is free to get back to normalcy, and make a full recovery from this Worldwide health pandemic crisis.

We would like to see President Biden call the Speaker of the House, Nancy Pelosi and Democrat Senate Leader, Chuck Schumer the Senate Majority Leader of the House and say, I had a personal bright light encounter with the Lord Jesus, and He told me to rise up and call you two. He told me to address The U.S. Nation back to God in repentance and faith, and stop our radical agenda against the Christian Church, and against the good people of the United States. I said, "Yes Lord".

At this juncture, we would like to hear that President Joe Biden, Nancy Pelosi, and Chuck Schumer all began to call upon the Name of the Lord in repentance and faith with godly sorrow. Their collective united prayer meeting with the Lord of Glory, that they have been fighting against and persecuting without their spiritual dull senses aware of just Who they have been in opposition to and treating with total disrespect and condescension, The Lord Jesus Christ the Son of the Living God.

They suddenly had a moment of great conviction with genuine change of mind and heart, and began to clearly see that when they have been persistently persecuting the Christian Church by effectively utilizing and weaponizing the pandemic Covid-19 Coronavirus by preventing, controlling, and holding power over the Christian Churches times of when they would like to assemble for freedom of worship, and choose not to be subservient to the Governors and Mayors of certain U.S. States and cities that decided to take and hold jurisdiction, and legal judgments and decisions over their subjects, wherein they erroneously think they have the right to do whatever they want to against The Lord's chosen, His called out people.

President Joe Biden, Nancy Pelosi, and Chuck Schumer all had a softening of their hardened hearts, and collectively experience their personal encounter with the Lord Jesus, and turned their lives over to follow the righteous ways of the Lord, and chose to reconcile with the Christian Churches, all U.S. American citizens, and non-U.S. citizens of The United States of America through an executive order by President Joe Biden.

The three Socialist Democrats made a complete 180 degree turn around and were completely transformed in their hearts and minds, and no longer conformed to be 100% opposed to The Christian Church and conservative America, and no longer were in one accord with the Progressive Socialist Democrat Party's agenda and policies. They were all radically saved, loved Jesus Christ, and wanted to be baptized with the Holy Spirit and Fire, and they all began to meet frequently to watch Jimmy Swaggart on SBN Broadcasting Network. There has been a positive change in America's political leadership!!

They truly enjoyed watching The Classics and hearing Jimmy Swaggart's evangelistic crusades where Christians were energized to witness and win souls for Jesus Christ, and they began celebrating to gether watching souls experience their new life born again glorious salvation experiences through faith in Jesus Christ and Him Crucified, having their sins forgiven through the blood of the Lamb of God and His sinless once and for all death of Christ Jesus on the Cross of Calvary.

Their lives were totally changed by the Lord, and they in one accord desired to do God's will without controversy, hesitation, and chose not to be in agreement with and controlled by the Progressive Socialist Democrat Party any longer. To God be all the glory, honor, and praise for the great things He has done. May this political fantasy become a wonderful reality in real time soon!!

Bud recently shared with me concerning the Roman Catholic teachings. He went on to say,

The Roman Catholic hierarchy claims that they have the authority to change the wafer that is put on the tongues of the kneeling worshipers, into the real body of Jesus, and the wine cups that they drink from is changed into the real blood of Jesus. This teaching or dogma is called transubstantiation.

Faithful Roman Catholics claim that they have received Jesus because of the wafer and wine changing into the actual blood of Jesus. They also claim in that they were sprinkled as babies by the priests, the Roman Catholic Church claims the authority to pronounce babies Christians based on their faithfulness in attending mass and attending confessions this means perpetual mass cards. Roman Catholic priests pray for the dead in Purgatory and the person having the perpetual mass card, the priest prays for the family member of that Roman Catholic that are in Purgatory.

The Roman Catholic priest when asked if the person they are praying for is out of Purgatory yet, the priest will shrug and say, "Nobody can know that". This teaching of Purgatory like so many other Roman Catholic teachings are not found in The Holy Bible, but are based upon Roman Catholic traditions which is basically considered extra non-Biblical teachings prescribed by the Roman Catholic Church and its faithful followers.

Any non-Roman Catholic that marries a Roman Catholic, the marriage ceremony is held in the Roman Catholic Church. A legal document has to be signed by the non-Roman Catholic and the Roman Catholic that has had any children conceived in the marriage must be raised according to Roman Catholic teachings and attend Roman Catholic Parochial School. If the non-Roman Catholic chooses or refuses to raise the children as Roman Catholics the Roman Catholic spouse will take away the children from the non-believing spouse.

The Roman Catholic Church has a lot of Roman Catholic lawyers. Let the reader be aware. The Roman Catholic Church believes that Mary is the holy mother of God, she is the co-mediator and to make request of Jesus she has the ear of Jesus for them. Thus, the Roman Catholic Church does not have the Holy Trinity, but believes in the Holy quartet. The Roman Catholic Church also believes in prayers to the dead saints because the dead saints have more light than we mortals on earth do. All of these teachings are in direct violation and deviation of the Word of God as recorded in The Holy Bible.

The Roman Catholic Church teaches the Virgin Mary remained a virgin until she ascended into heaven and that she is the Co-Redemptrix wherein she is believed upon as the holy mother of God. She intercedes on the behalf of the Roman Catholics and Jesus listens to mother Mary in answer to prayers.

Roman Catholic teachings which are based upon Roman Catholic traditions violate and deviate from the exegesis whereas there is no private interpretation of the infallible Word of

God. The Roman Catholic hierarchy believe they are developing the Word of God by adding to, taking away from, or ignoring the finished work of the cross of Calvary.

Semiramis, the mother of Nimrod who was the founder of Babylon. The same site where the tower of Zigerot which is the tower of Babel and it stood where the people were speaking one language had gathered in what would be considered the global village thinking of that day and building it higher and higher in order to worship the sun, the moon, and the stars. This is the early form of astrology and the people were worship ing the creation and not the Creator God.

The Roman Catholic Church advocated and were part of torturing and murdering Christians, Jews, and Muslims who objected to the Roman Catholic teachings. The Christians were also in defiance against the teachings of indulgences which was the teaching of perpetual mass cards in order to ransom loved ones out of Purgatory.

The Roman Catholic inquisition ordered by the Pope was against all those who opposed the Roman Catholic teachings. Thousands of faithful and devout Christians were murdered in cold blood by barbaric Roman Catholic torturers and executioners in the 15th and 16th centur-ies in front of yelling, cheering, and excited people. Peradventure you would like to know more about Roman Catholic doctrines and teachings of the church we recommend Catholicism & Christianity by Jimmy Swaggart.

May the above wishful thinking scenario become a reality in the lives of the three Socialist Democrat political adherents provided the Christians, citizens of America, and all non-U.S. citizens fervently pray daily for the three mentioned above, and all other deceived Democrat Party political leaders to have a divine personal encounter with the Lord Jesus Christ in a powerful way whereby they might be radically saved, regenerated and circumcised in their hearts, totally born again, and transformed in mind-heart-and spirit in and through Jesus Christ and Him crucified.

At this juncture we would like to share Bud's Words of Experience and the Journey of his Life that he shared with me recently regarding his early life's beginnings and what he experienced growing up as young child. In 1948 the Salvation Army when we were living in Lytton, California and during the summer time all of us kids were taken to a camp named, Mendocino in another county. It was way out in the woods and the boys had their cabins and the girls had separate cabins.

There was a creek running through the area and us boys would take off our tennis shoes, roll up our pants legs, and we would run down to the creek and kick at the rocks and stuff as we chased and catch crawdads. They also had in the area Red-Legged frogs which were good sized frogs that had red legs on them. The name of the game that we played was you would take a long piece of grass and use it as a lasso to put over the neck of a frog and catch it live.

When we were doing that there came a time to cook the frog legs and the crawdads that we caught. They were quite tasty for us boys to eat and at that same camp we would make a camp fire in the woods and there were a couple of male staffers which would oversee our activities in the woods.

The male staffs would end up telling scary stories and stuff that captured all of us boy's attention as you can imagine. And while we were sitting around the campfire that was probably a half a mile from our cabins when we were in the woods, but anyway, these girls came up and they stood on the other side of the campfire and they sang a song I'd never heard before in my life until that moment.

I remember the song which was, Ghost Riders in the Sky. And those girls sang in perfect harmony and I've never forgotten that after all these years. We ran all over in the woods at Camp Mendocino like boys will do. We had a lot of fun which were good times I can still recall.

I was born November 16th, 1938 in the old Community Hospital in Monterey, California. The medical doctor that assisted and helped my mother giving birth to me, the hospital staff almost lost me twice. While I was still a baby my mother placed me on an ironing board in Richmond, California to change my diaper and she walked out of the room and left me laying on the ironing board. I fell off the ironing board and landed on my head. I still have the scar from the incident.

My dad came home later from work that evening and became very angry about what had happened to me. Post-hospital care, early on in my school years I had trouble in the classroom with dizzy spells with the room going round and round and I was ignorant of God's helping hand at that time.

The dizzy spells gradually went away. I had struggles with my school subjects and a lot of the teachings and subject materials I learned on my own by reading and being self-taught over the following years. Anyway, then on January 3rd, 1976 and before I share about that I would like to talk about my sister, Roberta. We called her, Bert. We were in a Salvation Army home in Lytton, California north of San Francisco, California.

Anyway, my sister died when she was six years old in 1949. An African American kid named, Eddie Hudson who was a few years older than me, came to me and told me that my sister was dead. At first I didn't believe him. I didn't know that Bert had been even in the hospital and neither did our father know.

Our father worked and lived in Eureka, California north of Lytton. I went to the administration office which had a few concrete steps leading to the staff office front door and there was a male staff officer member sitting at his desk. I asked the man, what happened to my sister? He got up and responded to me in a loud voice, I don't want to talk about it and he slammed the door in my face. I was just a small boy approximately 10 to 11 years old at the time and this took place in 1949.

My sister, Roberta had been in the hospital and we didn't even know it. The Salvation Army didn't inform us about our sister's hospital stay and passing away. Anyway, I went back to the boy's cabins which were kept separate from the girl's dormitory, and there were offices overhead the administration building.

The girls had their own rooms up there. Anyway, two days later we had a staff member pound on the door where we were staying in the cabin and he told me and my brother to take a bath, and put on clean clothes because you are going to your sister's funeral. So my brother and I got cleaned up and got dressed and went down and climbed into the back of the funeral home hearse, and we were taken to the funeral in Healdsburg, California where the mortuary was located. My sister, Roberta was 6 years old when her spirit left her body.

In the mortuary when people filed passed the open casket I walked up and I placed my right hand on my sister's chest because the casket was open. I could feel her cold formaldehyde dead body. When I put my hand on her body I heard a voice speak to me in a commanding voice and say, Bert isn't there anymore. Nobody was standing there, but just myself when I heard this voice speak to me and let me know my sister wasn't there anymore. I yanked my hand back from my sister's body when I heard the voice speak.

I didn't know it at the time about spiritual things of a person's spirit being gone, but one thing I know over the years that I was saved January 3rd, 1976 as an atheist who was planning on killing myself, when the Lord came into my apartment through a closed door in Harmonyville, Idaho.

Trapped By A Psycho Doctor

I was an atheist and I was getting ready to commit suicide because I had a lot of things come down on me. I had a full load so to speak and I had a bunch of things that I had happened to me in my life. I was going to put my 357 magnum into my mouth and I was getting ready to kill myself. When all of a sudden the Lord came through a shut door which was the hallway door off of the kitchen in my apartment.

He came through that door and I felt His presence powerfully, I mean powerfully. It was not some psychological trip thing. It was real. In fact, it was very real to me, meaning His presence was very real in a tangible way what I was experiencing and I dropped to my knees and I asked Jesus Christ to become my Lord and Savior.

I didn't know how to pray back then, but I found myself bursting forth the words that I came forth from a heartfelt prayer that I hadn't memorized or rehearsed what I would say to God in a moment of desperation.

When I got up I felt like I was standing two feet off of the floor and I felt God's presence all over me. I mean all over me and I accepted the whole shebang. I accepted the Trinity and I personally accepted Jesus Christ. I was positively saved at that place and time. Oh, what He did for me that glorious day and over the years I have learned by studying the Word of God, and the Lord would reveal and open my mind to God's wonderful truths that has blessed me beyond measure.

During this time King David went through a period of mourning. He took off his robe and covered himself with ashes and he put on sackcloth on himself which was a sign of extreme humility and brokenness before the Lord. After a period of great sorrow and mourning over the loss of his son for which God had dealt with his heart, he got up and called for bath water to be drawn.

When the water had been drawn for him he took off the sackcloth and climbed in the bathing tub and washed all of the ashes off of his face and his body. Then he dried himself off and put on a new robe. Those in attendance were astounded that he had stopped mourning over his dead son.

They asked him why he had quit mourning and he responded by saying, I shall go up unto him, but he shall not return to me. (2 Samuel 12:14-23). This story bears witness with me of what the Lord had said to me in the mortuary in Healdsburg, California in 1949 when I had laid my hand on the body of my sister Roberta. We called her Bert and she was six years old when she left her earthly body.

Anyway, the Lord has revealed and shown me a lot of things over the years, like for instance the Gospel of (Mathew 12:36-37) it speaks about every idle word that comes out of your mouth and when you stand before God, you will be justified or you will be condemned based upon your words spoken upon this earth. Words that need to be repented of that you had uttered in your past, you better repent of them now, and ask the Lord to forgive you for your idle and vain words you have spoken that came from your mouth.

The revelations I have received from the Lord are powerful insights into the spiritual realm and faulty reasoning's of men and women Worldwide. God revealed to me how the most brilliant minds of men and women, and their laws do attack and show the ability of humans to suppress the truths of God, rationalize away God's truths that convict the hearts and consciences of the elite United States Supreme Court rulers, so that they willfully override their own consciences and usurp their own laws over the laws of God to satisfy sinful men and women.

By this, the U.S. Supreme Court makes laws that permit ungodly and carnal thinking people to live with blood on their hands, especially when they purport to supersede God's laws with man's intellectual court rulings having the fallen sin nature.

In January 1973, The United States Supreme Court legalized abortion on demand in a ruling known today as Roe verse Wade. The Christians that had come to protest the Roe verses Wade debate were kept in a separate Antechamber.

The U.S. Supreme Courts ungodly ruling was totally 100% without God's will be done, God's wisdom, and God's voice or the Christians voice being heard. The Christians were kept in a separate room while the U.S. Supreme Court was making their ruling, the Christians were told to keep silent and they were not allowed to present the Christian evidences against the horrors of abortion, the Roe vs. Wade decision. The Lord has shown me that when babies are murdered in the abortion clinics by cold blooded abortion assassins, that had they been allowed to be born they would have inherited the Adamic sin nature which is the fallen nature of mankind just like everybody else.

They were not given a chance to say "yes" or "no" to Jesus Christ because they were murdered, but the spirits of the babies are taken to heaven to be with the Lord. God is gracious, kind, understanding and merciful.

God's revelations to mankind found in the Holy Scriptures let us know that we have recorded in the Holy Scriptures in (2 Samuel 12:14-23), which hold all of the opinions of this world's system. King David's infant son had died, that meant his spirit had left his body, meaning his body had experienced life and death during his short life's span on earth. His body was sleeping the sleep of death.

Melisa Ohden, is a survivor of a botched abortion. I remember hearing her powerful real life testimony regarding her harrowing survivor story and that she had shared her survivor experience with a large gathering that had cheered when they heard she was a survivor of a botched abortion. When Melisa told the crowd of people that had President Obama been the president at that time she wouldn't be alive today and the group of people turned against her and became angry and upset with Melisa when Obama's name was associated with her botched abortion narrative. Hearing the truth can be painful if your thinking is totally opposite of God's truth revealed and manifested in human flesh who is Jesus Christ the embodiment of real truth in spirit and the giving of true life.

How pathetically tragic that so many misguided and spiritually blind American citizens can't recognize or accept the fact that President Obama twice had voted for the botched abortion bill and that he had become known as the abortion president. Thanks to the Lord there are strong advocates for the right to life movement in America like Melisa Ohden.

American citizens should not only celebrate the right to life that God has so wonderfully and graciously given to all the right to life and liberty to every human life conceived and born into the human family, but there is a counter culture that this very day are making themselves known in Hollywood and all around us in society that has been horribly brain washed and programmed by the likes of Planned Parenthood and other abortion groups of supporters in the world that are deceived by the god of this world.

We need to be wise as serpents and harmless as doves as Jesus said, (Matthew 10:16 NKJV), in today's anti-Christ culture and cancel culture trends among certain narcissistic psychopathic groups of people in society these days. Tax payer dollars are taken from hard earning American citizens to support these Anti-Christ groups.

I was watching and listening to a YouTube Video on the subject of conservative actors who are being punished by the Hollywood Elites relative to the cancel culture. Some of the best things that actors such as, Kevin Sobro, Antanio Sabato, and John Rich are doing is to fight against this rising trend in the American society that they know of, and keep doing what they are doing as methods of standing against the ones that want to cancel them out from societies way of life by endeavoring to positively influence society the best way they know how to.

To clarify and qualify their agenda to help influence society in the ways that will greatly benefit society for God's Kingdom on earth is to rise up and stand strong for God, country, faith, family, and Godly Christian conservative principles, values, and everything that God loves, treasures, and values.

We know that the Progressive Socialist Democrats want to silence every Christian voice of having a Godly influence that doesn't agree with their way of thinking. The Liberal Socialist Democrats think they are doing a good job of monitoring Christians and conservative thought in society today. Well God is monitoring what the Socialist Democrats have been up to, and He sees how they want to change society to think and agree totally with them.

We encourage Elon Musk as a champion and warrior of freedom of thoughts expressed in his quest to restore free speech to The Twitter Platform. We are thankful and grateful for everyone who has a high regard for and believes fully in The Word of God, The Lord Jesus Christ, The Holy Bible, and The U.S. Constitution of the United States of America. We are forever thankful for the freedoms we enjoy in America, and for The Lord God who gave our founding fathers the inspiration and wisdom to pen the great truths and principals of The American amendments which are historically recorded in The U.S. Constitution.

The Progressive Socialist Democrat Party is completely out of touch with society and their thoughts are radically opposite, and contrary to the Lord's thoughts and His will for all Christians and American citizens. The Lord's thoughts and plans for those He loves are thoughts for the good, thoughts of peace, and to give His people a good future. (Jeremiah 29:11-13 NKJV).

Anyway, for example when you take the Lord's name in vain the devil and the demons laugh with you, and the other people that are laughing with you need to take into consideration the seriousness of your words spoken in jest in your mind, but God takes those words uttered as a sin for which you are disrespecting, dishonoring, and devaluing His Holy Name with profanity in an empty manner, and by God you will be held accountable for. In other words if you take God's name in vain or in profanity you will be judged by the Lord accordingly. (Exodus 20:7; Deuteronomy Chapter 5: 11; Isaiah 52: 5, Psalm 19:14;
James 5:12; Ephesians 4:29 NKJV).

There are other verses that go along with Mathew's Gospel relating to (Chapter 12:36-37 NKJV).

Like what Jesus said to the Jews when He walked this earth, "You are of your father the devil, and the desires of your father you want to do. He was a murderer from the beginning, and does not stand the truth, because there is no truth in him. When he speaks a lie, he speaks from his own resources {his nature}, for he is a liar and the father of it." (John 8:44 NKJV).

We encourage everyone that has been programmed by what you heard spoken on Cable Television, the movies, sitcoms, and from an ungodly society that we all are surrounded by, be sure to ask the Lord to forgive you for your sin, and determine by God's help and grace not to be conformed to this world, but be transformed by the renewing of your mind, that you may prove what is that good and acceptable and perfect will of God. (Romans 12:2 NKJV).

Anyway, I just want you to know that your salvation was bought and paid for by Jesus Christ on the Cross of Calvary. That saying, all the centuries of law keeping turned people off with dismal failure. When Jesus walked this earth He kept the laws that He had given to Moses 436 years after Abraham. Abraham was justified by faith. Moses was given the laws on Mt. Sinai which were the 10 Commandments on tablets and they are the mirror of God's holiness.

And when the people of Israel looked at the laws written on the tablets given by God to Moses they were seeing God's holiness that man could not measure up to. (Romans 3:23-24 NKJV) says, "for all have sinned and fall short of the glory of God being justified freely by His grace through the redemption that is in Christ Jesus".

The very things Jesus said about the devil to the Jews being a liar and the father of it, well that is exactly what this world's system is doing today. And to die without Christ is to go into the flames of eternal burning hell, the Lake of Fire. And many people have died in stark terror in half moments on this earth. They were in stark terror before they died, but now it is too late.

In many hospitals throughout America, nursing homes, emergency center units, hospices, the staff are forbidden by the people in charge from praying over the sick or the person that is dying. The RN's will even tell the Christian(s) doing the praying that it is against the law. They also threaten to fire any staff that pray over the sick or the person that is dying.

It is imperative that we face the facts of reality of this fallen world's system psychologized by many deceived disciples of falsehood telling lies, but many hospital and nursing home staff will keep the patients medicated into a deep sleep so that they do not have a chance to receive Jesus into their hearts and lives. And that is denying them an opportunity to make heaven their eternal home by receiving Jesus Christ, and what He did for them individually and the whole world on the Cross of Calvary.

There has to be a special place in hell for people that forbid other people from being prayed for and allowed to receive Jesus Christ as their personal Lord and Savior.

And when the people of Israel looked at the laws written on the tablets given by God to Moses they were seeing God's holiness that man could not measure up to. (Romans 3:23-24 NKJV) says, "for all have sinned and fall short of the glory of God, being justified freely by His grace through the redemption that is in Christ Jesus,".

So the only way to make heaven is not by religion, not by denominations, and not by anything else on this earth. Anybody or anything that adds to, takes away from the finished work of the Cross of Calvary, that includes psychology, psychiatry, hypnotherapy, psychotherapy, situational ethics or any other thing that adds to the Cross will keep that person out of heaven where Jesus is seated at the right hand of the heavenly Father.

We have gotten out of the habit of studying the Bible on our own and researching and checking things, but instead of that we have gotten into a flow of going along with the entertainment industry and the news media. And at the very start of Trump's election the first time before he even got into office media, and the Democratic social media was cranked up for anti-President Trump rhetoric, and President Donald Trump propaganda.

The Socialist Media would make snide jokes, and make negative claims against President Trump throughout his presidential term. And the American people used to be able to recognize the school yard bully, and the bully was the one picking on the smaller kids was not popular, like in a chicken pen where a bunch of chickens would gather around one chicken and pick it to death, and that is exactly what the Socialist Democrats were doing to President Donald Trump.

And the majority of society went along with it because the people in the media are reading off of the teleprompters shoving Covid-19, rioting, looting, and all the violence in America resulting in tearing down of statues, historical buildings, attacking and demolishing the whole American business structure, and destroying America's historical foundations. God in His foreknowledge said, "If the foundations are destroyed, What can the righteous do." (Psalm 11:3 NKJV).

We need to keep in mind that George Soros, and other haters of the same thought were involved in paying the anti-American domestic activists regardless of the names they go by.

There were anti-President Trump rude insults, and all kinds of ugly things being shoved down the throats of the American society. The American votes were swayed away from President Trump because of it, and sad to say even many Christians in Christian churches throughout America were caught up in it too.

The religious cults offer their followers false promises with phony and deceptive lies that they can make heaven if they will only follow their religious practices, ceremonial rituals, and perform the works they prescribe. If they will perform certain religious observances in accordance with their belief system they will make heaven their eternal home one day. What the cults offer their followers faithful will lead to their eternal doom.

The finished work of the Cross of Calvary is the only answer for fallen humanity and the only solution that God will accept. The doctrine of the Holy Trinity means that God in three being distinct personages within the One Divine essence or nature of God. All three personages or persons are co-equal in nature and co-eternal. That is the Triune God, and when we pray to the father in Jesus name (John 16:23 NKJV) that is exactly what Jesus told His disciples to do before He went to the cross.

Anyway, thank you for listening to the truths I felt I needed to share that are so vitally important to Christian doctrines and teachings which we all recognize are part and parcel of the righteousness of the grace and goodness of God, which we believe and accept by faith in Christ Jesus. Bud had finished his closing remarks concerning the basic truths of life.

I remember attending a Josh McDowell's seminar years ago in Seattle, Washington. There was a large group of people in attendance while Josh shared with the audience concerning the historical accuracy and reliability of The Holy Bible. I recall Josh providing an excellent comparison of several religious leaders to the person of Jesus Christ. He said, you can take Muhammad and put him over here by himself apart from Islam and when you look back at Islam you see that Islam remains intact because Islam is based on a system of beliefs not based on its founder Muhammad.

He went on to share, you can put Buddha of over here with Muhammad and when you look back at Buddhism you see that Buddhism remains intact because its teachings are based on a system of beliefs, and not on its founder Buddha.

He again went on to share, you can take Confucius and place him over here with Muhammad and Buddha and when you look back at Confucianism it remains intact because Confucianism is based on a system of beliefs and not on its founder Confucius. He then said, you can take Jesus Christ and place Him over here with the other religious leaders and when you look back at Christianity it crumbles because Christianity is not based on a system of beliefs, but is based on its founder Jesus Christ.

I have appreciated being able to share Josh McDowell's religious leaders comparison to Jesus Christ with unbelievers over the years because I know it is an effective tool the Lord can use to open the hearts and minds of human souls that need to be evangelized for Christ Jesus.

Keep in mind, it also is imperative for Christian believers to always pray for the individuals and groups of unconverted souls we may witness to so that the Holy Spirit will continue to convict and work on each heart to help them recall and keep the Word of God shared with them as sown with good spiritual examples, illustrations, and applications so the hearers might have their understanding enlightened, and come to have saving faith to receive and believe on Jesus Christ as their Savior and Lord.

Coming to a saving faith in the Lord Jesus Christ will make all the difference in every person's life in a world going through a health crisis with heightened fears, troubling doubts, and great uncertainty. One of the positive consequences of the Covid-19 pandemic which is also referred to as the Coronavirus disease has been the increase of the purchasing and reading of The Holy Bible.

The Word of God can produce a harvest of faith in one's life to overcome adversity, and provide strength to persevere when we experience set backs on the road to experiencing success and prosperity in a person's life. Smith Wigglesworth had written a book on, "Ever Increasing Faith" and he had experienced incredible, and amazing miracles during his ministry whenever he placed his determined faith in the God of miracles.

When I look at all the things this nation is facing today in these critical times, I especially know we need to place our faith, trust, and hope in the Great Big God found in The Holy Bible. We can and will experience the miraculous in this generation and in our day and time in history if our faith is pointed to the finished work of Jesus Christ on the Cross of Calvary.

Always remember that nothing is impossible to Him, and when we place even a little bit of faith in God He can and will perform the miraculous in our hearts and lives in todays troubled world. For anyone that needs faith for salvation, a word of encouragement, and faith for the saving and redemption of your soul the following verses will edify your heart and life as you give Jesus Christ charge of your life. "In whom we have redemption through His blood, the forgiveness of sins, according to the riches of His grace".

"For by grace you have been saved through faith, and that not of yourselves; it is the gift of God, not of works, lest anyone should boast.", "not by works of righteousness which we have done, but according to His mercy He saved us, through the washing of regeneration and renewing of the Holy Spirit, whom He poured out on us abundantly through Jesus Christ our Savior," (Ephesians 1:7; 2: 8-9 NKJV; Titus 3:5-6 NKJV).

Josh McDowell was a brilliant university student and I remember him sharing with the seminar attendees that there was nothing more he liked to do was to put down Christians that thought they knew the answers in a university classroom. Josh shared that he had been challenged before to examine the claims of who Jesus Christ said that he was.

One day Josh went into the cafeteria and he said there were Christian professors in the cafeteria and a pretty university student that challenged Josh to examine the claims of Jesus Christ and who He claimed to be. Josh took the challenge very seriously and he researched Jesus Christ's claims for two years.

He went on to share that after two years of extensive research of Jesus Christ's claims about Himself, Josh said he came to the inevitable conclusion that either Jesus Christ was the biggest liar or lunatic this world has ever seen or He had to be who He claimed to be, the Son of God.

Josh's research to disprove the resurrection of Jesus Christ led him to discover the evidences that demand a verdict. In fact, Josh shares his evidence he discovered from all of his research by writing, Evidence That Demands a Verdict and a sequel, More Evidence that Demands a Verdict.

Bud and I recommend that everyone takes the opportunity to read the two books by Josh McDowell to have your questions answered that skeptics would have for reasons why they can't believe that a loving God would ever send His only begotten Son into the world, became a man that took on human flesh incarnate in bodily form, and died for the sins of all of humanity.

I have provided a better clarification of what I had experienced at the handiwork of the non-medical specialist, and the devastating results that followed my cosmetic surgeries. Some might speculate why I have had passengers hastily exit or deboard my carrier shuttles, and I would say there are people that have a lot of problems which may affect their perception as to what is happening on my carrier coaches.

The following quote by Jimmy Swaggart taken from, The Classics in Orlando, Florida 1985:

"Poor old America is in the same shape. We've wandered, we've wasted, we've lost our way and the nation is dying from sin and moral rot, but I believe God the Holy Ghost is going to reach down and pull us back". We believe and know that the Lord God is fully able to do the impossible and bring America back from its wayward ways and restore this nation, provided we will humble ourselves and return to the Lord in repentance and faith through Jesus Christ and Him crucified".

Donnie Swaggart shares the following timely message with the congregation and with the TV viewers on SBN Broadcast. "What I'm trying to tell you this is every man and every woman, every boy every girl. I don't care if you're black. I don't care if you're white. I don't care if you're red. I don't care if you're brown. I don't care if you're biracial. Jesus Christ died on Calvary in order for you to be saved and filled with the Holy Spirit.

Now here is my prophecy right now. The evil one is trying to destroy this nation through anarchy and socialism, but the Word of God says, in the last days I will pour out of my Spirit upon {all flesh}. The greatest days of the church are not behind us, but they are ahead. A move of God is coming. Hallelujah!"

I would like to share a gospel tract with the readers titled, YOU'RE A WINNER, and how you can benefit from its message and become a winner in Jesus Christ. "Recently it was reported that the winner of Canada's richest lottery jackpot of over $11 million U.S. had not collected his sudden wealth a week after the winning ticket had been announced! The world waited in amazement for the mystery winner to claim this great fortune. Finally a truck driver and his wife came forward with the winning ticket.

But there is an even greater mystery! Did you know that you are the winner of far greater wealth? In fact, the riches are so great that it would be impossible to tabulate the value in dollars and cents. You may be one of the winners who has not yet collected your bonanza.

Did you know that you're a winner? So many people today think of themselves as losers, and if you are one of them – you are wrong! For you are a winner! You may ask: Please tell me about my winnings! I am glad you asked! For I have good news for you . . . By and large, men and women in this world have lost about everything before they realize that they are personally bankrupt. They can actually be looked upon as lost. Jesus Christ said of them: "For what shall it profit a man, if he gain the whole world and lose his own soul?" (MK. 8:36).

This statement implies that it is possible to gain the wealth greater than the value of "the whole world." Such prospects make an $11 million dollar bonanza seem paltry. What does such an immense wealth include? The answer is that a lifetime is too short to learn about all the riches, and the human mind is incapable of fully comprehending the full value. But even in this brief good news release several fabulous riches can be mentioned.

First of all by accepting Jesus Christ as the One who suffered the penalty of death in our stead, and by asking Him to forgive our sin we are restored to man's original relationship to God. This means that we can with full confidence in all situations of life look to God as our Heavenly Father.

Can any one measure the wealth of peace, of contentment, of joy, of satisfaction, of meaning, and of purpose which this brings into a person's life? It means that our earthly life becomes enriched beyond comprehension!

Then on top of that the believer in Christ Jesus, God's Holy Son is assured an eternity in fellowship with God, with the angels and all the saints. Jesus Christ said, "Let not your heart be troubled: ye believe in God, believe also in me. In my Father's house there are many mansions . . . And if I go and prepare a place for you, I will come again, and receive you unto myself, that where I am, there you may be also" (Jn 14:1-3). YOU'RE A WINNER! – and you ought to begin to collect now! How can you begin to collect?

First of all believe in your heart that Jesus Christ died in you stead on Calvary's cross and that God raised Him from the dead, thereby proving that He was and is the Son of God. Then ask Him to forgive your sin in a simple prayer; in fact, you can talk to Jesus as you would to a friend. Acknowledge that Jesus is your Lord and live by His Word! And you have just begun to collect your fabulous wealth!

YOU'RE A WINNER! Paul Zettersten

We recommend Richard Roberts book titled, THE GOOD NEWS is The Bad NEWS IS WRONG! Richard shares, "Now it's time to put your faith to work! Maybe you've tried by yourself to straighten the bad situations out, yet the tears are still flowing. You may have tried everything you know to do, in the natural. Now it's time to put your faith to work in the midst of your troubles, and to call the things that are not as though they were!

It's time to declare before God and His mighty angels and all the hosts of hell itself, 'I believe by faith that the bad news is wrong and the good news of God's Word is true.' If you'll begin doing that, I believe you can begin to see some 'raising-up' miracles like you've not seen up until now in your life!"

At this juncture, I would like to share something I have declared and sang about over the years which seems very appropriate at this moment in time. Glory be to Jesus, Let the hallelujahs roll, Let me ring my Savior's praises far and wide, For I've opened up towards heaven all the windows of my soul, And I'm living on the hallelujah side!

In closing, we recommend that everyone takes the time to read what the Apostle Paul wrote to his faithful son in the faith, Timothy and as a warning to all, and what he had to say concerning the forth-telling of the last days which even now in our modern days of time and history, we can recognize that we are living in the last days before the return of the Lord Jesus Christ for His bride, the psychologized Church of today.

Paul writes, "But know this, that in the last days perilous times will come: For men will be lovers of themselves, lovers of money, boasters, proud, blasphemous, disobedient to parents, unthankful, unholy, unloving, unforgiving, slanderers, without self-control, brutal, despisers of good, traitors, headstrong, haughty, lovers of pleasure rather than lovers of God, having a form of godliness but denying its power.

And from such people turn away! For of this sort are those who creep into households and make captives of gullible women loaded down with sins, led away by various lusts, always learning and never able to come to the knowledge of the truth." (2 Timothy 3:1-7 NKJV).

Bud shares, "(2 Timothy 3:1-7) this exposes the modern teachings of the tax payer supported psycho-babble teachings of counseling which is the enemy of the cross of Christ."

The Apostle Paul provided the real purpose for his calling in the ministry: "For Christ did not send me to baptize, but to preach the gospel, not with wisdom of words, lest the cross of Christ should be made of no effect. For the message of the cross is foolishness to those who are perishing, but to us who are being saved it is the power of God." (1 Corinthians 1:13-14, 17-18, 23; 2:1-2; Galatians 6:14 NKJV).

For the man or woman, boy or girl, grandpa or grandma that is believing on the Lord Jesus Christ they are instantly saved at the moment of conversion, are being saved, and shall be saved provided they remain in the faith of Jesus Christ the Son of God. (John 8:31; Colossians 1:23 KJV).

I was listening to Todd Herman one morning the radio talk show host on 770 AM as I was going to get some gas at a local Costco Store in the Pacific Northwest. Todd mentioned that the critical race theory has it foundation in Marxism. This is the same racism theory that the Democrat Progressive Socialist Party want to indoctrinate the American citizen's students with in the public schools throughout this great Nation, and they are very determined to carry out their educational agenda directly into the minds of the youth of America as all part of their radical policies and sinister plans along with their hostile ideas to change American Society as aggressively as they can.

This is extremely upsetting too many parents and especially to the mothers of America who are strongly opposed and willing to fight back to save their sons and daughters from the Marxists and their educational pursuits.

I liked what Kelsey Bolar WF Senior Policy Analyst said on the Fox News Channel: "Americans across the board generally supported withdrawal from Afghanistan, but you know what they disliked more than endless wars losing was leaving American civilians our allies behind and Afghan women behind with hardly a chance to fight for themselves their right. We were there for 20 years, we had their backs, we abandoned them over night and now they face severe consequences of this decision that were completely avoidable and unforgiveable."

Meghan McCain: Biden "UNFIT TO LEAD" "I am furious our President was so incompetent not to see what every expert on the planet could have seen coming… The shame, dishonor, and embarrassment the Biden administration has brought to our country will take generations to undo…Biden is unfit to lead and I am nothing short of disgusted he and his staff can't seem to be bothered to leave their vacation…during an international crisis of our own creation."

American citizens according to, Finance Intelligence Report, "Biden's Weakness Abroad Imperils Us All". Bud and I agree that the Progressive SocialistPolitical Democrat Party has used our U.S. Armed Forces as a social experiment for years in Iraq and now in Afghanistan. It is time to impeach President Biden and Vice President Kamala Harris, use the powerful verdict of former President Donald Trump, YOU'RE FIRED!!

Bud and I would very much like to tell the socialist media planners and socialist activists for deceiving, twisting the narrative, and manipulating the American citizens and non-U.S. citizens into voting against President Donald Trump who should be serving out his second presidential term as I type, and stolen and destroyed ballots, YOU'RE FIRED TOO!!

It is time tell all of the Progressive Socialist Democrat Party leaders practicing political double speak, political deception, and political correctness along with their critical race and woke theories, critical anti-God and anti-Christian theories, and stop hindering the operation of the Holy Spirit in this world against God's chosen people.

The gates of hell shall not prevail against the Church of Jesus Christ no matter the arsenal of carnal weapons that the devil and the world may use against God's blood bought redeemed, new creations in Christ Jesus, and His royal priesthood.

We demand the Progressive Socialist Political Democrats put an end of continuing to deceive the spiritually ignorant people throughout this world's system. America and all International Countries, WAKE UP AND VOTE THESE CHARACTERS OUT OF OFFICE!!!

BUD AND I ARE TIRED OF HEARING TALK THAT IS CHEAP WITH NO ACTION. BRING ALL OF OUR U.S. ARMED FORCES AND ALL OF THE AFGHAN ALLIES THAT SUPPORTED OUR U.S. ARMED FORCES DURING THEIR 20 YEAR AMERICAN MILITARY RESCUE OPERATION AND BRING THEM HOME FROM THE TERROR OF THE TALIBAN IN AFGHANISTAN AND THE TERROR OF THE ISIS FIGHTERS IN IRAQ. OUR AMERICAN NATIONAL LEADERS CAN STEP UP AND DO MUCH BETTER THAN THEY HAVE BEEN DOING FOR DECADES.

Something we need to also keep in mind is the growing subversive tactics and influence of the Muslim population in America. A true follower of Islam hates Jesus Christ of the Bible.

It is imperative that America Wakes Up to the fact that we are under siege by the tyranny of our national leaders that demonstrate by their political decisions for the nation that they are united against God, Christians, America, and The U.S. Constitution. We must do everything in our united powers as a nation to take America back for God, Country, for all future generations, and for the world's sake. The battle for human souls is at stake for time and eternity.

I happened to hear a news pundit state over the radio on 770 am that he was concerned regarding the Afghan refugee immigrants coming into America when he mentioned that 99% had acknowledged when questioned however long ago that they preferred living under Sharia Law. For American Christians and all conservatives Sharia Law is diametrically opposed to the Bible and The United States Constitution. The Islamic Sharia Law is absolutely incompatible with American principles, values, and the American way of life.

Once more, we encourage all true Christians and conservatives to stand up, rise up, and speak up against the rebels that are in positions of leadership, which have the power of leadership of The United States Government backing and supporting their governing political decisions over the majority of American citizens.

I listened to the co-host on Spicer & Co aired on NewsmaxTV state, "There are 450 Americans left behind in Afghanistan". Rep. Greg Murphy stated that this administration is clueless about running the government. He also said, "Inflation is a tax". I totally agree with Rep. Murphy with his 100% accurate political analysis of the Progressive Socialist Democrat Party's current administration. I found him to be very knowledgeable of the facts, and policies of President Biden's Administrations senseless political decisions which fly in the face of wise business practices totally contrary to common sense, and smart choices for the good of America.

I listened to one Republican politician on YouTube Videos and he was speaking concerning the Progressive Socialist Democrat Party that see things through perception and not from a basis of reality. Another Republican pundit stated, The Democrats deal with things through emotion, and I recognize they are not thinking things through cause and effect factors with sound logic and reasoning elements without knowing their radical policies and the end results lead to socialism for America.

I recognize the American citizens are now having to face and deal with the hard realities of daily life experiences when they see the rising prices at the gas station pumps, high rising costs for groceries at the local stores, supermarkets, all the places of commerce, and a host of other rising costs shoved onto the American citizens. It effects all arenas.

There is also the cargo ship supply chain backup problem with all of the containers simply piling up out at sea, not having enough workers and truck drivers to get things up and running again as it was before President Biden's mask mandate, and his administration's rules and regulations they have placed on all the personnel involved in supply and demand. I observed a message recently on Cable TV that there is a shortage of 80,000 truck drivers. A lot of truck drivers have decided to retire, and they will need to be replaced with new truck drivers over the next number of years.

There are vast numbers of personnel that are sick and tired of President Biden's Administration's rules and regulations demands, and because of this governmental mandate and the need to be vaccinated and forced to wear a mask at work. Countless of first emergency personnel have decided to step aside. President Biden's Administration requires that all border patrol agents need to be vaccinated while allowing the multitudes of illegals not to be vetted or vaccinated. This ruling is a double standard to all intelligent thinking people.

Bud and I know the Progressive Socialist Democrat National Party is doing their level best at changing America which is destroying the American way of life through a systematic series of socialist leaning agendas and policies.

President Biden likes to say, "Build back better". From what I see the Progressive Socialist Democrat Party doing to America, their war on energy policies, tax and spend agendas, and senseless spending practices the better motto {which is a slogan} and very appropriate for the PSDP an acronym mentioned above is, "Build America back broke".

Bud and I recommend for everyone to watch on YouTube Videos, Gold Star father outraged as Biden considers paying $450K to taken from Fox News.

Bud and I recommend watching, Rep. Dan Crenshaw on Dems' Split Over Spending Agenda.

I'm positive if the radicals in charge of the decision making in The White House providing President Biden advice on all he should say and do for the good or the worst he could do to America and asked the following question, "Would you adopt and apply the crazy business policies and spending practices President Biden's Administration wants for Biden to apply to American corporations, the rich, middle class and the poor, and small businesses in your own life and business practices?

I know for a fact that many when asked the hard question individually, and not as a massive government power force they would have a blood vessel Wake Up to their cognizant mental faculties, and begin to smell the sobering, disgusting, bad coffee smells and tastes of the godlessness of socialism in America, and cause the drunken sailors spending tendencies in President Biden's Administration to receive a solid knuckle sandwich, Hawaiian punch, hurts donut metaphorically speaking, and the right foot of fellowship applied briskly in an upward motion to the seat of learning.

Bud and I are not advocating nor recommending physical violence be applied against President Joe Biden nor against Vice President Kamala Harris or against any Progressive Socialist Democrat Party member in any sense of the word. The above mentioned metaphor is only to get a political point across to the very ones doing all of the unwise spending of our U.S. monetary capital.

Remember President Biden and his administration are law breakers, and we recognize no one is above the law. The Progressive Socialist Democrat Party have suspended the immigration law, and now we have the open border policy thanks to President Biden and his radical borderless policy.

Bud has a word to extend to President Joe Biden and Vice President Kamala Harris which is, "Now hear this!! Now hear this!! Our American U.S. Ship is sinking!! Dog the hatches we are taking on following seas!! All crew on deck!!" I add, "Spend your remaining days on this earth President Biden and Vice President Harris, and enjoy living with the illegal immigrants you say you love and want a better life for them until you permanently fix the open U.S. borders".

Attention all U.S. Congress members and citizens: God forbid if Title 42 is rescinded or lifted at the U.S. southern border. The negative impact consequences will be colossal, and the humanitarian crisis which will result in negative repercussions on our U.S. economy, health care system, job market, Law Enforcement Agencies morale, an increase in criminal activity, and putting all American lives in grave danger.

The Progressive Socialist Democrats want all illegal immigrants to be able to vote in the next presidential election, and we say, "Their votes would be irresponsible based upon their expectation of favors from the Democratic Party. All U.S. citizens need to recognize, and know for a 100% fact that there are legal safe guards guaranteeing there will not be stolen ballots allowed after they vote.

It is high time for President Joe Biden and Vice President Kamala Harris to demonstrate their love to the illegal immigrants by making an appearance at the U.S.-Mexico border, and remaining with them for the rest of their political careers while they feign endeavoring to fix the U.S. border crisis or they become emboldened in their resolve, and actually shackle the U.S.-Mexico border crisis by seeking to impose new southern border controls by ordering the continued President Trump's building the wall policy.

Get a grip President Joe Biden and Vice President Kamala Harris and get serious about addressing the U.S. border crisis, visiting the U.S. southern border points, and get tough about building the wall that President Trump had started.

The Socialist psycho-heresy trained people in charge diminish and avoid the comments by Christians, conservatives, and Republican parents that attend the parent teachers meetings in the schools throughout America. They steer the people into more global village thinking. Christians need to be wise as serpents and harmless as doves, and as Loren Larson said on The Message of the Cross aired on SBN Broadcast Network, "Not to hate". Bud added, Christians are to supposed to hate sin, but love the sinner.

Remember for the evils of Socialism, Marxism, and Communism to triumph and thrive throughout the American population and its masses is for good people to remain silent, dumbed down, divided, and ignorant of what the nation's people can do to bring about the harvest of spiritual righteousness and holiness in the fear of the Lord, in order to obtain the pathway to successful right living for every U.S. citizen and all non-U.S. citizens living in The United States of America.

It would be wonderful for America's national leaders and educators to turn from their wicked ways in humility and contrition of heart and soul before the Lord, and enter into a true spirit of revival that would powerfully result in bringing about a mighty harvest of souls which would transform and reshape America for God in these last days like never before. Wise men and women, boys and girls still seek the Lord for His wisdom, guidance, and direction in these perilous times our nation is facing.

What better time could you think of than to spend time seeking the Lord in His Divine presence for the answers and solutions you may need at this very moment for your own personal, family, and national needs than right now and every day. The answer you are seeking for is found through faith in Jesus Christ and Him Crucified, and the price He totally paid for to redeem our salvation, and everything else Jesus Christ has done for us on the Cross of Calvary. To God be the glory, honor, and praise.

The best thing Bud and I would like to do for all of our readers at this moment is to wish you would come into a personal relationship with The Lord Jesus Christ, and for you to know how much He loves you. Jesus demonstrated His great love for you by willingly laying down His life so that you might find life in Him through faith in His shed blood on the Cross of Calvary, have your sins forgiven, and experience a spiritual new birth whereby being born again with eternal life which is resurrection life in the Spirit of Christ in Him. Bud and I wish you Jesus more than anything.

Bud and I recommend for everyone to listen to, I Wish You Jesus by Scott Wesley Brown on YouTube Videos.

Bud and I also encourage everyone to watch, Last Ounce of Courage -Full Movie on YouTube Videos.

All American citizens and non-U.S. citizens serious about preserving and saving our voter rights during our next presidential election we recommend for everyone to go to American VotersAlliance.org. Judicial Watch and other conservative groups have concrete evidence that the November 3rd, 2020 presidential election was hacked from within.

We concur with their fact filled based findings, and absolutely know the presidential election was stolen from President Donald John Trump with the applause of the Marxist Media and Big Tech Companies.

11

I FOOD FOR THOUGHT

In life, there are those who make things happen, those who watch things happen, and those who ask, "What happened?" Perhaps you see yourself falling into one of these categories. Perhaps you have a natural curiosity about how any person could ever be victimized by a cosmetic surgeon who was not a caring medical doctor. Perhaps you are interested in watching and reading about criminal cases and the mystery of how the police end up solving cases.

I never had a brother named Steven S. Scone, but let's imagine I did. Steven would have taught the uncaring doctor a lesson on the doctor's nose and ears, as payback for Dr. Cutter's words to me: "It didn't turn out as I envisioned." Steven would have said to the doctor, "Let's see if this turns out as I envision."

Steven would then have introduced the doctor to flying lessons into the wall and then onto the floor. Steven Scone would have had a series of private, hands-on counseling sessions with Dr. Cutter. Dr. Cutter not only would have learned how to fly, but he also would have learned some new dance steps.

Of course, the above is a fictitious scenario because as I said, I never had a brother named Steven S. Scone. We wrote this book with the earnest hope that patient victimization will become a thing of the past. My fictitious character named Steven only acted out a fantasy event as food for thought for the reader.

Our wish is that all who read this book will come to the knowledge of God and will openly accept Jesus Christ as Savior and Lord the only one who can truly help us through any circumstance we may encounter.

Bud and I recommend an excellent read by D. JAMES KENNEDY AND JERRY NEWCOMBE titled, WHAT IF JESUS HAD NEVER BEEN BORN?

One final life's important principles of formulas to help anyone dealing with un forgiveness issues in your family or personal relationships that we have to offer the readers is as follows:

OUR FAMILY

God made us a family. We need each other. We love and forgive one another. We work together and play together. We worship together and use God's Word together. Together we grow in Christ and learn to love all men. Together we serve our God and seek to know His will. These are our hopes and ideals. Lord, we ask for grace to attain them. In the precious name of Jesus.

Amen!

Decide to forgive. Choose to forgive. For resentment is negative. Resentment is poisonous. Resentment diminishes and devours the self. Be first to forgive, to smile, and to take the first step toward forgiveness. And you will see happiness bloom on the face of your brother or sister. Be always the first to forgive, and show it by your sincere words and actions.

Do not wait for others to forgive. For by forgiving you become the master of your own destiny in Christ Jesus. The fashioner of life and the doer of miracles. To forgive is to be like your Heavenly Father. Most beautiful form of love. In return you will receive untold peace and happiness!

Do not wait for others to apologize. For by asking for forgiveness we show our desire to maintain a clear conscience before God, and our brother and sister. Being the first to rightfully apologize we can reconcile communication breakdowns. The most basic quality needed for friendships is sincere humility. This is the quality which is sure to result from a clear conscience. How true God is on this point: "He that cover this sins shall not prosper, but whoso confesses and forsakes them shall have mercy." (Proverbs 28:13 KJV)

Readers, we offer you a loving schedule for achieving a forgiving heart to please the heart of the Father:

Sunday: Forgive yourself.

Monday: Forgive your Family members. Tuesday: Forgive your friends and associates.

Wednesday: Forgive across economic lines within your own nation. Thursday: Forgive across cultural lines within your own nation.

Friday: Forgive across political lines within your own nation.

Saturday: Forgive other nations and everyone that you might have ought against.

Only the brave know how to forgive. A coward never forgives. It is not in his nature.

A final thought--and a favorite quotation of mine. It's a line from George Roemisch's poem on

"Forgiveness": "Forgiveness is the fragrance of the violet which still clings fast to the heel that crushed it."

It's good to know that we are called to honor Christ Jesus our God, and Savior as ambassadors of reconciliation. God has given to us the ministry of reconciliation. 2 (Corinthians 5:18-20). What joyful blessings await those who are reconciled with their loved ones.

We thought that our Families and relatives would like to receive a copy of these biblical principles to maintain good and harmonious relationships. We desire that through your wise investments you will continue to grow strong family relationships. May God help you to harvest the best of family relationships. We offer these wonderful formulas mentioned above as our gifts to you, and special credits to George Roemisch for his formula on forgiveness.

On a humorous note: One day I took Bud with me to Life's Final Stop Funeral Home in Resurrection Life Ville where I had a part time job. I remember Bud touching a cadaver body lying in a casket in a viewing room, and he mentioned that the body was cold to the touch. We also decided to take the elevator to the downstairs basement to see the crematorium where we did see a crushed skull and the skeletal remains of a dead body inside. Bud and I also were able to view six dead men lying on cooling trays inside of one room, and behind a large separate door that had the sign which read: Preparation Room. When we opened the preparation room door that was cold and pitch dark inside, we were able to observe a large Asian man that Bud said was of Japanese American ethnicity.

The man was lying on a white porcelain preparation table. I walked back to the elevator and pulled out a five-dollar bill and twenty to twenty-five cents in change from my pants pocket, and placed it on a small bench inside of the elevator. I told Bud that I would give him the money inside of the elevator if he would walk over, and put his hand on the dead man with the lights off with the door being shut. I would then open the door and see that he was touching the dead body, and Bud would become the recipient of the money I promised him lying on the elevator bench. While Bud was engrossed viewing the dead man in the preparation room I quickly ran back to the elevator, and began to close the grating before closing the elevator door to make a fast get away upstairs, when here came Bud on the fly quickly darting back inside of the elevator where I was safely inside. I remember Bud saying to me, "Hey, don't do that to me man".

It became obvious to me that Bud was not in the frame of mind to stay one second or one minute more with the dead body inside that preparation room. It was time to give up our viewing practices for the day. We made our escape by taking the elevator back upstairs from that spooky situation.

Bud and I recommend for all readers to follow Journalist & Author, Alex Newman's documented knowledge and insights by going to Liberty Centinel.org regarding the United States Government's involvement and connections with the United Nations designs on changing America away from God, Country, our American way of life, and our families now and the U.S. Nations movements towards the future of 2030. We need for all Christians to unite and uphold in prayer all governing bodies, and politicians that hold decision making powers over all nations to the Heavenly Father in Jesus Name. (John 16:23)

We encourage all to contact SBN and request Journalist & Author, Alex Newman and his incredible researched findings regarding The United Nations agenda for America and worldwide in 2030 aired on July, 30th 2022. For the full interview with Alex Newman on Francis & Friends Go to: Watch SonLifeTV. Com

We recommend a great read for all of our readers entitled, The Battle For The American Mind by Pete Hegseth with David Goodwin.

We also recommend another great read by David and Barbara Cerullo entitled, INSPIRATION PROMISE BOOK

Chris Salcedo on NewsMaxTV says, "America Can No Longer Afford Democrats: The Cost To The Culture Edition"

Please keep in mind a good guiding principle to test whether President Biden and his Administration is helping or hurting America's citizens, and every other non-American is to watch what they do and not to swallow hook, line, and sinker what they say they are doing for the good of America. Do not continue to believe the speeches President Biden, appropriately name "Divider-in-Chief" or any other radical Progressive Socialist Democrat speaks on Nationwide Cable TV while leading America from behind, and allowing all illegal immigrants entering our U.S. Southern entry border checkpoints with national freedoms and plenty of benefits which should be given and awarded to legal U.S citizens. It is more than evident by their radical policies the Progressive Socialist Democrats want the illegal immigrant's votes.

Bud and I encourage all U.S. citizens, non-U.S. citizens, and illegal immigrants (if permitted) to do your patriotic duty, and vote during all midterm and national Presidential elections without compromise and choosing to skip out on voting whether you're discouraged in thinking your single vote will be hijacked, made void, and stolen by the National Progressive Democrat Party to appear as if your vote was strictly for their self-centered and radical political motives, agendas, and ideologies.

When it comes your time who to vote for during the upcoming 2022 midterms and the 2024 U.S. Presidential Elections we recommend that you take into consideration Rep. Congressman Allen West in April of 2012 had heard that there are up to 80 U.S. House of Representative Party members of the Communist Party. We encourage everyone to do a fact check whether the Congressional Representative that represents the State of the Union you live in might be a card-carrying Communist Party member. Remember to take a close look at their voting record, and their current policies peradventure they firmly stand for themselves remaining in office, power, and control over the American people from the womb to the tomb and from the cradle to the grave. Are their policies the very best and what is good for every American citizen or are their policies only good and acceptable to advance the Progressive Socialist Democrat Party and its radical ideologies.

Keep in mind as you're doing your fact checks on your State Representative there are social media planners eager to distract, and deceive American citizens from knowing the whole truth and nothing but the truth. The Neo-Marxist Media will do their level best at rope-a-dope keeping the American citizens sidetracked on the ropes away from the real truth of finding and knowing the answers to the subject matters you are searching for regarding your State Representatives. The media is very good at helping the Progressive Socialist Democrats at providing counterfeit nothing burgers that don't satisfy, and not allowing a crisis to go to waste. Be careful of their flowery speeches, but their policies leave Americans in a world of hurt.

We need to recognize right spiritual doctrines found in The Holy Bible, and false doctrines that ultimately lead us astray from Jesus Christ and Him crucified. It is imperative that you think right about the concept of a living Savior ready to meet your daily needs, and what you come to believe in has shown to have lasting consequences toward your eternal destiny, the legacy you leave behind for the direction of this great nation, and those who follow your steps to a better life. For all of the young Americans that have been influenced into believing in Socialism, Marxism, and Communism as being so great for America we hope you have Woke Up to a good dose of reality that these systems are fully corrupt, destroy, and do not bless and satisfy the lives of those pursuing these anti-God, anti-Christ, and anti-Bible systems which are leading to the destruction of everything good concerning America.

Has the free things the Progressive Socialist Democrats promised you in exchange to control every aspect of your life brought the true meaning and purpose of life you have been seeking for? Have these systems of beliefs truly met your premium expectations you have set for your lives?

Has atheism = belief there is no God; agnosticism = the reality of God is unknown; paganism = spiritual beliefs other than Christianity, Islam, and Judaism; pantheism = belief that all is God and His cosmos and He are One in the same. Secular humanism = the belief system that man is his own god, and he can produce his own morality and have self-attainment and fulfillment without the need to believe in God the Creator apart and distinct from man His creation; psychology = the study of the mind and behaviors of mankind from a scientific perspective; sociology = when men and women study the functioning, structure, and development of human society and its social problems. Have these systems of beliefs brought true meaning, purpose, and satisfaction you were seeking for into your families and your whole life?

None of the world's systems of beliefs has a corner on truth, but the truth is found only in Jesus Christ and the cross of Calvary. The world's systems of beliefs will lead you down the primrose path to disastrous consequences apart from eternal life and peace with God in Jesus Christ. Always keep in mind: "There is a way that seems right to a {person}, But its end is the way to {spiritual which is the second} death." (Proverbs 14:12 NKJV) The Biblical truth that eliminates the false doctrine of reincarnation: "And it is appointed for {humans} to die once, but after this the judgment." (Hebrews 9:27 NKJV) Jesus is the Prince of Peace and He offers His peace to all who will believe on Him. (Isaiah 9:6 NKJV) "Peace I leave with you, My peace I give to you; not as the world gives do I give to you. Let not your heart be troubled, neither let it be afraid." (John 14: 27 NKJV)

America is a great nation all because Jesus Christ who is the rock of our nations foundations, and what He has done through His Christian body of Christ worldwide born again believers to make America great from its inception. Jesus gave us the keys to make America great again if we will choose to follow His teachings and ways of successful living in our spiritual pursuits, business principles and practices, education, and harmonious relationships with God and our fellow humans.

God the Father = Father of Truth; Jesus Christ = the Truth, God Incarnate, Son of God, Savior and Lord = Resurrection Life = only way to come to God the Father; Holy Spirit = Spirit of Christ Jesus the Anointed Messiah; Satan = Lucifer = father of lies, sin, and death.

When men and women have researched and studied every subject matter and field of study known to the human family on earth if your conclusions have led you away from having a relationship with God through Jesus Christ and Him crucified then your prideful studies have separated your mind and heart from knowing true wisdom in Christ Jesus, and having the knowledge of the Lord God Almighty to guide, guard, and govern your life from infancy to the day your spirit leaves your body on earth.

For the young adults that have been won over by the propagandist lies, deceptions, and liars of this world that don't care one iota about your life, destiny, and future, you will one day find when you really need help in this life, and the provisions and benefits the anti-God, anti-Christ, and anti-Bible revolutionists you thought truly loved and cared about you and your friends were truly masters of deceptions that really hate, despise, and wished you were dead, buried, and gone from taking up space and being a useless eater on this planet as the Nazi's believed regarding their Jewish captives during The Holocaust. From their perspective you have unknowingly opened up your life to being a total sucker, and another of the world's biggest losers which deserved to be lied to, deceived, and ripped off royally of all of your life's unique individuality qualities, exceptionalism, Biblical talents and giftings, possessions, and freedoms.

We recommend Jonathan Cahn's book, The Return OF THE GODS which he so powerfully and in a persuasive manner explains how America has opened herself up to demon spirits that are even now working in and through false emissaries to deceive Americans into believing their narratives are for America's good. Ancient mysteries and events brought into our modern American lives and homeland of the free.

We encourage all who have forsaken the Lord God to repent and turn back to the Lord of Glory in godly sorrow: "All we like sheep have gone astray; We have turned, every one, to his own way; And the Lord has laid on Him the iniquity of us all." (Isaiah 53:6 NKJV); "And he went out to meet Asa, and said to him: "Hear me, Asa, and all Judah and Benjamin. The Lord is with you while you are with Him. If you seek Him, He will be found by you; but if you forsake Him, He will forsake you. ..."but when in their trouble they turned to the Lord God of Israel, and sought Him, He was found by them." (2 Chronicles 15:2-4 NKJV). "For godly sorrow produces repentance to salvation, not to be regretted; but the sorrow of the world produces death." (2 Corinthians 7:10 NKJV)

When Jesus confronted the twelve disciples whether they wanted to walk away and leave Him as many other of His disciples had done, Simon Peter recognized the seriousness of the choice they were being forced to make and the hard facts of the matter. "Then Jesus said to the twelve, Do you want to go away?" (John 6:67 NKJV). Having experienced walking with God in Christ Jesus on earth Peter was now facing the most serious dilemma of his life, what life would be like for him and the other eleven disciples should they also walk away from Jesus. I appreciate Peter speaking up with boldness, and making the right choice and confession concerning who Jesus truly was, "Lord, to whom shall we go? You have the words of eternal life. Also we have come to believe and know that you are the Christ, the Son of the living God." (John 6: 67-69 NKJV)

We have reached a very critical point in American history, and we as a nation must repent of our sins against the Lord our God and return to Him, and pray for a mighty Holy Spirit revival from The White House to the poor houses of America for Divine mercies from sin and shame, grace unto salvation by faith in Christ Jesus and Him crucified, and true reconciliation with God and our fellow humans.

Has the high price of losing your freedoms and leaving the decision making to the ever controlling governmental institutions for your life been really worth the propagandist lies, deceptions, and every false and corrupt system of humanity's beliefs in the god whether of self or the deity's you end up choosing for your life over and above the finished work of the cross of Calvary? We hope you are tired of being lied to, deceived by every evil person, and conned out of everything that you have worked hard for and rightfully earned? It is high time we all send President Biden and Vice-President Harris along with all of the Progressive Socialist Democrat Party members packing that only knows how to deceive, lie, steal, and cheat their way to destroy America with their radical ideology and policies.

President Biden is good at browbeating, intimidating, and using stern abusive words in his speeches endeavoring to put American citizens on a guilt trip over the illegal immigrant open border crises or bashing the MAGA/Make America Great Again Republicans who voted for former President Trump. President Biden looks like a pathetic presidential leader of the United States that the American citizenry does not need now or ever.

Greg Kelly on Newsmax TV gave the most accurate analysis on President Biden by using acrostics, and we would like for every Presidential Election Voter to think about Greg's great analysis when it comes your turn to vote in The 2022 United States Midterm elections & The United States 2024 Presidential elections. Greg shared his analysis as the following:

Everything Wrong In America Boils Down To This Liberal + Chaos = Biden

Biden-Border Inflation Disunity Energy (gas) No respect Liar Crime

Incompetent Hunter Bizarre Afghanistan Erratic Obscenity Racist Supply Chain Angry Lazy

After Greg provided the three acrostic analysis of President Biden mentioned above he said, "Other than that everything is going fine." 9/7/2022

Jonah Jon Jefferys

On behalf of the Great MAGA Movement Advocates & Supporters for returning America to its greatness again under God we say, It is time for President Biden to give himself a long break from the Oval Office right along with the Neo-Marxist Media, and resign as the current President of the United States of America coupled with the fake news reporters and pundits. Give it up Joe!! Give up the Presidency now Joe, and think of what is the best thing you could do for everyone looking to America for faith, hope, and love!!

A lot of nations that open their doors to their nations policies follow the slippery slopes downward by trying the anti-God systems of Socialism, Marxism, and Communism only to reverse course when these systems reach strangulation proportions on their spiritual leadership, governing political bodies membership, and economic and financial business practices, but President Biden and Vice-President Harris have stubbornly refused to change directions for the good of all American citizens and choose to steer The U.S. American Ship right into the rocks of shipwreck demilitarized destruction zones and beyond only to follow headlong on the impulses providing political guidance headings of radical left-wing ideology and destruction policies. As a great nation we desperately need a mighty move of God to lead us in the right direction to be ready for the future harvests the Lord has planned for us.

The fallen sin nature working through men and women in America is causing our nation to go deeper off course, and gullible shallow carnal women are leading gullible shallow carnal men to the nation's destruction. The sin nature is conniving, and it also operates through children and adults. God has much better thoughts and plans for America than we could ever have faith, hope, and trust for in these last days. "For I know the thoughts that I think toward you, says the Lord, thoughts of peace and not of evil, to give you a future and a hope. Then you will call upon Me and go and pray to Me, and I will listen to you. And you will seek Me and find Me, when you search for Me with all your heart." (Jeremiah 29:11-13 NKJV)

It is way beyond time to send all of the National Progressive Democrat Party members completely away from being in any capacity to make national decisions that affect our nation's decision making process regarding our great countries national, and state laws that negatively impact all living human beings in America. We have to guarantee the safety of all American people and the way of life, liberty, and the pursuit of the will of God.

Now is the time to send the above mentioned Progressive Democrat Party members where they will never be heard from or seen again occupying a political decision making capacity in The U.S. White House, The U.S. Congress, and all of the State Houses in every State of the Union. We must think right, believe right, and vote right concerning the very best Presidential candidate who would be the best President to lead America especially now. We must all make our united voices to be bold, loud, and clear when it comes to Saving America and Making America Great Again as the former President Donald Trump had desired, wished for, and wanted for all Americans and non-Americans alike. President Trump was a great President because he loved, cherished, and desired from the heart the very best for all Americans and Israelis.

It is for the above mentioned powerful words of warnings to the American citizens by the 16th President of the United States of America the very reasons, and there are many more why I literally can't understand the reasons for American citizens would ever want to vote for a Democrat for the Presidential Oval Office of this great U.S. Nation when the Socialist Democrat Political Party are known for taxing and spending the American citizens. Out of concern for the welfare of the people of this nation, and based upon the events of November 3rd, 2020 we remind you and know that the Socialist Democrat Party stole the election from President Donald Trump and thereby the American citizens were robbed of their voting rights.

For all of the deniers and naysayers to the factual truths, and maximum numbers of evidence that the 2020 Presidential election was stolen from President Donald Trump, we would like to recommend the readers to watch the 2020 Presidential Debates between President Trump and Senator elect Joe Biden on YouTube Videos. The readers can do a simple fact check themselves or merely recollect from memory the number of times presidential hopeful elect Biden had denied he knew nothing of his son's business dealings overseas. During the 1st Presidential Debate Joe Biden repeatedly stated that he knew nothing about his son's business dealings with Burisma, Ukraine.

Since then more and more of the facts have become evident that Hunter Biden's business dealings were not only making money for him and Senator Biden in Ukraine, but also they received money from China and Russia back in 2014. Senator elect Biden had undeniably lied to the American citizens on nationwide Cable TV, and as a negative consequence he is the current U.S. President. America had been duped by his lies, and they ended up voting for Senator Biden. Elect Joe Biden now President Biden is a "lying dog-faced pony soldier" who chronically lied to the American citizens as his predecessor, President Obama had.

Had Senator elect Biden told the truth during the Presidential Debates, America wouldn't have voted for him. I would like to think with all of his numerous disasters, crisis, and chaos created by President Biden and the Progressive Socialist Democrat Party has created for America to deal with in an ongoing basis, America would have awoke and rejected voting for Senator elect Biden.

He at one point during the Presidential Debates had referred to the business dealings of his son Hunter and stated, "It was Russian Collusion." It was a lie. As a negative consequence President Trump lost the presidential election, and America and Ukraine, and how many other nations have been victimized and put into national jeopardy including painfully suffering ever since then.

Senator elect and current U.S. President Biden had sold gullible America a bill of goods then, and he continues to deceive millions of the American citizenry today. Keep in mind America, there were millions of Americans that were alive when the voting ballots were stolen, and millions of American citizens allowed the vast numbers of criminals to get away with their thievery without spending serious time in jail or serve prison time for the crimes against America, The U.S. Constitution, President Trump, Make America Great Again election voters, and having destroyed the election process in America.

The stolen ballots that America was aware of were found to be true, and was validated with solid evidence in 2020 and 2021. And now American citizens are being lied to, and told that it didn't happen.

The powerful truths reported and all of the evidence America needs of the stolen election case has been presented in this book for everyone to read, and rightfully know that the presidential election in 2020 was positively stolen from President Trump and the American citizens. The Progressive Socialist Democrats used Senator Biden's lies during the 2020 presidential debates to steal the second term from President Trump when he was fully ready to serve out his second American presidency as the U.S. Commander in Chief. What are the American people going to do about it?

America, you may not want to revisit the stolen election ballots issue mentioned above and there are many other issues that face us as a nation, but you are being royally ripped off and robbed every day President Biden remains in the U.S. presidency.

There are many American's that think to themselves that all things continue as they were from the beginning of creation, but that simply is not true. The Progressive Socialist Democrat Party is not the same today as during the days when President John F. Kennedy was the U.S. President or when President Dwight D. Eisenhower served in the U.S. Oval Office. When the Coronavirus Pandemic (Covid-19) lockdown was enforced on the American citizens by the Democrat Party, people had lost sight of how Senator Biden had become the President of the United States?

We appeal to the readers to take another look and reconsider the 2020 presidential election debates on YouTube Videos, and what had transpired during the three presidential oral exchanges between President Trump and Senator Biden. We hope America has a momentous and wholehearted Wake Up during, after watching, and reviewing them over again!!

Bud and I know for an absolute certainty and we want all of the citizens of America to positively and emphatically know for themselves that with all of the mounting facts, and evidence that then Senator elect Biden had lied to the American people during the presidential election debates. Senator Biden continuously lied to America during the presidential election debates between President Trump and Senator Biden in 2020. Senator Biden had repeatedly lied to the American people by his continuous denials to President Trump who was pressing elect Biden for him to tell America the truth concerning his son's business dealings in Burisma, Ukraine.

The presidential election moderators had helped Senator Biden to not have to tell the truth, and nothing but the truth about his son's money making firm in Ukraine.

During one of the presidential election debates President Trump urged Senator Biden to tell the American citizens what he was going to do in reference if he should become the next U.S. President, and Senator Biden dogmatically said, "I'm not going to tell them." America, now you know and have been experiencing to your abject horror all of the hidden radical policies and agendas President Biden kept quiet about along with his Progressive Socialist Democrat Administration had in mind, and up their sleeves which American citizens have been forced to deal with on a daily basis. President Biden has become a national disgrace and dishonor as "Divider-in-Chief" of America.

Josh Rosenstern said today on, Insight a SonLife Broadcast Ministry, "I sit here today with more contempt for the Federal Reserve Bank, not the individual members so much, but the entire system because it is very clearly it is very clearly a destructive power. And is has done more to, I think the Federal Reserve Bank which was created by Congress has more to destroy the wealth and prosperity of our country than I think Congress has actually done. I think the Fed is at this point is very much to blame. Now Congress could, could hold them more accountable, but they don't. I think part of that reason of that dad is one or two things. Most of the Congressional members are, they're either just ignorant, uh or they actually think it works, but we have very few people".

John Rosenstern speaks up, "I'll tell you why the Congressional world does not disrupt the Federal Reserve because they like to get their little money deals in on bills, and when that's all approved and when Congress says, OK, we need money. They don't have any money so either they have to raise taxes, they got to deal with fiscal policy or they got to deal with monetary policy, and it's a lot easier to go to the Federal Reserve Bank window and say, John knocks three times in sound effects: "I'm here, I need more money". Josh, "Right". John, "And they create more debt cause that's how they get money is they create it out of debt which has increased the deficit".

"By the way this president for all income tax payers has in the last two years has increased their debt $33,000.00. Forty-seven percent of the people of this country pay federal income taxes. That means those that pay federal income taxes have now gone into more debt that the government has taken from us of $33, 000.00 per income tax payer. That brings them up to if I'm not mistaken around, what was the number it was outrages number around several hundred thousands. Josh, "It was close to a quarter million dollars depending on you say it".

John, "The debt that we now have this is creating more inflation which is what the feds are trying quote and quote". Josh, "Spending". John, "Right". Josh, "Spending creates inflation". John, "Right". Josh, "Yeah, exactly, exactly. The reason that I sit here". John takes charge and says, "And I blame, I want the people to hear me because we have some that don't understand us. Joe Biden is at fault. The majority Congress and Senate has allowed this to happen".

Josh, "Oh, they've been yeah, absolutely they've been". John, "They are at fault, and we cannot blame Trump. We cannot blame anybody else right now, they are doing everything wrong that can be done wrong to make this problem and they're going to make it worse. The whole student debt thing would make it worse, the health care issues things they want a resolution to that, the money". Josh, "Well all of the packages that were passed, the infrastructure bill and the inflation reduction act, all of these things have done nothing to help this economy".

Moving ahead Josh adds, "And now to clarify what I mean by contempt, I listened yesterday to the chairman and I listened what he said, it's very evident that here's what the Federal Reserve Bank wants to do to America. They want to slow our economy down by raising interest rates that means everyone who has credit card debt or any type of variable loan debt any type of variable interest rate your interest rate is going to keep going up". John, "Right". Josh, "So the amount of debt that you have you're going to be paying more interest on it.

It's already happened this year and you know that because you're seeing it. It's not ending any time soon apparently. So that's one thing we have to look at. People that have existing debt trying to afford it now is going to be more and more of their pay check".

Fast forwarding Josh adds, "To addition to that, folks who would like to get a home, folks who would like to get a car or do any type of financing at all, now it's going to be far more expensive, but that part because interest rates are going up, but that part really didn't even get me because I understand that part. What hit me very hard yesterday, was they made it in my opinion if you talk about feds speak, you have to interpret what they say sometimes whatever, but that's what we're supposed to be doing so here's how I interpreted it. They want unemployment to go up. They want to see Americans lose their jobs and get laid off". John, "Yeah". Josh, "And we're starting to see that".

Josh adds, "The fact is Americans are working, therefore Americans are spending, and they're blaming Americans spending for inflation when it's the spending of our government that caused the inflation. So now they're going to basically strangle and choke Americans who are working. They're going to have more people laid off which means more people are going to have to go on unemployment and government assistance which means more government spending. I have much great contempt for the Federal Reserve. They are stealing the wealth of Americans".

"They're going to cause, they will cause more people to get laid off and be out of work, mark my word that will be aired". John, "That's their intention". Josh, "And now they're not being shy or bashful or beating around the bush. They're being very emboldened by it. So ladies and gentlemen I know that when you hear the Federal Reserve Bank and interest rates it makes you want to just, you know your eyes glaze over because that's financing and economics I don't think about that. Well you need to, you need to because now it's going to start hurting you".

John, "Yeah". Josh, "And your family on every level if it hasn't already, and so far their nice little moves with interest rates, and all their balance sheet unwinding that they've done. We haven't seen it play out yet, they're still doing it".

John and Josh share additional information and then John says, "I don't want them to be in panic". Josh says, "We do need the people to understand is when you read the headline news and you see, Federal Reserve Bank raises rates three quarters of a percent. Oh, what does that mean? It means a lot, and the number one thing is what all you are seeing is exactly true. The number one thing that hit me yesterday was they want people to be out of work".

John, "… so they can create economic crisis, they can also destroy the U.S. economy". John asks Josh what can be done about it and recommending do what? Josh responds by saying, "You need to get informed on this number one and talk to your Congressman and Senator, and make sure they understand the significance of this and maybe they need to get learned on it too". John asks Josh about next Tuesday which is November 8th, 2020 and Josh answers, "Vote".

We recommend watching the entire Insight Program with John and Josh on SonLife Broadcast aired 11/3/22.

America, the January 6th Committee is an outright fraud, sham, and 100% bogus that needs to be exposed for their devious and sinister designs to destroy President Trumps hopes of ever serving out a second presidential term of the United States. The Speaker of the House of Representatives, Nancy Pelosi is also a corrupt politician who has done her best to cloud the minds of Americans, and she needs to be exposed and denounced as a devious shyster who revealed her true character when she ripped up a copy of President Trump's State of the Union Address February 4th, 2020.

Speaker Pelosi should have been arrested, and put in jail for committing such a despicable act of treason to the citizens of America and The Constitution. By the expression on her face, Speaker Pelosi thought she was so defiantly clever behind President Trump.

In 2020 when President Trump had requested of Speaker of the House, Nancy Pelosi 20,000 Army National Guard troops to be posted at the Capital Building on January 6th because President Trump suspected there could be trouble that would ensue in Washington D.C. concerning the presidential election results.

Speaker Pelosi rejected President Trump's needful appeal for the 20,000 U.S. Army National Guardsmen, and as a negative consequence chaos erupted at the U.S. Capital Building, and five people were killed before or after the dreadful event including, Ashli Babbit a twelve year
U.S. Air Force Veteran Marine. Ashli was a true patriot and supporter for President Trump.

The total denial of President Trump's U.S. Army National Guard Soldiers request to Speaker Nancy Pelosi resulted also in President Trump being falsely accused for causing an insurrection of the U.S. Capital Building on January 6th, 2021.

The American citizens need answers for the reason(s) why the Speaker of the House of Representatives refused to grant President Trump's appeal for 20,000 Army National Guard troops to protect the
U.S. Capital Building for the upcoming January 6th, 2021 presidential election outcome. President Trump recognized there should be protection secured for the demonstrators on January 6th, 2021 that were executing their rights to protest peacefully.

We know Speaker Pelosi was an anti-Trump activist for the Progressive Socialist Democrat Party. President Trump supporters were hoping for a positive outcome in favor of President

Trump. Speaker Pelosi was delusional, biased, and twisted in her thinking, and they have allowed Speaker Pelosi to remain in power as Speaker of the House.

We recommend watching the YouTube Video titled: Pelosi: must answer questions about Jan 6th intelligence: Rep, and hear Nancy refusing to allow Rep Jim Banks (R-IN) for Jan 6th Committee. Jim and another Republican Senator were blocked from joining the January 6th Committee.

Rep Banks recognizes Speaker Pelosi knows the line of questioning would lead back to Nancy Pelosi. Arizona Representative, Paul Gosar says, "Yeah", it is disturbing that Capital Police Officer that did the shooting actually appeared to be hiding, lying, and waiting in the gate. Not warning before killing her". Republican Gosar was referring to Ashli Babbit.

We know the Progressive Socialist Democrats have continued to stick, cram, and force feed the American people that President Trump is the culprit that caused all of the tragic mayhem on January 6th, and they like to keep the citizens of America distracted, and to focus into watching Cable TV News coverage about the U.S. Capital Building with the Pro President Trump's peaceful protesters on YouTube Videos.

The Progressive Socialist Democrats also have used Fake News pundits to falsely report the catastrophic historic events taking place that should have never have happened had Senator Biden told the truth during the 2020 presidential debates concerning his son's business dealings with Burisma, Ukraine.

The Progressive Socialist Democrats were pathetically all too anxious, and eager to take control of The White House and total authority and power over all of the America people. For this very reason mentioned Senator Biden although not really fit to serve with dignity, truthfulness, character, and as an honest leader became the president of choice regarding the United States and Commander in Chief led by the Progressive Socialist Democrat Party with corrupt Neo-Marxist Advisors.

I happen to have a gray poster of President Donald Trump that shows him sitting down with his forearm resting on his thigh, and his right finger pointing directly at the camera and it reads, "They are not coming for me. They are coming for you".

I have watched on Cable TV that there are Republican Representatives who are saying the Republican Party should move on, and put a stop to President Trump's re-election bid in 2024. I can fully understand President Trump's relentless frustrations and pursuit to regain the presidency in 2024.

I also recognize that there are a number of Republican Representatives which would very much like for the Republican Party to move away from supporting President Trump's re-election in 2024 concerning his mighty comeback to having his second presidential second term unjustly stolen from him by President Biden's outright lies, Neo-Marxist Media, Big Tech Companies, and a whole lot of deceived, duped, and programmed American citizens.

America, President Trump is a human being with fully charged emotions, and he recognizes there are those in the GOP Republican Party that have been programmed by other spineless Republican Party members that aren't willing to stand up, and fight for our great 45th President of the United States of America. Bud and I recognize all America needs to say is, "Let's give President Trump back his stolen second term presidency because he rightfully deserves to be reinstated to his lawful, and well deserved presidential position which the radical Progressive Socialist Democrat Party deviously and sinisterly stole from him.

Jonah Jon Jefferys

We call for a Giant American Red Wave all across America and say, Let's all give President Trump another chance, and go all-out with crowd swelling enthusiasm coupled with a grand reception in The White House followed with a huge rip-roaring standing ovation applause all across America along with everyone saluting President Trump.

A really good reason why President Trump should be reinstated as the U.S. President of America, and be able to honorably serve out his second presidential term simply because millions of Americans know that President Trump truly loves and cares for the whole human race in our nation, and he is willing to stand up and fight for all of us. We know we can fully trust President Trump and his Administration to lead America.

Florida's Governor, Ron DeSantis from what we can tell is an excellent Governor for all of the people in the State of Florida, but he hasn't been tested and tried as the Commander in Chief as President Trump has. For all of the citizens of America and the U.S. residents that has been blessed to live our lives under President Trump's Presidency we know full well he has been tested and tried as a great and excellent president, and found to be a strong leader and one that will stand up and fight for all, plus protect all of us from our enemies.

As far as all of the other U.S. presidential candidates we do not know if they would literally cave under the pressures to the radical ideologies, and strategies to all forms of demented Marxist, Socialist, and Communism forms of government.

President Trump would not allow the United States to be taken over by the above-mentioned governments!! President Trump respects and honors the Lord by the past principles and practices of his presidency, but President Biden and his administration have shown they do not truly love, honor, and revere the Lord God in all of their endeavors. We do not trust President Biden nor his Cabinet!!

President Biden with all of his executive orders, and rules and regulations that is hurting so many citizens of America today it reveals for most of the American people his administration doesn't care about the American citizenry. A lot of the citizens of America have faith, trust, and confidence in President Trump! You can now understand the reasons why a great number of Americans know President Trump should most assuredly be allowed to serve in the Oval Office again!!

We know the Progressive Socialist Democrats have a deep hatred for President Trump, and they have clearly shown their true colors by doing their level best to destroy this great man, and his chances of ever serving in the White House once more!!

President Trump is determined to stand up to the bullies, and he is totally against President Biden's Administration along with their globalist utopian vision for the world, its goals, and ideals to unite the earth's human family and remain in power. President Trump and his administration serves as a strong deterrent to the globalist's plans for uniting the world's population. We must eradicate their radical vision devoid of God's wisdom and plans, and vote for President Trump in 2024!!

Keep in mind there were other protesters that covertly mixed into the large gathering at The U.S. Capital Building with more sinister motivations to cause the mayhem, and with all of the chaos including all of the Cable News TV coverage that followed it clouded the minds of the American citizens into believing President Trump had called for the violent takeover by the protesters in order to remain in power.

We know the Progressive Socialist Democrats are actually the ones hiding behind the disastrous results at The U.S. Capital Building which is the major reason why there needs to be a criminal investigation into why things went horribly wrong at The U.S. Capital Building in the first place.

When the Republican Party regains the U.S. Senate and House they will hold the people accountable, and fully responsible for the fraudulent cover-up of the stolen presidential election ballots by having investigation trials.

I received a letter from Rear Admiral Luther F. Schriefer United States Navy-Retired and I read: "President Joe Biden is clearly picking up where Obama left off years ago and is stepping up the attacks on our veteran's faith…even their freedom of speech. I fear that if you and I don't act the Biden/Harris administration will be successful in their attempt to turn the military into yet another "woke" institution… a military where conservatives and religious individuals are punished is they share a bible, speak up or defend their values! I'm especially concerned that our military Christian brothers and sisters will be targeted and harassed for their faith yet again.

Why do I say this? First Joe Biden was there at Obama's side when attacks against our soldiers' religious liberties were happening. During the Obama years our soldiers were ordered: Not to talk openly about their faith! Not to Pray in Jesus' name while in uniform! Not to Share or distribute Bibles with fellow soldiers! Chaplains could no longer pray in Jesus' name and they could be punished if they approached a non-Christian soldier in crisis and share their faith with him or her. Bibles were only to be handed out if a soldier requested one. But I'm also seeing what's happening right now. In just over a year and a half we've seen several outrageous slaps in the face to our military service members by the Biden administration!

I probably don't have to remind you that in just the first few days of the Biden administration, National Guard members were forced on floors of parking garages… while the Biden administration spent 86 million on hotel rooms for illegal immigrants who crossed our border! Shameful! If that wasn't bad enough, the Pentagon – in an attempt to stop so-called "extremism in the ranks" – recently released a training manual that targets the free speech of religious service members and conservatives.

As reported by JP Media: "all personnel are being subjected to a Power-Point presentation packed with progressive ideology and misstatements of the Constitution, Designated officers are conducting the training on the bases. Stations, and ships at sea. It goes on… "The slides contain misstatements of the law characterizations of fellow citizens who believe in constitutional principles." Rear Admiral Schriefer had more for me to read consisting of six pages. There are a lot more important material and information to share with the readers, but we wanted all of the readers to know and to pass on to their family and friends that President Biden and President Obama are not friends to America nor to the U.S. Military Forces. What America can and should do about it read on?

America, it's time to vote President Biden and Kamala Harris, and all of the Progressive Socialist Democrats out of the political power scene. We are not seeing or hearing President Biden call America to a day of fasting and prayer as President Abraham Lincoln and President Ronald Reagan had when the nation needed healing, and guidance from The Lord God Almighty and from Providence as President George Washington our first U.S. President had done.

I recognize President Biden and his administration is very good at creating crisis after crisis for America, and then turning around and blaming President Trump or Vladimir Putin about the messes they are good about creating. It's time to vote the bums out, and let's help President Biden to swiftly retire where he can no longer trouble nor hurt America and its U.S. citizens. The same goes for Speaker Nancy Pelosi and Vice-President Kamala Harris!!

I was listening to Bill Hemmer on The Five with Fox News today, and Bill said the president speaking on the tarmac said, "We're going to win this time. I feel really good about our chances". President Biden is delusional in his thinking, and he can't perceive nor see the red wave election coming soon on November 8th, 2020. Bill went on to share that President Biden told America that President Trump didn't have the vaccine ready {inferring President Trump was incompetent and lacking all readiness to combat Covid-19}, but before President Biden took over the presidency in 2021 the vaccine was already rolling.

President Biden had lied to the citizens of America regarding President Trump, and the Covid-19 vaccines regarding the disease and control matter plus the insights and solutions to this U.S. and Worldwide international pandemic.

Another deceptive mind altering tactic, and ongoing practice of President Biden to deceive the American people as mentioned above is by telling the citizens of America radical left-wing ideology talking points. This current President has lock brain mentality when it comes to lying to the citizens of America which he as the pilot of The U.S. American Ship is fully in command, delusional, and weak, and yet he fully thinks he knows the right direction for all of America. Thankfully most Americans believe we are heading in the wrong direction as a country, and we must reverse course and allow The Republicans to Pilot The U.S. American Ship from this day forward.

President Biden had lied to the citizens of America regarding the Coronavirus vaccine too, and the disease control matter. May there be a mighty red wave tsunami which causes him to be shaken to the core of his being, seriously face reality, give up the presidency, and retire. There will be great rejoicing in America when that happens. For The Lord God has delivered America. Hallelujah!!

President Biden likes to identify himself as a Roman Catholic and its stance against abortion, and yet he goes right along with the pro-choice abortion rights for women in America so the Progressive Socialist Democrats can continue to receive the women's votes that strongly oppose the will and plan of God and the family institution. America, you deserve better in a President than what President Biden represents and depicts as the leader of a failed Democratic presidency. President Biden needs God, and the Republican GOP Party to help guide him to take the nation in a new and glorious direction for all of America. President Biden's Presidency would be greatly admired then!

We know that so many of the problems America is facing today is due to the fact that a lot of Americans were not raised in Christian homes where the parents taught the children the fear and admonition of the Lord. As a negative spiritual consequence a good share of American citizens do not believe on the Lord today, and they do not have an interest in getting to know God and His ways. They have been programmed to accept the free, and good things they enjoy in life without recognizing the Lord God is the very One who has blessed this nation's people with all of the good things and possessions they have gained in life. They take God's blessings as the giver of life for granted.

Our founding fathers made the choice to believe God's Word, and His promises to establish a new nation where they could obtain independence and freedom to worship the Lord God freely without being restrained by the British Empire controlled by The King of England's edict and rules. This turned out to be a very good foundational move on the part of our founding fathers, and for this new nation they called America. Millions of Americans know that as a nation we have gotten away from our founding principles and practices, and we have fallen away from the moral values which are essential to building good character and growing strong relationships. It is vital for the adults to leave a legacy for the children to follow.

We know we can't do this by ourselves. We must have God's help on this significant matter. As the Gospel singer Carman says, "We need God in America again" which is on YouTube Videos.

The Lord Jesus warns us that in the last days it will be as the days of Noah, and Jesus went on to describe what the existence on planet earth in the end times will be like. ""They ate, they drank, they married wives, they were given in marriage, until the day that Noah entered the ark, and the flood came and destroyed them all". (Luke 17:27) For the readers who are not familiar with what Noah's days were like Moses says, "And God saw that the wickedness of man was great in the earth, and that every imagination of the thoughts of his heart was only evil continually". "The earth also was corrupt, before God, and the earth was filled with violence. And God looked upon the earth, and, behold, it was corrupt; for all flesh had corrupted his way upon the earth". (Genesis 6:5; 11-12)

America, when you compare Noah's days with the behaviors, and events going on in America today you can see the need for serious positive changes for improvements concerning all U.S. citizens and U.S. residents.

God is a God of love, but He is also a God of judgment for them that disregard and disobey, and violate His commandments. America, let's return to the Lord in repentance, and faith for numerous mighty revivals to break forth throughout this nation, and begin to experience His bountiful blessings on this country once again. Unfortunately many American's do not choose to believe on the Lord, and as a most grievous consequence we are witnessing the breakdown in society, and a decline in cultural norms within America. The great national tragedies and ugly events have been aired for the citizens of America to watch on local and national Cable TV News Broadcasts.

America, as a great nation we must recognize that we are better than what we are witnessing daily on Cable TV, and we need to call on all Governors and Mayors to designate the best security officials in every
U.S. State of the Union with maximum election security measures in place to enforce totally protecting and securing our nation's free and fair election system as a hallmark of our U.S. Democracy.

The Lord and The Holy Bible has all of the answers, and the solutions to America's problems if we would only open our hearts to change by imploring and allowing Him to help us as individuals and as a nation. All citizens of America need to pray and ask the Lord to change our hearts and lives to be what He desires to make of us that pleases the Lord. May all Americans and worldwide take a step of faith, and make the right decision to look to Jesus Christ to make that glorious wonderful change in our lives through the transforming power and operation of the blessed Holy Spirit. Peradventure citizens of America see the importance of making the right decision as individuals, and for all of the family to give Jesus Christ who is our Ark of Safety and Protection total charge of your lives.

America, you can't expect God's hedge of protection when you throw God out from our Government Institutions, U.S News Media, Hospitals and Hospices, Schools, Nursing Homes and Convalescent Centers, Fire Departments and the EMTs, Medical Doctors, Coast Guard Recue Teams, Mountain Rescue Association, National Education System, and The U.S. Military. God cannot bless sin although America claims to be blessed by God. (2 Chronicles 7:14). It is naïve for people to claim God is blessing America when America is not obeying God and does not bless God themselves. American's must stop allowing themselves to be lied to, and constantly allowing themselves to be deceived. America, you must elect Godly Government leaders that are honest, Godly, and speak the truth about the facts of our domestic and international relationships with other nations.

I was speaking with Lorena's nephew, Santiago Gonzales at the breakfast table one morning and I asked him, "Who is Jesus Christ to you?" Santiago told me that what he believes is personal, so that was his way of not telling me what he thinks or believes who Jesus Christ truly is. It was kind of ironic because shortly after Santiago thought he had successfully moved beyond answering my question about the Lord Jesus, I brought up the Christian doctrinal teaching that Jesus Christ was virgin born. When I happened to mention that historic fact to Santiago about Jesus he immediately began to laugh over what I said to him. I immediately let Santiago know that he just told me what he believes about Jesus, and yet I didn't say it to him at the time that he was only fooling himself.

What Santiago believed who Jesus Christ truly is for from out of his heart he happened to reveal his belief system by the confession with his mouth whether he knew it or not.

I spoke with Bud in a recent personal phone call concerning my conversation with Santiago who is Lorena's nephew, and Medical Doctor from Michigan at the breakfast table when he responded to my question who is Jesus Christ to you, and he answered my inquiry that what he believed was personal. When Bud heard Santiago's response that his beliefs were personal he initially started to laugh over it. I followed up by asking him if he had been at the breakfast table at the time what he would have said to Santiago. Bud answered me, "Where in the Bible does it say it's personal. It says when He is in your heart you can't keep Him secret. I said, "There you go, very good Bud".

Bud, "He needs to know that. To me like my sons they have been given a real snow job from Charlotte and from Lucinda because the main crux of it hinges on Hebrews Chapter 6. Right there it's a crux because Lucas let me know that when he called me one time. It took me back and I hadn't prepared you know, but the thing is he came on real heavy about we have to go past the cross".

"The snow job that Charlotte and him both, you know?" I responded, "Yes! Yes!". "It has made things difficult for me to break through that to talk to my son, Jonah jon Jeffreys". I responded, "Yes!" you had a barrier. Charlotte and Lucas they built a barrier to block you out, and they thought they had scriptural proof of that with Hebrews Chapter 6 and you set them straight. Well I didn't have a chance to set them straight. I responded to Bud that I thought he had responded to Lucas, and let him know, uh". Bud said, "Oh, at that time I hadn't done any research on it. I said, "Oh, Oh I see. Oh, now that Lucas is gone, and". Bud said, "It took me back. I said, "Yes!" "I was going with the basic scriptures on the cross".

I said, "And it's unfortunate that Lucas has passed away before you could give him the answer, and set him straight". Bud said, "The thing is only God can break through that snow job that they piled on Jonah jon Jeffreys and Leo". I said, "There is not only wrong spiritual teaching that many pastors, a parents, the educational system, you name it politics, they've all done a snow job and with propaganda, wrong teaching, wrong doctrine. Bud said, "Yes!" I added, "And um, it's really sad". Bud, "Yes!" I spoke up, "And with the deprogramming of so many people in America". Bud, "Unless someone comes along and does research and speaks up". I said, "Thank goodness you did". Bud, "Basically sidelined".

I said, "Yes, I wish you had been at the table when Santiago was here with his daughter, both were at the table. I was at the head of the table, on the south side of our table. Santiago to my left and his daughter, Camila over to my right. I brought up to Santiago that Jesus was born again which is a historic fact. And what happened". Bud, "He was not born again". I said, "No, I didn't mean born again, I meant He was virgin born I'm sorry, uh. Bud, "Yes". I said, "If I misstated that, I'm sorry. He was virgin born, and as soon as I said that Santiago immediately responded by laughing. And then I responded, I let him know that, well that's what you believe who Jesus is. You just got through saying who Jesus is to you, what you think of Jesus".

Bud responded, "His philosophies like that uh, corrupt the minds of people around him, and probably the little children in Colombia too". I responded, "Yes, and um, Roman Catholicism has steeped and duped um, the Colombia people and Brazilian and you name it. South Americans, Central Americans, Mexico. Bud, "Yes!" "Yes!" "Yes!", but not only there, but America too. Roman Catholicism". I said, "Yes!" Bud, "You know I'll tell you something, infant baptism regeneration, infant baptism regeneration thinking they were Christian has in the Roman Catholic teachings been added to making it water baptizing". I said, "Yes!" "Yeah for infants, for infant baptizing and for the dead. Baptism for the dead and for infants. Infant baptism.

Now if you had been at the table with me and Santiago and Camila, and you heard Santiago laugh at Jesus being virgin born what would you say to him? Would you say you're fooling yourself, you're deceived or what would you say?" Bud answered, "I think I'd say something like, I'd point at the ceiling and I'd say, God is here right now, every word that you say you will pay for it. You're laughter at the virgin birth that is blasphemy! That is blasphemy!" I said, "That's exactly right. Wow, that is powerful Bud! I'm going to have you hang around with me all of the time because you bring up wow, powerful truths Bud! And um, thank you Jesus". Bud adds, "You know something, a lot of people that feel like that one that told you well, I don't want to go to heaven unless my dog goes there".

I said, "Yeah Chad! Lorena's brother-in-law. Amanda's husband." Bud said, "Yeah! Yeah! Regardless of his name as I pointed out that um, that he is saying, he's telling God how God should, who God should let in and what God should let into heaven".

I said, "Well, that's also the way he perceives and sees God, that God uh, that basically he's teaching pantheism because if he believes that Duke his former dog that passed away was God". Bud, "Yes! Yes!" I continued, "Then he's replacing the Creator with the creation". Bud, "Yeah, it's just like, it's just like the couple out on the patio from me, they're into pantheism.

And there's also women here that live next door that live next to them that interfere. When I've tried to talk with them before, this one old lady goes to them and says something, and they don't talk to me for quite a while". I said, "Wow! Well it's obvious they've been". Bud continued, "Something I've found out the Cherokee Indians we're into forms of pantheism because way back there when they were on the trail of tears, and they came to the Mississippi River, it was at flood tide. And they had two or three dogs a piece some of them. And the river boat captains told them because they were anchored in the river we don't allow dogs aboard. These are river boats, and there is just enough room for the people".

I said, "Right because they were packed". Bud, "So the Cherokee Indians got ready to cross hundreds and hundreds of them, and so they set there on the deck, and the dogs paced back and forth on the other river bank, paced back and forth as dogs will do. And uh, they used dogs to track and to hunt, and for personal pets. I said, "Yes!" Bud, "They believed that it was important for contact with ancestors to have those dogs. I said, "Wow!" Bud, "And so when those dogs finally because they kept crying and everything, and those dogs kept whining and everything. Finally the dogs jumped into the river and it tried to swim to the river boats, but the Mississippi River was so swift they drowned until there was only one dog left. And the Cherokee Indians were shouting out encouragement in their Cherokee language at the only dog left, and the dog finally went under. I said, "Oh no". Bud, "They broke down in tears".

I said, "I would think so that it was a trail of tears. In jest I added, "That was the water, the river of tears". Bud, "It was the part, a part of the start of the trail of tears". I affirmed Bud's narrative, "That was the beginning of the start of the river of tears, "Wow!". Bud, "Well, it was a little bit, they already had traveled maybe a hundred miles maybe, but uh. I added, "It was early in the start". Bud, "The Mississippi was at flood tide, you see upstream where the mountain snow had melted had made it into the river. The creeks and stuff had flowed into the Mississippi was at flood tide, and the river was flowing swiftly. I said, "Man!" Bud, "So the Cherokees were crying and bawling, and everything because they lost their dogs".

I said, "Boy! Well, I told you about". Bud added, "They were into that superstition". I said, "Yep! Yeah! They believed in the spirit of the wolf, the spirit of the bear, spirit of the dogs, spirit of the cats, whatever animal happened to be there" Bud, "Yes! Basically. It's no wonder that the continent was taken over, even though it was taken over by greedy people. I said, "Yes!" Bud, "In Texas you see at all cost, at all cost was his philosophy. At all cost, we will unite this country at all cost, in other words this in the manifest destiny". I said, "Brother". Bud, "And so anybody that got in the way was mowed down. Anybody against it was to be moved out of the way". I said, "That's really sad".

Bud, "And there were trappers that discovered easy passes for the wagon trains with less stress where they could get to the West Coast. And Jedidiah Smith was a man, a trapper, a mountain man that discovered a pass, and in other words it led into where the valley was which Salt Lake City later was, the great Salt Lake, everything. I said, "Man!" Bud added, "And so civilization spread, but like I heard this lady I was watching this video she was talking about it, she said, "Anybody that got in her way is eliminated". I said, "Wow"! Bud added, "It's called the South Pass". And you see back then they didn't have highways, cars, and all that, and so the Rockies were formitable cause they rose up like a giant wall in front of the wagon trains". I said, "Man!"

I asked Bud if Jedidiah Smith was something similar to Jeremiah Johnson?" Bud, "No! No! No! No way! Jeremiah Johnson that stupid movie, that was about a guy that was an animal lover, and you know that kind of a thing.

Jedidiah Smith was not that way, he was a mountain man. I said, "Wow!" Bud, "He hunted, he trapped, and he knew how to make his way through the woods". I said, "Man! He had to be an interesting" Bud spoke up, "Yes!" I said, "You would have enjoyed having a conversation with that man". Bud, "Yes! Yes!" He guided wagon trains through that pass. They called it the South Pass, and it got people down into a huge valley where the Great Salt Lake was.

The Great Salt Lake". I said, "Wow! Hey, so I really appreciate you sharing that you would have straightened Oh Santiago out in a hurry". Bud, "Oh Yeah", I would have jumped on that with both boots man because he's insulting my best friend. He's insulting my best friend. Jesus Christ sticks closer to me than a brother. I said, "Very good Bud! I like that!" Bud, "I'd say how dare you! That's my attitude. How dare you". I said, "That is an insult of treason to the Eternal Lord God". Bud, "It's blasphemy! It's blasphemy!" I said, "Yes!" In other words you better watch your step bud because He's hearing every word that you're saying right now".

I said, "Yes!" Bud, "He's in this room. I'd point right at the ceiling and say, He's in this room right now, He hears every word you're saying". I said, "Very good". Bud, "You're going to give an account of it. WATCH OUT BUDDY. WATCH OUT! WE TREAT GOD WITH RESPECT!" I said, "YES! HE IS THE BIG BOSS OF THE UNIVERSE!" Bud, "Yes!" "If he said, why doesn't He do something to me right now? I'd say to him, WATCH OUT. IT'S COMING BUDDY!"

I said, "Yes!" Bud, "Don't think for one minute because God is very very clear". I said, "It shows how darkened and deceived he really is. And especially with him being a Medical Doctor, a pediatrician knowing about the complexity of the human mind, and the human eye" which is in reference to the conflict of debates between what people happen to believe for or against their beliefs in Creationism vs. the theory of Evolution.

Bud, "Yeah!" "Romans (Chapter 12:19), "Vengeance is Mine, I will repay," says the Lord". "That right there". I said, "Yes!" And when we had company in the evening Santiago told the gathering that he wanted me to pray that President Trump would retire inferring that he wouldn't seek out the presidency in 2024, but he wanted me to pray with all ears listening. Bud, "I would look at him and I'd say, "You're talking like a fool". I said, "Yes!" Bud, "You are!" I said, "He was!" Bud, "And I'd say, you're talking like a fool!" I said, "He's fooling himself, he's deceiving himself". Bud, "No, I'd say you don't command me, and want me to pray against the will of God". I said, "Yes!" Bud, "And when you ask me to pray against the will of God dude, you are a fool!"

I said, "Hey, I like that". Bud, "You're going against the will of God". I said, "Yes!" Cause President Trump has made it known he". Bud, "I wouldn't get into all that about Trump. I said, "OK, good". Bud, "For the facts speak for themselves, but I would just lay that on him what I said. That's just what I would lay on him" I said, "Yes! Sounds good". Bud, "I wouldn't get into a long drawn out political conversation". I said, "No!" Bud, "I'd just tell him that right there". I said, "Yes!" And the Word of God doesn't return void unto Him, but it shall accomplish that which He sent it forth to achieve". (Isaiah 55:11)

Bud, "It does not return void". I said, "That's exactly right. Amen!" Bud, "The thing is we have a world full of people that are foolish". I said, "Yes! Very foolish!" Bud, "Very very foolish". I said, "Yes!" Bud, "That why I like to point up with my index finger, I point it up and I say, God is here right now. He hears every word you're saying". I said, "Very good. And just like when you're at the store, and you've let people know that God is watching you folks that are keeping a camera on us". Bud, "Yes!" That's what I tell them. I said, "Yes!" Bud, "The cameras that's monitoring us God is monitoring the person that is monitoring the camera". I laughed and said, "That's very good! Wow!"

Bud, "I do that, but you're probably afraid to do that because your wife is with you". I said, "No, I think it's important to be ready um you know, be apologetic and be ready to give an answer of the hope that is in us". (1 Peter 3:15) Bud, "Apoligia". I may not be able to jump to a Bible verse as quickly as some of them real quickly, but I have them in my heart, but I've read them. I may not be able to race to the verse when a Pastor asks for a certain verse as fast of some of the other people. I said, "But you have it in your heart, you have it on your car, and you have it on your shirt". Bud, "On my shirt and my car, and I speak up". I said, "Yes!"

Bud, "It doesn't make me popular with the women". I said, "So many have been programmed just like you say, and they've been very much deceived by the media, and this

Progressive SocialistParty, go head". Bud spoke up, The School System, The Government, The Neo-Marxist Media, everywhere you turn even where you worked at that personnel shuttle company. I said, "Yes!" Bud, "The restaurants and everything, and it's like you've got women bosses, and they don't want you talking about Jesus Christ. And just like years ago I went to work at Missouri Republic Express, and my boys were real-real small, and it's over in Pardonville here, this area. I would go to work there at four o'clock in the morning, take off from Amazing Grace Heights here.

I lived up the road from here back then. Anyway, I remember the first day I was getting broke in of all things, Cameron Cooper the boss had a woman as an instructor. And that woman, the first time I saw her I knew what she was. I knew it, I could see clean through her. Other people thought she was sweet. I saw a woman, a witch against the cross. I saw what she was. I said, "Wow!" We didn't even drive down the road a little ways, she was driving down the road and she said, "Oh, another thing. Don't talk about God or religion. I said, "Wow! She probably sensed the Spirit of Christ" Bud continued before I could finish ending my last statement with, in your life. Bud said, "She was talking about God. She was using God's name in vain constantly, but she was using her authority, she was abusing, I saw that.

I've learned to pick it up in the Spirit, you can pick it up from them". I said, "Yes!" Bud, "You can see them, you can tell". I said, "That's right!" Bud, "The spirit that's in them!" I said, "She probably sensed the Spirit of God, The Lord in your life, and it came to her thinking as you were riding down the road and she confessed it with her mouth. She declared it!" Bud, "I was sitting on the passenger side out it came, it didn't surprise me because when I first laid eyes on her I saw it! The Jezebel Spirit in other words! I could see it!" I said, "Yes!" It manifested clean through her!" I said, "Wow!" Bud, "The way she walked, the way she talked, the way she acted! I could see it". I said, "Man! Very sad!"

Bud, "Wherever we went, she was driving around, and she was showing me the route. The people oh, they thought she was miss wonderful". I said, "Yeah, she was the cat's meow". Bud, "Yeah!" I said, "And she thought she would use her position as top boss to say anything she wanted to even although she was speaking things" Bud, "She was speaking God's name in vain!" I said, "That is Big Time Trouble for her. She doesn't know how fortunate she was that God didn't strike her dead, but God in His grace and mercy". Bud, "And you know what?" I said, "Yep!" Bud, "And you know what since then I don't doubt that God hasn't dealt heavily with her". I said, "Wow!" Bud, "I don't doubt it!"

I said, "Yes!" Bud, "But I see a lot of women in society that way, in men too, but especially women". I said, "Wow!" Bud, "Women are controlling the men. I see in public places where women will take God's name in vain, and the men standing nearby cause they want to get along with the women. They ho-ho-ho-ho with her". I said, "Wow!" Bud, "Bunch of idiots!" I said, "Yes!" Bud, "Men need to grow a set, and act like men!" I said, "That's exactly right!" Bud, "Instead of letting women control them. When talking about Him, you're talking about your best friend! When you're talking with people in public, you talk about things that excite you!" I said, "Very good!"

Bud, "They are a very important part of your life, you talk about them". I said, "Yes!" Bud, "So if you're not a Christian you're talking about secular things" I said, "That's exactly right. They'll talk about the ball game, talk about sports, they'll talk about a new dress, new hairdo, eye lashes, whatever, manicuring your finger nails". Bud, "Etc., etc." I said, "Yeah".

Bud and I continued our conservation over the phone for a while longer. We both would like to see a positive change in society so it becomes more conscientious about taking the Lord's name in vain by asking the Lord Jesus to help everyone to break this sinful habit in God eyes especially since it has become common place worldwide, and so many people have been programmed to take God's name in vain because they simply have heard it used so often from friends, social media, sitcoms, the movies, etc. The Lord Jesus will answer your prayers for this grievous sin by His cleansing blood shed on the cross of Calvary, and the world will become a better place for it.

It is vital that the citizens of America return to following the Lord God Almighty by respecting, revering, and honoring His Word first through an act of observance, repentance, confession, and obedience before God Himself whereby we confess, and forsake our sins which we have been willfully and unknowingly committing, and breaking His commandments without the fear of the Lord before our eyes.

America we must have God's amazing grace again to help us through our trials and challenges we face as a nation through faith, and begin to experience His convicting power in our hearts and lives with Godly sorrow which is well pleasing before the Lord which will produce genuine fruits of repentance. The Lord has a bountiful harvest in store for all of us provided the size of the seeds we sow by an act of giving to the Lord and into His Kingdom.

American citizens, it's time to put an end of casting your election votes for political candidates based on their physical outward appearances, and falling for getting caught up in a personality binge. I'm concerned that many citizens of America have acquired a romantic fixation with endearing fantasy notions that the political party member will truly fulfill his or her promises that they have declared to the citizens of America. It's time to get a grip and recognize the difference between fantasy and reality in politics. Let's vote the Democrats out and the radical left-wing, and vote the Republican ticket all the way. And never again fall for the lies of the Progressive Socialist Democrat Party leaders.

Fox News had the following messaging yesterday: "MIDTERM MESSAGING OBAMA SAYS DEMOCRACY

MAY NOT SURVIVE UNDER REPUBLICANS". Citizens of

America, now you can understand the reason why President Biden follows his predecessor President Obama, and repeats the same messaging by telling the American people that democracy may not survive should the Republicans regain the U.S. Senate and the House of Representatives.

President Obama and President Biden are both delusional in their thinking, and they both have benefited from lying to the citizens of America. It's time to give them both the right foot of fellowship straight out the door from ever lying to America again!

I was watching Francis and Friends on SonLife Broadcast, and Francis Swaggart asked the panel a good question I'd like to share with the readers. She asked, "The reason why our military is not respected, and so disrespected today by so many different people and treated with disrespect today? John Rosenstern responded to the question Francis had asked by saying, "In part I think its ignorance. Most Americans don't know American History.

They don't understand the founding of our country or they have a misunderstanding of it because our schools have improperly educated young people especially about our past therefore our forefathers are considered nothing, but vicious slave owners. Those that sought for protection of our nation were colonizers that were just trying to expand America, and support a wicked and evil government. That's what's being taught in our public schools, and in our universities and in so many cases.

So because of that we have a misunderstanding of our soldiers. Now and I'm not going to sit here, and say I agree with everything America's done pertaining to wars, Afghanistan, Iraq, no I'm not saying that, but our soldiers that have been asked to fulfill a duty, and an obligation that they've made committing themselves to serving our nation with the probability of sacrificing of something of their life not just their physical life, but the complications that follow service. They've not been well respected, and we should respect our soldiers, we should respect our military personnel.

My father was a Veteran of two wars. World War 2, and the Korean War. And we grew up in a home that valued having a strong military. The U.S. having a strong military is beneficial not only to America, but also to the whole world. It's a deterrent.

If you have military power you have the capability to deter other nations from doing things that they would not do if they didn't feel that they had resistance from an outside source hence The U.S. have been The Police Force of the world. We have not asked for lands, we have protected lands, but we have fought for the freedoms of others, and I can say this from my dad who was an exile Jew that came to The U.S. became a U.S. Citizen, fought in two Wars, and asking him why did you join the military cause he waited to stand for freedom, and free his nation that was put under the tyranny of an Adolf Hitler and likewise. And all the different soldiers that I've known over the years and the military personnel.

They feel the same so lack of proper education number 1. Intentional lack of education. We have a group of young people today miss Francis that grew up in the sixties in our education system that are now professors and educators that grew up with Marxist, Socialist principles, and we're watching now the president I said on Insight and I'm not going to apologize for saying it again here. My dad said something to me many years ago when we were young, and I was always very interested. My dad was a man of many words so when he said something we paid attention. He said, "You can judge the character of a president by the way he treats the military".

And what we are seeing in our military today, and the way that he could say that is because the president has total control over our military so that's one thing. He has control over the help of necessarily Congress or the help of Senators or Representatives in the government now. If America does not retain the power that it has always been recognized for as far as modernity is concerned we're no longer going to be a deterrent the world needs to have tyranny checked. To have these tyrants such as China and in other places of the world, in Russia checked, they will continue to do what they want to do and they will do it without reservation, and yet this president and I blame Joe Biden who is solely responsible for what's going on in the military. He could stop it and he's not".

We encourage all readers to watch everything else John Rosenstern had to say on SonLife Broadcast aired on November 11, 2022. You can also go to: Watch. SonLife T.V..com

Fox New had these text messages,

"Elon Musk recommends voting for a Republican Congress, given the Presidency is Democratic". "Top Democrats say democracy will come to an end". It's obvious to Bud and me that the radical Progressive Socialist Democrats are fearful of losing their power and control over the citizens of America.

Judge, Jeanine Pirro had this to say regarding the Democrats, "The truth is the Democrats did not connect with the American people on the issue of safety, crime,

immigration, education, inflation, the economy, so I think the dissonance and the misalignment is going to be loud, and it's going to be across the country. And I think that after American's deliberate, and after they vote that verdict is going to be and more, it's going to be very painful for the Democrats".

I appreciate hearing from Elon Musk the Chief Executive Officer of Twitter, and Judge Jeanine Pirro who serves as a co-host on The Five with Fox News concerning their insightful perspectives, and evaluations of the midterm elections we are currently in at this time. We truly hope The U.S. American citizens will make the right choices in every State of the U. S. Union to cast their right to vote for the best midterm election candidate who is the most productive, and excels far above the voters expectations in getting things done for all citizens of America in 2022.

Texas Congressional U.S. Representative, Michael McCaul said, "You know as a conference we have an economic crisis, we have an energy crisis, we have a border crisis, and we have an international security crisis. I'll be focused on the international security crisis".

We appeal to the citizens of America concerning the 2022 midterm candidates whoever the citizens of America will choose to vote for, and concerning the presidential candidates in 2024 to make certain not to cast your vote according to a political candidate's race and ethnicity.

We recommend voting for the best qualified candidate whose political party is the closest to God, and to His will and plans for all of America. I asked Bud a sincere question why people continue to vote for Democrats and he responded, "It has to do with programming". Bud went on to say, "I don't put my hope in a politician. I put my hope in Jesus Christ". (Psalm 118:7-8 says), "It is better to trust in the Lord Than to put confidence in man. It is better to trust in the Lord Than to put confidence in Princes". This applies to political leaders too!!

America, it is futile to trust in man with his or her feet planted on the shifting sands of a political party that has chosen to remove God from their Progressive Socialist Democrat Party platform.

I recognize as human we have a tendency to be creatures of habit. A lot of people have a Wake Up in their lives by coming to their senses as the prodigal son had when he was feeding with the pigs in a far country. (Luke 15:11-32) Others learn from reading the Bible for themselves or when listening to a good news gospel sermon, a family member, a friend that truly cares about you as an individual or they have a Wake Up themselves, decide to vote for the best political candidate based on true facts, and not on biased indoctrination propaganda. Tony Perkins is the President of the Family Research Council, and he recognizes America is divided when looking at the 2022 U.S Midterm Elections.

Fox News reported on, Derrick F. Orden a Retired U.S. Navy Seal used, GAS, GROCERIES, AND GRANDKIDS. VAN ORDEN SAYS ELECTION ABOUT INFLATION to win the Wisconsin Midterm Election. An article by Catie Edmonson in the THE NEW YORK TIMES writes, Van Orden, Republican who attended Jan. 6 Rally, Wins Wisconsin House Seat.

He focused his campaign on the economy, but also leaned into the conservative culture wars, claiming on his website that Democrats were "taking the nation rapidly down the path to Socialism" and railing on a pod cast against what he described as the "woke ideology" seeping into the military. Down below it read, HOUSE SEAT TURNS RED REP-ELECT VAN ORDEN'S WISCONSIN WIN GIVES GOP A BOOST

Van Orden is the superior high class kind of U.S. Representative Election Leader that we need in America.

I recognize many citizens of America have allowed themselves to be programmed to vote for a political candidate that promises great things, and yet recognizing you have voted the same way year after year without that particular candidate doing his or her very best to satisfy the special interests you are most concerned about.

We know it is high time citizens of America make a radical switch from a political party and candidate change to see better voting results for all of American citizens, and not just think about yourself. You've been programmed to follow the crowd or you have a generational family traditional voting pattern. We urge all of the readers to dismiss the thought that your single vote won't matter one bit in any election, but rather decide to take action by making your vote count in every election the United States conducts including every second and fourth year, and vote in every U.S. Election Process for everyone's good.

Citizens of America you have made the choice, and taken the time to educate yourselves concerning politics, and political candidates at some time in your life by a parent or other family member, or an inspirational figure which produced a spark of interest to learn about different politicians that give great political speeches to your liking, agree or disagree with, and to follow or not to follow their lead.

I found out the hard way that there are predators in the medical fields, and I was left painfully devastated as a victim of finding the wrong medical doctor regarding my facial feature needs. We very much want to spare all of the readers that perceive, and see for yourselves moving from being a victim of voting for the wrong elected political leaders who care more about themselves remaining in power, their political party and position, and not about the real needs and concerns of most of the citizens of America.

I am concerned that a lot of Americans do not recognize as a nation we are in serious trouble with many threats within and without, and there truly was stolen election ballots from President Trump in 2020. We must face the facts, look at the evidence, and choose to fight back as true U.S. Americans, Patriots, and Conservatives.

In the final analysis, unless the American citizens push back, and deal with the proven facts of cases containing the solid evidence regarding the stolen election ballots, and demand to have the people responsible for stealing the 2020 election ballots for President Trump held accountable, then America can expect more stolen ballots; remain vulnerable, susceptible, and extremely likely to fall for more deceptions including more stolen election ballots in future elections. America can't afford to fall for another presidential candidate that will speak forth lies, falsehoods, and a magnitude of dark deception tactics to get you to continue to believe lies as Adolf Hitler did to his own citizens of Germany and to the Jews.

Adolf Hitler and the Nazi Officers were delusional in their thinking, and it led to over six million Jews being killed during the Holocaust.

The silence of those who disagreed with Adolf Hitler, and refused to speak up by warning others only encouraged more of the evil terror of the Nazi terrorism takeover. When Adolf Hitler was beginning to rise in power the silence of those who recognized who he really was, and they remained silent and refused to speak up which led to the evil violence that began ruling Germany. The Nazi symbol worn by the SS Nazi Military, and on the Nazi flags stood for Socialist Tyranny and Totalitarianism.

One of our U.S. Presidents actually admired Adolf Hitler's model that he created in Germany. The U.S. President I am referring to respected and admired Adolf Hitler's model of the citizens of Germany was before World War 2. Adolf Hitler admired and respected Margaret Sanger the founder of Planned Parenthood. Adolf Hitler read Margaret Sanger's biography, and he considered her a part of his purifying of the German race. You could say that Margaret Sanger's goals and Adolf Hitler's goals ran side by side. Jesus Christ recognized that if the blind leads the blind, both will fall into the ditch. (Matthew 15:14). People need to be warned concerning radical ideologies told to humanity that has led to a multitude of murders and violence against human souls worldwide.

Bud shared with me about a German student girl during World War 2, Sophie Scholl who when she was young had joined the Hitler youth. Later in life Sophie was captured by the Nazi soldiers. She was questioned by the Nazi officer who warned her that if she was found guilty she would be guillotined. Sophie had been passing out printed leaflets with a defiant message, and Bible verses on them warning the people about the evils of Adolf Hitler. Banging his fist on his desk he asked, "Would it be worth it"? Sophie responded, "It would be better to go the heaven than to live under your tyrant". Sophie was then led to the guillotine, and beheaded for treason as a resistance Nazism fighter.

We recommend buying and watching the DVD tilted, Death of a Nation. Beheaded by the Nazis at age 21, Sophie Scholl died fighting for passing out the anti-Nazi leaflets against sadistic Socialistic Tyrannical Nazism. Sophie had taken a bold Christian stand, and she was willing to die for her faith in Jesus Christ because she knew where her spirit would go when she was guillotined. She would be forever in heaven with the Father of Spirits. (Hebrews 12:9) Sophie Scholl had done her very best to Wake Up the German intellectuals and public.

Over nine million died during World War 1, and over twelve million died during World War 2 not counting the six million Jews that were murdered in the Holocaust. There are inevitable disasters awaiting those that believe lies spewed forth from national leaders whose lies are formulated by the father of lies who is Satan. America, you can simply learn from history of what happened to other nations gone with the passing of time, and the annuals of history or you can remain willfully ignorant. Thank God millions of American's have Woke Up to what is going on in America today, but millions more need to Wake Up from your willful deception, ignorance, and being dumbed down by spiritual and national leaders that speak lies.

When you do a search of what happened to those nations of the past that have fallen, they fell from within or they were attacked by other nations as Russia attacked Ukraine. When the body of Christ caves into the lies of the devil, and is corrupted from within, the nation follows suit, and so does the whole world.

We urge for America and Worldwide to pray earnestly and look to Jesus Christ, and His righteousness unto salvation by His saving grace through faith in the finished work of the cross of Calvary. Seek out wise and Godly leaders that have a gift of the Spirit of discernment who America can trust to lead this nation onto the right paths of spiritual maturity in Christ, strong faith in capitalism and economic freedoms to exercise an individual's rights, respect for law and order, respect for The Police and Law Enforcement, for America to have harmonious relationships with our allies, and fully know how to deal with our enemies with Godly wisdom. American citizens, please recognize that human lives are at stake in America and Worldwide.

Bud and I recommend reading an excellent book titled, Pray for Our Nation Scripture

Prayers To Revive Our Country by Keith and Megan Provance and sold by Harrison House Publishers in Tulsa, OK 74153

Each human soul can choose to follow Satan's lies or choose to follow the Lord God's plan of eternal happiness in heaven with Him.

Hebrews Chapter 6: verses 1-6 does not give us the excuse to add to or take away from the cross of Christ, and it does not tell us to go back under the Old Testament Law. (Colossians 2:14) tells us that Jesus nailed the Laws to His cross, and they were totally paid for in full. John (Chapter 19:30). Bud shared, in the original Koine Greek found in New Testament "tetelestai", Paid in Full. Nothing more needs to be paid for because Jesus Christ paid it all, and our debt of sins are gone when we confess and forsake our sins.

"He who convers his sins shall not prosper, But whoever confesses and forsakes them will have mercy." (Proverbs 28: 13) "If we confess our sins, He is faithful and just to forgive us our sins and to cleanse us from all unrighteousness." (1 John 1: 9)

Jimmy Swaggart says, "Sin is a form of insanity". When I mentioned that to Bud over the phone he responded, "It is a form of insanity". When an individual takes a moment to be alone or in a group, truly reflects, takes an account, and takes inventory of their lives whether their heart is right with God or not. The Bible says, "Examine yourselves as to whether you are in the faith. Prove yourselves. Do you not know yourselves, that Jesus Christ is in you?" (2 Corinthians13:5)

It is the most serious and sobering subject to think about when you consider eternity, give thought to the life you're living in the present, ponder your past sins you committed before God and man, and begin to face the big question everyone thinks about sooner or later.

That very sobering big important question happens to be, "What would happen to me if I died today?" Where will I spend eternity? It's easy to understand this thought provoking inquiry when you think about the brevity of life, and to realize there are a lot of people that find themselves thinking over the way they've lived, and whether their good deeds outweigh their bad deeds. God says, "The heart is deceitful above all things, And desperately wicked; Who can know it? I, the Lord, search the heart, I test the mind, Even to give every man according to his ways, And according to the fruit of his doings." (Jeremiah 17:9-10)

I would like to provide the readers with the answer from the Bible, "Not by works of righteousness which we have done, but according to His mercy He saved us, through the washing of regeneration and renewing of the Holy Spirit" (Titus 3:5)

I encourage all of the readers to ask themselves the following question: What if I should die today, and I stood before a righteous, just and holy God the eternal heavenly Father, and He asked you the question of the eternal ages as your Almighty Judge. God the Father asks you, Why should I allow you into heaven? What would your answer be? Do you want to be sure you are ready to go to heaven?

The answer to the sin problem and the sin nature is to receive The Lord Jesus Christ and Him crucified as your personal Savior and Lord, and to believe that His shed blood on the cross of Calvary will cleanse, wash away your sins, and all of your unrighteousness. Jesus Christ loves you more than the whole world, and He wants to have an intimate relationship with you as a friend that sticks closer than a brother. (Proverbs 18:24) Jesus wants to change your heart and life, give you a new birth in Christ, and make you into the person He wants you to be. Amen!!

I would very much like for all of the readers to come to an understanding that to please the Lord, "And be found in Him, not having my own righteousness, which is of the Law, but that which through the Faith of Christ, the Righteousness which is of God by Faith (Phil 3:9)" "If you Believer or unbeliever, will resolve at this moment to make Jesus the Lord of your life, realizing that every debt has been settled through the Cross, you truly can have a new beginning" (Galatians 6:14)

I remember sharing with a girlfriend, Josephine Kensington years ago regarding the spiritual touch that I could feel being manifested on my head. Josephine listened with interest as I took time to describe in detail this special true life ongoing experience which the Lord has so graciously put His anointing that I was literally feeling every day on my head. As a Christian, Josephine was not sensing or experiencing the physical manifested touch of the Lord at that time.

After Josephine and I had attended a number of miracle and healing services with Pastor and guest speaker, Jerry Gaffney I remember when Josephine shared with me that she was feeling the touch on her head as I was. Pastor Jerry had prayed over Josephine and myself, and as a special blessing the Lord Jesus had placed His gracious and loving anointed touch on her head too. Jesus Christ is amazingly wonderful!!

R.W. Schambach was a mighty man of God who had prayed for my father, Benjamin Scone many years ago in the city of Union when my dad had prostate cancer. Dad had even gone for radiation treatments to be cured of the serious deadly disease, and as a positive result my father was healed. I attribute dad's healing to the miracle working power of The Great Physician, Jesus Christ who with one touch or by a spoken word can heal a person who needs a miracle in their life and physical body when they ask in faith believing. They should expect to be healed of whatever physical need they may have. My dad had received his healing in his body from the Lord Jesus when brother R.W. Schambach had prayed a prayer of faith over him. Remember with Jesus Christ nothing is impossible with God, and to them that believe. (Matthew 19:26 & Luke 1:37)

R.W. Schambach says in his book title, EYEWITNESSES to Some of the GREATEST MIRACLES of Our Times, "As we have seen, the greatest miracle that can take place in an individual's life is when God reaches down His strong arm into the pit of sin, picks up a sinner, and washes him in the blood of Jesus Christ".

Bud and I recommend for all readers to watch the YouTube Videos, The Girl Who Believes in Miracles & I Can Only Imagine. They are both great inspirational movies for the whole family.

I was listening to Gabriel Swaggart today on SonLife Broadcast and I liked what he had to say, "And the moment we said yes to Jesus, we won the Eternal Super Bowl. When our Eternal Quarter Back Jesus Christ went to Calvary, and crushed the devil's head so how much more should we who are saved, and bought with the price rejoice because our names are written in the Lamb's Book of Life. And I'm glad about that. I mean it is and exciting time to be saved, and I'm born again. There's really been a change in me, born again just like Jesus said. Born again and all because of Calvary, I'm glad so glad that I've been born again".

Jimmy Swaggart who is Gabriel's grandfather said, "There is nothing in this world {that amounts to anything of eternal value} than the perfect will of God for your life. And God has a will for every single person …And it's a will of blessing. It's a will that can develop your life, develop your heart to where you can be of service and of use for the Kingdom of God. And the Lord said, Tell the people that they are now missionaries to the world".

On January 20th, 1961 President John Fitzgerald Kennedy gave "What many consider to be the most memorable and enduring section of the speech came towards the end when Kennedy called on all Americans to commit themselves to service and sacrifice": "And so, my fellow

Americans: ask not what your country can do for you – ask what you can do for your country." He then continued by addressing his international audience: "My fellow citizens of the world: ask not what America will do for you, but what together we can do for the freedom of man." Jonah jon Jeffreys and Bud have done their best to provide the citizens of America and Worldwide with a masterpiece of literary art with the non-fiction autobiography titled, which according to Bud Finnigan is, It's A Big Wake Up Call to the World

The last time Jonah jon Jeffreys and Lorena Scone were in Bogota, Colombia they were given a Buddhist statue by a family member to keep in their apartment. I didn't think the gift given to us out of good will was a good thing to have sitting erect and cross-legged under our console table with its back to the wall. Lorena told me that it was not an idol, but a decoration. Lorena and her sister-in-law, Alexandra had taken the time to paint the statue with precision colorful detail. I would observe the sculptured image in our apartment not able to speak, inability to hear or see us, and to communicate with us in an intelligent way or manner. In my thinking the Buddhist statue needed to be given back or thrown out because the Lord said in His Word that He is a jealous God, and not to have any graven images before Him. (Exodus 20:4)

Hi Doug,
I would appreciate your help on a very important following ministry subject that needs to be addressed. My wife, Lorena and I were visiting her family in Bogota, Colombia and a nephew of Luz

Marinas had given a Buddhist statue for us to have in our apartment. I had asked Lorena what good was that statue being in our apartment and she answered me with, It is for decoration. It is not an idol. I knew she didn't know what she was talking about according to my Christian background and training I had experienced back in the late 70's and early 80's. I would appreciate your knowledgeable theological & Bible based answer that the good people of Bogota, Colombia although ignorant of a solid scriptural based answer to set the record straight on this very important subject matter and most serious spiritual issue that millions of people worldwide may be confused over and need a good answer to.

So many of my wife's family think that a decorative Buddhist statue will bring good luck and financial prosperity into our lives and home, but the Lord God is a jealous God that needs no rival, and He alone is more than enough to meet our every need and is the answer to our financial needs in our lives, homes, and for all nations as well. The Lord says not to have other gods before him in a form of a graven image made in the likeness of anything in the heavens or any graven image on earth to worship or to serve them which would only take our hearts away from the Lord Himself. Lorena thinks that it is alright to have the Buddhist image in our apartment since it is only a decoration, and we're not worshipping or bowing down to it as a pagan idol. I think, believe, and know she is deceived and needs to know the truth to set the record straight and know that this is not right, and is 100% wrong in the sight of the Lord our God.

Thank you for your help to provide a good answer for my wife, Lorena to satisfy her thinking, and cover our lives with God's answer which the family in Bogota, Colombia needs a solution to what I see has opened their lives up to false image practices and non-Biblical teachings which will bring corruption into their hearts and lives. The family needs to know the truth found in the One True Lord God Almighty to avoid all deception, lies, and every sinful practice and ways of the world. Thank you for your Bible based answers for me to give to Lorena and her family in South America. In need of answers & God Bless

you.
   Best regards,

   Jonah jon Jeffreys

Dear Mr. Jonah jon Jeffreys:

Luck is a pagan concept, which should be shunned by Christians. Nothing brings good or bad luck. Rather, we follow Jesus Christ and commit our ways to him (Matthew 6). Why put a statue of the founder of a false, non-Christian religion in one's home? It sends the wrong message to anyone who would visit and there is no need for it. Moreover, it is an idol, and we must reject idols (Exodus 20:1-3). It is one thing to look at a Buddha statue in a museum, but to put it on one's home gives it domicile and endorsement. It does not belong there.

Best,

Doug Groothuis

Douglas Groothuis, Ph.D.
   Author of Christian Apologetics: A Comprehensive Case for Biblical Faith, 2nd (Inter Varsity Academic, 2022).Walking Through Twilight (Inter Varsity, 2017), Philosophy in Seven Sentences (Inter Varsity, 2016), and Truth Decay: Defending Christianity Against the Challenges of Postmodernism.

Professor of Philosophy

Jonah Jon Jefferys

Denver Seminary
6399 S Santa Fe Dr
Littleton, CO 80120
303-762-6895

I had sent an email and asked Pastor Mike Muzzerall of SBN Ministries the same question that I had asked Professor Doug Groothuis. Pastor Mike responded to my email in the following:

Greetings in the precious name of Jesus Christ our Lord and Savior. You have brought up a good question. If we follow the letter of the Law, we are to have no graven images at all in our homes. That would include pictures of Christ, clay book ends with the Dove of the Holy Spirit, or even a cross. However, I don't feel that this is the intent of that commandment. God knew that the heart of man is easily swayed to worship idols. For that reason, He simply said, "Thou shalt not!" In my apartment, I have a piece of pottery of children at the feet of Jesus, hugging his legs. I never pray to it, nor do I feel it brings me good luck or financial success. Here's where we have to make a distinction. First of all, the statue of Buddha is definitely an idol of a false god. It is no different than having a statue of Baal, Moloch, or Kimosh. Someone visiting you home would not know that you do not pray to the statue for in any other setting, it would be expected.

There are statues of Buddha all over the world. People travel there to pray and receive a promise of prosperity. The largest one at this time is the great reclining Buddha at Myanmar which is 1,365 feet long. The other issue is having anything that you feel brings "good luck". No matter what it is, it would be improper to have. Our source of blessing is Jesus Christ not pictures, statues, four leaf clovers, rabbit's foot, or shiny pennies. God would bless you as you seek Him. I hope I answered your question. God bless. Pastor Mike

I truly appreciated receiving the email responses from Professor Doug Groothuis and Pastor Mike Muzzerall regarding the Buddhist statues, and whether they bring good luck to all recipients that may have a Buddhist statue in their home, apartment, or any other type of dwelling space.

I brought to Bud's attention regarding Buddhist statues, sculptures, images and what he would answer the family in Bogota, Colombia that would say, Bud, we want to give you one of these Buddhist statues for you to place in your apartment to have financial prosperity. Bud spoke up and said, I won't have an idol in my apartment. It's demonic. These things have demons attached to them. I brought to Bud's attention a counter statement by saying what my wife, Lorena had said to me. It's only decoration. It is not a Buddha idol. Bud responded, Well, if you swallow that lie that's up to you, but I wouldn't swallow that lie. Jonah jon Jeffreys, No, what would you tell them? Bud, I just told you. It's an idol. I don't want to have anything to do with it.

Jonah jon Jeffreys, I shared with Bud. So you would say according to the Ten Commandments that He gave to Moses: Do not have any graven image before me, and that is a graven image made by the hands of the sculptor. Bud, Just like the silversmith in the New Testament that they bossed with the silver idols of the goddess of Diana.

(Acts 19:23-41) tells about a man named, Demetrius a silversmith, who made silver shrines of {the goddess} Artemis (Diana), was bringing no small profit to the craftsmen. I brought to Bud's attention, if the family mentioned-above it's only a decoration to beautify your. Bud quickly spoke up and said, Now the Indians say the same thing when you bring up Calcutta about the Hindu goddess on the outskirts of Calcutta with the all kinds of arms and everything all over the place. The goddess of Shiva, the goddess of death. Jonah jon Jeffreys, OK. Bud, You bring it up to them first the media, and they will quickly cover it over like, Oh, no, no, no, no. Jonah jon Jeffreys, Now wouldn't the Dalai Lama say, It's perfectly fine to have that in your home. You're going to have prosperity. You're going to have new teeth, new dentures. Bud, He's not my authority. Jonah jon Jeffreys, There you go. Very good! Bud reiterates, He's not my authority. My Authority is in heaven. He's in my heart. Jonah jon Jeffreys, Yes! Very good Bud!

I called attention to the Buddhist statue subject to Bud's mind once more by saying, So if the family in Colombia brought up that it is only for decoration. It is not an idol. You are not going to get down and worshipping this thing referring the Buddhist image. Bud responded, I would say, Why do you have it in your home for good luck? Or like in the case I was up there with a church group one time, I think it was Union. We walked into a Chinese Restaurant, and some of the elders in the church walked up and rubbed the belly of the Buddha that was in there for good luck.

Jonah jon Jeffreys, OK, that was some of the church folk? Bud, Yes! Jonah jon Jeffreys, And you said to them? Bud, Well, I didn't have much time to say anything to them because they were talking amongst each other. Jonah jon Jeffreys, OK, and when they saw you didn't do that and follow suit, and practice rubbing. Bud spoke up, I don't know my exact words, but I know that I resisted. Jonah jon Jeffreys, Oh yeah, but when they saw you didn't succumb, and go right along with their practice. Bud, They were uneasy with me. Jonah jon Jeffreys, OK. Bud, in other words I didn't fit in. Jonah jon Jeffreys, so if the family in Colombia brought up that it is decoration. It is not an idol. You are not getting down and worshipping this thing. Bud, I would say, why do you have it in your home for good luck? Jonah jon Jeffreys, Very good!

Bud, or like in the case I was with a church group one time I think it was up there in Union. We walked into a Chinese Restaurant and some of the elders in the church walked up, and rubbed the belly of the Buddha that was in there for good luck. Jonah jon Jeffreys, OK, so all this decoration practice stuff and lingo. It's just a decoration Bud. Don't get all. Bud spoke up, they can say all they want to, but they are calling God a liar. God is not a liar. He calls it an idol. I don't care what they say. The Authority of God's Word is Greater than what they say. Jonah jon Jeffreys, Very good! And any graven image that is made by hand or by a machine into some kind of an image that people are supposed to gain good luck, financial prosperity, protection. Bud, Exactly, Exactly! But you see the Bible calls them dumb idols that can't think, can't talk, a dumb idol! It's a dumb idol with demons attached to them!!

Jonah jon Jeffreys, Very good! So they need to repent and turn from it!! Bud, Yes! Get rid of it! So long as they are Catholics they are not going to because they are into a lot of superstitious stuff!! At this juncture Bud went on to share with me another Bible based philosophical idea to support his theological teachings with a Christian based world view.

Jonah jon Jeffreys and Lorena Scone had heard on the different news stations that a New York City District Attorney, Alvin Bragg DEFENDS DECISION TO CHARGE TRUMP; TRUMP INDICTMENT UNEALED; NEWSMAXTV STATES: TRUMP PLEAD'S NOT GUILTY TO 34 FELONY COUNTS; TRUMP CHARGED WITH FALSIFYING BUSINESS RECORDS; TRUMP ARRESTED, FACES 34 FELONY CHARGES; TRUMP: MY ONLY CRIME IS DEFENDING OUR NATION; TRUMP: OUR JUSTICE SYSTEM HAS BECOME LAWLESS; TRUMP: THERE'S NO CASE ON FOX NEWS; TRUMP: THE WORLD IS LAUGHING AT US; TRUMP: WE ARE NOW A NATION IN DECLINE

I appreciated hearing what Mike Pompeo, former U.S. Secretary of State had to say on FOX

NEWS TV when his former boss, President Trump was indicted on 34 criminal felony charges he said: "…He made them felonies. I think this suggests what we all feared. That this is a political prosecution, and the prosecutor should not have made such a judgment to bring these charges against the former President of The United States. I think it will divide American ways that are not good for our Republic".

I appreciated what Mike Pompeo had to say regarding the political felony charges made by D.A. Attorney Alvin Bragg against President Trump which by the sound of things will continue as a weapon to wear President Trump down so he would literally throw in the proverbial towel, and call it quits of ever running for The U.S. Presidency in 2024 and beyond. The Progressive Socialist Democrat Party doesn't know President Trump and his willingness to continue fighting for America until the battle is won with The Lord's Help to Make America Great Again under President Trump's leadership in The White House.

Mark Levin says that President Trump is a historical figure, and I concur 100% with Mark's powerful description of a great U.S. President that America and nations Worldwide needs to see at the helm of The

U.S. American Ship during these troubling times. The citizens of America do not need an inept, feckless, and weakened president that needs to be told what to think and say to the citizens of America by reading off a teleprompter. God Help Us!!

Bud and I encourage the citizens of America and non-U.S. citizens to continue to prayerfully believe, support, and stand for the re-election of President Trump in 2024. President Trump is willing to stand strong for America, and fight for everything that the U.S. citizens and non-U.S. citizens expects and trusts a fully committed and devoted U.S. President will live up to for all of America's good. We can know for an absolute certainty with The Lord's protection and guidance that America has a brighter future, and better days coupled with God's grace and rejoicing when the righteous are in power.

God says, "Delight yourself also in the Lord, And He shall give you the desires of your heart. Commit your way to the Lord, Trust also in Him, And He shall bring it to pass". "When the righteous are in authority, the people rejoice; But when a wicked man rules, the people groan". (PSALM 37:4-5; 29:2)

I saw on NewsmaxTV the following: Former President Hits Back At Biden Administration Over AFGHAN WITHDRAWAL through Truth Social with a scathing response by saying, These Morons in the White House, who are systematically destroying our Country, headed by the biggest Moron of them all, Hopeless Joe Biden, have a new disinformation fame they are Playing-Blame "Trump" for their grossly incompetent SURRENDER in Afghanistan. I watched this disaster unfold just like everyone else. I saw them take out the military FIRST, GIVE $85 BILLION of military equipment, allow killing of our soldiers, and leave Americans behind. Biden is responsible, no one else!

I listened to Admiral John Kirby the White House spokesman say, President Biden is very proud of the evacuation withdrawal out of Afghanistan. Even Admiral Kohn Kirby from his own perspective couldn't see a disastrous evacuation out of Afghanistan. PBS, Ap News, and CNN News recognize that President Biden after doing their review blames President Trump for the chaotic Afghanistan withdrawal. For anyone doing a fair and balanced intelligent review of the withdrawal from Afghanistan knowing all of the facts calculated into the most serious event and the potential consequences, I concur with President Trump 100% that President Biden is fully to blame for the chaotic Afghanistan evacuation.

President Biden went against his top military generals who recommended that they needed to keep and maintain at least 2,500 U.S. military troops in Afghanistan. President Biden thought 600 troops was sufficient which was once again delusional. And the most dangerous and deadly consequencial event occurred at the Kabul Airport as a result: "He detonated his suicide device, killing 13 American service members and an estimated more than 160 Afghan civilians".

When President Biden was a U.S. Senator of Delaware in The U.S. Congress according to his voting record he was always in the wrong when it came to Congressional Foreign Policy. Senator Biden's Congressional Affairs were messed up, and now as The U.S. President Joe Biden and his Administration are taking America into more Socialistic Totalitarianism where he acts more like a dictator than a president utilizing executive orders as his ruling edicts.

Citizens of America and non-U.S. citizens you have the voting election power to make a big positive difference in the next U.S. Presidential Election Process, and Vote for President Trump and Maintain a Straight-Ticket Voting Observance. After checking their Republican Party Ticket voting track record making absolutely positive they truly side with The Republican Party, Vote Republican Party right down the line!! We need everyone's vote!!

For everyone who loves and is mighty grateful for our U.S. Military Forces that have valiantly served and fought to keep the fierce battles in the Middle East of Iraq and Afghanistan rather than being fully engaged on The United States of America Homeland soil, we give a hearty salute and a thankful commendation for every brave soldier willing to pay the ultimate sacrifice for the freedoms we enjoy and the America way of life based on the principles of life, liberty, and the pursuit of happiness.

I happened to be listening to a Christian radio station in the Pacific Northwest as I was driving home from a dentist appointment, and I heard Michelle Bachmann a former U.S. House of Representatives of Minnesota talking with Dr. James Dobson who is an evangelical Christian author and psychologist. Dr. Dobson is the founder of Focus on the Family. Michelle Bachmann shared with Dr. Dobson that the Biden Administration has kept secretive information that they are planning of bringing The United States Sovereignty under The United Nations Health Organization Sovereignty which is run and operated by the Chinese Communist Party. Citizens of America we must do everything in our power to stop, prevent, and wrest The United States Presidency away from President Biden's Administration and their radical ideology especially during the next U.S. Presidential Election Process in 2024!!

Bud and I encourage all readers to call and request your U.S. State Representative in Congress to do everything in their power to reverse, revoke, and deny that the United States of America place or put our U.S. National Sovereignty under the power, and sovereignty of the United Nations Health Organization which is run and operated by the Communist Party of China. We urge you to call 202-224-3121 and make a positive difference for America's best interests!!

President Biden is so weak in the U.S. poll numbers that he has decided to hire a whole bunch of young people identified as influencers. They will be using TikTok to reach the large audiences of anyone and everyone they can capture their mental attention to help rescue and save President Biden's plummeting poll numbers.

America, I saw on Fox News TV that President Biden plans on running in 2024 although he thinks it is too early to announce it. I recognize it is high time to unseat, dethrone, and oust President Biden from ever doing any more harm and damage to America and its good citizens.

Jonah Jon Jefferys

From my perspective it is high time to fire President Biden and Vice-President Kamala Harris, and slam the presidential door shut on every Progressive Socialist Democrat Party members in agreement with and including all accomplices to the crimes they have been committing against America and its good people.

Bud and I recommend A Daily Devotional by Jimmy Swaggart entitled: the Expositor's Word for Every Day

Bud and I also recommend and encourage all readers to watch in English or Spanish the YouTube Video entitled: Unplanned Full Movie

Bud and I are pleased to know The United States Supreme Court Justices ruled in favor of Life for the unborn babies by reversing the unconstitutional decision in January of 1973 whereby The U.S. Supreme Court Judgment that established the Roe Verses Wade Court Case concerning women were granted the right to terminate the life of their unborn babies living in their wombs. God guided the U.S. Supreme Court Justices this time with bold courage to rule for life, liberty, and the pursuit of happiness regarding all of the babies to be born in the future to all family parents and single committed mothers.

This was a great decision by the U.S. Supreme Court Justices that not everybody in this day and age is happy with regarding this nearly fifty year old ruling that had a faulty U.S. Constitutional foundation and basis. May God Bless All Pro-Life Advocates.

Bud and I recognize The Supreme Court majority ruled in favor of allowing abortion advocates to look to their state representatives to determine their ruling on the abortion issue. Justice Samuel Alito wrote, "The Constitution does not confer a right to abortion; Roe and Casey are overruled; and the authority to regulate abortion is returned to the people and their elected representatives in the majority opinion of the court." We know the Lord God Almighty and His Christian Pro-Life Advocates were not allowed to speak when Roe verses Wade became a Federal Law Ruling in 1973.

May all become aware that when a woman or girl agrees to having an abortion and follows through with terminating the life of the unborn baby in their body it is a direct violation and an attack against God's Word in The Holy Bible that states in (Exodus 20: 13) "Thou shalt not kill" which literally means you shall not murder a living person. Also when a baby is aborted it is an attack on the man's genes or seed and his procreation rights that helped bring about through procreation the life of the unborn living creation within the woman's womb as God planned it.

We pray America and the nations Worldwide that practice the ongoing slaughter of millions of babies will Wake Up and know all such killings and all murderers will be judged by God without question. Let all such killings against innocent and defenseless babies be brought to a sudden halt throughout the world, "but leave it to wrath of God, for it is written, Vengeance is mine; I will repay, says the Lord." (Romans: 12:19, ESV)

Bud and I give all the praise, glory, and honor to God our Father and the Lord Jesus Christ for His eternal love, grace, and mercies He has shown and bestowed upon us through the long journey of writing this incredible book. We want to thank all of our readers that had the great opportunity to be introduced, and have a personal encounter with the greatest and very best friend, Lord, and Savior that we and the whole world could experience forgiveness of sins and be gloriously saved, healed, and delivered through the precious blood of the Lamb of God who John the Baptist boldly declared takes away the sins of the world, and now Christians are destined to be heaven bound. Paul the Apostle says, to be absent from the body is to be present with the Lord.

(John 1:29 & 36; 2 Corinthians 5:8)

Bud and I would be happy beyond measure to know you have come to meet and know you have been wondrously saved and born again through a personal encounter with the Lord Jesus Christ while reading our book. We recommend and encourage all readers to continue to seek and follow the Lord Jesus all the days of your life. Since God can and He is able to do all things we encourage everyone to go with God by faith in His Word, and He will go with you to the very end of your life and age of the world. Never give up believing and He will never give up on you, but stand on His promises whereby you will stand the test of time by living for God while faithfully preaching and sharing this glorious gospel of Jesus Christ and Him crucified. (1 Corinthians 2:2)

Printed in the USA
CPSIA information can be obtained
at www.ICGtesting.com
LVHW080324301024
795103LV00008B/25

Trapped By A Psycho Doctor

In this new non-fiction book titled, Trapped By A Psycho Doctor Author, Jonah Jon Jeffreys and co-author, Leo Finney have spent years on updating the manuscript to make their book into a must read for the entire world. When Jeffreys asked Finney what he would say to someone inquiring what our book is about without hesitation he responded, "It's A Big Wake Up Call to the World". We can see like millions of American citizens that America is heading in the wrong direction., and we have a U.S. Captain who is a law breaker, deceiver, and imposter who is at the helm of The U.S. American Ship, and as a consequence we are placed forever imperil unless we return to our Judeo-Christian Heritage, Foundation, and Principles. Let's Make America Great Again with President Trump!!

For everyone seeking, searching, needing, and desperate for answers concerning what the Progressive Socialist Democrat National Party has been doing to bring about the changes they are forcing on the citizens of America you need to read, Trapped By A Psycho Doctor. When America is strong the world is a safer place to live. Jeffreys and Finney recognizes the U.S. Nation and Worldwide was a much safer and better place to live when President Trump was The U.S. Commander in Chief. We want to help President Trump to be re-elected to the presidency in 2024.

Jonah Jon Jeffreys and his wife, Lorena, live in the Pacific Northwest.

Author
Jonah Jon Jeffreys

Co-Author
Leo Finney